CREATIVE CHAOS

Inside the CIA's Covert War
to Topple the Syrian
Government

WILLIAM VAN WAGENEN

The
LIBERTARIAN
INSTITUTE

Creative Chaos:
Inside the CIA's Covert War to Topple the Syrian Government

© 2025 by William Van Wagenen
All rights reserved.

Cover Design © 2025 Andrew Zehnder

Published in the United States of America by

The Libertarian Institute
612 W. 34th St.
Austin, TX, 78705

LibertarianInstitute.org

ISBN-13: 979-8-9896246-6-9

Advance Praise
for *Creative Chaos*

"Truth is the first casualty of war," and the 2011–present war in Syria is no exception. For Western audiences, weaved a deceptive tale about an evil and brutal dictator suppressing a legitimate democratic uprising, William Van Wagenen's detailed analysis will cause the scales to fall from their eyes.

Creative Chaos skillfully documents the nefarious and very deliberate drives to cultivate dissent in order to lay the groundwork for Salafist extremists to wreak havoc in the country, creating a "chaotic, jihadist dystopia." Emerging from the post -9/11 neocon alliance with Gulf States allies, Turkey, and Israel, and utilizing covert operations by intelligence agencies such as the CIA and MI6, every opportunity was taken to overthrow the Syrian government.

And when "regime-change" strategies faltered, the ultimate deception, by way of the Ghouta nerve gas attack in August 2013, was executed. The circumstances surrounding this still controversial event are forensically unpacked and a compelling case made that it was most likely a false flag designed to trigger full-scale military intervention.

Creative Chaos is essential reading for those still mired in the pervasive propaganda surrounding the war against Syria. "Truth is the daughter of time, not of authority," and I suspect that, in the not-too-distant future, the full truth about the West's dirty war against Syria will come to be widely known. This book is an essential step along the way.

– Dr. Piers Robinson, Co-Director of the Organisation for Propaganda Studies and Research Director for the International Center for 9/11 Justice.

Anyone interested in what a dirty war really looks like these days ought to hurry to a quiet corner with William Van Wagenen's encyclopedic *Creative Chaos*. It's all here: the quiet Americans who inflict their idealism on a faraway country, the immense sums required to sustain such an effort, the malevolent local figures, the evil genius of the social media networks, and the breathtaking misery such forces can visit on an otherwise functioning third world country. The story would be depressing if it were not so well told. One question that is likely to linger in readers' minds: The signs of an impending disaster were apparent from the beginning, as every page of *Creative Chaos* shows, so why did the architects of this tragedy refuse to read them?

– Theo Padnos, American journalist and author who was held prisoner by Jabhat al-Nusra from 2012 to 2014. He is the author of *Blindfold: A Memoir of Capture, Torture, and Enlightenment.*

While Syria for many years drove global headlines during the height of the tragic war which unleashed so much death and suffering on an entire population, the mainstream Western press has largely moved on. Washington might have conveniently "forgotten" its role in sparking and stoking the decade-long nightmare, but Syrians have not, and neither has William Van Wagenen. He has brought the receipts in this hard-hitting, sweeping indictment of the U.S. national security state.

– Brad Hoff, co-author of *Syria Crucified: Stories of Modern Martyrdom in an Ancient Christian Land.*

I've been documenting the Syrian crisis since it began in 2011. Initially, like many others, I was swept up in the excitement of the "Arab Spring," hoping for political liberalization in Syria. However, as the crisis unfolded, my perspective shifted dramatically. It became clear that what was being portrayed as a revolution or a civil war rooted in domestic unrest was, in fact, deeply influenced by foreign intervention, aimed at destabilizing a multi-ethnic and multi-religious nation for geopolitical gains that favored U.S. and Israeli interests in West Asia.

It has taken me over a decade to unravel the complex web of covert operations and regime-change operations orchestrated by the CIA and regional intelligence agencies, all of which were framed by the mainstream media as a "democratic revolution against the tyrant Assad."

Van Wagenen's book, *Creative Chaos*, provides a compelling and insightful examination of these U.S. operations in Syria, challenging the conventional narratives endorsed by many Western analysts who often acted as extensions of intelligence apparatuses, legitimizing Washington's dirty war.

The book is crucial in highlighting the U.S.'s role in instigating an al-Qaeda-led insurgency against the Syrian government, in collaboration with regional powers, including Qatar, Turkey, and Saudi Arabia. Van Wagenen documents how self-proclaimed opposition activists and human rights groups, often funded by the U.S., obscured the Salafist and undemocratic nature of the so-called "Free Syrian Army." This militia, in reality, served as a conduit for funneling billions of dollars' worth of weapons to al-Qaeda and its affiliates.

If you're seeking a thought-provoking book that challenges mainstream narratives and delves into one of the costliest covert operations in CIA history, *Creative Chaos* by William Van Wagenen is an essential read.

– Kevork Almassian, political analyst from Aleppo, Syria, specializing in Middle East and Mediterranean affairs. He is the founder of the Syriana Analysis platform.

CREATIVE CHAOS

Inside the CIA's Covert War
to Topple the Syrian
Government

WILLIAM VAN WAGENEN

Table of Contents

Foreword by Kevork Almassian...i

Introduction..iii

1. The Neocon Plan to Destroy Syria 1

2. America and Israel's Jihadist Proxies 13

3. Astroturfing 'Revolution'...33

4. Daraa, the Cradle of Regime Change 51

5. 'Mostly' Peaceful Protests...69

6. Latakia and Banias, Khaddam's Playground.............................91

7. Homs, the Capital of Regime Change 103

8. Idlib, Home of the 'Moderate Rebels'.................................119

9. The Propaganda War 145

10. Al-Qaeda Shows Its Face 155

11. 'Democracy' Comes to Damascus and Aleppo 171

12. The Mask of the 'Free Army' Falls Off.............................189

13. The Destruction of Yarmouk 205

14. Nusra and the Free Army Pave the Way for ISIS 221

15. Israel's Red Line...245

16. The Ghouta False Flag 273

17. The CIA Doubles Down on Dirty War 301

18. Syria's Missing 313

Conclusion 331

Endnotes 335

Acknowledgments...407

The Libertarian Institute 409

Foreword by Kevork Almassian

As a third-generation descendant of Armenian genocide survivors, I was raised in a deeply politicized environment where the memory of that atrocity was ever-present. In my community, the younger generation is continually reminded of the horrors of the genocide and taught the importance of resilience and survival. This upbringing instilled in me a strong sense of justice and a desire to contribute to a fairer world. It is, perhaps, one of the reasons why I became so deeply engaged with the Palestinian struggle for freedom, following the Second Intifada closely and being profoundly affected by it. However, the pivotal events that truly shaped my political perspective were the U.S. invasion of Iraq in 2003, Israel's invasion of Lebanon in 2006, and the onset of the regime change war in Syria in 2011.

What few people know is that, in 2011, I initially viewed the Arab Spring and the protests in Syria through a different lens. During the early months of the crisis, I was cautiously optimistic, hoping that the protests might lead to positive political change. With a background in international relations and diplomacy and a specialization in Middle Eastern politics, I believed that political liberalization could be a step forward, both for Syria and for the broader region. Like many at the time, I was influenced by the coverage of Al Jazeera, which held considerable credibility, particularly in Syria. I even supported the return of the exiled opposition figure, Haytham Manna, believing he could play a role in a peaceful transition of power.

However, my perspective shifted dramatically after the Jisr al-Shughur massacre in June 2011, when 120 government personnel were brutally killed by elements of the so-called unarmed opposition. This event marked a turning point for me. I began documenting the atrocities committed by sectarian insurgents and soon realized the stark contrast between the political rhetoric presented on television by well-dressed politicians and the actual goals of these insurgents, who sought the establishment of an "Islamic caliphate." The unfolding violence and sectarian motivations brought back painful memories of the Armenian genocide, which my family had passed down through generations. Hearing about such crimes was one thing, but witnessing similarly horrific acts in real time, on smartphones, was a chilling wake-up call.

Compounding this realization was the blatant involvement of foreign powers — the same forces responsible for the oppression of Palestinians and the occupation of Iraq — now supporting the insurgents in Syria. This prompted me to question the motives of these so-called "friends of the Syrian people." Could the very powers who had a hand in oppressing Palestinians and Iraqis truly have the best interests of the Syrian people at heart? It didn't take long for me to reach a conclusion. From that moment on, I knew where I stood — and that decision has shaped my path ever since.

Introduction

In December 2010, Muhammad Bouazizi, a Tunisian fruit seller, lit himself on fire to protest the indignity of having his cart confiscated by a police officer. His death sparked anti-government protests in Tunisia, which quickly spread throughout the Middle East, deposing Presidents Zine El Abidine Ben Ali of Tunisia, Hosni Mubarak of Egypt, and Ali Abdullah Saleh of Yemen. In March 2011, these protests, collectively known as the "Arab Spring," then spread to Syria, with observers expecting Syrian President Bashar al-Assad to be quickly deposed as well.

Shortly after the protests began, President Assad claimed that Syria was the victim of a "conspiracy" by Western imperialist powers seeking "to fragment Syria, to bring down Syria as a nation, to enforce an Israeli agenda."[1] Nine months later, as the country was descending into full-scale conflict, Assad claimed that the "external conspiracy which is being tailored in dark rooms is no longer hidden but now has become crystal clear and visible to anyone."[2]

Such a view was ridiculed by opponents of the Syrian government, who argued that U.S. and allied intelligence agencies had played no role in the eruption of the 2011 anti-government protests, which they termed the "Syrian Revolution." Instead, as described by the *New York Times*:

> Syrians, like other peoples across the region, rose up peacefully against their authoritarian government. Mr. Assad cracked down violently. Communities took up arms to defend themselves, then fought back in what became a civil war. Some soldiers joined the rebels, but not enough to win.[3]

Pro-opposition activists and authors Robbin Yassin-Kassab and Leila al-Shami argue that if one challenges this narrative and considers the role of foreign powers in sparking protests in Syria, this necessarily leads "ever deeper into conspiracism. For such people, not only the Syrian revolution but the whole Arab Spring was a foreign plot," while efforts to blame the protests on Western intelligence agencies, such as the CIA, "remove the agency of the peoples concerned," casting Syrians as "innocents pleased to suffer poverty, torture, and humiliation until some devilishly clever Westerner whispers in their ears" to rebel.[4]

Further, pro-opposition activists criticized the U.S. government, not for manufacturing the anti-government protests and armed rebellion that followed, but for U.S. "inaction" in Syria, alleging that President Barack Obama had stood idly by and refused to intervene militarily against Assad, a dictator they claimed was committing genocide against the Syrian people.[5]

However, as I will illustrate in the pages below, claims of U.S. inaction are a myth. U.S. planners did intervene massively in the conflict. They did so by covertly pumping what one former U.S. official described as a "cataract of weaponry" into Syria to arm the al-Qaeda-dominated insurgency fighting to topple the Syrian government.[6] CIA officials did this both directly and via allied regional intelligence agencies, in what the *Washington Post* acknowledged as "one of the agency's largest covert operations, with a budget approaching $1 billion per year."[7]

More importantly, there is clear evidence that U.S. planners not only intervened in the Syrian conflict after it erupted, but that they covertly sparked the conflict itself. U.S. planners began preparations as early as 2001 to effect regime change in Syria, and they successfully engineered the anti-government protests that erupted a decade later, in March 2011.

U.S. planners then used these protests as cover to launch the simultaneous al-Qaeda-led insurgency that quickly enveloped the country. It was hoped that this would ignite a sectarian civil war and pave the way for the fall of Syria's Baath-led government, possibly even through direct U.S. military occupation of the country.

Any honest effort to understand the origins of the Syrian conflict must take account of the covert role played by U.S. planners and their regional allies, in particular their support for the major al-Qaeda-affiliated groups that fought the Syrian government, namely the Nusra Front and Islamic State of Iraq and Sham (ISIS).

The covert U.S. effort to effect regime change in Syria was articulated by Saliba Mourad, a longtime critic of Syria's Baathist government. Mourad explains:

> I have been a refugee for 37 years due to my political engagement against the ruling Baath party. I cannot go back to Syria without being punished. But I see what the Western countries, Turkey, and the Gulf states are now trying to do to my country. It has nothing to do with human rights or democracy. They want to divide the country and get rid of an opponent to the U.S.'s plans for the region.[8]

Unfortunately, most Western observers continue to believe that the protests and armed insurgency against the Syrian government that erupted in 2011 were grassroots and popular, and that the U.S. and its allies played a benevolent role in the conflict, seeking to support the Syrian people against a brutal dictator. This is because of the sophisticated and unrelenting propaganda campaign launched by U.S. and British planners, with the complicity of the Western and Gulf press. It is this wall of propaganda that I wish to break through in the pages of this book.

In the chapters that follow, I detail the previous history of U.S. efforts for regime change in Syria, dating to shortly after the founding of the CIA in the 1940s, followed by the development of the more recent plan for regime change in Syria, which began in the wake of the 9/11 attacks.

I detail how these plans intensified starting in 2005 and how U.S. planners concretely implemented them on the ground by sparking anti-government protests in the Syrian border town of Daraa in March 2011.

I show how U.S. planners simultaneously launched an al-Qaeda-led insurgency against the Syrian government by partnering with their Saudi and Lebanese allies to infiltrate militants from two al-Qaeda-affiliated groups, i.e., the Islamic State of Iraq (ISI) and Fatah al-Islam, into Syria, and how these militants partnered with local Salafist militants to attack Syrian security forces, soldiers, and police under the cover of the earliest protests.

I discuss how these Salafist and al-Qaeda militants coalesced to form the various armed groups which formed the backbone of the Free Syrian Army (FSA), and how U.S.-funded opposition activists and human rights groups sought to obscure the Salafist nature of the FSA by portraying it as an army of defected Syrian soldiers fighting for freedom and liberal democracy.

I detail how ISI leader Abu Bakr al-Baghdadi created the Nusra Front and later the Islamic State of Iraq and Sham (ISIS), and the close relationship between these terror organizations and the FSA groups enjoying direct U.S., Gulf, British, Israeli, and Turkish support.

I discuss the intimate relationship between the FSA, the Nusra Front, and ISIS, and how the Nusra Front's victories were portrayed as victories for the FSA for public relations reasons. I discuss the U.S. effort to provide vast amounts of weaponry to the Nusra Front, and how this was done indirectly, by way of the FSA, to maintain plausible deniability.

Finally, I give attention to a series of false-flag assassinations and massacres, which were blamed on the Syrian government to mobilize support for direct Western military intervention. I devote particular attention to the August 2013 chemical attack in the Damascus suburbs of Ghouta. I detail how the Ghouta chemical attack, alleged to have killed over 1,400

Syrians, including many women and children, was perpetrated not by the Syrian government, but by a Saudi-backed Salafist armed group, Liwa al-Islam.

I discuss the pinnacle role this false-flag attack played in the broader Western regime change effort, an effort which has finally succeeded.

As I write this, Saliba Mourad's warning that the U.S. and its allies planned to topple the Syrian government and divide the country have come true.

On December 8, 2024, militants from the latest iteration of al-Qaeda in Syria, led by Abu Mohammad al-Jolani, conquered Damascus, largely without a fight. Jolani, responsible for countless sectarian massacres, now wears a suit and is being hailed in the Western press as the new moderate and diversity-friendly ruler of Syria.

After Damascus fell and Assad was deposed, Israel quickly occupied large swaths of additional territory in southern Syria, including in the strategic Golan Heights and water-rich Yarmouk Basin. Israeli tanks are now positioned less than 20 kilometers from Damascus.

Israel immediately launched hundreds of airstrikes, one of its largest bombing campaigns ever, to destroy the entirety of Syria's military infrastructure and weapons. The Syrian army has been destroyed and will never pose a threat to Israel, just as the Iraqi army under Saddam Hussein was destroyed after the 2003 U.S. invasion.

Turkish proxy forces, known as the National Army, occupy large swaths of northern Syria. President Recep Tayyip Erdoğan now publicly states that Aleppo, Syria's second-largest city and industrial engine, belongs to Turkey, and that the Ottoman Empire must be restored.

The U.S. Army, in partnership with Kurdish proxies known as the Syrian Democratic Forces (SDF), occupy north and east Syria, home to Syria's oil fields and wheat-producing regions. U.S. Forces continue to help transport stolen Syrian oil to the Kurdish region of northern Iraq, for further export to Turkey, and then Israel.

In other words, the U.S. plan "to fragment Syria, to bring down Syria as a nation, to enforce an Israeli agenda" has finally succeeded, over two decades after it began.

1. The Neocon Plan to Destroy Syria

Early Experiments in Covert Action

The role of U.S. planners in sparking the conflict in Syria in March 2011 was not immediately apparent to outside observers because it was, of course, deliberately obscured. As philosopher Gabriel Rockhill observes, intelligence services such as the CIA

> want to remain beneath the radar of history. They do not want to participate in or be identified as the heroes of history. But in a very paradoxical and quite pernicious way, they are often precisely those that are most powerful in the constitution of the visible histories we have and in the legacies that have been left.[1]

Covert U.S. efforts to destabilize Syria have a long history, dating to the period of Syria's independence from French colonial rule in the 1940s. Attorney and international law expert Ernesto Sanchez observed that "during the Cold War's early years, the United States tried to overthrow the Syrian government in one of the most sustained covert-operations campaigns ever conducted,"[2] while historian Douglas Little explained that "this newly independent Arab republic was an important staging ground for the CIA's earliest experiments in covert action."[3]

It is important to emphasize what motivated U.S. planners to intervene in Syria during this early period. Historian William Blum notes that according to declassified National Security Council documents, U.S. planners were responding to the "popular leftward trend" in the Syrian government, which was allowing "continuous and increasing Communist activities." While moving left politically, the Syrian government was also rejecting U.S. military aid, which would have obligated Syria to support U.S. efforts to "encourage the efforts of other free nations… to foster private initiative and competition [i.e., capitalism]."[4]

The CIA began intervening in Syria in 1949, barely a year after the agency's creation, by directing a coup directed against Syria's democratically elected president, Shukri al-Quwatli.

The Syrian president had opposed the U.S. policy regarding the establishment of the state of Israel and blocked the passage of the Arabian American Oil Company (ARAMCO) Trans-Arabian Pipeline from Saudi Arabia to the Mediterranean.[5]

Douglas Little adds that the CIA-planned coup installed General Husni al-Za'im in power, whom U.S. officials viewed as a "banana republic dictator type" with a "strong anti-Soviet attitude." A State Department political officer in Damascus, Deane Hinton, admitted that the successful 1949 coup was "the stupidest, most irresponsible action a diplomatic mission like ours could get itself involved in," and that "we've started a series of these things that will never end."[6]

As Hinton predicted, Syria underwent a long period of instability marked by additional coups in 1954, 1961, 1963, and 1966. Some measure of stability finally emerged in 1970 after another coup, in which a young Baathist air force officer, Hafez al-Assad, took power in what was known as the "Corrective Revolution."

A Bid to Seize Power

U.S. covert intervention in Syria intensified in the years after Hafez al-Assad came to power in 1970. In his book *Asad: The Struggle for the Middle East* (1989), historian Patrick Seale details how from 1977 to 1982, the Syrian government was subjected to a horrific campaign of bombings and assassinations by militants from the Islamic Front, an opposition coalition led by the Muslim Brotherhood, which very nearly toppled the government, and to which Assad responded with considerable brutality.

Founded in Egypt in 1928 by Islamic scholar and schoolteacher Hassan al-Banna, the Muslim Brotherhood is a transnational Sunni political movement with branches in various countries and whose aim is the establishment of states ruled by Sharia law.

According to Seale, some of the victims of the Islamic Front terror campaign in Syria

> were prominent officers and government servants, but others were professional men, doctors and teachers and the like, who were not involved with the regime and were therefore undefended. Most of them were Alawis which suggested that the assassins had targeted the community and were deliberately setting out to sharpen sectarian differences.[7]

Seale emphasizes the importance of the June 1979 Aleppo Artillery School massacre, in which Islamist militants murdered 32 Alawite army cadets: "A member of staff, Captain Ibrahim Yusuf, assembled the cadets in the dining hall and then let in the gunmen who opened fire indiscriminately." At the time, Syrian Muslim Brotherhood ideologue Sa'id Hawwa was advocating violence against Syria's Alawites based on the religious rulings of Ibn Taymiyya, the 14th-century religious scholar who urged the extermination of Alawites as heretics.[8]

Seale notes that in June 1980, President Assad himself narrowly escaped death after Islamist militants threw two hand grenades and shot bursts of machine gun fire at him while he waited to welcome an African dignitary. In response, Assad's brother Rif'at sent army units to the prison in Palmyra, where soldiers under his command murdered some 500 Muslim Brotherhood detainees held by the government.

The Muslim Brotherhood terror campaign and brutal Syrian government response infamously culminated in a showdown in the town of Hama in 1982. On February 2, Islamist militants ambushed an army unit in the city, with rooftop snipers killing some 20 soldiers. When army reinforcements were sent in, the local Islamist commander put out the call for a general uprising throughout Hama. According to Seale: "At this signal hundreds of Islamic fighters rose from their hiding places. Killing and looting, they burst into the homes of officials and party leaders, overran police posts, and ransacked armories in a bid to seize power in the city."[9]

Crucially, the Islamist militants enjoyed external support from both the Jordanian and Israeli governments, who wished to see Assad overthrown. As a result, the militants "had a fortune in foreign money, sophisticated communications equipment, and large arms dumps." Further, Seale writes that Assad was convinced of U.S. support for the militants, given the "discovery of U.S. equipment in the hands of the guerrillas, and especially sophisticated communications equipment of a kind, he claimed, that could only be sold to a third party with U.S. government permission."

By the time the Syrian army was able to crush the uprising three weeks later, thousands of Syrians lay dead, whether Islamist militants, Syrian security forces, or civilians living in the city. Muslim Brotherhood sources claimed that the battle at Hama was a massacre, resulting in 20,000 or more civilian deaths, while the U.S. Defense Intelligence Agency (DIA) estimated a much lower number, some 2,000, including 300–400 Brotherhood militants, suggesting an urban battle between two combatant groups.[10]

The events at Hama influenced the motivations of the Syrian opposition when the initial protests and attacks by armed groups against Syrian security forces began in the spring of 2011. Writing for the pro-opposition *al-Jumhuriya*, Arwa Khalifa observes, for example:

> The conflict between the Salafi movements in Syria and the political regime did not start with the Syrian revolution. Rather, this conflict, which historically possessed its own mechanics and self-causes, was initially part of the battle of the al-Assad regime with the movements of political Islam and its military branches [stretching back to the 1977–82 insurgency].[11]

In other words, the conflict that erupted in 2011 was in many ways a continuation of the events of 1982. For many in the Islamist-dominated opposition, taking revenge for Hama three decades before was an important motivation to partner once again with U.S. planners to topple Syria's Alawite-led government.

The events in Hama colored the views of the Syrian government as well. When the first protests erupted in March 2011, Syrian military and intelligence officials were keenly aware that they were facing an Islamist-dominated opposition not only driven by hatred of Alawites, but also enjoying the support of the U.S. and other foreign powers, including Israel, just as they had in 1982. Most observers of the Arab Spring were ignorant of this history, and this led them to imagine that the Syrian opposition was fighting for democracy, freedom, and human rights against a brutal and unpopular dictator.

The American Project

U.S. hostility to the Syrian government continued in the decades following the CIA's early regime change efforts. In his 2005 book *Inheriting Syria*, Flynt Leverett, former Senior Middle East Analyst at the CIA and Senior Director for Middle East Affairs at the National Security Council (NSC) during the first George W. Bush administration, explained why U.S. planners wished to effect regime change in Syria.[12] Leverett noted that Syria is a "swing state" in the Middle East, and that since Hafez al-Assad came to power in 1970, U.S. policy toward Syria has been motivated by an interest in bringing Syria into the pro-U.S. camp and thereby "tipping the regional balance of power against more radical or revisionist actors." Leverett complained that the U.S. has "had to cope with Syrian resistance on a variety of fronts" since 1970, which resistance included opposition to U.S. support for Israel's annexation of the Syrian Golan Heights, Syria's "largely successful campaign to repulse Israel's 1982 invasion of Lebanon," and Syria's "inauguration of a strategic alliance with Iran" which "ran against American moves throughout the 1980s to

4

bolster Saddam Hussein's Iraq as a bulwark against the Islamic Republic's revolutionary influence."

When Hafez al-Assad died in 2000, he was replaced as leader of the country by his son, Bashar, who continued Syrian resistance to U.S. policies in the region. Leverett noted further: "As the Bush administration launched its military campaign against Saddam's regime in 2003, Bashar not only opposed the war but authorized actions that worked against the U.S. pursuit of its objectives in Iraq." Leverett also discussed Syrian support for Palestinian resistance groups — such as the Popular Front for the Liberation of Palestine–General Command (PFLP-GC), Hamas, and Islamic Jihad — and the fact that Syria "has for many years been the principal conduit for Iranian military supplies going to Hezbollah fighters in southern Lebanon" who were resisting Israel as well.

Leverett then wondered whether the best course for "changing problematic Syrian behaviors" should entail efforts to "ratchet up economic, political, rhetorical pressure on Damascus" on the one hand, or "coercive regime change" on the other.

In short, as Syria expert David Lesch observed, Syria "did not give in to what, in the region during the Bush years, was often called the 'American project.'"[13]

Cleaning Up the Middle East

U.S. threats against Syria as described by Leverett were not new. According to former NATO Supreme Military Commander Wesley Clark, then U.S. Under Secretary of Defense for Policy Paul Wolfowitz told him after the First Gulf War in 1991 that "we didn't get rid of Saddam Hussein and we should have… We've only got five or ten years to clean up the middle east. These old Soviet surrogate regimes like Syria and Iraq, get rid of them before the next superpower comes along to challenge us." According to Clark, the efforts of Wolfowitz and other neoconservatives in the Bush administration to use force to change regimes aggressively "appeared full-blown after 9/11."[14]

In other words, neoconservatives sought to use the so-called War on Terror as a pretext to justify attacks on any state viewed as an enemy of the U.S. and Israel. As Samer Arabi observes, neoconservatives from the Project for the New American Century (PNAC) accused Iran and Syria of being "state sponsors of terrorism," even though neither played any role in the

9/11 attacks. PNAC then advocated "retaliation" if their support for Hezbollah in Lebanon, Israel's nearest enemy, did not immediately cease.[15]

In March 2003, U.S. planners launched the illegal U.S. invasion and occupation of Iraq, a country which also played no role in the 9/11 attacks. Wesley Clark famously revealed as well that the Iraq invasion was part of a larger plan developed by U.S. Secretary of Defense Donald Rumsfeld's office "to take out seven countries in five years," including Iran, Libya, and Syria.[16]

Clark's claims were confirmed by then Secretary of Defense Colin Powell's Chief of Staff Lawrence Wilkerson, who explained, "In my first briefing in the Pentagon from an Air Force three-star general in February of 2001, I almost fell off my chair." Wilkerson further describes the briefing:

> Hey, when we do Iraq, we're going to do Syria, Lebanon, and we're going to do Iran and maybe Egypt. I'm a military professional. They are doing contingency planning... but this was more than that, I listened to it, and this was more than that. Wes Clark was right. They had these plans. They were going to go right through all these countries they felt threatened Israel.[17]

This was further confirmed by documents released by the U.K. Iraq Inquiry showing British Prime Minister Tony Blair and U.S. President George W. Bush planning a possible attack on Syria in the same context.[18]

Syrian planners understood this threat well. David Lesch notes that

> in the fresh glow of the Bush administration's "mission accomplished" in 2003, several implicit threats were directed at Damascus — threats that Syrian officials took *very seriously*: Syria could be next on the Bush doctrine's hit list.[19] (emphasis in original)

Not only Syrian planners but also average Syrians were aware of these threats. Journalist and former U.S. Marine Brad Hoff notes that during a lengthy stay in Damascus in 2005, many of his Syrian acquaintances expressed the view that "a war on Syria is coming. The Americans are coming here — whether in a few years or more, they will target Damascus."[20]

A Clean Break

The threat of regime change was reinforced in October 2005 by CNN reporter Christiane Amanpour during an interview with President Assad. Warning Assad that U.S. planners were actively seeking to depose him, she stated:

> Mr. President, you know the rhetoric of regime change is headed towards you from the United States. They are actively looking for a

new Syrian leader. They're granting visas and visits to Syrian opposition politicians. They're talking about isolating you diplomatically and, perhaps, a *coup d'etat* or your regime crumbling. What are you thinking about that?[21]

As Brad Hoff observed, Amanpour was married to former U.S. Assistant Secretary of State James Rubin, who later advised both President Obama and Secretary of State Hillary Clinton. Amanpour was therefore not likely speculating, but instead appeared to be delivering a direct threat on behalf of U.S. planners.[22]

In December 2005, the *Wall Street Journal* reported that within U.S. government circles, the "pressure for regime change in Damascus is rising," and that according to Richard Perle, prominent neoconservative and architect of the U.S. invasion of Iraq, "Assad has never been weaker, and we should take advantage of that."[23] Perle, a member of the U.S. Defense Policy Board which advises the Department of Defense, made his comments in the context of a U.S.-sponsored effort to blame the Syrian government for the assassination of Lebanese Prime Minister Rafiq Hariri.

Perle's advocacy for regime change in Syria stretched back at least a decade. In 1996, Perle and other prominent neoconservatives had recommended to then incoming Israeli Prime Minister Benjamin Netanyahu that Israel

> shape its strategic environment, in cooperation with Turkey and Jordan, by weakening, containing, and even *rolling back Syria*. This effort can focus on removing Saddam Hussein from power in Iraq, an important Israeli strategic objective in its own right, as a means of foiling Syria's regional ambitions.[24] (emphasis added)

This recommendation was articulated in "A Clean Break: A New Strategy for Securing the Realm," a policy document co-authored by David Wurmser, a colleague of Perle's at the American Enterprise Institute (AEI). Flynt Leverett notes that because both Perle and Wurmser obtained influential positions in the Bush administration (with Wurmser becoming Middle East advisor to Vice President Cheney's staff) it was "thus not surprising that the Office of the Secretary of Defense became the principal agent advocating coercive regime change strategy toward Damascus, supported by the Office of the Vice President."[25]

Wurmser had also long been hostile to Syria's Baathist government, arguing in 1996 that the U.S. and Israel should "expedite the demise of

Baathism in Syria," and of secular Arab nationalism generally, to create new states in the region based on "tribal/clan/familial alliances."[26]

Wurmser's views were themselves reminiscent of the 1982 Yinon Plan, which viewed the breakup of the Baathist-led Syrian and Iraqi governments into weak, sectarian mini-states as beneficial for Israel. In an article titled "A Strategy for Israel in the Nineteen Eighties," Israeli journalist and former foreign ministry official Oded Yinon wrote:

> The dissolution of Syria and Iraq later on into ethnically or religiously unique areas such as in Lebanon, is Israel's primary target on the Eastern front in the long run, while the dissolution of the military power of those states serves as the primary short-term target. Syria will fall apart, in accordance with its ethnic and religious structure, into several states such as in present day Lebanon, so that there will be a Shi'ite Alawi state along its coast, a Sunni state in the Aleppo area, another Sunni state in Damascus hostile to its northern neighbor, and the Druzes who will set up a state, maybe even in our Golan, and certainly in the Hauran and in northern Jordan. This state of affairs will be the guarantee for peace and security in the area in the long run, and that aim is already within our reach today.[27]

The strategic benefit Israel would enjoy from the "Lebanonization" and "dissolution of the military power" of both Iraq and Syria, as expressed in the "Clean Break" and Yinon Plan documents, helps explain the prominent role played by Bush administration neoconservatives not only in the effort to topple the Syrian government, but also in launching the 2003 Iraq invasion, which led to accusations that the war had been fought almost solely on Israel's behalf, rather than, for example, for the benefit of American corporate interests in the oil and defense sectors.[28]

Wurmser and Perle's recommendation in the 1996 "Clean Break" document that both the Syrian and Iraqi Baathist states be dismantled suggests that Israel's strategic interests were still paramount in the minds of these same men when they advocated the invasion of Iraq in 2003.

Political scientists John Mearsheimer and Stephen Walt also argue that consideration of Israeli interests played a key role in the decision to invade Iraq in 2003. Walt notes that British Prime Minister Blair acknowledged as much in his testimony to the U.K. Iraq War Inquiry Committee. Blair explained that in his conversations with President Bush, "the Israel issue was a big, big issue at the time. I think, in fact, I remember actually, there may have been conversations that we had even with Israelis, the two of us whilst we were there. So that was a major part of all this."[29]

Given the prominence of neoconservatives in the Bush administration, this is to be expected. After all, as neoconservative commentator Max Boot asserted, steadfast support for Israel is a "key tenet of neoconservatism."[30]

Unsurprisingly, as Walt further notes, top Israeli leaders, including Benjamin Netanyahu, Shimon Peres, Ehud Barak, and Ariel Sharon, became important "cheerleaders for the invasion, and they played a prominent role in helping sell the war here in the United States," including by lobbying the U.S. Senate and writing op-eds in the *New York Times* and *Wall Street Journal*. Further, former President Bill Clinton explained that "every Israeli politician I knew believed that Saddam Hussein should be toppled, even if he did not have weapons of mass destruction."[31]

Both the 2003 Iraq invasion and subsequent regime change effort in Syria that unfolded in 2011 should therefore be considered part of a broader neoconservative effort to secure Israeli interests.

Creative Chaos

Part of the neoconservative effort to impose regime change in Syria was the creation of the Syria Reform Party (SRF), led by Farid Ghadry, shortly after the 2003 invasion of Iraq. Ghadry had left Syria with his family for Lebanon at a young age before immigrating to the United States, where he attended American University in Washington, D.C., and became a successful businessman. Ghadry enjoyed support from Richard Perle and other neoconservatives centered around then Vice President Cheney's office. Ghadry viewed Iraqi exile Ahmed Chalabi's role in promoting the U.S. invasion of Iraq as a positive model. Ghadry told the *Wall Street Journal* that "Ahmed paved the way in Iraq for what we want to do in Syria."[32]

In an indication of how deeply Ghadry reflected the interests of his neoconservative U.S. sponsors, and how little popularity he would ever enjoy among Syrians, Ghadry became a member of the American Israel Public Affairs Committee (AIPAC), the most powerful Israel lobby in Washington, and wrote a column on his website titled "Why I Admire Israel."[33]

According to Syrian journalist Salim Abraham, Ghadry claimed to want "regime change by any means," including a direct U.S. invasion and occupation of the country. Ghadry also hoped to dismantle Syria's largely socialist economy and replace it with a completely free-market system.

Abraham reports further that in November 2005, Ghadry met with both Perle and Chalabi in Washington, where they discussed "the next steps in

Syria" for regime change. Ghadry later described his plan to gather all Syrian opposition groups to create a government in exile, and then to "take people to [the] streets. Some people get killed. The international community gets further angry at the regime. Then, have NATO forces protect a safe zone in northern Syria," on the border with Turkey, after which "we will move right away into Syria."[34]

The regime change desired by Ghadry and his American handlers depended not only on an Iraq-style invasion and occupation, but also on inciting a sectarian civil war of the sort raging in Iraq at the time. In reviewing an essay written by Ghadry, Syria expert and academic Joshua Landis observed:

> Ghadry stipulates that by opening up a sectarian war inside Syria, the regime will fall. He encourages Washington to facilitate this and to "stir trouble amongst the Sunnis of Syria" — with the goal of causing the collapse of the Asad regime, preferably by a coup.[35]

Landis notes further that Ghadry

> takes the neocon policy of "creative chaos" to its logical conclusion, which is to fan the flames of the sectarian war being waged in Iraq to bring down the neighboring regimes and break the Middle East wide open. He presumes that Washington will end up siding with the Sunnis in Iraq against the Shiites and harness Saudi Arabia to this task.

Ghadry's strategy to use sectarianism to destabilize the Syrian government likely did not originate with him, but with his neoconservative U.S. handlers such as Richard Perle. U.S. planners had long viewed inciting sectarian tensions in Syria that would culminate in civil war as beneficial.

This strategy was articulated in a 1986 CIA memo, uncovered by Brad Hoff, entitled "Syria: Scenarios of Dramatic Political Change."[36] The memo is worth quoting at length due to the emphasis the document places on inciting anti-government protests in Syria of the kind seen in 2011. The memo states that "we believe that a renewal of communal violence between Alawis and Sunnis could inspire Sunnis in the military to turn against the regime," and that

> disgruntlement over price hikes, altercations between citizens and security forces, or anger at privileges accorded to Alawis at the expense of Sunnis could foster small-scale protests. Excessive government force in quelling such disturbances might be seen by Sunnis as evidence of a government vendetta against all Sunnis, precipitating even larger protests by other Sunni groups... A general

campaign of Alawi violence against Sunnis might push even moderate Sunnis to join the opposition. Remnants of the Muslim Brotherhood, some returning from exile in Iraq, could provide a core of leadership for the movement. Although the regime has the resources to crush such a venture, we believe brutal attacks on Sunni civilians might prompt large numbers of Sunni officers and conscripts to desert or stage mutinies in support of dissidents, and Iraq might supply them with sufficient weapons to launch a civil war.[37]

Watching the Carnage in Iraq

According to a December 2006 U.S. State Department cable leaked by WikiLeaks, U.S. embassy officials in Damascus similarly suggested that the U.S. should use sectarianism to destabilize the Syrian government, in this case by playing "on Sunni fears of Iranian influence." The cable explains:

> There are fears in Syria that the Iranians are active in both Shia proselytizing and conversion of, mostly poor, Sunnis. *Though often exaggerated*, such fears reflect an element of the Sunni community in Syria that is increasingly upset by and focused on the spread of Iranian influence in their country through activities ranging from mosque construction to business. Both the local Egyptian and Saudi missions here (as well as prominent Syrian Sunni religious leaders), are giving increasing attention to the matter and *we should coordinate more closely with their governments on ways to better publicize* and focus regional attention on the issue.[38] (emphasis added)

This resulted in a Salafi propaganda campaign originating from the Gulf countries, in which Qatari-owned Al Jazeera played a key role. As Iraqi-British author Sami Ramadani notes, Qatar's rulers "saw in Al Jazeera a vehicle for spreading their political influence," just as

> Qatar became the headquarters of U.S. military operations throughout the Middle East. Al Jazeera remains one of the root sources of constant scares about a supposed sectarian threat from Iranian and "Shia" influence in the region.[39]

As Robert Naiman observed, the December 2006 State Department cable advocating the exaggeration of a Shia threat "was written at the height of the sectarian Sunni-Shia civil war in Iraq," and therefore, "no one working for the U.S. government on foreign policy at the time could have been unaware of the implications of promoting Sunni-Shia sectarianism."[40]

U.S. planners realized that a sectarian war in Syria like that in neighboring Iraq would be in the interests of both the U.S. and Israel. A leaked email to Hillary Clinton from her advisor Sidney Blumenthal explained that the fall of the House of Assad could well ignite a sectarian war between the Shiites and the majority Sunnis of the region drawing in Iran, which, in the view of Israeli commanders, would not be a bad thing for Israel and its Western allies [because it] would distract and might obstruct Iran from its nuclear activities for a good deal of time [and possibly] even prove to be a factor in the eventual fall of the current government of Iran.[41]

It should further be noted that U.S. planners were not promoting sectarianism in Syria for the sake of toppling an unpopular leader. As Syria analyst Camille Otrakji observed: "Had President Assad been so unpopular with 'the Sunnis'… why did America's embassy need to manufacture Sunni anger?"[42] U.S. planners were aware that although President Assad did not come to power via democratic elections, he was nevertheless extremely popular. Veteran *Washington Post* reporter David Ignatius wrote in November 2005, for example, that "it's hard to find a Syrian who doesn't want Assad to remain at least as a figurehead. He's a symbol of stability for a country nervously watching the carnage in Iraq." Ignatius reports further that, according to the Syrian analyst Sami Moubayed, "the president would win in a landslide if there was an election."[43] Nevertheless, U.S. planners were willing to spark a sectarian war in the country to depose Assad.

2. America and Israel's Jihadist Proxies

The Brotherhood Option

Farid Ghadry enjoyed good relations not only with neoconservative U.S. planners but also with the Syrian Muslim Brotherhood and its leader, Ali al-Bayanouni, who himself was seeking to foster better relations with Bush administration officials.[1] The Muslim Brotherhood was seen as crucial to help "stir trouble amongst the Sunnis of Syria." Although the Brotherhood had only an underground presence in Syria and membership in the group was punishable by death, Salim Abraham notes that nevertheless, "the brotherhood is believed to be able to mobilize the already high religious sentiment in the country."[2]

Ghadry's hopes of coming to power in Syria on the back of American tanks floundered, however, when a more useful proxy to act on behalf of U.S. interests emerged. In December 2005, Syrian Vice President Abd al-Halim Khaddam shocked observers when he announced his defection from the Syrian government. Khaddam had been a member of the Baath's Regional Command for 30 years and had controlled the government's Lebanon file, which gave him significant influence over Lebanese politics.

According to *Al-Sharq al-Awsat*, when Hafez al-Assad transferred this file to his son Bashar in 1998, this "did not sit well with Khaddam and his allies in Lebanon."[3] Khaddam was briefly Syria's nominal leader after the death of Hafez al-Assad in 2000, before the transfer of power to Bashar. In 2005, Khaddam formally defected and accused the Syrian government of assassinating his friend, Lebanese Prime Minister Hariri. Khaddam moved to Paris and began organizing for regime change in the country he left behind. Khaddam then partnered with Brotherhood leader Bayanouni, who turned his back on Ghadry to form a new opposition group in exile, the National Salvation Front (NSF), in March 2006. The group immediately called for anti-government demonstrations within Syria.[4]

The NSF's status was elevated in October 2006, when several of its members met with Michael Doran of the U.S. National Security Council, who was a close associate of prominent neoconservative and Bush administration official Elliott Abrams.[5] Representatives of the NSF were also given a meeting with Saudi King Abdullah bin Abdul Aziz that same month.[6] The *Wall Street Journal* reported that Abrams warmed to the idea of partnering with the Brotherhood after Iranian-backed Lebanese Hezbollah fought Israel to a standstill in the summer of 2006, which caused Washington to become "increasingly concerned about Syria's military alliance with Iran, and the threat it posed to U.S. interests in the region."[7]

Time reported in December 2006 that U.S. officials were already "supporting regular meetings of internal and diaspora Syrian activists" in Europe and were considering a proposal to meddle in the upcoming 2007 Syrian legislative elections. This led one U.S. official to suggest that "you are forced to wonder whether we are now trying to destabilize the Syrian government." Framing it as "democracy promotion," *Time* reported that the destabilization campaign was led by Abrams in the National Security Council, and by Liz Cheney, Dick Cheney's daughter, in the State Department. To coordinate these efforts with additional government agencies, including the U.S. Treasury, intelligence services, and Pentagon, the Iran Syria Policy and Operations Group (ISOG) was created.[8]

Though gaining in popularity with U.S. planners, the NSF — and the U.S.-backed Syrian opposition broadly — had little credibility among Syrians themselves. As leading opposition figure Riad al-Seif explained in April 2007: "The image of the U.S. is so bad that if you're against the regime, you're an American spy." According to Seif, Syrians had no desire for regime change, in part because they wished to avoid the societal collapse and sectarian war taking place next door in Iraq courtesy of the 2003 U.S. invasion and occupation.[9]

Additionally, the Syrian government had been softening its approach to dealing with internal critics. Ammar Qurabi, director of the Syrian Human Rights Organization, noted during the same period that

> repression in Syria these days is not nearly as brutal as under the senior Assad, noting that the number of political prisoners had decreased sharply, their treatment in jail had improved, and prisoners of opinion were now facing civil tribunals instead of security courts.[10]

U.S. efforts to fund opposition activists to destabilize the government during this time could therefore have only the opposite effect, namely to encourage the government to tighten any repressive security measures once again in response.

Joshua Landis notes that when the NSF collapsed in 2009, the group had been so discredited that it "caused hardly a murmur among Syrians."[11] U.S. planners nevertheless continued to work with both the Brotherhood and with Khaddam to effect regime change in Syria by triggering a sectarian civil war.

Salafis Throwing Bombs

Hezbollah's surprisingly strong performance during the 2006 war against Israel, coupled with the rise of Iranian influence in U.S.-occupied Iraq, prompted what journalist Seymour Hersh described as a "redirection" in U.S. policy in the Middle East. This shift in policy was led by Dick Cheney, Elliott Abrams, and Saudi National Security Advisor and former Ambassador to the U.S., Prince Bandar bin Sultan.[12]

The redirection involved working with Washington's Sunni regional client states "to counteract Shiite ascendance in the region." As part of this effort, the "Saudi government, with Washington's approval, would provide funds and logistical aid to weaken the government of President Bashir [sic] Assad, of Syria." Hersh notes further that "there is evidence that the Administration's redirection strategy has already benefited the Brotherhood," and that, according to a former high-ranking CIA officer, Khaddam and the NSF were receiving both financial and diplomatic support from the Americans and Saudis.[13]

Hersh reports as well that, according to a U.S. government consultant:

> Bandar and other Saudis have assured the White House that "they will keep a very close eye on the religious fundamentalists. Their message to us was 'We've created this movement, and we can control it.' It's not that we don't want the Salafis to throw bombs; it's who they throw them at — Hezbollah, Moqtada al-Sadr, Iran, and at the Syrians, if they continue to work with Hezbollah and Iran."[14]

Seizing the Opportunity

In December 2006, the *chargé d'affaires* of the U.S. embassy in Damascus, William Roebuck, had already acknowledged the possibility of exploiting Salafist militants to promote regime change in Syria. Roebuck wrote in a cable to Washington that "we believe Bashar's weaknesses are in how he chooses to react to looming issues, both perceived and real," including

> the potential threat to the regime from the *increasing presence of transiting Islamist extremists*. This cable summarizes our assessment of these vulnerabilities and suggests that there may be actions, statements, and signals that the USG can send that will improve the likelihood of such opportunities arising. These proposals will need to be fleshed out and

converted into real actions, and we need to be ready to move quickly to take advantage of such opportunities.[15] (emphasis added)

This danger was illustrated by two waves of terror attacks in Syria, between 2004–06 and 2008–09. Terrorism expert Peter Neumann writes that "representatives of European intelligence services stationed in Syria at the time say that they received reports about terrorist incidents 'on a monthly basis.'"[16] The deadliest terror attack occurred in 2008, when a car bomb exploded in a Damascus suburb near the Sayyida Zeinab shrine. The shrine is revered by Shia Muslims and contains the grave of Zaynab, the granddaughter of the Prophet Muhammad. The *Los Angeles Times* quoted Syrian state media as reporting that the "vehicle was loaded with more than 400 pounds of explosives and blew up between 8 a.m. and 9 a.m. in a busy pedestrian area often filled with Lebanese, Iraqi, or Iranian religious tourists," killing 17 and injuring 14.[17]

This raises the question of whether U.S. efforts to convert the opportunities provided by "transiting Islamist extremists" into "real actions" involved sponsorship of these bombings.

As a result of these terror campaigns, the Syrian government initiated a far-reaching crackdown on Syria's Salafist community. A 2009 Human Rights Watch (HRW) report states for example that "the largest group of defendants before the [Supreme State Security Court] in the last three years can broadly be categorized as 'Islamists' — proponents of an Islamic state where Sharia (Islamic law) would be enforced." The HRW report went on to state that in many cases, the security court "relied solely on the defendants' possession of CDs and books by fundamentalist clerics as 'evidence' of belonging to groups planning terrorist acts" and that the court

> has cast the net too wide in its prosecution of Islamists and has blurred the lines between holding or expressing fundamentalist religious opinions or beliefs (which is protected by international law) and actual acts which warrant being criminalized, such as involvement in violence.[18]

Syrian government repression of the country's Salafist community is further illustrated by the career of the well-known Syrian human rights lawyer Razan Zaitouneh. According to a former colleague, Zaitouneh was

> one of the team of lawyers representing regime opponents in court. The regime is most fearful of political Islam and the Kurds, so the majority of political prisoners in Syria are Islamists, who, like the Kurds, are treated particularly badly. Zaitouneh therefore also

defends Salafists, whose views she personally rejects. But like all prisoners, they have earned the right to a fair trial.[19]

As a result, most of the political prisoners languishing in Syria's prison system were Salafists, and it was Salafists who suffered the most at the hands of the internal security apparatus. As detailed below, it was therefore Salafists who were at the forefront of the anti-government protests erupting in 2011, Salafists who fought in the earliest armed groups later known as the Free Syrian Army (FSA), and Salafists who comprised the majority of political prisoners whose release was a principal demand of opposition activists.

Jihadi University

Not only Syria but also Iraq provided a reservoir of Salafist militants that U.S. and Saudi planners could draw from to execute regime change in Syria. This included former detainees of the U.S.-run prison, Camp Bucca. The prison, located near the southern Iraqi city of Basra, held some 26,000 detainees at its height in 2007. According to Lt. Col. Kenneth Plowman, a spokesman for Task Force 134 which ran the prison, al-Qaeda members (who by that time referred to their organization as the Islamic State of Iraq, or ISI, which was the predecessor to ISIS) were effectively functioning as a gang within the camp's walls. Islamic State militants ran "jail house Sharia courts... despite the presence of U.S. guards, to enforce an extreme interpretation of Islamic law. They were then used to convict moderate inmates, who were then tortured or killed."[20]

In 2008, Marine Major General Douglas Stone was tasked with running Bucca. He concluded that the prison had become a "jihadi university," giving the al-Qaeda leadership the opportunity to recruit, organize, and plan within the prison. General Stone conducted extensive screening to identify which prisoners did not pose a security threat and could be released, and which were extremists, or "takfiris," that should be isolated from the broader prison population. He estimated that one third, or roughly 8,000, constituted "genuinely continuing and imperative security risks."[21]

An Islamic State member held in Bucca later told *The Guardian*:

> We had so much time to sit and plan... It was the perfect environment. We all agreed to get together when we got out. The way to reconnect was easy. We wrote each other's details on the elastic of our boxer shorts. When we got out, we called. Everyone who was important to me was written on white elastic. I had their phone

numbers, their villages. By 2009, many of us were back doing what we did before we were caught. But this time we were doing it better.[22]

The Great Prison Release

Islamic State militants were by this time "doing it better" because of what Craig Whiteside of the U.S. Naval War College dubbed the "Great Prison Release of 2009." That year, 5,700 detainees were released from Bucca. Whiteside writes that "an unknown number of these men were destined to return to [the Islamic State of Iraq], to execute operations as part of cells assembled during their time in Bucca." Whiteside, himself a former U.S. Army infantry officer and Iraq War veteran, was puzzled by the release plan, which did not meet the usual preconditions for the early release of prisoners after a conflict, including that the "population must support the release." He notes that support for the release of these militants was likely low, even among Iraq's Sunnis, given that the country's Sunni tribes had formed the Awakening Movement to fight al-Qaeda alongside U.S. forces two years before. Whiteside notes further:

> The United States is often unjustly blamed for many things that are wrong in this world, but the revitalization of ISIL [ISIS] and its incubation in our own Camp Bucca is something that Americans truly own… The Iraqi government has many enemies, and the United States helped put many of them out on the street in 2009. Why?[23]

Those released from Bucca in 2009 included many of the Islamic State's most prominent future leaders, including ISIS Caliph Abu Bakr al-Baghdadi, who was first detained there in 2004. *The Independent* reported in 2014 that, according to the terrorism analyst firm the Soufan Group:

> In all, nine members of the Islamic State's top command did time at Bucca… Apart from Baghdadi himself, who spent five years there, the leader's number two, Abu Muslim al-Turkmani, as well as senior military leader Haji Bakr (now deceased) and leader of foreign fighters Abu Qasim, were incarcerated there.[24]

The Soufan Group's claim that Baghdadi was held for five years starting in 2004 means that he was released by U.S. officials in 2009. A guard at the camp, U.S. Army Colonel Kenneth King, confirmed that Baghdadi was released at this time. Colonel King explained in 2014 that he recalled the day of Baghdadi's 2009 release, and that Baghdadi had jokingly told him, "I'll see you guys in New York." Anonymous U.S. officials tried to discredit King's claim, asserting that Baghdadi was released from Bucca no later than 2006.

This was likely to limit the embarrassment of such an admission, given that Baghdadi was by then the most notorious terrorist in the world. However, Colonel King insisted, "I know my detainees as well as my guards... I could be mistaken... but I'm 99 percent. He's a dead ringer for the guy I had the run-in with... His face is very familiar."[25]

Baghdadi's later successor as head of ISIS, Abdullah Qardash, known in the organization as Abu Ibrahim al-Hashimi al-Qurashi, was also held in Camp Bucca and released in 2009. BBC journalist Feras Kelani writes that in early 2008, U.S. forces raided Qardash's residence in Mosul and arrested him, and that for months, Qardash was subjected to intense interrogation by the Americans, some of which Kelani gained access to through Iraqi intelligence. Kelani explains further that "Qardash also told his captors he was chosen as a deputy to the emir, Abu Omar al-Baghdadi," but that in 2009, "Qardash was released under unclear circumstances."[26]

Shockingly, Kelani's reporting makes clear that U.S. officials released Qardash despite clear awareness that he was the deputy emir to then Islamic State leader Abu Omar al-Baghdadi (the predecessor to Abu Bakr al-Baghdadi), as their own interrogation transcripts indicate. It therefore cannot be said that U.S. officials released Qardash due to ignorance of his membership and importance in the organization.

Abu Muhammad al-Adnani was another prominent future ISIS leader held in Bucca. Adnani fought against U.S. forces. He was captured and then detained at Bucca in 2005 but then released by U.S. officials in 2010. Adnani went on to become the official spokesman for ISIS, announcing the establishment of the so-called Caliphate in 2014, and then became head of its Emni division, which recruited, trained, and dispatched ISIS operatives to carry out attacks abroad, including in Paris and Brussels.[27]

Abu Muhammad al-Jolani, the future leader of the al-Qaeda affiliate in Syria, the Nusra Front, was also among those Islamic State leaders held in Camp Bucca. He was detained in 2006 and released by U.S. officials in 2008. After his release, Jolani was appointed head of Islamic State operations in Mosul Province and in August 2011 was dispatched to Syria by Abu Bakr al-Baghdadi to establish the Nusra Front.[28]

Planting Flowers

The folly of releasing Camp Bucca's most dangerous prisoners was immediately apparent to Iraqi officials. In March 2009, *Washington Post* journalist Anthony Shadid visited the town of Garma, some 16 kilometers from Fallujah, a former al-Qaeda stronghold in Anbar Province. Shadid asked the local police chief about the nature of the released detainees. The police chief replied that when these men were detained, they "weren't planting flowers in a garden. They weren't strolling down the street." The police chief admitted to being overwhelmed by the return of hundreds of former Bucca inmates to the area, while estimating that 90 percent would return to the fight. The deputy police chief in Garma noted that the one-time driver of former al-Qaeda in Iraq leader Abu Musab al-Zarqawi was among those who had been released, and had already carried out a car bomb attack that had killed 15. An Iraqi Ministry of Interior official further told Shadid that "Al-Qaeda is preparing itself for the departure of the Americans. And they want to stage a revolution."[29]

The "Great Prison Release of 2009" was followed by the escape of several additional top al-Qaeda leaders from another U.S. prison, Camp Cropper, near Baghdad International Airport, in two separate incidents in 2010. Circumstances surrounding the events in both cases suggest that the al-Qaeda militants didn't escape, but rather were deliberately released by U.S. officials.

In July 2010, Camp Cropper was handed over to Iraqi officials and renamed Karkh Prison. Five days later, four Islamic State members escaped, including the organization's justice minister, finance minister, and interior minister. The prison's warden, Omar Hamadi, disappeared as well, suggesting that he facilitated the escape from the otherwise highly secure prison simply by driving the detainees out of the gates in his car.[30]

This was suspicious because U.S. officials had insisted that Hamadi, who had worked with the U.S. military since 2006, be appointed warden. Martin Chulov of *The Guardian* reported that Hamadi was "a protégé of the American taskforces who had run the jail" and that, according to the Iraqi justice minister, "we were surprised by this man... We were told that we could trust him."[31]

Despite the handover of the prison to Iraqi officials, the U.S. military still maintained control of a maximum-security section of the prison, known as Compound 5, holding some 200 of the most dangerous and high-value detainees in the country. In September 2010, four additional Islamic State members inexplicably escaped from this U.S.-controlled section of Karkh. The AP reports that an Iraqi military spokesman said the Americans had notified them of the escape, but that "it was not clear exactly when or how they escaped." A U.S. military spokesman "confirmed there was an escape, but provided no details."[32]

Such prison releases were crucial because the Islamic State had been all but defeated by 2010. But after their release by U.S. officials, these Islamic State leaders were able to resurrect the notorious terror organization. CIA Director John Brennan acknowledged the near death and subsequent revival of the Islamic State. Brennan explained in 2015 that ISIS

> had its roots in al-Qaida in Iraq. It was, you know, pretty much decimated when U.S. forces were there in Iraq. It had maybe 700-or-so adherents left. And then it grew quite a bit in the last several years, when it split then from al-Qaida in Syria, and set up its own organization.[33]

With the dramatic rise of ISIS in Syria in 2014, the *New York Times* acknowledged the U.S. role in incubating the ISIS leadership in its own prisons but claimed that this was inadvertent. The *NYT* wrote that ISIS leader Baghdadi had indeed been held at Bucca, but that the United States had only "*unintentionally* created the conditions ripe for training a new generation of insurgents" (emphasis added).[34]

Even if the U.S. actions which incubated the Islamic State leadership in U.S. prisons were unintentional, the release of these Islamic State militants in 2009–10 was not.

As mentioned above, Saudi Prince Bandar bin Sultan had assured his U.S. counterparts that he controlled Salafist militant groups in the region ("We've created this movement, and we can control it"), and that these groups could be directed against the U.S. and Israel's enemies: Iran, Syria, and Hezbollah. For Prince Bandar to reconstitute an essentially defeated Islamic State organization and unleash it in the direction of Syria, a large-scale release of U.S.-held al-Qaeda prisoners of the sort seen in 2009–10 would have been needed. In other words, the Islamic State leaders released by U.S. planners would be used to "stage a revolution" — but one which would begin in Syria, rather than Iraq.

Firing Up the Old Sunni Network

Evidence that the resurrected Islamic State in Iraq was preparing an operation to topple the Syrian government comes from a 2012 U.S. Defense Intelligence Agency (DIA) memo which noted that "AQI [al-Qaeda in Iraq] supported the Syrian opposition *from the beginning*, both ideologically and through the media. AQI declared its opposition of Assad's government because it considered it a sectarian regime targeting Sunnis" (emphasis added).[35] The document notes further that AQI spokesman Abu Muhammad al-Adnani (released from Bucca in 2010 as noted above) "declared the Syrian regime as the spearhead of what he is naming Jibha al Ruwafidh [Forefront of the Shiites] because of its [the Syrian regime's] declaration of war on the Sunnis."

A better translation of *Jibhat al-Ruwafidh* is the "Front of the Rejectionists," with "rejectionist" being a derogatory reference to Shiites. The "Front of the Rejectionists" identified by AQI spokesman Adnani paralleled the "Shiite Crescent," namely the alliance between Iran, Syria, and Hezbollah, which was feared by U.S., Israeli, and Saudi planners. The interests of the U.S., its allies, and AQI were at this time aligned, making cooperation against the Syrian government beneficial for all.

The DIA document notes further:

> AQI had major pockets and bases on both sides of the [Iraq-Syria] border to facilitate the flow of materiel and recruits. There was a regression of AQI in the western provinces of Iraq during the years 2009 and 2010. However, after the rise of the insurgency in Syria, the religious and tribal powers in the regions began to sympathize with the sectarian uprising. This (sympathy) appeared in Friday prayer sermons, which called for volunteers to support the Sunnis in Syria.[36]

In other words, before the eruption of protests in March 2011, the infrastructure was in place (i.e., pockets and bases on both sides of the border to facilitate the flow of materiel and recruits) for al-Qaeda to launch an anti-government insurgency in Syria.

American journalist Theo Padnos, who was kidnapped and then held hostage by the Nusra Front for two years, pointed to al-Qaeda's preparations to launch a "revolution" in Syria before the eruption of protests as well, in this case by sending fighters into Syria.

After the Islamic State of Iraq and Nusra Front formally split and became rivals in 2013, with the Islamic State of Iraq becoming ISIS, Padnos was often held in cells with ISIS militants captured by Nusra. Padnos explained that the

> ISIS commanders and foot soldiers with whom I was sometimes imprisoned believed that their leaders, directing matters from planning rooms in Anbar Province in Iraq, dispatched fighters into Syria in late 2010, long before any child in Deraa scrawled his graffiti on a schoolyard wall.[37]

Padnos explained further that, "in probably late 2010, before all the demonstrations in Deraa, at the very beginning of things, before the beginning of things, they made this point to me often, they came into Syria in order to destroy the country."[38]

This means that, rather than simply supporting the so-called revolution in Syria as the DIA memo suggests, al-Qaeda actively helped to spark it.

The early military involvement of al-Qaeda fighters in the so-called Syrian Revolution is further confirmed by the fact that the first declared armed group to begin fighting the Syrian government was Harakat Ahrar al-Sham al-Islamiya, or "the Islamic Movement of the Free Men of Sham," which enjoyed an early endorsement from the global al-Qaeda leadership, presumed at that time to be in Pakistan.

Rania Abouzeid of *Time* magazine reported that according to one fighter from the group, the Ahrar al-Sham leadership "started working on forming brigades 'after the Egyptian revolution'... *well before March 15, 2011*, when the Syrian revolution kicked off with protests in the southern agricultural city of Daraa" (emphasis added).[39]

Writing in the Lebanese *As-Safir*, journalist Abdullah Suleiman Ali also indicates that Ahrar al-Sham was active in the early months of the uprising. He reports that according to his source within the group, a number of foreign fighters, "including Saudis, were in Syria as the Ahrar al-Sham movement was emerging, i.e., since May 2011." Suleiman Ali notes that these Saudi fighters joined Ahrar al-Sham during this early period based on recommendations from senior al-Qaeda figures, and that longtime al-Qaeda operative and former Fighting Vanguard member Abu Khalid al-Suri played an important role in establishing the group.[40]

Ayman al-Zawahiri, the global al-Qaeda leader, later named al-Suri as his representative in Syria. Al-Suri attempted to mediate the dispute between the Nusra Front and ISIS at the time the two al-Qaeda groups split. Al-Suri had previously been a courier for Osama bin Laden in Afghanistan, and Spanish officials allege that he received surveillance tapes of the World Trade Center from the operative who made the videos and delivered them to al-Qaeda's senior leadership in Afghanistan.[41]

Ahrar al-Sham's connection to Zawahiri and the global al-Qaeda leadership was further noted by opposition activist and later McClatchy journalist Mousab al-Hamadee, who explained: "One of my friends who is now a rebel leader told me that the moment the group announced itself in

2011 it got a big bag of money sent directly from Ayman al-Zawahiri, the leader of al Qaida."[42]

Saudis constituted the largest contingent of foreign militants fighting for al-Qaeda in Iraq and were among the prisoners released by U.S. forces from Iraqi prisons in 2009–10. This means that Abu Khalid al-Suri would have likely turned to this pool of Saudi fighters in Iraq to establish Ahrar al-Sham during this early period. Abdullah Suleiman Ali reports further that "it is likely that the influx of Saudi jihadists into Syria began with the start of the crisis there." This likely included Saudis entering Syria from Saudi Arabia itself, rather than just from Iraq.[43]

Shortly after Ahrar al-Sham was established, Bush administration official and neoconservative John Hannah alluded to Bandar's control of a Sunni militant network, and the utility this network could provide to U.S. planners. Hannah wrote in *Foreign Policy* on April 22, 2011, of the possibility that "the [Saudi] Kingdom might once again fire up the old Sunni network and point it in the general direction of Shiite Iran," and that

> Bandar working without reference to U.S. interests is clearly cause for concern. But Bandar working as a partner with Washington against a common Iranian enemy is a major strategic asset. Drawing on Saudi resources and prestige, Bandar's ingenuity and bent for bold action could be put to excellent use across the region in ways that reinforce U.S. policy and interests: through economic and political measures that weaken the Iranian mullahs; undermine the Assad regime.[44]

'We Have a Liberal Attitude'

Another reservoir of al-Qaeda-affiliated militants to be leveraged by U.S. planners was in Lebanon. Seymour Hersh notes that according to a 2005 International Crisis Group (ICG) report, pro-Saudi Lebanese politician Saad Hariri (son of the assassinated Prime Minister Rafiq Hariri) had helped release four Salafist militants from prison who had previously trained in al-Qaeda camps in Afghanistan and were arrested in Lebanon while trying to establish an Islamic state in the north of the country. Hariri also used his influence in parliament to obtain amnesty for another 29 Salafist militants, including seven suspected of bombing foreign embassies in Beirut the year before. Hersh notes that according to a senior official in the Lebanese government, "we have a liberal attitude that allows Al Qaeda types to have a presence here."[45]

Charles Harb of the American University of Beirut similarly observed in May 2007 that Saad Hariri was giving "political cover" to "radical Sunni movements." He explains that in order to attract Sunni voters in the 2005 national parliamentary elections, Hariri had "pardoned jailed Sunni militants involved in violence in December 2000." Harb also warned that "courting radical Sunni sentiment is a dangerous game," while noting the involvement of Saudi intelligence in cultivating these groups. He explained that "several reports have highlighted efforts by Saudi officials to strengthen Sunni groups, including radical ones, to face the Shia renaissance across the region. But building up radical Sunni groups to face the Shia challenge can easily backfire."[46]

Harb was writing in response to the eruption of violence in the Nahr al-Bared Palestinian refugee camp on May 19, 2007. The camp, located in northern Lebanon, had been occupied by militants from the al-Qaeda-affiliated group Fatah al-Islam. Fighting had erupted between the militants and members of the Lebanese security forces, allegedly after an attempted bank robbery. The fighting continued for months, leaving the camp almost entirely flattened and its Palestinian refugee population homeless.

Two months before the outbreak of violence in Nahr al-Bared, the *New York Times* had interviewed Fatah al-Islam's leader Shakir al-Abssi, a former associate of Abu Musab al-Zarqawi. The *NYT* reports that, "despite being on terrorism watch lists around the world, he has set himself up in a Palestinian refugee camp where, because of Lebanese politics, he is largely shielded from the government."[47] Major General Achraf Rifi, general director of Lebanon's Internal Security Forces, told the *NYT* that to enter the camp and detain al-Abssi, "we would need an agreement from other Arab countries."[48] In other words, Abssi was being shielded by Saad Hariri and Saudi intelligence.

As will be discussed further below, Salafist militants from Lebanon, including militants from Fatah al-Islam, flooded across the border in 2011 to join the U.S.-backed war against the Syrian government.

The British Connection

Britain provided another reservoir of al-Qaeda-linked militants who could be deployed to effect regime change in Syria on behalf of U.S. planners, courtesy of their counterparts in British intelligence.

This is not surprising, given that Britain has long served as a haven for al-Qaeda-affiliated jihadist groups. *The Guardian* reports that "[Osama] bin Laden's British connection dates back to the early 1990s, when he founded a London-based group, the Advisory and Reform Committee, that distributed literature against the Saudi regime."[49] Academic Christopher Davidson details early British support for al-Qaeda in his book *Shadow Wars* (2016). Davidson notes, for example — per New York federal court documents indicting bin Laden for carrying out 9/11 — that bin Laden visited the U.K. personally and considered applying for asylum there; meanwhile, his London office

> was designed both to publicize the statements of Osama bin Laden and to provide a cover for activity in support of al-Qaeda's "military activities," including the *recruitment of military trainees* [emphasis added], the disbursement of funds and the procurement of necessary equipment including satellite telephones and necessary services.[50]

Prominent jihadist theoreticians who lived in the U.K. for extensive periods in the 1990s included Abu Qatada al-Filistini, Abu Musab al-Suri, and Abd al-Hakim Belhaj.

Abu Qatada al-Filistini, known as "al-Qaeda's spiritual ambassador to Europe," received asylum in Britain in 1994 after leaving Pakistan, and became a prominent supporter and fundraiser for jihadist causes around the world, including in Algeria and Chechnya. According to Raffaello Pantucci of the International Institute for Strategic Studies (IISS) in London, Abu Qatada faced an "apparent litany of allegations by continental European intelligence services" of involvement in terror plots, including in Jordan where he was sentenced to life imprisonment *in absentia*. Abu Qatada nevertheless enjoyed haven in Britain and was long suspected of having links with British intelligence, including providing assurances that no terror attacks would occur in Britain.[51]

Abu Musab al-Suri, a Syrian known as the "architect of global jihad," also confirmed to prominent Palestinian journalist Abd al-Bari Atwan that "a tacit covenant was in place between MI6 [British intelligence] and the extremists," which allowed them haven in Britain during this period.[52]

Al-Suri was born in Aleppo and joined the Muslim Brotherhood while a student. He then rose to become a member of the Brotherhood's military command al-Talia al-Muqatila, or "the Fighting Vanguard," as the group fought the Syrian government at Hama in 1982. Al-Suri is implicated in the train bombings in Madrid in 2004 and London in 2005, as well as in helping to shape Abu Musab al-Zarqawi's terror campaign in Iraq.[53]

Abd al-Hakim Belhaj was the founder of the al-Qaeda-affiliated Libyan Islamic Fighting Group (LIFG). In his book *Secret Affairs: Britain's Collusion with Radical Islam* (2012), journalist Mark Curtis explains that Belhaj formed the LIFG in 1990 in Afghanistan with 500 Libyan jihadists then fighting the Soviet-backed Afghan government. The LIFG then went on to fight with the Armed Islamic Group (GIA) against the Algerian government as well, before turning their attention back home to Libya to topple President Moammar Qaddafi. According to the British Home Office, the LIFG's "aim had been to overthrow the Qaddafi regime and replace it with an Islamic State," while the U.S. government described the LIFG as an "al-Qaeda affiliate known for engaging in terrorist activity in Libya and cooperating with al-Qaeda worldwide."

Curtis reports further that in 1996, British intelligence partnered with the LIFG in a failed assassination attempt against Qaddafi, and that prominent members of the LIFG were allowed to establish a base for logistical support and fundraising in Britain. Curtis notes that the group's communiques calling for the overthrow of the Libyan government were issued from London, where several prominent LIFG members, including Belhaj, were living after having received political asylum.[54]

Another prominent Islamic extremist living in London in the 1990s was the exiled Syrian cleric Muhammad Sarour Zein al-Abbedine. Writing for the Combating Terrorism Center at West Point, Raffaello Pantucci writes that Muhammad Sarour was

> one of the more under-reported but highly important figures to have emerged from the United Kingdom… A British passport holder, Surur was based in the United Kingdom for almost two decades after moving there in the 1980s… A former Muslim Brotherhood activist, Surur was an innovator in Salafist thinking and established with his followers the Center for Islamic Studies in Birmingham, from where he published magazines and later ran the alsunnah.org website.[55]

Muhammad Sarour was infamous for writing, under a pseudonym, the book *Then Came the Turn of the Majus*, which later inspired al-Qaeda in Iraq leader Zarqawi to call for genocide against Iraq's Shia population.[56]

As will be discussed below, Sarour and his followers later played a prominent, though often unacknowledged, role in the early protest movement that erupted in Syria in 2011, including in Daraa.[57] Pantucci notes for example that, according to journalist Malik al-Abdeh, Sarour would later establish "himself as one of the key conduits for Qatari money to the anti-Assad rebels."[58]

Convoys of Murder

Mark Curtis also detailed the role played by U.S. and U.K. intelligence in dispatching young men from Britain's Salafist community to fight in the war in Bosnia in the early 1990s.[59] This was later acknowledged even in the mainstream U.K. press. In 2005, British Parliament Member (MP) Michael Meacher wrote in *The Guardian*:

> During the Soviet occupation of Afghanistan in the 1980s, the U.S. funded large numbers of jihadists through Pakistan's secret intelligence service, the ISI. Later the U.S. wanted to raise another jihadi corps, again using proxies, to help Bosnian Muslims fight to weaken the Serb government's hold on Yugoslavia. Those they turned to included Pakistanis in Britain.[60]

British jihadi recruits and weapons were smuggled into Bosnia under the pretext of humanitarian aid efforts, specifically through so-called "convoys of mercy." In one notable case, British-Pakistani and London School of Economics graduate Omar Saeed Sheikh joined an aid convoy to Bosnia, which he acknowledged in his journal was for "organising clandestine support for the Muslim fighters."[61] Upon reaching the Croatian port town of Split near the Bosnian border, Sheikh joined a jihadist group called the Harakut-ul-Mujaheddin (HUM) and was sent to Pakistan for training. Sheikh was later convicted of kidnapping *Wall Street Journal* reporter Daniel Pearl in Pakistan. Pearl was beheaded, and his death was captured on video.[62] As noted by *The Guardian*, Sheikh also wired $100,000 to 9/11 hijacker Muhammad Atta, allegedly at the behest of Pakistan's intelligence service.[63]

In the late 1990s, British intelligence also dispatched British-Pakistani jihadis to Kosovo under the cover of humanitarian convoys to continue the war against Serbia. MP Meacher writes further:

> For nearly a decade the U.S. helped Islamist insurgents linked to Chechnya, Iran, and Saudi Arabia destabilise the former Yugoslavia. The insurgents were also allowed to move further east to Kosovo...

> The former U.S. federal prosecutor John Loftus reported that British intelligence had used the al-Muhajiroun group in London to recruit Islamist militants with British passports for the war against the Serbs in Kosovo.[64]

The al-Muhajiroun group was established in 1996 in Britain by exiled Syrian cleric Omar Bakri Mohammed, who, as journalist Nafeez Ahmed details, was a longtime informant for Britain's domestic intelligence service, meeting regularly with his handlers throughout the 1990s.[65] Bakri himself acknowledged his role in training jihadists to be dispatched abroad. He explained to *The Guardian* in May 2000 that al-Muhajiroun has a network of centers around the world, divided into two wings: "There is the da'wah (propagation) network, and there is the jihad network." *The Guardian* noted that Bakri "admitted that there is a global network of agents with connections to the military camps, some of whom work from Britain."[66]

Reflecting on this period, Mark Curtis observed that:

> London had by [1998] become, along with Taliban-controlled Afghanistan which housed bin Laden, the principal administrative centre for global jihad, where authorities were, at the very least, turning a blind eye to terrorist activities launched from their soil.[67]

Muhajiroun founder Bakri left Britain for Lebanon one month after the 7/7 attacks, in which suicide bombers targeted the London transit system, killing 52, on July 7, 2005. Although former Muhajiroun members participated in the attack, British officials strangely allowed Bakri to leave Britain, while banning him from returning to the country. By 2009, Lebanese security forces were accusing Bakri of training al-Qaeda members, while Bakri himself boasted, "Today, angry Lebanese Sunnis ask me to organize their jihad against the Shi'ites... Al-Qaeda in Lebanon... are the only ones who can defeat Hezbollah."[68]

Leadership of the Muhajiroun movement was taken over in Bakri's absence by Anjem Choudary, who subsequently founded various related front groups, including Islam4UK, Sharia4UK, al-Ghurabaa, and Sharia4Belgium, which later sent many Belgian jihadis to fight in Syria after 2011.[69]

According to Nick Lowles, chief executive of anti-racist organization "Hope not hate," Choudary "has influenced some of the most well-known terrorists of the last decade and he has helped to send British and European Muslims to war zones around the world to engage in jihad," and also has links to major international terrorist groups, including al-Shabaab in Somalia and Ansar al-Islam, the northern Iraq group which is affiliated with al-Qaeda. Choudary was bizarrely promoted as a credible voice representing Islam in the British press, suggesting links of his own to British intelligence. Choudary has appeared frequently on a wide range of television shows in the U.K., including the BBC's flagship *Newsnight* program, which led to widespread frustration among British Muslims, who complained that Choudary in no way represents mainstream Muslim opinion.[70] Choudary has been promoted in the U.S. press as well, making appearances on Fox News to give an allegedly Muslim perspective on controversial events involving terrorism, including the Charlie Hebdo attacks in Paris.[71]

Despite his links to terrorist groups over many years, Choudary was not convicted on terrorism charges by U.K. authorities until 2016, after expressing support for ISIS in private social media conversations and online sermons. He was released from prison in 2018.[72]

Seek and Destroy

In 2009, the same year al-Muhajiroun's Omar Bakri Mohammed was training al-Qaeda militants in Lebanon and U.S. planners were helping to resurrect al-Qaeda in Iraq via prison releases, former French Foreign Minister Roland Dumas was told by top British officials that "they were preparing something in Syria… Britain was organizing an invasion of rebels into Syria." Dumas continued, "They even asked me, although I was no longer minister for foreign affairs, if I would like to participate." When asked why the British would undertake such a plan, Dumas responded, "Very simple! With the very simple aim! To overthrow the Syrian government, because in the region, it's important to understand, that the Syrian regime makes anti-Israeli talk." Dumas further claimed that he had previously been told by an Israeli prime minister that the Israelis would "seek to 'destroy' any country that did not 'get along' with it in the region."[73]

It is doubtful that U.K. planners would undertake such a project without guidance from their U.S. counterparts. This suggests that U.K. efforts to organize "an invasion of rebels into Syria" was part of the broader U.S. effort to promote regime change in the country. Dumas did not indicate, or perhaps did not know, who exactly would constitute the so-called rebels that would invade Syria. It appears, however, that British officials speaking to Dumas were referring to militants from both the LIFG and al-Muhajiroun, given the groups' long histories of cooperation with British intelligence.

However, this British "rebel army" of the LIFG and al-Muhajiroun was first dispatched not to Syria, but to Libya, at the start of the so-called Arab Spring in 2011.

LIFG activities had been harshly curbed by British authorities in 2004 after the "Deal in the Desert" between then British Prime Minister Tony Blair and President Qaddafi led to a rapprochement between the two countries. The British government then placed the LIFG on its terror list in 2005 and assisted in the rendition of two senior LIFG leaders, Abd al-Hakim

Belhaj and Sami al-Saadi, to Libya. The British security services allowed other LIFG members to remain in the U.K. but placed them under surveillance, house arrest, or detention.[74]

But British foreign policy regarding Libya pivoted once again in 2011. Middle East Eye (MEE) quotes Ziad Hashem, an LIFG member granted asylum in Britain: "When the revolution started, things changed in Britain."

MEE reports further that "the British government operated an 'open door' policy that allowed Libyan exiles and British-Libyan citizens to join the 2011 uprising that toppled Muammar Qaddafi." LIFG members under counterterrorism control orders in Britain were allowed to travel to Libya with "no questions asked," and many had their passports returned to them for this purpose. One British-Libyan speaking with MEE explained:

> These were old school LIFG guys, they [the British authorities] knew what they were doing… The whole Libyan diaspora were out there fighting alongside the rebel groups.

> [Another] described how he had carried out "PR work" for the rebels in the months before Qaddafi was overthrown and eventually killed in October 2011. He said he was employed to edit videos showing Libyan rebels being trained by former British SAS and Irish special forces mercenaries in Benghazi, the eastern city from where the uprising against Qaddafi was launched.[75]

LIFG leader Belhaj had himself been released from prison by Libyan authorities in 2010 as part of a reconciliation deal arranged by Qaddafi's son, Saif al-Islam.[76] With the start of the U.K.-backed Islamist insurgency in 2011, Belhaj commanded the Tripoli Brigade, which played a key role in toppling the Libyan government on behalf of NATO, spearheading the ground assault on the Libyan capital.[77]

The Tripoli Brigade was itself formed by Mahdi al-Herati, who lived for 20 years in exile in Ireland, and had fought against U.S. occupation forces in Iraq in 2003. Herati returned to Libya from Ireland at the outset of anti-government protests in February 2011 and partnered with his Irish-born brother-in-law Husan al-Najar and other Libyan exiles to organize the Tripoli Brigade.[78] According to fellow anti-government fighters, Herati's group received assistance from French, Qatari, and CIA intelligence officers.[79] As mentioned above, Irish special forces mercenaries were on the ground in Benghazi, suggesting that Herati and his fighters were among them.

Once the NATO-backed LIFG campaign to topple Qaddafi in 2011 was successful, many of these same Libyan exiles, including Herati and al-Najar, were dispatched to fight in Syria, as will be discussed in Chapter 10.[80]

3. Astroturfing 'Revolution'

Neoconservatives Embrace 'Non-Violence'

In addition to supporting opposition politicians and al-Qaeda-affiliated militants, U.S. planners also funded and trained a network of political and media activists to agitate for regime change in Syria by organizing protests and producing anti-government propaganda.

The *Washington Post* reported in April 2011:

> The State Department has secretly financed Syrian political opposition groups and related projects, including a satellite TV channel that beams anti-government programming into the country, according to previously undisclosed diplomatic cables. The London-based satellite channel, Barada TV, began broadcasting in April 2009 but has ramped up operations to cover the mass protests in Syria as part of a long-standing campaign to overthrow the country's autocratic leader, Bashar al-Assad. Barada TV is closely affiliated with the Movement for Justice and Development [MJD], a London-based network of Syrian exiles. Classified U.S. diplomatic cables show that the State Department has funneled as much as $6 million to the group since 2006 to operate the satellite channel and finance other activities inside Syria.
>
> [The MJD], which is banned in Syria, openly advocates for Assad's removal. U.S. cables describe its leaders as "liberal, moderate Islamists" who are former members of the Muslim Brotherhood.[1]

This suggests that the MJD was a Muslim Brotherhood front group created to receive U.S. funding. The *Wall Street Journal* reported in 2007, for example:

> The U.S. has traditionally avoided contact with the Brotherhood across the Middle East. But now the State Department and National Security Council have begun to hold regular strategy sessions on Syria policy with the NSF and is funding an organization *linked to it*.[2] (emphasis added)

As noted in Chapter 2, the National Salvation Front (NSF) was an opposition coalition founded in part by the Muslim Brotherhood.

The founder and director of Barada TV was Ausama Monajed, who was also director of public relations for the MJD. In 2008, Monajed attended a "Syria in Transition" conference in Washington, D.C., as well as a luncheon with President Bush where he was photographed with Secretary of State Condoleezza Rice. Monajed later partnered with journalist Michael Weiss of the Henry Jackson Society (HJS), a neoconservative British think tank, to produce reports advocating U.S. military intervention in Syria. The HJS counts various prominent American neoconservatives among its patrons, including Richard Perle, former CIA Director James Woolsey, and Project for a New American Century (PNAC) founders and Iraq War advocates William Kristol and Robert Kagan.[3]

The connection between U.S. financing of "activities inside Syria" and regime change was tacitly acknowledged by U.S. officials themselves. The *Washington Post* noted further that the leaked cables "show that U.S. Embassy officials in Damascus became worried in 2009 when they learned that Syrian intelligence agents were raising questions about U.S. programs," and that Syrian authorities "would undoubtedly view any U.S. funds going to illegal political groups as tantamount to supporting regime change."[4]

The *Post* reports as well that much of the funding for Syrian opposition groups discussed in the cable, including the MJD, was provided via the Middle East Partnership Initiative (MEPI), a program established by neoconservative members of the Bush administration in 2004, and overseen by Vice President Cheney's daughter Liz, who held the post of Deputy Assistant Secretary of State for Near Eastern Affairs.[5] As mentioned in Chapter 2, these activities were coordinated through the Iran Syria Policy and Operations Group (ISOG).

Syrian opposition activists received training specifically from the Center for Applied Nonviolent Action and Strategies (CANVAS). The center was founded by U.S.-funded Serbian activists from a group called Otpor, who had helped to overthrow Slobodan Milošević in 2000.[6] At that time, Otpor activists were trained through a State Department program run out of the U.S. embassy in Hungary using philosophies of non-violence adapted from the teachings of academic Gene Sharp.[7]

Otpor co-founder Srdja Popovic had close ties with U.S. planners, having attended a December 2009 National Security Council meeting to discuss events in Iran. Popovic also gathered intelligence for Stratfor, the private intelligence firm that bills itself as a "Shadow CIA" that provides services to corporate clients including the American Petroleum Institute, Archer Daniels Midland, Dow Chemical, Duke Energy, Northrop Grumman, Intel, and Coca-Cola. A Stratfor analyst who worked with Popovic described how activists from Otpor "basically go around the world trying to topple dictators and autocratic governments (ones that U.S. does not like)."[8]

MJD public relations director Ausama Monajed was apparently among those Syrian activists trained at CANVAS. In April 2011, just after the outbreak of protests in Syria, Al Jazeera reported that Monajed was

> inspired by the writings of University of Massachusetts professor Gene Sharp on non-violent struggle against totalitarian systems, and by the Serbian pro-democracy movement that brought down Slobodan Milošević. He now runs a team of volunteers in Europe and the U.S. lobbying policy makers to pressure the Syrian regime and publishes a daily digest of news and videos on the protest movement gathered from inside the country.[9]

As will be discussed below, Monajed and his team of volunteers (i.e., Muslim Brotherhood activists) controlled the Syrian Revolution 2011 Facebook page that was crucial in organizing early anti-government protests.

The Sugar Daddy of Overt Operations

Similar training programs were also organized for activists in Egypt, providing a further window into the type of support Syrian opposition activists like Monajed received. The *New York Times* reports that according to cables leaked by WikiLeaks, opposition activists in Egypt received training from organizations funded by both the National Endowment for Democracy (NED) and State Department.[10]

The NED has a long history of openly funding opposition groups in countries targeted by Washington for regime change. These overt activities often complement the largely covert activities of the CIA. *Washington Post* reporter David Ignatius described the NED in 1991 as the "sugar daddy of overt operations," while quoting NED co-founder Allen Weinstein who explained that "a lot of what we do today was done covertly 25 years ago by the CIA."[11]

The *New York Times* notes further:

> Some Egyptian youth leaders attended a 2008 technology meeting in New York, where they were taught to use social networking and mobile technologies to promote democracy. Among those sponsoring the meeting were Facebook, Google, MTV, Columbia Law School, and the State Department…

> Affiliating themselves with the American organizations may have tainted leaders within their own groups. According to one diplomatic cable, leaders of the April 6 Youth Movement in Egypt told the American Embassy in 2009 that some members of the group had accused Ahmed Maher, a leader of the January [2011] uprising, and other leaders of "treason" in a mock trial related to their association

with [State Department-funded] Freedom House, which more militant members of the movement described as a "Zionist organization."[12]

The 2008 technology meeting referenced by the *New York Times* was the Alliance for Youth Movements Summit, organized by State Department staffer Jared Cohen.[13] Cohen had been recruited to the State Department in 2006 and became an aide to then Secretary of State Condoleezza Rice, in part due to his insight that emerging technologies such as Bluetooth could be used in innovative ways by Iranian activists to bypass government surveillance and communication shutdowns, and that such technologies could play a role in political transitions (i.e., regime change).[14] Cohen came to this realization while traveling in Iran as part of a research trip in which he sought to interview Iranian opposition leaders, but ended up spending most of his time hanging out with young, tech-savvy Iranians.[15]

The Great Right Hope

When Barack Obama took office in January 2009, he appointed Hillary Clinton as secretary of state. Neoconservatives applauded Clinton's appointment due to her hawkish foreign policy views, calling her the "Great Right Hope," conservatives' "Woman in Washington."[16]

Under Clinton, the State Department remained a bastion of neoconservative hostility toward Syria within the broader U.S. foreign policy establishment. Lee Smith of *The Weekly Standard* wrote in 2010 that the Syrian government was "a regime that much of Washington loves to hate" and that "many of those who are most contemptuous of the Syrian regime are to be found in the State Department."[17] This included Assistant Secretary of State for Near Eastern Affairs Jeffrey Feltman, who as the Bush administration's ambassador to Lebanon from 2004 to 2008 became known as an anti-Iran and anti-Hezbollah hawk.[18] Feltman became a point man for the Obama administration's relations with Damascus and was viewed as a "hardliner" on Syria.[19]

As journalist Rania Khalek observed, Clinton's alliance with the neoconservative movement would grow over time and win her its strong support. During her 2016 presidential campaign, Clinton's outspoken neoconservative supporters included Iraq War architect Robert Kagan[20] and former Deputy CIA Director Michael Morell,[21] who praised Clinton for her hawkish stance on Syria. CIA support for Clinton is unsurprising, given that her husband, former President Bill Clinton, had close ties to the CIA

36

stretching back to at least the 1980s. As governor of Arkansas, Bill Clinton was involved in the CIA operation to transport weapons to the agency's proxy army, the Contras, that sought to terrorize Nicaraguan society and topple the socialist Sandinista government.[22]

Jared Cohen was one of the few members of Condoleezza Rice's State Department Policy Planning division retained by Secretary Clinton, and he continued to advise on policy in the Middle East. Cohen played a crucial behind-the-scenes role in helping Iranian opposition activists use emerging social media technology, in particular Twitter, to coordinate protests during the so-called Green Revolution in June 2009.[23] Some Iranian opposition activists had also been trained in Serbia by Otpor in non-violent tactics for regime change.[24]

Secretary Clinton bragged about the State Department's role in discreetly facilitating the protests, even though this undermined President Obama's policy of non-intervention in Iranian affairs at the time.[25] According to *Wall Street Journal* reporter Jay Solomon, Obama wished to engage Iran in talks for a deal to end its nuclear energy program, and had allegedly even ordered the CIA to sever its contacts with Iran's Green Movement supporters.[26]

Cables later released by WikiLeaks made clear that Obama and Clinton's differing views on intervention within Iran were simply tactical. The *New York Times* reported:

> When Mr. Obama took office, many allies feared that his offers of engagement would make him appear weak to the Iranians. But the cables show how Mr. Obama's aides quickly countered those worries by rolling out a plan to encircle Iran with economic sanctions and antimissile defenses. In essence, the administration expected its outreach to fail, but believed that it had to make a bona fide attempt in order to build support for tougher measures.

These "measures" included "an array of sanctions considerably harsher than any before attempted."[27]

By the time of the so-called Arab Spring in 2011, the Obama administration's obsession with regime change in Iran was made explicit. David Sanger of the *New York Times* noted in April 2011 that "containing Iran's power remains their central goal in the Middle East," and that "every decision — from Libya to Yemen to Bahrain to Syria — is being examined under the prism [of how to] slow Iran's nuclear progress, and *speed the arrival of opportunities for a successful uprising there*" (emphasis added).[28] Promoting regime change in Syria played a key role in such calculations because, "as some in Mr. Obama's war council have noted, *if protestors succeed in Syria, Iran could be next*" (emphasis added). Sanger notes further that the NATO bombing of Libya was undertaken in part to send a threatening message to Iran and to illustrate U.S. military capabilities to Iranian planners.

Regime Change at Heart

In his book *Surveillance Valley* (2018), journalist Yasha Levine details how U.S. planners facilitated the training of anti-government activists in Arab countries, Iran, and elsewhere during this period in the use of a privacy software called Tor. The concept upon which Tor was based was discovered by U.S. Navy researchers and developed into usable software by military contractor and U.S. intelligence agency consultant Roger Dingledine. The Tor project was spun off as a non-profit led by Dingledine, but by 2008 was still operating almost entirely on grants from the U.S. government, including from the Defense Advanced Research Projects Agency (DARPA), the Navy, the State Department, and the Broadcasting Board of Governors (BBG), an outgrowth of the CIA's propaganda arm.

In 2008, a hacker named Jacob Appelbaum joined Tor and was tasked with marketing the product to the broader hacker community and to cyber dissidents from countries viewed as U.S. enemies. For Tor to provide anonymity for elements of the U.S. intelligence services using the software, it was necessary that many unrelated users also employ Tor, whether they be hackers, criminals, drug dealers, or child pornographers. Ironically, Jacob Appelbaum's marketing campaign helped Tor gain credibility as a useful tool to fight U.S. government spying and privacy overreach, despite its U.S. government origins and funding, as did later endorsements from National Security Agency (NSA) whistleblower Edward Snowden, and from WikiLeaks founder Julian Assange, whose organization relied on the software to receive and disseminate leaked documents. Appelbaum and Assange met in 2005 and became good friends, with Appelbaum joining WikiLeaks in 2010 as its only member from the United States.

Appelbaum's association with WikiLeaks allowed him to obscure his activities on behalf of the U.S. government (even portraying himself as a victim of U.S. government surveillance and harassment) and to disassociate Tor in the public mind from its creators and ongoing funders in the U.S. military.

Internal Tor email communications obtained by Yasha Levine via FOIA request also show that Appelbaum and Dingledine passed on information about their relationship with WikiLeaks and the "inner workings of WikiLeaks's secure submission system" to their government handlers at the BBG. This information was presumably then passed on further to other government agencies who also had an interest in WikiLeaks's activities. Levine notes that "it's not clear whether Assange knew that Appelbaum's salary was being paid by the same government he [Assange] was trying to destroy."[29]

In December 2009, Appelbaum toured several countries in the Middle East to train activists in the use of Tor, including as part of an Arab Bloggers Workshop in Beirut.[30] Appelbaum attempted to visit Syria during this time as well, presumably for similar purposes, but was unsuccessful for unknown reasons.[31]

Appelbaum also visited U.S.-allied Qatar during the same trip to train employees from the state-owned Al Jazeera satellite channel in the use of the software.[32] The U.S. partnership with the Muslim Brotherhood discussed above naturally extended to partnering with Al Jazeera, which was widely regarded as a Brotherhood mouthpiece due to the Qatari monarchy's support for the group.[33] As mentioned in Chapter 1, Al Jazeera was a source of anti-Shia propaganda meant to create sectarian divisions in Syria.

The U.S. partnership with Al Jazeera later became explicitly evident when a 2012 email from Jared Cohen (by that time at Google) to Hillary Clinton was leaked by WikiLeaks. Cohen informed Clinton of a tool that Google had developed to track defections from the Syrian government, and that Google had partnered with Al Jazeera to broadcast updates from the tool into Syria.[34] Al Jazeera later took credit for the development of the tool, while acknowledging assistance from Movements.org, the successor to Cohen's State Department-funded Alliance for Youth Movements.[35]

Jacob Appelbaum's activities promoting Tor, and the broader promotion of what U.S. planners called "Internet Freedom," may seem innocuous at first glance, but it played a crucial role in promoting U.S. efforts at regime change in Syria and elsewhere. Jillian Yorke of the Electronic Frontier Foundation (EFF), which also promoted Tor and participated in the 2009 Arab Bloggers workshop in Beirut, later admitted, "I do fundamentally believe that the State Department's 'Internet freedom agenda' is at heart an agenda of regime change."[36]

As Levine points out, such a view was later confirmed by *Rolling Stone*, which wrote:

> By using Tor in place of another browser, protestors and journalists can log on to Twitter or surf dissident chat rooms with far less risk of being tracked by a government that might imprison them or worse... During the Arab Spring, Tor helped facilitate protests throughout the Middle East.

Rolling Stone cited Mauritanian activist and Tor proponent Nasser Weddady as explaining that "there would be no access to Twitter or Facebook in some of these places if you didn't have Tor... All of [a] sudden, you had all these dissidents exploding under their noses, and then down the road you had a revolution."[37]

Director of Regime Change

In June 2010, Jared Cohen and his State Department colleague Alec Ross led a delegation of tech executives on a trip to Syria. Under the pretext of promoting business investment, Cohen sought to convince Syrian officials to allow increased penetration of the social media tools that would later be needed to topple the Syrian state. The *New York Times* reported:

> Their delegation, which included representatives from Microsoft, Dell, Cisco Systems, and other companies, met with Syria's president, Bashar al-Assad, and other senior officials, as well as *younger entrepreneurs who are bucking their country's tight control of the Internet*. The delegation told Mr. Assad that companies would invest more in Syria if it stopped blocking social media websites like Facebook and YouTube, and did a better job of protecting intellectual property.[38] (emphasis added)

Alec Ross made the real purpose of his and Cohen's trip explicit four months later. In a September 2010 internal State Department email he wrote:

> When Jared and I went to Syria, it was because we knew that Syrian society was growing increasingly young (population will double in 17 years) and digital, and that this was going to create disruptions in society that we could potentially *harness for our purposes*. In what is *the first of what I predict will be many interesting cases in the future*, this past week a campaign went viral on Facebook in Syria (even though Facebook is outlawed in Syria it is widely accessed through proxies) showing teachers in Syria abusing their pupils. Thousands of Syrians made public their support on Facebook (the fact that people made their identities known is notable) for the campaign to remove these teachers, and the Ministry of Education intervened and fired the

teachers. This is the first known case of a successful social media campaign in Syria. *More will come.*[39] (emphasis added)

Shortly after Cohen and Ross's trip to Syria, *Fortune* noted that Cohen "advocates for the use of technology for social upheaval in the Middle East and elsewhere."[40]

In September 2010, Cohen left the State Department to join Google, not to transition away from promoting regime change, but "because he wanted a different avenue of attack," in the words of *Greenwich Magazine*. In a fawning profile of Cohen, *Greenwich* described Cohen's Google division, known as Google Ideas and later Jigsaw, "as a sort of free-floating state department with private sector efficacy," and that "Cohen quite suddenly sits at a great nexus of technology and power and influence."[41]

Julian Assange later observed that Cohen's activities at Google in triggering anti-government protests in Egypt in January 2011 amounted to "active corporate intervention in foreign affairs at a level that is normally reserved for states," and that "Jared Cohen could be wryly named Google's 'director of regime change.'"

Cohen and Google CEO Eric Schmidt had visited Assange to interview him under the pretext of working on a book they were co-writing, initially called the *Empire of the Mind*, but later changed to *The New Digital Age: Reshaping the Future of People, Nations and Business*. It was only after the interview that Assange became aware of how closely linked Google had become to the U.S. military and intelligence agencies. Assange pointed to the "explicit digital imperialism" expressed through the updated title of the book and "the conspicuous string of pre-publication endorsements from famous warmongers like Tony Blair, Henry Kissinger, Bill Hayden, and Madeleine Albright on the back."[42]

Rolling the Dice

Cohen's efforts coincided with an Obama administration decision to formalize the policy of sparking the protests and unrest needed to bring the Muslim Brotherhood to power, not only in Syria, but in the Arab world broadly.

In August 2010, Obama tasked a team of advisors led by National Security Council (NSC) official Samantha Power and Middle East specialist Dennis Ross to issue a report known as Presidential Study Directive 11 (PSD 11), which laid the blueprint for regime change in four Arab countries, including Egypt and three others left unnamed. According to the *New York Times*, Obama "pressed his advisors to study popular uprisings in Latin America, Eastern Europe, and Southeast Asia to determine which ones worked and which did not." The report, the result of weekly meetings involving experts from the State Department and CIA, then "identified likely flashpoints, most notably Egypt, and solicited proposals for how the administration could push for political change in countries with autocratic rulers who are also valuable allies of the United States." Obama was particularly concerned about Egypt due to the expected succession crisis to the rule of its aging and unpopular president, Hosni Mubarak.[43]

Syria analyst Camille Otrakji points out that according to Michael McFaul, a study participant and later U.S. Ambassador to Russia, the report looked at cases of "aging authoritarians" and "negotiated transitions between elites." McFaul asks, "If a country like Egypt went up in flames, should the United States engage whatever rose out of the ashes?"[44] Or would it instead be preferable to negotiate a transition between elites in advance of any possible crisis?

The obvious implication of the policy would be to welcome the rise of Islamist groups to power, including the Muslim Brotherhood, which in the case of Egypt anyway constituted the only significant organized opposition to Mubarak. The *Washington Post* reported in March 2011, shortly after Mubarak had been toppled through street protests, that "the Obama administration is preparing for the prospect that Islamist governments will take hold in North Africa and the Middle East." Tacitly endorsing the Brotherhood, a senior administration official argued: "If our policy can't distinguish between al-Qaeda and the Muslim Brotherhood, we won't be able to adapt to this change."[45]

French planners similarly prepared to welcome Islamist groups to power in the region. Journalists Christian Chesnot and Georges Malbrunot report that Patrice Paoli, head of the Middle East division of the French foreign ministry, was an enthusiastic advocate for political Islam. Along with fellow diplomat Ludovic Pouille, Paoli had gone to Geneva on many occasions before the Arab Spring to meet secretly with Islamist leaders from several Arab countries. When Alain Juppe was appointed foreign minister in February 2011, Paoli convinced him to support the Muslim Brotherhood publicly in Egypt and Tunisia, and from behind the scenes in Syria.[46]

Many commentators find it controversial that the policy set forth in PSD 11 would effectively endorse a U.S.-Muslim Brotherhood partnership across the Arab world. However, this was simply a broadening of the policy initiated by Elliott Abrams and other neoconservatives in the Bush administration regarding Syria.

Encouraging regime change in states not only viewed as enemies, such as Iran, Libya, or Syria, but also in close allies, such as Egypt, seemed to mark the beginning of a new approach. David Ignatius of the *Washington Post* therefore characterized the recommendations of the report as risky and a "roll of the dice."[47]

As Camille Otrakji observes as well, President Obama described in his autobiography how "by mid-December [2010] the documents laying out the [PSD 11] strategy were just about ready for my approval." Of course, this was just as anti-government protests were erupting in Tunisia. Obama suggests that this was just a coincidence: "If only our timing had been a bit better. The same month in the North African nation of Tunisia, an impoverished fruit vendor set himself on fire outside a local government building," sparking anti-government protests of the so-called Arab Spring.[48]

Obama seems to be obscuring the timing of his approval of PSD 11 here, presumably to avoid admitting any connection between his policy, which David Ignatius described as "low-key," and subsequent events in Tunisia and Egypt.[49] Obama needed the "negotiated transitions between elites" in Tunisia and then in Egypt to be viewed as grassroots, democratic revolutions with no Western support in order for them to have any legitimacy.

It is further clear that the policy shift set forth in PSD 11 had already been approved by this time, because U.S. efforts to topple Mubarak in Egypt had long been underway, under the direction of Jared Cohen, as further described below. It is hard to imagine, given Obama's stated objective of creating "political change in countries with autocratic rulers who are also valuable allies of the United States," how the timing of PSD 11 could have been any better from Obama's perspective.

While U.S. regime change efforts to topple the unpopular leaders of close allies such as Egypt and Tunisia would focus on soft methods, such as sparking peaceful street protests, in the case of America's enemies (namely Syria and Libya), these protests would be supplemented by harsher methods, including unleashing extreme violence from Salafist armed groups, as well as the possibility of direct Western bombing campaigns, as later chapters of this book will illustrate.

Human Rights, or Propaganda?

The U.S. government funded not only Muslim Brotherhood and cyber dissident activists to prepare the ground for regime change in Syria, but also organizations that claimed to be neutral Syrian human rights observers. Instead, these groups served as organs for disseminating U.S. government propaganda under a seemingly credible guise.

One such group was the Damascus Center for Human Rights Studies (DCHRS). DCHRS was not based in Damascus as one might presume, but in Washington, D.C., while the group's founder, Radwan Ziadeh, held fellowships with various U.S. and U.K. think tanks and universities. In 2010, shortly before the outbreak of war in Syria, he was a fellow with the CIA cutout NED (National Endowment for Democracy).[50] Ziadeh later became the director of foreign relations for the Syrian National Council (SNC), which represented the U.S.-, British-, and Gulf-backed political opposition abroad.[51] In February 2012, Ziadeh joined prominent neoconservatives including Max Boot, Liz Cheney, and John Hannah to sign a letter to President Obama advocating Western military intervention in Syria.[52]

Another allegedly independent and neutral Syrian human rights activist was Razan Zaitouneh, who defended Salafist prisoners at Syria's State Security Court, as mentioned in Chapter 2, and was based in Damascus, enjoying close ties with the U.S. embassy there. After anti-government protests began in March 2011, Zaitouneh and several organizations she founded became prominent sources of biased and fabricated information for the Western press.

Leaked State Department cables note that Zaitouneh was providing reports to U.S. embassy personnel and had secretly met with U.S. officials, including State Department Foreign Affairs Officer Joseph Barghout, as early as 2009.[53] Zaitouneh was also in contact with Robert Ford, who became U.S. Ambassador to Syria in 2010. Zaitouneh secretly met with Ford in person in May 2011, shortly after the crisis erupted.[54] According to *Deutsche Welle*, Zaitouneh was using a computer provided by a State Department-funded program.[55] This suggests that she had access to software for communicating with U.S. officials securely.

It is also clear that Zaitouneh was among the activists receiving U.S. funding as part of the broader regime change effort long before 2011. Zaitouneh partnered with another well-known opposition activist, Mazen Darwish, to form the Local Coordination Committees of Syria (LCC). Darwish told fellow opposition activist Zaina Erhaim that the LCC was first established in 2009, at the time of the so-called Green Revolution in Iran, and that the LCC intensified its activities after anti-government protests toppled the Tunisian government in January 2011. Darwish explained:

> We were hiding behind the others' movements, supporting them, knowing that Syria was next... In February 2011, we organized a meeting with Razan and some Kurdish parties to discuss the possibility of using the occasion of Nowruz (the Kurdish New Year) as the spark for the Syrian revolution.[56]

Zaina Erhaim herself notes the U.S. funding the group received, explaining that "during its active years, the LCC got its funding from the French and U.S. governments."[57]

The LCC was a spin-off from an earlier group, the Syrian Center for Media and Free Expression (SCM), which was also founded by Darwish, in this case in France in 2004, and which received funding from the NED and George Soros's Open Society Foundation (OSF).[58] The OSF was a donor to the Democratic Party known for its prominent role in promoting the so-called Color Revolutions in Georgia in 2003 and Ukraine in 2004 on behalf of the U.S. government.[59]

Razan Zaitouneh also formed the Violations Documentation Center (VDC), which started as an LCC project but became an organization of its own after the Syrian crisis began. The VDC also became a source of biased and false information for Western journalists regarding the conflict.[60]

The case of Razan Zaitouneh is a reminder that, as Syria commentator Camille Otrakji observed, "the United States finds it normal that it should influence, organize, promote, or brainwash local activists" in Syria.[61]

Wissam Tarif, the executive director of a group called Insan, was another allegedly neutral human rights campaigner. Like Mazen Darwish's SCM, Insan also received funding from George Soros's OSF, indicating that Tarif was also working on behalf of U.S. interests.[62]

When interviewed by Western media outlets, Tarif, who is Lebanese, was typically presented as Syrian, and Insan as a Syrian human rights organization. For example, in an appearance on CNN with Anderson Cooper on March 23, 2011, five days after the first major protest in Syria,

Cooper vaguely described Tarif as a "human rights activist in Syria" while Tarif spoke as if he had lived in Syria his whole life, stating: "We have been living in this country for 50 years under emergency law. This element of fear has to be broken."[63]

Tarif was wrongly identified as Syrian in the early weeks of the conflict by the *New York Times*[64] (April 13, 2011), the *Christian Science Monitor*[65] (May 3, 2011), *Die Welt*[66] (June 24, 2011), and *The Guardian*[67] (March 2, 2012), while the *Washington Post*[68] and *New York Times*[69] wrongly described Insan as a Syrian human rights group (April 23, 2011, and May 10, 2011, respectively). *Atlantic* journalist Uri Friedman was virtually alone in identifying Tarif as Lebanese and in pointing out that Insan was based in Spain rather than in Syria.[70]

Tarif claims that he moved to Syria in 2002 to establish an institute to teach computer science and languages.[71] The institute was renamed Insan in 2007 and supposedly became an advocacy group. Tarif was then deported by the Syrian government a few months later for the activities of his organization. There is no indication that Tarif returned to Syria until March 2011. Tarif claims that he entered Syria twice, in March and again in April 2011, without the knowledge of the authorities, and that he visited both Daraa and Douma.[72]

Uri Friedman noted the ubiquitous presence of both Tarif and Zaitouneh in Western coverage of the early protests when discussing death tolls and how clashes between protestors and security forces transpired.[73]

The fact that so many Western media outlets relied on the same two people, Tarif and Zaitouneh, as their chief sources of information suggests coordination with the intelligence services to platform only those voices that would reliably promote the preferred U.S. narrative.

Just a few weeks after protests erupted in Syria, Tarif was working directly for another OSF-funded advocacy group, Avaaz. According to Avaaz's website, the organization was founded by, and modeled on, MoveOn.org, an Internet-based advocacy group established to campaign for the Democratic Party.[74] MoveOn.org is in turn funded by Soros's OSF.[75]

Writing for the *New Republic*, journalist Simon van Zuylen-Wood reports that Avaaz is a New York-based advocacy group founded in 2007 that "distributed proxy servers to dissidents during Iran's Green Revolution," and "was one of the first NGOs to react to murmurs of rebellion in [Syria]."

According to Avaaz co-founder Ricken Patel, "everyone told us that Syria wasn't going to blow up. We didn't buy that."[76]

According to Wissam Tarif, in April 2011, "Avaaz got in touch with me, and asked about what was needed — cameras, satellite phones, SAT modems, DSL phones. Avaaz ran a fundraiser and sent the stuff into Syria."[77] According to a Western analyst quoted by NPR, Avaaz "flooded the place with [satellite] phones and computers, and they have their own contacts with the Western media and connect the two."[78] Tarif then

> oversaw the training of ordinary Syrians who subsequently re-entered their country to report on what was going on. As Syria became increasingly dangerous and difficult to penetrate, Western journalists came to rely ever more on Avaaz's daily email briefings, which compiled information from 200 such Syrian "citizen journalists." (About 600 reporters receive Avaaz's briefings).[79]

In other words, so-called human rights groups — such as Insan led by Wissam Tarif, the Local Coordination Committees (LCC) and Violations Documentation Center (VDC) led by Razan Zaitouneh, and the Damascus Center for Human Rights Studies (DCHRS) led by Radwan Ziadeh — were not independent human rights groups seeking to document human rights violations objectively. Instead, these groups were founded to promote anti-Syrian government propaganda in concert with U.S. objectives. By portraying U.S.-funded activists as neutral human rights campaigners, and by relying on the information these groups provided, the Western press promoted the narrative preferred by U.S. planners surrounding the early events in Syria.

As the Syrian conflict progressed, two additional ostensibly independent human rights groups, the Syrian Network for Human Rights (SNHR) and Syrian Observatory for Human Rights (SOHR), were created and became prominent sources for the Western press for news about events in Syria. Both are similarly based in and funded by states that were belligerents in the conflict, namely Qatar and the U.K., respectively. As journalist Max Blumenthal observes, these groups have been a major source of information (or misinformation) pertaining to the war for virtually every Western media outlet and human rights group, including the *New York Times*, *The Guardian*, and Amnesty International, among many others. The SNHR has been the source of the most egregiously false accusations against the Syrian government and has openly and aggressively campaigned for Western military intervention.[80]

'God Forbid the Baath Falls'

When anti-government protests erupted in several Arab countries, collectively known as the Arab Spring, starting in December 2010, the necessary infrastructure was therefore in place to manufacture a crisis in Syria. U.S. planners were able to draw on a variety of human resources to implement their regime change project, including secular and Muslim Brotherhood activists using social media technologies, sham human rights monitors, sectarian Salafist preachers, and armed al-Qaeda militants managed by regional U.S. allies. These actors all variously worked to "stir trouble" among at least a segment of Syria's Sunni population, namely the Salafist community, and thereby attempted to spark a sectarian war meant to lead to regime change, in accordance with U.S. objectives.

For many Syrians, it was easy to perceive the looming danger. This fear was particularly acute within Syria's Christian community, who had some foreknowledge that the U.S. effort to provoke sectarian war and regime change was near implementation. Brad Hoff, who lived in Syria periodically between 2004 and 2010, and whose wife is a Syrian Christian from Damascus, explains that he received

> confirmation from a handful of Syrian Christian individuals that in 2010 into early 2011 (just before the conflict started in Syria), U.S. intelligence officers were contacting them and very aggressively seeking their assistance — trying to make them assets… Suffice it to say that some Syrian Christians had been essentially tipped off by U.S. intelligence operatives that something big was coming for Syria, again, significantly prior to the actual start of the war (basically there were some "work for us or we won't be able to protect you" kind of arrangements being pitched… or rather "threats" perhaps). In one glaring instance, an official from the then existent U.S. Embassy in Damascus (it closed in February 2012) tried to convince a well-liked local Syrian Christian man who had spent a career working for major American news outlets in the Middle East (thus he had a lot of high-level media contacts across the globe) to become part of the U.S.-recognized "political opposition" in Syria. Keep in mind this was *before* such an "opposition" body was even brought into existence.[81] (emphasis in original)

Hoff also notes that the ramifications of a possible regime change war in Syria were clear to the Christian community. He quotes Ghattas Hazim, the Antiochian Orthodox bishop of Baghdad and Kuwait, who stated after the 2003 U.S. war to depose Saddam Hussein that "Christians are being slaughtered in Iraq … the West does not lift a finger to protect them."

Time journalist Rania Abouzeid similarly noted on March 6, 2011, less than two weeks before the first major anti-government protest, that "Syrians don't have to look far to see what wholesale regime change looks like. It isn't pretty." She quoted one Syrian as warning, "God forbid, God forbid the Baath falls here. We will wish we were as unstable as Iraq... Iraq will look like a paradise."[82]

Sadly, the cogs of Washington's regime change machine had already long been set in motion. As *Guardian* journalist Charlie Skelton later observed: "This has been brewing for a time. The sheer energy and meticulous planning that's gone into this change of regime — it's breathtaking." The first step was to "take people to [the] streets [so that] some people get killed."[83]

4. Daraa, the Cradle of Regime Change

Taking People to the Streets

Large-scale anti-government protests erupted in Tunisia on December 18, 2010, and in Egypt on January 25, 2011. In keeping with this trend, opposition activists in Syria used Facebook to call for demonstrations as part of a "Day of Rage," demanding the "fall of the regime" on February 4, 2011. The BBC reported that "the organizers behind the [Syria Revolution 2011 Facebook] page claimed they were not from any political group but were simply activists and rights campaigners from Syria and Europe."[1]

However, as Syria expert Joshua Landis reports, the Syria Revolution 2011 Facebook page was controlled by Muslim Brotherhood activists. The administrator of the site was a Brotherhood member based in Sweden.[2] AFP also noted the connection between the Syria Revolution 2011 Facebook page and the Brotherhood via Ausama Monajed, the public relations director of the Movement for Justice and Development (MJD), a U.S.-funded Brotherhood front group. AFP reported that Monajed was "one of the most prominent coordinators of the 'Syrian Revolution' pages on Facebook." Monajed explained to AFP that he was responsible for coordinating with the international media, including Al Jazeera and Saudi-owned Al Arabiya, and to help them contact sources inside Syria.[3]

As noted in Chapter 3, Monajed had close ties with U.S. planners. He attended a lunch with President Bush in 2008 and attended non-violence trainings from the State Department-funded Serbian activist group Otpor.

As a result of Brotherhood control of the Syria Revolution 2011 Facebook page, calls to protest on February 4, 2011, did not appeal to Syrians' desires for democracy, as many imagined, but rather to desires for revenge against the government for defeating the Muslim Brotherhood's armed insurgency decades before, which culminated in the 1982 battle for Hama. Camille Otrakji observed that "Syria's Islamists talk about 'justice' (politically correct way to express their lust for revenge). The original date set by the organizers of the Syrian revolution coincided with the 29th anniversary of the events of Hama," and the comments on the Syrian Revolution 2011 Facebook page calling for protests on February 4 were "easily 90%+ sectarian and revenge driven."[4]

Otrakji further observed:

If you read the older posts on the Syrian Revolution Facebook page (before they got a facelift and professional PR help), you wouldn't believe how much religious language you find, and also how much deception there is. They were trying to whip up sectarian hysteria, to radicalize Syria's Sunnis so as to bring down the regime. This is not what most Syrians want, but they have enough Syrians they can potentially influence.[5]

In other words, the U.S.-funded Brotherhood activists controlling the Syrian Revolution 2011 Facebook page were calling for protests hoping to "stir up the Sunnis," in accordance with U.S. objectives.

Ribal al-Assad, a cousin of President Assad, but also an opposition figure and head of the London-based Organization for Democracy and Freedom in Syria, similarly observed:

The campaign was a bit outrageous. First, they've chosen a date that reminds people of the uprising of the Muslim Brotherhood. People don't want to be reminded of the past. They want change, but they want it peacefully. And the picture they used on Facebook, a clenched fist and red color like blood behind. It was like people calling for civil war and who in his right mind wants that?[6]

The use of the clenched fist logo was another indication of the foreign origins of the protest movement, as this was the logo used by U.S.-funded Otpor activists in Serbia who had trained Ausama Monajed and other anti-government activists abroad.[7]

Refusing the Call

According to BBC Arabic, calls for protest on February 4, 2011, "did not succeed," however.[8] This was not only due to the sectarian messaging visible on Facebook, which appealed only to a small segment of Syrian society, including only a small segment of Syrian Sunnis, but also due to the popularity of President Assad himself. Rania Abouzeid observed on March 6, 2011, that Assad "has outlasted U.S. neocon threats of regime change," and that "even critics concede that Assad is popular," in part because "Assad has a hostile foreign policy toward Israel and stridently supports the Palestinians and the militant groups Hamas and Hizballah."

In other words, Assad was popular for many of the very reasons U.S. planners wished to topple his government.

Abouzeid further quoted opposition activist Ammar Qurabi as acknowledging that, rather than Iraq-style regime change, the "majority want and request that the President undertake reform within the [Baath] party, the government, and the security agencies. That is important."[9]

The failed call for protests on February 4 was followed by additional efforts to bring the so-called Arab Spring to Syria. Rania Abouzeid writes:

> On Feb. 19, the son of a store owner in Hariqa, near Souq Al-Hamidiyah in Damascus, was insulted and allegedly beaten by a traffic cop. Nothing unusual so far. But then hundreds, and by some accounts more than 1,000 people, quickly massed into an angry crowd, chanting, "The people will not be humiliated." Within half an hour of the incident, the country's powerful interior minister was on the scene, apologizing and promising that the alleged culprit would be reprimanded.[10]

Activists organized another protest in Damascus on February 23 in front of the Libyan embassy. In this case, they were demonstrating in support of anti-government protests in Libya. When the protestors ignored police warnings not to move closer to the embassy, they were confronted by riot police, who hit and verbally abused them. Fourteen were arrested and taken to the political security division of the interior ministry. According to Abouzeid, one of the detainees remarked, "I was thinking if this is the beating I get outside, in the open, what will they do to me once they get me inside?" Abouzeid notes, however, that once they reached the ministry, the detained protestor

> was surprised. The group was offered water, the use of the bathroom, and the chance to wash up before being addressed by an officer who seemed to be in charge. "He didn't introduce himself to us, but he said, 'We are all the sons of this country, we don't doubt your nationalism or your love for your country, but we would prefer that this episode not be repeated.'"[11]

Activists again used Facebook to call for anti-government protests to take place on March 15, but according to Syrian sociologist Muhammad Jamal Barout, "the call was not answered" once again. Barout writes in his book *Syria in the Last Decade: The Dialectic of Stagnation and Reform*:

> On March 15, a demonstration began in Damascus, with a gathering of five people in front of the Umayyad Mosque. The protestors then marched in the Hamidiya market, and when they approached the Hariqa neighborhood, dozens of other demonstrators joined and were dispersed by security forces, who arrested six of them.[12]

The following day, Razan Zaitouneh and Mazen Darwish organized a small sit-in at the Ministry of Interior in Damascus, and Darwish was arrested days later.[13] Well-known opposition activist Suhair al-Atassi, who comes from a prominent family from Homs, was arrested at the demonstration.[14]

The decision to protest in March was made in part to encourage Syria's Kurdish population to revolt, as this was when Syria's Kurds hold annual commemorations of Saddam Hussein's 1988 gassing of Iraqi Kurds in Halabja, the 2005 Kurdish revolt against the Syrian government in Qamishli, and the Newroz holiday. Barout notes, however, that the "Kurds responded negatively to these activist requests." Like most Syrians, "they wanted to achieve their goals through methods of understanding, and not by methods of pressure on the regime."[15]

Saleh Muslim, leader of the Kurdish Democratic Union Party (PYD), later explained that what the Kurds wanted was a "secular Syria" and that is why "we chose a third way; we are opposed to the regime; but we refused to join a revolution that starts from mosques."[16]

Although anti-government demonstrations thus far had virtually no popular support, this was not necessarily an obstacle for U.S.-funded activists seeking regime change. All that was needed was a spark. As Barout observed, what was important about the March 15 demonstration in Damascus "was not the modest number of demonstrators, which did not exceed dozens, but its slogans. This is the logic of the growth of the 'snowball' or 'fireball'... A fire can be started under favorable conditions with a match."[17]

Creating the Snowball

As Jared Cohen of the U.S. State Department and later Google observed, "revolutionary triggers can be very superficial," and if a government makes a mistake and overreacts to something that otherwise might just be "noise," it may create "grievances that weren't there to begin with," which then can lead to a real revolution. While referring to this dynamic as the "Dictator's Dilemma," Cohen went on to cite an example from Singapore, which is governed under a multi-party parliamentary system. Cohen noted that a dispute between two residents about which days they were allowed to cook curry quickly erupted into street protests over broader questions of immigration, after government overreaction to the initial dispute.[18]

Wael Ghonim, a Google marketing executive who wrote algorithms based on the idea of the "attention economy," explained in 2017 how social media platforms like Facebook can amplify these grievances and create divisions in a society that can lead to mob like behavior and violence. Ghonim explained:

> I used to think that the algorithms which operate, which I actually was part of teams building such tools, were democratic because it's based on engagement. If you like it, more people are going to see it. If you don't like it, less people are going to see it. But I grew into thinking that these are actually mobocratic algorithms, from mobocracy or the rule of the mobs… we are very emotional creatures and when the tools are all about agreeing, so the more you are polarizing, the more you are sensational, the more you are against the other… then the algorithms are going to give you all the distribution you want. What are you going to do next? You are going to be more polarizing because that's how it works.[19]

Cohen and Ghonim's observations illustrate that Facebook was not a means to facilitate a popular revolution for democratic change, but rather to create triggers that incite division among different groups in a society. In the case of Syria, this was particularly dangerous, as the country has more religious and ethnic diversity than Egypt or Tunisia, for example. Facebook was therefore extremely effective in promoting anti-Alawite sectarianism and, by extension, anti-government sentiment in Syria that could be used to spark civil unrest and potentially civil war.

Ghonim had himself created the "We are all Khalid Said" Facebook page, which he used to help organize the first major anti-government protest in Egypt on January 25, 2011, in coordination with his Google colleague Jared Cohen.

Khalid Said was a young Egyptian man who was brutally beaten to death by police near his home in Alexandria on June 6, 2010, after being wanted by police for petty drug possession. Anti-government Egyptian activists then decided to make Said's death the focus of their organizing campaign.[20]

Wael Ghonim's coordination with Cohen is illustrated by Ghonim's detention by Egyptian authorities two days after the January 25, 2011, protest that triggered events in Egypt. According to Ghonim, his interrogators "were 100% convinced that foreigners are behind us, that someone manipulates and finances us." Ghonim denied this, claiming that he had tricked Google into giving him a leave of absence for personal problems to leave his offices in Dubai to return to Egypt as the revolution erupted.[21]

It was clear, however, that Ghonim and his fellow protest organizers from the April 6 Youth Movement were being directed and funded by U.S. planners. Ghonim was detained because he had met with Cohen, who had entered the country a day before and was being tracked by Egyptian security services.[22]

While Ghonim claimed that Cohen's visit to Egypt was simply a coincidence and had nothing to the with the outbreak of protests, such a coincidence is implausible, given that Cohen's entire career at the State Department and Google had focused on promoting just such an event, and that the April 6 Youth Movement, which had also played a crucial role in organizing the January 25 protests on Facebook, was part of Cohen's Alliance for Youth Movements and had been coordinating directly with the State Department since 2008.[23]

Cohen's role behind the protests in Egypt was also made clear in leaked emails from Fred Burton of the private intelligence firm Stratfor. Burton, who was himself a former State Department security official, observed that "Google is getting WH [White House] and State Dept support and air cover," while noting what he viewed as "Google's covert role in foaming [sic] uprisings."[24]

Ghonim later acknowledged that he viewed it as his "role to create the snowball" that would lead to the fall of Egyptian president Hosni Mubarak.[25] As in Tunisia, the outbreak of protests leading to regime change in Egypt was in line with the strategy laid out in President Obama's PSD 11, with Ghonim and Cohen playing crucial roles.

The Writing on the Wall

It is widely assumed that the spark that started the Syrian crisis came from several young boys who, in a brave act of political defiance, painted anti-government graffiti on the walls of their school in the southern Syrian town of Daraa in February 2011. The graffiti read, "It's your turn, Doctor," suggesting that President Assad, trained in Britain as an ophthalmologist before coming to power, would be the next dictator to fall as a result of the Arab Spring protests. The boys were then detained for several weeks and allegedly tortured by Syrian intelligence, including by having their fingernails pulled out. When the boys' family members met with Syrian intelligence officers to appeal for their release, one officer allegedly humiliated the families further by threatening to rape the boys' mothers. The first major protest in Syria then took place on March 18, 2011, in Daraa as family members and other residents protested to demand the release of the boys and ask that other local grievances be addressed. As news of the boys' torture spread, the spark of the Syrian Revolution was lit.

The story as described above has some basis in fact but was distorted and exaggerated in several important ways by activists seeking to stoke anger against the government.

To begin, the boys did not write anti-government graffiti as an act of willful and spontaneous protest. Instead, opposition activists had previously started a campaign to paint anti-government graffiti in a variety of Syrian cities. As part of this campaign, opposition activists in Daraa manipulated several younger teenage boys into writing political slogans on the school wall, the meaning of which the boys themselves did not understand.

Further, there is an indication that the activists knew that the boys would be arrested and mistreated, and they sought to use such an incident to spark anti-government protests in Daraa in the same way the deaths of Khalid Said and Muhammad Bouazizi had been used to spark demonstrations in Egypt and Tunisia.

Azmi Bishara, a well-known Al Jazeera analyst and the general director of the Qatar-based Arab Center for Research and Policy Studies, investigated this issue in his book *Syria: A Path to Freedom from Suffering* (2013).

Bishara explains that after protests in Tunisia and Egypt led to the fall of Ben Ali and Mubarak on January 14, 2011, and February 11, 2011, respectively, hope spread in Syrian activist circles that Syrian president Bashar al-Assad could be deposed as well. As a result, these activists undertook to write slogans on walls in public spaces such as "It's your turn, Doctor" and "God, Syria, Freedom, that's all" and "The people want the downfall of the regime." Bishara notes that according to opposition activist Ra'id Abu Zeid, activists from the Syrian National Party, the Socialist Union Party, and the Communist Action Party graffitied these slogans on walls in multiple Syrian cities, including in Damascus proper, in the town of Tel in the Damascus countryside, and in Daraa.

Bishara notes as well that writing political slogans on walls was not a new tradition in Syria, and that similar campaigns had been undertaken during the period of conflict between the Muslim Brotherhood and Syrian government in the early 1980s and after Bashar succeeded his father Hafez as president of Syria in 2000. At that time, slogans appeared on walls of mosques such as "The country was ruined when it was taken over by a boy," mocking Bashar's then young age, which required amending Syria's constitution to allow him to become president.[26]

Bishara writes that according to interviews that his research team carried out with relatives of the boys in Deraa, no information confirmed that any of them had written political slogans on the walls. Rather, most of the testimonies his team collected suggested that this was instead done by what Bishara called "party activists." An uncle of one of the detained boys indicated that they had been throwing rocks at policemen manning a checkpoint in the Daraa al-Balad neighborhood and were detained because a policeman submitted a political security report claiming they had also thrown Molotov cocktails. According to one narrative, the boys were then wrongly accused of writing on the school wall after they were already in detention. Other reports indicated they were accused of this because the names of some of them were found written on the school wall under the graffitied slogan "The people want the downfall of the regime."[27]

The *New York Times* similarly reports that one of the boys detained for allegedly writing the graffiti, aged 15, described how his cousin had set fire to a police kiosk on the same day the graffiti was written. That some in the group were attacking police kiosks suggests as well that they were political activists in their late teens rather than young, non-political boys.[28]

However, while several teenagers were detained for throwing Molotov cocktails at the police, several younger boys did paint anti-government slogans on their school wall and were detained as a result. They did not paint the graffiti as an act of political defiance, however, as is commonly claimed. Instead, opposition activists told them what to write and pressured them to do so.

This is evident through reporting by Mark MacKinnon for the *Globe and Mail*, who managed to locate one of the young teenage boys years later and interview him. MacKinnon writes:

> Naief Abazid had no inkling that he was about to launch a revolution, or anything else that has followed. *He was just doing what the bigger kids told him to.* Trying to make them laugh. "It's your turn, Doctor Bashar al-Assad," he painted, just under the window of the principal's office of the all-boys al-Banin school in his hometown of Daraa. The date was Feb. 16, 2011... "I was the youngest one in the crowd. *They told me what to write,*" Naief recalled.[29] (emphasis added)

MacKinnon reports that Naief was detained the next day when a Syrian intelligence officer pulled him out of class. It was apparently easy to identify the handwriting of Naief and several other boys because their names were painted elsewhere on the school wall, as Bishara had also suggested. According to MacKinnon, the security officer

> said he wanted to talk to Naief about some graffiti on the school wall, and told the boy to follow him outside. (Naief later realized that he had written his name a year earlier on another part of the school property; that sample of his handwriting was all the evidence the security forces would need)…

> At the *mukhabarat* office, Naief was hung by his wrists from the ceiling, his feet dangling several inches off the ground. Then, the security men started to whip the wispy 14-year-old with thick cables. Through his pain, the boy counted 40 strokes. After being arrested and tortured, Naief Abazid was taken from Daraa to a security office in Suwayda, and then to the feared Palestine Branch's headquarters in Damascus, the Syrian capital. Next, his body was folded into the inside of a tire — a particularly cruel piece of torture already made infamous by the Assad regime's interrogators — and rolled forcefully down a hallway until the tire slammed into a concrete wall with Naief inside. For the next 10 days, he was kept in an isolation cell that he remembers as a metre and a half long and just a half-metre wide. Every hour or half-hour, he was subjected to another session in the tire, or another round of lashes… Eventually, [Naief] gave his torturers the names of five boys who had been in the crowd that urged him to write the graffiti. Those five would in turn be arrested and tortured into giving up the names of others who had been at the school that night, as well as some who weren't, until there were 23 boys in custody.

Activists Leading the Crowd

MacKinnon also managed to locate and interview one of the opposition activists, known as Abu Fuad, who at the age of 18 pressured 14-year-old Naief into writing the anti-government slogans on the school wall. MacKinnon writes:

> Abu Fuad also isn't a real name. It's a *nomme de guerre* adopted by a [then 18-year-old] who, even living in faraway Germany, is still tormented by the al-Assad regime. Wiry, bearded, he pulses with an angry revolutionary vibe that neither Naief nor Jamal possess… He is also still a wanted man in Daraa. He was jailed once, in October 2011, after his spray-paint smuggling operation was discovered by soldiers. The police later found that he had a Jordanian mobile phone and, more incriminating still, a memory card full of videos he'd taken during the early protests against the regime.[30]

In other words, Abu Fuad was an opposition activist who took part in the broader anti-government graffiti campaign. MacKinnon reports further:

> After 12 days of being hung from his wrists, Abu Fuad admitted to having painted anti-regime graffiti, and to having helped organize demonstrations... The whole family fled immediately to Jordan, except for Abu Fuad, who stayed to do what he could to help the revolution. He says that he never fired a weapon, but instead used his motorcycle to help transport Free Syrian Army fighters who were wounded in battle... Naief says it was Abu Fuad who led the crowd that encouraged him to write "It's your turn, Doctor al-Assad" on the wall of al-Banin school. Abu Fuad agrees that it was Naief who wrote those words, and that someone else put them in his head. But he swears he wasn't at the school that day.

This indicates that Abu Fuad, or some other opposition activist leading the crowd, pressured Naief, a younger, non-political schoolboy, into writing the anti-government slogans on the wall, including telling him what to write, as part of a broader opposition graffiti campaign.

Amplifying and Promoting Rumors

Rumors soon spread about the torture that several of the boys were allegedly subjected to. Much of this was apparently exaggerated by opposition activists to spark protest, however. Bishara writes:

> There are many accounts and rumors that have emerged about the torture of the children, mentioning that the detained children were exposed to burning, and hot irons, and ripping out their fingernails. And these accounts are all exaggerations and incorrect, it appears... It is correct that the children were exposed to torture in the security branch in Suwayda, but what was said about burning and pulling out their fingernails were rumors that were not confirmed by any source. And they were later exploited for tactical political purposes; for example, the incident was used politically against the Syrian regime to provide a symbol and provide moral significance to the boys' detention resembling that of Muhammad Bouazizi in Tunisia and Khalid Said in Egypt. And this makes clear the influence of the Arab Spring, including amplifying an event and promoting it in a way that motivates people to protest.[31]

Bishara's view about the exaggerated reports of the torture was confirmed by journalist Rania Abouzeid, who reported from within Syria for several years during the war. Writing for *Time*, Abouzeid concluded:

> The "Daraa children," as they were dubbed in the media, weren't children, and many had nothing to do with the writing on the walls,

but tales of their harsh treatment in custody (real and embellished) sparked protests for their release, demonstrations that ignited the Syrian revolution in mid-March and christened Daraa as its birthplace.[32]

An opposition activist from Daraa similarly claimed that he had seen reports in the French media and from Al Jazeera about the boys, but that "there was some exaggeration in them."[33]

This raises the question of whether Naief and Abu Fuad were in fact subjected to the torture they described to MacKinnon years later, or whether their accounts also contained some exaggerations. Once the mythology of the boys' torture was established, it would be hard for Naief to contradict this when speaking later of these early events. It would also excuse his giving up the names of the fellow boys at the school that day. As Abu Fuad was an opposition activist, it would make sense for him to exaggerate the brutality of his treatment as well. However, it is clear that the detained young men and boys involved in the graffiti incident were treated harshly.

In response, a delegation of local elders and religious clerics met with the head of the political security branch in Daraa, Atef Najib, who is a cousin of President Assad, to request the release of the young men and boys. Opposition sources reported that one security official responded to this request by humiliating the members of the delegation, saying, "Forget your children. If you really want your children, you should make more children. If you don't know how to make more children, we'll show you how to do it."[34]

It appears that this threat to rape the mothers of the detained boys was also an exaggeration. Of this meeting, Bishara writes that "rumors spread like fire" that the delegation of elders and clerics "heard words that stabbed the honor of their women, and that they responded to this humiliation with great anger." However, Bishara continues:

> The truth is that *we were not able to confirm the truth* of these anecdotal rumors. But it is clear that the delegation was exposed to humiliation, which caused a dynamic of protest, according to a formula of traditional solidarity representing local and tribal pride against humiliation.[35] (emphasis added)

These events of course require us to ask: Why did opposition activists pressure several non-political young boys into writing anti-government slogans on the wall of their school? Why were boys pressured to write political graffiti when they had already graffitied their own names on the school walls previously? Presumably, these activists would know that the boys were likely to get caught and would face severe punishment and, if the stories are true, even torture. It is understandable if the activists themselves wished to take the risk of expressing anti-government views using graffiti or any other method. But why would they seek to include unwitting young boys who had no idea what they were writing? Further, why would opposition activists spread false rumors that the boys had had their fingernails ripped out, or that security officials had threatened to rape the boys' mothers?

As mentioned earlier in this chapter, opposition activists had used Facebook to call for demonstrations as part of a "Day of Rage" demanding the "fall of the regime" already on February 4, some two weeks before the boys were pressured to write on the school walls, and that these calls to protest "did not succeed."

Opposition activists therefore needed to manufacture an incident resembling the horrendous deaths of Muhammad Bouazizi and Khalid Said in order to create sufficient anger against the government to encourage people in Daraa and elsewhere to protest. The hope was to portray the government as waging a war on Sunnis, to convince at least a segment of the country's Sunni community to take to the streets to demand the fall of the government. The nature of the harsh treatment (and possible torture) of the young boys in Daraa was therefore exaggerated to stoke this anger further and was exploited to encourage people to protest out of solidarity for fellow tribal members, as noted by Azmi Bishara.

Opposition activists may have also strategically chosen which boys to pressure into writing on the walls. According to Abd al-Qader al-Dhoun, an opposition activist from Daraa:

> The children who had been arrested for drawing slogans against the president were from several families or clans, Aba Zeid, Mahamid, and Masri. But the majority were from the Aba Zeid family, which is famous because it has always had bad relations with the government. Basically, half the family belongs to the Muslim Brotherhood, and the other half is Communist.[36]

By ensuring that boys from the Abu Zeid clan were detained, including Naief Abazid, the activists were able to amplify any pre-existing hostility between the clan's members and the government.

But why did Najib detain, allegedly torture, and then refuse to release the boys? Najib's motivation was apparently to obtain information about the activists behind the graffiti campaign and broader calls for the overthrow of the government. The interrogation of the boys yielded the names of several of these activists. Najib apparently feared that Daraa would be used as a base for overthrowing the government in the same way the city of Benghazi had been used to overthrow the Libyan government of Moammar al-Qaddafi. Benghazi fell to opposition control on February 21, 2011, just five days after the boys graffitied the school wall and while they were still in detention.[37] The fall of Benghazi was later cited by Syrian authorities as a reason to prevent protestors from establishing a headquarters in the Omari Mosque in Daraa.[38]

For Najib, the graffiti campaign and calls on Facebook to overthrow the government in February represented the early stages of such a conspiracy. Phil Sands of the UAE-owned *National* explains that according to one Syrian security official, Najib "is a hero. He really was the first one to discover the conspiracy against Syria; he saw it before the rest of us."[39] Najib's paranoia regarding the efforts of outside powers to carry out regime change in Syria eventually proved to be justified.

Ironically, his harsh treatment (and possible torture) and lengthy detention of the boys in Daraa played a role in turning many Daraa residents against the government and opened the door for the very intervention of foreign powers Najib apparently thought he was preventing. In other words, Najib faced the "Dictator's Dilemma" that U.S. planners such as Jared Cohen wished for him to face, and Najib overreacted in a way that helped cause events in Syria to snowball out of control.

'Some People Get Killed'

The strategy of Syrian opposition activists and their U.S. funders ultimately proved successful. Najib's actions, combined with anti-Alawite and anti-Shiite sectarian messaging on social media from opposition activists, created sufficient anger among some of Daraa's residents to set the stage for the first significant anti-government protest in the country on Friday, March 18, 2011.

According to Abd al-Qader al-Dhoun, the anti-government activist from Daraa, protests began in the southern Syrian city that Friday, when a small group of young men gathered in front of the Hamza bin al-Abbas Mosque and began chanting "God Is Great" and "Freedom." Within a half-hour, the mayor came to speak with the protestors, after which the governor of the province came as well. The young men presented their demands to the governor, including the demand to release political prisoners, including

Islamists, and to restore female employees of the education ministry to their teaching positions. These women had been forced to leave their teaching posts and work in other ministries alongside male employees because they had insisted on wearing face coverings that leave only the eyes uncovered (known as *niqab*, which is customary among Salafists). The young men soon became angry and began chanting against the governor and throwing rocks at him, forcing him to flee. Many of the young men were religious students of Sheikh Ahmed al-Siyasna, the blind imam of the nearby al-Omari Mosque. After the governor fled, the protestors went to al-Omari for the Friday sermon and started a new protest there with a larger group of some 1,500 people.[40]

Activists called for this protest in part using Facebook as well. AFP reported that after Friday prayers on March 18, Daraa residents responded to calls for protest by the Syrian Revolution 2011 Facebook page, which declared a "Syrian Day of Rage," calling for "revolution until freedom."[41]

It should be noted that activists within Sheikh Siyasna's circle were in touch with Jacob Appelbaum during this period. As mentioned in Chapter 3, Appelbaum had toured through the Middle East in 2009 on behalf of the U.S. government to promote the use of Tor among activists in the region, and Tor played a crucial role in allowing these activists to avoid government surveillance while using social media to plan protests and disseminate propaganda in the so-called Arab Spring countries. Appelbaum tweeted just five days after the first protests in Daraa that "if media is looking for the leader of the Syrian revolution in Daraa — I'll pass contact information for [Ahmed Siyasna] — DM me."[42]

Sheikh Siyasna became the symbolic head of the protest movement in Daraa and the point man for negotiating with the government and conveying the protestors' demands. Siyasna was not an activist demanding democracy, however. In a May 2012 speech to a conference of the fundamentalist religious group Hizb al-Tahrir in Lebanon, Siyasna spoke of the protest movement as a "revolution of believers" to defend Islam against the secular and allegedly atheist Syrian government and its Shia allies Iran, Hezbollah, and the Mahdi Army.[43] The conference was organized to promote the goal of establishing an Islamic state in Syria.[44]

It is also no accident that the first major protest was in Daraa, rather than the larger cities such as Damascus or Aleppo. French journalists Georges Malbrunot and Christian Chesnot write that it was well known that many

Islamists who had left Syria to earn a living in Kuwait and Saudi Arabia had returned and were now living in Daraa and the surrounding villages. The journalists cite a Syrian government intelligence report from 2009 that concluded that Daraa had the largest concentration of Salafists in the country, and that Salafism had replaced Baathism as the dominant ideology for many young Syrians. This was in part because Saudi clerics had established a network of imams across the country to whom they were providing funding.[45]

Despite the religious, and in most cases Salafist, orientation of the early protestors, the Western press would nevertheless portray the so-called Syrian Revolution as a movement for democracy.

The fact that Appelbaum was in touch with activists within Siyasna's circle in Daraa is also an indication that the first protest in Daraa was at least in part organized by activists who had received previous training and funding from U.S. agencies, and that they were coordinating with U.S. planners via intermediaries such as Appelbaum. As noted earlier in this chapter, it was supporters of Siyasna who started the first protest in Daraa and began throwing rocks at the governor while he tried to listen to the protestors' demands. Additionally, this protest was promoted by the Syria Revolution 2011 Facebook page, which was controlled by Brotherhood activists led by Ausama Monajed.

Recall that Monajed received training by the State Department-funded activist group Otpor in Serbia. Siyasna's relationship with Hizb al-Tahrir also raises additional questions about the role of Western intelligence agencies in the early period of the Syrian conflict. As journalist Nafeez Ahmed details, Hizb al-Tahrir was long since penetrated by the U.K. intelligence services.[46]

Elements from Outside

After Friday prayers on March 18, the crowd of protestors then marched from the al-Omari Mosque to the Political Security office of Atef Najib. Reuters claims that three men — Wissam Ayyash, Mahmoud al-Jawabra, and Ayhem al-Hariri — "were killed when security forces opened fire on Friday on civilians at a peaceful protest demanding political freedoms and an end to corruption in Syria."[47] BBC Arabic similarly claimed that according to sources in Daraa, "four demonstrators were killed by security forces during a peaceful demonstration demanding political freedom and an end to corruption."[48]

However, Syrian security forces did not simply open fire on peaceful protestors to crush dissent. A closer look at events of the day suggests that the deaths occurred in the context of violent riots and attacks on Syrian security forces. Furthermore, there is evidence that these first deaths may have been false-flag killings carried out by Salafist militants.

Regarding the rioting, Sheikh Siyasna told the government-run *Tishreen* newspaper: "There were elements from outside Daraa determined to burn and destroy public property... These unknown assailants want to harm the reputation of the sons of Hauran... The people of Daraa affirm that recent events are not part of their tradition or custom."[49] It is possible that supporters of Siyasna instigated the rioting, and that Siyasna was simply blaming the violence on unknown, outside elements to shield his own supporters from blame, but he does not deny that violent rioting occurred.

Muhammad Jamal Barout provides a rather detailed account of the March 18 protest that broadly supports Siyasna's admission. Based on his interview with Al Jazeera's then Damascus bureau chief, Abd al-Hamid Tawfiq, Barout writes that

> protestors, with the families of the children at the front, headed towards the al-Omari Mosque. They chanted "Where are you, oh people of *al-Faz'a*?" and "God, Syria, freedom, that's all," and "There is no fear after today," and they also chanted against the head of the political security branch, Atef al-Najib and against the governor, Faisal Kalthum, and against business tycoon Rami Makhlouf... Then they *headed to the political security branch building to burn it down.* After about two hours, at about three thirty in the afternoon, four helicopters arrived that had been called in by the head of the security branch, and they were carrying counter-terrorism soldiers dressed in all black.[50] (emphasis added)

It is after this rioting and the arrival of the counterterrorism forces by helicopter that the first killings allegedly occurred. Sheikh Youssef Abu Roumieh, who resigned as representative from Daraa in the Syrian People's Assembly in support of the protests, acknowledged that the first protestors were shot after these anti-terrorism units arrived to contain the riots. He nevertheless claimed that "they immediately went down to shoot the civilians in Daraa," and were "preventing ambulances transporting the wounded to

---

* *Faz'a* is a Syrian slang word referring to one's obligation to come to the aid of others in distress.

the hospital. So, they [the protestors] took the Omari Mosque as a hospital for the wounded."[51]

Burn It Down

It is not surprising that Syrian security forces, including the counterterrorism forces, would intervene to stop the rioting in Daraa. This was to prevent the destruction of public property generally but also to safeguard the lives of any people still inside the buildings that rioters were seeking to burn down.

Subsequent protests illustrate the dangers involved in situations of this sort, where events can quickly spin out of control. Three are worth highlighting here. During an anti-government protest on June 4, 2011, armed protestors threw an incendiary device inside the front doors of the post office in the northern Syrian town of Jisr al-Shagour, setting it on fire and burning eight people to death inside.[52] Two days later, on June 6, protestors in the Yarmouk Palestinian refugee camp in the Damascus suburbs attempted to burn down the headquarters of the Popular Front for the Liberation of Palestine–General Command (PFLP-GC), a pro-Syrian government Palestinian political party. In the process, one PFLP-GC official was stabbed to death by protestors, and a PFLP-GC guard was burned to death inside the building, while PFLP-GC guards shot and killed two protestors.[53] On February 18, 2011, during the first days of anti-government protests in Libya, protestors in the eastern city of Derna burned to death several government supporters after locking them in holding cells in the local police station, and then setting it on fire.[54]

If Syrian security forces did shoot and kill four protestors on March 18 as claimed by sources speaking with the Western press, it is possible that this was due to the chaos resulting from the riots, rather than due to the security forces simply wishing to stop protestors from peacefully expressing dissent.

5. 'Mostly' Peaceful Protests

Armed Protestors

Israel National News also pointed to rioting in Daraa in subsequent days, reporting:

> On Friday [March 18, 2011], police opened fire on armed protestors killing four and injuring as many as 100 others. According to one witness, who spoke to the press on condition of anonymity, "They used live ammunition immediately — no tear gas or anything else." At the funerals of two of those killed, opposition leaders handed authorities a list of demands, which included the release of political prisoners. In an uncharacteristic gesture intended to ease tensions, the government offered to release the detained students, but seven police officers were killed, and the Baath Party Headquarters and courthouse were torched, in renewed violence on Sunday.[1]

Like Abu Roumieh who resigned from the People's Assembly, the Israeli news site assigns blame to Syrian security forces for immediately using live fire to kill four protestors, but adds two crucial details, that police opened fire on *armed protestors* and that *seven policemen were also killed* at some point between Friday and Sunday.

As academic Michel Chossudovsky observes:

> From the initial casualty figures (Israel News), there were more policemen than demonstrators who were killed: 7 policemen killed versus 4 demonstrators. This is significant because it suggests that the police force might have been initially outnumbered by a well-organized armed gang. According to Syrian media sources, there were also snipers on rooftops which were shooting at both the police and the protestors. What is clear from these initial reports is that many of the demonstrators were not demonstrators, but terrorists involved in premeditated acts of killing and arson. The title of the Israeli news report summarizes what happened: "Syria: Seven Police Killed, Buildings Torched in Protests."[2]

This calls into question whether the four demonstrators who were killed were in fact peaceful civilian demonstrators. It is possible that they were instead armed militants killed in clashes with the counterterrorism forces but portrayed by opposition sources as unarmed civilians. Armed clashes certainly continued in subsequent days so that by Sunday, March 20, "seven police officers were killed."[3]

Such a scenario occurred three months later in the town of Jisr al-Shagour. According to journalist Rania Abouzeid, an armed militant named Basil al-Masry was killed while attacking a government checkpoint. Masry's death angered many residents of the town, who believed rumors that Masry had been unarmed when he was killed, rather than carrying out an armed operation. As a result, his funeral on June 5, 2011, doubled as an anti-government demonstration, providing cover for Salafist militants to attack the security forces (discussed in more detail in Chapter 8).[4]

A Soldier's Story

Independent journalist Gail Malone interviewed a Syrian soldier who was present in Daraa and who also claimed that protestors were armed and opening fire on Syrian security forces on Friday, March 18, 2011. The soldier explained:

> So, we go that Friday 1:00 p.m. after they finished the prayers. We were surprised that they didn't come from the Mosque only; they came from other neighbourhoods and they were surrounding us. They took over the house [roofs], any street entrance, everything. And they started shouting Allah Akbar! So, they surrounded us, and they started throwing Molotov cocktails and rocks on us from every corner. We were surprised. We only had the Fire Engine, the hose water, and the Civil Police formed the first line having riot shields and batons. We were surprised to hear the sound of machine guns, not just Kalashnikovs, AKs or something like this, but things that shoot a lot of bullets and all my friends were falling around me. Lots of people were injured, and ambulances were not enough to take them to the hospitals. They ran out of ambulances to take them to the hospital.[5]

The soldier also claims that he and his fellow soldiers were not allowed to carry weapons, such as Kalashnikovs, but were limited to batons and riot shields. The soldiers were therefore terrified to confront the protests in subsequent weeks. Soldiers who refused to do so were detained and transferred to Damascus as a result.

For the authorities in Damascus then to dispatch the counterterrorism forces by helicopter to Daraa in the afternoon of Friday, March 18, would make sense in this context.

That Syrian security forces were initially unarmed, and were shot at by armed demonstrators, is likely difficult to accept for many observers, because it runs so counter to the accepted narrative about the origins of the Syria conflict. However, there is video of just such an incident in the city of Homs

70

in subsequent weeks. A member of the Syrian security forces, Muhamad Yusuf Ateeq, was shot and killed by snipers while armed only with a baton and plastic shield for riot control.[6]

Additionally, the soldier's claim that the security forces were initially using a water hose from a fire engine rather than weapons to control the riots was confirmed by opposition sources. The Muslim Brotherhood website itself published a video of the police in Daraa using "water cannons belonging to fire engines" to disperse the demonstrators.[7] This also suggests that the government's first reaction was not simply to open fire with live ammunition on peaceful demonstrators, as the narrative provided in Western reporting would suggest.

It should be remembered that in February 2011 young men in Daraa had already been attacking Syrian police kiosks with Molotov cocktails and trying to burn them down. As discussed in Chapter 4, this was confirmed by the *New York Times* and Azmi Bishara during their investigations of the detention of the young boys who had graffitied the school wall. This means that it is probable that protestors were also attacking the security forces in a similar way on March 18, as described by the soldier.

The possible involvement of al-Qaeda in the events in Daraa on March 18 must also be considered at this time. Recall that American journalist Theo Padnos, who was kidnapped and then held as a hostage of the Nusra Front for two years, was told by fellow ISIS prisoners that the Islamic State leadership had "dispatched fighters into Syria in late 2010, long before any child in Deraa scrawled his graffiti on a schoolyard wall."[8] Padnos explained further that, as the wave of demonstrations swept the country,

> these al-Qaeda people from Iraq infiltrated as many demonstrations as they could. And with the weapons they brought into Syria from Iraq they started shooting at the police and they started murdering the police officers and surrounding the police stations and throwing smoke bombs and waiting until the police guys come out and then shooting the policemen and then capturing the weapons and going off to the next police station. They told me about this from the beginning; they are very proud of this. They do not believe that the Syrian revolution really began with demonstrations. For them, it began because they made it begin by killing the police officers. They were the ones who launched the whole thing. It's important for them to feel it's a jihad and they are leaders of the jihad.[9]

Recall as well that prominent al-Qaeda member Abu Khalid al-Suri was gathering these fighters to form the militant group Ahrar al-Sham in the weeks before the first major protest on March 18, 2011, and that Saudi intelligence was allowing al-Qaeda members still under travel ban orders to leave Saudi Arabia to fight in Syria.

This lends credibility to the soldier's claim that he and fellow soldiers were fired upon by well-organized armed groups, most likely comprised of al-Qaeda militants, on March 18 and during subsequent protests.

Responding to Protestors' Demands

Amidst the chaos in Daraa on Friday, March 18, the Syrian government attempted to defuse the situation by sending a top government official from Damascus to negotiate with a group of prominent Daraa elders representing the protestors, led by Sheikh Siyasna. Muhammad Jamal Barout writes:

> At the same time, a high-level political delegation arrived, led by Hisham Ikhtiyar, head of the Office of National Security, who was known for dealing with crises and putting out fires. The Central Security Committee, led by Ikhtiyar, agreed with the elders of Deraa on 13 points, foremost among them the resignation of the political security head [Atef al-Najib] and the governor of Deraa [Faisal Kalthum]. Ikhtiyar also agreed to expel the companies of Rami Makhlouf from Deraa, apologize to the local people, and allow a meeting between Deraa's elders and president Bashar al-Assad, and also to political reform, and more freedoms, and the return of teachers who wear the niqab to their teaching posts, and to repeal unjust laws regarding the buying and selling of land, such as law 48 and law 26, and to lower the prices of fuel, and to some other local demands. Ikhtiyar further informed the elders of Deraa that the president had agreed to these demands, and the people now awaited them being carried out.[10]

Regarding the "unjust laws regarding buying and selling of land," one Daraa resident explained to CNN that Political Security chief Najib

> made it difficult for people to sell their land, citing national security when denying approval for sales, because of Daraa's proximity to Israel, a sworn enemy... Najib would send his proxies to offer to buy the land at half the price and take on responsibility for obtaining the approvals, swindling people out of their livelihoods.[11]

The demands of the protestors mentioned above indicate that locals in Daraa had many legitimate reasons to protest the corruption and authoritarianism of the Syrian government. Hisham Ikhtiyar's efforts to negotiate with the elders of Daraa, however, showed a willingness on the part of the Syrian government to make the concessions needed to defuse the situation peacefully, rather than attempt to use violence immediately to suppress any sign of dissent. Barout acknowledges this, explaining that Ikhtiyar was sent "to try to contain this situation, and to agree to apologize to the families of the martyrs, to establish an investigation into events and to hold the responsible officials accountable, to release the detainees, and to deliver orders from the president not to open fire on the protestors." Barout notes as well that Ikhtiyar and Siyasna "came to an understanding, including to release the boys who had written on the walls, as they had not been released yet."[12]

In other words, sending security forces to contain the protests and riots in Daraa, coupled with efforts to address the protestors' legitimate grievances, mirrors the response we would expect from any government. Further, it is doubtful that Syrian security forces would have opened fire intentionally on peaceful protestors in Daraa on Friday, March 18, simply to prevent them from expressing their demands. This does not mean that Syrian security forces never used violence or committed abuses. It does mean, however, that the portrayals of the Syrian government in the Western press as uniquely evil due to its response to the early protests in Daraa are not justified.

The Motorcycle Men

So far, we have discussed several ways the killings in Daraa on March 18 may have occurred. However, there is evidence of yet another possibility: that the four protestors were killed in a false-flag attack.

Muhammad Jamal Barout reports that according to Abd al-Hamid Tawfiq, the Al Jazeera Damascus bureau chief,

> a few hours after the agreement between Ikhtiyar and Siyasna, a group of masked militants riding motorcycles opened fire on the demonstrators, killing four people between the hours of six and eight in the evening, including Ahmad al-Jawabra, who was considered the first martyr.[13]

And who were the masked militants riding motorcycles? Barout takes for granted that they were from the government side, but it is far from clear that this was the case. Even if the government wished to suppress the protests with violence, it is likely that it would have used either the counterterrorism forces that had arrived earlier that day from Damascus or local plainclothes security men (known by opposition supporters as *shabiha*) to confront and disperse the protestors. For example, plainclothes security men beat protestors to disperse a small demonstration outside the Umayyad Mosque in Damascus on the same day.[14] It is unclear why the government would instead resort to using masked men on motorbikes in Daraa.

One possibility is that the masked men on motorcycles were "saboteurs" or "infiltrators" from a third party such as al-Qaeda. Prominent opposition leaders later acknowledged the presence of such third-party infiltrators, and subsequent events show that armed militants from the opposition side commonly used motorbikes to conduct hit-and-run attacks against the Syrian security forces and army. This raises the possibility that the killers of the first protestors on March 18 were saboteurs from a third party of this sort.

Evidence of armed opposition militants using motorbikes to carry out attacks in this way comes not only from pro-government sources, but also from independent and opposition sources. For example, on April 19, 2011, the Syrian interior ministry issued a circular in Homs Province to prevent the entry of motorbikes into the city, "because some armed groups in the province implement their criminal plans using motorbikes."[15] On the same day, the pro-government *Akhbariya* news channel claimed that "masked men" riding in "GMC vehicles and on motorcycles" opened fire on a funeral tent, shooting at both civilians and the security forces and police, injuring 11 policemen.[16]

On May 5, 2011, the *Christian Post* reported that "protestors are being led by hardline Islamists and that Christians have come under pressure to either join in protests demanding the resignation of President [Bashar] Assad, or else leave the country." Additionally, "eyewitnesses report seeing around 20 masked men on motorcycles open fire on a home in a Christian village outside Daraa, in southern Syria."[17]

Barout himself notes that on June 3, 2011, dozens of masked young men from the area of Jabal al-Zawiya in Idlib Province arrived in the town of Jisr al-Shagour on motorcycles with weapons they had purchased on the black market or had captured from government caches. These men were among those who attacked the Popular Army headquarters in the town to capture additional weapons. Two days later, on June 5, opposition militants attacked the local post office and military security headquarters, leading to a 36-hour gun battle.[18]

Human Rights Watch (HRW), which has links to the U.S. government and is supportive of the Syrian opposition, reported that an opposition activist witnessed a protest in the city of Homs on July 8, 2011, in which "several defectors showed up on motorcycles and killed 14 or 15 members of the security forces using Kalashnikovs and pump-action shotguns."[19] Although HRW described the opposition militants carrying out this attack in Homs as army defectors, in fact defectors among the armed opposition were relatively few in number. Instead, the security forces were likely killed by Islamist militants, as a Salafist armed group known as the Farouq Brigades was dominant in Homs at that time (discussed in more detail below).

Opposition sources also acknowledged the possibility of saboteurs and infiltrators playing a role in early events of the uprising. As noted in Chapter 4, Sheikh Siyasna also acknowledged that there were "unknown assailants" present at the protest on March 18 in Daraa who were "determined to burn and destroy public property."[20] These may have been Siyasna's supporters, but if not, who were they?

Further, journalist Alix Van Buren of Italy's *la Repubblica* newspaper reported on April 13, 2011, that "several Syrian dissidents believe in the presence and the role of 'infiltrators.'" Among these dissidents was prominent opposition intellectual Michel Kilo. Although Kilo accepted that possibility, he "cautioned that the issue of 'infiltrators and conspiracies' should not be exploited as an obstacle in the quick transition towards democracy."[21]

Significantly, the claim that the first protestors were killed in Daraa by militants on motorcycles, rather than by Syrian security forces, comes from an "against interest" source, namely an Al Jazeera bureau chief. The Qatari-owned channel had a clear agenda to demonize the Syrian government, in cooperation with U.S. planners. Because of the editorial line of his employer, Abd al-Hamid Tawfiq was incentivized to relay a story that blamed the government for the first killings, but he instead made a claim, at least privately, that would appear to exonerate the Syrian security forces and suggest the possibility of false-flag killings.

Interestingly, Tawfiq resigned from his post in May 2011, citing only vague "pressures," which many assumed to be coming from the Syrian government side.[22] However, this period would see several prominent Al Jazeera journalists resign from the channel to protest what they viewed as coverage that was biased against the Syrian government and in favor of the Muslim Brotherhood. On April 24, 2011, Ghassan Bin Jeddo, the head of Al Jazeera's Beirut office, resigned because of the channel's "alleged abandonment of professional and objective reporting, as it became 'an operation room for incitement and mobilization."'[23] Al Jazeera journalist Ali Hashem resigned in 2012, citing the channel's censorship of his Syria reporting during this early period, which revealed armed groups crossing from Lebanon into Syria in late April 2011 (discussed in detail in Chapter 7).[24] The subsequent Al Jazeera Beirut bureau chief, Hassan Shaaban, resigned shortly after Hashem in 2012 as well.[25]

It's a Sabotage

But why would saboteurs from a third party want to kill protestors during the first major day of anti-government protests in Daraa on Friday, March 18? As discussed in Chapter 4, opposition activists demanding the fall of the Syrian government needed a spark (or several sparks) resembling the deaths of Khalid Said in Egypt and Muhammad Bouazizi in Tunisia to unleash public anger against the government and to encourage people to protest. The strategy relied on getting protestors to take to the streets, and for people to be killed, to unleash a sectarian civil war that could topple the government. A false-flag killing during the first major day of protests could of course provide such a spark.

Killing protestors at this critical juncture and blaming it on the government would also sabotage Sheikh Siyasna's efforts to win concessions from the government through negotiations, in exchange for putting an end to the protests and rioting. Recall that Abd al-Hamid Tawfiq reported that the first protestors were killed by the masked men on motorbikes "a few hours after the agreement between Ikhtiyar and Siyasna." This was the perfect opportunity to ensure that any agreement between the two sides would fall apart. The father of one of the boys detained for writing the graffiti one month before indicated that the conflict could have been resolved peacefully, but that as the deaths of protestors mounted, "people became uncontrollable."[26]

Because al-Qaeda militants sought to create chaos by attacking Syrian security forces under the cover of protests to launch their so-called revolution, they were incentivized to carry out a false-flag killing, in this case against civilian protestors, to accomplish this goal.

An end to the protests in exchange for government efforts to answer local grievances was a disaster scenario not only for al-Qaeda elements, but for hardline elements of the opposition broadly, who demanded the "fall of the regime" and wanted "revolution" from the start. This attitude was evidenced when local supporters of the exiled Salafist preacher Muhammad Sarour Zein al-Abbedine later accused Sheikh Siyasna of treason for his willingness to negotiate with the government to end the crisis peacefully. Sarour's supporters tried to pressure Siyasna to radicalize his position and abandon negotiations, but Siyasna refused.[27] Sheikh Anas Sweid, a pro-opposition Sunni cleric from Homs, similarly stated a few weeks later that any clerics who stood against "the street" would be attacked, so they therefore had no ability to calm the protestors as government officials had demanded of them.[28]

The Men in Black

Additionally, opposition activists exploited the killings of the first protestors on March 18 in Daraa to incite sectarian tensions further and to try to turn the Sunni community against the government. They did this by spreading rumors that militants from Hezbollah, the Lebanese Shiite resistance group, had participated in suppressing the protests.

Azmi Bishara writes for example that, according to opposition activists Abu Anas al-Shami and Bilal Turkiya:

> After hours from the protests in Deraa on March 18, 2011, the regime called in the Rapid Intervention forces and the counter-terrorism forces from Damascus, to take the sports stadium in Deraa al-Balad as a base for its operations. And it is worth mentioning that these teams are not familiar to Syrian citizens, as they had only been formed in 2005, but they did not appear internally in the country until 2010, and the regime rarely used them in security raids and prosecuting smugglers in late 2010. Members of these forces were wearing military uniforms that were black in color, which differs from the clothes that the army and security forces and police wear in Syria. And the people of Deraa were surprised by these forces and many people thought that elements of Hezbollah were invited by the regime to suppress the demonstrations, and this is what led to the appearance of the slogan "No to Iran, no to Hezbollah" and for some of the activists of Deraa to make the accusation that Hezbollah was participating in the suppression of the demonstrations in the beginning of the revolution.[29]

However, the slogan "No to Iran, no to Hezbollah" emerged from the Saudi government's effort to publicize the alleged threat of Shiite and Iranian influence in Syria.

Muhammad Jamal Barout writes:

The merging of hostility for the [Syrian] regime and Hezbollah was the result of the Salafi propaganda campaign originating from the Gulf countries which targeted Shiites generally, and which focused on the concept of the Shiite-Nusayri [Alawite] alliance, as expressed in the writings of Muhammad Sarour Zein al-Abbedine.

Barout pointed to the "Shia-Nasayri Alliance" episodes on Muhammad Sarour's website as evidence for this.[30] As noted in the 2006 State Department cable discussed in Chapter 1, this was done in order to create sectarian divisions in the country.

Further, it would be odd for residents of Daraa to mistake the rapid intervention forces for Hezbollah militants, as Bishara suggests, solely from the color of their uniforms. More likely, opposition activists were actively spreading the rumor that Hezbollah was suppressing the protest on Friday, March 18, in Daraa to discredit the Syrian government, to incite sectarian tensions, and to bring more Sunnis into the streets to protest thereby.

Evidence for this comes from the fact that opposition activists did attempt to spread false rumors about a supposed Hezbollah massacre in Damascus on the same day. While speaking to Saudi-owned *Al-Arabiya* satellite channel, opposition supporter Mahmoud al-Homsi claimed that thousands of Hezbollah members entered the Umayyad Mosque in Damascus on Friday, March 18, and assaulted, killed, and injured dozens of people with knives. Barout notes that this was a complete fabrication, and that al-Homsi was attempting to exploit the fact that most of the protestors were Sunni.[31]

As mentioned in Chapter 4, there was indeed a small protest on March 18 outside the Umayyad Mosque in Damascus, following calls for protest on Facebook. According to journalists from AFP, the protest was dispersed when plainclothes members of the security forces beat protestors emerging from the mosque after Friday prayers and detained two protestors. This once again illustrates that the security forces at times used harsh tactics, but no one was killed, and Hezbollah was of course not involved.[32]

Al-Homsi later gained notoriety for his anti-Alawite hate speech, threatening in December 2011:

From this day on, you despicable Alawites, either you renounce [Syrian president] al-Assad, or we will turn Syria into your graveyard... I swear that if you do not renounce that gang and those killings, we will teach you a lesson that you will never forget. We will wipe you out from the land of Syria.[33]

Flesh to the Dogs

Another opposition figure known for his calls for violence against Alawites was the Salafist preacher Adnan al-Arour. Originally from Hama and a former member of the Muslim Brotherhood, Arour had a significant following in Syria despite living in exile in Saudi Arabia, thanks to his popular satellite television programs.

As Islamic scholar and opposition supporter Thomas Pierret notes, Arour had

> made a name for himself over the previous five years with his anti-Shiite programs. As soon as demonstrations started in Deraa, Al-'Ar'ur reoriented his media effort to support the uprising with the programme *With Syria Until Victory*... Al-'Arur rapidly acquired considerable popularity among the protestors: he was frequently praised by crowds during demonstrations.[34]

Muhammad Jamal Barout notes that Arour studied under Salafi scholars Sheikh Nasir al-Din al-Albani and Sheikh Abd al-Aziz bin Baz in Saudi Arabia, and

> became famous among some strict Salafists who seem to think that God created them only for the sake of killing the Shia, due to his debates with the Shia and Sufis [and that] Arour, who possesses a certain influence in the ranks of popular religious groups broadly through his satellite channel "Sifa," changed from forbidding rebellion against the sovereign power before the outbreak of the protest movement, to supporting [rebellion] and aiding it, and inciting participation in it.[35]

Then Al Jazeera journalist Nir Rosen reported that Arour's "name is often chanted in demonstrations" and that Arour spoke at early protests via satellite feed from Saudi Arabia, where many of the opposition media coordinators were based. Rosen also notes that Arour was popular in Sanamain, a conservative town near Daraa and an early site of protests.[36]

UAE-owned *Al-Bayan* newspaper explained that

> Arour's instructions to the demonstrators to form barricades and civilian checkpoints and to shout "God is great" from rooftops at night received a great response in a number of Syrian cities, so that some of his supporters inside [Syria] described him as the inspiration and first guide of the revolution.

Al-Bayan quoted a protestor from the town of Douma in the Damascus countryside, who claimed that Arour's strong words through the Safa and Wesal [satellite] channels had a major role in giving motivation and raising the morale of young people and urging them to continue the revolution... These words resonated with the rebellious Syrian street despite the repression practiced by the regime, and accordingly, the demonstrators chanted to Sheikh Arour in the squares with the phrases: Preach, preach, preach, ya Arour![37]

Al-Bayan further quoted a university student from the city of Rastan near Homs who explained that

no one in the Syrian opposition has the same influence as Sheikh Adnan, especially in Homs and its countryside, and the pictures of Arour that they raised in their protest marches are only an appreciation of his support for the demands of the people.

Adnan al-Arour notoriously warned in June 2011 that

those Alawites who remained neutral will not be harmed. Anyone who supported us will be on our side, and will be treated as a citizen just like us. As for those who violated all that is sacred, by Allah, we shall mince them in meat grinders and we shall feed their flesh to the dogs.[38]

Hidden Militias and Mysterious Attacks

There are several possibilities, then, to account for the four deaths during the protests in Daraa on March 18, 2011. One possibility is that Syrian security forces killed the first protestors in the chaos of the rioting that accompanied the demonstrations. A second possibility is that those killed were not civilian protestors, but armed militants clashing with the security forces. A final possibility is that protestors were killed by infiltrators or saboteurs — from al-Qaeda, for example — who wished to sabotage any agreement to end the crisis and to turn residents against the government.

It should be noted here that there was significant confusion among locals in Daraa about who was killing whom during this early period. Just being present in Daraa at the time, including at a protest where killings took place, does not necessarily mean that one could determine the source of the violence. Additionally, first impressions can change once more evidence emerges.

For example, in 2014, journalist Sharmine Narwani interviewed a member of the large Hariri family in Daraa. The Hariri family member, who was present in Daraa as events unfolded in March and April 2011, said that people were confused and that many "loyalties have changed two or three times from March 2011 till now. They were originally all with the government. Then suddenly changed against the government — but now I think maybe 50 percent or more came back to the Syrian regime." Narwani reports further that

> as Hariri explains it, there were two opinions in Daraa. "One was that the regime is shooting more people to stop them and warn them to finish their protests and stop gathering. The other opinion was that hidden militias want this to continue, because if there are no funerals, there is no reason for people to gather... At the beginning 99.9 percent of them were saying all shooting is by the government. But slowly, slowly this idea began to change in their mind — there are some hidden parties, but they don't know what."[39]

But the al-Qaeda fighters comprising the "hidden militias" and "hidden parties" carrying out attacks were then joined by local young men from the protest movement to form the growing anti-government insurgency.

Summarizing the situation in Syria as of one month after the beginning of anti-government protests, Muhammad Jamal Barout writes:

> There were signs of an initial and simple armament process for some groups of young men, "mysterious" attacks on some army and police units, and the emergence of some Salafi players abroad, especially the "Sarourists," who have bases of influence among the youth of Houran [Deraa], to develop the protest movement into an overall revolution against the regime.[40]

This means that it was the supporters of Muhammad Sarour who constituted the hardline elements of the opposition and comprised the groups of young men who were becoming militarized to turn the protest movement into an "overall revolution." As mentioned in Chapter 2, Sarour, who spent 20 years in Britain, would later emerge as "one of the key conduits for Qatari money to the anti-Assad rebels."[41]

The merging of these two groups — foreign al-Qaeda fighters and local supporters of Muhammad Sarour — would seem to explain the attack on Syrian security forces in the town of Nawa, near Daraa, on April 22, 2011. Human Rights Watch (HRW) confirmed that seven members of the security forces were shot to death under the cover of protests that day. The witness cited by HRW tried to emphasize the peaceful nature of the protestors, claiming that they approached the political security building in Nawa holding olive branches to demand the release of two detainees, and that political security officers opened fire on the protestors, killing four. The witness nevertheless acknowledged that some of the protestors were at least lightly armed, and that once the protestors succeeded in storming the building, "they saw seven members of the security who had apparently been shot and killed by the protestors during the confrontation."[42]

The number of political security men who died in the confrontation (seven) compared to protestors who died (four) resembled the ratio of protestors to police killed in the first weekend of protests in Daraa. This again suggests that the four dead protestors may have instead been armed militants.

We have clear evidence of an al-Qaeda attack near Daraa four days before the events at Nawa. This comes from V.P. Haran, the Indian ambassador to Syria, who noted that on April 18, 2011, Syrian media reported that between six and eight Syrian soldiers were killed when an armed group raided two security posts on the road between Damascus and the Jordanian border. After visiting the area two days later and speaking with locals, Haran had the impression that something even more serious had taken place. U.S. Ambassador to Syria Robert Ford and the Iraqi ambassador to Syria both expressed their view in private conversations to Haran that the Syrian security forces had been not merely killed, but beheaded, and that al-Qaeda in Iraq was responsible for the killings.[43]

According to Haran, al-Qaeda had carried out attacks even earlier as well, on March 25 in Syria's northwest port city of Latakia.[44] Syrian government sources claimed that twelve people were killed in Latakia that weekend, including security personnel, after unidentified gunmen shot at crowds from rooftops.[45]

Fake Massacres

The confusion about who was killing whom was compounded for Syrians due to claims of fake massacres and killings spread by U.S.-trained opposition activists using social media and encryption tools. The dissemination of propaganda of this sort began in coordinated fashion just as the protests erupted in Daraa. For example, Rania Abouzeid reports:

> A Facebook page entitled "The Syrian Revolution 2011," which has more than 56,000 fans, appears to be emerging as a key virtual rallying point for pro-democracy supporters. On Saturday [March 19] it posted a 39-second video purportedly shot in Daraa of a group of men gathered around a bloodied youth in a black t-shirt who appeared to be dead. A volley of gunshots is heard, scattering the crowd. There was no date on the video, nor any way to verify where the footage had been obtained.[46]

While few questioned the veracity or credibility of such unverifiable videos at the time, as the Syrian conflict progressed, it became clear that, as journalist Patrick Cockburn observed, many of the videos of this sort published on Facebook and YouTube amounted to "black propaganda" from the opposition. These unverifiable videos were passed on by the Western and Gulf press in a manner resembling the simple spreading of rumors. Cockburn notes that, "of course, people who run newspapers and radio and television stations are not fools. They know the dubious nature of much of the information they are conveying."[47]

On April 2, 2011, *Newsweek* journalist Mike Giglio published an interview with an activist using the pseudonym Malath Aumran, who had been organizing online against the Syrian government for three years (in other words, since the time that the U.S. State Department had partnered with the large tech firms to fund and train Syrian, Egyptian, and Iranian cyber dissidents). *Newsweek* writes of Aumran:

> The photo he uses for public consumption evokes an eerie sense of familiarity, but isn't real. A computer-generated amalgam of many men, it is everyone and no one at all. Even his virtual presence is a specter, concealed behind encryption… When demonstrations broke out in Daraa recently, phony activists on Twitter blasted out videos of massacres, which were duly picked up by dissidents including Aumran. The videos turned out to be fakes, discrediting the type of social-media elite who were crucial news sources in countries like Egypt and Tunisia.[48]

Although Gigli blames the fake massacre videos on the Syrian security forces, it is more likely that such videos were created by foreign intelligence services and spread by opposition media activists to turn public opinion against the Syrian government. It was certainly not in the government's interest to spread fake videos suggesting its own security forces were carrying out massacres. The usefulness of spreading such propaganda is precisely why U.S. planners had spent years promoting the use of Twitter, Facebook, YouTube, and Tor among activists.

Days after Gigli's *Newsweek* article, Aumran was identified by the Syrian government as Rami Nakhle, a Syrian activist who had fled the country in January 2011. Nakhle had been interrogated multiple times by the security services, who were "suspicious of him due to his travels abroad and contacts with the activist and media communities."[49] By his own account, Nakhle had worked for years with U.S. clients Razan Zaitouneh and Mazen Darwish to establish the LCCs (Local Coordination Committees) before the outbreak of protests in 2011.[50]

During the first months of the so-called revolution, Nakhle carried out his cyber activism from Beirut, and in August 2011 was spirited out of Lebanon by UN officials. Further illustrating his U.S. government links, Nakhle was then brought to Washington, D.C., where he began working for the U.S. government-funded U.S. Institute for Peace on a project known as the "Day After," led by academic and Syria specialist Steven Heydemann. Nakhle then went on to become a member of the Syrian National Council (SNC), a U.S.-, Gulf-, and Turkish-backed opposition group.[51]

One role of the LCCs led by Zaitouneh, Darwish, and Nakhle was to inflate, or even to fabricate, death counts. Hafiz Abdul Rahman of Maf, a Kurdish human rights group in Syria, explained that his group could not rely on information reported by the LCC-run Facebook pages because he viewed the group as partisan. He explained that "the tansiqiyaat [LCC] might report five deaths when really there were three and two injuries. In some cases, individuals hunted by the regime used Facebook to falsify their own deaths."[52]

Using Tanks Against Protestors?

Because Salafist militants, including militants from al-Qaeda, were infiltrating protests and attacking Syrian soldiers and police, the opposition and Western press were able to portray the government's military operations against these militants as efforts to crack down on peaceful protests. For example, Anthony Shadid of the *New York Times* reported on April 25, 2011, that

> a handful of videos posted on the Internet, along with residents' accounts, gave a picture of a city under broad military assault, in what appeared to mark a new phase in the government crackdown. *Tanks had not previously been used against protestors*, and the force of the assault suggested that the military planned some sort of occupation of the town.[53] (emphasis added)

Shadid quoted a Daraa resident as claiming, "It's an attempt to occupy Daraa." The resident further explained how

> soldiers had taken three mosques, but had yet to capture the Omari Mosque, where he said thousands had sought refuge. Since the beginning of the uprising last month, it has served as a headquarters of sorts for demonstrators. He quoted people there as shouting, "We swear you will not enter but over our dead bodies."

Even opposition sources confirmed, however, that armed clashes between the Syrian army and unknown militants were taking place, meaning that the tanks were sent against armed militants, rather than against protestors as Shadid suggested. Al Jazeera quoted a Daraa resident on April 27, 2011, as noting that "the army is fighting with some armed groups because there was *heavy shooting from two sides…* I cannot say *who the other side is*, but I can say now that it is so hard for civilians" (emphasis added).[54]

Opposition activists Sally Masalmeh and Malek al-Jawabra also confirmed to *Wall Street Journal* reporter Sam Dagher that during the Syrian army's assault on the al-Omari Mosque in April 2011, opposition militants had barricaded themselves inside the mosque and were stockpiling weapons there. Masalmeh and Jawabra resorted to conspiracy theories to explain the presence of weapons in the mosque, suggesting that "there were people among the protestors working secretly with the Mukhabarat [Syrian intelligence] and that it was they who facilitated the procurement of weapons and urged confrontation with the army."[55]

These claims of conspiracy are not credible, however, given additional admissions from other pro-opposition sources. For example, the activist from Daraa, Abd al-Qader al-Dhoun, was proud to acknowledge that two of his cousins fought and died in clashes with Syrian security forces at the al-Omari Mosque during this period. He stressed to the interviewer that claims that they were "terrorists" were false, but that they were indeed armed militants using Kalashnikovs and pump-action shotguns.[56]

Other pro-opposition sources also detailed efforts to smuggle weapons to militants in Daraa during March 2011, further contradicting the conspiracy theories.

Prominent opposition and human rights activist Haytham Manna provided evidence that elements close to pro-Saudi Lebanese politician Saad Hariri were funneling weapons to militants in Syria, including in Daraa. Manna publicly disclosed in an interview to Al Jazeera on March 31, 2011, that "he had received offers to arm movements from Raqqa to Daraa three times by parties he did not identify in the interview."[57]

Muhammad Jamal Barout additionally writes that, according to Manna, there were secret communications between some Syrian businessmen abroad who found themselves in a battle of revenge with the Syrian regime because their interests had been harmed by the network of the pro-regime businessman Rami Makhlouf, and that these groups were willing to fund and arm opposition movements throughout the country. Barout notes that these businessmen apparently had relations with professional networks capable of delivering weapons to any location in Syria, and that some members of the Future Movement (a prominent political party in Lebanon led by Saad Hariri and known to have strong Saudi support) were among those arranging these weapons shipments.[58]

Manna confirmed further details to journalist Alix Van Buren of Italy's *la Repubblica* newspaper, speaking "about three groups having contacted him to provide money and weapons to the rebels in Syria":

> First, a Syrian businessman (the story reported by Al Jazeera); secondly, he was contacted by "several pro-American Syrian opposers" to put it in his words (he referred to more than one individual); thirdly, he mentioned approaches of the same kind by "Syrians in Lebanon who are loyal to a Lebanese party which is against Syria,"

presumably referring to the Future Movement in Lebanon as well.[59]

To Arm a Resistance

Further evidence of the armed nature of the opposition in Daraa comes from Anwar al-Eshki, a former Saudi general, who alluded to his government's arming of militants in Syria as well. In an interview with the BBC, Eshki explained that he had been in contact with opposition militants in Daraa, and that they were stockpiling weapons in the al-Omari Mosque, apparently against the wishes of the mosque's imam, the blind Sheikh Ahmed Siyasna, who rejected the idea of using violence. Eshki also described the Saudi rationale for providing weapons to opposition militants as the conflict went on, explaining:

> We saw on different occasions how to arm small groups to form a "resistance." To arm a "resistance" doesn't necessarily mean to give them tanks or heavy weapons like what happened in Libya. However, you give them weapons, so they can defend themselves and exhaust the army. The goal is to drive the government forces outside the cities to the villages.[60]

Foreign efforts to spark an insurrection covertly from Daraa, as described by Eshki, are unsurprising, given the city's location near the Jordanian border. CIA plans to spark an insurrection in Syria all the way back in 1957 recommended the same strategy. Historian Matthew Jones writes that the creation of an incident along the Syrian-Jordanian border was seen as the most promising scenario to spark outside military intervention. King Hussein's [of Jordan] cooperation and influence could be enlisted to induce one or two of the Bedouin tribes residing in southern Syria to stage a rising of sufficient scale to provoke a Syrian army counter-attack… In addition, SIS [British intelligence] and CIA should gather Syrian opposition groups together in Jordan under the aegis of a "Free Syria Committee," while "Syrian political factions with paramilitary or other actionist capabilities should be prepared for execution of specific tasks suited to their talents."[61]

Flynt Leverett, the former CIA and NSC official cited in Chapter 1, acknowledged the crucial early U.S. role in arming militants launching attacks against Syrian government targets in 2011. Leverett told journalist and author Scott Horton that the Obama administration was "looking for a place where regime change would do harm to Iran's regional position," and that Syria "seemed to fit the bill." As a result,

from early on, the administration started encouraging and supporting the opposition, coordinating with allies, whether European allies, the Saudis, the Turks, the Qataris *to fund and equip armed oppositionists* in Syria, a big percentage of whom it turns out, *aren't even Syrian but had been brought in from outside Syria*, and very early on [President Obama] declared Bashar al-Assad must go.[62] (emphasis added)

This was despite the fact that, as Leverett acknowledged, "Assad has the support of a significant majority of Syria's population."

As discussed in Chapter 2, Saudi intelligence had "fired up the old Sunni network" and brought in many al-Qaeda militants from outside Syria during this early period. Leverett seems to be referencing this effort here, and that it was done with U.S. approval.

Qatari Prime Minister Hamad bin Jassim bin Jaber Al-Thani also discussed the U.S. role, stating that a security committee was established with representatives from the U.S., Saudi Arabia, Qatar, Turkey, and Jordan to coordinate the Syria file, namely the effort to topple the Syrian government. Al-Thani notes that Qatar was in charge of this file in the early months of the conflict.[63] Al-Thani had met with Saudi King Abdullah, who told him, "We are with you. Take the lead, and we will coordinate." Al-Thani then explained: "All distribution was done through the U.S. and the Turks and us and everyone else that was involved, the military people."[64]

The Martyr Hamza al-Khateeb

It was in this context that one of the most controversial early events of the war occurred, namely the killing of 13-year-old Hamza al-Khateeb in April 2011. The BBC summarized events, reporting that

> Hamza went missing after a demonstration at an army barracks near Deraa in the south at the end of April. Activists say he was captured and tortured to death, and that his mutilated body was handed back to his family four weeks later. The government says he received three fatal gunshot wounds during the protest and died on the spot, but there was a delay in handing over his body because he was not identified.[65]

Providing the opposition view of events, Al Jazeera cited one of Hamza's cousins, who said the teenager was not political, "but everybody seemed to be going to the protest, so he went along as well," and that Hamza walked with friends and family 12 kilometers along the road from his hometown of Jeezah to Saida [near Daraa city], where Syrian security forces began opening fire on the protestors. According to the cousin, "people were killed and wounded, some were arrested. It was chaotic. We didn't know at that point what had happened to Hamza. He just disappeared."

A month later, Hamza's body was delivered to his family by Syrian authorities. The cousin explained further that, "when Hamza's mother came to see the body she was only shown his face," and that "we tried to tell the father not to look, but he pulled the blanket back. When he saw Hamza's body he fainted. People ran to help him and some started filming — it was chaos."[66]

Those who started filming were activists who had gained access to the body. The activists released a video showing Hamza's body with the narrator saying:

> In the name of God the all-merciful, we present to you another martyr among the martyrs of freedom, from the city of Jeezah and the province of Deraa, and his name is Hamza Ali al-Khateeb, and his age is 13 years old when he went out in the "Friday of anger" to lift the siege of the sons of Deraa, and he was detained at the Saida housing complex and he was tortured in the ugliest ways.[67]

Al Jazeera described the activist-produced video showing Hamza's body, and alleged it was mutilated due to the torture before his death. Al Jazeera claimed that

Hamza's eyes were swollen and black and there were identical bullet wounds where he had apparently been shot through both arms, the bullets tearing a hole in his sides and lodging in his belly. Hamza's mutilated, castrated corpse was riddled with bullet holes and burn marks. On Hamza's chest was a deep, dark burn mark. His neck was broken and his penis cut off.[68]

In contrast, Syrian state television claimed that after Friday prayers on April 29, people began to gather in some villages of Daraa countryside responding to calls for jihad, and that "armed members showed up among the crowd and succeeded in misleading many young children into going with them to fire at the [military housing] compound's guards, whose chief was martyred."

The report cited an alleged friend of Hamza's, who claimed that he, Hamza, and two other friends had joined a group of protestors, and "we headed to the military residences in Saida accompanied by armed men. As we reached there, some demonstrators opened fire toward the compound injuring one soldier. Later, there was a heavy fire exchange and we had to hide behind trees." The friend added that Hamza was among the injured and "fell to the ground and I didn't know what happened to him."

The Syrian state television report then claimed that Hamza's body was found in the area surrounding the military housing compound and was transferred to the National Hospital in Daraa along with others killed in the clashes. A coroner then analyzed and took photos of Hamza's body, but because the body could not be identified, it was placed in the morgue. Finally, roughly a month later, the body was able to be identified, and authorities returned it to the family.[69]

The coroner who examined Hamza's body, Akram al-Shaar, claimed that Hamza had been killed by three gunshots, the wounds of which had caused significant bleeding, and that there were no signs of torture at the time of his death. Shaar claimed that the apparently mutilated state of the body shown by the activist video was a result of natural decay that occurred between the time of Hamza's death on April 29 and when the body was delivered to the family on May 21. This was evidenced by comparing photos of the body taken by the coroner at the time of death with the video of the body as filmed by the activists. In the activist video, the body was extremely bloated, and the skin had turned much darker in color.[70]

Syrian authorities provided Hamza's family with the coroner's report, and President Assad met directly with Hamza's father and uncle to offer condolences and to discuss what happened. Speaking with Syrian state television, Hamza's uncle commented that

> we do not care about foreign media; what we care about is to get the truth, and to get it correct and complete. We have received martyr Hamza's body from the National Hospital in Deraa, and everything has been documented in the doctor's report which is now in the attorney general office, and we have a copy of it... [The president] cares about Hamza as if he was his own son, what can we say more.

Hamza's father commented further: "Yes, it is true, [President Assad] wanted to meet me, Hamza's father personally, to make sure all of it is true."[71]

In the state television report, both Hamza's uncle and father appear to be speaking freely and under no duress. Both appear grateful to have met President Assad. This was despite claims by Al Jazeera that, according to Hamza's cousin, Hamza's father had wanted to press charges against the army and security forces, and that he and his wife were visited by the secret police and threatened.[72]

Amid these conflicting claims, opposition activists established a Facebook page in Hamza's honor and drew parallels between the death of Hamza and that of Khalid Said, the young man murdered by police in Egypt whose death had been used by U.S.-funded activists as a rallying cry for anti-government protests.

The *Washington Post* reported four days after the emergence of the video that although "details of exactly what happened to Hamza are sketchy and cannot be independently confirmed," Hamza's death had reinvigorated Syria's protest movement. The *Post* reported that "activists believe Hamza will become the Khaled Said of Syria," while quoting Wissam Tarif of Insan as explaining: "This boy is already a symbol... It has provoked people, and the protests are increasing."[73]

6. Latakia and Banias, Khaddam's Playground

Latakia

The armed nature of the opposition was also evident in Latakia. On March 25–26, 2011, protests and violence also erupted in the northern coastal town, home to both Sunnis and Alawites. As elsewhere, conflicting reports emerged about the source of the violence. Human Rights Watch reported that "anti-government demonstrators in Latakia who spoke to television outlets accused the security forces of opening fire on them, while officials and pro-government protestors accused the anti-government protestors of having guns and shooting at police."[1] Government sources claimed that 12 were killed — including civilians, members of the security forces, and two unknown gunmen who allegedly opened fire from rooftops — and that the army was dispatched to the city in response to the violence.[2]

On March 27, 2011, *Al-Quds Al-Arabi* reported that an organized effort was in place to spread rumors that Alawites would be murdered by Sunnis, and Sunnis murdered by Alawites, and that the security services had arrested several foreigners, most likely Jordanians. The paper also reported that gunmen had been roaming through Latakia in cars, some carrying fake plates, while firing shots at homes and in the streets, leading to three deaths. This resulted in locals forming self-defense committees to prevent strangers from entering their neighborhoods.[3]

The general government version of events was supported by the Indian ambassador V.P. Haran, who, as noted in Chapter 5, claimed that al-Qaeda militants had carried out attacks in Latakia on March 25.[4]

On March 29, 2011, the Lebanese newspaper *As-Safir* detailed unconfirmed reports from an Arab diplomatic source who claimed: that Syrian authorities had confiscated seven boats loaded with weapons coming from the northern Lebanese coast; that Syrian and Lebanese militants had entered Syrian territory through the Bekaa Valley and at some points in northern Lebanon; and that these militants had allegedly carried out military operations, including sniping and shooting using night vision equipment and sniper rifles.[5]

Time journalist Rania Abouzeid similarly reported that al-Qaeda-affiliated militants were active in Latakia Province early in the crisis. She reports that a Salafist militant named Muhammad

> enlisted a small group of Salafi friends from Latakia who, along with a few local men he'd armed, overran half a dozen small police stations in villages dotted around the city. The first raid was in mid-April… Mohammad said he netted nine Kalashnikovs and ammunition. It wasn't hard.[6]

Muhammad had previously recruited fighters to go to Iraq to fight with al-Qaeda in 2003 and went on to become a commander in the Nusra Front.

Fighting in Latakia between the army and opposition armed groups would continue through the summer of 2011. Starting on August 13, 2011, the Syrian army carried out operations in several neighborhoods to defeat the militants. Anthony Shadid of the *New York Times* reported claims from Syrian government sources that the security forces were fighting men armed with "machine guns, grenades, and explosive devices" in several neighborhoods, including in the al-Ramel al-Janoubi neighborhood, and that two members of the security forces were killed and 41 wounded. Despite reporting the Syrian government's claims, Shadid nevertheless portrayed the operation as a response to peaceful anti-government protests in Latakia and claimed that the defiance of the demonstrators "prompted the attack on some of the city's neighborhoods populated by Palestinian refugees and poor Syrian Sunnis." Shadid claimed that "for the first time… gunfire was coming from navy vessels anchored off the coast."[7] This claim — that Syrian warships were bombarding civilian neighborhoods in response to peaceful protests — was echoed by Al Jazeera,[8] the BBC,[9] and United Nations Relief and Works Agency for Palestine Refugees (UNRWA) representative Chris Gunness,[10] who claimed that the Palestinian camp in the al-Ramel neighborhood had been bombed, and that this had caused some 5,000 Palestinians to flee, whose whereabouts were unknown.

Like the *New York Times*, Khaled Yacoub Oweis of Reuters also portrayed the Syrian military operation in Latakia as an attempt to "crush protests," rather than an effort to defeat armed militants who had infiltrated the city.[11] Further, Oweis cited Rami Abdul Rahman of the U.K.-funded Syrian Observatory for Human Rights (SOHR) as claiming that Syrian authorities were using the local soccer stadium as a mass detention center for civilians. This claim was repeated by the *Los Angeles Times* as well, which cited a local doctor who claimed that Syrian forces had stormed the Palestinian refugee camp, and that "what we know and what we have seen is that the April 7 football stadium and Sports City stadium have turned into a detention facility."[12]

All of these claims proved to be false, however — part of the broader propaganda campaign against the Syrian government. Tarek Homoud of the Muslim Brotherhood-funded Action Group for Palestinians in Syria (AGPS) visited the al-Ramel Palestinian camp at the time and acknowledged that while there was a Syrian army operation against militants in the broader al-Ramel neighborhood, the Syrian army was not targeting the al-Ramel Palestinian camp itself. Homoud also confirmed that the Syrian navy was not bombarding the al-Ramel area, and that the football stadium was not being used as a mass detention center, but as housing for internally displaced persons (IDPs) fleeing the violence. Homoud explains that the

> Syrian army sent warning to the residents of the camp to leave. Thousands of its inhabitants left immediately in different directions. The sport city in Latakia city opened its doors to the IDPs. The bombing that took place targeted the Syrian neighborhood [al-Ramel] and not as what was described officially which was that the Syrian armed boats shelled the Palestinian camp. Only small parts of the camps were shelled when fighters entered it. This resulted in three persons being killed in the camp. The destruction was limited, and some houses were exposed to live bullets.[13]

The Secretary of the Palestinian Forces Alliance in Damascus, Khaled Abdel Majid, also confirmed that the al-Ramel Palestinian camp had not been singled out for attack, and denounced the statement issued by Gunness of UNRWA. Majid explained that

> the Palestinian neighborhood of Raml was not bombed at all, and that military and security operations are taking place in the neighborhoods of al-Skantouri and Quneis, adjacent to the Palestinian neighborhood of Ramel... The Palestinian neighborhood of Ramel is a small part of the area that witnessed security operations.[14]

Journalist Sharmine Narwani also confirmed that Syrian warships had not bombarded the city, explaining that "three separate sources — two opposition figures from the city and an independent Western journalist — later insisted there were no signs of shelling."[15] As reported by the Lebanese newspaper *al-Akhbar*, even "U.S. State Department spokeswoman Victoria Nuland indicated that she could not confirm published reports that Syrian warships had bombed the coastal city of Latakia."[16]

Despite credible reports that the Syrian army was simply doing its best to root out armed militants from the city, the narrative promoted by the *New York Times*, Reuters, and SOHR — namely that the Syrian government was carrying out mass detentions and using navy warships to bombard residential areas to crush peaceful dissent and protest — persisted.

Banias

In the coastal town of Banias, the government also deployed tanks — though not to suppress protests, but rather to respond to opposition attacks on Syrian soldiers and to prevent a sectarian war from erupting between Alawite and Sunni residents. In this case, the agent working on behalf of U.S. and Saudi interests was former Syrian Prime Minister Abd al-Halim Khaddam. As discussed in Chapter 2, Khaddam defected from the Syrian government in 2005 and began working toward regime change at that time with both the Muslim Brotherhood and neoconservatives from the Bush administration.

According to researcher Sabr Darwish of the EU-funded and pro-opposition *SyriaUntold*, protests in Banias also began on March 18, 2011 — as in Daraa — and were organized and led by Sheikh Anas Ayrout, a local Sunni cleric and imam of the al-Rahman Mosque, with activist Anas al-Shaghri also playing a prominent role.[17] Ayrout later became a member of the Western-backed Syrian National Council (SNC) and in 2013 called for killing Alawite civilians to create a "balance of terror" to compel them to abandon support for the government.[18]

According to opposition activist Bissam Walid, the demands of the protestors in Banias included: the release of detainee Ahmed Hudhayfa, who had been arrested in Damascus; the return of female teachers who, for wearing the niqab, had been transferred to jobs in other ministries; the lowering of electricity prices; and segregated education of boys and girls.[19]

During the first protest on March 18, demonstrators attacked an Alawite truck driver before Sheikh Anas Ayrout intervened to stop them. According to Sabr Darwish, protests in Banias were otherwise peaceful and allowed to go forward unsuppressed by the security forces over the following three weeks, while government officials were responsive to protestors' demands. During protests on April 1, demonstrators chanted slogans against Iran and Hezbollah, criticizing their alleged intervention in Syria. The next week, demonstrators began a sit-in at the central square of the city.[20]

If They Shoot at You

Events in Banias became violent on Saturday, April 9, 2011, when nine Syrian soldiers were killed. Regarding the attack, *The Guardian* reported:

> Syrian soldiers have been shot by security forces after refusing to fire on protestors, witnesses said, as a crackdown on anti-government demonstrations intensified. Witnesses told al-Jazeera and the BBC that some soldiers had refused to shoot after the army moved into Banias in the wake of intense protests on Friday.[21]

The Guardian also quoted Wissam Tarif of Avaaz to support their account. Tarif claimed that a conscript from Madaya village named Mourad Hejjo was one of those shot by government snipers, and that "his family and town are saying he refused to shoot at his people." *The Guardian* also linked to footage on YouTube that it claimed "shows an injured soldier saying he was shot in the back by security forces."[22]

Prominent Syria expert and academic Joshua Landis quickly showed the claims made by *The Guardian* and Wissam Tarif to be false, however. Landis demonstrated that the soldiers were instead killed by opposition militants using sniper rifles from a distance as the soldiers' bus was entering Banias.

Landis writes:

> Video of one soldier purportedly confessing to being shot in the back by security forces and linked to by *The Guardian* has been completely misconstrued. *The Guardian* irresponsibly repeats a false interpretation of the video provided by an informant… The video does not "support" the story that *The Guardian* says it does. The soldier denies that he was ordered to fire on people. Instead, he says he was on his way to Banyas to enforce security. He does not say that he was shot at by government agents or soldiers. In fact, he denies it. The interviewer tries to put words in his mouth, but the soldier clearly denies the story that the interviewer is trying to make him confess to. In the video, the wounded soldier is surrounded by people who are trying to get him to say that he was shot by a military officer. The soldier says clearly, "They [our superiors] told us, 'Shoot at them *if* they shoot at you.'"[23] (emphasis in original)

Landis notes further that the

> interviewer tried to get the wounded soldier to say that he had refused orders to shoot at the people when he asked: "When you did not shoot at us what happened?" But the soldier doesn't understand the question because he has just said that he was not given orders to shoot at the people. The soldier replies, "Nothing, the shooting started from all directions." The interviewer repeats his question in another way by asking, "Why were you shooting at us, we are

Muslims?" The soldier answers him, "I am Muslim too." The interviewer asks, "So why were you going to shoot at us?" The soldier replies, "We did not shoot at people. They shot at us at the bridge."[24]

Azmi Bishara later confirmed that opposition militants killed the soldiers as well. Bishara cites a political activist from the Together Movement in Banias as explaining how opposition militants had fired on the soldiers from an observation bridge on the international highway which links Latakia and Damascus.[25]

Bishara links the attack on the soldiers' bus to "the ongoing arms smuggling operation across the Lebanese border," which was used to smuggle weapons into both Homs and Banias. Bishara writes that

> Muhammad Ali al-Biyassi (one of the people working with Abd al-Halim Khaddam) requested arming the people which went out in protests in the beginning of April 2011. And this person led the operation to send weapons to Banias. And the operations to smuggle weapons led to military confrontations with the Syrian army and security forces.[26]

Bishara cites as his source "a person from the family of al-Biyassi who witnessed these operations and who soon was among those who carried weapons and told the witness the details of the operations."

Making the Decision

The attack on the soldiers on April 9, 2011, was the first effort to launch an armed insurrection to take control of Banias. Pro-opposition activist Sabr Darwish acknowledges that Sheikh Anas Ayrout's supporters sought a violent takeover of the city. Darwish tries to portray it as defensive in nature, despite the killing of the nine Syrian soldiers and weapons smuggling that preceded it. Darwish writes:

> There is no real consensus about the exact day the decision was made to liberate the revolutionary neighborhoods. However, according to many testimonies, it is agreed that Sheikh Anas Ayrout played a crucial role in every aspect of the events. Following Ayrout's recommendation to self-defense and the subsequent blockades created by the youth, entire neighborhoods fell to the control of the residents.[27]

Darwish claims that Ayrout ordered his supporters to arm themselves, set up roadblocks, and take control of several neighborhoods. This came after the government had allegedly cut electricity and phone lines in Banias and amidst rumors that Syrian security forces would soon invade the city. Darwish writes further:

> Although there was no clear sign that the regime was about to storm the city, with no increase in security presence in the streets or military reinforcements surrounding the city, the people were still worried. Rather than use his clout to ask about the power and communications, Ayrout called for the residents to practice self-defense, and made things worse. The citizens mobilized, carrying their arms, and the youth erected checkpoints and roadblocks, cutting off access to public roads with garbage. The atmosphere of the city was charged with anticipation and concern.

Muhammad Jamal Barout also noted that armed men took control of the city. He writes that on Saturday, April 9, the day the soldiers were shot, an

> angry demonstration took place, where several of the demonstrators were wearing shrouds, as symbolic evidence of their willingness to be martyred, which the speaker made as the ultimate goal of achieving freedom. And in the evening of the same day, an armed group took control of the city and called for jihad, and provoked the neighborhoods with a majority Alawite and Christian population by chanting sectarian slogans.[28]

Regarding the protestors wearing shrouds, Barout cites Al Jazeera as reporting that the "Syrian Revolution 2011" movement had broadcast on its Facebook page a videotape of a demonstration in the city in which dozens participated, some of whom wore white shrouds. Preachers of mosques in the city had urged citizens in Friday sermons to exercise their right to demonstrate.[29]

On Sunday, April 10, the day following the attack on the soldiers and after Ayrout's followers took over several neighborhoods, sectarian tensions erupted. Pro-opposition lawyer Haitham al-Maleh reports that "a group barricaded themselves in the Abu Bakr al Siddiq Mosque. It was shortly after dawn, the dawn prayer. Armed with sticks, they mounted the defense around the shrine to face the security forces."[30]

Plainclothes security forces in speeding cars coming from Alawite neighborhoods then opened fire on Sunni men guarding both the Rahman and Abu Bakr al-Siddiq Mosques, injuring 12, according to opposition sources.[31] Reuters reported that one of the injured, Osama al-Sheikha, died from his wounds a week later.[32]

Sabr Darwish reports further armed sectarian clashes between Alawite and Sunni young men on the same day. He reported that amidst the atmosphere of fear and anticipation, sounds of heavy fire were heard from the bridge. Later, people learned that a group of youth from the Alawite villages surrounding Banias had clashed with some of the activists stationed at the entrance of the city... The intruders fled following the clashes, leaving behind a young Alawite man. The activists decided to detain this man, and videos emerged of them beating him. On the way to hand him to Sheikh Ayrout, the man was stabbed multiple times with sharp knives which led to his death several hours later.[33]

The man stabbed to death by Ayrout's supporters was Nidal Janoud, an Alawite vegetable seller. Janoud's murderers filmed the killing and uploaded the video to the Internet. The shocking footage was later shown on Syrian state television and led to the arrest of two of the killers and also to widespread outrage among government supporters.[34]

The *New York Times* claimed that on the same day Janoud was murdered, Sunday, April 10, "four protestors were killed by state security forces during pro-democracy demonstrations in Baniyas."[35]

These were not pro-democracy protests, however. Ayrout and his supporters were demanding segregated education for boys and girls, and that female employees of the ministry of education wearing the niqab be restored to their teaching positions. Additionally, the *NYT* provided no details of the circumstances of these deaths, nor of the source of the claim, but appeared to be relying on information from both Wissam Tarif and Razan Zaitouneh, both of whom were quoted in the report regarding other aspects of events in Banias that day.[36]

The vague nature and lack of sourcing of this claim make it questionable whether those killed that day were protestors. More detailed accounts of events in Banias from opposition sources, including from Sabr Darwish and Bissam Walid, do not mention the deaths of any protestors on that day, but do report on armed sectarian clashes between Alawite and Sunni young men and the attack on the al-Rahman Mosque.[37]

This suggests that any deaths that day, beyond Nidal Janoud's, were likely of armed supporters of Anas Ayrout engaging in clashes with Alawite gangs or security forces. It is also possible Nidal Janoud was wrongly counted as among those killed by Syrian security forces that day. As Sharmine Narwani observed, Janoud's name appeared on an early list of Syrian victims compiled by the SOHR, in which the victims were presumed to have been killed by government forces.[38]

98

In response to the violence in Banias, local security forces then rounded up hundreds of Sunni men, causing a group of some 350 women to block a road in protest to demand their release.[39] According to the *New York Times*, "YouTube postings said to be of the protest showed women, most wearing head scarves, some wearing full veils and many with children, pumping their fists and calling for the release of their relatives."[40]

Video later emerged, broadcast on Al Jazeera, of Syrian security forces kicking and beating a large group of detained men lying on their stomachs with their hands tied behind their backs in a public square in the nearby town of Baida.[41] Barout writes that this "provoked an angry emotional response among the protest street, and promoted a criminal image of the security men, and strengthened the feelings of hatred against them, and the legitimacy of taking revenge against them."[42]

'We Are Happy It's the Army'

To avert further sectarian violence, government authorities struck a deal with notable local community members to withdraw the security forces from Banias and replace them with units from the army to maintain order. After Syrian army units entered Banias on Monday, April 11, 2011, one resident told the AP that "schools and shops were closed because people feared more clashes," and that "the army's arrival was met mostly with relief." The resident explained further that "we are happy it's the army and not security forces who are like regime-hired gangs."[43]

Reuters reported that "the deal, struck in Damascus between a Baath Party official and imams and prominent figures from Banias, was intended to help calm the city," while citing Rami Abdul Rahman of SOHR as explaining that "Banias residents arrested over the past several weeks are already being released," and that "the army will go in but there is also a pledge to pull out the secret police… and improve living conditions."[44]

Al Jazeera reported further that "the army's entry into the city was preceded by the release of 200 people on Wednesday and 150 Thursday who were arrested in connection with the events witnessed in the city in the past weeks." However, "Those found to have carried a weapon and were involved in violence remained in detention."[45]

Sectarian tensions still remained high. On April 14, Syrian state media claimed that "a group of armed snipers shot today a number of army members while they patrolled the city of Banias… One was martyred and another wounded."[46] After additional anti-government protests in Banias the next day, Friday, April 15, Muhammad Jamal Barout noted that

> the culture of this period took on a changed character, with religious slogans and speeches, blessing the victims and expressing readiness for martyrdom, and some protestors wore shrouds, which symbolized the readiness to militarize the conflict and mobilize for jihad.[47]

Despite the clear Salafist nature of the protests in Banias, Daraa, and elsewhere, Razan Zaitouneh claimed on April 16, 2011, to *The Guardian* that the crisis in Syria was erupting because Assad had "ignored the main demands of the people: freedom and democracy."[48] Zaitouneh was either completely ignorant of the dynamics of the protests she claimed to be objectively reporting on, or, more likely, was sticking to the script written for her by her handlers at the U.S. embassy in Damascus.

Meddling with the Blood of Innocents

It soon became clear that former Syrian Vice President Abd al-Halim Khaddam, who had been working for years with U.S. planners and the Muslim Brotherhood to topple the Syrian state, was behind the attacks that killed the nine Syrian soldiers on April 9, 2011, and the subsequent armed insurrection that threatened to spark a sectarian war in Banias.

As mentioned above, Azmi Bishara reported that the person responsible for smuggling weapons into Banias, Muhammad Ali al-Biyassi, was an associate of Khaddam.[49]

Additionally, when asked by *la Repubblica* journalist Alix Van Buren about events in Banias, prominent opposition figure and lawyer Haythem al-Maleh blamed the government for sectarian violence, but also acknowledged that the "elements that want to poison the relationship between the people and the regime: those who shoot demonstrators and soldiers to sow terror." When asked further whether he gave credibility to rumors of "infiltrators," Maleh asked, "How can you not, given the ambushes against the army?" Maleh directed blame at Khaddam, stating, "His fiefdom is Banias. Today two of his men were arrested for having stirred up protests and criminal gangs."[50]

Maleh's statement — that infiltrators were shooting not only soldiers but also demonstrators to sow terror — suggests further that the killings of the four protestors on March 18 in Daraa may have been a false-flag attack.

Van Buren notes that another opposition source had pointed to Khaddam's role in arming militants in Banias:

> The veteran blogger Ahmed Abu ElKheir, unfortunately now in prison for the second time in less than a month, and not yet released, has links to Banyas. The first, peaceful demonstration of Saturday morning was also sparked by the request for his release. In his Facebook profile, before being arrested, he too lashed out against Khaddam. Several commentators from that area agreed with him, cursing Khaddam for meddling "with the blood of the innocents."[51]

Although the army was trying to de-escalate a sectarian war in Banias sparked by an armed attack by opposition militants on Syrian soldiers themselves and exacerbated by the subsequent abuses of the local security forces and Alawite gangs, Razan Zaitouneh characterized the army's deployment to the city as an invasion to suppress peaceful protest. Zaitouneh wrote on April 12, 2011, that "Baniyas is still surrounded by army and security... There is fear that it will be attacked this night."[52]

7. Homs, the Capital of Regime Change

Homs

Another place where al-Qaeda-affiliated militants were deployed by Washington's regional proxies was in Homs, Syria's third-largest city. Homs is populated by Sunnis, Christians, and Alawites, and it lies near the Lebanese border.

Homs was one of the early epicenters of anti-government demonstrations and later became known as the first "capital of the revolution." According to Muhammad Jamal Barout, secular, middle-class activists such as Najati Tayyara made Homs an early protest center. These activists created Facebook pages to encourage residents to protest the detention of a young woman named Tel al-Malouhi.[1]

According to Azmi Bishara, Malouhi was detained in 2009 after criticizing the Syrian government on her blog. Syrian authorities accused her of spying on behalf of the U.S. government due to her relationship with an Austrian officer working for UN forces in the Israeli-occupied Golan Heights. The officer was accused of having sexual relations with Malouhi and weaponizing her for the benefit of the U.S. embassy in Cairo. Malouhi's detention became a symbol for the opposition in Homs to rally around.[2]

Bedouin tribes also played a significant role in the early protest movement in Homs due to their anger against the government after a wave of detentions in late 2010. The detentions came as part of a government effort to crack down on fuel smuggling. Significant profit could be made smuggling government-subsidized fuel across the nearby border to sell at higher market rates in Lebanon. Fuel smuggling was of concern to the government, which had struggled to maintain fuel subsidies in recent years due to the drain on the budget these subsidies had caused — some $9 billion, as of 2008.[3] But many Bedouin tribes in Homs had come to rely on income from fuel smuggling after declines in the livestock sector. As a result of their smuggling activities, many of the tribes in Homs were already armed prior to 2011.[4]

'We Don't Want to See Alawites'

On March 18, 2011, a small demonstration of some 200 people was organized in front of the Khalid bin al-Walid Mosque in Homs. The following week saw another anti-government demonstration by the Bedouin tribes in the al-Bayadha neighborhood.[5]

More protests followed on Friday, March 25, dubbed the "Friday of Glory" by opposition activists. According to Azmi Bishara, security forces surrounded the Khalid bin al-Walid Mosque to prevent protestors from gathering there. Instead, protestors gathered at several different sites, including the Nur Mosque in the Khalidiya neighborhood, and mosques in al-Bayadha and Deir al-Ba'lba. The protestors then converged on the square of the old clock tower in the center of Homs, while some also went to the nearby officers' club. Bishara notes that

> security forces were disciplined and didn't disperse demonstrations with force in Homs on March 25. Officers talked with protestors to get them to end the demonstration peacefully, in which they ripped up a picture of [Hafez] al-Assad. Officers wanted to disperse the demonstration peacefully to avoid sectarian clashes in the city which would entail a new dynamic.[6]

However, according to AFP, demonstrators attacked the officers' club, and a Syrian official confirmed that "an employee of the officers' club died as a result of an attack by the demonstrators."[7] On the same day, President Assad's advisor, Bouthaina Shaaban, claimed that she was personally present when Assad gave orders not to shoot at protestors, but that "this does not cancel out that there may be some mistakes."[8]

Bishara claims that after the protests on March 25, sectarian polarization intensified, with Alawite gangs attacking the Khalidiya Mosque, and Sunni protestors responding with chants of *"Biddna nahki ala' al-makshouf, al-alawiya ma biddna inshuuf!* (We want to say the obvious, we don't want to see Alawites)!"[9]

The sectarian tensions of this period were accompanied by tit-for-tat kidnappings between the city's Sunni and Alawite communities. Katie Paul of *The Daily Beast* described a resident of a religiously mixed neighborhood in Homs who later became an opposition fighter. Paul reports that "within days of the start of the protests in the southern city of Daraa, Alawis in Karm al-Zeitoun [a neighborhood in Homs] began kidnapping Sunnis for money, and vice versa." According to the resident, "everyone used to live mixed, but it became like war in the streets."[10]

On Friday, April 1, 2011, which activists dubbed the "Friday of the Martyrs," a 23-year-old woman named Tahani al-Khalidi was shot and killed by the security forces. She was apparently killed on a balcony while filming a demonstration originating at the Khalid bin al-Walid Mosque.[11] Bishara notes that Syrian authorities, on orders from the governor Iyad Gazal, tried to calm the situation by establishing a mourning tent for Khalidi and offering payment of money to the family of the girl, but the heads of the al-Bayadha neighborhood, who were of Bedouin origin, rejected this.[12]

Signs of Militarization

The opposition movement in Homs became militarized on Sunday, April 17, 2011, in the wake of the death of a local tribal leader named Sheikh Badr Abu Musa. Reuters cited an unnamed "human rights defender" as explaining that

> protests against the rule of the Baath Party intensified in Homs after the authorities handed over the body of Sheikh Badr Abu Musa of the Al-Fawara tribe to his family for burial on Saturday [April 16]. A 12-year-old boy was killed at Abu Musa's funeral, which turned into a demonstration on the same day. Abu Musa was arrested a week ago in front of a mosque after he participated in a pro-democracy demonstration.[13]

Reuters's unnamed source in Homs explained further that on Sunday, April 17, "Syrian forces killed eight protestors during the night in Homs in clashes after the killing of [Abu Musa]."

But those killed on Sunday, April 17, in the wake of Abu Musa's death were not peaceful protestors. Muhammad Jamal Barout and Azmi Bishara both describe the clashes between Abu Musa's supporters and the security forces on that day as armed confrontations, rather than peaceful demonstrations attacked by security forces. Bishara also describes these clashes as the first "signs of popular militarization" in the Baba Amr neighborhood, which became the epicenter of fighting between opposition militants and the Syrian army in Homs in late 2011.[14]

Bishara writes that

> security forces delivered the body of Sheikh Bader Abu Musa, one of the leaders of the Fawa'ara tribe who was killed under torture after his detention. And this resulted in *military confrontations* between youths from Abu Musa's group and security forces in which 14 people were killed and 50 others were wounded.[15] (emphasis added)

According to Barout, "the death of the revered Sheikh in this context led to the eruption of heavy clashes."

Further evidence of armed opposition activity comes from the killing of several Syrian army officers during this time. As journalist Sharmine Narwani reports, Syrian Brigadier General Abdo al-Tallawi was assassinated on Sunday, April 17, alongside his two sons Ahmad and Khader and his nephew Ali.[16] Large crowds attended the funeral procession of the four victims the following day, with attendees chanting pro-government slogans.[17] Syrian state media claimed that the bodies had also been mutilated.[18]

It should be noted here that it is not likely that Abu Musa was a democracy activist or arrested at a pro-democracy protest as reported by Reuters. As we have already seen in Daraa and Banias, the protestors demonstrating at mosques were not demanding democracy; rather, they were making conservative religious demands. Furthermore, Abu Musa's death happened in the context of tit-for-tat Alawite and Sunni kidnappings and the smuggling of both weapons and fighters into Homs from nearby Lebanon (discussed in more detail below), making it possible that he was involved in these activities and had been detained as a result.

But did Syrian authorities torture Abu Musa to death, as opposition and Western sources claim? Some government supporters would deny that the security services committed any crimes of this sort during its response to the unrest, but if this were the case, Bouthaina Shaaban would not have acknowledged that "mistakes" had indeed been made during this early period, and Abu Musa's supporters would likely not have engaged in armed clashes with local security forces the day after his body was returned, leading to 14 more deaths. This suggests that Abu Musa was tortured to death as claimed. If so, Abu Musa's death illustrates one of the crimes committed by the security forces that stoked legitimate anger against the government and led to the kind of sectarian hatred against Alawites in Homs that U.S. planners were counting on.

The Clock Tower Fabrication

Reports of events on the following day, Monday, April 18, were once again distorted by local opposition activists, and uncritically passed on by the Western press. Funerals for the armed supporters of Sheikh Abu Musa who were killed on Sunday, April 17, were held on Monday, April 18, and turned into protests. Activists then took the decision to march to the square of the new clock tower, located in the center of Homs, and to establish a sit-in there resembling that established in Egypt's Tahrir Square previously. The sit-in would set the stage for another alleged massacre that was used to suggest that the Syrian government was using appalling levels of violence to suppress peaceful dissent.

Human Rights Watch obtained testimony from an alleged defected intelligence officer who claimed that

> we were there with Air Force security, army, and *shabiha*. At around 3:30 a.m. [early Tuesday morning, April 19], we got an order from Colonel Abdel Hamid Ibrahim from Air Force security to shoot at the protestors. We were shooting for more than half an hour. There were dozens and dozens of people killed and wounded. Thirty minutes later, earth diggers and fire trucks arrived. The diggers lifted the bodies and put them in a truck. I don't know where they took them. The wounded ended up at the military hospital in Homs.[19]

Al Jazeera similarly reported claims by activists of a "real massacre," and that "shooting was being carried out directly on the demonstrators."[20]

It turns out that there was no massacre, however. *Time* journalist Rania Abouzeid reported that the alleged clock tower massacre "was a turning point in the struggle for Homs, although years later some of the men present that night would admit that claims of a massacre were exaggerated, even fabricated, by rebel activists to garner sympathy."[21]

Instead, the violence at the new clock tower likely involved armed clashes between opposition militants and Syrian security forces under the cover of the protests and sit-in, as was the case in the wake of the death of Sheikh Abu Musa two days prior.

On Friday, May 6, dubbed the "Day of Defiance," armed clashes portrayed as peaceful protests suppressed by the security forces continued. Anthony Shadid of the *New York Times* reported that "the worst violence was reported in Homs, Syria's third largest city, where activists described a chaotic, bloody day, as tanks entered the town." Shadid reported that "the government said 10 soldiers had been killed there by what it described as 'terrorists,' while activists said at least 9 soldiers had defected to their side" and that sixteen protestors had been killed. Shadid reported that according to residents in Homs, "we answered the call to protest today, but the intelligence forces attacked us right away by opening fire on us," and that "the security forces fired without provocation."

However, the deaths of the nine soldiers suggest activists were trying to hide opposition attacks on Syrian security forces by claiming that the dead soldiers had defected. This was a pattern which would often be repeated.

Events such as the alleged massacre at the clock tower in Homs led even French diplomats to complain privately about the level of bias in Western media reporting. While the foreign press was denouncing the Syrian government for carrying out massacres, one French diplomat in Syria wrote a colleague in Paris to warn, "Don't believe what the TVs say," while French Ambassador to Syria Eric Chevallier took advantage of a visit to Paris to lecture the management of France 24, the country's flagship news station, telling them that they did not understand anything happening in Syria, and that the channel was misinforming its viewers. Chevallier also noted that foreign media, including Saudi-owned pan-Arab newspapers *al-Hayat* and *Al-Quds Al-Arabi*, were exaggerating the size of protests. Reports from France's internal intelligence service, the DCRI, also contradicted Western and Gulf news reporting. While Razan Zaitouneh and others claimed that the protestors were entirely peaceful, secular, and seeking democracy, the DCRI very quickly saw the hand of the Salafists and jihadists in the uprising and suggested that support for the protestors merited caution. French diplomats reported that most young people demonstrated spontaneously, but also observed the presence of well-organized Islamists with connections outside Syria.[22]

Such a view is consistent with the observations made by Father Frans Van der Lugt, a Dutch Jesuit priest who lived in Homs for nearly fifty years. As detailed by journalist John Rosenthal, Van der Lugt explained in a letter published in January 2012 on the Dutch-Flemish *Mediawerkgroep Syriëwebsite*:

> From the start, the protest movements were not purely peaceful. From the start I saw armed demonstrators marching along in the protests, who began to shoot at the police first. Very often the violence of the security forces has been a reaction to the brutal violence of the armed rebels.

Rosenthal notes that in September 2011, Van der Lugt had similarly written:

> Moreover, from the start there has been the problem of the armed groups, which are also part of the opposition... The opposition of the street is much stronger than any other opposition. And this opposition is armed and frequently employs brutality and violence, only in order then to blame the government. Many representatives [or supporters] of the government... have been tortured and shot dead by them...

> Personally, I expect little good to come from the opposition, which, moreover, has been instigated and paid by foreign interests.[23]

Fr. Van der Lugt's testimony is valuable because he was a neutral, on-the-ground source. Van der Lugt refused to leave Homs despite the violence of the subsequent years and was respected by both government and opposition supporters at the time of his assassination by an unknown gunman in 2014.[24]

Islamist Style

Instead of a massacre of demonstrators in Homs, opposition militants were once again carrying out attacks on Syrian police and security forces. Al Jazeera's report from April 19 also quoted an eyewitness who reported "heavy shooting near the police command center in the city and said that the shooting was like 'rain showers.'" The eyewitness also indicated that calls for jihad and to support the protestors were launched through loudspeakers from mosques near the clock tower square and the Bab Seba' neighborhood.[25] In the wake of these armed clashes, the Syrian interior ministry issued a circular in Homs Province to prevent the entry of motorbikes into the city, as mentioned in Chapter 5, "because some armed groups in the province implement their criminal plans using motorbikes."[26]

In addition to the gun battle at the police station, Major Iyad Harfoush, an off-duty commander in the Syrian army, was killed by opposition militants on Monday, April 18.[27] Sharmine Narwani reports that according to his wife, "someone started shooting in the mostly pro-regime al Zahra neighborhood of Homs — Harfoush went out to investigate the incident and was killed."[28] Another Syrian officer, Colonel Mu'een Mahalla, was assassinated in al-Zahra the same day.[29] According to Muhammad Jamal Barout, both Mahalla and Harfoush were Alawite, and their killings led to further sectarian tensions in the mixed-sect neighborhoods of al-Humaydia and al-Wa'er, and also the neighborhoods of al-Khalidiya and al-Zahra.[30]

The calls for jihad, the attack on the police station, and the assassination of the three Syrian officers on April 17–18 coincided with the formation of a Salafist militia known as the Farouq Brigades, which went on to become an early and prominent faction of the so-called Free Syrian Army (FSA). French journalist Jonathan Littell visited Homs in 2012 and met an FSA commander with a "thick beard, moustache shaved, Islamist style," who claimed that "in April [2011] already, they were trying to organize themselves militarily…"[31]

Walid al-Faris, an opposition activist from Homs, noted that the Farouq Brigades were founded by Amjad Bitar, a young student of Islamic law with a Salafi orientation who had begun supporting various armed groups, most notably in the neighborhoods of al-Khalidiya and Baba Amr, which were the two most important gathering points for opposition fighters in Homs. Among the fighters were some who had fought in Iraq previously. Training camps for the fighters and bomb-making factories were set up in orchards on the outskirts of the city. These orchards provided cover for the fighters and facilitated their movements.[32]

Just as in Banias, the flow of arms into Homs was facilitated by Saad Hariri, a close ally of both U.S. and Saudi intelligence. Azmi Bishara noted that "the circles close to the people who took up arms confirm that arms smuggling from Lebanon began in late April 2011" and that "Saad Hariri appears to have funded the smuggling of arms from Lebanon, as evidenced by the naming of some battalions by his name or by his father's name."[33]

Further confirmation of Hariri's involvement in arming Salafist militants fighting the Syrian government emerged from reporting by Lebanese journalist Radwan Mortada. In December 2012, Mortada reported that his newspaper, *al-Akhbar*, had obtained audio recordings of Future Movement parliament member Okab Sakr organizing weapons transfers to armed Syrian opposition groups at the behest of Saad Hariri. Mortada's reporting indicated further that Sakr was directing attacks against the Syrian army from operations rooms in both Lebanon and Turkey, and that he enjoyed close relations with intelligence officials from Qatar, Turkey, and Saudi Arabia.[34]

Saad Hariri was facilitating the flow not only of weapons into Syria, but of Salafist militants as well. As discussed in Chapter 2, starting in 2005, Hariri had partnered with Saudi intelligence in the northern Lebanese city of Tripoli to cultivate Salafist groups, including Fatah al-Islam, which battled the Lebanese army in the Nahr al-Bared Palestinian camp in 2007.[35]

As part of the "redirection" in U.S. policy in the region, Fatah al-Islam militants were then sent to fight in Syria. Dr. Haytham Mouzahem, director of the Beirut Center for Middle East Studies, explained that "when the uprising in Syria began in 2011, many of the remaining Fatah al-Islam members crossed the border and joined groups in the Free Syrian Army."[36]

Starting in April 2011, Al Jazeera journalist Ali Hashem witnessed what were likely Fatah al-Islam fighters crossing from Lebanon into Syria from the Wadi Khaled area.[37] Hashem explained that

> we saw armed men just crossing the river, the great northern river, which is the only, you know, natural barrier between Lebanon and Syria. They were just crossing that barrier and going into Syria, and

then clashing with the Syrian Army. That was in May. And even something similar happened in April, but it wasn't on camera. But in May it was on camera and we had the footage, and, you know, no one wanted to have them on air… I'm not sourcing or quoting; I just saw with my eyes, and it was in the beginning of the revolution, it was just, like, one month and a half from the revolution. And things were, you know, I was seeing a lot of weapons, people with RPGs, people with Kalashnikovs, you know, just crossing from the borders. And they were not one or two; they were a big number; they were just dominating the whole village that we were on the borders with. So, you know, the militarization of the revolution started early.[38]

In a rare admission of the armed nature of the opposition during this early period, Anthony Shadid of the *New York Times* reported on May 8, 2011, that "American officials acknowledge that some protestors have been armed" and that "Syrian television is suffused with images of soldiers' burials."[39] By this time, at least 81 soldiers and police had been killed.[40]

That the fighters witnessed by Ali Hashem crossed into Syria from the Lebanese town of Wadi Khaled was significant, given that the town quickly became a Salafist stronghold. In 2012, Lebanese news agencies al-Jadeed, Murr Television (MTV), and Lebanese Broadcasting Corporation (LBC) all reported on Sunni Islamist and Salafist demonstrations and rallies in Lebanon's northern regions, including in Wadi Khaled, which showed "footage of bearded men waving black flags of al-Qaeda."[41]

Hashem later resigned from Al Jazeera in protest of the channel's refusal to broadcast his reports of armed militants crossing into Syria. He speculated that Al Jazeera's editors were attempting to obscure the violent nature of the uprising, as there were those who wanted to portray Assad as using weapons to crack down on dissent, "while the others on the revolution side are kind of peaceful people, are not holding weapons."[42]

This is unsurprising, given that Al Jazeera had been coordinating its news coverage with U.S. planners since at least 2010. Lebanese academic Asad Abu Khalil noted for example that

> the head of Al Jazeera told me in 2010 that the U.S. embassy in Doha, Qatar, sends a weekly report in which they provide a critique of every program that appears on Al Jazeera in order to have them change their tunes, to change it towards America.[43]

The flow of Salafist foreign fighters crossing from Lebanon into Syria continued in subsequent months. The German magazine *Der Spiegel* reported that Sheikh Masen al-Mohammad, a prominent Salafist cleric in Tripoli, was sending fighters into Syria as early as the summer of 2011. Sheikh Masen explained that, in his view, "Assad is an infidel," and "there is a holy war in Syria and the young men there are conducting jihad. For blood, for honor, for freedom, for dignity." According to one of the fighters interviewed by *Der Spiegel*, around 60 percent of the Lebanese fighters crossing the border from Tripoli to Homs had already fought in Iraq.[44]

Der Spiegel reported further that Salafist fighters infiltrated Qusayr, a town between the Lebanese border and nearby Homs. Leila, a Christian resident of the town, explained that "despite the fact that many of our husbands had jobs in the civil service, we still got along well with the rebels during the first months of the insurgency." However, Leila's daughter Rim explained further that "last summer [2011] Salafists came to Qusayr, foreigners. They stirred the local rebels against us" and began a campaign to target Qusayr's 10,000 Christian residents.

According to Rim:

> They sermonized on Fridays in the mosques that it was a sacred duty to drive us away… We were constantly accused of working for the regime. And Christians had to pay bribes to the jihadists repeatedly in order to avoid getting killed.

Rim's husband was murdered by the jihadists in February 2012. Rim detailed how

> he was stopped at a rebel checkpoint near the state-run bakery… the rebels knew he was a Christian. They took him and then threw his dead body in front of the door of his parents' house four or five hours later.[45]

The treatment of Christians in Qusayr was a manifestation of attitudes expressed in many of the early protests. A common slogan chanted by demonstrators throughout Syria was "Alawites to the grave, Christians to Beirut."[46] Journalist Harout Ekmanian, an Armenian Christian from Aleppo, explained further:

> "Alevis to the grave, Christians to Beirut" was a slogan invented during the first days of the rebellion, and it is still commonly used. However, back then, it was condemned, because there were people with different views in the opposition. Once the opposition started to carry arms and became militarized, this slogan [has] started to be used more commonly.[47]

The foreign jihadists occupying Qusayr included militants from Fatah al-Islam. This was confirmed in April 2012 when a well-known Fatah al-Islam commander from Lebanon, Abdel Ghani Jawhar, was killed in the town after he accidentally blew himself up while building a bomb. Jawhar was an explosives expert and had been in Qusayr sharing his expertise with the militants occupying the city.[48]

Before his death, Jawhar had been one of Lebanon's most wanted men. He had allegedly killed 17 Lebanese soldiers in Tripoli and had fought against the Lebanese army in the Nahr al-Bared Palestinian camp, where 168 Lebanese soldiers were killed, including Jawhar's own cousin.[49]

As a result of Salafist threats, most of Qusayr's Christians fled to Lebanon. The *Los Angeles Times* interviewed Christian refugees from the town in 2012, who said they were "tired of threats and public taunts of being 'unbelievers' and 'dogs of Assad,'" and they recounted being forced to attend rallies against the government. One woman told the paper that "if the [government opponents] had acted peacefully, maybe we would have sided with them... But they were terrible. They looted and robbed."[50]

The Nakba and Naksa Protests

Yarmouk, with a pre-war population of some 150,000 Palestinians and 650,000 Syrians, was the largest Palestinian refugee camp in Syria, lying in the southern outskirts of Damascus. Yarmouk was established in 1957 for Palestinians ethnically cleansed from their homes by Zionist militias as part of the establishment of the State of Israel in 1947–48, events known by Palestinians as the *Nakba*, or "Catastrophe." Some of these refugees were resettled in Yarmouk, which soon came to be considered the capital of the Palestinian diaspora. As Palestinians were granted all the rights of Syrians except for citizenship and the ability to vote, Palestinians from the camp quickly integrated into the social and cultural life of the country. Over time, many Syrians came to reside within the borders of the camp as well, and as the population of Damascus grew, Yarmouk gradually became a suburb of the capital.

Prominent in the camp was the Palestinian faction, the Popular Front for the Liberation of Palestine–General Command (PFLP-GC), led by Ahmed Jibril. The PFLP-GC is an offshoot of the larger Popular Front for the Liberation of Palestine (PFLP), a Marxist political party and a member of the Palestine Liberation Organization (PLO). The PFLP was founded by George Habash, a Palestinian Christian who became a refugee in Lebanon as a boy after Zionist militias expelled his family from their home during the Nakba.

Jibril, a former officer in the Syrian army, criticized the PFLP for allegedly placing too much focus on theoretical discussion and too little emphasis on actual armed struggle against Israel. Jibril split from the PFLP in 1968 and formed the PFLP-GC, which maintained bases in both Syria and Lebanon and remained close with the Syrian government, enjoying the strong support of Hafez al-Assad.

Due to the PFLP-GC's close ties with the Syrian government, the group became a target of a propaganda campaign meant to delegitimize its role in representing Palestinians in Yarmouk soon after the crisis in Syria began in the spring of 2011.

This propaganda campaign began after a series of controversial events in May and June 2011. On May 15, large demonstrations were organized by Palestinian youth activists in the occupied West Bank and Gaza, as well as in Egypt, Lebanon, and Syria, to commemorate the Nakba and to agitate for the right of Palestinian refugees to return to their homes in Israeli-occupied Palestine.

In Syria, thousands of Palestinians marched to the border of the Israeli-occupied Golan Heights waving flags and braving Israeli land mines. Several Palestinian protestors then scaled the Israeli border fence and were welcomed by local Druze residents of the town of Majdal al-Shams on the other side. Israeli troops responded by opening fire on the protestors, killing four. Israeli soldiers killed another ten Palestinian protestors on the Lebanese-Israeli border in separate protests there as well.[51]

The Nakba Day protests were followed three weeks later, on June 5, by protests commemorating the *Naksa*, or "Setback." On that day in 1967, Israel defeated the Arab states in the Six-Day War, and thereby conquered the West Bank, Gaza, Golan Heights, and Sinai. The Israeli victory set the stage for 50 years of occupation of additional Palestinian land. During the Naksa Day protest on the Syrian border in June 2011, protestors once again tried to cross the border fence. This time, Israeli forces responded even more harshly, killing some 22.[52]

Israeli planners observed preparation for the protests in advance (which took place openly through social media) and sought early to establish a narrative claiming that the Syrian government was behind the protests, and that Assad supposedly wished to use them to deflect attention from the anti-government protests he himself faced. The same claims were later repeated by U.S. government officials, as well as by opposition activists in Syria, who argued that Assad was really to blame for the deaths of protestors killed by the Israeli army, since Syrian security had allegedly manipulated Palestinians into marching to the border. However, the Palestinian protests in Syria were clearly popular and organically organized, as similar protests also took place in Lebanon, Gaza, the West Bank, Jordan, and Egypt.[53]

Similar protests also occurred in Gaza in 2018, with Israeli snipers targeting Palestinians marching to the border fence with live fire. Israeli snipers targeted unarmed protestors from safe distances, several instances of which were caught on video, including the shooting of Palestinian footballer Mohammad Khalil in the knee, and of Abdel Fattah Abd al-Nabi in the back. Israeli snipers also shot and killed female Palestinian medic Razan al-Najjar. Israeli Brigadier General Zvika Fogel acknowledged that Israeli snipers were deliberately targeting protestors, including even children, with live bullets. In that case, Israel sought to deflect responsibility by blaming Hamas for orchestrating the protests, just as they had blamed Assad for orchestrating the 2011 protests in Syria.[54]

The Funeral Turned Demonstration

Another controversial event occurred on the day after the June 2011 Naksa protest. On June 6, a funeral was held in Yarmouk for several of the Palestinians killed by Israeli snipers the day before. Pro-opposition activists then turned the funeral into a demonstration during which some Yarmouk residents expressed anger at the Syrian government and Palestinian factions, including the PFLP-GC, for failing to support the Naksa protest.

The *Los Angeles Times* reported claims that the PFLP-GC "used live ammunition to shoot at young protestors in Yarmouk camp as they were participating in a funeral procession," killing up to 20.[55]

Such a summary of events gives the impression that the PFLP-GC killed many protestors for simply participating in a funeral procession. This view would be promoted by Syrian opposition activists to claim that both the Syrian government and PFLP-GC were enemies of the Palestinians in Yarmouk and of the Palestinian cause generally.

This was a misleading view of what occurred, however, as rioting once again accompanied the protest. Reuters reports that

> mourners threw stones at Palestinian figures who had praised Assad. Hundreds of refugees armed with sticks and stones then headed to the PFLP-GC headquarters and tried to storm it. Several protestors managed to get in and killed one PFLP-GC gunman,

after which the headquarters was burned down.[56] The *New York Times* quoted a shopkeeper from Yarmouk as explaining that "the crowd began to throw stones at the organization's headquarters. Then, he said, 'the building guards began to shoot at us.'"[57]

Opposition activist and Yarmouk resident Nidal Bitari provided a similar account, but suggested that the PFLP-GC guards opened fire first after a group of angry protestors had broken from the procession route and surrounded the PFLP-GC headquarters, known as the Khalsa. He explains that

> one of the PFLP-GC guards fired at the unarmed crowd and killed a fourteen-year-old boy named Rami Siyam, and other GC militants began shooting from the roof. People went mad. They began setting fire to cars, and thousands stormed the building. Ahmad Jibril and his top deputies had to be rescued by the Syrian army, and PFLP-GC reinforcements were called in from Lebanon. At some point in the melee, gas bottles inside the building exploded, starting a fire, and by nightfall the four-story building was badly charred.[58]

Bitari notes that three people were killed that day, including the young boy and also a PFLP-GC guard who died in the fire, explaining that the "press articles the next day reported that twelve or thirteen people had been killed during the demonstration, but this was totally false and some press agencies later corrected the story."

Ibrahim al-Ali of the Muslim Brotherhood-funded Action Group for Palestinians in Syria (AGPS), lists a lower number of dead as well, claiming that four were killed, including two protestors who were shot — the young boy Rami Siyam and also Jamal Ghutan — and two PFLP-GC members — the guard Khalid Rayyan, who was burned to death in the fire, and Naser Mubarak, the PFLP-GC head for the Syria region who was allegedly stabbed to death by protestors.[59]

Journalist Tarek Homoud, also of AGPS, reported on the killing of the PFLP-GC members as well, explaining that Mubarak (whom he refers to as Abu al-Abed Nasir) "was killed by knives as a group arrested him while he tried to calm them down. He was stabbed 50 times." Also, reports Homoud, "one of the building's guards was killed by burning alive in his corner."[60]

Other reports suggest that armed groups may have been involved in attacking the Khalsa, not merely angry protestors with sticks and rocks. Journalist Sharmine Narwani reports that according to a Hamas official with whom she spoke, "some Free Syrian Army (FSA) fighters went to Ahmad

Jibril's offices — the Khalesa compound — during the funeral and started shooting."[61]

Al-Akhbar pointed to Salafist elements attempting to incite Palestinians against the PFLP-GC, and suggested that this is what led protestors to try to breach the confines of the Khalsa.[62] Lebanese academic Asad Abu al-Khalil also notes that according to an eyewitness with whom he spoke, the confrontation at the Khalsa "resulted in an armed clash."[63] If armed clashes took place, this suggests that there were armed men among the protestors and that weapons were not limited to the PFLP-GC guards.

While accounts conflict regarding who attacked first, the PFLP-GC guards were attempting to protect the PFLP-GC headquarters and party officials inside from an angry crowd. This does not justify firing live ammunition into the crowd, but it does suggest that the PFLP-GC did not simply open fire on civilians in order to crack down on peaceful protests, as suggested by the *Los Angeles Times*, and as the mainstream narrative regarding Syria would over and over claim.

For example, Razan Zaitouneh's Violations Documentation Center (VDC) continued to claim years later that the PFLP-GC killed "more than 20 people" at the funeral "on what was known later as 'Al Khalsa Massacre.'" This narrative would prove helpful in denigrating later efforts by the PFLP-GC to protect the camp from the foreign-backed Salafist armed groups (some of which, as we shall see later, were supported by Israel) and to encourage some Palestinians to abandon their neutral stance and join the opposition in trying to topple the Syrian government.

8. Idlib, Home of the 'Moderate Rebels'

A Curious Mixture

While the Syrian government faced a curious mixture of non-violent protest and armed insurrection, Western reporting focused only on protests, implying that any deaths occurring in Syria resulted from the government killing peaceful demonstrators demanding democracy.

Certainly, the government did kill some peaceful protestors. Journalist Hala Jaber of the *Sunday Times* observed in June 2011 that according to one Syrian security official, the security forces

> see demonstrators in the hundreds or thousands, chanting anti-government slogans or tearing pictures of Assad — something that only a few months ago would have landed people in jail — and they react heavy-handedly and shoot randomly.[1]

While reporting from Syria in the summer of 2011, journalist Nir Rosen described how he had

> been to about 100 demonstrations in Syria. In many of them I had to run for my life from live gunfire. I was terrified. The demonstrators who go out every day since March know they are risking their lives. It helps them to believe in paradise and martyrdom.[2]

However, this was only half of the story. The other half — that Salafist militants, including from al-Qaeda, were infiltrating protests and killing members of the security forces, police, and army — was ignored. Nir Rosen explained further:

> Many of those reported killed are in fact dead opposition fighters, but the cause of their death is hidden and they are described in reports as innocent civilians killed by security forces, as if they were all merely protesting or sitting in their homes. Of course, those deaths still happen regularly as well.[3]

Also ignored was that third-party infiltrators from al-Qaeda were killing demonstrators to "sow terror" and "poison the relationship between the people and the regime," as acknowledged by opposition figure and lawyer Haythem al-Maleh.

As a result, outside observers received a distorted picture of the conflict and its causes. The conflict in Syria was not, as claimed by Avaaz's Wissam Tarif in September 2011, "between peaceful protestors and an army."[4]

This was further demonstrated by events in Idlib Province in June 2011. Hala Jaber reported that Islamist gunmen used the cover of a demonstration to attack Syrian security forces in the town of Ma'arat al-Nu'man. According to tribal elders from the town, men armed with rifles and rocket-propelled grenade launchers joined some 5,000 protestors demonstrating outside a military barracks in the middle of the town. The armed men attacked the barracks, where roughly 100 police were barricaded inside, causing a military helicopter to come to the aid of the police. Four policemen and 12 of the armed men were killed, while 20 policemen were wounded. The barracks was then ransacked by a mob and set on fire, as were the local courthouse and police station.[5]

Islamist militants attacked Syrian security forces under the cover of protests during this time in the town of Jisr al-Shagour as well. As noted in Chapter 5, on June 3, 2011, dozens of masked young men from the area of Jabal al-Zawiya in Idlib Province arrived in Jisr al-Shagour on motorcycles toting weapons. Two days later, Islamist militants attacked the local post office and military security headquarters, leading to a lengthy gun battle with security forces.[6]

According to Rania Abouzeid, the violence began when an armed militant named Basil al-Masry was killed while attacking a government checkpoint. Masry's death angered many residents of the town, who believed rumors that Masry had been unarmed when he was killed, rather than carrying out an armed operation. As a result, his funeral doubled as an anti-government demonstration. As protestors approached the local post office, several hundred Islamist militants emerged from among the protestors and opened fire on government snipers stationed atop the post office roof. The militants then threw incendiary devices inside the post office doors, lighting the building on fire and burning eight people to death, before turning to attack the nearby military security building, where state security and political security personnel were holed up inside. When the Syrian authorities sent a convoy of soldiers to come to their assistance, the Islamist militants ambushed the convoy, allegedly killing some 120 of the soldiers.[7]

Whose Mass Graves?

Opposition activists spread the false claim that the slain soldiers were defectors killed by their own Alawite superiors in the army, despite evidence to the contrary provided by Syria expert Joshua Landis, who showed that the soldiers had been killed by opposition gunmen.

Landis reported that the Syrian government published tapped phone calls of opposition activists from before the massacre in which they discussed a plan to send all the women and children of the city to Turkey and then to tell foreign journalists that Syrian military personnel had shot their own soldiers. As Landis explained, "When enlisted men refused to shoot on unarmed demonstrators, their Alawi officers mowed them down — that was the story to be told to the Western press." The activists also discussed how to obscure the Salafist nature of the opposition movement, and how any killings must be blamed on the army in order to hide the armed nature of the opposition. Landis also challenged the government claim that 120 of its soldiers had been massacred by opposition militants, arguing instead that the Syrian government had likely inflated the death toll, and "that only a single mass grave turned up 10 dead soldiers." Ominously, however, "four had their heads cut off."[8]

As Rania Abouzeid reported, it was only years later that activists involved in the incident acknowledged that the story of the soldiers defecting was fabricated. Abouzeid had herself reported on the incident at the time and unwittingly passed on the false claim that the dead soldiers had first defected.[9] Abouzeid later reversed her reporting and provided full details of the event after interviewing an Islamist militant who had participated in the attack, as well as other civilians who were present in the initial protest outside the post office. The militant, a man named Muhammad, who had first organized armed groups in Latakia as discussed in Chapter 6, acknowledged to Abouzeid that he and his men filmed the bodies of some of the security forces whom they had killed and presented the videos so as to show "mass graves full of the regime's victims."[10]

The Free 'Army'

After the killing of the Syrian soldiers in Jisr al-Shagour, cracks were beginning to emerge in the narrative of a peaceful uprising being crushed by a ruthless dictator. To reinforce the narrative that these soldiers had been killed by their own officers after defecting, interviews were quickly arranged for journalists in the Western and Gulf press with Colonel Hussein Harmoush, who claimed to have defected from the Syrian army with 30 of his soldiers to protect civilians in Jisr al-Shagour after the alleged mutiny.[11]

These same outlets began airing YouTube videos of other alleged Syrian officers, including of Riad al-Asaad and Abd al-Razzaq Tlass, defecting to the opposition.[12] Tlass's defection was deemed important because he is a relative of Manaf Tlass, the then brigadier general and also childhood friend of Bashar al-Assad, and Mustafa Tlass (Manaf's father), the former Syrian defense minister and close advisor to Hafez al-Assad.[13]

The publicity given to Harmoush, Asad, Tlass, and other defectors paved the way for the announcement of the establishment of the Free Syrian Army (FSA) on July 29, 2011, thereby providing cover for a nascent Salafist and al-Qaeda-led insurgency that had already been active for months. The myth of a secular rebel army comprised of defected officers fighting for democracy and to protect civilians was officially born.

Rather than a people's army of defected soldiers, the FSA was initially just a small group of defected Syrian officers in Turkey, which provided a brand under which a loose conglomeration of foreign-backed Salafist armed groups was able to fight, both for public relations reasons and to gain access to weapons supplied by U.S., Gulf, and Turkish intelligence agencies.

As Syria expert Aron Lund observed, the "FSA doesn't really exist" as an actual army, but was simply a "branding operation," likely run by Turkish intelligence.[14] According even to the BBC, the small number of defected army officers who initially founded the FSA in July 2011 were based in Turkey and "had little or no operational control over what was happening on the ground in Syria."[15]

Instead, the FSA leadership was tasked with issuing press releases for Western media consumption and coordinating weapons shipments to the armed groups fighting on the ground in Syria. Joseph Holliday of the Institute for the Study of War noted in December 2011, for example, that "there is little hard evidence to suggest that the Free Syrian Army is anything more than a media outlet" and potential weapons conduit.[16]

Azmi Bishara similarly observed that the media reported statements from the leadership of the FSA as though this leadership knew what was happening on the ground in Syria — when in fact they did not — and that some of the FSA officers spoke from Istanbul about events they themselves had only heard about from the media.[17]

Furthermore, it was members of Syria's Salafist community, as opposed to religiously mainstream Sunnis, who formed the backbone of the FSA groups that emerged from the protest movement. Muhammad Abu

Rumman of the University of Jordan explains that "Salafists deeply penetrated the armed revolution, thus defining the revolution's social role," while noting only "modest Sufi presence in the armed factions in particular and in the peaceful revolution in general."[18]

Journalist Bisam Nasir similarly observed that "Salafist groups in the Syrian arena top the list of armed groups, organizations, and movements fighting the Syrian regime and its allies, as they are the most present and the most powerful on the military level." Although the Western journalists and think tank analysts later characterized the insurgency as divided into secular "moderates" from the FSA on the one hand and Islamist "extremists" such as from the al-Qaeda-affiliated Nusra Front on the other, Nasir notes that according to the Kuwaiti Islamic writer and researcher Ali al-Sanad, the primary distinction between the various armed groups fighting the Syrian government was in the kind of Salafism they adopted, whether quietist, activist, or jihadi.[19]

Nasir further cites Syrian preacher and Islamic researcher Jamal al-Farra as noting the influence on the broader insurgency of "Surouri Salafism," an innovative and radical ideology that married the concern with politics and organization of the Muslim Brotherhood with the theological creed of traditional Salafism.[20]

The Salafist orientation of the armed groups fighting under the FSA banner was problematic, due to the sectarianism inherent to Salafist ideology, especially when merged with political activism favored by the Muslim Brotherhood. Syrian dissident Nidal Nuaiseh wrote, for example, that "Salafist calls for the murder of Alawites are not new, but are at the core of the Salafist ideology, and have been at its core for hundreds of years."[21]

The Sarouri Salafism described by Jamal al-Farra is derived from the thought of Muhammad Sarour, the sectarian Salafist cleric from Daraa whose followers played a key role in the early demonstrations in Daraa, as discussed in Chapter 5. Sarour provided not only the ideological inspiration for many of the armed groups fighting to topple the secular Syrian government, but "was quietly active in the Syrian uprising" itself and was eulogized by the U.S.-backed opposition Syrian National Council (SNC) upon his death in 2016.[22]

Sarour's influence is an indication that not only the armed insurgency but also the anti-government protest movement itself had largely Salafist roots. Muhammad Abu Rumman explains further:

When the Syrian popular protests broke out in March 2011, Islamic symbols — and their material manifestations — were conspicuously present. Their visibility and influence increased further with the ascendance of spiritual discourse, the elevated role of mosques and their preachers, and the contribution of religious scholars. The Islamic groups and the militant Islamists have become key players in the ongoing military and security struggle.[23]

Tending to the Necessary Details

The Salafist orientation of the early FSA groups is illustrated by the cases of two prominent FSA commanders, Hassan Aboud and Ahmed Abu Issa al-Sheikh.

Hassan Aboud was a militant from the town of Sarmin in Idlib Province who had traveled to Iraq to fight against U.S. occupation forces in 2004 and was seen in a video with Abu Musab al-Zarqawi in Fallujah. After returning to Syria in 2005, Aboud led an apparently unremarkable life as a mason and laborer, though locals from his hometown speculated that he was sent back to Syria as part of an al-Qaeda sleeper cell.[24]

Aboud participated in anti-government protests starting in March 2011 and took part in the ambush of the Syrian army convoy near Jisr al-Shaghour in June 2011. Aboud's friend Daoud al-Sheikh was killed in the fighting, leading Aboud to establish Liwa Daoud, or "the Daoud Brigade," in his honor. C.J. Chivers of the *New York Times* writes:

> His brigade started small. But it set up a guerrilla base among olive groves and caves, where it trained, manufactured weapons, and extended its fight... Many early rebel groups lacked experience, money, training, and cohesion. The [Daoud] Brigade was different, Mr. Aboud's townspeople said. It tended to details necessary to become a fighting force.[25]

Aboud had expertise in using improvised explosive devices (IEDs) from his time in Iraq, and later became a double amputee after an improvised rocket accidentally exploded near him.[26]

Aboud and his Daoud Brigade soon joined Saqour al-Sham, or "the Falcons of the Levant," a Salafist militia fighting under the FSA banner. Formally founded in September 2011 in the town of Sarjeh in Idlib Province, Saqour al-Sham was led by Ahmed Abu Issa al-Sheikh, who was the brother of Aboud's deceased friend Daoud al-Sheikh.

Before the start of the 2011 conflict, Ahmed Abu Issa al-Sheikh was a relatively unknown figure. He had been imprisoned in 2004 for 11 months by the Syrian government in the Palestine Branch for his Salafi proselytizing activities,[27] while his father was killed by the Syrian government in Tadmur Prison during its conflict with the Muslim Brotherhood in the early 1980s.[28]

Saqour al-Sham became a magnet for funding from the Gulf, and Ahmed Abu Issa quickly became one of the most prominent commanders and most powerful men in Idlib Province.[29] In a sermon he delivered in late April 2012, Abu Issa

> called on the Syrian people to turn toward their religion and to view politics as a vehicle for elevating God's word. He also said that Muslims had lost their honor because they had abandoned Jihad, replacing aspirations for martyrdom with a fear of death.[30]

Journalist Wael Essam notes that the most prominent religious advisor for Saqour al-Sham was an Egyptian jihadist who later joined Ahrar al-Sham.[31] Aron Lund notes that Saqour al-Sham "has used suicide bombers and frames its propaganda in religious rhetoric," while its website

> features a link to the Levant Islamic Commission, an Islamic aid organization set up by supporters of the Deraa-born Salafi scholar Mohammed Surour Zeinelabidin, which is presumably another source of funding for the group.[32]

Hassan Aboud of Liwa Daoud became one of the most important military commanders in Saqour al-Sham and participated in several key battles against the Syrian army in subsequent years, including at the Taftanaz military airport, Shabiba military base, Air Defense College, and Madajin checkpoint in Aleppo; at the Jadida checkpoint in Hama; and at the Hamishu checkpoint in Idlib.[33]

Hassan Aboud and his fighters later joined ISIS, bringing with them their weapons and a convoy of armored vehicles and tanks. Aboud became a prominent commander in the terror group and led the ISIS assault on the Aleppo countryside in August 2014. He was known for singing songs in which he threatened to kill his former FSA counterparts. Aboud also helped lead the attack to capture the ancient town and heritage site of Palmyra, after which ISIS publicly murdered Khaled al-Asaad, the retired director of antiquities for the site. Aboud was killed in March 2016 when his convoy struck a roadside bomb.[34]

Although Salafist militants such as Hassan Aboud and Ahmed Abu Issa al-Sheikh formed the backbone of FSA groups fighting on the ground, the small number of defected officers based in Turkey, such as Hussein Harmoush, allowed the Western press to present the FSA falsely as secular and democratic. Like Aboud, many of the commanders and fighters of these early FSA groups then went on to fight for al-Qaeda-affiliated groups, whether ISIS, the Nusra Front, or Ahrar al-Sham, all of which shared the FSA's same Salafist orientation.

Defectors?

The false narrative that Syrian officers were killing their own soldiers for refusing to fire on protestors, as claimed by Hussein Harmoush in Jisr al-Shagour, was spread by the organizations that claimed to be local, neutral human rights observers, but which were in fact created and funded by the U.S. and other governments seeking regime change in Syria.

As noted in Chapter 3, one such group was the Damascus Center for Human Rights Studies (DCHRS), led by Radwan Ziadeh and funded by the U.S. government via the NED. The BBC reported on May 5, 2011, for example, that sources within the DCHRS said that up until that point in the conflict, "81 bodies of soldiers and army officers had been received. Most were killed by a gunshot to the back. DCHRS says it strongly suspects that the soldiers were killed for refusing to shoot civilians."[35]

These same claims also found their way into the report issued in November 2011 by the UN Independent International Commission of Inquiry on the Syrian Arab Republic. In preparing the report, the UN commission put out a "public call" to "all interested persons and organizations to submit relevant information and documentation that would help the commission implement its mandate." As a result, the commission appears to have relied on claims from the DCHRS and other opposition activists, rather than conducting its own independent investigation into events.[36] This provides an example of how U.S. government propaganda can be laundered into UN reports, via allegedly independent sources.

Even some opposition sources questioned the implausible narrative that soldiers were being killed by their own officers for refusing to shoot civilians. Rami Abdul Rahman of the U.K.-funded SOHR privately told journalist Sharmine Narwani that "this game of saying the army is killing defectors for leaving — I never accepted this because it is propaganda."[37]

The perception that any dead soldiers were killed by their own officers, rather than by U.S.- and Gulf-backed Salafist militants, persisted in part due to the Violations Documentation Center (VDC) led by Razan Zaitouneh. As Narwani noted in February 2012:

The VDC — another of the UN's OHCHR sources for casualty counts — alleges that 6,399 civilians and 1,680 army defectors were killed in Syria during the period from 15 March 2011 to 15 February 2012. All security forces killed in Syria during the past 11 months were "defectors"? Not a single soldier, policeman, or intelligence official was killed in Syria except those forces who opposed the regime? This is the kind of mindless narrative of this conflict that continues unchecked. Worse yet, this exact VDC statistic is included in the latest UN report on Syria issued last week.[38]

The apparent reason for U.S.-funded propagandists like Zaitouneh and Ziadeh to spread rumors about fake defections was not only to hide the early armed nature of the opposition, but also to sow confusion in the Syrian army and to encourage thereby actual defections, an objective of U.S. planners.

Writing for the Brookings Institution, Michael Doran and Salman Sheikh explained in July 2011 that the U.S. "must promote defections from the Syrian security services." The authors outlined five policies they argued would "hasten the rate of defections from the regime."[39] As noted in Chapter 2, Doran was a neoconservative close to Dick Cheney and also Elliott Abrams, who starting in 2006 participated in planning for regime change in Syria with Abd al-Halim Khaddam and the Muslim Brotherhood.

Google executive and former State Department official Jared Cohen later partnered with Al Jazeera to "create a visualization tracking the defections of diplomats, senior military officials, and members of parliament from Syrian President Bashar al-Assad's regime," further illustrating that U.S. planners hoped to see large-scale defections from the Syrian army and government.[40]

The desired mass defections never materialized, however. French academic and Syria expert Fabrice Balanche writes:

> The media were happy to highlight the hundred or so Syrian generals who had defected, but omitted to mention that the Syrian army includes around 1,200 brigadier generals (amid), and that there had been no desertions from the army's hundred major generals (liwa) who form the backbone of the system. Defections primarily took place among officers who were on the verge of retirement, yielding to petrodollars, and had been relegated to management or technical posts.

Balanche notes further that "it is primarily conscripts who have deserted, and more through fear for their lives than refusal to endorse the regime."[41]

In other words, these conscripts feared for their lives because of attacks from heavily armed and foreign-backed Salafist militias adopting the FSA brand, rather than from being shot in the back by their own officers.

Furthermore, any Syrian soldier or officer trying to defect to the FSA was just as likely to be tortured and killed by FSA militants as to be embraced by them. Writing for pro-opposition *Syria Direct*, Michael Pizzi and Nuha Shabaan explained:

> Defection is not so simple, however. Every defecting or captured soldier must stand for an ad hoc trial in a Free Army military court. These courts are neither highly organized nor consistent in how they rule or operate, but most apply some version of Islamic jurisprudence... The very real possibility of execution, however, looms for those who have committed "crimes" on behalf of the regime.[42]

Pizzi and Shabaan cite an opposition media activist from Deir al-Zour who explained that "certain prisoners in FSA custody will pay the price for their involvement in the regime's brutality, an almost certain deterrent to defection for those Sunnis who feel they may be implicated." Of course, any soldier could be viewed as complicit in the "crimes on behalf of the regime" simply for serving as a conscript in the army.

If these Sunni Syrian soldiers had any doubt, they could simply turn to YouTube to watch videos of their comrades being tortured by the Salafist militias constituting the FSA. As Camille Otrakji notes:

> Syrian opposition "rebels" frequently torture soldiers and civilians they capture to force them to either admit to things (true or not) or to appear on a YouTube video saying they were stupid to serve in Assad's army and that they now join the FSA which is militarily stronger and, more importantly, God's favorite in Syria.[43]

Pizzi and Shabaan explain further that

> while activists increasingly blame the Alawite-led *shabiha* and mercenary Hezbollah forces for keeping the Assad regime in place, it is in fact *the Sunni population that is quietly propping it up*... The internecine Sunni-Sunni divide grows every day on the battlefield... [because] Sunnis continue to fight in the regime's military.[44] (emphasis added)

The fact that Syria's Sunnis, a majority of the population, were supporting the government gives an indication of how little popular support the foreign-backed Salafist insurgency actually enjoyed.

Journalist Nir Rosen, who was initially sympathetic to the opposition and spent several months among FSA groups in Syria in 2011, similarly noted:

> The issue of defectors is a distraction. Armed resistance began long before defections started. While fighters are often portrayed in the

media as defectors from the Syrian military, the majority are civilians who have taken up arms. The opposition believes it will have more legitimacy if fighters are dubbed "defectors," and described collectively as the Free Syrian Army.[45]

Even pro-opposition sources acknowledged that claims of widespread defections to the FSA were simply untrue. Azmi Bishara notes, for example, that

> the firm truth that has accompanied the revolution since the beginning of militarization is that most of the revolutionaries that became armed were civilians that were not trained with carrying weapons, and not soldiers or officers who had fled, in contrast to what spokespersons of the revolution claimed.[46]

Clear Sectarian Overtones

By July 2011, shortly after the founding of the FSA, Homs had emerged as the epicenter of the conflict. As mentioned in Chapter 5, opposition militants fighting in the city coalesced to form *Kata'ib Farouq*, or "the Farouq Brigades," which began fighting under the FSA banner. As with Saqour al-Sham, Farouq's ideology was explicitly Salafist. This means that it was also explicitly sectarian and anti-Alawite and anti-Shia.

One of the founders of Farouq, a lawyer named Abu Sayyeh, explained to journalist Rania Abouzeid that the group chose a name with "clear sectarian overtones tied to Assad's alliance with Shiite Iran." The Farouq Brigades were named for Farouq Omar bin al-Khattab, a companion and father-in-law of the Prophet Muhammad who, as the second caliph, conquered the Sassanid Persian Empire. Abu Sayyeh explained further that "we wanted to be called Farouq as an indication of our desire to confront Persian ambitions in our Arab lands."[47]

This sectarianism is not surprising, given the dominant role played by Salafists generally in the establishment of Farouq. Opposition activist Walid al-Faris notes that

> the biggest part of the financial support came from religious students of the Salafi methodology in Homs and outside it. This was confirmed by the announcement of the actual leadership of the brigade, which originally belonged to the Salafi methodology, and this was not apparent initially.[48]

As mentioned in Chapter 7, the most important founder of the Farouq Brigades was Salafi preacher Amjad Bitar, who was able to fund the group via donations from Salafi networks in the Gulf states.[49] But the Salafist orientation of the Farouq Brigades was not "apparent initially" because the group was publicly led not by Bitar, but by the defected Syrian army officer Abd al-Razzaq Tlass.[50]

After a trip to Syria in August 2012, opposition activist Ammar Abd al-Hamid confirmed that although Farouq was apparently "run by a charismatic young defector, Captain Abdurrazzaq [Tlass], it was guided from behind the scenes by a Salafi scholar by the name of Amjad Bitar."[51] This allowed Farouq, like the FSA broadly, to be viewed wrongly as secular, democratic, and moderate in the Western press.

Furthermore, Farouq, like other FSA groups, did not consist primarily of army defectors who had refused to fire on peaceful civilian protestors. Rania Abouzeid reports that "opposition media activists pushed the idea that Farouq and the broader Free Syrian Army were largely comprised of defectors, but they were mainly armed civilians." She quotes a Farouq commander named Abu Azzam as explaining that they were "a civilian revolution, not a revolution of defected soldiers."[52]

Walid al-Faris observed further that "the number of defected officers in Homs remained small, and the [opposition] fighters feared dealing with them in the beginning due to security reasons," and that although the defected army officer Abd al-Razzaq Tlass "played a prominent role in the training of the revolutionaries" in Homs, "most of the defected officers went outside of Syria, as most officers wanted a large salary and administrative roles far away from the front and from the war, and this made benefiting from their expertise difficult." Al-Faris notes that the armed groups in Homs benefited most from local jihadists who had previously fought abroad, explaining that "on the other hand, a number of Syrians participated in the defense of Iraq during the American occupation and gained expertise from both theoretical and practical training exercises," and that those militants who had a large role in training the fighters in the use of weapons and laying mines and military tactics were "Islamist-Jihadists."[53]

McClatchy journalist David Enders, who spent time with a unit of Farouq fighters in April 2012, also noted the role of al-Qaeda militants fighting in the Farouq ranks. Enders explained that several Farouq fighters eagerly acknowledged to him that they had fought in Iraq against U.S. occupation forces, including in 2004 in Fallujah, after Enders indicated that he himself had reported from Fallujah at the time.[54] Similarly, Al Jazeera journalist James Bays observed that the Farouq Brigades unit he was embedded with in

Qusayr in May 2012 "includes many more civilian volunteers. Many don't wear uniforms, and some cover their faces with the keffiyeh, or Arabic scarf. We were told some of these fighters had fought in Iraq."[55]

Given the early influence of al-Qaeda-affiliated fighters in Farouq, it is unsurprising that, after several schisms, the majority of the group's original militants joined ISIS in late 2013. Journalist Wael Essam notes that

> the most important contingent of the Farouq Brigades joined the organization [ISIS]. Farouq was the most prominent [armed group] at the beginning of the revolution in Homs. In addition, a number of prominent revolution activists, such as Abu Yazen al-Homsi, joined the organization [ISIS] early on.[56]

Despite the Salafist and explicitly sectarian orientation of Farouq, with its attendant "calls for the murder of Alawites," and despite Farouq's connections to al-Qaeda-affiliated militants who had previously fought in Iraq, *Foreign Policy* magazine nevertheless described the group as "at one point, the lynchpin of the West's effort to build a 'moderate' opposition" in Syria.[57]

Serving the Revolution

By July 2011, Syrian police and security forces were engaging in regular clashes with Farouq militants in Homs. Nir Rosen described the situation as follows:

> Spend enough time in Homs and you will be confronted with the battles between security forces and their armed opponents. On July 21 Syrian security forces clashed with opposition fighters in the city's Bab Assiba neighbourhood. The following day I met several members of state security. They were saddened by the loss of a captain in the Ministry of Interior's SWAT unit — he had been shot in the neck just above his vest. I was told that the day before, opposition fighters had used a rocket-propelled grenade in Ashiri on the outskirts of Homs. One state security man called Shaaban complained that Bab Assiba had become its own state. The day before, he had taken part in heavy fighting there and helped transport 35 wounded soldiers out. "It was like a wedding," he laughed as he described the shooting.[58]

Assassinations became commonplace during this period as well, which fit with broader U.S. plans to destabilize the Syrian government. According to Amnesty International, on July 24, Rida Drei', a 31-year-old Shia supermarket owner from the al-Bayadha neighborhood in Homs, was abducted and murdered by opposition militants. His body was found with a bullet wound in the upper neck, cuts to the head and nose, and bruised lips, while his car was found burned in a graveyard.[59] Azmi Bishara noted that in just one day in July 2011 in Homs, about 30 people were kidnapped and killed by opposition militants, but that the public appearance of weapons in the streets did not begin until August 2011.[60]

Opposition activists accused the Syrian government of assassinating several prominent civilians in Homs during this time.[61] However, according to Bishara, it was known that opposition militants were responsible for the killings. He provides as examples: the head of the chest surgery division of the National Hospital, Hassan Eid (Alawite, killed on August 24); the deputy director of the faculty of chemistry in Homs University, Na'il al-Dakhil (Christian, killed September 26); the vice dean of the faculty of architecture in the Ba'ath University in Homs, Muhammad Ali Aqil (Shiite, also killed September 26); and the nuclear engineer Aws Abd al-Kareem Khalil (Alawite, killed September 28). Bishara notes that while the above-mentioned men had participated in a national dialogue organized by the Syrian government, the men had nevertheless rejected Syrian government efforts to end the crisis militarily via a "security solution" and had demanded real democratic reforms. Opposition militants assassinated them anyway. Bishara noted further that opposition activists justified passing unconfirmed, exaggerated, and fabricated information of this kind (falsely blaming the Syrian government for such killings) to the media because of their belief that it "served the revolution."[62]

Friday of the Children of Freedom

The city of Hama, which in the summer of 2011 had become another center of protests, saw instances of both government brutality against demonstrators and opposition assassinations of government supporters. The events in Hama were also noteworthy for the visit of the U.S. Ambassador to Syria Robert Ford in July to witness the protests, and because anti-government sentiment was said to be high as a legacy of the bloody confrontation between the Syrian army and the Muslim Brotherhood in 1982.

Tensions escalated in Hama after a protest on Friday, May 20, 2011. Protestors wrote the slogan "We demand dissolving the army of traitors and the establishment of a national army" on a wall on the road near the Omar bin al-Khattab Mosque, which was a reference to the events of 1982.[63]

During the protests, young men began throwing stones at riot police armed with plastic shields and batons. Several of the police seized Amran Daweek, a protestor who had been throwing rocks, and brutally beat him with batons in the head as he lay on the street bleeding. Daweek later died from his injuries, and video of the beating spread through social media, angering residents in Hama and providing a catalyst for further protest.[64]

On Friday, June 3, activists used the slogan the "Friday of the Children of Freedom," with activists claiming that some 50,000 had protested at al-Assi Square in Hama, and that Syrian security forces had opened fire, killing at least 53 demonstrators. Syrian state television in turn claimed that protestors were "trying to clash" with the security forces; that protestors had attacked and set fire to public buildings; that armed men had used the cover of the demonstration to carry out attacks; and that three "saboteurs" had been killed.[65]

According to a report published years later in the Lebanese newspaper *Ad-Diyar*, which is viewed as pro-Syrian government, the head of Hama's Military Security division, Major General Muhammad Mufleh, had until that time successfully contained the demonstrations by setting up checkpoints which protestors were not allowed to pass. However, as the protests grew, Mufleh became concerned that the security services would not be able to contain them, and that they would spread throughout the entire city of Hama, leaving the local security forces and army spread too thin to maintain control of the city. Mufleh then asked his superiors in Damascus how he should respond in such a scenario and allegedly received a cable directing him to "use force" in that case.

On June 3, when the large demonstration procession reached the checkpoints and wanted to pass through them, members of the Syrian army and members of the intelligence services opened fire in the direction of the demonstrators. Some of the demonstrators also used weapons against the army and intelligence. Their weapons were not visible at the beginning of the demonstration, however, as the armed men among the protestors were in the back rows. The clash resulted in the deaths of 63 civilians and nine soldiers. When the violence ended, the demonstration had been dispersed, and a night curfew was imposed on the city.

Apparently in response to the killings on June 3, allegations of corruption and treason were directed at Major General Mufleh in the Syrian media, leading to calls for his dismissal. However, General Assef Shawkat, President

Assad's brother-in-law, intervened to clarify that Mufleh had dealt with the protests in Hama according to the written cable sent to him from Damascus. Mufleh was then appointed head of the Military Security division in Aleppo Province. According to some reports, Mufleh would later play a crucial role in the fall of Aleppo to Salafist insurgents roughly one year later.[66]

If the *Ad-Diyar* report is correct, this would provide an example of when Syrian authorities did authorize the use of force to control protests (albeit protests with some armed elements), in this case due to fears that Hama, one of Syria's major cities and a provincial capital, would be lost to state control. The specter of another Benghazi was again apparently on their minds.

This contrasts with contemporaneous efforts elsewhere to ensure that Syrian security forces did not use force against protestors. In a lengthy report claiming to detail the responsibility of top Syrian government officials for issuing orders to kill peaceful protestors, journalist Ben Taub of *The New Yorker* nevertheless provides evidence to the contrary. Taub claims to cite Syrian government documents smuggled out of the country by a defector which detail internal deliberations of the military intelligence branch in Deir al-Zour, led by Brigadier General Jameh Jameh, in April 2011. Taub writes:

> Even as the committee discussed the importance of showing restraint, the violence escalated. Jameh said that protestors were courting "bloodshed, in preparation for summoning a foreign military intervention," an outcome that he said he desperately wanted to avoid. Early the next morning, he sent a one-sentence cable to all military-intelligence sections in the province: "You are requested to instruct your agents to strictly refrain from opening fire indiscriminately and killing people."

> In May, security in the province rapidly deteriorated. Men armed with bats, pistols, and incendiary bombs burned two police stations, four police cars, and six police motorcycles. Intelligence agents learned that someone had tried to recruit volunteers to detonate a car bomb

outside Jameh's house. The head of the Deir Ezzor political-security branch warned, "There may be a wave of assassinations."[67*]

Brigadier General Jameh's strict orders to avoid the use of force in Deir al-Zour, coupled with orders received by Major General Mufleh to use force to contain protests if they exceeded certain limits in Hama during roughly the same period, show a difference in opinion among top Syrian officials about how to deal with the protests and the foreign-backed Salafist insurgency that they understood themselves to be facing. Some hardliners — such as Asef Shawkat, who supported Mufleh in the wake of the Hama killings on June 3 — advocated resorting to force, while those who tried to remove Mufleh by initiating a campaign accusing him of corruption apparently objected to such harsh methods.

Syria's Kandahar

Shortly after the bloody events in Hama on June 3, 2011, the army pulled out of the city, while protests were allowed to continue uninterrupted by the security forces. The *Christian Science Monitor* reported that a protest on July 1 was the largest to date, while "activists said police were thin on the ground and that the roads to the city were not sealed off, as had been done in the past." This was apparently a gamble by the government "that more violence, at this point, will only enrage the populace more."[68]

It was in this context that U.S. Ambassador to Syria Robert Ford chose to visit Hama. State Department spokeswoman Victoria Nuland claimed that the intention of Ambassador Ford's July visit "was to make absolutely clear with his physical presence that we stand with those Syrians who are expressing their right to speak for change, who want a democratic future and who are expressing those views peacefully."[69]

In an exchange with Camille Otrakji, Ford later claimed that from April to June 2011, "the protests were almost entirely peaceful. I saw them myself

---

* Taub writes further that "Jameh's scruples apparently waned in the summer of 2011," and that "Jameh personally participated in many of the interrogations" in which detainees were brutally tortured. However, Taub bases this accusation on what he says is "evidence obtained by" the Commission for International Justice and Accountability (CIJA), a group funded by Britain and the European Union to collect documentary evidence of Syrian government war crimes. Taub gives no indication what evidence CIJA has for this accusation against Jameh, despite claiming that the evidence CIJA had compiled was, according to Stephen Rapp, United States Ambassador-at-Large for War Crimes Issues, "much richer than anything I've seen, and anything I've prosecuted in this area."

at Hama and believe me, not the Baath HQ, not the police HQ, not the municipal building, nothing touched. Police were drinking tea in white plastic chairs in the shade."[70]

In response, Otrakji wrote that "Ambassador Ford remembers so well the many stories that support his convictions, including what happened when he visited Hama. But there are many other stories that are inconsistent with his account of a fully peaceful Hama revolution." Otrakji then provided three sample accounts from Hama when opposition militants controlled the city after the army had pulled out. He explains that Lebanese journalist Ghadi Francis reported in mid-July 2011 from revolution-controlled Hama and "described it as 'Syria's Kandahar' where revolutionaries, mostly Islamists, carry weapons and knives and control the city's check points." Otrakji pointed to "a video showing a Salafi who stabbed an old Alawite man at one of those checkpoints. You can see the bleeding old man is scared and trying to calm down the Salafi revolutionary." Otrakji also notes a video of opposition militants which shows a "celebration where they are throwing the bodies of those they killed in the river outside Hama."[71]

Nir Rosen reported:

> I met with the family of Issa Bakir, an 11-year veteran police sergeant serving in Aleppo. After visiting his family in Rabia on July 5, Issa was driving back to Aleppo via Hama. On the outskirts of Hama he was stopped at a checkpoint. He was hit on the head with a club and his throat was then slit. "They stopped him, burned his car, slaughtered him, and we found him next to the mosque," his father told me.[72]

On July 20, Anthony Shadid of the *New York Times* reported that in Homs,

> episodes of lawlessness and vengeance have punctuated the city's experiment. An informer was hanged from an electricity pylon last month; the bodies of three or four others were thrown into the Orontes River, residents say. These days, Hama is represented by Mustafa Abdel-Rahman, the 60-year-old cleric in charge of the Serjawi Mosque. Islamists populate and perhaps dominate the ranks of protestors, and by some estimates, a fourth of the city has fled, fearing a showdown more than the brand of rule the Islamists might impose.[73]

The Flower and the Nightingale

In perhaps the most shocking case of opposition violence in Hama, militants murdered Ibrahim Qashoush, a young illiterate man with a clubbed hand who worked as a security guard at the local fire department, claiming that he was an informer. On July 3, 2011, opposition militants slit his throat and dumped his body in the Orontes River. Opposition activists from the LCC in Hama then spread photos and video of the corpse to claim that Qashoush had been a non-violent demonstrator famous for writing songs mocking President Assad which became popular in local anti-government protests.[74]

The activists alleged that government thugs known as *shabiha* had murdered Qashoush and ripped out his vocal cords as punishment for his songs — without explaining, however, how they could have been on hand to film his corpse as the blood was still flowing from his neck.[75]

Journalist James Harkin confirmed in a report for *GQ Magazine* years later that the protest singer was actually another man, Abdul Rahman Farhood, who was still alive and living as a refugee in Europe. One Syrian human rights investigator acknowledged to Harkin that "some of the opposition were telling lies [about Qashoush] because they thought it would be helpful. It was because of this that I fell out with them." The false claim that the Syrian government killed Qashoush did help the revolution, according to Harkin, as Qashoush's slaying became a "rallying point for protestors" in Hama, who considered him "the nightingale of the revolution."[76]

The false-flag killing of Ibrahim Qashoush was soon followed by another similarly shocking claim of Syrian government brutality. Amnesty International claimed in a September 2011 report that an 18-year-old woman named Zeinab al-Hosni had been murdered by Syrian security agents, who had decapitated, skinned, and cut off the arms of her body. Amnesty then used the claim of Zeinab's murder to advocate action against the Syrian government at the UN Security Council.[77] Zeinab had allegedly been detained several weeks before, on July 27, by security agents to pressure her brother, Mohammed, who had been active in organizing anti-government protests in Homs, to turn himself in. Mohammed was allegedly told by telephone that Zeinab would be released only if he stopped his activities. He was arrested, and on September 13, his mother was summoned by security forces to pick up his body, which allegedly showed bruises, burns, and gunshots.[78]

Opposition activists then posted graphic video footage online of a mutilated body said to be that of Zeinab, which triggered outrage among the opposition. Protestors carried the picture of the dead woman and dubbed her the "flower of Syria."[79]

However, Amnesty and opposition activists' claims fell apart two weeks later, on October 5, when Zeinab appeared alive on Syrian state television, showing her identification card and saying that she was alive but that she had run away from home and stayed with a relative because her brothers had been abusing her. Zeinab's mother and brother Yousef confirmed that it was indeed Zeinab in the video, and that they had somehow misidentified her body at the morgue.

In acknowledging the error, Amnesty researchers said that their initial statements on Zeinab's death had been based on "information provided by sources close to the incident itself, who passed Amnesty International video footage of a dismembered body."[80] Because Amnesty's initial reporting was based on the sources "close to the incident" (i.e., opposition activists) rather than from the family itself, this suggests that the story of Zeinab's alleged death originated with opposition activists seeking to manufacture anger against the government. *GlobalPost* noted that activists were the source of the video, stating that

> the video activists made of the corpse is too graphic to publish. It shows a bone sticking through from a severed arm, barely recognizable, its hand having also been hacked off. The decapitated head, blackened and burned, its eyes and lips sealed shut. The stump of an arm and the gaping hole in her shoulder where a blade was wielded to cut the woman into pieces.[81]

The cases of Ibrahim Qashoush and Zeinab al-Hosni are reminiscent of the case of Hamza al-Khateeb discussed earlier. In all three cases, activists gained early access to the bodies and quickly released videos presenting a narrative of almost unimaginable government brutality. The later false opposition claims regarding Qashoush and al-Hosni therefore suggest a pattern that points further to the likelihood that the Syrian government account of Hamza al-Kateeb's death is the correct one.

Despite the outrage caused by such false claims of Syrian government atrocities, many Syrians who were initially enthusiastic about a peaceful movement for change nevertheless abandoned the protest movement during this time, as its violent and sectarian trajectory became increasingly clear.

One Alawite from Homs named Fadi explained that "when the revolution started, I was really excited," and that in April 2011 he had joined an anti-government demonstration in which "secret service people were brutal with the demonstrators. And that same night, they started shooting at people." However, after soon hearing calls for jihad, which he viewed as a call for violence against Alawites, "suddenly I became scared and I changed my mind, as I realized that what was happening was no longer a revolution." Fadi noted that a turning point for him was when opposition militants killed three young Alawite boys in July 2011.

Sunday Times journalist Hala Jaber described a similar phenomenon. Jaber reported that Syrian journalist and opposition activist Mohammed Hamadah changed his view of the so-called revolution after he was detained and tortured by opposition gunmen on June 10, 2011, in his hometown of Ma'arat al-Nu'man. After hitting him on the back with electric cables, dripping burning plastic over his back, thighs, and ankles, and electrocuting him through his toes, Hamadah's captors found the name George among the contacts in his mobile phone. Jaber writes:

> This led to another beating for mixing with "a Christian infidel, a crusader and a pig." Hamadah was warned that if he turned out to be from the Alawite minority that forms Syria's elite, his baby daughter would be cut to pieces in front of him. Finally, he was hung upside down while electrodes were applied to his back and buttocks.[82]

'Protecting' Civilians

Once the reality of armed struggle to topple the Syrian government became apparent, it then became common to acknowledge that FSA militants were using violence, but only to protect civilians. However, Nir Rosen wrote in September 2011 that according to an opposition activist in Homs, the militants publicly said that they were fighting "to defend the civilians but most of their operations involve[d] attacking checkpoints." According to the activist, "they say 'we attack the ones who attack us; this is our way of defending civilians.'"[83]

This success was in part attributable to covert assistance from British and Qatari special operations units which, according to a February 8, 2012, report from the Israeli news site Debka, were present in Homs during this period:

> [They] are tactical advisors, manage rebel communications lines, and relay their requests for arms, ammo, fighters, and logistical aid to outside suppliers, mostly in Turkey... Our sources report the two foreign contingents have set up four centers of operation — in the northern Homs district of Khalidiya, Bab Amro in the east, and Bab Derib and Rastan in the north. Each district is home to about a quarter of a million people.[84]

The Debka claims were apparently confirmed by leaked emails from Reva Bhalla, director of analysis of the private intelligence firm Stratfor, which explained that special operations units, presumably from the U.S., U.K., France, Jordan, and Turkey, were on the ground in Syria since at least December 2011. Bhalla's email provided details of a December 6 Pentagon meeting attended by members of the U.S. Air Force Strategic Studies Group. In the meeting, it was discussed that foreign intelligence officers were in Homs with the mission to train opposition fighters to "commit guerrilla attacks, assassination campaigns, try to break the back of the Alawite forces, elicit collapse from within."[85]

These offensive attacks continued over subsequent months in Homs, allowing FSA militants to expand their control of larger and larger sections of the city. After an interview with Farouq commander Abd al-Razzaq Tlass on January 24, 2012, French journalist Jonathan Littell wrote:

> Tlass is leaving to launch an attack against some army checkpoints and things might go sour, and we leave... In twenty minutes more or less, we're in Khalidiya. There, first surprise: an FSA checkpoint at the entrance of the neighborhood, with sandbags and armed guys. Ra'id is surprised, that didn't exist in November; it means the FSA has gotten seriously stronger, if they dare show themselves openly here, so close to the center.[86]

The Syrian army responded by launching a counter-offensive against opposition militants in Khalidiya which included the use of heavy artillery. Nir Rosen writes that the Syrian army operation

> was interpreted by leaders of Homs's uprising as a response to their recent gains... [Opposition fighters] announced that they attacked security forces in Rastan, expelled them from Talbiseh, and took control of more territory in Homs city, launching two attacks on the State Security and Military Security headquarters. On February 3 [2012], the day government forces began their offensive, opposition fighters attacked at least three army checkpoints, including one at Homs's Qahira roundabout, where they reportedly seized a large armoured vehicle — either a personnel carrier or a tank. They also captured many Syrian soldiers and released a video of interviews with the officers of the captured unit.[87]

Rosen also quoted a member of the Homs Revolutionary Council, who declared, "We control most of Homs." As a result of Farouq's gains in late 2011 and early 2012, Homs came to be viewed as the "capital of the revolution."[88]

The Daily Beast reported that during the same Syrian army offensive, three groups of FSA fighters from the Farouq Brigades successfully attacked two high-rise buildings occupied by the Syrian army, "killing about 60 security forces and capturing another six, whom they handed over to the brigade's interrogators."[89]

Farouq often then executed most of the Syrian soldiers it captured. Amnesty International reported that, according to one armed opposition commander linked to the FSA who was active in the Homs,

> out of every 10 captured soldiers, around six would be usually killed. [The opposition commander] went on: "When we were still in control of Baba Amr, every time we killed a captured soldier or officer, we kept his military ID, his cell phone, and other possessions all in a safe place. The soldier would be buried in Basateen Baba Amr [Baba Amr's orchards]. But in the last few months, we stopped being as organized… the government started using airstrikes, so we have to leave the battlefield as quickly as possible… and captured soldiers would slow us down. So [the FSA] would just kill them on the site and leave."[90]

Journalist Sharmine Narwani reports that according to a leaked email dated March 25, 2012, which summarized a meeting of armed opposition groups in Homs, the groups' leaders acknowledged that more recent Syrian army shelling in the Khalidiya neighborhood was also in response to a Farouq attack on a Syrian army checkpoint, and that Farouq's financial backers in Saudi Arabia were "urging the targeting of loyalist neighborhoods and sectarian escalation."[91]

The Syrian army was not alone in deploying heavy weapons in urban areas. Farouq was also shelling pro-government neighborhoods while battling the army, despite claims from Ambassador Robert Ford that armed opposition groups were not in possession of such weapons. In February 2012, Ford and CNN had released satellite images allegedly showing Syrian government use of heavy artillery, and of whole neighborhoods that had been destroyed due to shelling, including one appearing "like a ghost town — with no cars at all, there's damage in the roads and so much damage on the top of the buildings." However, Bernard of the *Moon of Alabama* (*MOA*) blog showed that the artillery allegedly deployed by the army in civilian areas was instead being used in training areas,[92] while Sharmine Narwani showed that the CNN satellite photos showing heavily damaged areas were of the pro-government al-Zahra neighborhood, rather than, say, pro-opposition Baba Amr, indicating that it was opposition militants from the Farouq Brigades who had caused the destruction using their own artillery instead.[93]

One victim of Farouq and FSA shelling was French journalist Gilles Jacquier, who was killed in Homs on January 11, 2012, along with eight

Syrians who had gathered to form a small pro-government protest when the journalists arrived in the city. Jacquier and other foreign journalists had been invited to Syria by Sister Marie-Agnès, a Lebanese nun living near Homs known for her reconciliation efforts. The group was visiting Akramah, a majority Alawite neighborhood, when a mortar landed near the group.[94]

French authorities immediately suggested that the Syrian government had carried out the attack as part of a "manipulation," claiming that "only Syrian officials knew that a group of Western journalists were visiting Homs that day, and which neighborhood they were in."[95]

However, a Lebanese photographer working for AFP who survived the attack claimed that the shell was launched from the Bab Sbah neighborhood, which was known to be pro-opposition. This suggested that the FSA was responsible for the death of Jacquier and the eight Syrians who died with him. This was confirmed when *Le Figaro* reported that a member of a local human rights group in Homs told a Syrian opposition leader in France that the opposition had committed "a big blunder" in launching the mortar that killed Jacquier; and that "shortly after the attack, we knew quite quickly" who had fired the mortar, and that this information had been passed on to the Arab League, which had observers in Syria at that time.[96]

Civilians in both pro-government and opposition neighborhoods suffered terribly from the violence from both sides. Jonathan Littell reports that in the al-Bayadha neighborhood, government snipers "shoot at everyone, women, children, first aid workers, for no reason whatsoever." Littell witnessed several civilians who had been targeted by snipers being brought to a makeshift medical clinic:

> The first wounded man is brought in just before noon, his abdomen pierced by a bullet as he was trying to protect his children from the shots of a sniper hidden on the roof of the neighbourhood post office; his son soon follows, with two fingers shot off. Another man has already been killed in the same place, we are told. Two hours later, it's a 10-year-old boy, whose thick black hair I stroke as the doctor binds his hands with gauze. The bullet, which went through his chest, killed him on the spot. His cousin gazes at the little body and sobs: "Praise to God, praise to God." There will be a last one before evening, a man shot through the lungs, who will barely survive.[97]

Littell noted as well: "No one denies that Alawite civilians have already been the victims of murders or kidnappings, often for use as bargaining chips."

Although heavy weapons were being used and atrocities committed by all sides, opposition activists, whenever speaking with the Western press, nevertheless ignored the role of the Farouq Brigades and their foreign sponsors in instigating the violence, and characterized the Syrian army as simply massacring civilians.[98]

This gave foreign leaders the pretext to call for regime change in Syria, a long-standing U.S. foreign policy objective.[99] Referring to the violence in Khalidiya in February 2012, President Obama omitted any mention of opposition violence and described Syrian army actions as "indiscriminate violence," while claiming that "Assad must halt his campaign of killing and crimes against his own people now. He must step aside and allow a democratic transition to proceed immediately."[100]

Also ignored by Obama and the Western press broadly was the ethnic cleansing of Christians from Homs by sectarian opposition armed groups. Only years later did *Newsweek* report that Christians faced a "total purge" from Syria, and that this had begun in Homs during this time, noting that "a clergyman who led a parish in Homs before the war said Free Syrian Army (FSA) fighters and other Islamic armed groups expelled 15,000 Christian families from their homes in the old city of Homs in February 2012."[101]

9. The Propaganda War

Media Capture

The violent aspects of the Syrian opposition in Homs were largely obscured from outside observers, due to the sleight of hand used by opposition activists when reporting events on the ground. These activists deliberately sought to obscure the role of armed opposition groups in the conflict, while highlighting Syrian government violence. NPR reported that one opposition media activist from Homs "admits that he and his colleagues tailored their information to show as much of the civilian misery, and as little rebel activity, as possible."[1]

Western journalists making brief visits to opposition-held areas of Syria similarly provided a distorted picture, as they were typically accompanied by media activists affiliated with the FSA and were only allowed to see what the media activists allowed them to see. Jonathan Littell explained that members of the opposition's "local information bureau insisted on supervising all journalists' access to Baba 'Amr [an opposition-held neighborhood in Homs], and within the neighborhood access to strategic places, like a demonstration or the [health] clinic." Littell was able to avoid this supervision to some degree by embedding with FSA fighters directly, noting that when accompanied by the media activists, "we'd see only what they want us to see, and they'd be acting as if the FSA didn't exist."[2]

Littell notes further that he met a cameraman in Homs, named Abu Yazen al-Homsi, who provided a lot of images to Al Jazeera and other networks:

> [Yazen al-Homsi] regards himself as an activist, not a journalist. "I could never send an image that might harm the revolution." He can almost never film the FSA. Once, he filmed the destruction of a tank, but the FSA forbade him from sending out the images. The FSA is afraid of showing there are civilians who joined their ranks. For them, that would be giving credit to the regime's claims of "terrorism"... Abu Yazen al-Homsi confirms that all foreign journalists (except for us) work with the Information Bureau. "It's because they can't have access to certain information. The Bureau controls them."[3]

As noted in Chapter 8, Abu Yazen was one of many activists who joined ISIS early after its establishment in April 2013.[4]

The success of the information bureau in shaping the reporting about events in Homs was illustrated clearly in the case of prominent American war correspondent Marie Colvin, who visited Homs in February 2012, where she was tragically killed by a Syrian army mortar. Photographer Paul Conroy, who accompanied Colvin, relates in his book that, according to Colvin: "At least in Libya we could get a driver and go where we wanted and see what we wanted... Here, it's pretty much up to them what we see. I'm slightly uncomfortable with that. Our lives are in their hands, and we just have to go with it." Conroy writes further, "We agreed that it was going to be difficult to remain nonpartisan. We relied on the FSA and the activists for everything. Coupled with our inability to move independently, this would make both reporting and surviving here far more complex than anything we had experienced in Libya."[5]

It was in this context that Colvin reported in her last on-air interview from Homs before her death that she had seen a baby die. "The baby's death was just heartbreaking," she told CNN's Anderson Cooper. "We just watched this little boy, his little tummy heaving and heaving as he tried to breathe. It was horrific. My heart broke." Colvin explained further: "There are no military targets here... The Syrian Army is basically shelling a city of cold, starving civilians."[6]

In reality, Colvin had no way to confirm how the child had died, under what circumstances, or where, as she had only seen a video of the baby dying on a computer laptop screen, which was shown to her by media activists from the information bureau. Paul Conroy writes that in

> Baba Amr, Syria, during the early hours of Tuesday [February 21, 2012] morning, Abu Hanin called everyone into the main room of the media center. We all watched in hushed silence as the baby boy on the laptop's screen gasped and struggled hopelessly towards his final, dying breath. The scene galvanised Marie, stabbing at the raw nerves that fueled her need to bear witness. "Paul, we have to get this out. This can't be allowed to slip by and disappear into the ether. They're murdering babies, for Christ's sake. We have to tell the world. It's why we're here," she said, her furious gaze locked on me.[7]

In the same attack that killed Colvin, French photojournalist Remi Ochlik was also killed; Conroy was injured, and so apparently was French reporter Édith Bouvier (of *Le Figaro*). Controversy then arose over efforts to evacuate Conroy and Bouvier. According to AFP, the International Committee of the Red Cross, in partnership with the Syrian Red Cross, had tried to evacuate the journalists but had been blocked, not by the Syrian government but, surprisingly, by the FSA.[8]

Noting this strange fact, Bernard of the *Moon of Alabama* blog provided evidence that Bouvier was not in fact injured, but had instead faked her injury alongside a prominent opposition journalist, Khaled Abu Saleh, who had himself faked injuries in multiple videos in the past. Bernard suggests that Bouvier faked her injuries to provide a pretext for French President Nicholas Sarkozy's proposal of opening humanitarian corridors in Syria, which, if enforced by the French military, could serve as a Trojan Horse for further intervention and the breaching of Syrian sovereignty.[9]

Georges Malbrunot and Christian Chesnot of *Le Figaro* report that the French foreign intelligence service, DGSE, sought to evacuate Bouvier to Lebanon (50 kilometers away) with the help of Lebanese Internal Security Forces, which were close with the FSA. Unaware of the DGSE effort, French Ambassador Chevallier had himself encouraged Bouvier to accept evacuation by the Syrian Red Crescent to Damascus, after which he would escort her to Paris. Chevallier had wished to repeat his success in returning home the body of the journalist Gilles Jacquier.

Chevallier later learned, however, that Bouvier could not be evacuated via Damascus because she was not alone, as she was accompanied by a group of French mercenaries also in need of evacuation, who were in Homs fighting alongside the FSA's Abu Baqir group. The DGSE then successfully exfiltrated both Bouvier and the mercenaries to Lebanon via Qusayr, Syria.[10] This suggests that Bouvier was not only a journalist, but also that she was fulfilling obligations for French intelligence, which, as we shall see later, was the case with other *Le Figaro* journalists as well. This raises the question of whether these French mercenaries were working with FSA groups at the time they launched the mortar that killed the French journalist Jacquier.

The case of Marie Colvin illustrates that many journalists covering the Syria war, even those with the courage to visit the war zone rather than file reports from the safety of Beirut, were often simply passing on rumors told to them by their opposition media activist handlers.

Parachuting into conflict zones for short periods, with no Arabic language ability, under the watch of opposition media activists, and with little understanding of the context of the conflict, many journalists were only able to convey a distorted picture of events on the ground. In the reports filed by Colvin, there was no indication of opposition militants attacking Syrian army checkpoints, detonating car bombs in urban neighborhoods, or assassinating Syrian army officers and pro-government civilians — *or* of the presence of the French mercenaries. Opposition efforts to invade neighborhoods, towns, and cities — and the Syrian army's efforts to defend the same from these assaults — were invisible. Instead, only evidence of government violence (much real, but also much imagined) was presented to viewers, with the violence of armed opposition militants completely erased from the picture, because this was all the opposition media activists wanted these journalists to see.

Black Propaganda

But the fog surrounding reporting of the war was not simply due to the manipulation of Western journalists. Instead, it was the result of years of advanced preparation by U.S. planners to control the narrative of the conflict once it began. In addition to Razan Zaitouneh and Wissam Tarif, other so-called "citizen journalists" provided a major source of this disinformation.

As Bernard of *MOA* notes, citizen journalists supported by Avaaz became notorious for creating fake videos to blame violence on the government. A notable example includes Danny Abdul Dayem, a British citizen of Syrian descent, whose reports were regularly featured by Anderson Cooper on CNN and on Al Jazeera. Bernard cites academic Asad Abu Khalil as observing that some unedited videos created by Abdul Dayem and later leaked to the Syrian government

> show the correspondent or witness (for CNN or from [Al Jazeera]) before he is on the air: and the demeanor is drastically different from the demeanor on the air and they even show contrived sounds of explosions timed for broadcast time. I have to say that [Al Jazeera] and the affiliated Ikhwan [Muslim Brotherhood] media win the award for the largest volume of lies in this crisis. Their lies have been rather helpful to the Syrian regime which now fills its airtime with exposing the lies and exaggerations of the Ikhwan-led Syrian opposition.

> [One video in particular] shows the footage prior to [Al Jazeera] reports: they show fake bandages applied on a child and then a person is ordered to carry a camera in his hand to make it look like a mobile footage. It shows a child being fed what to say on [Al Jazeera].[11]

Syrian journalist Rafiq Lutf and British journalist Vanessa Beeley also documented fabricated media reports of government violence from Abdul Dayem, including an alleged attack on an oil pipeline in Homs. In that case,

CNN journalist Arwa Damon, who was on the ground in Homs, participated in faking reports of the attack.[12]

Journalist Patrick Cockburn similarly noted the Al Jazeera role, writing that the Qatari-owned channel

> has become the uncritical propaganda arm of the Libyan and Syrian rebels… The purpose of manipulating the media coverage is to persuade the West and its Arab allies that conditions in Syria are approaching the point when they can repeat their success in Libya. Hence the fog of disinformation pumped out through the Internet.[13]

The private security and intelligence firm Stratfor concluded that the fog of disinformation often began with opposition activists. As Sharmine Narwani reports, Stratfor concluded in December 2011 that pro-opposition groups were spreading propaganda in the hope of "convincing external stakeholders, such as the United States, Turkey, and France, that the regime is splitting and is prepared to commit massacres to put down the unrest, along the lines of what the regime carried out in 1982 in Hama." This was, of course, meant to pave the way for U.S. military intervention in Syria, as had by that time just occurred in Libya under the same pretext. Stratfor concludes further that "most of the opposition's more serious claims have turned out to be grossly exaggerated or simply untrue, thereby revealing more about the opposition's weaknesses than the level of instability inside the Syrian regime."[14]

British historian and Syria expert Patrick Seale therefore argued in *The Guardian*:

> The strategy of the armed opposition is to seek to trigger a foreign armed intervention by staging lethal clashes and blaming the resulting carnage on the regime. It knows that, left to itself, its chance of winning is slim. For its part, the regime's brutality can be explained, if not condoned, by the fact that it believes it is fighting for its life — not only against local opponents but also against an external conspiracy led by the United States (egged on by Israel) and including Saudi Arabia, Qatar, Britain, and France. The regime's strategy is to prevent — at all costs — its armed opponents from seizing and holding territory inside the country, as this might give foreign powers a base from which to operate. As soon as it identifies pockets of armed opponents, it sends in its troops to crush them. That it often uses disproportionate force is not in doubt: this is all too predictable when a conventional army faces hit-and-run opponents. Trapped between opposing forces, civilians inevitably pay the price.[15]

It should be noted that U.S., British, and French planners were the originators of false atrocity claims, via the opposition activists and citizen journalists whom they themselves were funding. This means that fabricated stories about Syrian government atrocities were instead meant to influence Western public opinion, which otherwise stood in the way of direct U.S. military intervention anywhere in the Middle East due to the unpopularity of President Bush's 2003 invasion of Iraq.

The British government played an outsized role in covertly creating this propaganda, under the guise that it was coming independently from Syrian activists and FSA groups themselves. In May 2016, *The Guardian* reported that the British Foreign and Commonwealth Office had for years been "waging information warfare in Syria" by hiring contractors to

> produce videos, photos, military reports, radio broadcasts, print products, and social media posts branded with the logos of fighting groups, and effectively run a press office for opposition fighters. Materials are circulated in the Arabic broadcast media and posted online with no indication of British government involvement.[16]

The Houla Massacre

Patrick Seale made his observations regarding the opposition's efforts to trigger foreign intervention in the wake of the Houla massacre. On May 25, 2012, opposition activists spread videos showing victims of a mass killing, allegedly at the hands of pro-government Alawite *shabiha* militiamen, in the town of Taldou in the Houla region near Homs.[17] According to the UN, 108 people were killed, including 34 women and 49 children, some by artillery, while others were shot or had their throats slit.[18]

The same day, U.S. National Security Council spokeswoman Erin Pelton blamed the Syrian government, stating that the killings served as a "vile testament to an illegitimate regime," while U.K. Foreign Secretary William Hague called for an emergency session of the UN Security Council in response, claiming that "our urgent priority is to establish a full account of this appalling crime and to move swiftly to ensure that those responsible are identified and held to account."[19] Secretary of State Hillary Clinton also demanded that "those who perpetrated this atrocity" be identified and held to account.[20] She then blamed the Syrian government, stating that President Assad's "rule by murder and fear must come to an end."[21]

Two days later, the BBC implied that the Syrian government was responsible for the massacre and published an article with the heading "Syria massacre in Houla condemned as outrage grows." The article featured a photo of a young boy jumping over dozens of white body bags. The photo was accompanied by a caption stating that the photo is "believed to show the bodies of children in Houla awaiting burial." *The Telegraph* quickly reported, however, that the photo in the BBC article was not from Syria at all, but had been taken by photographer Marco di Lauro in Baghdad during the 2003 Iraq War. Di Lauro commented:

> What is amazing [is] that a news organization has a picture proving a massacre that happened yesterday in Syria and instead it's a picture that was taken in 2003 of a totally different massacre. Someone is using someone else's picture for propaganda on purpose.[22]

Efforts to blame the Syrian government came despite the fact that Major General Robert Mood, head of the UN observer mission to Syria, had visited the site of the massacre in Houla on May 26, the day after it occurred, and had refused to attribute responsibility for the killings, stating that "the circumstances that led to these tragic killings are still unclear," and that "as we speak now, I have other teams on the ground in Houla trying to establish more of the facts."[23]

Mood reiterated in a subsequent press conference that "we have been there with an investigative team. We have interviewed locals with one story, and we have interviewed locals that have another story. The circumstances leading up to al-Houla and the facts relating to the incident itself still remain unclear to us."[24] Mood explained further, on June 15, that a report containing details of these two contradictory accounts from locals had been submitted to the UN Security Council, which had not made the report public, for reasons that were not clear to him.[25]

Once evidence emerged from Mood's UN observers that opposition militants may have been responsible for the horrific massacre, Clinton and Hague's demand that a "full account of this appalling crime" be established was suddenly nowhere to be found. The failure of the UN Security Council to make Mood's report public, and the subsequent lack of interest in investigating the events in Houla to confirm responsibility for the massacre, allowed the perception of Syrian government responsibility, as promoted by the BBC and other Western media outlets, to persist. This was reinforced by comments made by Rupert Colville, the spokesman for the Office of the UN High Commissioner for Human Rights (OHCHR), who claimed from Geneva that the Syrian government was likely responsible for the Houla massacre, while ignoring the evidence from the UN's own observer mission on the ground in Syria led by Mood.[26]

However, reporting from journalist Rainer Hermann on June 7 in the *Frankfurter Allgemeine Zeitung* provided evidence from opposition sources that in fact armed opposition groups were responsible for the massacre, and that among the victims were a Shiite family who had converted from Sunni Islam and a Sunni family viewed as government supporters (one family member had been elected to the Syrian parliament). Hermann writes:

> Based on credible witness statements, Syrian opposition activists who come from the region have in recent days been able to reconstruct the likely course of events in Hula. Their result contradicts the claims made by the rebels who accused the *shabiha*, acting under the protection of the Syrian army, of the crime.[27]

On July 23, *Der Spiegel* contradicted Hermann's conclusions by publishing a report supporting the view that Alawite *shabiha* militias did indeed carry out the massacre. *Der Spiegel* sent a team that managed to visit Taldou, the village in Houla where many of the killings took place, to interview witnesses of the massacre. *Der Spiegel* did not say how its team managed to get access to Taldou but noted that the village was still under control of the FSA. *Der Spiegel* claimed that the Syrian government was still bombing the town at times and wished to prevent any foreigners from visiting.[28]

This means that the *Der Spiegel* team likely gained access to the village with permission of the FSA. This also means that anyone speaking with the *Der Spiegel* team would likely be constrained from saying anything contradicting the FSA claims about government culpability.

As discussed in Chapter 7, FSA brigades in Homs employed media committees to control tightly what journalists could see and to shape any news provided by Western journalists in areas they controlled. There is no reason to believe that in Taldou, under FSA control, the media committees would not also tightly control the narrative presented by locals to the *Der Spiegel* team. This is even more likely, given the huge amount of international media attention that had already resulted from the massacre. Whoever could be blamed, whether the opposition or the government, would lose a huge battle in the ongoing propaganda war.

For this reason, as journalist John Rosenthal observes, the most reliable testimony about culpability for the massacre in Houla is that obtained by Rainer Hermann of the *Frankfurter Allgemeine Zeitung*.[29] Crucially, it was against the interest of these opposition activists speaking to Hermann to acknowledge the culpability of their own side, meaning that it is unlikely that they would fabricate such claims. Furthermore, Hermann is a respected journalist for one of Germany's largest newspapers and did not represent any side in the conflict. This makes it unlikely that he would deliberately fabricate the admissions made to him by those opposition activists, who wished to remain anonymous for obvious safety reasons.

The timing of the Houla massacre and accompanying propaganda in the Western press is also important. UN head Kofi Anon had negotiated a ceasefire that started April 12, some six weeks before the massacre in Houla. Patrick Cockburn notes that

> the Houla slaughter makes Syria once again the centre of international attention and a possible target for some form of foreign intervention.
>
> The ceasefire was only sporadically implemented from the beginning. The government has always had more interest in its successful implementation, which would stabilize its authority, than the insurgents, who need to keep the pot of rebellion boiling. The UN monitoring team says that during the ceasefire "the level of offensive military operations by the government significantly decreased" while there has been "an increase in militant attacks and targeted killings." But any credit the Syrian government might be hoping for in showing restraint will disappear if the latest atrocities are confirmed.[30]

A week after the Houla massacre, WikiLeaks released a memo written by a military officer who described a December 2011 meeting he attended at the Pentagon with four U.S. military intelligence officials, as well as British and French liaison officers, in which the question of imposing a Libya-style NATO no-fly zone in Syria was discussed. The memo mentioned that the officers present "don't believe air intervention would happen unless there was enough media attention on a massacre, like the Qaddafi move against Benghazi."[31]

Although allegations that Qaddafi intended to massacre civilians in Benghazi later proved to be propaganda, as shown by Alan Kuperman in *Foreign Affairs*, these allegations were nevertheless successful in triggering a no-fly zone that immediately expanded into a broad-based NATO bombing campaign resulting in regime change.[32]

Benghazi therefore provided a model to emulate for opposition militants in Syria and their backers in U.S. and allied intelligence agencies, a theme that would emerge often in the conflict moving forward.

10. Al-Qaeda Shows Its Face

Jolani Returns to Syria

In August 2011, after al-Qaeda elements had been already active in Syria for at least five months, Islamic State in Iraq (ISI) leader Abu Bakr al-Baghdadi dispatched his deputy, Abu Muhammad al-Jolani, from Iraq to extend the group's franchise formally into Syria, which became known as Jabhat al-Nusra, or "the Nusra Front."

The AP published a report providing an outline of Jolani's life based on information from Iraqi and Jordanian intelligence and from a prominent Jordanian Salafist leader. The report explains that Jolani, a Syrian,

> was once a teacher of Arabic before moving to Iraq, where he turned to militancy and eventually became a close associate of Abu Musab al-Zarqawi, the Jordanian-born leader of the militant group al-Qaeda in Iraq. After al-Zarqawi was killed by a U.S. airstrike in 2006, al-Golani left Iraq, briefly staying in Lebanon, where he offered logistical support for the Jund al-Sham militant group, which follows al-Qaeda's extremist ideology, the officials said. He returned to Iraq to continue fighting but was arrested by the U.S. military and held at Camp Bucca, a sprawling prison on Iraq's southern border with Kuwait. At that camp, where the U.S. military held tens of thousands of suspected militants, he taught Classical Arabic to other prisoners, according to the officials, who spoke on condition of anonymity because they were revealing information from secret files. After his release from prison in 2008, al-Golani resumed his militant work, this time alongside Abu Bakr al-Baghdadi, the head of al-Qaeda in Iraq — also known as the Islamic State of Iraq. He was soon appointed head of al-Qaeda operations in Mosul Province. Shortly after the Syrian uprising began, al-Golani moved into Syrian territory and, fully supported by al-Baghdadi, formed the Nusra Front, which was first announced in January 2012.[1]

These same details of Jolani's life were confirmed in July 2015 by Al Jazeera, which noted that Jolani had returned to Syria from Mosul specifically in August 2011.[2] Al Jazeera is in a good position to know the outline of Jolani's past, including his 2008 release from the U.S. prison in Bucca, given that Jolani granted two major interviews to the network, one in December 2013 (Jolani's first),[3] and the other in 2015.[4]

These reports from the AP and Al Jazeera contradict pro-opposition propaganda claiming that Jolani was held by the Syrian government in

155

Sednaya Prison and deliberately released in 2011 to Islamize and militarize an otherwise peaceful and secular uprising.[5]

Jolani's presence in Syria initially remained secret, as did that of other foreign jihadists working with FSA groups during this period. For example, Aaron Zelin, an expert on Tunisian jihadism, observed:

> In 2011, before jihadist groups officially announced their presence in Syria, foreign fighters began mobilizing to Syria with the non-jihadist Free Syrian Army... As for the announcement of foreign fighter martyrs, this began in February 2012, with the posting of the first recorded martyrdom notice on the jihadist forum Shamukh al-Islam. This announcement was long delayed, with the fighter in question, a Kuwaiti named Hussam al-Mutayri, having died August 29, 2011, while fighting with the FSA in Damascus.[6]

Although al-Qaeda had not yet formally announced its existence in Syria, al-Qaeda-affiliated foreign jihadists from Iraq, Saudi Arabia, and Lebanon had of course entered Syria as early as late 2010 and had helped sparked the conflict itself in March 2011, as discussed in Chapter 2.

This means that Jolani was far from the first al-Qaeda leader present in Syria, and much of the infrastructure needed by Jolani to establish the Nusra Front was already present when he returned to the country. As discussed in Chapter 2 as well, Ahrar al-Sham was established before March 2011 by longtime al-Qaeda figure Abu Khalid al-Suri, with many Saudi foreign fighters joining his group.

Abdullah Suleiman Ali of *As-Safir* reports:

> The majority of these "migrants" [foreign fighters] had secretly joined Ahrar al-Sham, since it was a faction recommended by al-Qaeda leaders. Yet, the majority of these "migrants" moved to Jabhat al-Nusra, when the latter was established. As for [Abu Khalid al-Suri], he remained with Ahrar al-Sham, in a move that may have been intended to strengthen the "al-Qaeda movement" in Ahrar al-Sham, to be used at the right time.[7]

One al-Qaeda figure who successfully traveled to Syria from Saudi Arabia, despite a Saudi government travel ban, was Sheikh Abdel Wahed, who was known as Saqr al-Jihad, or "the Hawk of Jihad." Suleiman Ali notes that Abdel Wahed

> may be the first leader of the first generation of Afghan Arabs who arrived in Syrian territory a few months following the outbreak of the crisis. He settled in the mountains of Latakia and worked on establishing the Soqqor al-Ezz battalion, through which Abdel Wahed attracted prominent figures of the jihadist work in

Afghanistan. These included Abdel Malak al-Ihsa'i (Abu Leen), Zaid al-Bawardi (Abu Ammar al-Makki), and Abu Mohammed al-Halabi, who were all from the first generation and spent more than 25 years in fighting — from Afghanistan to Bosnia, and Chechnya to Iraq — and the three of them were killed in Syria. The Soqqor al-Ezz battalion assumed another role of working on receiving "the migrants" at the Turkish-Syrian border, and provided them with shelter until they were assigned to battalions… The frequency with which Saudi nationals were collectively mobilized to fight in Syria increased after Jabhat al-Nusra was established and started carrying out its suicide operations. Convoys of jihadists were crossing over the Turkish border continuously all the way to the headquarters of Soqqor al-Ezz battalion in the mountains of Latakia. From there, these convoys either enrolled in Jabhat al-Nusra or stayed with the Soqqor-al-Ezz battalion. Yet, the majority of these Jihadists joined Jabhat al-Nusra, since the sheikhs of al-Qaeda recommended Jabhat al-Nusrah instead of Ahrar al-Sham.[8]

A Daily Diet

The Nusra Front first made its presence in the Syria conflict apparent with a suicide bombing in Damascus on December 23, 2011. Suicide car bombers targeted the General Security Directorate and another branch of the security services, killing 44, including civilians and security personnel. Opposition activists claimed that this was a false-flag attack carried out by the government to discredit the armed opposition.[9] However, Syria expert Joshua Landis cast doubt on this view, noting, "I am only surprised that we haven't seen the use of suicide bombing sooner." With the continued breakdown of law and order, radical groups would be able to spread, and "the chances are that the daily diet of suicide bombings, that have become a part of political life in Iraq, will also become common in Syria."[10]

As Landis expected, more such bombings quickly followed. According to Syrian state television, a suicide bomber detonated explosives near a bus, killing some 26, including both civilians and security personnel in the Midan district of Damascus on January 6, 2012. Opposition activists once again claimed that the attack was a false flag carried out by the government.[11]

Three weeks later, al-Qaeda's Syrian affiliate, the Nusra Front, made its role in the conflict public and explicit. On January 24, Al Jazeera reported that Abu Muhammad al-Jolani had announced the formation of the "Support Front for the People of the Levant," or the Nusra Front, whose fighters he called "the Mujahideen of al-Sham," pointing to his hometown of al-Shuhail in Deir al-Zour Province "as a starting point for the work of this front." In his statement, he also called on Syrians "to wage jihad and take up arms to bring down the Syrian regime."[12]

To the embarrassment of the U.S.- and Gulf-backed political opposition, Jolani's Nusra Front soon claimed responsibility for the Midan attack, as well as for another mass casualty suicide bombing in Aleppo that killed 28 on February 10, 2012. Furthermore, U.S. Director of National Intelligence James Clapper suggested that the attacks bore the hallmarks of al-Qaeda in Iraq, and that militants from the group had infiltrated into Syria to join the fight against the government.[13]

Clapper's acknowledgement of al-Qaeda's operations in Syria coincided with warnings from Iraqi security official Adnan al-Assadi that "a number of Iraqi jihadists went to Syria," and that "weapons smuggling is still ongoing." Al-Assadi explained that the "prices of weapons in Mosul (the province's capital) are higher now because they are being sent to the opposition in Syria," including through a border crossing near al-Bukamal, a town in Syria's Deir al-Zour Province on the Euphrates River and opposite the Iraqi town of al-Qaim.[14]

Cradle of the War

Iraqi security official al-Assadi's statements point to the early importance of Deir al-Zour Province, which was the epicenter of al-Qaeda's activities in Syria. *Guardian* journalist Leith Abdul-Ahad was one of the few journalists to visit the province, and in July 2012 he noted:

> Al-Qaida has existed in this parched region of eastern Syria, where the desert and the tribes straddle the border with Iraq, for almost a decade. During the years of American occupation of Iraq, Deir el-Zour became the gateway through which thousands of foreign jihadis flooded to fight the holy war. Many senior insurgents took refuge from American and Iraqi government raids in the villages and deserts of Deir el-Zour.

Abdul-Ahad contends that the Syrian government had "for years played a double game, allowing jihadis to filter across the borders to fight the Americans while at the same time keeping them tightly under control at home." Abdul-Ahad writes further that "in the pre-revolutionary days when the regime was strong it would take a year to recruit someone to the secret cause of jihad," but according to a Nusra fighter, who had himself fought in Iraq as a young man after 2003 and participated in early demonstrations against the Syrian government in 2011: "Now, thanks to God, we are working in the open, and many people are joining in."[15]

Nusra leader Jolani's hometown of al-Shuhail played a particularly important role, as noted in his announcement of the Nusra Front's establishment. Abdul-Ahad also visited al-Shuhail and noted that the town "has become the de facto capital of al-Qaida in Deir el-Zour. More than 20 of its young men were killed in Iraq. In Shuhail the al-Qaida fighters drive around in white SUVs with al-Qaida flags fluttering."[16]

Theo Padnos, who was held for ten months in al-Shuhail during his captivity with Nusra, also pointed to the importance of Deir al-Zour in the anti-government insurgency that erupted in 2011. According to the fighters, fellow prisoners, and civilians with whom he managed to speak while held captive, the so-called Syrian Revolution was not about democracy or human rights, but rather about waging war against the Alawites in the Syrian government and establishing an Islamic state. Padnos writes:

> I suspect now that the true cradle of the war in Syria wasn't Deraa, where the famous graffiti "The People Want the Fall of the Regime" first appeared on a schoolyard wall, but rather the Euphrates River Valley, especially the eastern portions of it, downstream from Raqqa, where Syria's oil and gas fields lie…
>
> I suspect I quizzed dozens if not hundreds of Deiris, as people from this region are known (after the provincial capital, Deir Ezzor)… As it happened, I did not encounter a single person in the eastern half of Syria who believed that peaceful demonstrators in Deraa — or mosque goers in the restive suburb of Duma or citizens anywhere else in the west — were the true fomenters of a rebellion in Syria. The true fomenters, in the opinion of my prison interviewees, were the men of the jihad.[17]

After his release from captivity, Padnos was asked by *Guardian* journalist Owen Jones, "Do you think, looking back, what we saw in the early parts was a genuine revolution of people who wanted democracy and freedom that was hijacked by Islamist terrorist organizations?"

Padnos responded, "No, I don't see that. That is the conventional narrative that's what many people believe… So much of the incentive or initiative for the West to support the revolutionaries is because we say Bashar al-Assad started it. But the revolutionaries themselves say, 'No, no, we started it.'"[18]

The full name of the group established by Jolani suggests that Nusra, which means "support," was meant to nurture the Salafist armed groups fighting under the FSA brand. Ghaith Abdul-Ahed interviewed a Nusra commander named Abu Khuder in the town of Muhassan in Deir al-Zour, who explained that

> his men are working closely with the military council that commands the Free Syrian Army brigades in the region. "We meet almost every day," he said. "We have clear instructions from our [al-Qaida] leadership that if the FSA need our help we should give it. We help them with IEDs and car bombs. Our main talent is in the bombing operations."[19]

Abdul-Ahad notes further that the origins of the so-called Syrian Revolution in Deir al-Zour were not secular, as was typically assumed, and that FSA commanders were exploiting religion to manipulate the young men fighting in their ranks. He writes that "religious and sectarian rhetoric has taken a leading role in the Syrian revolution from the early days." He quotes an FSA commander in Deir al-Zour city as explaining that "religion is the best way to impose discipline. Even if the fighter is not religious, he can't disobey a religious order in battle." He quotes a local activist as well, who described how "religion is a major rallying force in this revolution. Look at [Adnan] Ara'our [a rabid sectarian preacher] — he is hysterical and we don't like him, but he offers unquestionable support to the fighters and they need it."[20]

An Open Secret

In early 2012, FSA groups were not only receiving assistance from al-Qaeda in the east of the country in Deir al-Zour, but also in the northwest, near the border with Turkey. The assistance came in the form of al-Qaeda-affiliated militants from the Libyan Islamic Fighting Group (LIFG), including many who were British of Libyan descent, as well as shipments of Libyan weapons facilitated by the CIA and British intelligence, MI6.

Seymour Hersh reports that after Qaddafi's fall in September 2011, the CIA began running a "rat line" to ship weapons looted from Libyan army stockpiles to opposition militants in Syria. Hersh reports that

> the rat line, authorized in early 2012, was used to funnel weapons and ammunition from Libya via southern Turkey and across the Syria border to the opposition. Many of those who ultimately received the weapons were jihadists, some of them affiliated with al-Qaida.[21]

Hersh notes further that, according to a classified annex to the Senate Intelligence Committee report on the attack on the U.S. consulate in Benghazi, Libya, in September 2012, an

> agreement was reached in early 2012 between the Obama and Erdoğan administrations. It pertained to the rat line. By the terms of the agreement, funding came from Turkey, as well as Saudi Arabia and Qatar; the CIA, with support of MI6, was responsible for getting arms from Qaddafi's arsenals into Syria. A number of front companies were set up in Libya, some under the cover of Australian entities. Retired American soldiers, who didn't always know who was really employing them, were hired to manage procurement and shipping. The operation was run by [CIA Director] David Petraeus.

Although Hersh reports that the CIA weapons shipments began in early 2012, they likely began earlier, in at least November 2011, when "volunteer" fighters from the NATO-backed interim Libyan government began traveling to Syria to fight with FSA groups after they had successfully toppled Qaddafi. On November 29, 2011, *al-Bawaba* reported that

> 600 rebel fighters have already gone from Libya to Syria in order to support the Syrian opposition… The Libyan rebels entered Syria through Turkey, to join "the Free Syrian Army"… The door is still open to more volunteers in Libya in case they wish to fight.[22]

One prominent Libyan commander who traveled to Syria was Mehdi al-Herati, a Quran teacher with Irish citizenship who had previously fought against U.S. occupation forces in Iraq in 2003.[23] As noted in Chapter 2, Herati traveled from Ireland to Libya in February 2011 to form the Tripoli Brigade, which spearheaded the invasion of the Libyan capital, along with LIFG founder Abd al-Hakim Belhaj.[24]

Belhaj and other former LIFG militants were in turn partnering with British intelligence during the Libyan conflict. Middle East Eye (MEE) reported that U.K. Foreign Office Minister Alistair Burt acknowledged that the British government was in communication with Libyan insurgents during this period, and it was "likely that this included former members of Libyan Islamic Fighting Group." MEE reports further that according to Salafist activist and former Guantanamo detainee Moazzam Begg, the "British government's use of and support for former members of the LIFG during the Libyan uprising was a 'pretty open secret.'"[25]

After traveling to Syria, Mahdi al-Herati founded a fighting brigade called Liwa al-Ummah. Herati first entered Syria in October 2011, just two months after the fall of Qaddafi, under the pretext of providing humanitarian aid.

After crossing the border from Turkey, Herati went to the Jabal a-Zawiya region of Idlib Province and met with leaders from Ahrar al-Sham. According to Herati, he was welcomed "as a brother" by the al-Qaeda-affiliated group.[26]

Foreign Policy notes that the Facebook page for Liwa al-Ummah promoted a

> video clip of the late Abdullah Azzam, a Palestinian religious scholar who provided the theological underpinning for the jihad against the Soviets in Afghanistan in the 1980s, outlining when jihad becomes *fard ayn*, meaning an individual duty. A message bylined by Harati contains an invitation to "join the jihad in the land of al-Sham."[27]

Herati's men were well armed, with 12.5mm and 14.5mm anti-aircraft guns, rocket-propelled grenades, and rifles including PKCs and M16s at their disposal. Herati was able to recruit fellow Irish nationals to fight in Syria due to his standing in Ireland's Salafist community. One young Irish fighter admitted that his plan to come fight in Syria initially worried his family, but that "they respect and trust Sheikh Mahdi, so when they learned I was coming to join him here, they felt a little better."

Herati claimed that Liwa al-Ummah was almost entirely Syrian but that he and fellow Libyans who established the brigade were providing "training and organization," as well as "playing a combat role and providing our Syrian brothers with our experience of the Libyan revolution."[28]

In 2013, Ibrahim al-Mazwagi, a Brit of Libyan descent who had fought for Herati and Belhaj's Tripoli Brigade, became the first British jihadist to die in the Syrian conflict.[29] *The Independent* reported:

> According to the Facebook page set up in his honour, the North Londoner had fought in Libya in 2011 before heading to fight alongside his "brothers in Syria" last August [2012]... "He took part of [sic] a major operation against the Assad regime forces yesterday and passed in the ensuing battles."[30]

MI6 John

In Syria, Mazwagi fought as part of an armed group known as Katibat al-Muhajireen, or "the Emigrants' Brigade," which consisted primarily of foreign fighters, including many British citizens.[31] The group was led by Abu Omar al-Shishani, a red-bearded ethnic Chechen who went on to become one of the most prominent military commanders in ISIS.[32] As a former member of the Georgian military, Shishani had received training from U.S. special forces.[33]

Another Brit who fought for Katibat al-Muhajireen was Muhammad Emwazi, who joined the group after traveling to Syria in August 2012 with Mazwagi.[34]

Later known in the British press as "Jihadi John," Emwazi joined ISIS in 2013 and gained notoriety after beheading journalists James Foley and Steven Sotloff, aid workers David Haines, Alan Henning, and Peter Kassig, and 22 Syrian soldiers.[35]

As *The Guardian* reported, Emwazi came to Britain with his family from his native Kuwait as a young boy. After attending the University of Westminster to study information technology, Emwazi became politically active as part of a group of West Londoners who followed a local Islamic preacher named Hani al-Sibai. Some members of Sibai's West London group took part in jihadi training camps in the North of England and Scotland and were being monitored by MI5, Britain's domestic intelligence arm.[36]

Sibai was an open supporter of al-Qaeda who fought in Afghanistan with the so-called mujahideen in the 1980s. He was living in a 1-million-pound home in London and receiving an annual 50,000-pound disability benefit from the British government.[37]

In 2009, Muhammad Emwazi traveled to Tanzania with two friends from the group, Bilal el-Berjawi and Mohamed Sakr. Assumed to be traveling to Somalia to join al-Shabaab, an Islamist group fighting to control the country, the men were detained in Dar es Salaam by MI5. They were subjected to lengthy interrogations before being forced to return to the U.K. Both Berjawi and Sakr later succeeded in traveling to Somalia but were killed in U.S. drone strikes. Emwazi continued to be monitored by MI5 and was prevented from traveling to his native Kuwait in 2010, where he allegedly wished to marry.[38]

Emwazi claimed that he was interrogated and harassed by MI5 at the Heathrow Airport in London, and he complained of his treatment to CAGE, a Salafist advocacy group led by former Guantanamo detainee Moazzam Begg. CAGE then began an advocacy campaign on Emwazi's behalf.[39]

In August 2012, Emwazi was then somehow able to travel to Syria and join Katibat al-Muhajireen with Mazwagi. *The Daily Beast* reported that this seemed odd, given that Emwazi had been "described as a core member of an extremist network linked to the al Shabab group in Somalia during a court hearing as far back as 2010" and had been tracked by MI5 for at least five years. "His links to terror networks were well known — and yet, he was released by the authorities" to travel to Syria.[40]

Crucially, Katibat al-Muhajireen enjoyed direct support from British intelligence during the time Emwazi fought for the group. This is evidenced by the terror trial of Swedish citizen Bherlin Gildo, who also fought for Katibat al-Muhajireen during the same period as Emwazi.[41]

The Guardian reports that Gildo was detained while transiting through Heathrow Airport. He was accused by British prosecutors of attending a terrorist training camp and receiving weapons training between August 31, 2012, and March 1, 2013, as well as possessing information likely to be useful to a terrorist. However, the terror trial collapsed, in the words of *The Guardian*, "after fears of deep embarrassment" to the British security services. This was because, as Gildo's lawyer explained, "British intelligence agencies were supporting the same Syrian opposition groups as he [Gildo] was."[42] The *Daily Mail* reported that Gildo, who was "stopped at Heathrow with a guide to jihad," was allowed to walk free after the British "intelligence services 'refuse[d] to hand over evidence'" related to the case.[43]

Kidnapped by the One Who Killed Him

Muhammad Emwazi became infamous after carrying out the horrific murder of James Foley in 2014. An American freelance journalist who had reported from Iraq and Afghanistan, Foley traveled to Libya in 2011 to cover the NATO-led war on Moammar Qaddafi's government. While in Libya, a close colleague of Foley's was shot and killed by members of the Libyan security forces, who also detained and imprisoned Foley for 44 days.

After leaving Libya, Foley began making trips into Syria to report on the conflict for *GlobalPost* and AFP. In November 2012, he was returning to Turkey after a reporting trip with British journalist John Cantlie. After stopping at an Internet café in the town of Binnish, the pair's taxi began heading for the border when it was overtaken on the road and forced to stop by a van full of armed men.

Journalist James Harkin explains that according to two European hostages who had been held with Foley but later freed, the kidnapping gang that took Foley and Cantlie was led by Emwazi. "[Foley] was kidnapped by the one who killed him," one of the freed Europeans told Harkin. "I am sure of that."

Emwazi participated in Foley's abduction just two months after arriving in Syria in August 2012. According to a U.S. Department of Justice indictment, Emwazi was joined by two of his fellow Brits, Alexanda Amon Kotey and El Shafee Elsheikh, in the operation to abduct Foley.[44] Emwazi, Kotey, Elsheikh, and one other Brit, Aine Davis, were later collectively known as the "Beatles" in the Western press.

While Emwazi became infamous for allegedly murdering James Foley in 2014 as a member of ISIS, it is not well known that Emwazi also abducted Foley while a member of Katibat al-Muhajireen, and that the group was at that time receiving support from British intelligence, as shown by the periods when Bherlin Gildo attended a Katibat al-Muhajireen training camp. This means that not only ISIS but also British intelligence bears responsibility for Foley's abduction and subsequent murder.[45]

Shades of Bosnia

Emwazi and Mazwagi's cases illustrate the role played by U.K. intelligence in the pipeline that facilitated the travel of British jihadists to Syria. Journalist Nafeez Ahmed reports:

> According to former British counterterrorism intelligence officer Charles Shoebridge... [U.K.] authorities "turned a blind eye to the travelling of its own jihadists to Syria, notwithstanding ample video etc. evidence of their crimes there," because it "suited the U.S. and U.K.'s anti-Assad foreign policy."[46]

Ahmed further notes:

> This terror-funnel is what enabled people like Emwazi to travel to Syria and join up with IS [ISIS] — despite being on an MI5 terror watch-list. [Emwazi] had been blocked by the security services from traveling to Kuwait in 2010: why not Syria?

U.K. planners were once again relying on the jihadist networks they had built in London starting in the 1990s. As Raffaello Pantucci observed:

> The most striking aspect about the Syria-U.K. connection is its similarity to past events. Not only are there shades of Bosnia in the ease with which Britons can join the war in Syria, but there are also similarities in the structures that have nurtured the conflict.[47]

As discussed in Chapter 2, these structures revolved around al-Muhajiroun Movement founder and British intelligence asset Omar Bakri Muhammad, who had facilitated the flow of British jihadists to Bosnia and Kosovo in the 1990s. Bakri then left Britain for Lebanon in 2005 in the wake of the 7/7 bombings, and by 2009 was wanted by Lebanese security forces for training al-Qaeda militants. Lebanon's state-run National News Agency reported on November 12, 2010, that Bakri had been sentenced to life in prison with hard labor, but, strangely, a retrial was ordered and Bakri was released on bail.[48]

Bakri continued training jihadists and in November 2012 gave an interview to the British *Sun* newspaper describing the training camp he had established on the Lebanon-Syria border. Bakri claimed to have trained fighters from various European countries, including Britain, and that "after their training they will do their duty of jihad (holy war) in Syria and maybe Palestine."[49] Bakri's fighters were of course never sent to Palestine, as Israel was an ally, rather than a target, of British planners.

The "shades of Bosnia" included the ostensibly humanitarian "convoys of mercy" that served as a cover for the flow of fighters from Britain to Syria. Pantucci himself observed several of these convoys organized by British charities and described how by

> using a blend of videos, magazines, flyers, stalls in city centers, charity boxes inside and outside mosques, and sponsored events, these charities turn the money they raise into goods which they then drive — in convoys usually with donated ambulances — to refugee camps in Turkey.[50]

One Salafist activist traveling from Britain to Syria as part of a humanitarian convoy in mid-2012 was former Guantanamo detainee and CAGE founder Moazzam Begg. According to *Foreign Policy*, one of Begg's close CAGE colleagues acknowledged that Begg had provided physical training to foreign fighters from Katibat al-Muhajireen in Aleppo.[51]

Like Bherlin Gildo, Begg was arrested by British police in 2014 on terrorism charges for his participation in a Katibat al-Muhajireen training camp, but the case against him was also dropped after British intelligence intervened, illustrating to the prosecutors that Begg's support of jihadist fighters had been in accordance with U.K. foreign policy objectives at the time. *The Guardian* reported that Begg was freed after MI5 "belatedly gave police and prosecutors a series of documents that detailed the agency's extensive contacts with him before and after his trips to Syria," and which showed that MI5 told Begg he could continue his work for the so-called opposition in Syria "unhindered."[52]

The fact that Begg had been released from Guantanamo years before, specifically at the request of British Prime Minister Tony Blair, and had been in close contact with MI5 regarding his activities in Syria, led author Nu'man Abd al-Wahid to ask whether "British intelligence was funneling jihadis through Mr. Begg on an individual basis and/or through the aid convoy he was travelling with," and whether Muhammad Emwazi, the eventual ISIS militant responsible for some of the most shocking atrocities in the Syria conflict, was among those Katibat al-Muhajireen foreign fighters trained by Begg.[53]

Eran Benedek and Neil Simon of the Combating Terrorism Center at West Point noted how "there have been networks of British-Libyan Islamists in Manchester and Libya, some of whom had connections to global jihadi groups, over two generations."[54]

Return of the Safari Club

In July 2012, Saudi Prince Bandar bin Sultan became head of Saudi intelligence. As Bandar was already serving as head of the national security office, this doubled his responsibilities and allowed him to take an even greater role in the U.S.-backed regime change effort in Syria. CIA officials enthusiastically welcomed his assistance. The *Wall Street Journal* reported that CIA officials

> believed that Prince Bandar, a veteran of the diplomatic intrigues of Washington and the Arab world, could deliver what the CIA couldn't: planeloads of money and arms, and, as one U.S. diplomat put it, wasta, Arabic for under-the-table clout,

with one senior U.S. intelligence official calling the Saudis "indispensable partners on Syria."[55]

The *WSJ* notes further that with backing from then CIA Director David Petraeus, Bandar set to work in the summer of 2012 establishing a joint operations center in Jordan, complete with an airstrip and warehouses for arms, while sending his younger half-brother and then Deputy National Security Advisor Salman bin Sultan to direct the operation. This was part of an aggressive Saudi shift to operate largely out of Jordan instead of Turkey.

Petraeus was at the same time arguing for escalating the war by directly arming the Salafist militias of the FSA in conjunction with Bandar. The *New York Times* reported that in August 2012, Petraeus "presented a plan to begin arming and training small groups of rebel forces at secret bases in Jordan." Secretary of State Clinton backed the plan, saying that it was "time for the United States to get 'skin in the game.'" However, President Obama did not wish to take drastic action in Syria with presidential elections looming that fall, fearing that it would hurt his chances of re-election, and therefore resisted pressure from Clinton and Petraeus.[56]

Ambassador Robert Ford also played a role. According to journalist Michael Gordon of the *New York Times*, Ford traveled to Langley, Virginia, to meet with CIA Director David Petraeus in 2012 to discuss plans to provide weapons covertly to the Syrian opposition.[57]

Petraeus's plan to topple Assad during this period included a covert operation — about which we unfortunately have few details — which was apparently never carried out. In his book *Left of Boom* (2016), CIA case officer Doug Laux explains that as part of a Syria task force he had been asked to "find ways to remove President Assad from office." By September 2012, Laux had developed plans for a covert operation which had "gained traction in Washington." However, because the plan "relied heavily on political contingencies," it was not approved at that time. Laux explained that "President Obama and Secretary of State Clinton were on the defensive in the aftermath of the Benghazi disaster" in Libya.[58]

Obama and Clinton were facing criticism from Republican leaders for the events in Benghazi, where Islamist militants had attacked the U.S. consulate and nearby CIA annex on September 11, 2012. U.S. Ambassador to Libya Chris Stevens and three other U.S. officials were killed in the attack. As journalist Aaron Maté details, Ambassador Stevens had been involved in operating the CIA "rat line" to ship weapons from Libya to FSA militants in Syria.[59]

The *Wall Street Journal* noted further that while Bandar was working closely with Petraeus to escalate the war, the Saudi ambassador to the U.S., Adel al-Jubeir, began "courting members of Congress who could pressure the administration to get more involved in Syria." Jubeir and Bandar were coordinating closely with Republican Senators John McCain and Lindsey Graham. In September 2012, Prince Bandar met with McCain and Graham in Istanbul, where McCain complained to Bandar that the Salafist militias of the FSA were not getting sufficient weaponry. According to McCain, in the succeeding months he saw "a dramatic increase in Saudi involvement, hands-on, by Bandar."[60]

As discussed in Chapter 2, Bandar had been involved since 2006 in planning to topple the Syrian government using al-Qaeda-affiliated Salafist fighters, in partnership with American neoconservatives close to then Vice

President Dick Cheney — including Richard Perle, Elliott Abrams, and Michael Doran.

New York Times journalist Mark Mazetti reports that Bandar and the Saudi kingdom were

> the same partner the CIA has relied on for decades for money and discretion in far-off conflicts… The CIA and its Saudi counterpart have maintained an unusual arrangement for the rebel-training mission, which the Americans have code-named Timber Sycamore. Under the deal, current and former administration officials said, the Saudis contribute both weapons and large sums of money, and the CIA takes the lead in training the rebels on AK-47 assault rifles and tank-destroying missiles.[61]

Mazetti notes further that

> the roots of the relationship run deep. In the late 1970s, the Saudis organized what was known as the "Safari Club" — a coalition of nations including Morocco, Egypt, and France — that ran covert operations around Africa at a time when Congress had clipped the CIA's wings over years of abuses.

The U.S.-Saudi partnership continued during the 1980s, with Prince Bandar, then the Saudi ambassador to the U.S. and a close friend of the Bush family, assisting the CIA to arm and fund the so-called mujahideen fighting the Soviets in Afghanistan, as well as the Contras fighting the socialist Sandinista government in Nicaragua. *Slate* reports that Prince Bandar also held accounts at Riggs Bank, long known to have ties to the CIA.[62]

Bandar's close cooperation with the CIA leadership continued in the months leading up to the attacks on the World Trade Center and Pentagon on September 11, 2001. As Aaron Good, Ben Howard, and Peter Dale Scott detail, Bandar provided funds (via his wife) to two presumed Saudi intelligence officers, Omar al-Bayoumi and Osama Basnan, who in turn arranged housing and flight lessons for two of the 9/11 hijackers, Khalid al-Mihdhar and Nawaf al-Hazmi. Before the attack, the two hijackers in turn enjoyed protection from top CIA officials, Richard Blee and Tom Wilshire, who intervened with the FBI to prevent their surveillance and possible detention. Blee and Wilshire were protégés of then CIA Director George Tenet, who met regularly with Bandar during this period. Tenet visited Bandar's Virginia home monthly, and the two would frequently exchange information, the details of which Tenet would not reveal even to other officials at the CIA.[63]

11. 'Democracy' Comes to Damascus and Aleppo

Operation Volcano in Damascus

Bandar's accession to the role of Saudi intelligence chief in July 2012 coincided with two major FSA offensives, in Damascus and Aleppo. On July 14, the FSA launched a large offensive to take Damascus, dubbed "Operation Damascus Volcano and Syrian Earthquake," which was made possible by weapons shipments organized by U.S. and Saudi planners two months before.

In May 2012, the *Washington Post* reported:

> Syrian rebels battling the regime of President Bashar al-Assad have begun receiving significantly more and better weapons in recent weeks, an effort paid for by Persian Gulf nations and coordinated in part by the United States, according to opposition activists and U.S. and foreign officials… [Materiel] is being stockpiled in Damascus.[1]

The *Post* quotes an opposition figure: "Large shipments have got through… Some areas are loaded with weapons."

Reuters notes that the July 14 offensive began when so-called rebels attacked Syrian security forces in al-Hajar al-Aswad, a district of southern Damascus adjacent to and south of Yarmouk. The operation involved 2,500 militants, many of whom had been redeployed from other parts of the country. The fighting spread to three other districts the next day, including Midan in the heart of Damascus, with battles flaring within sight of Assad's presidential palace. Militants hid in narrow alleyways and battled government tanks using rocket-propelled grenades and roadside bombs.[2] The offensive was highlighted by the bombing of the National Security Building in Damascus on July 18, which killed four top Syrian security officials, including Defense Minister Dawoud Rajha, National Security chief Hisham Ikhtiyar, and Assad's brother-in-law, Deputy Defense Minister Assef Shawkat.[3] Recall, from Chapter 5, that Hisham Ikhtiyar had led the government's negotiations with Sheikh Ahmed Siyasna in Daraa after the first protest there in March 2011.

The *New York Times* noted that

> the attack on the leadership's inner sanctum as fighting raged in sections of the city for the fourth day suggested that the uprising had

reached a decisive moment in the overall struggle for Syria. The battle for the capital, the center of Assad family power, appears to have begun.[4]

FSA leaders claimed the bombing was "a turning point in Syria's history" and the "beginning of the end" for the government.[5] One FSA commander was more cautious, however, suggesting that "it is more ebb and flow; these skirmishes are just a test as our fighters infiltrate then withdraw... The Free Syrian Army has a hit-and-run strategy. This is urban warfare. It favors the rebel forces and not the conventional forces."[6]

The Syrian army was able to repel the offensive, however, retaking control of the Midan district on July 20, 2012.[7] But the FSA retreat from the heart of Damascus was merely tactical, and opposition militants would try to take the capital again in the coming months. *Al-Monitor* reported that "the regime appears to have won round 1 in the fight for Damascus, but the war is far from over."[8]

The Islam Brigade

The FSA group that took credit for the bombing of the National Security Building was Liwa al-Islam, or "the Islam Brigade." Liwa al-Islam was founded by Zahran Alloush, a Salafist activist from the town of Douma in the eastern Ghouta region, in the Damascus suburbs. Alloush's father Abdullah was a prominent Salafist preacher and the imam of Douma's Tawhid Mosque before he emigrated to Saudi Arabia in the mid-1990s.

As Syria expert Aron Lund details, after beginning his studies in Saudi Arabia under prominent Salafi scholars, including Ibn Baz, the Saudi Grand Mufti, Alloush returned to Syria and completed a degree in Sharia at Damascus University. Alloush also engaged in underground Salafi missionary activity and in 2009 was detained at Sednaya Prison by Syrian authorities as a result. When anti-government protests began in March 2011, Alloush was still in prison, but was released as part of a presidential amnesty in June 2011. Alloush immediately joined the nascent anti-government armed insurgency, and by September 2011 had organized his own armed group, Saraya al-Islam, or "the Islam Company," which began with a core group of 14 religious students and received support from local Salafist preacher Sa'id Delwan.

By early 2012, Alloush's group, now known as Liwa al-Islam, had become the most powerful armed group in eastern Ghouta. As an FSA faction, Liwa al-Islam was able to procure weapons that had been collected in Libya by the

Muslim Brotherhood and smuggled to Syria with the help of Qatari and Turkish intelligence. Alloush's control over the distribution of these weapons helped Liwa al-Islam to become the most powerful armed group in the Damascus suburbs, at the expense of the rival Douma Martyrs Brigade.[9]

Zahran Alloush soon became notorious for his sectarianism. In 2013, he called for "cleansing Damascus" of all Alawites, while calling Shiite Muslims, of which Alawites are considered an offshoot, "unclean." Speaking to Alawites, he threatened to "destroy your skulls" and "make you taste the worst torture in life before Allah makes you taste the worst torture on Judgment Day."[10]

Why Was Alloush Released?

Much has been made of Alloush's release from Sednaya Prison in June 2011. Syrian opposition members have attempted to cite this as proof that Assad released various Islamist prisoners early in the conflict to "Islamize" and militarize an otherwise secular and peaceful uprising. Presumably, this was a way for Assad to discredit the protestors as terrorists, and to shift the conflict to a military arena, where the Syrian government would more easily prevail.[11]

This explanation makes little sense, however. There was no way for the Syrian government to know in advance that Alloush would become a prominent guerrilla commander upon his release, as Alloush did not have an obviously violent past. Aron Lund explains that "Alloush was arrested in 2009 and charged with gun possession, though the main reason for his arrest seems to have been his Salafi activism."[12]

As mentioned in Chapter 2, the Syrian government had imprisoned many Salafist activists for peaceful activities in the years leading up to the 2011 conflict. According to Human Rights Watch, most Syrian political prisoners were Salafists as of 2009.[13] This is confirmed by the fact that most clients of Razan Zaitouneh were Salafists imprisoned by the Syrian government.[14]

The Syrian opposition was calling for the release of all political prisoners throughout the early months of the protests.[15] Because most political prisoners were Salafists, this meant that the opposition was calling for the release of Salafist political prisoners and not just secular human rights activists, as was commonly assumed. The government was therefore incentivized to release Salafist political prisoners such as Alloush to diffuse pressure from the protest movement, which included the Salafi community.

Khaleej Online reports, for example, that Alloush was released due to popular pressure, as his father was a well-known Salafist preacher based in Saudi Arabia.[16] The prominence of the Alloush family in Douma, a town considered a Salafist hotbed in Syria, explains why local activists and protestors would demand his release.

Saqour al-Sham founder Ahmed Abu Issa al-Sheikh himself rejected rumors that he and Alloush had been imprisoned together in Sednaya, which formed part of the conspiracy theory claiming that Assad had deliberately released both men together to militarize and Islamize the insurgency. Ahmed Abu Issa himself denied that he had met Alloush while in prison, as Ahmed Abu Issa had been imprisoned at the Palestine Branch in 2004, while Alloush was imprisoned in Sednaya from 2009 to 2011.[17]

Some jihadists were released from Sednaya as part of presidential amnesties in 2011, but this does not mean that these men were released deliberately in order to strengthen the nascent al-Qaeda-led insurgency, which had already been created by the U.S. and its regional allies. Possible reasons for the release of such men by the Syrian government include incompetence, corruption, or efforts to infiltrate the Salafist insurgency that was carrying out attacks against Syrian security forces in the first months of the protests. For example, according to Saudi-owned *al-Hayat*, ISIS leader Abu Bakr al-Baghdadi initially advised his deputy and Nusra leader Abu Mohammad al-Jolani not to accept former prisoners from Sednaya as members of Nusra "for fear of penetration (by the regime forces)."[18]

Furthermore, opposition circles never sought to exclude Alloush or Liwa al-Islam from the broader political opposition, including after Liwa Islam dropped the FSA moniker. Instead, Alloush and Liwa al-Islam were considered key players in the Western- and Gulf-backed insurgency, enjoying particularly strong support from Saudi Arabia. This indicates that the opposition accusations — that the Syrian government sought to Islamize an otherwise secular insurgency — were not sincere. Alloush remained a key player in the mainstream Syrian opposition until his assassination by a Russian airstrike in December 2015. The *New York Times* viewed Alloush's death at the time as "a significant blow to the armed opposition."[19]

Additionally, as we shall see in Chapter 12, opposition political leaders also openly embraced al-Qaeda's Syria franchise, the Nusra Front, as part of the "revolution," demonstrating that they had no reservations about the Salafist nature of the armed groups that they were supporting. Without the

Salafist militias comprising the FSA and Nusra, there would have been no "revolution" to speak of at all.

More Fog than Light

Salafists like Alloush were deeply embedded not only in the armed insurgency, but in opposition political and media groups as well, which also made opposition claims that Assad was responsible for the "Islamization" of the insurgency illogical. For example, the Local Coordination Committees (LCC) Facebook pages regularly posted content in support of the Salafist armed groups once the violent aspects of the so-called revolution began to be publicized. For example, in October 2012, the International Crisis Group wrote:

> The leading activist Facebook page dedicated to the Damascus suburb of Douma, a key opposition stronghold, regularly posts material released by Liwa al-Islam and actively encourages users to follow the group's online material... Similarly, material released by Kata'ib Ahrar al-Sham regularly is posted by Idlib and Tartous-based activist groups; Liwa Saqour as-Sham's propaganda appears on the pages of Idlib- and Aleppo-based groups; and Katibat al-Ansar's material is posted on a range of Homs activist pages.[20]

As noted in Chapter 4, the Syria Revolution 2011 Facebook page was managed by Muslim Brotherhood activists, making its support for the Salafist armed groups expected. However, it may seem surprising that the LCC, founded by U.S.-funded secular activist Razan Zaitouneh, would also promote these same Salafist armed groups.

The LCC consisted of a mixture of Islamist and secular activists. The LCC was run by anonymous activists in various parts of the country, each having their own page dedicated to a specific city or region. LCC activist Zeina Erhaim notes that these ideological differences eventually emerged into the open. She notes that the representative of the LCC in the Aleppo suburb of Bza'a later joined ISIS, while another LCC representative "joined the FSA in a Damascus suburb and ended up carrying out a suicide attack on a regime barricade near his hometown of Domair."[21]

When Lebanese journalist Ghadi Francis interviewed members of the LCC in Hama, she asked about the role of Salafist preacher Adnan Arour. They explained that they considered Arour important, calling him the "trumpet of the revolution," even though when they saw Arour's picture being held up by a protestor in a demonstration, they quickly forbade it. "We said to him 'get rid of the picture, go hang a picture [at home].'"[22]

It is unsurprising that Razan Zaitouneh was working so closely with Islamist members of the LCC, given that Zaitouneh, as discussed in Chapter 2, had spent much of her career as a lawyer advocating the release of Salafist political prisoners.[23] For this reason it is also unsurprising that when Zaitouneh sought to avoid detention by Syrian authorities in 2013, she took refuge in Douma, then under the control of Zahran Alloush's Liwa al-Islam. In a tragic but also ironic twist, Liwa al-Islam is widely viewed as responsible for her later disappearance and killing.[24]

Both the secular opposition and Western journalists were aware of the Salafist orientation of many of the early opposition activists, but they sought to obscure it and portray them as pro-democracy activists for public relations reasons instead. Even the International Crisis Group, itself pro-opposition and U.S.-funded, acknowledged:

> From day one, the question of Salafism within opposition ranks has been more of a political football than a subject of serious conversation. Assad backers played it up... [but r]egime detractors played it down, intent on preserving the image of a pristine uprising; people sympathetic to their cause, whether in the media or elsewhere, likewise were reluctant to delve too deeply into the issue, anxious about playing into regime hands. The net result has been more fog than light.[25]

'Aleppo, Where Are You?'

Shortly after the July 2012 FSA assault on Damascus, attention turned to Aleppo, Syria's second-largest city, which had until then largely avoided the violence seen elsewhere in the country.

In the early days of the Syrian conflict, Aleppo was considered a "regime stronghold," indicating loyalty among its residents to the Syrian government and to President Assad. At the start of the anti-government protests in March 2011, lack of support from the residents of Aleppo was a source of frustration for those demonstrating in other parts of the country. A common refrain among protestors at that time was "Aleppo, where are you?"[26]

This was particularly frustrating, given that Aleppo is a majority Sunni city, and it was primarily Sunnis whom opposition activists and U.S. planners sought to mobilize for demonstrations.

When protests finally appeared in Aleppo in August 2011, this was almost six months after the beginning of protests in other Syrian cities. *The Guardian* reported that the biggest protest that day, in the Sakhour neighborhood, consisted of just 1,000 people (in a city of 2 to 3 million), and described Aleppo as "more invested" in the Syrian government than other cities.[27]

An important event in the early period of the conflict in Aleppo was the double car bombing of the Military Security Headquarters in February 2012. The *New York Times* reported on the bombings:

> In Aleppo, a bastion of government support, the dual explosions wounded about 235 people... 14 of them critically. State television repeatedly broadcast images of disemboweled victims lying amid jumbled concrete wreckage. One of the buildings appeared flattened, and the other was a rose-colored, five-story expanse of shattered windows and cracked masonry.[28]

AFP reports that the bombing was later claimed by the Nusra Front.[29] It was unlikely that this type of horrific violence further increased support in Aleppo for an already unpopular protest movement and Salafist insurgency.

In the wake of the February 2012 Military Security Headquarters bombing, an armed opposition group known as Liwa al-Tawhid, or "the Monotheism Brigade," began capturing towns and villages in the northern Aleppo countryside.

Liwa al-Tawhid quickly became one of the most important FSA brigades. Al Jazeera notes that, while fighting under the FSA banner, the group's leaders, Abd al-Qader al-Saleh and Abd al-Aziz Salama, were inclined towards the Salafi ideology.[30]

After visiting Syria in August 2012, opposition activist Ammar Abdulhamid pointed to the Salafi orientation of the group as well, writing that, "as for Al-Tawhid Brigades, their Salafi orientation is known to all, but their funding comes from both the MB [Muslim Brotherhood] as well as Salafi sympathizers in the Gulf."[31]

The AP similarly noted that Tawhid was "strongly backed by the Muslim Brotherhood, the fundamentalist political organization that is closely allied to Qatar."[32] Reflecting language consistent with Muslim Brotherhood ideology, Tawhid proclaimed its mission was to establish a "civil state in Syria with Islam being the main source of legislation."[33]

Pro-opposition *al-Dorar al-Shamiyya* noted that before the war, Tawhid leader Abd al-Qader al-Saleh had been a grain merchant from the town of Marea in the Aleppo countryside and had previously done missionary work in Jordan, Syria, Turkey, and Bangladesh after completing his military service in a chemical weapons unit in the Syrian army. Saleh was one of the first organizers of anti-government demonstrations in Marea. He transitioned to armed action a few months later and was chosen as commander of a local brigade in Marea, before being chosen to lead Liwa al-Tawhid.[34] Saleh then became a member of the Staff of the FSA as a representative of the Northern Front.[35]

Just as the role of Salafists in the earliest FSA brigades was often overlooked, so was their role in the early anti-government demonstrations. Acknowledging this, Saleh told the *New York Times*: "We were secretive… The public knew there was someone named Hajji Marea who led the demonstrations. But nobody knew who he was," referring to himself.[36]

'Aleppo Is with the Regime'

On July 19, 2012, shortly after the FSA assault on Damascus and bombing of the National Security Building there, Liwa al-Tawhid partnered with the Nusra Front to launch an invasion of Aleppo. Tawhid leader Abd al-Qader al-Saleh appeared in a video with a Nusra commander to announce the operation, which they named "Aleppo Volcano."[37]

The FSA and Nusra militants attempting to take control of Aleppo were not from the city itself, but rather from the surrounding rural areas. *The Guardian* reported that in July 2012, "opposition sources said fighters from rural areas around Aleppo had been converging on the city of 3 million people," and that "dozens of FSA rebels had penetrated deep inside the city."[38]

The entry of the militants was allegedly facilitated by the betrayal of Aleppo's Military Security division chief, Major General Muhammad Mufleh, mentioned in Chapter 8 in connection with the bloody events in Hama of June 3, 2011.

According to Lebanese newspaper *Ad-Diyar*, the situation in the Aleppo countryside had been boiling, and Major General Mufleh began sending warnings to Damascus about the emergence of both peaceful and armed demonstrations in Aleppo city, as well as the growing presence of jihadist cells in the Aleppo countryside and the town of Azaz on the nearby Turkish border. Fearing that Aleppo would fall in a repeat of events in Hama, Mufleh sought to launch a military operation in the Aleppo countryside and again asked for direction from his superiors in Damascus. Mufleh received conflicting answers, however, with some directing him to use weapons but in a measured way, while others directed him to solve the problems in Aleppo using only dialogue.

Mufleh sent one final cable warning that the situation in Aleppo was dangerous, and he urgently requested authorization to carry out a military operation. As Mufleh awaited a response, the security situation in Aleppo deteriorated further, with car bombs and other attacks targeting the city. The orders apparently never came, and Mufleh then passed authority to his subordinate and fled the city for Turkey. Officers in the Syrian army later alleged that Mufleh had received $5 million in bribes from the opposition to allow Liwa al-Tawhid and Nusra militants to enter the city.[39]

Al-Haqiqa newspaper provides a somewhat different account, reporting that according to Turkish sources, Mufleh had met with Turkish Consul Adnan Kajiji and a Turkish intelligence officer on July 16, 2012, to arrange his defection. In exchange for a security guarantee that he would not be killed by the opposition for his role in the events in Hama the year before, the intelligence officer demanded that Mufleh hand over the "security keys" to Aleppo and allow 7,000 opposition militants to enter the city through the specific access road under Mufleh's control. Turkish intelligence then arranged with Muslim Brotherhood leader Muhammad Farouq Tayfour to gather the necessary fighters to invade the city days later. These included not only Liwa al-Tawhid fighters under Brotherhood control, but also fighters from the Nusra Front and Ahrar al-Sham. Turkish intelligence then handed over control of the Bab al-Hawa border crossing to these al-Qaeda groups to allow additional militants in Turkey to join the looming assault. Mufleh then allowed thousands of opposition fighters to enter the Salaheddine neighborhood of Aleppo, under the pretext that they were displaced persons from other parts of Syria, before himself fleeing by car to Turkey via Azaz.[40]

Rumors swirled surrounding Mufleh's fate, variously suggesting that he had resettled in Canada, that he had been betrayed by the Turkish consul and killed by Muslim Brotherhood militants as he approached the Turkish border by car, and even that he had long been coordinating with Liwa al-Tawhid and that his death had been faked to facilitate his defection.[41]

Over the course of the next few months, Liwa al-Tawhid and Nusra managed to capture large portions of eastern Aleppo, while the Syrian army successfully defended Aleppo's western districts, keeping most of the city under government control. This created a bloody stalemate that would last for years.

Most residents were opposed to the Tawhid and Nusra occupation of large areas of Aleppo, however. An FSA commander acknowledged this, telling *The Guardian*: "Yes, it's true... Around 70% of Aleppo city is with the regime. It has always been that way. The countryside is with us, and the city is with them."[42]

James Foley reported that a junior FSA commander had joked to him shortly before the invasion that "while the war raged all around it, the people of Aleppo were only concerned about their barbecues," and that the commander "promised Aleppo would burn." Foley noted that "three months later, Aleppo is on fire. The 1,000-year-old market has been gutted."[43]

Robert Worth of the *New York Times* also reported that the so-called rebels had little popular support. Worth reported that according to Adnan Hadad, a member of Aleppo's Revolutionary Military Council, in the spring of 2012,

> weaponry was flowing in from across the Turkish border and battalions were being formed... Tawheed's members began pushing for a military takeover of Aleppo, accusing the council of excessive caution and even secret deals with the regime. The council resisted, saying they should move only when it was clear that the city's people wanted them to. In July [2012], Tawheed took matters into its own hands. Armed insurgents flooded eastern and southwestern parts of the city, taking over civilian houses as well as police stations in the name of the revolution. Hadad considered the move a "fatal mistake."[44]

Rania Abouzeid, who reported from on the ground in Syria for years, also noted how unpopular the FSA and Nusra were in Aleppo. She wrote that what she called the revolution "had devolved into anarchy," and that "perhaps nowhere was the chaos more evident than in the great northern metropolis of Aleppo," which was "dragged into the uprising in July 2012 like a hostage" by men who "weren't welcomed by locals — men with little camaraderie, undisciplined groups, some of which looted the homes of civilians they claimed to be protecting."[45]

Even those Syrians supportive of the so-called revolution often did not welcome the FSA and Nusra presence in Aleppo, because they knew that the fighting with the Syrian army would come to them. For example, pro-opposition *Al-Dorar al-Shamiyya* acknowledged that "at the beginning of the revolution, there were some reservations from the people of Aleppo about the entry of Liwa al-Tawhid into the city, fearing the response of the strong Syrian regime and its impact on it."[46]

Tawhid leader Saleh dismissed these fears and justified the civilian suffering and destruction that resulted from the FSA presence in Aleppo. Saleh explained that this was the "price of freedom" required to "liberate" the people "from the regime of Bashar al-Assad," without stopping to wonder whether the people of Aleppo wanted to be liberated, and if so, by him and his Muslim Brotherhood-sponsored Salafist fighters.[47]

'We Are Together'

The close integration of Liwa al-Tawhid (fighting under the FSA banner) and the Nusra Front (fighting under the al-Qaeda banner) was illustrated by comments from a Nusra commander in Aleppo in August 2012. The Nusra commander suggested that he and his militants were fighting in the ranks of Liwa al-Tawhid itself. According to the *Washington Post*, which surprisingly had journalists embedded with Nusra:

> Abu Ibrahim said his contingent included men from Morocco, Libya, Tunisia, and Lebanon, as well as one Syrian who had fought in Iraq against the Americans… Abu Ibrahim said his fighters are part of Liwa al-Tawhid, or "the Unity Brigade," a newly formed battalion of rebel groups fighting in and around Aleppo. "We are together," he said. "There is good coordination."[48]

The *Post* also quoted Abu Feras, a spokesman for the Aleppo Revolutionary Council, who claimed that Nusra fighters were regarded "as heroes" in Aleppo, and that "they fight without fear or hesitation."

FSA commander Abd al-Jabbar al-Okaidi, leader of the Revolutionary Military Council in Aleppo, also confirmed that Nusra fighters were essentially part of the FSA itself. Okaidi spoke positively of Nusra and stated in an interview with pro-opposition Orient TV that Nusra fighters "constitute perhaps 10% of the FSA in the city of Aleppo and in Syria."[49]

Okaidi became an intermediary between the Salafist fighters on the ground in Aleppo and U.S. and other foreign intelligence agencies using them as proxies to topple the Syrian government. Okaidi enjoyed close relations with former U.S. Ambassador to Syria Robert Ford, and in this way was able to provide a secular façade for the FSA-branded but Salafist Liwa al-Tawhid. This then allowed the Western powers to channel aid to armed groups that would under other circumstances be viewed as terrorists and extremists.[50]

In August 2012, correspondents from *The Guardian* observed fighters from other parts of the Islamic world, including Saudi Arabia, Pakistan, Algeria, and Senegal, further suggesting that the FSA and Nusra operation to take Aleppo was an invasion by outsiders and foreigners who were not welcomed by the city's residents.[51]

The importance of foreign jihadis in the battle for Aleppo was underscored in September 2012, when French doctor Jacques Bérès spoke with France 24 after returning from his third trip to Syria to help treat wounded opposition fighters. Bérès, who worked at one of the two main hospitals in Aleppo for the French NGO Doctors Without Borders, explained:

> More than fifty percent of the warriors I had to take care of were jihadists, not just foreigners, but with the look of jihadists, with the beard and Koranic verses on the forehead. Their fellow soldiers, when they came to visit them at the hospital, said quite frankly, "We are Jihadists."[52]

Two French jihadists with whom Bérès spoke said that they were trying to follow the example of Mohamed Merah, a 23-year-old jihadist shot dead by French police after he murdered seven people, including Jewish schoolchildren, in a terrorist attack in Toulouse in March 2012.

The Christians Are Protesting

The invasion of Aleppo by Nusra and FSA fighters, who shared the extremist and sectarian religious views of Adnan Arour and Muhammad Sarour, was particularly devastating for Aleppo's large Christian population. Persecution of Christians throughout Syria had been widespread since the start of the crisis in the spring of 2011.

While reporting from Syria in August 2012, journalist Robert Fisk quoted a Syrian friend who noted:

> The Christians are protesting... The Greek Catholic Archbishop of Aleppo has just made an appeal to the Western powers not to send weapons to the fundamentalists. The Syrian Catholic church in Aleppo has now been bombed.[53]

FSA and Nusra control of Aleppo city and its surrounding countryside quickly resulted in a wave of kidnappings of Christians. In April 2013, two Orthodox Christian bishops, Gregorius Yohanna Ibrahim of the Syriac Orthodox Church and Boulos Yazigi of the Greek Orthodox Church, were themselves kidnapped while traveling from Aleppo to the Turkish border to help negotiate the release of two priests, Michael Kayyal and Maher Mahfouz, who had previously been abducted.[54]

Before the conflict, Aleppo's Christians numbered some 250,000, whereas by November 2014, some two years after the jihadist capture of the eastern section of the city, the number had dwindled to roughly just 100,000, predominantly in the government-held west.[55]

Aleppo's Sunni Muslims, the majority of the city's population, did not appear to welcome the takeover of their city by religious extremists either. Several Western journalists provided early descriptions about so-called rebel-controlled areas of Aleppo, including Martin Chulov (August 2012),[56] James Foley (October 2012),[57] and Steven Sotloff (February 2013).[58] All described disillusionment among civilians with life there under jihadi rule.

Nor was kidnapping limited to the Christians, as the phenomenon soon became a defining feature of life in Aleppo under FSA and Nusra rule. Peter Bouckaert of Human Rights Watch discussed the rise of kidnapping for ransom in Syria, tracing the rise of the phenomenon to the period when Nusra and the FSA invaded Aleppo. He explained in June 2013:

> The kidnappings have been going on for about a year, it's really intensified. It started mostly when fighting broke out in Aleppo… In cities like Aleppo, the kidnappings for ransom that are taking place have very significantly undermined support for the opposition. Because in general, civilians are very fearful of these kinds of kidnappings, especially people with wealth. Assad's regime was known for brutality, but this kind of insecurity didn't exist for wealthy business people. They knew if they stayed out of politics, they could live secure lives.[59]

Destroy the Country to Change the Regime

Furthermore, the presence of the Salafist militants led to the widespread destruction and depopulation of many areas under their control, due to government efforts to root them out, causing terrible suffering and displacement. *Independent* journalist Kim Sengupta described how by August 2012, the Salaheddine district of Aleppo was largely empty, as FSA factions fought Syrian government forces there:

> There are very few civilians to be seen in Salaheddine, whose deserted streets are filled with fallen masonry, shattered glass, and twisted metal. The dead are much more in evidence, bodies lying in the open, the rising stench from the ones buried in debris.[60]

According to one FSA militant with whom Sengupta was embedded, Syrian forces in Salaheddine "have been firing from the tanks, but all they are hitting are empty buildings." Sengupta writes as well that "the only human voices, however, were hurried conversations in doorways between fighters; the people who lived here have gone." Sengupta notes that the Bustan al-Qasr neighborhood in Aleppo had a population of 300,000 before the FSA and Nusra took control of the area, but that it had fallen to "around 40,000 as the exodus rises," while quoting a resident who said that "the MiGs and helicopters [of the Syrian government] are the reason we're leaving."

Veteran Middle East correspondent Patrick Cockburn, who spent a significant amount of time reporting from Syria, described the result of the FSA takeover of any given Syrian city this way:

> The military tactics of both sides ignore the well-being of civilians in the cities. Armed rebel units move into the suburbs, whether they are welcome or not. In some places, like the large township of Douma on the outskirts of Damascus, the Muslim Brotherhood has always been strong and the FSA is popular. In others, particularly in Aleppo, the arrival of the FSA is regarded with dread. Local people know what will happen next. Government artillery opens fire, and bombs are dropped from the air. The population flees and the contested district becomes a ghost town. The rebels loot government offices, schools, factories, and shops.[61]

The so-called rebels were themselves responsible for significant destruction as the battle for control of Aleppo continued. James Foley quoted one Aleppo resident who explained: "We don't like Bashar. We don't like the regime. We want them to go out. But there is an easier way. Kill everybody? Destroy the country just to change the regime? It's too much." As an example of this, Foley pointed to a series of four "massive suicide car bombings, which leveled blocks of the government center [and] left craters some 10 feet deep" in October 2012.[62]

The AP reported that the car bombings had targeted Saadallah al-Jabri Square, home to a famous hotel and a coffee shop, as well as an entrance to Aleppo's historic old city, with its famous markets, killing 40 and wounding 90, including both civilians and members of the security forces.[63]

Foley noted that the government often showed similar disregard for civilian life because they assumed that any civilians left in the conflict zone were supporters or family members of the so-called rebels. According to Foley, after the suicide bombings in Saadallah al-Jabri Square, the "Syrian army retaliated by launching an air assault on a school housing refugees. Witnesses called it a massacre, 10 civilians killed and about 60 wounded."[64]

Steven Sotloff quoted an Aleppo resident who initially welcomed the FSA and Nusra into the city, but who was soon not happy about their presence: "We organized food deliveries for them at the front. We were so happy to finally be doing something for the revolution. But after a few months, we saw who these people really were." Sotloff also noted the shortages of bread, gas, and cooking oil that characterized life after the so-called rebels' arrival. Many residents reported waiting in line for four hours or more to buy bread. When Sotloff asked a local grocer, Anwar Khuli, about his thoughts on allegations that the FSA had recruited children as fighters, the grocer responded, "These guys will do anything to win, even if it means destroying our youth... They have already destroyed our country."[65]

Another account from inside Aleppo comes from Syrian journalist Edward Dark (a pseudonym), who was active in the early months of the protest movement, but quickly became disillusioned by the so-called rebels. In May 2013, he described how

> Aleppo was raided by the rebels [who] would systematically loot the neighborhoods they entered... They would strip factories and industrial zones bare, even down to the electrical wiring, hauling their loot of expensive industrial machinery and infrastructure off across the border to Turkey to be sold at a fraction of its price. Shopping malls were emptied, warehouses, too. They stole the grain in storage silos, creating a crisis and a sharp rise in staple food costs.[66]

Dark also described how the destruction in Aleppo was not limited to government airstrikes. Dark notes that the so-called rebels

> would incessantly shell residential civilian neighborhoods under regime control with mortars, rocket fire, and car bombs, causing death and injury to countless innocent people, their snipers routinely killing in cold blood unsuspecting passersby. As a consequence, tens of thousands became destitute and homeless in this once bustling, thriving, and rich commercial metropolis.

Dark summarized his feelings, concluding that the coming of the FSA and Nusra "was a shock, especially to those of us who had supported and believed in the uprising all along. It was the ultimate betrayal."

A Liberal, Tolerant System of Government

In March 2013, Liz Sly of the *Washington Post* reported that Liwa al-Tawhid had joined with Nusra to create the *Hayaa al-Sharia*, a civil authority in Aleppo based on fundamentalist interpretations of Islamic Law. Sly wrote:

> Based out of the city's former Eye Hospital, which was damaged during the fighting and then occupied by Jabhat al-Nusra as its headquarters, the Hayaa is also backed by other rebel units, including the Tawhid Brigade, the city's biggest fighting force.[67]

The Aleppo Eye Hospital included a basement prison for the *Hayaa*, where American journalists Theo Padnos and Matt Schrier, as well as Syrian prisoners, were being held and regularly tortured at the time of Sly's visit.[68] James Foley and British journalist John Cantlie were also later imprisoned at the hospital, in July 2013.[69]

The type of governance imposed by the *Hayaa* in Aleppo was illustrated by several men who were regular visitors to Padnos's cell. Padnos notes that these men later videotaped themselves publicly executing a woman after accusing her of prostitution. They shot her in the back of the head in the middle of the street and allowed her blood to leak across the pavement.[70]

Perhaps most shockingly, in July 2013, Salafist militants in the poor Shaar district of Aleppo publicly shot and killed a 14-year-old boy, Mohammad Qataa, three times in the face for making what they considered to be an insulting comment about the Prophet Muhammad. The boy had been selling coffee in the street and was asked by someone for a free cup. The boy responded that no one gets a free cup, not even the Prophet. This was enough for three militants standing nearby to accuse the boy of blasphemy, drag him away, and execute him publicly just a half-hour later in the street. The video of his face, with a hole where his nose and mouth should have been, went viral on Facebook and Twitter.[71]

Although Aleppo quickly descended into a chaotic, jihadist dystopia, author Nu'man Abd al-Wahid observes that Western-based opposition activists nevertheless bizarrely sought to romanticize the 2012 FSA and Nusra invasion and looting of Aleppo, describing it as a socialist revolution led by freedom fighters struggling on behalf of Syria's working class. For example, Robin Yassin-Kassab bizarrely suggested that

> On the night of 19 July 2012, as a battle erupted in the Salahudeen neighbourhood, thousands of fighters poured into the city from the northern and eastern countryside. Videos of the convoy filled distant

revolutionaries with enthusiasm to echo that of the men on the backs of trucks… brandishing Kalashnikovs and freedom flags.[72]

12. The Mask of the 'Free Army' Falls Off

Perfected in Iraq

While militants from the FSA's Liwa al-Tawhid were working with Nusra to invade Aleppo in July 2012, FSA groups in the eastern province of Deir al-Zour were capturing territory with the help of Nusra as well. As noted in Chapter 10, Deir al-Zour was the "cradle of the war," and al-Qaeda in Iraq had infiltrated fighters into the province in late 2010, before the outbreak of anti-government protests the following spring. These al-Qaeda militants further had instructions to help the FSA groups emerging in the wake of the protests by supplying them with suicide bombers and bomb-making expertise.

The *New York Times* reported on July 24, 2012, that

> while leaders of the Syrian political and military opposition continue to deny any role for the extremists, Al Qaeda has helped to change the nature of the conflict, injecting the weapon it perfected in Iraq — suicide bombings — into the battle against President Bashar al-Assad with growing frequency.[1]

The *NYT* noted that rumors of the presence of al-Qaeda fighters in Deir al-Zour had been circulating for months, "after a massive truck bomb exploded near a military base — which the resistance attributed to the Assad regime, claiming it had bombed itself." The *NYT* also quoted an FSA commander in Deir al-Zour who hardly bothered to dispel the rumors: "'If Al Qaeda comes to get rid of him,' Sayid said, referring to Mr. Assad, 'why not? But I personally have seen none of them.'"

An FSA brigade known as the Alwiya Ahfad al-Rasoul, or "the Ahfad al-Rasoul Brigades," was particularly strong in Deir al-Zour Province, home to the country's largest oilfields. *Al-Quds Al-Arabi* described Ahfad al-Rasoul as a group "with an Islamic orientation but linked to the Free Syrian Army, which forms an umbrella for most of the opposition fighters and is linked to the National Coalition of Revolution and Opposition Forces."[2] The AP described the group as among the brigades with a "conservative religious ideology" that enjoyed strong backing from Qatar.[3] Middle East analyst Nicholas Heras noted that in Idlib and Raqqa, Ahfad was working with the Nusra Front to "institute 'Salafist' civil administration" and "is frequently referred to as part of the Salafist current in the ideological development of Syria's armed opposition groups."[4]

Ahfad al-Rasoul units originating in Deir al-Zour included the al-Qaqaa' Brigade, led by Ali al-Matar from the town of al-Qawriah, and the Allahu Akbar Brigade, led by Saddam al-Jamal from al-Bukamal, a smuggling town on the Iraqi border. The al-Qaqaa and Allahu Akbar Brigades were joined by smaller FSA brigades from the town of Muhassan to fight under the Ahfad al-Rasoul umbrella.[5]

On November 17, 2012, fighters from the Allahu Akbar Brigade captured the Hamdan airport, allowing them to take control of the town of al-Bukamal. The offensive was led by Saddam al-Jamal, a local smuggler turned FSA commander.[6] Jamal gave a celebratory speech atop a captured tank in which he dedicated the victory to the "heroic mujahideen."[7]

Jamal claimed that he organized an armed group in the early months of the conflict in response to the killing of six protestors by Syrian military intelligence. He noted that because al-Bukamal is a border town, many residents like himself had long been involved in smuggling and were therefore already well armed.[8]

Ziad Haj Obaid emerged as the leader of Ahfad al-Rasoul, and both Obaid and Jamal enjoyed prominence in the FSA. Obaid was appointed to the Arms Committee for the U.S.-backed Supreme Military Council (SMC), while Jamal became the top FSA commander for the whole of Syria's eastern region.[9]

Jamal infamously defected to ISIS with his fighters and military equipment in late 2013[10] and became notorious for some of ISIS's most notorious atrocities, including burning alive the Jordanian fighter pilot Moaz al-Kasasbeh and massacring 700 members of the Shaitat tribe in Deir al-Zour.[11]

Another FSA group, Liwa Janud al-Haqq, or "the Soldiers of Truth Brigade," helped Jamal's Allahu Akbar Brigade capture al-Bukamal and the nearby Hamdan airport. Janud al-Haqq was led by Firas al-Salman, who had joined al-Qaeda to fight against U.S. occupation forces in Iraq in 2003, and who had a close relationship with Abu Musab al-Zarqawi. After the start of protests in 2011, Salman formed Janud al-Haqq, which was active in planting land mines and bombs targeting the Syrian army. Salman and his fighters later pledged allegiance to Nusra in 2013, and then to ISIS in 2014.[12]

The FSA's November 2012 capture of Hamdan airport and al-Bukamal city was part of the broader FSA and Nusra campaign to capture Deir al-Zour Province in eastern Syria. McClatchy reported on November 21 that

> Syrian rebels have captured two of the three major oilfields in the country's southeastern Deir al Zour Province and are extracting oil that they say is helping to support their rebellion… Among the groups profiting from the wells are Jabhat al Nusra.[13]

The next day, McClatchy reported that FSA and Nusra fighters had captured an air base in the nearby city of Mayadeen, and that

> the flags that were hoisted by the rebels at the base were not the one used by rebel groups that have pledged allegiance to the secular Free Syrian Army. Rather it was a black flag flown in particular by Islamist groups that are heavily involved in the fight against the government in this province. One building at the captured base flew the flag of Jabhat al Nusra, a group of fighters that have called openly for the establishment of a Syrian state based on Islamic law and that some fear has ties to al Qaida. "They are just one of the groups that is fighting here," said a rebel commander after the capture of the base.[14]

The Invasion of Ras al-Ayn

While the Syrian opposition spread conspiracy theories suggesting that Assad had deliberately released Islamist militants from Sednaya Prison in order to "Islamize" the so-called revolution, former and current FSA groups continued to help al-Qaeda's Nusra Front rampage across the country, wresting more and more territory from government control.

Fighters from the FSA's Ahfad al-Rasoul, led by FSA Colonel Khaled al-Mustafa, participated in the November 2012 Nusra Front-led assault on the majority Kurdish city of Ras al-Ayn, or *Serekaniye* in Kurdish, which lies on the Turkish-Syrian border and was controlled at the time by Kurdish militias known as the People's Protection Units (YPG), the armed wing of the Democratic Union Party (PYD).[15]

Consistent with the typical pattern, most Western and Gulf media coverage focused on the role of the FSA in capturing Ras al-Ayn, while omitting the fact that Nusra had led the operation. For example, in its coverage, Al Jazeera made no mention of the Nusra role, while quoting a local Syrian tribal leader who claimed that "the Free Syrian Army has completely seized control. The last remnants of the regime were terminated yesterday, and they captured weapons that were being used against the revolutionaries."[16]

McClatchy later noted, however, that "shortly after rebels seized control of Ras al-Ayn from government forces last November [2012], it became clear that Nusra made up the bulk of the fighters that had taken over. Within days, Nusra and Kurdish militias were battling."[17]

As in Aleppo, residents quickly turned against the joint FSA-Nusra occupation of their city. *Syria Deeply* reports that according to Kurdish journalist Muhyideen Isso,

> residents welcomed the Free Syrian Army at first, but then the Assad regime launched airstrikes on the city and the rebels were asked to leave. The FSA ignored the request and in a display of the increasingly Islamist nature of those fighting the Syrian government, the rebels burned down liquor stores and a church... The PYD and other Kurdish militias decided to fight back.[18]

YPG militants managed to block the Nusra/FSA advance, which led to the division of the city between the two sides before a ceasefire was reached stipulating that the YPG end its alliance with the Syrian government.[19]

When clashes erupted again in January 2013, NPR reported that "activists say the Free Syrian Army is launching mortars and using tanks to fire into civilian areas, and more than 50 people have been killed." They quote Kurdish residents who fled the shelling:

> "I'm shocked. I'm shocked by FSA's behavior... We thought it is a national army, defending our homeland, not shelling civilians." ... [Kaniwar, the first resident] says that in the early months of the uprising he was with the opposition, marching alongside Arab Syrians in peaceful protest. But now, he has lost faith.

> "I think we are all stunned," [Sally] Ali [the second resident] says. She too once supported the FSA rebels, but not anymore. "It's obvious that the FSA is helping create conflict between Arabs and Kurds."[20]

FSA and Nusra shelling of Ras al-Ayn caused the local civilian Kurdish council to beg for "an immediate end to this war and the indiscriminate shelling with tanks and artillery in order to preserve the lives of civilians."[21]

The *New York Times* noted local opposition to the FSA and Nusra as well: "The Kurds say the rebel fighters that came to Ras al-Ain, some of whom they say belonged to an extremist Islamist group, burned and looted their village."[22]

The FSA/Nusra occupation of Ras al-Ayn upset the traditional cooperation and tolerance which had long allowed various ethnic and religious groups, including Arabs and Kurds, and Christians, Yezidis, and

Muslims, to live together. The AP interviewed a Christian resident whose home had been confiscated by the FSA:

> "As a Christian I am very afraid," she said.

> She described the life before the war as harmonious, saying there was no difference between Muslims and Christians, and that people paid no attention to which religious group anyone belonged to.

> "Now there is no trust," she said. "A lot of Christians have been kidnapped."[23]

A YPG spokesman noted that over time, "the Islamists became more and more aggressive. They destroyed places where alcohol was for sale. They started to forbid women to walk on the street without a veil. What kind of revolution is that?"[24]

Rather than liberating Ras al-Ayn as part of a popular revolution, FSA and Nusra militants invaded and occupied the city as a proxy force acting on behalf of Turkey. *Al-Sharq al-Awsat* reported that according to both the SOHR and Kurdish officials, FSA and Nusra attacks on Ras al-Ayn in both November 2012 and January 2013 originated in Turkey, with Nusra and FSA fighters accompanied by tanks and artillery crossing the border to bombard the city.[25]

Lebanese *al-Akhbar* observed that the attack on Ras al-Ayn was part of the Turkish effort to solve the "Kurdish question." When the Syrian army agreed to withdraw from Kurdish areas in northeastern Syria early in the conflict, granting Kurdish political parties a measure of local autonomy, this allowed "Western Kurdistan" to become dominated by the YPG, which were affiliates of the Kurdistan Workers Party (PKK). The PKK had fought an off-again, on-again insurgency against the Turkish government for decades, and YPG control of areas near the Turkish border was viewed by Turkish planners as constituting strategic depth for the PKK, and therefore unacceptable.[26] The same concerns that caused Turkey to support the jihadist assault on Ras al-Ayn in November 2012 later led Turkey to support ISIS's infamous assault on Ayn al-Arab, or *Kobani* in Kurdish, another Kurdish majority town on the Syrian border, in September 2014.[27]

Despite the terror experienced by locals in Ras al-Ayn at the hands of invading Salafist militias, secular Syrian dissident and activist Michel Kilo painted the invasion in a positive light. After Kilo visited the town to help negotiate a ceasefire on February 5, 2013, Turkish state media reported that

Kilo revealed that a group affiliated with the armed groups in the city, including Ahfad al-Rasoul and Nusra, had received him

> with great affection, and showed him all respect and appreciation, and thanked him for his efforts in resolving the crisis with the Kurdish militias, noting that Jabhat al-Nusra does not pose a threat to the political arena in Syria, and that the United States of America is working to cause Syrians to fear Jabhat al-Nusra, which only constitutes 7 or 8 percent of the Free Army's ranks.[28]

Because secular opposition figures such as Kilo consistently signaled approval for Salafist militias, including Nusra, in this way, the nature of the insurgency facing the Syrian government remained largely obscured from Western observers. This allowed the myth of a secular and democratic FSA fighting for democracy to persist.

'We Are Proud Islamists'

While the Salafist origins of the FSA were initially murky and obscured from outside observers, the Lebanese *Daily Star* further pointed to the nature of the groups comprising the FSA:

> More than one FSA battalion has named itself after Ibn Taymiyya, the 14th-century Sunni Muslim scholar who urged the extermination of Alawites as heretics. This kind of act cancels out any favorable rhetoric or actions by other elements of the FSA, some of whose spokesmen often promise to establish a Syria that is pluralist and civil, and not religious in character.[29]

Furthermore, in an October 2012 meeting to announce the unification of Revolutionary Military Councils in several major towns, the "guest of honor" had been "Sheikh Adnan Arur, the regime's favorite target of spite — a hard-line Sunni cleric who has been vicious in his rants against the Alawites."

Just days later, on October 11, Liwa al-Tawhid, Liwa Islam, Kata'ib al-Farouq, and Saqour al-Sham all abandoned the FSA brand and instead formed the Syrian Islamic Liberation Front (SILF), thereby openly acknowledging their Islamist orientations. Saqour al-Sham leader Ahmed Abu Issa al-Sheikh was made head of the SILF coalition. He explained of the SILF: "We are proud of our Islamism, and we are Islamists… We want a state with Islamic reference, and we are calling for it."[30]

Reuters reported that the groups forming the SILF had abandoned the FSA brand because "many rebel leaders were angered" that FSA head Riad al-Asaad "was based in Turkey, saying it stripped him of any legitimacy among fighters who were dying inside the country," and that according to Ahmed Abu Issa, whose son had been killed in the fighting six months before, "we are tired of paper tigers outside the country who have no link to the battlefield."[31]

The FSA groups that publicly announced their Islamist orientation at this time were not fringe FSA factions, but rather the most powerful FSA groups fighting on the ground against the Syrian government. Syria expert Aron Lund noted at the time that the SILF was "pretty much the new mainstream face of the insurgency."[32]

Lund also described the general demise of the FSA brand at this time, explaining that

> the heyday of the FSA was in early/mid 2012, when new factions were being declared at a rate of several per week. But by mid-2012, the brand seemed to have run its course, as people soured on Col. Asaad and his exiles. The FSA term slowly began to slip out of use. By the end of the year, most of the big armed groups in Syria had stopped using it altogether, and one by one, they dropped or redesigned the old FSA symbols from their websites, logotypes, shoulder patches, and letterheads. Their symbolic connection to the FSA leaders in Turkey was broken — and since no connection at all had existed outside the world of symbols, that was the end of that story.[33]

This abandonment of the FSA brand was not the result of a sudden transformation of these early FSA groups from secular to Islamist, but rather an admission of their ideological orientation from the outset.

Although the member groups of the SILF had abandoned the FSA brand and asserted their Islamist orientations, they continued to receive support from Western and Gulf nations, including the United States. In December 2012, the U.S. and other Western and Gulf powers created the Supreme Military Council (SMC) of the FSA, based in Turkey. The establishment of the SMC allowed U.S. planners to keep the FSA brand alive and also to continue supplying weapons to the Salafist armed groups of the newly formed SILF.

The BBC notes that the SILF members, "which ranged from moderate Islamist to ultraconservative Salafist in outlook, recognised the SMC and made up the bulk of its fighting force,"[34] while the *New York Times* reported that the SMC, led by Salim Idris, "effectively replaced the loose network of defected officers who were considered leaders of the Free Syrian Army, many of them outside the country," including Riad al-Asaad.[35]

Despite the "moderate Islamist to ultraconservative Salafist" nature of the armed groups being supplied by the SMC, the secular opposition based abroad continued to demand that the U.S. and other foreign powers escalate SMC weapons shipments.

For example, opposition leader George Sabra, who is both a Christian and communist, was elected as head of the U.S.-backed Syrian National Council (SNC) in November 2012, one month after the creation of the SILF. Upon his appointment, Sabra immediately called for the Syrian "rebels" to be armed, telling the Saudi newspaper *al-Hayat*: "Quite clearly, we want weapons."[36] That Sabra had no issue arming Islamists was made clearer still when in December 2012 he explained that al-Qaeda's Syrian franchise, the Nusra Front, was "part of the revolutionary movement."[37] This is perhaps not surprising, given that Islamists appeared to hold sway even over the secular opposition leaders based abroad. The SNC was widely acknowledged as being dominated by the Muslim Brotherhood, and prominent Muslim Brotherhood leader Mohammed Farouq Tayfour was named George Sabra's deputy, further suggesting that Sabra was largely a figurehead.[38]

During this time, the Western press and think tank analysts continued to describe the Salafist armed groups supported by the U.S. and its Gulf allies as "moderate" due to their connection to the SMC, while Riad al-Asaad continued to command a small number of fighters who continued to use the FSA brand. Efforts to portray the sectarian Salafist fighters receiving weapons from the U.S.-backed SMC as moderate were promoted by Analysis Research Knowledge (ARK), a public relations firm contracted by the British Government.

Journalist Ben Norton writes that, according to leaked documents from ARK, the firm "oversaw the PR strategy for the Supreme Military Council (SMC)" and

> created a complex PR campaign to "provide a 're-branding' of the SMC in order to distinguish itself from extremist armed opposition groups and to establish the image of a functioning, inclusive, disciplined and professional military body."

> ARK admitted that it sought to whitewash Syria's armed opposition, which had been largely dominated by Salafi-jihadists, by "Softening the FSA Image."[39]

U.S. intelligence analysts were privately more forthright about the nature of the armed groups that they were backing. The U.S. Defense Intelligence Agency (DIA) issued a memo in August 2012 assessing that "the Salafists, the Muslim Brotherhood, and AQI [al-Qaeda in Iraq] are the major forces driving the insurgency in Syria."[40]

One Purpose, Many Flags

Shortly after the formation of the SILF, these former FSA groups also publicly acknowledged their alliance with al-Qaeda's Syria branch, the Nusra Front, which they had previously sought to downplay.

They did so in response to the U.S. State Department placing Nusra on its official list of terror groups in December 2012. The *New York Times* reported at the time that "the lone Syrian rebel group with an explicit stamp of approval from Al Qaeda has become one of the uprising's most effective fighting forces," and that the group had been placed on the terror list because it was "a direct offshoot of Al Qaeda in Iraq, Iraqi officials and former Iraqi insurgents say, which has contributed veteran fighters and weapons."[41]

In response, the Syrian opposition organized nationwide protests with the slogan "The only terrorism in Syria is Assad's," which according to *Time* journalist Rania Abouzeid was "a clear rebuke to the naming" of Nusra as a terrorist organization. Abouzeid noted further that dozens of anti-government armed groups also publicly declared, "We are all Jabhat al-Nusra," and that "even the leadership of the political opposition in exile has condemned the terrorist label."[42] Opposition leaders extending moral support to Nusra included Sheikh Moaz al-Khatib, head of the newly formed and U.S.-backed Syrian National Coalition of Revolutionary and Opposition Forces.[43]

Liwa al-Tawhid leader Abd al-Qader al-Saleh was also among those who condemned placing Nusra on the terror list, declaring as well that

> there is no terrorism in Syria except the terrorism of Bashar al-Assad… We participate in the fighting with [Nusra] and may disagree with some political ideas and visions, but we do not accept that they or other fighters be placed on the terrorist list.[44]

Saleh's reference to fighting with Nusra referred to the two groups' joint invasion and occupation of eastern Aleppo five months previously, in July 2012.[45] Fellow Tawhid and FSA commander Abd al-Jabbar al-Okaidi also defended Nusra, stating that "they fight side by side with the Free Syrian Army, we have only seen good things from them."[46]

Correspondents for the pro-opposition *Zaman al-Wasl* reported that the activist street movement in Aleppo and the Idlib countryside organized demonstrations calling for "Victory to Nusra," and that pictures were circulating in recent days of FSA officers in Aleppo raising banners reading such slogans as "Nusra fights with me in the battlefield. We are not terrorists." *Zaman al-Wasl* further noted the close collaboration between FSA groups and Nusra in laying siege to the Menagh air base in the Aleppo countryside.[47] One Nusra fighter explained to Reuters the reason for such close cooperation with the FSA: "Our aim is to depose Assad, defend our people against the military crackdown, and build the caliphate. Many in the Free Syrian Army have ideas like us and want an Islamic state."[48]

Summarizing the alliance between the FSA factions and Nusra, the Pan-Arab newspaper *Al-Quds Al-Arabi* noted that 2012 was a time when "there was no enmity between Nusra and the FSA. Everyone was fighting for one purpose, even if there were many flags."[49]

Why Now?

This raises the question of why the U.S. placed Nusra on the terror list at this specific time. CIA analyst and targeting officer Nado Bakos notes that Nusra's link to al-Qaeda in Iraq had been widely acknowledged almost one year before, in February 2012, when Director of National Intelligence (DNI) James Clapper had testified in front of the Senate Armed Services Committee that "we believe al-Qaeda in Iraq is extending its reach into Syria."[50]

Waiting a full year to classify Nusra formally as a terrorist organization suggests that political considerations — rather than an objective analysis of the group's origins, ideology, and activities — dictated the making of the designation.

But why did the Obama administration wait so long to add Nusra to the terror list? Why did this occur in December 2012 specifically? If one acknowledges that Nusra was "one of the uprising's most effective fighting forces," as noted by the *New York Times*, the obvious takeaway for those with real concerns about terrorism would be to place Nusra on the terror list and then to halt weapons shipments to the insurgency entirely.

Instead, it appears that the State Department placed Nusra on the terror list for the exact opposite reason: to *increase* support for the Nusra-led insurgency. From the spring of 2011 to December 2012, most military and financial support for anti-government armed groups flowed from U.S. allies, in particular the intelligence agencies of Saudi Arabia, Qatar, and Turkey, with CIA head David Petraeus playing a supervisory and coordinating role. For U.S. planners to provide even indirect material support to an insurgency dominated by an al-Qaeda affiliate would create clear legal and public relations difficulties. By placing Nusra on the terror list, however, U.S. planners were able to create an artificial dichotomy in the Syrian insurgency. With the insurgency now split between allegedly "moderate" and "extremist" wings, U.S. planners could claim to provide weapons and aid to the "moderate" elements of the insurgency, while at the same time publicly dissociating itself from the "extremist" elements in al-Qaeda. This was despite the obvious awareness that increasing aid and providing weapons to groups fighting and cooperating closely with al-Qaeda would also benefit and strengthen al-Qaeda.

As a result, the *New York Times* explained the purpose of placing Nusra on the terror list this way:

> The hope is to *remove* one of the biggest obstacles to *increasing* Western support for the rebellion: the fear that money and arms could flow to a jihadi group that could further destabilize Syria and harm Western interests.[51] (emphasis added)

In short, when U.S. planners placed Nusra on the terror list, they were using concern over terrorism as a pretext to give themselves political and legal cover to arm an insurgency dominated by terrorists. U.S. planners of course knew that the Nusra Front, al-Qaeda's formal Syrian affiliate, would be the ultimate beneficiary of the weapons that they and their regional allies were pumping into Syria. This was desirable because U.S. planners were using al-Qaeda as a proxy to topple the Syrian government and terrorize the Syrian people. To do this, plausible deniability was needed, however, and placing Nusra on the terror list provided this.

A Cataract of Weaponry

Just as Nusra was placed on the State Department terror list, the CIA was undertaking a massive effort to increase weapons shipments to the FSA, with many of the weapons predictably falling into Nusra's hands. This came as part of a new push by U.S. planners to help the jihadists take the Syrian capital of Damascus.

The *New York Times* reported of this period that

> with help from the CIA, Arab governments and Turkey have sharply increased their military aid to Syria's opposition fighters in recent months, expanding a secret airlift of arms and equipment... [which] expanded into a steady and much heavier flow late last year [2012], the data shows... Most of the cargo flights have occurred since

November [2012], after the presidential election in the United States.[52]

The same *NYT* article quotes Hugh Griffiths of the Stockholm International Peace Research Institute, who notes the massive amounts of weaponry FSA groups received. Griffiths explains:

> A conservative estimate of the payload of these flights would be 3,500 tons of military equipment... The intensity and frequency of these flights... are suggestive of a well-planned and coordinated clandestine military logistics operation...

> Arms and equipment were being purchased by Saudi Arabia in Croatia and flown to Jordan on Jordanian cargo planes for rebels working in southern Syria... [forming] what one former American official who was briefed on the program called "a cataract of weaponry."

The *NYT* also reported of this period that, according to U.S. officials, the bulk of these weapons shipments were going to "hard-line Islamic Jihadists." U.S. officials at the same time claimed incompetence, suggesting that the military assistance they were sending via their own partners in Saudi and Qatari intelligence, under the supervision of the CIA, was somehow reaching exactly those armed groups that "we don't want to have it."[53] Such statements, while patently false, were part of an effort by U.S. officials to establish plausible deniability for their activities.

In addition to providing weapons, the CIA began training FSA militants directly as well, in camps in Jordan. McClatchy reports that one so-called rebel participant in the training program

> said men he believed were American intelligence officers observed what was taking place. Another said he believed British officers were helping to organize the training. The training itself was handled by Jordanian military officers, the rebels said. By November [2012], another rebel said, the training had expanded to anti-tank weapons and Stinger anti-aircraft missiles.[54]

The *Los Angeles Times* reported that FSA militants from Damascus were among those receiving training, and that

> CIA officials declined to comment on the secret training programs, which was being done covertly in part because of U.S. legal concerns about publicly arming the rebels, which would constitute an act of war against the Assad government.[55]

In March 2013, the AP reported that the U.S. and its regional partners had "dramatically stepped up weapons supplies to Syrian rebels" in recent weeks as part of a "carefully prepared covert operation" to help "rebels to try and seize Damascus." Despite claims that the weapons were meant for "secular" fighters, and that U.S. officials were "wary of arming the rebellion, fearing weapons will go to Islamic extremists," the AP observed that in fact

> there is little clear evidence from the front lines that all the new, powerful weapons are going to groups which have been carefully vetted by the U.S.

> Many videos have appeared online showing militants from the various Islamic extremist rebel factions — including Jabhat al-Nusra, which the U.S. has officially labeled a foreign terrorist group — with such weapons in recent weeks.[56]

The U.S.- and Saudi-supplied Croatian weapons began reaching Nusra in Daraa Province almost immediately and helped the terror group achieve significant gains in southern Syria over the course of the next year. Eliot Higgins of the *Brown Moses* blog noted that FSA brigades and Nusra jointly assaulted a Syrian government military base outside of al-Sahweh in December 2012. Higgins located images showing Nusra fighters using these Croatian weapons, presumably because FSA groups had shared them with Nusra during the joint operation.

Higgins, who later founded Bellingcat.org, an investigative website with ties to Western intelligence, also noted that in March 2013, the FSA and Nusra jointly attacked the Syrian army outpost of Hajez Barad in the town of Busr al-Harir in Daraa Province. He located images of Nusra fighters using the same Croatian weapons during that operation as well.[57]

In March 2013, the *Washington Post* reported that the FSA-affiliated Yarmouk Martyrs Brigade had cooperated with Nusra to seize the 38th Division air base of the Syrian army in Daraa Province.[58]

The *New York Times* reported that by the summer of 2013, the U.S. was itself sending weapons to so-called rebels in southern Syria, in addition to those being sent via Saudi and Jordanian intelligence.[59] *The National* reported that these weapons were distributed via an operations command center in Amman, Jordan. These distributions included vehicles, sniper rifles, mortars, heavy machine guns, small arms, and ammunition to FSA units. Western and Arab military advisors based in the operations center offered tactical advice on attacking Syrian government targets.[60]

In September 2013, Al Jazeera reported that so-called rebels, among them fighters from Nusra, wrested control of the Ramtha border crossing to Jordan from the Syrian army.[61]

On October 4, 2013, the Lebanese *Daily Star* reported that according to a source in the opposition Joint Military Council, Saudi-supplied anti-tank missiles sent to FSA groups in Daraa had reached Nusra "within days" of delivery to the FSA. The source stated that "Nusra paid $15,000 for each. So they are going in, and immediately being sold on."[62]

That Nusra regularly purchased weapons from the Western-backed military councils supplying the FSA was further confirmed one year later. In October 2014, the *New York Times* reported that Shafi al-Ajmi, a Nusra fundraiser, told a Saudi news channel that "when the military councils sell the weapons they receive, guess who buys them? It's me."[63]

On January 5, 2014, *The National* interviewed opposition activists and FSA fighters and commanders in Daraa.

One FSA fighter explained how "[Nusra] offer their services and cooperate with us, they are better armed than we are, they have suicide bombers and know how to make car bombs."

A local opposition activist described how "the FSA and Al Nusra join together for operations, but they have an agreement to let the FSA lead for public reasons... Operations that were really carried out by Al Nusra are publicly presented by the FSA as their own."

An FSA commander further explained that assistance from Nusra to the FSA had been crucial during several battles against the Syrian government in the south of the country, and that the FSA and Nusra had an agreement to share weaponry captured during successful operations. The commander added that this fact is rarely acknowledged because "the face of Al Nusra cannot be to the front. It must be behind the FSA, for the sake of Jordan and the international community."[64]

Although Nusra was the ultimate recipient of U.S.-supplied weapons, Reuters reported that Congress approved sending additional small arms and anti-tank rockets to FSA groups in southern Syria in late January 2014, with a budget that would extend weapons shipments through September 2014.[65]

While the symbiotic relationship between the FSA and Nusra became clear by the end of 2012, this had previously been obscured by opposition propaganda, which had turned reality on its head and blamed the Syrian government for creating Nusra. Writing for McClatchy, David Enders observed in December 2012, for example:

> At first, many anti-Assad activists denied that [Nusra] was working
> with the rebels, claiming that the Syrian government had created it to
> discredit the opposition. Now, however, Nusra's influence has surged

over the rebellion, not only with bombings in Damascus and other cities, but in more traditional military operations where battalion-size Nusra units have been instrumental in insurgent successes across the country.[66]

13. The Destruction of Yarmouk

War Comes to Yarmouk

The "cataract of weaponry" provided to the FSA and Nusra by U.S. planners between November 2012 and March 2013 was part of a broader U.S. effort to refocus the insurgency on taking Damascus.

One FSA commander told the *Washington Post* that these weapons shipments were part of an effort to "shift the focus of the war away from the north toward the south and the capital, Assad's stronghold." Another commander, Saleh al-Hamwi, indicated that "the shift was prompted by the realization that rebel gains across the north of the country over the past year were posing no major threat to the regime in Damascus," and that weapons shipments would flow through Jordan into Syria because the "province of Daraa [in southern Syria] controls a major route to the capital and is far closer." Al-Hamwi added that "Daraa and Damascus are the key fronts on the revolution, and Damascus is where it is going to end."[1]

Although FSA militants had succeeded in penetrating the heart of the capital and in killing top Syrian government officials by bombing the National Security Building during the July 2012 offensive "Operation Damascus Volcano," they had nevertheless failed to hold territory and could only engage in hit-and-run attacks.[2] The Syrian army was then able to force the FSA to retreat. Reuters reported that according to one FSA commander, the July 2012 offensive failed because it had been disorganized and lacked proper resupply lines.[3]

If the FSA and Nusra were to succeed in taking Damascus, better supply lines therefore needed to be established, and the Yarmouk Palestinian refugee camp, located in the southern suburbs of Damascus, was crucial for this effort. Yarmouk is bordered to the south by the town of al-Hajar al-Aswad, an FSA stronghold that itself is bordered to the south by the Damascus countryside, and easily reachable from Daraa. If the FSA and Nusra could capture Yarmouk, this would help establish a reliable supply line stretching from Jordan all the way to Damascus and provide a reliable base from which another major offensive on the capital could be launched.[4]

The FSA Declares War on the PLA

Of course, if the FSA could capture Yarmouk, this would also drag Syria's Palestinians into the conflict, the majority of whom wished to remain neutral. FSA efforts to involve the Palestinians had already begun months before. Nidal Bitari, the opposition activist from Yarmouk, writes that in the spring of 2012, "the FSA began floating the idea of planting car bombs inside the camp to get residents to invite them in for protection," and that even pro-opposition Palestinian activists in the camp sought to end coordination with the FSA because "everyone knew that once the FSA was nearby, tanks and mortars would soon follow."[5]

The FSA did detonate a car bomb in Yarmouk, while also carrying out bombings in Damascus more broadly. The *Electronic Intifada* noted that in March 2012, "a car exploded in one of the quietest thoroughfares of the camp on the same day that two bombs ripped through downtown Damascus, killing those inside the car."[6]

FSA militants also began a campaign of assassinations against Palestinians to intimidate them into withdrawing support for the Syrian government. The *Electronic Intifada* noted as well that

> in yet more ominous developments, there have been reports of the mysterious killings of Palestine Liberation Army cadres of various ranks — a brigade of the Syrian army in which all Palestinian men in Syria over the age of eighteen are required to carry out military service.[7]

The Palestine Liberation Army (PLA) was founded in 1964 as the military wing of the Palestine Liberation Organization (PLO). Brigades of the PLA were created in Gaza, Egypt, Iraq, and Syria. All branches of the PLA were later incorporated into the Palestine National Authority (PNA) except for the Syrian branch, which became an all-Palestinian branch of the Syrian army.

Journalist Sharmine Narwani visited Yarmouk and spoke with two PLA commanders, General Hassan Salem and General Nabil Yacoub, who provided details of the assassinations of several of their PLA comrades in 2012. These included Major Basil Amin Ali, assassinated on January 5 in the Damascus suburb of Aarbin; Colonel Abdul Nasser Mawqari, assassinated on February 29 in Yarmouk; Colonel Rida Mohyelddin al-Khadra, assassinated on March 6 in Qatna, 20 kilometers south of Damascus; Brigadier General Anwar Mesbah al-Saqaa, assassinated on June 5 in

Damascus; Colonel Ahmad Saleh Hassan, assassinated on June 26 in Sahnaya, also in the Damascus suburbs; and General Abdul Razzak Suheim, assassinated along with his son, and a soldier guarding them, on July 26 in the Yalda neighborhood near Yarmouk.[8]

Opposition activists attempted to blame these killings on the government. However, AFP reported on July 18, 2012, that the FSA's joint command had issued a public statement warning "that pro-regime Palestinian leaders on Syrian soil were 'legitimate targets,'" making such assassinations expected.[9]

Furthermore, Palestine's ambassador to Syria Anwar Abd al-Hadi attributed the killings to the FSA, claiming that

> rebels killed some PLA officers to force Palestinians to help the Syrian revolution — to intimidate them. And they blamed the Syrian army. The target of this crisis is the Palestinian case. They think when they occupy Palestinian camps in Syria and divide them, they will forget Palestine.[10]

Sharmine Narwani further described FSA efforts to target Palestinians in the PLA. On July 11, 2012, FSA militants kidnapped and killed 14 Palestinian soldiers who were heading back to the Nairab Palestinian refugee camp on a weekend break from training exercises near Hama. According to the PLA generals whom Narwani interviewed,

> the soldiers were divided into two groups — half were shot, while the other half were tortured and then beheaded. Many Palestinians I interviewed told the story of the driver of the PLA van — who was not a soldier himself. Ahmad Ezz was a young man from the Nairab camp in Aleppo. The rebels spared him — temporarily — then strapped him into a vehicle rigged with massive explosives, and ordered him to drive into a Syrian army checkpoint. According to multiple Arabic news reports, at the very last minute, Ahmad veered sharply away from the checkpoint. The rebels detonated the explosives and Ahmad died, but by changing course he spared the Syrian soldiers. In what perhaps speaks to Palestinian sentiment about the Syrian conflict more than many of the "contested" incidents, the residents of Nairab camp turned out en masse for Ahmad's funeral. Says Mohammad, a young Palestinian whose family lives outside Yarmouk in one of the neighboring suburbs — and who first told me the story of Ahmad — "We saw him as a hero for saving the [Syrian] soldiers."[11]

Although opposition activists also blamed the Syrian government for killing its own Palestinian conscripts from Neirab camp, Ahrar al-Sham and the FSA's Saqour al-Sham later released video showing the explosion and taking responsibility for the attack on the checkpoint Ahmed had veered away from.[12]

The FSA assassination campaign extended to alleged informants as well. In November 2012, the well-known Syrian-Palestinian actor Mohammed Rafeh was assassinated in the Damascus suburb of Barzeh. The AP reports that according to the pro-opposition SOHR, Rafeh "was killed for apparently giving information to the regime about rebels and antigovernment protestors." The AP notes, however, that "Mr. Rafeh's death comes after a campaign began on social media calling for actors who support Syrian President Bashar Assad to be punished."[13] This suggests that Rafeh was assassinated simply for his outspoken public criticism of the so-called rebels.

Such assassinations were commonplace in the Damascus area during this period. Amnesty International cited a relief worker involved in transporting the dead and wounded in the Damascus suburb of Douma as describing how

> in July and August 2011, one man was "executed" around every two weeks… We would go and pick them up. The most common reason given for the killings was that the victim served as an informer for the security. The number of those "executed" gradually increased to one every week, then two or three every week. By July 2012, three to four people were being "executed" every day, and we stopped knowing the exact accusation. People just referred to them as informers.[14]

Amnesty reported as well that "Ali al-Zamel, a Palestinian refugee accused by armed opposition groups of acting as an informer for the Syrian authorities, was abducted in July 2012 and killed around five days later," and that his body was dumped in the "hole of death," a hole 15 meters long, 6 meters wide, and 5–7 meters deep, dug for the foundation of a building in an area south of al-Tadhamon, near Yarmouk. The hole "was apparently used by armed opposition groups to dump bodies of people they had summarily killed. Residents frequently checked the hole… to see if further bodies had been dumped there."[15]

In the spring of 2013, a hole of this sort in al-Tadhamon was the site of a massacre, but carried out by the government side. In 2022, video emerged of Syrian intelligence officers massacring 41 detainees, at least some of whom were blindfolded and told to walk forward until falling in the hole, after which an intelligence officer machine guns them, dumps gasoline on the bodies, then lights fire to the pit.[16]

Two researchers from the University of Amsterdam, Annsar Shahhoud and Ugur Umit Ungor, later identified the intelligence officer visible in the video, Amjad Yousef. After posing as a government supporter and developing an online relationship with Amjad through Facebook, Shahhoud duped Amjad Yousef into acknowledging his role in the massacre. Amjad had lost his younger brother three months before to the war and admitted: "I killed a lot. I took revenge."[17]

One victim, a Palestinian-Syrian named Wassim Siam, was identified in the video by his parents. They described how Wassim had disappeared on April 14, 2013, after he left Yarmouk to get flour for a family-owned bakery. They suspected that their son had been detained, and hadn't given up hope of seeing him again, before seeing the video of his brutal killing.[18]

Neutrality Falls Apart

In the summer of 2012, as the FSA assassination campaign against the PLA was well underway, reports first emerged of Palestinians with Ahmed Jibril's PFLP-GC fighting alongside the Syrian army, as well as of Palestinians fighting with the FSA. Palestinian neutrality in the conflict was now falling apart.

On July 18, AFP quoted an opposition activist known as Abu al-Sakan as claiming that "many Palestinian youth have joined the FSA, and they are fighting side by side with the Syrian revolutionaries in the Tadamon and Al-Hajar Al-Aswad districts."[19] *The Guardian* noted on July 20 that a source in Yarmouk

> said members of the Free Syrian Army were fighting tanks in the area and trying to prevent the security forces from entering. But they have been overrun after Palestinian factions, close to the regime, sided with the government troops.[20]

The fighting in these districts caused a massive influx of displaced persons into areas viewed as neutral and safe, such as Yarmouk and the nearby Khan al-Sheih Palestinian refugee camp. Those fleeing the violence were graciously hosted by camp residents, whether in UNRWA schools, mosques, or private homes. *Al-Akhbar* reported that the common feeling among the displaced was one of sadness mixed with anger:

> Says Abu Muhammad, the father of four children, "We are not guilty of anything but wanting to live in peace, far away from the game of the current war. My house lies in the Hajr al-Aswad area and missiles destroyed it, and I was hit by shrapnel in my hand, and I also broke three ribs in my chest. I still can't remember the details of leaving Hajr al-Aswad and arriving at this school with my family."[21]

Yarmouk did not remain safe for long, however. Fighting spilled over into the camp more and more during July 2012. Civilians lived in fear, often not knowing whether the bombs falling on their homes were from the hands of the FSA or the Syrian army. One elderly Yarmouk resident described how when he had once fought as a guerrilla for the PLO against Israel, Palestinians had had a clear enemy. However, "if I am now killed in my home, I will not know the source of the bullet or missile or who fired it. We are living in a dirty and frustrating time now."[22]

One Fatah supporter emphasized his party's efforts to remain neutral during this period, while also acknowledging the risks of doing so:

> Palestinians have also paid the price of Arab countries' struggles for decades. So most Fatah supporters are trying to stay on the fence... But it is difficult because even if they do not go to the revolt, the revolt is coming to them.[23]

Arming the Popular Committees

In the wake of the July 2012 FSA offensive on Damascus and increased fighting in neighborhoods adjacent to Yarmouk, the PFLP-GC leadership was keenly aware of the threat of a jihadist takeover of the camp and argued that remaining neutral was no longer a viable option. Ahmed Jibril began distributing weapons to Palestinians in Yarmouk to create "popular committees" to defend the camp against the FSA. These popular committees were comprised of about 500 men from a variety of Palestinian factions, excluding Hamas.

Al-Akhbar noted, however, that many Palestinians in the camp opposed these actions because they considered

> the participation of supporters of Ahmed Jibril in preserving the security of the camp a clear violation of the agreement made by all factions of the Palestine Liberation Organization, in the beginning of the events in Syria, which declared that all Palestinian resistance factions refrain from engaging in the internal Syrian conflict and remain committed to neutrality.[24]

Anwar Raja, the PFLP-GC's media director, was unapologetic about arming the popular committees, however, feeling that it was a necessary measure, despite opposition from the other Palestinian factions. Raja explained that

> we warned Palestinians in 2011 and 2012 about rebels coming to occupy Yarmouk, and increased these calls as rebels took control of surrounding areas in Tadamoun, Hajar al-Aswad, Yalda. We said the

groups should arm themselves in defense of the camp, but they ignored us.[25]

During this time, *Al-Akhbar* reports that a group of Yarmouk businessmen also sent a delegation to the Damascus police chief to request that walking police patrols be established to protect the camp from the so-called rebels, the cost of which these businessmen offered to pay from their own pockets. FSA militants assaulted the Damascus police headquarters later that same evening, killing all the officers present.[26] Al Jazeera reported on the attack as well, claiming that the FSA militants killed and injured dozens of security men and *shabiha* during the assault, while also capturing the weapons cache inside.[27]

Pro-opposition Palestinians began to accuse the popular committees themselves of constituting *shabiha*. *Al-Arab* quoted some Palestinian refugees from Yarmouk as calling on the UN, rights groups, and the PLO to "save them from the *shabiha* of the Syrian regime and its snipers."[28]

One member of a local humanitarian group, the Jafra Foundation, described how the neutrality of the camp slowly fell apart during this period:

> The Palestinian camps were a safe haven for internally displaced persons and for the wounded, especially in Yarmouk camp. Now, this wasn't appreciated by either side — the Assad regime or the opposition. The opposition wanted us to participate more in protests and militias and side with them. At the same time, the regime used the same logic — they accused us of allowing "terrorists" to enter the camps and of not fighting with the Syrian regime, which, they say, was always with us and supported our rights. This confusion from the two sides also found its voice within the Palestinian people. Some people began to participate in demonstrations and [rebel] military actions. On the regime side, the Popular Front for the Liberation of Palestine–General Command and Fatah al-Intifada began to recruit for Assad. In the beginning, the idea was just to protect the camps. That changed.[29]

The Ramadan Massacre

It was in this context that several mortars landed in Yarmouk on August 2, 2012, tearing into a busy street during the height of Ramadan celebrations, killing twenty. *Al-Akhbar* quoted an eyewitness to the bombing as saying:

> A state of terror and chaos filled the place after the first bomb fell. We immediately tried to help the injured. After only two minutes the second bomb fell in the same place, which caused a large number of dead and injured.[30]

Saudi-owned *Al-Sharq al-Awsat* reported claims from the local representative of the Palestinian Center for Human Rights (PCHR) that the "massacre that was committed was intentional," because three shells fell "within two minutes in the same place within Ja'una Street in the camp" and that "we have verified the source of the shells and found they were fired from the site of regime artillery on Qasioun mountain above the Republican Palace." According to *Al-Sharq al-Awsat*, the Syrian army supposedly carried out the massacre because of the "dissatisfaction of the Syrian regime with the Palestinian movement, especially after the uprising of the camp, and the support it presented to oppressed Syrian families" displaced due to fighting in nearby neighborhoods.[31]

Despite opposition and PCHR claims that the Syrian government was responsible, the *New York Times* reported that "details surrounding the attack suggest it may not be that simple," and that the FSA may have carried out the attack in retaliation for PFLP-GC efforts to arm the popular committees. The *NYT* quoted one spokesperson for a local Palestinian opposition group who described Jibril's efforts to distribute weapons as "provocative," while the *NYT* also noted that

> the blasts appear to have hit near the office of a faction that was distributing weapons, the Popular Front for the Liberation of Palestine–General Command. A well-placed opposition activist who declined to be identified publicly because of political considerations said the bombings might have been the work of rebels who had aimed for that office but missed.[32]

Such a view seems reasonable, given that the FSA had a few weeks earlier declared that pro-government Palestinian leaders were legitimate targets. This, on top of Jibril's efforts to distribute weapons, could easily have prompted the FSA to target the PFLP-GC headquarters in retaliation. Furthermore, if the Syrian government did wish to retaliate against Palestinians broadly for their supposed support of the opposition, as *Al-Sharq al-Awsat* claims, it would still not make sense for the Syrian army to bomb areas of Yarmouk under the control of its own allies (areas near the PFLP-GC headquarters). More likely, FSA militants targeted the PFLP-GC headquarters on August 2, missed, and accidentally killed 20 people.

Importantly, opposition activists viewed the alleged killing of Palestinians by the government as positive, as it would supposedly help break the bond between the Palestinians and the Syrian government, causing them to come to the opposition side and end their neutral stance. The *New York Times* described how "trying to break that bond has been a primary goal of the opposition," and that "other activists blamed the government [for the August 2 bombing] although they acknowledged that they wanted to draw the Palestinians into the conflict."[33] The *NYT* also quoted an opposition activist as saying, "Let [the Palestinians] show the world how they don't want to get involved after many of them were killed by Assad," revealing the disdain that many in the opposition felt towards Palestinians for their attempts to remain neutral. This resembled opposition anger at residents of Aleppo during the same period for their lack of support for the "revolution."

The bond between Palestinians and the Syrian government proved difficult to break, however. The *New York Times* reported in late June 2012 that

> Syria prides itself on being one of the few Arab countries to offer Palestinians full civil rights. They can own property and hold government jobs, for instance. "It is hard for us to forget that Syria deals with us as ordinary citizens," said Abu Mohammad, 40, another refugee, who runs a candy store in the Yarmouk camp. "If Assad is gone, no Arab or foreign state will host us," he said. "We want to live in peace and look after our sons, not to live in tents again."[34]

The fighting that began in Yarmouk in the summer of 2012 intensified further in the fall. In late October 2012, the FSA brigade known as Suqour al-Golan, or "Falcons of the Golan," announced the formation of a special unit allegedly made up of all Palestinians, specifically for the purpose of fighting the pro-government Palestinian cadre of the PFLP-GC and the popular committees. An FSA commander declared to Reuters: "Now they are targets for us, targets for all the FSA. All of them with no exceptions."[35]

Zero Hour

The stage was now set for an all-out assault on Yarmouk as part of the broader FSA push toward Damascus. Nidal Bitari notes that

> the FSA, by that time joined by the extremist Jabhat al-Nusra, had long set their sights on Yarmuk camp as the "gateway to Damascus." Since the autumn of 2012, they had been talking more and more openly about the "zero hour" for liberating Damascus, and everyone knew that Yarmuk was the intended launching pad... And with the PFLP-GC now fighting the rebels outside the camp, the FSA could claim that the camp's neutrality had ended and use that as an excuse to go in.[36]

Writing for the Institute of Palestine Studies (IPS), Mustafa al-Harash claims that on the evening of December 15, 2012, news from a source in the Syrian armed opposition reached the PLO that so-called rebel groups had decided to storm the camp and had designated a zero hour for doing so, which was just hours away. After holding an emergency meeting, the PLO factions decided to send a delegation to meet with the leadership of the rebel groups and to discourage them from storming the camp. The rebel groups had already made the decision, however, and would not retreat from it, indicating that they were not concerned with the consequences of assaulting the camp, in terms of death and destruction and displacement of civilians. According to Harash, the rebels viewed this as simply the "price of jihad" (*dharibat al-jihad*) that civilians must pay. The rebel leadership further insisted that assaulting Yarmouk was justified because the camp was on "Syrian land," and necessary for gaining an advantage against the Syrian security apparatus and its Palestinian allies in the PFLP-GC popular committees.[37]

PFLP-GC officials alleged that then director of Saudi intelligence, Prince Bandar bin Sultan, was the chief planner of the assault on Yarmouk.[38] This seems reasonable, given the role of Saudi intelligence in organizing weapons shipments to the FSA on behalf of the CIA during this period, and given that, according to a leaked National Security Agency (NSA) document, Bandar was personally giving orders to FSA groups to "light up Damascus" and "flatten" the Damascus airport with missiles just three months later.[39]

Bombing of the Abd al-Qader Mosque

Nusra and the FSA initiated the assault and entered Yarmouk camp on the night of Saturday, December 15, 2012. The jihadi assault of the camp and subsequent clashes with PFLP-GC militants defending it set the stage for perhaps the most infamous incident in Yarmouk of the entire war. On Sunday, December 16, the Syrian air force bombed the camp's Abd al-Qader al-Husseini Mosque and a UNRWA school. The SOHR reported eight killed, while opposition activists claimed at least 25 dead.[40]

The *New York Times* described the scene of the bombing:

> In Yarmouk, burned body parts littered the ground at the Sheik Abdul Qader Mosque, which had offered shelter to Palestinians and others displaced by fighting in other areas. Minutes before, a Syrian fighter jet fired rockets at the camp. Women, crying children, and white-bearded men thronged the streets with hurriedly packed bags, not sure where to look for safety.[41]

The *NYT* also interviewed a fleeing Yarmouk resident who was "shocked on Sunday at the speed of the government assault, in which fighter planes and artillery were used to attack the area hours after rebel fighters entered Yarmouk."[42]

The victims of the horrific mosque and school bombings appear to have been residents who were not able to flee the camp after the Syrian government had warned residents to do so. *The Guardian* quotes an elderly woman named Um Hassan as explaining that many had left Yarmouk after warnings broadcast from mosques early on Sunday morning, but that

> others had sought refuge in a mosque and remained behind. Syrians who had fled from battle zones elsewhere in Syria were staying in a nearby school. They also chose to stay. Both groups were hit by bombs dropped from jets.[43]

The government claimed that the bombing of the school and mosque was a mistake, made in the context of attacking the FSA positions to prevent their further advance on Damascus (perhaps assuming that most civilians had fled or that FSA militants were using the mosque and school as bases).[44] In contrast, opposition activists claimed the Syrian air force bombed the mosque and school on purpose, and wished to target civilians directly, in an effort to punish Yarmouk's Palestinians for supposedly supporting the FSA and Nusra.

On Monday, December 17, *al-Akhbar* quoted a prominent Popular Front for the Liberation of Palestine (PFLP, not to be confused with the PFLP-GC) leader who described the situation as "extremely dangerous. The FSA has taken total control over wide sections of the south of the camp, such as Square 15 and the area surrounding the Khalsa," the PFLP-GC headquarters, resulting in a PFLP-GC withdrawal. The PFLP leader speculated that

> the worst is yet to come. If the camp falls under the control of the Free Army and the extremist Islamic jihadist groups, it will become the launching pad for military operations, and the camp residents will pay a heavy price.[45]

The New Nakba

As the fighting continued between the government and the jihadists in Yarmouk, camp residents continued to flee to safety. Before the war, the population of Yarmouk had been roughly 650,000, with some 160,000 Palestinian refugees, and the remainder Syrians. One PFLP official estimated that the number in the camp by December 2012 had been much higher, perhaps 1.5 million, due to the number of displaced who had sought refuge in the camp while fleeing violence in adjacent neighborhoods.[46]

However, within days of the fighting in December 2012, the camp had become largely depopulated. This caused many to draw parallels between the mass displacement of residents from Yarmouk, the capital of the Palestinian diaspora, and the mass displacement of Palestinians during the original Nakba, when Zionist militias ethnically cleansed some 750,000 Christian and Muslim Palestinians in 1947–48 to capture land for the creation of the Jewish state.

Thousands of Palestinians fleeing Yarmouk gathered in front of the immigration and passports office in the Ain Karsh district of Damascus to obtain permission to travel to the Palestinian camps in Lebanon.[47] Others found refuge in other Palestinian camps in Syria, in particular Khan al-Sheih.

Al-Akhbar quoted one Palestinian father as saying:

> It was a difficult decision I took with my family to settle our affairs to head toward Ain al-Hilwah camp in south Lebanon and to live with our relatives there. I do not possess the money to travel to ensure securing work in Lebanon to support my family. But the scenes of death after the bombing of the Abd al Qadir al-Husseini Mosque were enough to leave the camp and never return.[48]

Al-Akhbar described this time as "the new chapter in the exile of the Palestinians from their homeland," stating that

> the residents of the camp have lived through a state of terror and fear in recent days, as the scope of the destruction in the camp increased as a result of bombing with mortars from the side of the Free Army and artillery shells and missiles from airplanes of the Syrian regime army. The mutual bombing led to tens of dead and injured and resulted in large material damages, which caused a mass exodus estimated at thousands of families which recently decided to leave their homes, carrying with them anything they could, in a scene harking back to memories from the Nakba of 1948... Yesterday morning, the residents of the camps in Khan al Sheih, al-Sabina, and Jaramana awoke to the arrival of tens of thousands of displaced persons from Yarmouk camp. Some were transported in trucks collectively, while others arrived walking by foot after the paths were blocked before them.[49]

Those few Palestinians not able to flee the camp after the FSA and Nusra invasion and Syrian air force bombing soon caught a glimpse of the nature of the armed men now occupying Yarmouk, who quickly began to loot property, impose their extremist religious views on residents, and express disdain for the Palestinian cause. Nidal Bitari explains that

> the rebels became more and more abusive toward those who remained. Some brought in friends and relatives to squat in empty houses; looting and robberies became common. Jabhat al-Nusra set up Islamic courts, and Palestinian activists were arrested and tried. There were rumors of assassinations. The most serious abuses were committed by the FSA's Eagles of the Golan and Ababil Hawran brigades, which the FSA leadership, located outside the camp, said it was unable to control... After the FSA entered the camp, residents were shocked to hear rebel fighters telling them to go back where they had come from. A similar attitude was reflected later at the official level: during negotiations for lifting the siege on Yarmuk, the FSA reportedly rejected a proposal that all armed men leave the camp on the grounds that the rebels were fighting for their land, and that camps were on their land.[50]

Similarly, *Syria Deeply* published an interview with an unnamed activist from Yarmouk who explained that after the so-called rebels came,

> the FSA broke into houses of the [PFLP]-GC and Syrians who they claimed were working for the regime. They looted and occupied the houses. They took over our hospitals and stole medicine. People felt it was the same as the Nakba.[51]

This hostility toward the Palestinian cause is unsurprising, given that the armed groups that invaded Yarmouk in December 2012, including Nusra, enjoyed not only Saudi and American, but also Israeli, support. The *Wall Street Journal* reported that Israel was secretly paying salaries and providing munitions to armed opposition groups in southern Syria, in particular the Knights of the Golan, starting as early as 2013. The group's spokesman explained that "Israel stood by our side in a heroic way... We wouldn't have survived without Israel's assistance."[52]

According to a May 2014 report from the United Nations Disengagement Observer Force (UNDOF), armed Nusra-led opposition groups were in contact with the Israeli army across the Golan ceasefire line, including during clashes with the Syrian army, and that opposition fighters were being transported across the ceasefire line to be treated in Israeli hospitals.[53]

The *Wall Street Journal* reported in March 2015 that Nusra fighters were being treated in Israeli hospitals near the border, and that Israeli officials justified this by claiming that they did not screen for fighters before admitting them for treatment. The *WSJ* also quoted retired Brigadier General Michael Herzog as justifying tacit cooperation with Nusra because they are "a unique version of al-Qaeda" and "totally focused on the war in Syria, and not focused on us."[54]

Israeli authorities had attempted to keep their support for Nusra covert. As a result, Israeli police detained Sidqi Maqt, a Syrian Druze from Majdal al-Shams in the Israeli-occupied Golan Heights, in February 2015. Maqt, who had been imprisoned by Israel for 27 years for his resistance to Israeli occupation of the Golan, was released in 2012 and began documenting the relationship between the Israeli army and Nusra. Upon his detention, Israeli authorities placed Maqt in solitary confinement and charged him with espionage and assisting the enemy during wartime for posting videos and photos of Israeli-Nusra collaboration to Facebook and for giving interviews to Syrian state media. Maqt documented meetings between Israeli military personnel and Nusra militants, and in one video documented two white buses with Nusra fighters entering an Israeli army base.[55]

In June 2015, Israeli Defense Minister Moshe Ya'alon confirmed for the first time publicly that Israel had been providing aid to armed opposition groups. This aid had previously been kept secret because "it is not in the rebels' interest to publicize the fact that Israel assists them."[56]

The Siege Begins

In response to the December 2012 invasion and occupation of Yarmouk, and to prevent the FSA and Nusra from advancing further on Damascus, the Syrian army and its allies in the PFLP-GC established checkpoints at the northern edge of the camp, imposing a partial siege. The siege was only partial because the FSA and Nusra controlled entrances to the south of the camp, connecting it to al-Hajar al-Aswad, which they also controlled. Syrian and allied Palestinian forces monitored what went in and what went out of the camp entrances that they controlled, while civilians were able to access UNRWA assistance at the Zahra entrance to Yarmouk.[57]

The government tightened the siege further during the summer of 2013 to protect Damascus, but with little concern for civilians remaining in Yarmouk. Months went by when very little aid was able to reach the camp. UN efforts to deliver aid were hampered by Syrian government bureaucratic red tape. Ben Parker of the United Nations Office for the Coordination of Humanitarian Affairs (OCHA) in Syria complained that officially, the UN was allowed to deliver aid anywhere, "but every action requires time-consuming permissions, which effectively provide multiple veto opportunities."[58]

UNRWA Commissioner-General Filippo Grandi detailed how

> entry and exit were tightly controlled by the warring parties, but residents continued to receive some assistance. Access became tighter until it was all but sealed in September [2013], [after which residents began living] as in a medieval siege, [subsisting] on grass, spices mixed in water, and animal feed. They burned furniture on their balconies to keep warm; they suffered severe malnutrition and dehydration. Many died from readily treatable conditions.[59]

During this time, the Syrian government also swept up many innocent people while trying to target jihadists and their supporters ensconced in Yarmouk. Writing for *al-Akhbar*, journalist Qassem Qassem suggests that it is an "undeniable fact" that the Palestinian filmmaker from Yarmouk, Hassan Hassan, was "killed in the regime prisons," that he was not a terrorist or "takfiri," and that he "never carried a gun nor blew himself up with an explosive vest." Qassem notes that the four-minute film for which Hassan was detained, first by Nusra and later by the government, had criticized the pro-Syrian government Palestinian factions and popular committees on the one hand, as well as the anti-government Islamists in Yarmouk on the other.[60]

Jonathan Steele of *The Guardian* writes: "In October 2013, in a sign of how bad things had become, the imam of Yarmouk's largest mosque issued a fatwa that permitted people to eat cats, dogs, and donkeys."[61] Steele notes further that according to a woman from Yarmouk whom he interviewed, the FSA and Nusra were not allowing male residents to leave the camp. Steele writes that the woman

> had been given permission to leave Yarmouk three months earlier with her three teenage daughters. The oldest one was pregnant. Owing to malnutrition, she was suffering from anemia so severe that she was at risk of losing her baby. The other two girls also had medical problems. But leaving the camp had meant splitting the family. The husband of the pregnant woman could not leave the camp, nor could Reem's husband, or her 16-year-old son. Rebel groups were eager to keep people in the camp, she said, particularly men and boys. Their departure was seen as defection from the opposition cause as well as potentially making it easier for government troops to enter the camp by force and regain control.

Not only the government but also the FSA and Nusra bore blame for preventing food and aid from reaching residents. The International

Committee of the Red Cross (ICRC) claimed that both sides had blocked medical aid to the sick and wounded because "whatever medical aid is brought to one part or the other is interpreted as an indirect military support to the other side."[62] Similarly, the Palestinian Ma'an News Agency explained that so little food and medicine had reached the camp during 2013 "because of the siege of the regime forces from outside, and the sniper operations which the armed groups inside the camp undertake."[63]

The *New York Times* noted that Palestinians in Yarmouk were not only "blockaded and bombarded by the Syrian government," but at the same time "ruled internally by a tangled web of armed groups, including Syrian insurgents and Palestinian factions, said by residents to siphon scarce food to their own fighters and families."[64]

As a result of the government siege and FSA and Nusra hoarding of food, many civilians in Yarmouk eventually starved to death. *Newsweek* interviewed Ram Heramic, a 24-year-old resident of Yarmouk:

> "I remember the first person to starve to death… He was a 6-year-old boy called Abd Alhay Yousif. It's ironic — his name means 'one who worships immortal gods'… The immortal gods did not protect him. He never grew up."

> Heramic and others from Yarmouk compile what they call the Starvation Death List. It has 177 names of people who have died of hunger [between 2013 and May 2015], during the period of siege when hardly any goods have been able to reach the camp.[65]

14. Nusra and the Free Army Pave the Way for ISIS

War of the Airports

While FSA groups were helping Nusra occupy parts of Deir al-Zour, Aleppo, Ras al-Ayn, Daraa, and Yarmouk as 2012 came to an end, they were at the same time helping Nusra launch a new offensive, which led to what was known as the "War of the Airports." Targets of the months-long offensive included the Taftanaz, Wadi al-Deif, and Abu Duhoor air bases in Idlib Province, as well as the Menagh air base in the Aleppo countryside.[1]

According to *Time* journalist Rania Abouzeid, armed opposition groups hoped to capture these targets before turning their focus toward Idlib city and Jisr al-Shughour, the two main cities still under Syrian government control in Idlib Province at the time.[2]

The FSA and Nusra offensive began with an operation known as Ma'rakit al-Bunyan al-Marsous, or "the Battle of Reinforced Structures," which opened various new fronts in the fight against the Syrian army near the town of Ma'aret al-Numan on the strategic M5 Motorway linking Damascus and Aleppo. In preparation for the campaign, opposition activists formed a special media room to distribute news updates and photos via the major Arabic satellite news channels and social media.[3]

On January 2, 2013, the FSA announced that the battle to control Taftanaz air base, the first phase of the al-Bunyan al-Marsous operation, had begun. Al Jazeera reported that the "Free Army brigades had begun bombing the airport since the morning in preparation for storming it," and that the air base included thirty aircraft and was guarded by about 400 soldiers.[4]

As fighting raged at Taftanaz, FSA head Salim Idris took credit for planning the assault. On January 6, the Saudi newspaper *Okaz* reported that Idris

> manages, through the central operations room, all military operations inside Syria and on the five fronts. In his first interview with an Arab newspaper, he said that the battles that the rebels are fighting are planned by the [FSA] General Staff, stressing that he is working from inside Syria in coordination with all the battalions on the ground.[5]

When opposition forces successfully captured Taftanaz days later, on January 11, the *Washington Post* described it as possibly "the biggest strategic victory yet for rebel fighters," while estimating that some 100 Syrian soldiers and 20 opposition fighters had been killed. Many of the Syrian soldiers had been executed, their bodies dumped en masse in a shallow hole.[6] Opposition forces were also able to capture large amounts of heavy weapons and ammunition, and they destroyed large numbers of Mi-8/17 transport helicopters.[7]

While Salim Idris and the FSA publicly took credit for the assault on Taftanaz, the so-called rebels fighting on the ground were from Nusra and other Salafist militias. The *Washington Post* reported that according to a media activist embedded with opposition armed groups during the battle,

> some of those who helped capture Taftanaz were members of the rebel Free Syrian Army, [but] the bulk of the attacking force was made up of fighters from the al-Nusra Front, along with Ahrar al-Sham and Talia al-Islamiya, two other religious extremist groups.[8]

Writing in *Time*, journalist Rania Abouzeid explained:

> In coordination with the Salafist Ahrar al-Sham brigades, [Jabhat al-Nusra] shepherded the final two-week phase in the months-long battle for the strategically important Taftanaz military airport that fell to the rebels in mid-January. The participation of other groups in those final stages of the fight was only at Jabhat's invitation. Jabhat al-Nusra also established a committee that first itemized and then distributed the war spoils. Still, the sheer scale of Marakit il Bina il Marsoos, its multiple fronts and the pledges to the Sharia court mark it as a new battlefield experiment the rebels hope will be emulated by others if it is successful.[9]

The only faction with public links to the FSA that fought at Taftanaz was itself a religious extremist group, namely Saqour al-Sham. Al Jazeera journalists who spoke to a commander on the ground in Taftanaz confirmed that Liwa Daoud had played a limited role in the assault alongside Nusra and Ahrar al-Sham.[10] As discussed in Chapter 8, Liwa Daoud was one of eight brigades constituting Saqour al-Sham and was led by Hassan Aboud, who later defected to ISIS. *Al-Quds Al-Arabi* reports that Aboud was one of the most important military leaders in Saqour al-Sham and participated in the siege of the Taftanaz military airport.[11]

FSA chief Idris's claiming credit for planning an operation that was actually led by Nusra and Ahrar al-Sham suggests that his involvement at Taftanaz was only cosmetic and for public relations purposes. This fit a broader pattern in the conflict. As discussed in Chapter 12, operations really carried out by al-Nusra were often "publicly presented by the FSA as their own."[12]

Events at Taftanaz therefore provided another indication that the "bulk" of the opposition was comprised of religious extremist groups and jihadi fighters, rather than secular democratic "rebels." This made it difficult to take seriously any assurances by the FSA leadership about protecting Alawites in areas that might be captured by the opposition. Just days before the launch of the al-Bunyan al-Marsous campaign at Taftanaz, Nusra had issued a video declaring their wish to exterminate Syria's Alawite population. The *Washington Post* reported on January 11, 2013:

> In a video posted online last week, more than two dozen fighters from the al-Nusra Front stand in front of a black flag with Koranic scripture, brandishing machine guns and rocket-propelled grenades. "O, you nusereyeen and your troops," the speaker says, using a derogatory reference for followers of the Alawite faith. "We dedicate ourselves only to battle you and exterminate you."[13]

This raises the question of whether "opposition" is an appropriate term for the Syrian government's adversaries. In most countries, the opposition is a political party or movement critical of the ruling party or elite, seeking to make changes through reform and political activity broadly. In the case of Syria, the "opposition" consisted primarily of a foreign-backed terrorist organization which advocated societal norms far outside the mainstream of Syrian thought, including mainstream Sunni religious thought. The "opposition" advocated the extremist sectarian religious ideology of Muhammad Sarour and Adnan Arour, which endorsed the genocide of Syria's Alawites and ethnic cleansing of its Christians. This contrasted with the mainstream Muslim belief of Syria's most popular and influential Sunni cleric, Muhammad Said Ramadan al-Bouti, which advocated peaceful coexistence between Syria's various religious groups.

This suggests that the armed groups described as the Syrian opposition should more accurately be referred to as foreign-backed Salafist mercenaries — or even as "Wahhabi contras," as suggested by journalist Leith Marouf — due to the extremist nature of their ideology and their role as proxies for their foreign sponsors.[14]

The Battle for Wadi al-Deif

Once Taftanaz was captured, the coalition of FSA, Nusra, and Ahrar al-Sham forces turned their attention to the Wadi al-Deif air base, also located in Idlib

Province near the town of Ma'arat al-Numan. The base also sits astride the strategically important M5 Motorway connecting Damascus and Aleppo.

Armed opposition groups had initially laid siege to Wadi al-Deif in October 2012. On October 9, fighters aligned with FSA Colonel and Idlib Military Council head Afif Suleiman overran Ma'arat al-Numan during a 48-hour gun battle with the Syrian army.[15] Suleiman's fighters were soon joined by Jamal Maarouf's Kata'ib Shuhada Suria, or "Syrian Martyrs Brigades." After the Syrian army was expelled from the town, the fighting shifted to the nearby Wadi al-Deif military base.[16] By October 26, when clashes again erupted at the air base, Suleiman and Maarouf's men had been joined by fighters from the Nusra Front to assist in imposing the siege.[17]

On January 19, 2013, shortly after Taftanaz fell, the Northern Front Command of the FSA announced that it had begun the second phase of the al-Bunyan al-Marsous campaign, which involved a renewed assault on Wadi al-Deif. The FSA leadership then announced that the battalions participating in the operation had cut off the supply road to the base from the area around the town of Khan Sheikhoun.[18]

As in Taftanaz, the FSA leadership claimed credit for the renewed assault on Wadi al-Deif. However, Nusra and Ahrar al-Sham were again leading the operation, with Liwa Daoud of Saqour al-Sham also playing a notable role.

Rania Abouzeid explained that the assault on Wadi al-Deif air base was "not the first time Jabhat al-Nusra has taken the organizational lead in a fight in Idlib," while quoting a Nusra commander at Wadi al-Deif as explaining that, as at Taftanaz: "We invited all of the leaders of the brigades here... They have all sworn to the [Sharia] court to work together. God willing, this will serve as an example to others."[19]

FSA Colonel Afif Suleiman was working with Nusra's Sharia court to decide how to divide weapons previously captured from the Syrian army, including at Taftanaz. Colonel Suleiman explained to Abouzeid that

> the Sharia court is empowered to try and hold accountable any side that breaks its pledge... In other battles, there were disputes and tension, people would take the booty that they wanted, so we decided that it is better that the ghanaim [spoils] would be in the hands of the Sharia court and it can distribute it based on the participants.[20]

Abouzeid also interviewed a Saqour al-Sham commander who was part of the operations team planning the battle at Wadi al-Deif, showing the group's participation in the assault as well. The commander also discussed the disputes about dividing weapons among the participating factions.

As head of the FSA's Idlib Military Council, Suleiman himself had little control over the fighters at Wadi al-Deif. He explained to Abouzeid that the fighters

> know that the councils are just a way to organize their activities; they don't expect anything else from them. If somebody says they fought in this battle, if there is no proof, if he was not registered, who will believe him? The council is a means to organize and to prove the participation of people and groups.[21]

Abouzeid then added that, in other words, Colonel Suleiman is "a record keeper that occasionally distributes arms and ammunition." Suleiman's presence nevertheless served to obscure the leading role played by Nusra jihadists, while also illustrating the extent to which the FSA leadership was dependent upon, and integrated with, al-Qaeda.

The fighting at Wadi al-Deif reached a stalemate as Nusra and its allies were short on the heavy weaponry needed to capture the base, in which 350 Syrian soldiers were barricaded, short on supplies, outnumbered, and isolated.[22]

After withstanding six months of coordinated attacks, the beleaguered soldiers received reinforcements and additional weapons when the Syrian army was able to break the jihadi siege on April 15, 2013.[23] This resulted in part because Nusra fighters had redeployed away from Wadi al-Deif to participate in the invasion of Raqqa, a provincial capital in the east of the country that would soon constitute an even more important prize.[24]

The War of Missiles and Artillery

Regarding the "War of the Airports," FSA head Salim Idris had explained that

> in fact we have no choice but to fight this war, as the regime is not superior to us except in the air, and we must control its airfields to neutralize the air force, and the revolutionaries have fought and are still fighting a violent war in the vicinity of Taftanaz airport in Idlib and Menagh military airport in Aleppo, and the rest of the other airports, and these airports are gaining strategic importance as a starting point for striking the countryside where the fighting brigades are in control… And let me tell you that once the war of the airports is over, the war of the missiles and artillery will begin, which is our next goal in our war with the regime forces.[25]

As noted by Idris, the assault on Taftanaz was accompanied by a similar effort to capture the Menagh air base in the Aleppo countryside. Abd al-

Qader al-Saleh of Liwa al-Tawhid partnered with the Nusra Front to lay siege to Menagh starting in December 2012.[26] Saleh was joined in the battle by U.S. favorite and FSA commander Abd al-Jabbar al-Okaidi.[27]

While pro-opposition sources claimed that the attack on Taftanaz was in response to the Syrian air force bombing civilians from the air, Idris's comments make clear that the Syrian military's air superiority was viewed by the FSA as a barrier to taking control of the country. If Salim Idris could put an end to airstrikes against FSA and Nusra fighters in the Idlib countryside, this would be followed by a "war of artillery and missiles" allowing them to conquer the province's urban centers, Jisr al-Shagour and Idlib city.

This was acknowledged by an alleged Syrian air force officer who defected to the opposition side months later. The officer explained to *Al-Dorar al-Shamiya*:

> In the event that the air force is neutralized, the people will be safe, and *an air embargo will be imposed, which will lead to progress towards the liberation of Syria*, which we promise the people to achieve in the coming period.[28] (emphasis added)

The above comments by Salim Idris and the defected air force officer show that Syrian air force bombing targeted armed opposition groups, retarding their efforts to take control of the country. If the military airports at Taftanaz, Wadi al-Deif, Menagh, and elsewhere could be captured and the Syrian air force grounded, this would open the way for further jihadist advances on the ground and a possible U.S.-imposed "air embargo" on the jihadists' behalf.

This contrasted with opposition propaganda, which suggested that the goal of Assad's air campaign was simply to bomb civilians as punishment for dissent, while omitting any reference to the targeting of the Salafist militias of the FSA and their Nusra jihadist allies. This then gave the impression that most deaths in the conflict resulted from Assad bombing civilians from the air, whether using conventional bombs and missiles, or improvised "barrel bombs," which were characterized as somehow uniquely deadly.

Focusing on civilian deaths from Syrian government airstrikes was also helpful to the opposition because the so-called rebels did not have any air power, and this therefore suggested the government was responsible for most, if not all, of the violence in the conflict.

This then led to claims by opposition supporters, most notably during the 2016 Syrian army campaign to liberate Aleppo — by which time it had been joined by the Russian air force — that Assad was carrying out a genocide.

For example, Nicolas Tenzer of the Paris School of International Affairs (Sciences Po) argued that Assad was carrying out a "war of extermination" in Aleppo and implied that he was responsible for the "massacre" of all 500,000 Syrians estimated to have died in the conflict by that time.[29]

Similarly, Jett Goldsmith of NATO-funded Bellingcat claimed that of these 500,000, "the majority, in fact, according to data compiled by the Syrian Observatory for Human Rights (SOHR), were victims of punitive, indiscriminate regime airstrikes on civilian populations."[30]

However, the SOHR article cited by Goldsmith made no such claim. It claimed a completely different total killed (some 370,000) and did not attribute responsibility for the deaths of civilians killed (122,997) to any one side. The SOHR report also noted the large numbers of Syrian soldiers and pro-government militiamen killed (93,088), as well as large numbers of foreign jihadists (44,254) who had also fallen in the fighting. The report also estimated that an additional 95,000 fighters from both sides combined may have been killed as well.[31]

That so many combatants on both sides died during the conflict contradicts claims that Assad was simply carrying out an air war against defenseless civilians. Such a view was confirmed by U.S. Chairman of the Joint Chiefs of Staff Martin Dempsey, who acknowledged that deaths from Syrian government airstrikes, whether of civilians or jihadist militants, while significant, never made up most of the casualties in the conflict. In April 2013, he explained that "airstrikes only account for roughly 10 percent of the total casualties in Syria, which by some estimates exceeds 80,000. Direct fire or artillery account for the remaining 90 percent."[32]

There were certainly instances, for example at the Abd al-Qader al-Husseini Mosque in Yarmouk, where the Syrian military showed a shocking disregard for civilian life when authorizing airstrikes in urban areas. But this was in the context of preventing the advance of jihadist militants.

Furthermore, the "cataract of weaponry" provided by U.S. planners and their regional allies allowed the so-called rebels to unleash mass violence, killing both Syrian soldiers and civilians by "direct fire or artillery," which was further complemented by Nusra's suicide bombers and truck bombs. This was illustrated by the FSA's shelling of pro-government neighborhoods in Homs in early 2012 and Nusra's use of artillery and suicide truck bombs in Aleppo later the same year. It is for this reason that FSA head Salim Idris felt that a "war of artillery and missiles" would be to the advantage of the al-Qaeda-dominated opposition he claimed to be leading.

Raqqa Falls to al-Qaeda

The firm alliance between the FSA and Nusra soon allowed these "Wahhabi contras" to conquer the eastern Syrian city of Raqqa in March 2013, which soon paved the way for the rise of ISIS in Syria.

Before the FSA and Nusra invasion of Raqqa, the city had been viewed as a haven from the violence and chaos raging elsewhere in the country. Rania Abouzeid writes that

> Raqqa city was once dubbed the "hotel of the revolution" because it became home to hundreds of thousands of people displaced from fighting elsewhere who sought refuge in a place considered firmly in the grip of Syrian President Bashar Assad.[33]

As a result, residents of Raqqa living under government control feared the coming "rebel" invasion of their city, while Syrians taking refuge in Raqqa feared becoming displaced by war a second time. As the invasion loomed, Al Jazeera reported that

> more than a half a million people are estimated to have fled to the northern city of al-Raqqa, doubling its population, and they now face another threat, because rebels are planning to take the city from government forces.[34]

The Al Jazeera correspondent interviewed a Raqqa resident who "made an appeal to the rebels," stating: "We can't go to another place; we fled from death and destruction. Do you want to destroy this city too? I am your sister from Deir al-Zour. Please, don't enter Raqqa."

The *Daily Star* similarly noted at the time that Raqqa's residents "had pleaded with rebels not to enter the densely built metropolitan area, fearing that Assad's war planes and artillery could target residential areas."[35] The BBC noted that even Raqqa's local representative in the opposition Syrian National Coalition (SNC) had pleaded with the Salafist armed groups not to enter the city, as "the fear now is that the regime will hit Scud missiles indiscriminately at Raqqa to punish the population."[36]

Despite clear signs that the so-called rebels had no popular support, and that most Syrian civilians preferred to live in government-controlled areas, if only for the sake of security, the Western press continued to suggest that the

Salafist militias comprising the "opposition" were fighting on behalf of the Syrian people broadly.

Despite local opposition, on March 2, 2013, Ahrar al-Sham initiated the assault on Raqqa, with help from a coalition of Salafist armed groups, including Nusra, the Farouq Brigades, and the Ahfad al-Rasoul Brigades, which were still fighting under the FSA banner.[37]

Two days later, Raqqa fell to the coalition of Salafist militias. The *Daily Star* reported that according to Mustafa Nawaf al-Ali of the opposition SNC, "Islamist brigades, including the Al-Qaeda-linked Nusra Front, Ahrar al-Sham, and the Sunni Hawks, entered Raqqa after overrunning an army position at its northern entrance."[38]

Prior to the invasion, Ahrar al-Sham apparently understood that they had little support among Raqqa's residents and sought to obscure this. Writing in *Syria Comment*, Syria researcher Matthew Barber reports that Ahrar al-Sham had created a brigade of local fighters just for the assault on Raqqa, to give the false impression of a local takeover of the city, rather than of an invasion by outsiders.[39]

This apparently did not fool the city's residents. Writing in the *New York Review of Books*, Sarah Birke, who visited Raqqa just two months after it fell, noted that the "takeover came from outside and many locals were unhappy about this."[40]

The capture of Raqqa by Salafist militias was widely celebrated by the Syrian opposition based abroad, however, despite the open participation of the al-Qaeda groups. Opposition activists viewed the fall of Raqqa as particularly significant because it was the first provincial capital to be controlled entirely by so-called opposition forces. Reuters reported that the opposition SNC claimed that the capture of Raqqa would prove "a decisive victory in the struggle for the downfall of the criminal Assad regime and to salvage Syria from the ugliest epoch in its history."[41] Some local pro-opposition activists then declared Raqqa the "icon of the revolution."[42]

U.S. officials also viewed the Salafist occupation of Raqqa, of which al-Qaeda played a prominent part, positively. On the same day Raqqa fell to America's presumed enemies, U.S. Secretary of State John Kerry announced from Riyadh that Washington would continue to work with its "friends to empower the Syrian opposition."[43]

Contrary to opposition claims, "the ugliest epoch" in the history of Raqqa was just beginning. Predictably, when the Salafist armed groups captured

Raqqa, civilians sought to flee the city en masse. *Al-Arabiya* reported that one month after Raqqa fell to opposition forces, "more than half of Raqqa residents and those who migrated to it before it was seized have fled, amounting to more than a million."[44]

Those who remained were immediately subjected to fundamentalist religious rule and terrorized by a wave of killings. Rania Abouzeid observed three weeks after the fall of the city:

> That Islamists now run this city is unmistakable. On Thursday, a massive black flag bearing the Islamic shahada ("There is no god but God and Mohammad is His messenger") was hoisted atop a flagpole in the square in front of the elegant multi-arched governorate building, near a fallen bronze statue of Hafez Assad in tribal garb... the townsfolk speak of Alawites being killed just for being Assad's coreligionists.[45]

The AP writes that even

> opponents of the Assad regime in the city have been put off by what they see as the extremists' unnecessary brutality. In the days after seizing the city, the Muslim brigades brought captured security forces into public squares, killed them and drove their bodies through the streets.[46]

Despite the harsh reality of al-Qaeda rule, secular opposition activists from the group "Raqqa Is Being Silently Slaughtered" attempted to idealize the first months after the fall of Raqqa, bizarrely claiming that the city's residents "enjoyed a period when we could work freely and walk in the streets carrying revolutionary flags."[47]

Europe Will Be Funding al-Qaeda

The fall of Raqqa to the Nusra Front, Ahrar al-Sham, and the FSA in turn paved the way for the rise of ISIS in the city, which later became the organization's Syrian capital. When Raqqa was captured by Nusra and its allies, ISIS did not have a formal presence in Syria. Then known as the Islamic State of Iraq (ISI), the group had been fighting a guerrilla war since the group's establishment in 2003 in the wake of the U.S. invasion of Iraq. Initially known as Tawhid wal-Jihad and led by Abu Musab al-Zarqawi, the group fought against U.S. occupation forces and the Shiite-led Iraqi government installed by U.S. planners. The organization was largely defeated after Zarqawi was killed in a U.S. airstrike in 2006, and after the Sunni tribes in Anbar Province waged a war against it, known as the "Awakening," in

2007. However, the organization was revived, when, as detailed in Chapter 2, Abu Bakr al-Baghdadi and other top ISIS commanders were released from U.S.-run Iraqi prisons in 2009–10. Baghdadi created the Nusra Front in the summer of 2011, when he sent a small cadre of his commanders, led by Abu Muhammad al-Jolani, to Syria in support of the already existing Salafist insurgency, in which al-Qaeda-affiliated fighters already enjoyed a strong presence.[48]

Although the Islamic State of Iraq was Nusra's parent organization, and Nusra leader Jolani was formally subordinate to ISI leader Baghdadi, in practice Nusra had become largely autonomous from ISI by the time Raqqa was captured in 2013. In response to Nusra's growing independence and power, Baghdadi sought to reassert control over Nusra, and in April 2013, shortly after the capture of Raqqa, he declared that the two groups had formally merged to form a new organization called the Islamic State of Iraq and Sham (ISIS). Jolani was apparently surprised by Baghdadi's merger declaration and promptly rejected it, causing the groups to split formally and become rivals.[49]

Journalist Theo Padnos reports that Baghdadi's effort to assert his control over Nusra resulted from a dispute over the division of oil revenues. Padnos writes that while held captive by Nusra:

> I gleaned that the two organizations were about equal in strength and that under no circumstances would the Islamic State be allowed to touch the oil fields, the real prize in Syria's east… The real issue between the Nusra Front and the Islamic State was that their commanders, former friends from Iraq, were unable to agree on how to share the revenue from the oil fields in eastern Syria that the Nusra Front had conquered.[50]

Baghdadi's effort to assert control over Nusra came two weeks after a Nusra-FSA campaign to capture the oilfields in Deir al-Zour Province had begun, suggesting that Baghdadi had anticipated Nusra's capture of these fields and the "huge money" that would soon accompany them.[51]

As the *Financial Times* reported on April 22, 2013, the prize of these oil fields became even more desired after European Union (EU) foreign ministers "lifted an oil embargo against Syria to allow rebels to sell crude to fund their operation." The *FT* quoted Guido Westerwelle, the German foreign minister, as stating, "We wish for good economic development in the areas controlled by the opposition; therefore we lift the sanctions that hinder the moderate opposition forces' work." The *FT* also quoted William Hague, the U.K. foreign secretary, as stating that while the security situation would make it difficult to export oil, it was still "important for us to send the signal that we are open to helping in other ways."[52]

Time reported:

> As part of the decision, the EU ministers also agreed to export technical equipment, insure the rebels' shipments of oil and invest in the rebel oil businesses… Since the regime controls the oil pipelines, as well as the existing export terminals on the Mediterranean, rebel groups would have to truck barrels of oil across rebel territory into Turkey, where the nearest refineries are situated and where they could — if they can produce enough oil — export to the rest of Europe.[53]

European officials were enthusiastic to help, even though it was clear that Nusra, not the FSA, was in actual control of the oilfields. *FT* noted this, reporting that, "according to activists, however, many of those oilfields are now under the control of Jabhat al-Nusra, the al-Qaeda-linked rebel group."[54]

Time similarly noted, almost as an afterthought, that "complicating the issue is the fact that several of the rebel-held oil fields are believed to be under the control of Jabhat al-Nusra, which has declared its allegiance to al-Qaeda."[55]

Three days later, on April 25, 2013, the FSA spokesman for the eastern region of Syria feigned exclusive control of oil fields jointly captured with Nusra and offered access to foreign investors in exchange for military protection, stating that "we will commit to any deal to invest in oil if air cover is provided."[56]

Lebanese *As-Safir* similarly reported over the next year that while the Turkish government

> facilitated the cross-border smuggling of oil, taking advantage of the European Union's decision to allow the purchase of oil from the Syrian opposition… the Nusra Front is the one dominating the oil trade, not the opposition "Syrian National Coalition."[57]

Syria expert Joshua Landis noted the importance of controlling the oil fields, explaining that "whoever gets their hands on the oil, water, and agriculture holds Sunni Syria by the throat," and that "the logical conclusion from this craziness is that Europe will be funding al-Qaida."[58]

ISIS later captured these oil fields and the concomitant smuggling infrastructure required to profit from them after taking control of Deir al-Zour Province from Nusra and the FSA in 2014. The smuggling of oil through Turkey became ISIS's main source of revenue, netting the group some $1.5 million per day at its height.[59]

The EU decision to lift sanctions and allow Nusra to export oil via Turkey therefore played an important role in the rise of both Nusra and ISIS. While ISIS's ability to smuggle and sell oil through Turkey later attracted considerable media attention, Nusra's previous ability to do the same, with explicit support from EU officials, was largely ignored, despite the group's recent terrorist designation.

Gaining a Foothold

Although Baghdadi's efforts to merge ISI and Nusra failed, he was nevertheless successful in allowing his organization, now named ISIS, to gain a strong foothold in Syria, starting in Raqqa. This foothold would soon allow ISIS to control much of eastern and northern Syria, laying the foundation for the so-called Caliphate.

Writing in U.S.-funded *Irfaa Sawtak*, Khalid al-Ghalli explains how ISIS gained control of Raqqa. Even though Nusra leader Jolani rejected the merger with ISI,

> this did not prevent the al-Nusra Front from losing many of its members in favor of the new organization, as well as important sources of its funding. In this way, ISIS has gained a foothold in Raqqa, with fighters, military headquarters, and checkpoints that were until recently affiliated with Al-Nusra Front... [As a result,] ISIS quickly transformed into the most powerful organization in the city, benefiting from the majority of al-Nusra fighters joining it and the support it brings from Iraq.[60]

On May 14, 2013, just six weeks after FSA and Nusra fighters captured Raqqa, making it the "icon of the revolution," NPR reported that ISIS

> executed three men in the town square in front of hundreds of people... It was a brutal display of power that announced their presence and set the tone for how ISIS would govern in Raqqa. ISIS allowed local media activists to post a video of the executions, showing fighters in black masks pushing the captive men to their knees and then shooting them at point-blank range.[61]

The AP reports further that according to a local activist, the men were Shiites who "were executed in front of everyone, young and old," and that "for several hours, nobody dared approach the bodies to take them for burial until a nurse did. The nurse, Mohammad Saado, was assassinated by unknown gunmen the next day."[62]

According to Omar al-Huwaidi, a prominent activist in Raqqa, ISIS began trying to implement a legal dress code for women and demanded the closure of shops during prayer times. Many leaders of the revolutionary movement were kidnapped and tortured by ISIS, as well as leaders in the local council and journalists.[63]

Reuters quoted an opposition activist from Raqqa, who described months later how "all the FSA cared for was stealing and accumulating money. From the first day of Raqqa's liberation they left it to the Islamic State." Reuters journalist Mariam Karouny further explained: "Residents say they know little about the fighters. They include Iraqis, Gulf Arabs, and Libyans, they say, but keep their identity hidden behind masks and avoid conversation," suggesting that Raqqa was essentially under foreign occupation by the jihadist militants.[64]

The influx of foreign jihadists and their families caused one former resident of Raqqa to tell Sarah Birke that "in a city where once neighbor knew neighbor, now many can't even speak the same language," and that "by the time I left I no longer recognized Raqqa as a Syrian town."[65]

Despite professing to be secular and democratic, the U.S.-backed Syrian National Coalition (SNC) continued to view ISIS as part of the "Revolutionary Forces" in Raqqa several months after the group made its influence in the city known.

When the Italian Jesuit priest and opposition supporter Father Paolo Dall'Oglio was kidnapped and presumed to have been murdered by ISIS after visiting Raqqa in August 2013, Wael Sawah wrote in *The Syrian Observer* that

> the National Coalition issued a poor statement on Thursday asking to uncover the fate of the pro-revolution celebrity in a province that theoretically falls under its authority. The statement did not even bother condemning the kidnapping of the priest and/or taking any political (or otherwise) action against the group that kidnapped him. The Syrian Coalition "urged" FSA battalions and the Local Council in Raqqa to "take any possible steps to ensure the safe return of Father Paolo. The Coalition stresses the need for all Revolutionary Forces to commit to the guiding principles of the Syrian Revolution including protecting civilians as well as journalists and clerics." But the farthest it could go was to emphasize "that public freedom must be enshrined in the Syrian Revolution's guiding principles and respected by all Revolutionary Forces."[66]

The SNC's celebration of the Nusra Front and Ahrar al-Sham capture of Raqqa in March 2013, and the later failure of the SNC to condemn the abduction, let alone apparent murder, of Father Paolo by ISIS, further highlighted the dirtiest secret of the entire war, namely that the foreign-backed and external political opposition had no influence on the ground in Syria. The "Syrian Revolution," with "freedom" as its "guiding principle" as articulated in SNC press releases, simply did not exist.

Winning Hearts, but Losing Minds

The Farouq Brigades, once the strongest of the FSA factions, began its slow decline at the time the Syrian Islamic Liberation Front (SILF), consisting of the major FSA groups, was created in late 2012. Part of this decline apparently resulted from its refusal to choose sides in the growing rivalry between foreign intelligence agencies jockeying for control of the insurgency. Without support from Qatar and Turkey on the one hand, nor from Saudi Arabia on the other, Farouq quickly lost influence, gaining only one position out of 30 in the newly created Supreme Military Council (SMC).[67]

Rania Abouzeid quotes Bilal Attar, the founder of the Sham News Network (SNN) and later a senior Farouq official, as describing how "the Farouq was left blowing in the wind" by its former Gulf sponsors, which chose to spend their funds supporting other armed groups.[68]

Farouq's conflict with the Nusra Front also contributed to the group's decline. The conflict was not due to ideological differences or a struggle between moderates and extremists. Rather, it revolved around the struggle for the resources and revenue that control of Syria's northern border crossings with Turkey afforded.

Opposition forces, including Farouq, had captured the Bab al-Hawa border crossing in July 2012, while Farouq captured the Tel Abyad border crossing in September 2012. Control of these crossings allowed Farouq to gain revenue from taxes levied on the passage of people, goods, and weapons across the border.[69] In September 2012, an independent jihadi commander known as Abu Mohamad al-Absi, who at one point controlled one of Bab al-Hawa's two gates, was kidnapped and killed, most likely by Farouq. Nusra retaliated in January 2013 by killing a Farouq commander in Bab al-Hawa known as Abu Ali.[70]

In March 2013, Nusra twice attempted to assassinate Farouq commander Mohammad al-Daher, better known as Abu Azzam, who controlled the Tel

Abyad border crossing for Farouq. Abu Azzam was seriously injured, while members of both Farouq and Nusra were killed in clashes between the groups.[71]

The Nusra brigade in Tel Abyad defected to ISIS in April 2013, and in May 2013 took control of the border crossing from Farouq, weakening the group even more. ISIS was then able to defeat Farouq easily because Farouq had sent many of its fighters to al-Qusayr, where FSA factions were trying to fend off an assault from the Syrian army and Lebanese Hezbollah.[72]

Once again, this was not a battle between so-called moderates and extremists. U.S. government-funded Voice of America (VOA) reported at this time that

> Farouq commanders describe the feuding as between Jihadists and more secular-minded fighters, but other rebel commanders say the strife appears to be as much a power struggle over control of the lucrative border crossings into Turkey at Tal Abyad and Bab al Hawa... Many of the Farouq fighters, especially those in northern brigades, have reputations for smuggling, looting, and extortion. Civilians in villages in Idlib and Aleppo Provinces spoke of their mistrust of Farouq fighters earlier this year to VOA, accusing them of corruption and robbery.[73]

Summarizing the demise of the previously much-vaunted Farouq, Syrian journalist Malek al-Abdeh wrote in November 2013 in *Foreign Policy*:

> Instead of making the necessary alliances needed to carve out their own fiefdom in resource-rich areas, Farouk's forces embarked on a disastrous war with two powerful families: Ahrar al-Sham and Jabhat al-Nusra. The war ended with Farouk's expulsion from oil- and grain-rich Raqqa Province; it also lost control over the vital border crossing at Tal Abyad that its fighters had liberated in September 2012. Confined to resource-poor and heavily contested Homs Province, it failed to draw smaller groups into its orbit and grew progressively weaker, eventually splintering into bickering factions of a few hundred fighters each.[74]

Farouq had also been weakened from defections, which plagued it starting in late 2012. One prominent Farouq commander, Abu Sakkar, split from the group in October 2012 to form the Independent Omar al-Farouq Brigade, which continued to fight under the FSA banner. Abu Sakkar had participated in early battles against Syrian government forces in Homs in 2011–12 and gained notoriety in April 2013 after video surfaced of him cutting out the heart and liver of a dead pro-government fighter. In the video, Abu Sakkar threatens to slaughter Alawites and cut out their hearts and eat them. He then appears to take a bite of the dead fighter's heart.[75] Abu Sakkar later joined the Nusra Front and was killed in battle in April 2016.[76]

More defections occurred when, in early 2013, Farouq co-founder and financier, the Salafi Sheikh Amjad Bitar, was asked to resign due to an internal dispute within the group. He took his significant funding and the majority of the group's fighters with him to form the Farouq Islamic Brigades, thereby weakening the original Farouq organization further.[77] Rania Abouzeid quoted an early civilian Farouq leader as claiming: "Amjad Bitar was like a bank… and when he was removed, the Bank of the Farouq collapsed."[78]

The Farouq Islamic Brigades led by Bitar remained a member of the SILF, which continued to receive support from the U.S.-backed SMC. According to its official media outlet, the group positioned itself "as a pious Islamist fighting organization waging jihad against the Assad government." In videos released by the group,

> Kata'ib al-Farouq fighters are referred to as mujahideen (those waging jihad) and are shown in prayer before battle. In some of its media content, [Farouq Islamic Brigade] fighters wave the black flag of jihad, and display the jihadist flag popularized by the Islamic State of Iraq.[79]

Pragmatic Reasons

Although Raqqa immediately became not a secular democratic paradise, but rather an Islamist dystopia, and the so-called armed opposition was dominated by openly Salafist groups such as the Farouq Brigades, opposition activists nevertheless performed the needed mental gymnastics to perpetuate the myth of a secular, democratic opposition wishing to free Syria from a brutal dictator.

In their book *Burning Country: Syrians in Revolution and War* (2016), Syrian-British authors Robin Yassin-Kassab and Lina al-Shami bizarrely cited a Gulf-funded study to claim that the majority of Syrian members of Ahrar al-Sham and the Nusra Front agreed that "democracy is preferable to any form of government," and that the role of both al-Qaeda-affiliated groups in the insurgency was of little concern because these fighters had joined only for "pragmatic reasons" and "it is probable that many of these men will leave the jihadist ranks once Assad falls."[80]

Although many young men did join Nusra, ISIS, and other Salafist militias for pragmatic reasons, they soon underwent a program of ideological indoctrination, causing them to become committed jihadists, ready to sacrifice and die for the cause.

Secular opposition leaders appeared to have pragmatic reasons of their own to support the Salafist armed groups forming the so-called armed opposition. These leaders hoped to ride the jihadist wave to take power for themselves should the Syrian government fall. For example, prominent secular opposition leader Suhair al-Atassi made a public appearance in Tal Abyad in October 2012, after the Farouq Brigades had taken control of the town. The Carnegie Middle East Center writes that Atassi "described her visit as a show of support for the Free Syrian Army and evidence that armed rebels are fighting for a civil state."[81]

As noted in Chapter 12, secular opposition activist Michel Kilo had similarly praised Nusra in February 2013 after the group captured Ras al-Ayn, and George Sabra had declared Nusra as "part of the revolutionary movement" in December 2012 after it was put on the U.S. terror list.

Observing the pronouncements of Atassi, Kilo, Sabra, and others, Syrian academic Mark Tomass explained that

> the secular opposition believed that a violent overthrow of the regime would still bring them to power. Since they had no armed groups representing them on the ground, they served with the blessings of their Western and Arab sponsors as the spokesmen for the Islamist fighters, including al-Qaida.[82]

Ambassador Ford's All-Stars

Despite Baghdadi's failed takeover of Nusra in April 2013, ISIS initially continued to cooperate closely with Nusra and various FSA factions, both in Raqqa and elsewhere. FSA commander Abd al-Jabbar al-Okaidi, the head of the U.S.-backed Revolutionary Military Council in Aleppo, described his close relationship with the two al-Qaeda affiliates during this time. As noted in Chapter 11, Okaidi stated in an interview with Orient TV that Nusra was itself part of the FSA, estimating that Nusra fighters "constitute perhaps 10% of the FSA in the city of Aleppo and in Syria."[83] Okaidi then told the interviewer that ISIS was an important partner of the FSA as well: "My relationship with the brothers in ISIS is good... I communicate almost daily with the brothers in ISIS to settle these disputes and issues" that emerged after the Nusra/ISIS schism. Okaidi further denied that ISIS was a "takfiri" organization (with *takfir* referring to the practice of excommunicating and then killing other Muslims for holding views Salafists consider heretical).[84]

This was of course bizarre, given that the misuse of takfir is what ISIS and its predecessor organizations were perhaps best known for, after a decade of sectarian barbarism against fellow Muslims in Iraq.

ISIS leaders in Aleppo had similarly kind words for the FSA. Al Jazeera reports that according to Abu Atheer, the ISIS commander for Aleppo Province at the time:

> We are buying weapons from the FSA. We bought 200 anti-aircraft missiles and Konkurs anti-tank weapons. We have good relations with our brothers in the FSA. For us, the infidels are those who cooperate with the West to fight Islam.[85]

Note that Abu Atheer was the same ISIS commander who by this time in the summer of 2013 was holding James Foley and other foreign journalists and aid workers captive.[86]

According to reporting by the *Los Angeles Times*, Konkurs missiles were provided to FSA groups via the CIA's regional allies, while CIA officers trained FSA fighters in the use of these weapons in Jordan and Turkey starting in November 2012.[87] In August 2013, one month after the Al Jazeera report, journalist Joanna Paraszczuk noted that video had emerged of Okaidi's Liwa al-Tawhid fighters using Konkurs anti-tank missiles to bombard Syrian army armored vehicles at Menagh air base.[88]

This suggests that both Liwa al-Tawhid and ISIS ultimately received these missiles from the same source in the FSA's Supreme Military Council (SMC). Colonel Okaidi was likely responsible for the sale of these weapons to ISIS commander Abu Atheer, as Okaidi was both the head of the SMC's Armament Committee for the Northern Front and acknowledged coordinating closely with ISIS.[89] Other Salafist militias, including Ahrar al-Sham and Jaish al-Islam, also managed to acquire the CIA-supplied Konkurs missiles.[90]

Importantly, Okaidi also enjoyed a good relationship with U.S. Ambassador to Syria Robert Ford. One month after FSA factions, ISIS, and Nusra conquered Raqqa, Ford took the risk to cross the border secretly from Turkey to meet personally with Okaidi in May 2013.[91]

Ambassador Ford had himself been involved in the CIA effort to provide weapons to the FSA via the agency's regional allies. As mentioned in Chapter 10, Ford had traveled to Langley, Virginia, to meet with CIA Director David Petraeus in 2012 to discuss plans to provide weapons covertly to the Syrian opposition.[92]

Ford was presumably meeting with Okaidi in May 2013 to coordinate the supply of Konkurs missiles, though Ford later claimed to be delivering only non-lethal aid to Okaidi and his men.[93]

Ford's Syria visit was followed by that of U.S. Senator John McCain, who met with FSA leaders in Turkey and briefly inside Syria the same month. The BBC reported that McCain had "repeatedly urged more forceful American support of Syrian rebels, calling for U.S. cruise missiles to target Syrian government forces," and that "he has also repeatedly urged that the insurgents should be armed." During the visit with McCain, FSA head Salim Idris "called for weapons to continue their fight," as well as for a no-fly zone and airstrikes on government targets and Lebanese Hezbollah.[94]

One week prior to McCain's visit, an FSA spokesman had threatened genocide against Syria's Shia and Alawite minorities. This was in response to reports that the town of al-Qusayr might soon be recaptured by the Syrian army, with the crucial assistance of Hezbollah fighters.

Bloomberg reported:

> Communities inhabited by Shiite Muslims and President Bashar al-Assad's Alawite minority will be "wiped off the map" if the strategic city of Al-Qusair in central Syria falls to government troops, rebel forces said.[95]

Colonel Abdel-Hamid Zakaria, a spokesman for the FSA in Turkey, explained further:

> The same applies to Alawite villages. We don't wish this thing at all, but it will be something out of control. Who would be able to control and restrain thousands of fighters full of the spirit of revenge? Who would be able to control all those people?[96]

Bloomberg further cited David Hartwell, senior Middle East analyst at IHS Jane's, who acknowledged:

> While it may suit states such as Qatar, Saudi Arabia, and even the United States to see this type of sectarian conflict develop as a means of retarding the regional influence of Iran (via Hezbollah) and al-Qaeda, the results in terms of long-term regional instability could be dramatic.[97]

White House Chief of Staff Denis McDonough also emphasized the importance of weakening Iran via Syria at this time, while acknowledging that the insurgency was dominated by al-Qaeda. The *New York Times* reported that according to McDonough, "the status quo in Syria could keep

Iran pinned down for years," and "a fight in Syria between Hezbollah and Al Qaeda would work to America's advantage."[98]

Prominent Sunni cleric Yusuf al-Qaradawi also escalated his rhetoric in response to Hezbollah's efforts to liberate Qusayr from its jihadist occupiers. Terrorism researchers Thomas Hegghammer and Aaron Y. Zelin noted at the time:

> A Pandora's box was opened in the Middle East in late May. That was when Yusuf al-Qaradawi, the Egyptian theologian who is perhaps the world's most influential Sunni cleric, called on Sunni Muslims worldwide to fight against the regime of President Bashar al-Assad and Hezbollah in Syria.[99]

A prominent member of the Muslim Brotherhood and the author of more than one hundred books, Qaradawi had left Egypt for Qatar in 1961 and became a celebrity through his weekly television show on Al Jazeera which enjoyed tens of millions of viewers.

In keeping with the policy of his Qatari sponsors, Qaradawi had called for toppling the Syrian government in April 2011, claiming in a Friday sermon that the "train of the revolution has reached its station in Syria." Qaradawi was criticized for his sectarianism at the time because he stated in the same sermon that "the people treat President Assad as if he is Sunni — he is educated, young, and can accomplish a lot — but his problem is that he is a prisoner of his entourage and of his [Alawite] sect."[100]

Qaradawi later sought to incite Syrian Sunnis against not only Alawites but also fellow Sunnis found to be supporters of the government. In December 2012, he claimed on Al Jazeera that it was necessary to fight anyone supporting the Syrian government, "whether combatants or civilians, religious clerics or the ignorant."[101]

During the interview, Qaradawi specifically criticized Muhammad Said Ramadan al-Bouti, the country's most prominent Sunni cleric and a staunch critic of Salafism, for his support for the Syrian government. Known as the "Shaykh of the Levant," Bouti was assassinated by opposition militants three months later, in March 2013.[102]

The Hatla Massacre

On June 5, 2013, the Syrian army and Hezbollah successfully recaptured Qusayr, as opposition leaders feared that they would. A week later, FSA and Nusra fighters made good on their previous threats and carried out a massacre in the Shia town of Hatla, near Deir al-Zour city.

The *New York Times* reported that the Syrian government called the killings "a massacre of civilians, saying that 30 died," but that

> antigovernment activists put the toll at 60 and said most of the dead were pro-government militia fighters who had attacked rebels one day earlier…
>
> Several battalions of Sunni rebels, including members of extremist Islamist groups, stormed the village and, in video posted online by antigovernment activists, could be seen setting houses on fire as they shouted sectarian slogans, calling Shiites dogs, apostates and infidels.
>
> "This is your end, you dogs," a man off camera said as he panned across what he said were the corpses of "pug nosed" Shiites, including one with what appeared to be a gunshot wound to the head. "We have raised the banner of 'There Is No God but God' over the houses of the rejectionist Shiite apostates," one fighter chanted in another clip as a black cloud billowed above the village and jubilant gunmen brandished black flags often used by the extremist Al Nusra Front and other Islamist fighting groups.[103]

Al Jazeera similarly reported that a video supplied by SOHR "showed masked fighters shouting, 'Here are the Mujahidin [Islamist fighters] celebrating entering the homes of the rejectionists, the Shias.' The fighters added that they 'burned the homes' of the Shia residents."[104]

The participation of FSA factions was confirmed by an opposition activist who told the AP after the killings that "the situation in the village is quiet, and the [rebel] Free Syrian Army is in full control."[105]

While acknowledging the role of the FSA, opposition activists at the same time sought to obscure the sectarian nature of the killings. *The Independent* reports:

> Activists denied that the killings were sectarian in nature, claiming instead that they were a response to an attack on a Free Syrian Army checkpoint by 30 armed villagers from Hatla. The activists claim the opposition fighters were incited by the Assad regime's decision to arm the population of Hatla, one of the only Shia villages in an area that has been firmly under rebel control for more than a year. However, the language used in the videos is explicitly sectarian. "This is the Shia, this is the Shia carcass, this is their end," the cameraman says as a blanket is lifted from one of the victims. That video, posted by a pro-Assad group, indicates those responsible were non-Syrians, possibly from Kuwait.[106]

Kuwaiti Salafi cleric and Nusra fundraiser, Shafi al-Ajmi, made it clear that the FSA and Nusra had attacked Hatla out of revenge for the loss of Qusayr. *The Independent* reports:

> In a speech in front of the Lebanese embassy in Kuwait, Salafi Sheikh Shafi al Ajmi, one of the most outspoken supporters of the Syrian opposition, said the attack was retaliation for the recent fighting in Qusayr,

and that Syria would be "a burying ground" for Hezbollah.[107]

Furthermore, in addition to the threats made by FSA spokesman Colonel Abdel-Hamid Zakaria that Shiite and Alawite villages would be "wiped off the map," FSA and Liwa al-Tawhid commander Abd al-Jabbar al-Okaidi had also threatened to target Shia civilians in response to the fighting in Qusayr. *Al-Quds Al-Arabi* reported that Okaidi had publicly threatened to launch advanced rockets at civilian areas in the southern suburbs of Beirut, known as Dahiya, where residents are primarily Shia and where Hezbollah enjoys strong support. Okaidi also claimed that his fighters would attack the bases of pro-government militias (*shabiha*), specifically in "the Shiite villages in Syria," mentioning the towns of Nubl and Zahra by name, in response to Hezbollah's role in Qusayr.[108]

The attack on Hatla further shows that the FSA groups in Deir al-Zour and elsewhere were not secular in orientation, nor fighting for democracy or human rights. Instead, they viewed themselves as fighting a sectarian war against Alawites and Shiites and for the establishment of a fundamentalist religious state.

Atmosphere of Crisis

The June 2013 opposition loss of al-Qusayr was a bitter blow to the Western-backed Salafist insurgency, as the town was located near the Lebanese border and was the doorway for supplying weapons to the FSA and Nusra in Syria's third-largest city, Homs. A Syrian general explained: "Whoever controls Qusayr controls the centre of the country, and whoever controls the centre of the country controls all of Syria."[109]

Not only jihadists and sectarian Salafist preachers but also U.S. planners began to panic as a result. The *New York Times* reported that the loss of Qusayr and the attendant "collapse of rebel positions in western Syria fueled the atmosphere of crisis" in the White House during this time.[110] *Politico* reports that during the second week of June 2013, Obama administration officials held a series of meetings to review U.S. policy toward Syria. The White House "concluded that a more direct U.S. intervention — one that includes arming the rebels or possibly imposing a no-fly zone — was needed to stem the tide of Assad victories in the past two weeks."[111]

Amidst this atmosphere, Reuters reported that the United States would deploy Patriot missiles and F-16 fighter jets to Jordan for military exercises, and that "U.S. officials left open the possibility they could remain in place" after the exercises had ended. Reuters notes further that "the decision to send Patriot missiles to Jordan is particularly controversial for Russia," which suspected that the missiles would be used to impose a no-fly zone over Syria, "heralding the first direct Western military intervention in the conflict."[112]

Preparations to impose a no-fly zone over southern Syria via Jordan complemented NATO's standing ability to enforce a no-fly zone over the north of the country using missiles based in Turkey. On March 19, 2013, NATO chief Admiral James Stavridis told Senator John McCain as a result that "we are prepared, if called upon, to be engaged as we were in Libya."[113]

On June 6, 2013, both McCain and Senator Lindsey Graham reiterated their desperation for intervention by again calling for President Obama to establish a no-fly zone. McCain claimed to CNN that "vital national security interests are at stake," and that "we should be able to establish a no-fly zone relatively easily."[114] One month before, McCain had made his motivations clear, explaining that "the fall of Bashar al-Assad would be the greatest blow to Iran in twenty-five years."[115]

The main obstacle preventing the Western military intervention demanded by Senators McCain and Graham as well as other hawks at this time was not Russia, however, but President Obama. While authorizing covert military support to the opposition, Obama at the same time refused to authorize direct U.S. military intervention, whether in the form of a no-fly zone or bombing campaign, against the Syrian army.

The desperation of these hawkish elements within the U.S. foreign policy establishment to intervene militarily on behalf of the FSA and Nusra was accompanied at this time by an increase in allegations claiming that Assad had used chemical weapons against civilians. Crucially, Syrian government use of chemical weapons was the one thing that could cause Obama to green-light Western military intervention, because of the infamous "red line."

15. Israel's Red Line

Whose Red Line?

In August 2012, almost a year before the Syrian army's liberation of Qusayr, President Obama had stated:

> We cannot have a situation in which chemical or biological weapons are falling into the hands of the wrong people... We have been very clear to the Assad regime but also to other players on the ground that a red line for us is, we start seeing a whole bunch of weapons moving around or being utilized.[1]

Obama stated further that any such use of chemical weapons "would change my calculus... would change my equation," and open the door to U.S. military intervention in the conflict.

According to the *New York Times*, the red line originated after

> American intelligence agencies began picking up communications with ominous signals that Mr. Assad's military was moving chemical weapons and possibly mixing them in preparation for use. Mr. Obama ordered a series of urgent meetings, and on Aug. 20 [2012] he made a comment that would come to haunt him.[2]

Surprisingly, however, the concept of the red line did not originate with Obama. The *Wall Street Journal* reported that

> the use of the "red line" expression in the context of Syrian chemical weapons started with Israeli officials, who used the phrase in private discussions with their American counterparts. It quickly became part of internal administration discussions. George Little, the Pentagon spokesman, used the phrase publicly in July 2012, and then-Secretary of State Hillary Clinton used it during a visit to Turkey. One top administration official was so worried about the "red-line" talk in the halls of the White House and State Department that he asked aides not to use the phrase.[3]

Worries about the "red line talk" were likely driven by the realization that this strongly incentivized the opposition to make false claims that the Syrian army had used chemical weapons, thereby pressuring Obama to authorize direct U.S. military intervention.

For example, journalist Charles Glass reported that a former U.S. Ambassador to the Middle East told him that Obama's "red line" was an "open invitation to a false flag operation."[4]

Secretary of State Clinton also began to promote the idea of a no-fly zone at this time, following her meeting with Turkish Foreign Minister Ahmet Davutoğlu in Istanbul. Clinton said that she and Davutoğlu agreed that a no-fly zone and other assistance for the so-called rebels "need greater in-depth analysis."[5]

Although the idea of imposing a no-fly zone sounds rather benign, and oriented at defending civilians, Michael O'Hanlon, a national security and defense policy specialist at the Brookings Institution, warned in response to Clinton's comments that "you have to consider the slippery-slope phenomenon... how this could evolve from a no-fly zone to a no-go zone" as the Libya intervention did. "If no-fly fails to stop Assad's attacks," O'Hanlon warned, "then there's a lot of pressure to strike at Syrian tanks and artillery."[6]

During a private speech to investment banking firm Goldman Sachs in 2013, Clinton acknowledged that a no-fly zone in Syria would lead to direct U.S. or NATO intervention that would kill many civilians. She explained that

> to have a no-fly zone you have to take out all of the air defense, many of which are located in populated areas. So our missiles, even if they are standoff missiles so we're not putting our pilots at risk — you're going to kill a lot of Syrians... So, all of a sudden this intervention that people talk about so glibly becomes an American and NATO involvement where you take [out] a lot of civilians.[7]

Despite her private reservations, Clinton continued to advocate a no-fly zone publicly. This suggests that the "slippery slope" phenomenon was clearly understood by Clinton and others in the Obama administration. Using the rhetoric of a no-fly zone was simply a way to rebrand what would be a politically unpalatable war of aggression killing many civilians as a humanitarian effort to protect civilians.

Another Model for Regime Change

But calls for a no-fly zone as part of a regime change effort in Syria were not new. As mentioned in Chapter 1, U.S.-based opposition activist Farid Ghadry, a favorite of neoconservative Bush administration officials, described his "practical plan to destabilize Bashar Assad's rule," which involved taking "people to [the] streets. Some people get killed. The international community gets further angry at the regime. Then, have NATO forces protect a safe zone in northern Syria... This way we will move right away into Syria."[8]

Opposition leaders made similar demands for Western intervention soon after the anti-government protests and accompanying Salafist insurgency began in March 2011. In September of that year, opposition activist Rami Jarrah (speaking under the pseudonym Alexander Page) was asked what the international community could do to help the opposition. Jarrah replied, "Well, what people actually want is pressure on the neighbouring countries so that they might do something, and what that may be is international intervention even of a military sort."[9]

In December 2011, during a bloody battle between the Syrian army and the FSA's Farouq Brigades in the Baba Amr neighborhood of Homs, Jarrah appeared on CNN alongside another activist from the city. The activist explained, "We want your help… We just need a no-fly zone, and more pressure on al-Assad's regime."[10]

In April 2012, as the fighting in Homs continued, Dr. Mousa al-Kurdi, a prominent opposition activist based in Britain, told Al Jazeera, "Either you defend us, or you arm the Syrian Free Army to defend us. You have the choice."[11]

Many outside observers have noted that provoking Western military intervention, as occurred in Libya, was the opposition's best strategy to topple the Syrian government. Azmi Bishara writes that "a number of [opposition] politicians were betting on international intervention to protect the revolution according to the Libyan model, which was present in their minds."[12]

Similarly, in June 2011, as the NATO bombing campaign in Libya was already underway, Syria expert David Lesch observed that the fall of Qaddafi would provide "another model for regime change" that could be applied to Syria, namely "that of limited but targeted military support from the West combined with an identifiable rebellion."[13]

The Libyan capital of Tripoli fell to Islamist militias fighting under the cover of NATO bombs three months later, on August 28, 2011. Qaddafi was taken captive and brutally murdered (sodomized with a bayonet and then shot in the head) by these same forces on October 20, 2011.[14]

Because of Libya, the Syrian opposition and its regional backers — in particular Saudi Arabia, France, and Turkey — were convinced that a U.S.-led intervention was imminent in Syria as well.

In September 2011, as fighting continued with the last vestiges of the Libyan army in Qaddafi's hometown of Sirte, Erdoğan visited the country and vowed that Assad would soon share Qaddafi's fate.[15] Erdoğan told a cheering crowd: "Today, Libya. Tomorrow, Syria."[16]

Christopher Phillips of Chatham House notes that as early as October 2011, Syrian opposition activists were calling for a no-fly zone at Friday demonstrations, and that leading members of the opposition Syrian National Council (SNC), such as Bourhan Ghalioun and Bassma Kodmani, "spoke of their preference for military intervention at the beginning of 2012, as if it was a realistic possibility." According to Kodmani, because intervention in Libya had succeeded, the regional powers were assuring the opposition: "It is coming, it is coming definitely, the intervention is coming."[17]

Prominent opposition activist Michel Kilo later observed, "We were naïve... people believed the Americans were going to intervene... Encouraged by the West — France in the lead — the insurgents believed it."[18]

Laughing Among Ourselves

This raises the question of what legitimacy opposition leaders such as Basma Kodmani and Bourhan Ghalioun had to justify their calls for Western intervention. It was assumed that because they were Syrian, they must be speaking on behalf of the Syrian people. However, neither Kodmani nor Ghalioun had any significant standing among Syrians.

A member of the French foreign ministry noted that "we laughed among ourselves when listening to these opposition figures," including Kodmani, Ghalioun, Suhair al-Atassi, and others, "who had their business in Arabia, their home in Paris, and for the most part had not set foot in Syria for years."[19]

Kodmani and Ghalioun were then recruited by the Muslim Brotherhood to put a secular face on the otherwise Islamist-dominated opposition, namely the SNC. Another secular opposition figure, Haytham Manna, recalled that in one of a series of meetings between April and June 2011,

> Ghazwan Masri, a businessman close to the Islamists, asked me to participate in a preparatory symposium for the transitional council. I told him that I would like to know the program. He then opened his computer and I saw the names of the sixteen participants: Fourteen Islamists or the like and only two secularists. I told him that Syria was not made up of 80% Islamists and 20% secularists. It was not serious.[20]

Bernard Henri Levy, the prominent French novelist and Israel advocate who took credit for convincing French President Nicholas Sarkozy to intervene in Libya in 2011, was also a strong voice for intervention. In June 2012, Levy sought to promote his view that the "successful intervention in Libya can serve as a blueprint" for intervention in Syria. In July 2012, Levy told Saudi-owned *Al-Arabiya*, "I think that it is even more doable in Syria than it was in Libya."[21]

Levy's appetite for Western military intervention was not unique to him. It was shared by the French foreign policy establishment generally, which had undergone dramatic change since 2003, when France had opposed the looming U.S. invasion of Iraq. Journalist Alain Gresh observed in *Le Monde Diplomatique* that since that time, France's foreign policy has been marked by "a closer strategic alliance with Israel and shifting toward the American neoconservative position on Iran." Gresh notes further that the 2012 "election of [Socialist] François Hollande to the presidency has changed none of this."[22]

In August 2012, Bernard Henri Levy slammed the newly elected Hollande's policy on Syria as "too passive," while explaining that "the attack plans are ready… Everyone knows it will not take much to deal the [Syrian] regime a death blow. All we need is a pilot."[23]

However, both Hollande and his appointment for foreign minister, Laurent Fabius, would later prove to be hawks regarding intervention in Syria. Fabius stated in August 2012 that "Bashar al-Assad does not deserve to be on earth," and also, in December 2012, that the "Nusra Front is doing a good job."[24]

Waiting for Washington

Not only French but also British officials were eager to apply the successful Libya model to Syria. As author Nu'man Abd al-Wahid details, it was not the U.S., but rather Britain, at the forefront of the NATO intervention in Libya, with British Prime Minister David Cameron and the right-wing U.K. press castigating President Obama for his hesitancy in authorizing military force.[25]

The first British cruise missiles and RAF Tornado warplanes were directed toward Libyan targets on March 21, 2011. A week later, on March 29, *Forbes* published a report from the private intelligence firm Stratfor detailing French and British motivations for intervention, including a desire for access to Libya's oil resources and to sell weapons to a pro-Western

Qaddafi successor regime. Stratfor concluded: "In a sense, France and the United Kingdom are replaying their 19th century roles of colonial European powers looking to project power and protect interests outside the European continent."[26]

The British role in Libya included not only bombing from the air, but also deploying al-Qaeda-affiliated militants to fight on the ground, militants which British intelligence had been harboring in the U.K., most notably in Manchester, for decades. As detailed in Chapter 10, U.K. intelligence had facilitated the travel of Libyan Islamic Fighting Group (LIFG) militants from Britain to Libya to fight against Qaddafi in early 2011.

After the U.K. destroyed the Libyan state and plunged the country into chaos, British General Sir David Richards prepared to implement similar plans in Syria. *The Telegraph* reports that General Richards prepared a plan for the British army "to build, train, and equip a 100,000-strong Syrian rebel army to overthrow President Bashar al-Assad," and that

> rebels would have been chosen over a 12-month period from groups already fighting the regime, and taken for training to neighbouring Jordan and Turkey, which both support the uprising. Those numbers would then, in theory, have been able to sustain the momentum of an attack on Damascus, particularly if backed by air power provided by the West and friendly Gulf countries. The plan would have been a larger-scale version of the intervention in Libya in 2011.[27]

Note that 2012 was the time when U.K. intelligence was facilitating the travel of British jihadists such as Muhammad Emwazi to Syria to fight for Katibat al-Muhajireen.

Prime Minister Cameron ultimately called off direct U.K. military intervention in Syria in 2012, claiming that "it would be unsellable to Washington as well as contrary to Parliamentary and public opinion." This led General Richards to complain later that Cameron didn't "have the balls" to go through with it.[28]

But with claims of Syrian government use of chemical weapons after the fall of Qusayr a year later, in May 2013, discussion of a possible British-American military intervention in Syria was revived.

Ludicrous Claims

The first claims of Syrian government chemical weapons use had already appeared the year before, shortly after Obama declared his famous red line, in August 2012.

Following a visit to Syria in September 2012, opposition activist Ammar Abdulhamid wrote for the neoconservative Foundation for the Defense of Democracies (FDD) that

> recently, and following a takeover by rebels of a missile base near Damascus, one of the people affiliated with the old operations room encouraged rebels to claim that some missiles had chemical warheads in the hope that this will show the Americans that their red line was being challenged. The claim, of course, was ludicrous.[29]

By "operations room," Abdulhamid was referring to the "Istanbul control room." Rania Abouzeid reported in September 2012 that

> a secretive group operates something like a command center in Istanbul, directing the distribution of vital military supplies believed to be provided by Saudi Arabia and Qatar and transported with the help of Turkish intelligence to the Syrian border and then to the rebels,

and that "Saudi Arabia's man" in the control room was Lebanese Future Party politician Okab Sakr.[30]

In other words, it was foreign intelligence agencies encouraging so-called rebels to claim that Syrian government missiles were armed with chemical warheads.

The issue of chemical weapons arose again in late November 2012, when Israeli officials claimed to have satellite imagery of Syrian troops mixing sarin at two storage sites and using it to fill dozens of 500-pound bombs that could allegedly be loaded onto airplanes. Obama administration officials were told that the sarin-armed planes "could be airborne in less than two hours — too fast for the United States to act, in all likelihood." According to the *New York Times*, the incident "renewed debate about whether the West should help the Syrian opposition destroy Mr. Assad's air force, which he would need to deliver those 500-pound bombs."[31]

Opposition leader George Sabra seized on these allegations to demand Western military intervention, claiming that Assad would not "hesitate to commit such atrocities as he approaches his inevitable end unless he faces firm and unequivocal international opposition," and that "we ask the countries of the world to act before disaster hits, not after."[32]

According to later reporting from journalist Seymour Hersh, the alleged filling of bombs with sarin was the result of activity picked up by a system of on-the-ground sensors used by Israeli and U.S. intelligence to monitor any movement of Syria's chemical weapon arsenals. Hersh later confirmed that the Syrian government was not preparing for a chemical attack, but that the "event was later determined to be part of a series of exercises," and that "all militaries constantly carry out such exercises."[33]

Two weeks later, on December 23, 2012, opposition sources claimed that the Syrian army had carried out a chemical attack using sarin in the city of Homs. Al Jazeera reported claims that at least seven people had died after inhaling a poisonous gas "sprayed by government forces in a rebel-held Homs neighbourhood," and that according to Raji Rabbou, an activist in the city: "We don't know what this gas is, but medics are saying it's something similar to sarin gas."[34] Opposition activists also released videos of the casualties from the alleged chemical attack.[35]

Claims of a chemical attack in Homs were apparently reinforced by reporting from journalist Josh Rogin in *Foreign Policy*. Rogin provided details of a leaked cable from the U.S. consulate in Istanbul, which supposedly confirmed the use of chemical weapons by the Syrian government after an exhaustive investigation. Rather than sarin, the cables suggested that another chemical, known as Agent 15, or BZ, was used.[36]

This claim was quickly called into question, however. Tommy Vietor, a White House spokesman, explained that Rogin's claims were not "consistent with what we believe to be true about the Syrian chemical weapons program," while a State Department spokesperson added, in response to the reporting by Rogin, that there was "no credible evidence to corroborate or to confirm that chemical weapons were used."[37]

CNN reported on January 16, 2013, that "the concern triggered a more extensive investigation by the State Department," and that according to a senior U.S. official,

> the gas was determined to be a "riot control agent" that was not designed to produce lasting effects... But just like with tear gas, if you breathe in an entire canister, that can have a severe effect on your lungs and other organs... That doesn't make it a chemical weapon, however.[38]

Yahoo News similarly reported:

> If recent media reports have left an impression that Syrian President Bashar Assad might already have used chemical weapons against his own people, think again, says arms expert Jeffrey Lewis. The scholar on weapons of mass destruction is assailing the credibility of Syrian opposition allegations that the chemical "Agent 15" was dispensed in the restive northern city of Homs on Dec. 23.[39]

Lewis himself noted that "the Istanbul consulate cable was based on accounts by a contractor, [Analysis] Research Knowledge or 'ARK,' which in turn used a Syrian group known as Basma to interview 'three contacts' about the alleged attack." ARK is in turn funded by the U.K. Foreign Office, meaning that, according to Lewis, "these appear to be U.S.- and U.K.-funded groups that produce anti-regime propaganda... Are we really surprised that they are alleging chemical weapons use?"

The role of the U.K.-funded contractor ARK in promoting false allegations of a chemical attack in Homs is important because it suggests the involvement of British intelligence in seeking to trigger Obama's red line.

Not only British but also Saudi intelligence was promoting questionable evidence of a chemical attack that would trigger the red line. The *Wall Street Journal* reported that

> the Saudis, who have close ties to rebel factions, played an important early role in collecting evidence, Arab diplomats said. This past winter [early 2013], the Saudis flew to the U.K. a Syrian who was suspected of having been exposed to a chemical agent.[40]

While momentum was building to blame the Syrian government for a chemical attack, U.S. Chairman of the Joint Chiefs of Staff General Martin Dempsey also pushed back against this narrative, arguing: "I think that Syria must understand by now that the use of chemical weapons is unacceptable. And to that extent, it provides a deterrent value."[41] Another senior U.S. defense official also noted: "I think the Russians understood this is the one thing that could get us to intervene in the war." In other words, there was no doubt on all sides who would benefit from the Syrian government carrying out a chemical attack, and it was not the Syrian government.[42]

The Khan al-Assal Chemical Attack

A few months later, the issue of chemical weapons emerged once again. On March 19, 2013, a rocket containing chemicals was fired at the town of Khan al-Assal in Aleppo Province in northern Syria. According to the U.K.-funded SOHR, the attack killed 25, including, crucially, 16 Syrian soldiers.[43]

Because Syrian soldiers had been killed, this suggested that opposition militant groups were responsible. However, opposition sources quickly claimed that the government had carried out the attack instead, killing its own soldiers. The pro-opposition Aleppo Media Centre, which, as journalist Vanessa Beeley details, received funding from the French foreign ministry,[44] claimed that there had been cases of "suffocation and poison" among civilians in Khan al-Assal after a surface-to-surface missile was fired at the town, and that it was "most likely" due to the use of "poisonous gases" by the Syrian government.[45]

Abd al-Jabbar al-Okaidi, head of the FSA's Aleppo Military Council, claimed that he had witnessed the attack, and that it was not a surface-to-surface missile, but "an errant strike on a government-controlled neighborhood by Syrian warplanes flying at high altitude."[46]

U.S. officials also sought to deflect blame from the opposition. Martin Chulov of *The Guardian* reported that

> Washington, which has for the past six months claimed that only the use of chemical weapons could lead it to overturn its opposition to direct intervention in Syria, later said it had "no reason to believe" rebels had been responsible but was studying claims that the regime may have been.[47]

Claims of Syrian government responsibility were immediately dubious. To believe them would mean that the Syrian government had done the "one thing" that could get the U.S. to intervene, while entrusting the operation to military commanders who were inept enough to kill 16 of their own soldiers accidentally in the process.

Assad's Slam Dunk

The Syrian government itself felt that opposition responsibility was clear and sent a letter to UN Secretary General Ban Ki-moon the day after the Khan al-Assal attack, on March 20, requesting that the UN "conduct a specialized, impartial, and independent investigation of the alleged [chemical] incident." Ban Ki-moon quickly agreed to launch an investigation, appointing Swedish professor Ake Sellstrom, a former weapons inspector in Iraq, as its head on March 26.[48]

However, as open-source analyst Adam Larson details, Western diplomats immediately sought to torpedo the Syrian government's request for an objective investigation into the Khan al-Assal incident.[49] British and French diplomats promptly demanded that the investigation focus not only on the March 19 attack in Khan al-Assal, but also on other alleged chemical attacks that might be blamed on the Syrian government. These included the December 2012 incident in Homs as well as a new claim of a Syrian government chemical attack in the Damascus suburb of Ataybah, which also allegedly took place on March 19, 2013, the day of the Khan al-Assal attack.[50]

The *New York Times* reported that

Britain and France have written separately to Secretary General Ban Ki-moon of the United Nations that there is credible information suggesting Syria's government has used chemical weapons in the civil war on multiple occasions since last December... There had been an exchange of letters with the secretary general starting on March 25 about the information, which they would not reveal in detail.[51]

Despite the British and French request, UN spokesman Martin Nesirky stated on March 26 that "work is already well under way so that the mission can be dispatched quickly."[52]

But by April 8, 2013, Ban had accepted the British and French request and "urged the Syrian government to accept an expanded UN probe into alleged chemical weapons use, saying he had concluded that an alleged attack in Homs in December [2012] warrants investigation."[53]

Syria's representative to the UN, Bashar al-Jaafari, claimed that an agreement had already been reached four days before, on April 4, 2013, with the UN's disarmament head Angela Kane, a former German diplomat and World Bank official, to deploy the UN mission only to Khan al-Assal. According to Jaafari, "Kane then went back on the agreement... and delivered a letter the next day contrary to the previous agreement." Kane justified this by claiming to have received new information about the alleged 2012 chemical attack in Homs, and that this increased the urgency of investigating not only the Khan al-Assal allegations, but the Homs allegations as well. Syrian state television noted that al-Jaafari wondered how the UN could so conveniently have new information available to it of an incident that had already taken place months ago.[54]

By insisting that other alleged chemical attacks be included in the UN investigation, British, French, and now UN diplomats were attempting to muddy the waters of the investigation. They apparently understood that any independent investigation focusing solely on the Khan al-Assal chemical attack would clearly implicate the Western-backed opposition; therefore, the investigation had to be expanded to include additional alleged attacks of dubious credibility which could still be blamed on the Syrian government.

If both sides could be blamed for perpetrating chemical attacks, opposition responsibility for Khan al-Assal could be diluted, and Western military intervention could still be justified by suggesting that the government was also guilty of crossing the red line. The French and British diplomats were clearly grasping at straws by demanding that the Homs incident be included, considering how even the U.S. State Department and Pentagon had already dismissed allegations against the Syrian government in that case as baseless.

Additionally, if the claims of a chemical attack in Homs had been credible, why did British and French diplomats wait to request that the UN investigate them only immediately after the Syrian government made such a request regarding Khan al-Assal? Unsurprisingly, when the Ake Sellstrom-led UN mission later reached Syria in August 2013, it declined to investigate the Homs attack. It was not one of the alleged attacks for which there was sufficient credible information to merit further investigation.[55]

Blaming the Victims

While discussing the controversy surrounding the pending investigation of the Khan al-Assal attack, Leslie Gelb of the Council on Foreign Relations (CFR) noted a historical precedent for the U.K. and French diplomatic tactic. Gelb explains that after helping Saddam Hussein carry out chemical attacks against both Iran and Iraq's rebellious Kurdish population during the Iran-Iraq War in the 1980s, U.S. diplomats sought to blame Iran falsely for chemical weapon attacks against Iraq.

Gelb recalled "the little matter of America's great ally in the 1980s, Saddam Hussein," who used chemical weapons against Iranian soldiers, killing between 50,000 and 100,000, as well as against Kurds in Halabja, killing some 7,000, primarily civilians. Gelb writes:

> Washington's response was to try and *place the blame for Halabja on Iran.* Throughout the war, the Reagan team blocked United Nations action against Iraq. After Halabja, it took seven weeks of back and forth before the U.S. finally agreed to a Security Council resolution condemning "the continued use of chemical weapons in the conflict between Iran and Iraq" and expecting "both sides to refrain from the future use of chemical weapons in accordance with their obligations under the Geneva Protocol." In other words, *the resolution implicated Iran as well as Iraq, even though no evidence was produced proving Tehran's culpability.*

> Let's face facts. Our nation's leaders wanted Iran's defeat and were prepared to accept almost any behavior by Saddam that furthered that goal. Even a truly ethical leader like the U.S. secretary of state at that time, George Shultz, admitted years later, "It's a very hard balance. They're using chemical weapons, so you want them to stop using the chemical weapons. At the same time, you don't want to see Iran win the war." Think about that kind of honesty regarding Syria...

I believe Assad is probably guilty of the crime, but history shows that evidence could pop up a year or so hence that the jihadi rebels planted the chemicals to foment Western military action against Damascus.[56] (emphasis added)

Gelb concluded by saying that "the screamers for U.S. military intervention [in Syria] are gaining traction," and that it would be difficult to "stop the hordes for long."

This means that there was a historical precedent for U.S. officials to tolerate the use of chemical weapons for the sake of undermining an enemy.

As Adam Larson details further, there was an additional objective of the French and British demands for an expanded UN investigation in Syria, namely the attempt to impose an all-pervasive inspection regime on the country comparable to that imposed on Iraq in the years preceding the 2003 U.S. invasion.[57]

On April 27, 2013, Syrian Information Minister Omran al-Zouabi claimed, for example, that by broadening the scope of the Khan al-Assal investigation to include additional sites and attacks, the aim of the Western powers was

first, to cover those who are really behind the use of chemical weapons in Khan al-Assal, and secondly, to repeat Iraq's scenario, to pave the way for other investigation inspections. To provide, based on their results, maps, photos of rockets and other fabricated materials to the UN, which as we know, opened the way to the occupation of Iraq.[58]

Syrian fears were not unfounded. As the *Washington Post* reported in 1999:

United States intelligence services infiltrated agents and espionage equipment for three years into United Nations arms control teams in Iraq to eavesdrop on the Iraqi military without the knowledge of the UN agency that it used to disguise its work.[59]

The resultant Syrian government rejection of the revised and expanded investigation proposal therefore delayed the launch of the Khan al-Assal investigation. This allowed U.S. officials to deflect culpability away from the so-called rebels and redirect it toward the Syrian government. State Department spokesman Patrick Ventrell disingenuously argued that "if the regime has nothing to hide, they should let the UN investigators in immediately so we can get to the bottom of this" and determine "whether or not the president's red line has been crossed."[60]

The delay in the deployment of Ake Sellstrom's team to investigate the Khan al-Assal attack in turn granted British and French intelligence additional time to manufacture new dubious claims of Syrian government chemical use that could be added to the baseless December 2012 allegation regarding Homs.

Chemical Attack at Sheikh Maqsoud?

In the wake of the March 19, 2013, Khan al-Assal attack, and the efforts by British and French diplomats to muddy the investigation thereof, came another dubious alleged chemical attack that again was blamed on the Syrian government. This occurred on April 13, 2013, in the majority Kurdish Aleppo suburb of Sheikh Maqsoud.

ABC News and the *Times of London* both published reports suggesting that a chemical attack had occurred in Sheikh Maqsoud, based on video footage of victims from a hospital, as well as on testimony from a man named Yasser who was allegedly injured in the attack.

Both outlets reported that Yasser claimed that he was awakened by a loud noise at roughly 3:30 a.m. His home then filled with smoke from a canister that had been dropped from the air, causing him to pass out. Yasser then woke up hours later in a hospital in Afrin, about 40 miles away, only to discover that his wife and young son had been killed in the attack.

However, the testimonies given by Yasser to ABC and the *Times of London* were contradictory. In the ABC account, Yasser claimed that he became dizzy and fell to the ground in his home, then crawled to his wife to hug her before passing out. He then woke up in the hospital in Afrin.[61] In contrast, in the *Times of London* account by journalist Anthony Lloyd, Yasser claims that he escaped to the street with one of his infant sons before passing out, after which he woke up in Afrin.[62] Both accounts cannot of course be true, and this suggests that he was embellishing or even fabricating his story in dramatic ways.

Doubts about the veracity of the *Times of London* and ABC reports quickly emerged. Journalist Tracey Shelton of *GlobalPost* visited Sheikh Maqsoud three days after the incident to try to confirm rumors that chemical weapons had been used.[63]

Shelton concluded, however, that Sheikh Maqsoud was a case of a "horrific chemical weapons attack that probably wasn't a chemical weapons attack" because the symptoms one would expect to see in the victims simply were not present. Shelton reported that "the telltale sign of a sarin gas attack is miosis, or constricting of the pupils," but that she and *GlobalPost* were unable to confirm that any of the victims had miosis.[64]

Experts soon contradicted the claims of the ABC and *Times of London* reports as well, suggesting that the video of victims at the hospital provided to the *Times* by the doctor treating them had been staged.

Eliot Higgins, by this time an open-source investigator for NATO-funded Bellingcat, asked several chemical weapons experts about the video of the victims in the hospital to see whether opposition claims appeared credible.

Higgins queried a consultant from the private threat intelligence firm Allen Vanguard, as well as Steve Johnson, Deputy Editor of *CBRNe World*, a magazine devoted to responding to chemical, biological, radiological, nuclear, or explosives (CBRNe) threats or incidents. Both concluded that the video showing alleged effects of nerve gas on the patients in the hospital had likely been staged.

The Allen Vanguard consultant explained that

> the presence of a camera person, lack of IPE [individual protection equipment] worn by the staff, lack of general panic and lack of recognised symptoms amongst the "victims" makes me think that the event has been staged. The symptoms that have been presented have probably been elaborated with single applications of foam; the foam has stopped emerging by the time the camera is shown at them.[65]

Both also questioned whether a chemical weapon such as nerve gas could have been used, since the gas was apparently delivered through a white handheld canister typically used to disperse riot gas. It made no sense for a very dangerous chemical to be delivered by a weapon thrown by hand, as whoever threw the canister would remain in close proximity to the gas and likely be exposed to it as well. Steve Johnson of *CBRNe* rhetorically asked, "Would you trust your ability *to throw* a nerve agent to keep you safe?"

Yet more strange is that the only image of such a canister that had previously emerged was not of a Syrian government soldier brandishing it, but rather a Nusra Front fighter, who had the canister attached to his tactical vest.

Whose Samples?

In short, allegations of a government nerve gas attack in Sheikh Maqsoud were fabricated. However, the British government still treated them as

259

credible, based on soil samples alleged to be from Sheikh Maqsoud, which were smuggled out of Syria and which subsequently tested positive for chemical agents at the U.K.'s Porton Down lab.

The veracity of the samples was also questionable, given later revelations that the samples had been provided by a chemical weapons specialist with links to British intelligence, Hamish de Bretton-Gordon. By his own later admission, de Bretton-Gordon engaged in a covert effort to smuggle soil samples out of Sheikh Maqsoud and to help the *Times of London* produce its report about the alleged attack there.

Journalist Kit Klarenberg of The Grayzone reports that de Bretton-Gordon, who previously claimed to be a member of the 77th Brigade, the British Army's official psychological warfare division, and who has been identified in the British press as a former spy, explained during a 2014 interview that

> last year there was a reported sarin attack in Sheikh al-Maqsood, and I helped the *Times* — chap called Anthony Lloyd who very sadly got shot two weeks ago — to cover this story and tried to get samples to the U.K. for analysis... I won't go into the details of that.[66]

In short, a British intelligence asset, de Bretton-Gordon, helped to plant a story in the U.K. press and provided samples to the U.K. government of unknown origin, to prove an alleged chemical attack for which there is clear video evidence of staging. This fabricated evidence was then used by U.K. officials to claim that the Syrian government had crossed Obama's red line.

While de Bretton-Gordon provided samples to the U.K. government, a U.S.-funded medical NGO provided samples from Sheikh Maqsoud to the U.S. government. Anthony Lloyd reports in the *Times of London* that according to local medical sources, "in the immediate aftermath of the attack a team from 'an American medical agency' arrived at the hospital in Afrin. They took hair samples from the casualties for testing at 'an American laboratory.'" Lloyd notes that these samples led U.S. Defense Secretary Chuck Hagel to suggest that "the Syrian regime had probably used chemical weapons, specifically sarin gas, on a small scale."[67]

CNN journalist Christiane Amanpour reports that the medical agency collecting these samples was the Syrian American Medical Society (SAMS), led by Dr. Zaher Sahloul.[68] SAMS was not an independent, non-political, humanitarian organization, however. Dr. Sahloul had himself campaigned strongly for U.S. military intervention in Syria. On July 26, 2013, three months after the fabricated Sheikh Maqsoud attack, Sahloul attended a White

House Iftar dinner, in which he hand-delivered a letter to President Obama urging him to establish a no-fly zone in Syria.[69]

As journalist Max Blumenthal later reported, SAMS has functioned as an arm of the U.S. foreign policy establishment to promote regime change in Syria. SAMS received millions in funding from the United States Agency for International Development (USAID), which boasts its own Office of Transition Initiatives to promote regime change in target countries, while former USAID staffers David Lillie and Tony Kronfli were among SAMS's directors. The group later played a key role in manufacturing false reports of Syrian government chemical attacks in Khan Sheikhoun in 2017 and in Douma in 2018. A former SAMS employee characterized the group to Blumenthal as "Al Qaeda's MASH unit."[70]

British and U.S. claims of Syrian government sarin use in Sheikh Maqsoud were accompanied by similar accusations from Israeli intelligence. During a national security conference in Tel Aviv on April 23, 2013, a senior Israeli military intelligence official, Brigadier General Itai Brun, had claimed:

> To the best of our professional understanding, the regime used lethal chemical weapons against the militants in a series of incidents over the past months, including the relatively famous [Khan al-Assal] incident of March 19… Shrunken pupils, foaming at the mouth, and other signs indicate, in our view, that lethal chemical weapons were used.[71]

Brun's evidence allegedly included "photographs taken of the area after the attacks" indicating sarin use.

Reuters reported three days later, however, that experts from the UN's Organisation for the Prohibition of Chemical Weapons (OPCW) made clear that the evidence claimed by the U.S. and Israel did not meet UN standards, and that the OPCW would only issue a judgment about the use of chemical weapons if inspectors were able to visit the site directly to collect soil, blood, urine, and tissue samples, maintain custody of the samples, and examine them in certified laboratories.[72]

The issue of the chain of custody was particularly important. OPCW spokesman Michael Luhan explained that even if samples were made available to the OPCW by the U.S. and Israel, the organization could not use them because "the OPCW would never get involved in testing samples that our own inspectors don't gather in the field, because we need to maintain chain of custody of samples from the field to the lab to ensure their integrity."[73] If samples were collected by opposition activists, journalists, or

Western intelligence agencies and then provided to the OPCW, it would be impossible to ensure that the samples came from the site of the attack in question and had not been manipulated for political purposes.

Despite the lack of any credible evidence of a Syrian government chemical attack in Sheikh Maqsoud, Khan al-Assal, Homs, or elsewhere, the Obama administration mimicked Israeli claims, suggesting that the "Syrian government is likely to have used chemical weapons on a small scale against its own people," even though, according to the *Washington Post*, the "administration provided no evidence in public... saying only that its conclusion was partly based on 'physiological' data."[74]

The *New York Times* was also skeptical, with the paper's editorial board noting on April 24, 2013, that while Assad "may be capable of using weapons of mass destruction, there is no proof that he has done so," and that "the case against Mr. Assad, so far, is thin."[75]

Unsurprisingly, when a UN mission later reached Syria in August 2013 to investigate a series of chemical attacks, it was not able to corroborate the allegation that chemical weapons had been used at Sheikh Maqsoud.[76]

Chemical Attack at Saraqeb?

The staged chemical attack on April 13, 2013, in Sheikh Maqsoud was quickly followed by additional allegations, this time in the town of Saraqeb, in Idlib Province, on April 29.

The BBC reported that the Syrian army had bombarded Saraqeb with artillery, and that according to local doctors, one woman named Maryam Khatib had died in the attack while eight others were admitted to the hospital who were suffering from breathing problems and vomiting and also had constricted pupils. BBC journalist Ian Pannell visited Saraqeb two weeks later. Opposition activists showed him videos of the alleged chemical attack. He also interviewed the dead woman's son, who explained that "it was a horrible, suffocating smell. You couldn't breathe at all. You'd feel like you were dead. You couldn't even see. I couldn't see anything for three or four days."[77]

In this case, opposition sources claimed that the government had used the same handheld grenade-like devices used in Sheikh Maqsoud, but this time enclosed in a concrete casing and allegedly dropped by helicopter. The BBC noted further that one device was said to have landed on the outskirts of Saraqeb, with eyewitnesses describing a box-like container with a hollow concrete casing inside. In another video, a rebel fighter holds a canister said to be hidden inside the devices. Witnesses claim there were two in each container. Another video shows parts of a canister on the ground, surrounded by white powder.[78]

The evidence for a chemical attack carried out by the Syrian government in Saraqeb was just as weak as in the case of Sheikh Maqsoud, given that the same type of canister was used in both locations. As noted earlier in this chapter, the security experts consulted by Eliot Higgins concluded that the canisters likely contained only riot control agents such as tear gas, and had previously only been seen in the possession of opposition fighters from the al-Qaeda-affiliated Nusra Front, who saw no need to wear protective equipment when handling them.

Tracey Shelton, who had investigated the Sheikh Maqsoud claims, also reported that Turkish doctors had tested the blood of victims of the alleged attack in Saraqeb, but that no sign of sarin was detected and the tests "did not find anything unusual."[79]

Despite this, French Foreign Minister Laurent Fabius later claimed the opposite: that samples taken by a local medical team in Saraqeb and sent to French intelligence had tested positive for sarin.[80] The samples were taken from four alleged victims who were treated in a field hospital run by the France-based Union of Syrian Medical Relief Organisations (UOSSM). The samples included those from Maryam Khatib, who died after being transported to a hospital in Turkey.[81]

Among the UOSSM doctors allegedly treating victims was a British-Syrian oncologist named Mousa al-Kurdi. He described Maryam Khatib as "completely unconscious, some evidence of froth on her mouth, no surgical injury whatsoever... red eyes, very hot... muscle twitching [and] I've never seen pupils so constricted, almost non-existent."[82]

Like SAMS in Sheikh Maqsoud, al-Kurdi was not a neutral and objective source. Al-Kurdi had helped coordinate medical logistics from inside Syria in the early days of the war and was involved politically with the Western-backed political opposition, the Syrian National Council (SNC). As noted earlier in this chapter, al-Kurdi appeared on Al Jazeera in April 2012 to make a special appeal to the international community: "Either you defend us or you arm the Syrian Free Army to defend us. You have the choice."[83]

It is an odd coincidence that a well-known British-Syrian doctor happened to be in Saraqeb at just this moment to treat victims and give testimony of an alleged chemical attack which could have triggered the very foreign military intervention he had been openly calling for.

It should be noted that Ian Pannell was the BBC reporter in Saraqeb relaying the opposition activists' claims of a chemical attack. This is significant because Pannell helped stage another fake chemical attack a few months later, with the help of al-Kurdi's daughter, another British-Syrian doctor named Rola Hallam, which will be discussed in the following chapter.[84]

Importantly, Western and Israeli intelligence and diplomatic officials did not appear particularly concerned with generating credible allegations of Syrian government chemical weapons use. Quantity rather than quality of claims was sufficient to create the perception of Assad's guilt, so long as these were repeated regularly in the Western press.

Stopping the Hordes

In the wake of Khan al-Assal, Sheikh Maqsoud, and Saraqeb, the "hordes" demanding Western intervention that Leslie Gelb had warned about included not only neoconservative Republicans, but also interventionist Democrats. On April 26, 2013, Anne-Marie Slaughter, a Princeton academic and the former director of policy planning during Hillary Clinton's term as secretary of state, published an op-ed in the *Washington Post* arguing that any reluctance to intervene in the Middle East caused by the 2003 Iraq War must be forgotten because "U.S. credibility is on the line," and that if Obama did not intervene in Syria, "the world would see Syrian civilians rolling on the ground, foaming at the mouth, dying by the thousands while the United States stands by." Slaughter cited the fabricated claims of chemical weapons use in Homs in December 2012 as proof that the Syrian government had crossed the red line, while claiming further that "similar evidence has been squelched again and again, until finally our allies — the British, the French, and even the Israelis — forced our hand."[85]

Slaughter's effort to pressure Obama to intervene was reinforced as well by *New York Times* columnist and former executive editor Bill Keller two weeks later. Keller also argued that the lessons of the Iraq War must be ignored, claiming that "Syria is not Iraq," while trying to shame Obama into launching an intervention. Keller recommended escalating weapons shipments to the so-called rebels, and that if Assad still refused to step down, "we send missiles against his military installations until he, or more likely those around him, calculate that they should sue for peace." Keller stressed the risks of inaction, including "the danger that if we stay away now, we will get drawn in later (and bigger), when, for example, a desperate Assad drops Sarin on a Damascus suburb."[86]

Both Slaughter and Keller displayed a curiously prescient knowledge of the alleged chemical attack that would take place almost four months later in the Damascus suburbs of eastern and western Ghouta.

Whose Sarin?

Just as pro-intervention propaganda intensified in the U.S. press, Syrian government claims about opposition use of sarin in Khan al-Assal in March 2013 were bolstered, in this case by the conclusions of Carla del Ponte, a member of the UN's Independent International Commission of Inquiry on the Syrian Arab Republic and a former war crimes prosecutor. *The Telegraph* quoted del Ponte on May 6 as explaining:

> According to the testimonies we have gathered, the rebels have used chemical weapons, making use of sarin gas… We still have to deepen our investigation, verify and confirm (the findings) through new witness testimony, but according to what we have established so far, it is at the moment *opponents of the regime* who are using sarin gas.[87] (emphasis added)

Del Ponte's claim was bolstered by communications between American journalist Matthew VanDyke and Eliot Higgins of Bellingcat. VanDyke had fought with NATO-backed Islamist militants against the Libyan government in the summer of 2011, before traveling to Syria, ostensibly as an independent journalist. Emails between the two were hacked and leaked. In one of the email conversations, VanDyke writes to Higgins:

> I have a source that has been reliable in the past, who gave me information about the rebels having acquired a small quantity a few months ago, and I know what building they came out of and I know some things about the building, having been to the site that give the information some additional credibility…

> The Syrian regime was openly contemplating the idea of letting inspectors into the Aleppo case for a reason. I'm just telling you so that you'll keep an open mind about these incidents and not have anything come totally unexpected to you in the future about chemical weapons use in Syria.[88]

To this warning, Higgins responded, "I'll keep an eye out then."

Journalist Seymour Hersh also reported that opposition forces, specifically al-Qaeda's Syrian affiliate, the Nusra Front, were in possession of sarin and able to carry out the attack against government soldiers in Khan al-Assal.

Hersh writes that in the spring of 2013, U.S. intelligence learned that the Turkish government "was working directly with al-Nusra and its allies to develop a chemical warfare capability," and that "Erdoğan's hope was to instigate an event that would force the U.S. to cross the red line. But Obama didn't respond in March and April." Erdoğan and Obama then met for a working dinner on May 16, 2013, with National Security Advisor Tom Donilon accompanying Obama, and Turkish intelligence chief Hakan Fidan accompanying Erdoğan. According to Hersh, "the meal was dominated by the Turks' insistence that Syria had crossed the red line and their complaints that Obama was reluctant to do anything about it." When Erdoğan pressed Obama on his reluctance, saying, "But your red line has been crossed!" Obama responded by pointing at intelligence chief Fidan and stating, "We know what you're doing with the radicals in Syria."

Hersh reported further that a classified U.S. Defense Intelligence Agency (DIA) briefing on June 20, 2013, indicated that "al-Nusra maintained a sarin production cell," and that Nusra was "attempting to obtain sarin precursors in bulk, tens of kilograms, likely for the anticipated large scale production effort in Syria." Hersh also noted that "more than ten members of the al-Nusra Front were arrested in southern Turkey with what local police told the press were two kilograms of sarin." According to a former senior U.S. intelligence official with whom Hersh spoke:

> We knew there were some in the Turkish government... who believed they could get Assad's nuts in a vise by dabbling with a sarin attack inside Syria — and forcing Obama to make good on his red line threat.[89]

The French Connection

A few weeks after UN investigator Carla del Ponte's claim that it was the opposition that likely deployed sarin in Khan al-Assal, new claims of Syrian government chemical use emerged, this time through reporting from the French newspaper *Le Monde*.

After spending March and April 2013 embedded with FSA fighters, *Le Monde* journalists published a report on May 27 which claimed to "bear witness to the use of toxic arms by the government of Bashar al-Assad." The journalists passed on accounts from FSA fighters alleging multiple chemical attacks during this period, including in the Damascus suburbs of Adra, Ataybah, and Jobar.[90]

McClatchy reported, however, that according to Jean Pascal Zanders, a leading expert on chemical weapons formerly of the European Union's Institute for Security Studies, much about the *Le Monde* report "bears questioning." Photos and a video accompanying the report showed FSA fighters preparing for chemical attacks by wearing gas masks, but these would not be helpful because

> sarin is absorbed through the skin, and even small amounts can kill within minutes. [Zanders] also expressed skepticism about the article's description of the lengthy route victims of chemical attacks had to travel to get to treatment, winding through holes in buildings, down streets under heavy fire, before arriving at remote buildings hiding hospitals…

Zanders noted that "had sarin been the chemical agent in use, the victims would have been dead long before they reached doctors for treatment," and that he was

> skeptical of sarin use because there have been no reports of medical personnel or rescuers dying from contact with victims. Residue from sarin gas would be expected to linger on victims and would infect those helping, who often are shown in rebel video wearing no more protection than paper masks.

McClatchy notes further that

> *Le Monde* reported that one doctor treated a victim with atropine, which is appropriate for sarin poisoning. But that doctor said he gave his patient 15 shots of atropine in quick succession, which Zanders said could have killed him almost as surely as sarin.

According to Zanders: "It's not just that we can't prove a sarin attack; it's that we're not seeing what we would expect to see from a sarin attack."[91]

Rather than confirming the use of sarin or another chemical weapon, the *Le Monde* report instead confirmed what the *New York Times* had already noted in March 2013, namely that during the Syria conflict, the "term 'chemical weapons' has sometimes appeared to be used loosely to include not just deadly nerve agents like sarin gas but also tear gas and other nonlethal irritants used for crowd control."[92]

On June 5, 2013, *Le Monde* claimed to have provided samples of blood, urine, hair, and even clothing from thirteen alleged victims of chemical attacks in Jobar and Ghouta to the Centre D'Études du Bouchet, the only laboratory in France certified to test for the presence of chemical weapons. Some of the samples tested positive for sarin, allowing French Foreign Minister Laurent Fabius to claim that the Syrian government had carried out multiple chemical attacks and that Obama's red line had been crossed.[93]

In addition to the problems noted by Jean Pascal Zanders, the claims based on the samples provided by *Le Monde* suffered from the same chain of custody issue discussed earlier in this chapter, and the samples were therefore not considered credible evidence by UN investigators.

When the UN mission later reached Syria in August 2013, it declined to investigate the alleged attacks in Jobar between April 12–14, 2013, as there was not sufficient credible information to merit further investigation.[94]

This raises the question of whether the *Le Monde* reporters were deliberately working with French intelligence to manufacture false claims of Syrian government chemical weapons use.

One indication of this is that, as the Working Group on Syria, Propaganda and Media (WGSPM) notes, the editor of *Le Monde* at the time, Natalie Nougayrede, later became part of the Integrity Initiative, a U.K. Foreign Office-funded project dedicated to "setting up covert networks ('clusters') of journalists, academics and military/foreign service StratCom practitioners" in various countries. The initiative was dedicated to "covert manipulation of the public sphere, including campaigns to smear and suppress dissenters" critical of U.K. foreign policy. WGSPM notes that

> Nougayrede had a role in information operations in Syria. Under her direction, two *Le Monde* journalists acted as couriers to transfer samples provided by the opposition, allegedly from chemical attacks, to French intelligence agents in Jordan. *Le Monde* was then given the scoop of reporting that these samples had tested positive for sarin at the French chemical weapon detection lab at Le Bouchet.[95]

This is not surprising, given that, as noted earlier in this chapter, elements of the French foreign policy establishment (represented by Bernard Henri Levy) had been advocating an attack on Syria since July 2012 and were promoting the view that the NATO intervention that destroyed the Libyan state could be repeated in Syria. The reporting in *Le Monde* in May 2013 clearly advanced that policy goal.

268

The Special Assessment

Despite uncredible and even fabricated reports of Syrian government use of chemical weapons, and the knowledge that Turkish intelligence was assisting the Nusra Front to develop a program to produce and use sarin, the White House nevertheless issued a special assessment on June 13, 2013, claiming that the Syrian government had used chemical weapons.

The Hill reported: "The White House for the first time says Syria has used chemical weapons, crossing the red line. The administration says it will arm the rebels in response."[96]

This was significant because it was the first time the White House itself formally declared that the Syrian government had used chemical weapons. However, the declaration was clearly made for political reasons, to justify increased U.S. arming of the al-Qaeda-dominated opposition in the wake of the Syrian army's liberation of Qusayr.

Politico reported that it was "a decision prompted by the realization that Syrian President Bashar Assad was on the cusp of gaining a permanent advantage over rebel groups," while an administration official with direct knowledge of the deliberations rhetorically asked, "Would we have made [the determination Assad had breached the red line] even if we didn't have the evidence? Probably."[97] But the White House didn't have credible evidence that Assad had used chemical weapons.

According to Deputy National Security Advisor Ben Rhodes: "Legally, we couldn't say what the support was; all I could say were things like: 'This is going to be different — in both scope and scale — in terms of what we are providing to the opposition.'"[98]

According to the AP, these weapons were likely to include small arms, ammunition, assault rifles, and a variety of anti-tank weaponry, including RPGs.[99] As noted in Chapter 14, CIA-supplied Konkurs anti-tank missiles began appearing in the possession of all the major armed groups at this time, including among ISIS fighters.

These new weapons shipments were apparently meant to supplement those still flowing to the so-called opposition via the rat line from Libya. The *New York Times* reported on June 21, 2013, that Qatar was obtaining weapons from militias in Libya and providing these to their proxies in Syria, with the CIA playing "at least a supporting role," according to Syrian opposition figures. According to a former Obama administration official: "We're watching it. The Libyans have an amazing amount of stuff." Although "the shipments from Libya have been very large," the *NYT* reported further that they "have not kept up with the enormous rebel ammunition expenditures each day," suggesting that the additional weapons shipments detailed by Ben Rhodes were necessary.[100]

White House efforts to escalate the war under the pretext that Assad had used chemical weapons were met with resistance from U.S. lawmakers, however, who expressed concerns about a plan that would effectively arm al-Qaeda. Reuters reported on July 8, 2013, that Secretary of State John Kerry and CIA Deputy Director Michael Morell were tasked with briefing the House and Senate intelligence committees about the White House plan, but both committees initially rejected it and put a temporary freeze on the funds earmarked for the weapons purchases. This was due to worries that "weapons could reach factions like the Nusra Front."[101] House and Senate officials later backed down and, despite "very strong concerns," agreed to move ahead with the White House strategy.[102]

But this was not enough to satisfy "the hordes" that Leslie Gelb had warned about. Senator John McCain applauded Obama's decision to escalate arms shipments, but he continued to demand supplying heavier weapons and establishing a no-fly zone over Syria.[103] McCain and Senator Lindsey Graham issued a joint statement on June 14, 2013, a day after the White House special assessment was issued, arguing that "we cannot afford to delay any longer. We must take more-decisive actions now to turn the tide of the conflict in Syria."[104]

When discussing the special assessment, Rhodes pointed to four alleged chemical attacks in the previous months: on March 19 in Khan al-Assal, on April 13 in Sheikh Maqsoud, on May 14 in the town of Qasr Abu Samra, and on May 23 in Adra.[105]

U.S. Ambassador to the UN Susan Rice at the same time sent a letter to UN chief Ban Ki-moon claiming that the Syrian government had used chemical weapons and requesting that the UN mission include the incidents in Sheikh Maqsoud, Qasr Abu Samra, and Adra in its ongoing investigation. The AP reported in response that Ban "opposes the U.S. decision to send weapons," and that he insists that "the validity of any information on the alleged use of chemical weapons cannot be ensured without convincing evidence of the chain-of-custody."[106]

In response to the special assessment, McClatchy published a report citing various chemical weapons experts who expressed doubts about the

White House claims, including Richard Guthrie, formerly head of the Chemical and Biological Warfare Project of the Stockholm International Peace Research Institute, and Philip Coyle of the Center for Arms Control and Non-Proliferation in Washington. McClatchy also reported that Greg Thielmann, a senior fellow at the Washington-based Arms Control Association, had raised questions about the lack of a "continuous chain of custody for the physiological samples from those exposed to sarin." McClatchy noted further that even Anthony Cordesman of the Center for Strategic and International Studies (CSIS), "a proponent of the United States providing military assistance to the rebels," had "raised doubts about the possible motive for announcing the chemical weapons conclusion." Cordesman stated that "the 'discovery' that Syria used chemical weapons might be a political ploy."[107]

By July 12, 2013, the UN mission had still not reached an agreement to enter Syria, and U.S. and European officials were now demanding that nine further alleged chemical incidents be investigated in addition to Khan al-Assal. Russian UN envoy Vitaly Churkin responded by accusing Western officials of inventing new and fake allegations of chemical weapons use in Syria to complicate an otherwise straightforward investigation of events in Khan al-Assal. Churkin explained:

> We need to look into credible allegations... Unfortunately, I think what our Western colleagues have been doing is trying to produce the maximum number of allegations with minimum credibility in an effort, one might think, to create maximum problems for arranging such [an] investigation.[108]

16. The Ghouta False Flag

The Ghouta Chemical Attack

The Ake Sellstrom-led UN mission finally arrived in Damascus on August 18, 2013, after an agreement on the contours of the UN investigation was reached with Syrian officials. The alleged use of chemical weapons would be investigated in just three areas: Khan al-Assal, Sheikh Maqsoud, and Saraqeb. There was also no mandate to determine responsibility for any attacks. The AP reported that although "diplomats and chemical weapons experts have raised doubts about whether they will find anything since the alleged incidents took place months ago," the Syrian government was nevertheless hopeful that its claim of opposition use of sarin at Khan al-Assal would be vindicated by the UN investigation.[1]

However, on the morning of August 21, just three days after the UN mission had arrived, reports began to emerge of a large-scale chemical attack in the Damascus suburbs of eastern and western Ghouta. The BBC reports:

> Within hours, dozens of videos were uploaded of large numbers of distressed and visibly sick adults and children with no external signs of injury. In some of the most graphic footage, dozens of bodies, including many small children and babies, were seen laid out in rows on the floors of clinics and mosques, and on streets.[2]

The videos allegedly documented a massive chemical attack by the Syrian government on civilians, with U.S. intelligence sources claiming that sarin was used and that 1,429 people died, including 426 children, while the SOHR claimed to have confirmed 502 dead.[3]

The alleged attack gave White House officials the pretext they had long needed to convince Obama to initiate military intervention. The *New York Times* reports:

> Within hours, administration officials began signaling that they were preparing for an immediate military strike to punish the Syrian government — an idea dismissed repeatedly in the past and a hard sell with some allies, a war-weary public and Congress.[4]

President Obama was nevertheless still hesitant, however. In a CNN interview recorded the following day, August 22, Obama highlighted the dangers of intervening with force in Syria without UN Security Council approval.[5]

At the same time, Ake Sellstrom's UN mission was quickly instructed to delay the Khan al-Assal investigation and to "focus [their] investigation efforts on the Ghouta allegations" instead.[6] This prompted Syrian state media to claim that reports of a chemical attack in Ghouta were "an attempt to divert the UN chemical weapons investigation commission away from carrying out its duties" to investigate what had happened in Khan al-Assal.[7]

Whose Intelligence?

The Syrian government was nevertheless open to the UN team investigating what happened at Ghouta, as were some U.S. officials, to help determine the veracity of reports of a chemical attack before taking military action.

The *Wall Street Journal* reported that one day after the attack, on Thursday, August 22, Secretary of State Kerry "took the unusual step of calling Syrian Foreign Minister Walid Moallem to demand immediate access to the areas."[8] However, access to the site of the attacks was not entirely in Syrian government hands, because, as Moallem told Kerry, those "districts weren't under government control." Kerry responded to Moallem, however, by saying that "rebel forces could ensure the safety of the UN investigators." According to Moallem, the call "ended in a cordial way." The *WSJ* reported further that "that same day [Thursday, August 22], UN Secretary General Ban Ki-moon also called on the Syrians to provide immediate access." However, a formal UN request strangely "wasn't made until Saturday," August 24. Angela Kane, the UN disarmament chief, met with Foreign Minister Moallem on Sunday, August 25, and arranged for the UN mission to begin its work, finally, on the following day, Monday, August 26.

White House officials tried to blame the Syrian government for delays in getting the UN mission access to the attack site, even though the UN had not submitted a request to visit the site until just the day before, Saturday, August 24. After Syrian state television announced on Sunday, August 25, that UN inspectors would be allowed to visit the site the following day, an Obama administration official bizarrely claimed that the decision was "too late to be credible." The official claimed further that the Syrian government wanted to delay an investigation "to give the evidence of the attack time to degrade," and that "the regime's continuing shelling of the site also further corrupts any available evidence of the attack."[9]

However, UN head Ban Ki-moon insisted that the investigation should move forward, while Ban's spokesman, Farhan Haq, reminded observers that an investigation was clearly worthwhile because "sarin can be detected for up to months after its use."[10]

In other words, the Obama official disingenuously blamed the Syrian government for a delay of just a few days in Ghouta, even though U.S., French, and British diplomats had worked to delay the investigation of Khan al-Assal for months.

This four-day delay was sufficient to allow Israeli intelligence to intervene politically to help overcome Obama's hesitance and keep the White House on course for intervention. The *Wall Street Journal* notes further that "the U.S. position changed rapidly," and that "Obama's position already had shifted by Saturday morning [August 24]" towards intervention, even absent a UN resolution. This "dramatic turnaround" was spurred by "a flood of previously undisclosed intelligence, including satellite images and intercepted communications, [which] convinced them the Syrian regime had used chemical weapons against its own people." According to the *WSJ*:

> One crucial piece of the emerging case came from Israeli spy services... The intelligence... showed that certain types of chemical weapons were moved in advance to the same Damascus suburbs where the attack allegedly took place a week ago, Arab diplomats said.[11]

The Guardian also noted the Israeli role, explaining that according to the German magazine *Focus*, "the bulk of evidence proving the Assad regime's deployment of chemical weapons... has been provided by Israeli military intelligence." The 8200 Unit of the Israeli army, which specializes in electronic surveillance, claimed to have intercepted a conversation between Syrian officials that proved the use of chemical weapons. *The Guardian* noted further that "senior Israeli security officials arrived in Washington on Monday [August 26] to share the latest results of intelligence-gathering, and to review the Syrian crisis with National Security Advisor Susan Rice."[12]

After receipt of the new Israeli intelligence, Rice then went to work trying to sabotage the UN investigation, so that the planned military intervention could proceed. The *Wall Street Journal* reports:

> In an email on Sunday [August 25], White House National Security Advisor Susan Rice told UN Ambassador Samantha Power and other top officials that the UN mission was pointless because the chemical weapons evidence already was conclusive... The U.S. privately *urged the UN to pull the inspectors out*, setting the stage for President Barack Obama to possibly move forward with a military response.[13] (emphasis added)

Brennan's Slam Dunk?

Some U.S. intelligence officials were skeptical of the Israeli intelligence claims, however, and sought to avoid responsibility for the looming U.S. military intervention.

On Monday, August 26, Director of National Intelligence James Clapper warned Obama that Syrian government responsibility for the attack was "not a slam dunk."[14]

The same warning was also given to journalists at the AP on Thursday, August 29. The AP reported:

> The intelligence linking Syrian President Bashar Assad or his inner circle to an alleged chemical weapons attack is no "slam dunk," with questions remaining about who actually controls some of Syria's chemical weapons stores and doubts about whether Assad himself ordered the strike, U.S. intelligence officials say.[15]

The AP noted further that some U.S. intelligence officials "have even talked about the possibility that rebels could have carried out the attack in a callous and calculated attempt to draw the West into the war."

Regarding the "slam dunk," Deputy National Security Advisor Ben Rhodes later noted that this was

> the exact phrase that George Tenet, then director of the CIA, had used to assure George W. Bush that Saddam Hussein had weapons of mass destruction. Clapper seemed to be signaling that he wasn't going to put the intelligence community in the position of building another case for another war in the Middle East that could go wrong.[16]

Clapper then refused to issue an assessment on behalf of the intelligence community regarding the Ghouta attack, seeking to shift liability onto the White House by recommending that Rhodes author an assessment for public release instead. Rhodes agreed but as a result explained: "I felt waves of anxiety, anticipating how I might be hauled before Congress if things went terribly wrong after a military intervention."

The Anti-Assad Operation Has Begun

One indication that the Ghouta chemical attack was a "callous and calculated attempt to draw the West into the war" is that armed opposition groups were at the same time preparing to launch an assault on Damascus with the help of U.S., Israeli, and Jordanian intelligence, the success of which depended on the sort of direct Western military intervention that only Assad's crossing of Obama's red line could open the door to.

One day after the Ghouta chemical attack, *Le Figaro* reported that "the anti-Assad operation has begun." The French newspaper reported on August 22:

> The first Syrian contingents trained in guerrilla warfare by the Americans in Jordan have been in action since mid-August in southern Syria, in the Deraa region. A first group of 300 men, probably supported by Israeli and Jordanian commandos, as well as by men from the CIA, would have crossed the border on August 17. A second would have joined them on the 19th.[17]

Le Figaro also quoted David Rigoulet-Roze, a researcher at the French Institute for Strategic Analysis (IFAS), as explaining that

> their thrust would now be felt as far as Ghouta, where the FSA formations were already at work… the idea envisaged by Washington would be the possible creation of a buffer zone from southern Syria, or even a no-fly zone, which would make it possible to train opponents in complete safety, until the relationship of forces changes. This is why the United States deployed Patriot batteries and F16s in late June in Jordan.[18]

Furthermore, Georges Malbrunot and Christian Chesnot note: "Apparently, the jihadists were already positioned to launch a massive assault on Damascus, taking advantage of the confusion that would then have gripped the regime" in the event of Western airstrikes. The French journalists report that Mokhtar Lamani, the UN representative in Damascus, sent a confidential note to his superior, UN Special Envoy to Syria Lakhdar Brahimi, stating that "the rebel Salafist group Liwa al-Islam, which is close to Saudi Arabia, had held a secret meeting indicating that it had positioned 8,000 fighters in Ghouta, supported by 4,000 men of the al-Nusra Front, to lead the offensive on the Syrian capital in the event of strikes."[19]

Preparations for attacking Damascus in the wake of the coming false-flag attack were simultaneously taking place in Turkey as well. According to a group of former U.S. intelligence analysts, known as Veteran Intelligence Professionals for Sanity (VIPS), "on August 13–14, 2013, Western-sponsored opposition forces in Turkey started advance preparations for a *major, irregular military surge*" (emphasis added). VIPS claims further that

> initial meetings between senior opposition military commanders and Qatari, Turkish and U.S. intelligence officials took place at the converted Turkish military garrison in Antakya, Hatay Province, now

used as the command center and headquarters of the Free Syrian Army (FSA) and their foreign sponsors. Senior opposition commanders who came from Istanbul pre-briefed the regional commanders on an imminent escalation in the fighting due to "a war-changing development," which, in turn, would lead to a U.S.-led bombing of Syria. At operations coordinating meetings at Antakya, attended by senior Turkish, Qatari and U.S. intelligence officials as well as senior commanders of the Syrian opposition, the Syrians were told that the bombing would start in a few days. Opposition leaders were ordered to prepare their forces quickly to exploit the U.S. bombing, march into Damascus, and remove the Bashar al-Assad government. The Qatari and Turkish intelligence officials assured the Syrian regional commanders that they would be provided with plenty of weapons for the coming offensive. And they were. A weapons distribution operation unprecedented in scope began in all opposition camps on August 21–23. The weapons were distributed from storehouses controlled by Qatari and Turkish intelligence under the tight supervision of U.S. intelligence officers.[20]

U.S. and allied plans to topple Assad in this way were reminiscent of the 2012 British plan from General Sir David Richards, discussed in Chapter 15, which called for training so-called rebels in Jordan and Turkey in numbers sufficient to "sustain the momentum of an attack on Damascus, particularly if backed by air power provided by the West and friendly Gulf countries," in a larger-scale version of the Libya intervention.[21]

FSA commander and Supreme Military Council (SMC) spokesman Qassem Saaddedine also acknowledged that preparations had been made to topple the Syrian government in concert with the expected Western bombing campaign. In an interview with Reuters published on Saturday, August 31 — the day the UN mission was expected to leave, opening the way for the bombing campaign to begin — Saaddedine explained that "his forces assessed that a Western attack would happen in the coming days and would last about three days." Saaddedine explained further:

> We ordered some groups to prepare in each province, to ready their fighters for when the strike happens... They were sent a military plan that includes preparations to attack some of the targets we expect to be hit in foreign strikes, and some others that we hope to attack at the same time.[22]

The targets that Saaddedine expected to be hit included "military sites such as the headquarters of military leadership, military airports, certain weapon storage areas, or launch pads and installations for large missiles such as Scuds," as well as bases belonging to the Fourth Armored Division and Republican Guard.

Saaddedine then claimed that "the plans had been prepared without any help from foreign powers." Recall, however, that senior opposition commanders in Istanbul and Antakya had received briefings of the coming bombing campaign, as reported by VIPS. Saaddedine himself conceded to Reuters: "There may have been [foreign] consultations with the head of our council, Salim Idriss, but I cannot confirm this."

Timing Is Everything

The timing of the "anti-Assad operation" to take Damascus is important to keep in mind here. Crucially, preparations for the operation began *before* the August 21 Ghouta attack, as the VIPS and *Le Figaro* reports show.

The success of the operation depended on a U.S.-led bombing campaign, which by this time could be triggered only by a "war-changing development," such as a chemical attack crossing Obama's red line. That preparations for this "major, irregular military surge" were underway a week before the Ghouta attack suggests foreknowledge of the attack itself, and therefore opposition and foreign intelligence agency responsibility for it.

It is improbable that Assad would by coincidence order a chemical attack, the one thing that could provide the pretext for Western intervention, just as the CIA and its regional partners were launching a covert operation to attack Damascus, the success of which depended entirely on such an intervention.

In arguing against the Syrian government's responsibility for the Ghouta attack, many have noted the irony of the timing, but for another reason. It is improbable that Assad would order a chemical attack just in time for the UN investigators, whom he himself had invited into the country, to be present to investigate it. The *Los Angeles Times* noted, for example:

> Several experts suggested that the timing of the alleged attack — just three days after the arrival of the UN investigators — further muddied the picture. It was unclear what Assad would gain from such an action, given that a deliberate chemical strike would enrage both his many international enemies and even his allies in Moscow.[23]

Foreign Policy similarly reported that Assad had no reason to order such an attack, "nor are U.S. analysts sure of the Syrian military's rationale for launching the strike, if it had a rationale at all."[24] Charles Heyman, a former British military officer, similarly explained that "we can't get our heads around this — why would any commander agree to rocketing a suburb of

Damascus with chemical weapons for only a very short-term tactical gain for what is a long-term disaster?"[25]

By contrast, if the Ghouta attack was a false-flag operation carried out by opposition militants with help from foreign intelligence agencies, the coincident timing of all these events makes perfect sense. A false-flag chemical attack would allow the Salafist militias of the FSA, Liwa al-Islam, and Nusra to march on Damascus under the umbrella of U.S., French, and British bombs in a repeat of the Libya intervention, while at the same time derailing any UN investigation of the Nusra sarin attack at Khan al-Assal.

Whose Rockets?

While circumstantial evidence available at the time suggested that Assad was not responsible for the Ghouta chemical attack, it took years before hard evidence finally emerged to confirm this conclusion. This evidence finally came from an analysis of the rockets used in the attack, which conclusively showed that Liwa al-Islam, the Salafist militia sponsored by Prince Bandar and Saudi intelligence, was in fact responsible.

Ironically, details about the rockets were initially used to suggest that Assad was responsible. On September 13, 2013, the Ake Sellstrom-led UN mission released its interim report on the Ghouta attack. The report confirmed that "surface-to-surface rockets containing the nerve agent sarin were used."[26]

Although the UN mission was not charged to apportion blame, the details it provided of the rockets, known as "volcanoes," appeared to confirm claims about Syrian government responsibility. For example, Eliot Higgins of Bellingcat claimed that "there is no evidence of Syrian rebel forces ever using this type of munition — and only Syrian government forces have ever been shown using them."[27]

The *New York Times* and Human Rights Watch also seized on details provided in the UN report to claim Syrian government guilt. The *NYT* writes that the report also

> identified azimuths, or angular measurements, from where rockets had struck, back to their points of origin. When plotted and marked independently on maps by analysts from Human Rights Watch and by the *New York Times*, the United Nations data from two widely scattered impact sites pointed directly to a Syrian military complex.[28]

If the attack originated from government-controlled territory, using rockets previously identified only in the possession of the Syrian army, this pointed to Syrian government culpability.

However, a few months later, in December 2013, this conclusion was refuted by Theodore Postol, a professor of science, technology, and national security policy at the Massachusetts Institute of Technology (MIT), and Richard Lloyd, an analyst at the military contractor Tesla Laboratories.

The *New York Times* reported that Lloyd and Postol showed that the maximum range of the rockets was less than 3 kilometers, rather than the 9-kilometer range assumed by the *NYT* and HRW. This suggested that the rockets did not come from deep inside Syrian government-held territory, but rather from areas that were contested between opposition militant groups and the Syrian army.[29]

Additionally, according to Postol, the large-caliber rocket used in the attack "was an improvised munition that was very likely manufactured locally," and was "something you could produce in a modestly capable machine shop."[30] In other words, an opposition faction such as Liwa al-Islam could have easily manufactured the rockets, meaning that it was irrelevant whether such rockets had previously only been identified in the Syrian government's possession.

Years later, it was confirmed that the rockets were indeed launched from opposition-held territory, specifically by militants from Liwa al-Islam. In a detailed report published by Rootclaim in 2021, open-source researchers Michael Kobs, Chris Kabusk, and Adam Larson were able to use azimuths to identify a common origin of the launch site of all seven rocket attacks targeting eastern Ghouta. They were also able to geolocate a previously known video showing Liwa al-Islam militants launching rockets of the same sort, while wearing gas masks, to the same location, which was firmly in Liwa al-Islam-controlled territory.[31] What happened at Ghouta was indeed a false-flag attack.

Taking a Walk

After the horrific videos of the Ghouta victims went viral on the morning of August 21, 2013, one crucial aspect of the anti-Assad operation remained: to pressure President Obama into ordering the U.S.-led bombing campaign. This pressure immediately came from CIA Director John Brennan. As a former senior U.S. intelligence official told Seymour Hersh:

The immediate assumption was that Assad had done it. The new director of the CIA [Brennan], jumped to that conclusion… drives to the White House and says, "Look at what I've got!" It was all verbal; they just waved the bloody shirt. There was a lot of political pressure to bring Obama to the table to help the rebels, and there was wishful thinking that this [tying Assad to the sarin attack] would force Obama's hand: This was the Zimmermann Telegram of the Syrian rebellion, and now Obama can react.[32]

Other U.S. intelligence officials also identified Brennan as not only jumping to conclusions about who had carried out the attack, but as attempting to perpetrate a fraud on President Obama. In the wake of the Ghouta attack, former intelligence officials from VIPS, led by Philip Giraldi and Matthew Hoh, published a statement on September 6, 2013, to warn President Obama about the trap being laid for him. VIPS writes that according to some current CIA officers with whom they had spoken, who were working on the Syria issue, the Syrian government had not carried out the Ghouta attack, and "CIA Director John Brennan is perpetrating a pre-Iraq-War-type fraud on members of Congress, the media, the public, and perhaps even you."[33]

The U.S. military intervention in Syria was set to commence sometime between Saturday, August 31, and Monday, September 2.[34] President Obama had already ordered the Pentagon to develop target lists, while five Navy destroyers were in the Mediterranean, ready to launch cruise missiles. French President François Hollande, the most enthusiastically pro-intervention among Europe's leaders, was preparing his forces to attack as well.[35]

Hersh reports that the initial scale of the planned attack was massive. He quotes a former senior U.S. intelligence official as explaining that the target list was meant to "eradicate any military capabilities Assad had."[36]

However, on Friday, August 30, the day before the bombing was possibly to begin, President Obama and his chief of staff, Denis McDonough, went for a walk on the White House lawn. *Politico* reports:

Most observers expected him to launch the strikes — until he came back from the walk, that is. Then, Obama surprised nearly everyone by deciding to force a vote in Congress on whether to do so, effectively putting the military action on hold.[37]

The Obama administration then launched a public relations offensive to continue to make the case for war, hoping to convince a reluctant Congress to authorize the intervention. However, skepticism of the White House case only grew.

On September 8, 2013, the AP published a scathing report asking why the Obama administration refused to show the evidence it claimed to have proving Assad's guilt, including satellite imagery and transcripts of intercepted communications provided by Israeli intelligence. According to the AP, so far, the Obama administration had not provided a "shred of proof."[38]

The Videos

But the CIA and White House push for war did not depend on proof, but rather on the emotional shock value of the Ghouta videos.

On the day of the Ghouta attacks, the *Los Angeles Times* noted, for example, that "the scale of the alleged carnage and the graphic videos of the dead and injured that surfaced Wednesday left many officials across the globe demanding action."[39]

This was no accident. The utility of using difficult-to-verify viral videos to manipulate political leaders had already been recognized by Jared Cohen, the State Department official later known as "Google's director of regime change," who had helped spark the anti-government protests in both Egypt and Syria in 2011.

Cohen had also played a role in facilitating the anti-government protests in Iran in 2009, known as the Green Revolution. While speaking at Stanford University about events in Iran during that period, Cohen explained that President Obama was forced by Western journalists to respond to a viral video of an Iranian woman named Neda Agha-Soltan, who was shot and killed, allegedly by a pro-Iranian government militia, during the protests. Cohen noted that

> within two hours, this video had reached millions of people around the world and was on the desks of some of the most powerful and least accessible people on the planet: presidents, prime ministers... At the time, the President had said there is going to be no meddling in Iran because the nuclear negotiations were on the horizon... So, what happened was some unknown Iranian got a virtual meeting because someone captured a video of a young girl being murdered and uploaded it to YouTube. And President Obama responded and at that moment changed the policy of the United States government.[40]

Cohen and his counterparts in the CIA and State Department pushing for regime change in Syria were therefore aware that shocking videos alleging

Syrian government atrocities could similarly be used to pressure Obama to authorize U.S. intervention.

President Obama himself referred to the importance of the Ghouta videos during a prepared statement he delivered on August 31, 2013, while seeking to rally public support for war:

> Ten days ago, the world watched in horror as men, women, and children were massacred in Syria in the worst chemical weapons attack of the 21st century... the world can plainly see — hospitals overflowing with victims; terrible images of the dead.[41]

It is possible that Obama deliberately cited the videos to manipulate the public into supporting U.S. intervention. However, given Obama's previous reluctance to authorize military action, another possibility is that Obama was himself manipulated into changing his stance due to the emotional effect of the shocking videos.

The horrific Ghouta videos were relied upon to convince not only the public, but also U.S. lawmakers, to support intervention. On September 5, 2013, U.S. Senators received a classified briefing in which they viewed a DVD compilation of images and videos of the Ghouta attack, with ABC News reporting that "the graphic images have become a rallying point for the administration."[42]

While the case for war depended on the shock value of the Ghouta videos, a closer look at the videos at the same time provided reason to doubt the White House narrative of events, rather than confirm it.

The *New York Times* reported:

> The videos, experts said, also did not prove the use of chemical weapons, which interfere with the nervous system and can cause defecation, vomiting, intense salivation and tremors. Only some of those symptoms were visible in some patients.[43]

The *Los Angeles Times* similarly noted that "experts raised some red flags, including signs that medical staff treating the victims didn't appear to be experiencing any symptoms, which would be expected if a pure nerve agent had been released."[44] The BBC reported that, according to Alexander Kekule of the Institute for Medical Microbiology at Halle University in Germany, none of the patients in one of the videos "showed typical signs of sarin or other organophosphorous nerve agents," and that "it also cannot be totally excluded that the whole video is a political staging. In this case, however, it would be a very good one."[45]

Although the videos did not show the symptoms that experts expected to see if the victims had been killed in a sarin attack, their shocking nature and the emotions they evoked made it difficult for many to question whether the videos could show something other than what the Syrian opposition and White House claimed. The idea that the videos could have been staged or fabricated was simply too difficult for most to imagine.

Whose Videos?

Due to the central role that the Ghouta attack videos played, it is necessary to consider who created them and how. While it would indeed have been difficult for Liwa al-Islam militants and their media activists to fabricate footage of a false-flag chemical attack and disseminate it so quickly throughout the international media, it would have been less difficult with help from the foreign intelligence agencies supporting them. Although it was not known at the time, the British government later acknowledged that it was running media operations on behalf of the so-called rebels, including Liwa al-Islam. This suggests that the flurry of shocking videos released in such quick and coordinated fashion in the aftermath of the Ghouta attack was part of a psychological operation run by British intelligence.

As noted in Chapter 9, *The Guardian* reported in May 2016:

> The British government is waging information warfare in Syria by funding media operations for some rebel fighting groups…

> Contractors hired by the Foreign Office but overseen by the Ministry of Defence (MoD) produce videos, photos, military reports, radio broadcasts, print products, and social media posts branded with the logos of fighting groups, and effectively run a press office for opposition fighters.

> Materials are circulated in the Arabic broadcast media and posted online with no indication of British government involvement.[46]

The Guardian reports further that U.K. government contractors, such as Innovative Communications and Strategies (InCoStrat), were to provide "media coaching to influential [rebel] officials" and run an around-the-clock "[rebel] central media office" with "media production capacity," and that "one British source with knowledge of the contracts in action said the government was essentially running a 'Free Syrian Army press office.'" *The Guardian* reported as well that the effort was meant to help the so-called "moderate armed opposition," and mentioned Jaish al-Islam (the successor to Liwa al-Islam) as among these moderate opposition groups. *The Guardian* claimed that this effort began in the autumn of 2013 and was part of a propaganda war directed not against the Syrian government, but against ISIS.

The autumn 2013 date claimed by *The Guardian* would appear to rule out a U.K. role in producing the Ghouta videos which emerged shortly before, in August 2013. However, *The Guardian* appears to be spreading misinformation regarding the date the propaganda effort began, and regarding its claim that ISIS was the target.

As discussed in Chapter 15, the U.K. Foreign Office-funded contractor Analysis Research Knowledge (ARK) was involved in promoting false claims about the alleged chemical attack in Homs in December 2012. Furthermore, as journalist Ben Norton reports:

> In a leaked document it filed with the British government, ARK said its *"focus since 2012* has been delivering highly effective, politically- and conflict-sensitive Syria programming for the governments of the United Kingdom, United States, Denmark, Canada, Japan and the European Union."[47] (emphasis added)

Further, ISIS was not formed until April 2013, meaning that the organization could not have been the target of a U.K. propaganda campaign that began in 2012. Rather, the target was the Syrian government.

By the time of the Ghouta attack in August 2013, U.K.-funded contractors such as ARK had long been working with the so-called moderate armed opposition, including Liwa al-Islam. They would therefore have been in a position to launch a sophisticated information operation on Liwa al-Islam's behalf, and thereby could upload dozens of videos "within hours" of the Ghouta attack that were immediately disseminated throughout the international media.

Unsurprisingly, the Ghouta videos were cited not only by President Obama, but also by U.K. Prime Minister David Cameron when he attempted to persuade the British Parliament to authorize participation in the looming U.S. intervention against Syria.[48]

Like the Walking Dead

One clear example of staged chemical attack footage produced by the U.K. government comes from British state media directly. On August 29, 2013, just one week after the Ghouta attack, the BBC aired footage of the aftermath of an alleged napalm attack carried out by the Syrian army in Atareb, a village near Aleppo. The aftermath was apparently witnessed and filmed by BBC journalist Ian Pannell and his cameraman, Darren Conway, with the BBC describing the victims as "like the walking dead."[49]

The video footage, which became part of the BBC documentary *Saving Syria's Children*, is clearly fabricated, as activist Robert Stuart has detailed, with crisis actors wearing makeup to appear as burn victims and responding to directions from the camera crew to begin behaving as if in terrible pain. The footage is immediately reminiscent of a low-budget Hollywood zombie movie, as even the BBC description of the victims suggested.[50]

The Atareb napalm video was a collaboration between British elements that had attempted to create the perception of a sarin attack in Saraqeb three months before, as discussed in Chapter 15. In the Saraqeb case, BBC journalist Pannell had reported on the alleged attack, detailing video footage passed to him by opposition activists. Dr. Mousa al-Kurdi, the British-Syrian gynecologist who had lobbied for Western military intervention, claimed to have been present in Saraqeb and to have treated victims of the attack in a field hospital run by a French medical charity.

In Atareb, Pannell was present once again, this time conveniently in the direct aftermath of the alleged attack and able to produce a live-action video report showing the chaos during the initial treatment of the injured. In this case, Dr. Mousa al-Kurdi was not present, but his daughter, a Syrian-British doctor named Rola Hallam, who worked for a U.K.-registered charity called Hand in Hand for Syria, conveniently was. She oddly stopped in the middle of the chaos to speak on camera with Pannell's team, rather than seek to aid the alleged victims.[51]

Importantly, the zombie-style BBC footage was released just one day ahead of the U.K. parliamentary vote to authorize military action against Syria. The timing of the video's release was clearly meant to influence British parliamentarians to vote in favor of military action. However, the BBC's efforts in Atareb were not successful, as the U.K. Parliament narrowly voted against intervention in Syria, 285–272, on August 30.[52]

The fake BBC documentary from Atareb, coupled with the false claims of chemical attacks in Sheikh Maqsoud and Saraqeb, as well as the carefully planned release of the Ghouta videos within hours of the alleged attack, all appear to have been part of a broader psychological operation created by U.K. intelligence to mold U.S. and U.K. public opinion for the sake of triggering Western military intervention.

Whose Victims?

Two weeks before the alleged Ghouta chemical attacks, another similarly violent incident occurred, which received considerably less attention in the Western press. On August 4, 2013, militants from Nusra, ISIS, and the FSA participated in the massacre and mass kidnapping of Alawite civilians in ten villages in Latakia. Human Rights Watch investigated the incident in detail and reported that the jihadist militants overran a Syrian army position, killing some 30 Syrian soldiers, and then massacred 190 civilians, including 57 women, 18 children, and 14 elderly men. The jihadist militants also kidnapped and held hostage some 200 additional civilians, the majority women and children.[53]

The Telegraph reported that the U.S.-backed Syrian National Coalition (SNC) "praised" the ISIS-led offensive, justifying the killings by claiming that "the villages had been used as launching posts from which pro-government militias had shelled rebel held villages."[54] The *New York Times* reports that FSA commander Salim Idris, who headed the U.S.-backed Supreme Military Council (SMC), insisted on video that his forces had played a leading role in the attack, in response to criticism from the other participating jihadist groups suggesting that his FSA fighters had been hanging back.[55] Rania Abouzeid reported for Al Jazeera as well that the field hospital supporting the ISIS, Nusra, and FSA militants who carried out the massacre was funded by U.S. and U.K. charities and staffed by a Syrian-British doctor named Rami Habib, who had previously worked for the National Health Service (NHS) in Leicester, U.K.[56]

Abouzeid interviewed a fighter who participated in the campaign and described the aftermath of the massacre. He explained, "I was there… I walked into a room, a small room. It was full of men they had killed. They were fighting-age men, I wasn't sad for them, it's war." In another room he entered, ISIS militants

> had gathered women and girls in this room, from the ages of what looked like six or seven to the elderly. It was odd. There were only very young or old, there weren't any young women. They'd killed them all, and piled them on top of each other. There is no religion, no morals, no ideology that could accept that. That's what [ISIS] did, and in the name of Islam. It made me sick.[57]

Abouzeid further quoted a Nusra commander as bragging that in the Alawite villages they "killed everything in them, took everything from them, burned everything in them."[58]

Journalist Vanessa Beeley interviewed a survivor of the massacre from the town of Ballouta, Ramez Badea Saleem. Beeley writes that Saleem tells her

> that his wife threw herself off the rooftop of their home, only to be shot dead by the terrorists on the ground. An elderly man, 90 years old, had his throat slit while he was sleeping. Two of Ramez's nieces were murdered in their car. He speaks of the dismemberment of corpses, the discovery of mass graves containing body parts, severed arms and legs among the discarded bodies of men, women, and children.[59]

While the events in Ghouta, of which responsibility was far from clear, received wide attention in the Western press, the FSA, ISIS, and Nusra massacre and kidnapping of Alawites in Latakia, which was not disputed, even by opposition sources, and which took place just two weeks prior to the Ghouta attack, was effectively ignored.

The Telegraph reported on these events on August 11, 2013, one week after they occurred, but the *New York Times*, BBC, and *The Guardian* provided no coverage until October 2013, after the Human Rights Watch report had been released. I was unable to find any mention of the massacre by the *Washington Post*, even after the October HRW report.

The *Post* did note on October 2, however, that the "CIA is expanding a clandestine effort to train opposition fighters in Syria," and that the program "is aimed at shoring up the fighting power of units aligned with the Supreme Military Council, an umbrella organization led by a former Syrian general that is the main recipient of U.S. support."[60]

In other words, not long after the massacre had been reported by *The Telegraph*, the CIA announced additional support for the SMC, and its head, General Idris, who had participated alongside ISIS and Nusra in carrying out one of the war's most horrific atrocities.

'Sarin Doesn't Slice Throats'

This mass kidnapping of Alawites in the weeks prior to the alleged chemical attacks in Ghouta led some government supporters to speculate that the victims shown in the Ghouta videos were some of the Alawite women and children who had just been kidnapped in Latakia, and that Liwa al-Islam had murdered these captives and used their corpses in pre-prepared propaganda videos portraying them as Syrian government victims.

It was never confirmed that Alawite victims of the Latakia massacre were among the corpses in the Ghouta videos. However, such speculation raises the question of the identity of the victims in Ghouta. Research from pharmacologist Denis O'Brien suggests that the victims shown in the Ghouta videos were not local Sunni residents, but rather Alawite captives and prisoners of Liwa al-Islam, who were murdered as part of the false-flag massacre blamed on the government.

O'Brien concluded this after carrying out a detailed review of videos showing roughly 100 victims of the alleged Ghouta sarin attack, namely those appearing in a building turned makeshift morgue in the eastern Ghouta town of Kafr Batna. O'Brien concludes that the victims shown in the videos were not killed by sarin at all. Even though a sarin attack did occur in Ghouta, this is not what killed the victims, at least not those appearing in the Kafr Batna videos. Rather, O'Brien argues that these victims were killed by the so-called rebels themselves, most likely through carbon monoxide or cyanide-induced asphyxiation. O'Brien concluded this due to the primarily pink shading of the skin of the victims (rubicundity), rather than the blue-shaded skin (cyanosis) which would be expected if the deaths were caused by sarin. The differences in skin color result from the different ways these chemicals affect the oxygen levels in the blood of a victim. O'Brien speculates that the victims were initially locked in a basement room of the makeshift Kafr Batna morgue complex (video of the basement shows several victims who are still alive) where they were suffocated to death with carbon monoxide or cyanide, after which their corpses were brought up to the ground floor room and lined up in rows to be filmed.

O'Brien also shockingly observes how the videos from Kafr Batna show at least one victim who was alive in the sun-lit, ground floor room of the morgue even hours *after* the time of the alleged sarin attack, but who later bled to death while under the supervision of the medical workers allegedly trying to treat him and other victims. O'Brien observed this by looking at several videos and photos taken at different times showing the same victims lying dead on the floor. The earliest images show a man lying on the floor, apparently dead, while a later image shows the same man, but this time with a clenched fist and a white cloth covering his neck, as well as a separate blue blanket underneath his head that has become saturated with blood. Furthermore, the blood has also spread on the floor underneath other victims. This suggests that the man was still alive, but unconscious, after the initial attempt to kill him via asphyxiation in the basement. After bringing him to the sun-lit ground floor room, his captors realized that he was not dead, and slit his throat to finish the job. He was then left to bleed out, as those alleging to be medical workers calmly carried on withdrawing blood samples from other corpses.[61]

In short, the roughly 100 victims shown in the videos from Kafr Batna were not killed in a sarin attack, but in a managed massacre. As Adam Larson observed: "Sarin doesn't slice throats."[62]

Academic Paul McKeigue outlines further why the possibility of a managed massacre carried out by the so-called rebels is the best hypothesis for explaining the available evidence regarding the Ghouta incident. He observes that "of at least 150 videos uploaded, badged as coming from 18 different media outlets, not one shows [any] search and rescue operation," that all the "victims were in day clothes though the alleged attack occurred at about 2 a.m.," and that no video emerged of "interviews with bereaved survivors who would be able to document, with family photos, that they were relatives of victims seen dead in morgues." McKeigue uses probability theory to show that these observations would be unlikely if the government had indeed carried out a sarin attack, especially an attack that killed so many people, and that a managed massacre of the victims better explains the events in question.[63]

Some have claimed that a managed massacre is not plausible, arguing that opposition militants would not murder their own, including many women and children, for political gain.

However, we have already seen that Liwa al-Islam militants launched the sarin-filled rockets in the direction of eastern Ghouta. Additionally, if the victims in the videos were not pro-opposition Sunni civilians, as is typically assumed, but rather pro-government Sunni or Alawite civilians, the willingness of Liwa al-Islam to murder large numbers of men, women, and children to trigger the U.S. intervention they desired would be expected, given the existing incentives. The willingness of opposition groups, including the FSA, to kidnap and massacre Alawite civilians in large numbers has already been demonstrated earlier in this chapter.

This would be further unsurprising, given that Liwa al-Islam's leader, Zahran Alloush, has called for genocide against Alawites,[64] and given that in 2015 Liwa al-Islam (by that time known as Jaish al-Islam) was parading Alawite captives in cages in public squares, as reported by AFP.[65]

Years later, it further became clear that Liwa al-Islam would have had many captives to draw from for a false-flag massacre of the sort alleged by O'Brien and McKeigue. As Reuters reports, when the Syrian army was finally able to defeat Jaish al-Islam in 2018, the Syrian government gave the group's fighters free passage from Ghouta to the northern Syrian city of Jarablus in exchange for releasing some 3,500 captives then being held in Jaish al-Islam's Tawba Prison.[66]

Dead Men Tell No Lies

O'Brien's finding that the victims in Kafr Batna did not die from sarin raises the question of whether victims from other sites identified as part of the Ghouta attack also died from something other than sarin. Shockingly, the UN mission led by Ake Sellstrom consciously chose not to exhume bodies of the victims to test for sarin exposure when they visited two of the seven sites of the alleged Ghouta attack, preferring instead to follow the White House narrative and assume that sarin was the only possible cause of death.

A doctor in Ghouta who worked with the UN team told *The Guardian*: "We asked the [UN] committee to exhume the bodies for checking them. But they refused. They say that there was no need to do that."[67]

During an interview with Russia Today, UN disarmament chief Angela Kane, who accompanied the inspectors to Damascus, gave a tortured explanation as to why. When asked whether the UN investigators had requested access to bodies of victims of the alleged Ghouta attack, or had seen any of the bodies, Kane replied that "there were so many victims who are still alive that there was really no need to exhume bodies... a dead body can't tell how the person dies... a living person can tell you that."[68]

As Adam Larson points out, Kane's logic was "bizarre and completely incorrect." As the saying goes, it is "dead men who tell no lies." Witnesses can be curated and coached to tell a specific story, or they may be confused about what had happened to them during the chaos of the attack. But the body of a victim can be tested definitively for proof of sarin exposure significant enough to cause death.[69]

Had the UN team exhumed some bodies in Ghouta to obtain samples, the chain of custody would have remained intact, and this could have settled the question of whether the victims died of sarin, or something else. Because no bodies were exhumed, emphasis was shifted to physiological evidence derived from the alleged survivors of the attack, and the verbal testimony they provided when interviewed by the UN team.

According to the interim UN report on Ghouta, there seems to be no doubt that many people were exposed to, and suffered from, sarin exposure. This was confirmed not only through interviews and medical records of survivors, but also through blood and urine tests carried out by the UN team from the same survivors.[70]

This confirms that an attack with sarin-filled rockets occurred, but it does not confirm whether those who died on August 21 also died from sarin exposure. It is possible that the rockets contained enough sarin to affect many people and show up in samples, but not enough to kill many people.

Not Logical

The failure to exhume and test the bodies of the deceased again came under scrutiny after the interim UN report regarding Ghouta was released on September 13, 2013. Journalist Sharmine Narwani noted a crucial oddity in the report. The UN mission had gathered environmental samples from two areas in Ghouta: Moadamiyah in western Ghouta on August 26, and Ein Tarma and Zamalka in eastern Ghouta on August 28–29. Narwani notes that a closer look at the charts in appendix 7 of the report

> shows a massive discrepancy in lab results from east and west Ghouta. *There is not a single environmental sample in Moadamiyah that tested positive for Sarin…* Yet it is in Moadamiyah where alleged victims of a CW attack tested highest for Sarin exposure… *It is scientifically improbable that survivors would test that highly for exposure to Sarin without a single trace of environmental evidence testing positive for the chemical agent.*[71] (emphasis in original)

This suggests that in Moadamiyah in western Ghouta, no chemical attack occurred at all, and the survivors presented to the UN team were exposed to sarin somewhere else. As journalist Robert Parry points out, it is likely that the victims in Moadamiyah who tested positive for sarin were exposed in Zamalka, Ein Tarma, or elsewhere, but were brought to field hospitals in Moadamiyah for treatment. Parry notes that this possibility was raised even in the White House assessment written by Ben Rhodes and released on August 30 just before the U.S. intervention was to begin.[72]

Journalist Gareth Porter noted another anomaly in the interim UN report. Porter explains that the UN mission had asked an opposition leader to help identify survivors of the alleged chemical attack, and that this opposition leader chose the doctors who in turn identified the patients to be interviewed. The 36 individuals ultimately selected for detailed profiles of symptoms described themselves as among the most seriously exposed to sarin.[73]

Strangely, only 5 of these 36 patients thought to be most seriously exposed to sarin exhibited miosis, or constricted pupils. Porter reports that according to Dr. Abbas Faroutan, who treated Iranian victims of Iraqi nerve gas attacks during the Iran-Iraq War in the 1980s, it was "not logical" that only 5 of the 36 reported experiencing miosis if they had all been exposed to sarin.

To Porter, this "suggests a much less lethal attack with munitions that were less effective and perhaps even using much less sarin than was initially assumed," and that the 50-liter warheads on the rockets used in the eastern Ghouta attacks were likely not filled with pure sarin, but with a mixture of sarin and water. This would perhaps be enough to cause the survivors to have some exposure to sarin, but not enough exposure to cause mass casualties.

MIT professor Theodore Postol concluded as a result that perhaps "the objective was not to kill people, but to terrify people... Or it was to look as much like the Syrian government [attacking] as possible."[74]

In other words, for militants from Liwa al-Islam to carry out a false-flag attack to be blamed on the Syrian government, they did not need to produce or acquire enough sarin to cause mass casualties. Instead, they needed to acquire and use just enough sarin for it to be detected in at least some human and environmental samples collected by the UN mission.

That opposition militants in the Damascus suburbs were in possession of at least small amounts of sarin was later confirmed with the release of the Ake Sellstrom-led UN mission's final report in December 2013. The report concluded that sarin had been used on a small scale *against* Syrian soldiers during clashes with opposition militants just days after the August 21 Ghouta attack, namely on August 24 in the Jobar neighborhood in Damascus and on August 25 in Ashrafiah Sahnaya in the Damascus countryside.[75]

Due to the difficulty of producing sarin, even in small amounts, it is possible that the opposition militants acquired this from the Nusra Front. Seymour Hersh reports that according to a U.S. intelligence document issued mid-summer 2013, a Nusra militant named Ziyaad Tariq Ahmed was operating in eastern Ghouta, and that he was an "al-Nusra guy with a track record of making mustard gas in Iraq and someone who is implicated in making and using sarin."[76] In other words, Nusra may have been supplying sarin in limited amounts to local militants from Liwa al-Islam to use in their battles with the Syrian army, and potentially as part of the August 21 false-flag attack.

As noted in Chapter 15, Seymour Hersh reported that "the Turkish government was working directly with al-Nusra *and its allies* to develop a chemical warfare capability" (emphasis added). This means that if Nusra was providing Liwa al-Islam with sarin, it did so with the blessing of Turkish intelligence.

That only small amounts of sarin were used in the Ghouta attack undercuts the conclusions of the U.K. Joint Intelligence Committee assessment regarding Ghouta, issued on August 29, 2013, which claimed that "it is not possible for the opposition to have carried out a CW attack *on this scale*" (emphasis added).[77] While the killings in the Ghouta attack were indeed on a mass scale (100 killed in Kafr Batna alone), the chemical attack itself was not.

But if the amount of sarin in the rockets fired in Ghouta was not sufficient to cause the mass casualties attested to in the videos, how then did hundreds of people die? The answer, of course, is that the victims presented in the videos were killed in another way, likely by asphyxiation from exposure to carbon monoxide or cyanide, as Denis O'Brien concluded.

Chemical weapons expert Jean Pascal Zanders had similarly concluded that the victims were likely exposed only to small amounts of nerve agents, and that they had died of asphyxiation that was unrelated to this exposure. Zanders explained that

> if one looks at the symptoms [shown in the YouTube videos], *they are not very strong in terms of exposure* [and] if you watch the clips closely, you will see [parts] where people clearly show signs of asphyxiation but show no signs of exposure to neurotoxicants such as sarin or VX gas.[78] (emphasis added)

Intervention, but for Whom?

Like President Obama, U.S. Chairman of the Joint Chiefs of Staff Martin Dempsey was reluctant to initiate a U.S. bombing campaign in the wake of the Ghouta massacre, knowing that an intervention *against* the Syrian government was in turn an intervention *for* al-Qaeda.

The *Los Angeles Times* reported that, according to Dempsey, while U.S. forces could easily defeat Assad's air defenses and tilt the conflict in favor of the rebels, the United States should avoid even limited military engagement because the rebels, who include fighters loyal to Al Qaeda, don't back U.S. interests. Syria today is not about choosing between two sides but rather about choosing one among many sides.[79]

While Dempsey was right to point out that any direct U.S. military intervention would be done on behalf of al-Qaeda, he was wrong to suggest that the terror group did not back U.S. interests. As discussed in Chapter 2, U.S. officials had worked closely with Prince Bandar to use al-Qaeda to launch the war against Syria in 2011 in the first place.

Further, U.S. officials had also privately acknowledged that al-Qaeda was indeed fighting on behalf of what they considered to be U.S. interests multiple times. In February 2012, Hillary Clinton aide Jake Sullivan had indicated in an email that "AQ [al-Qaeda] is on our side in Syria."[80]

Similarly, the August 2012 Defense Intelligence Agency (DIA) report had made clear that Salafists, the Muslim Brotherhood, and al-Qaeda were the driving forces of the U.S.- and Gulf-backed insurgency, and that the U.S. and its regional allies supported the establishment of a "Salafist principality" in eastern Syria as part of the effort to topple Assad and divide the country.[81]

Washington's dependence on al-Qaeda-affiliated groups to execute its covert war against the Syrian government had come into public focus just two weeks before the Ghouta chemical attack. On August 5, 2013, U.S.-backed FSA leader Colonel Abd al-Jabbar al-Okaidi appeared in a video next to an ISIS commander celebrating the successful capture of the Menagh air base near Aleppo in a culmination of the "War of the Airports" discussed in Chapter 14.

Of the fall of Menagh, the *New York Times* reported that weeks of "relentless suicide vehicle bombings on the walls of the base" had turned the tide in the battle.[82] U.S. Ambassador to Syria Robert Ford, a strong supporter of arming the so-called rebels, writes:

> One morning in early August [2013], I came to the office at the State Department to see reports that Menagh had finally fallen and pictures of Akaidi standing next to ISIS field commander Abu Jandal al-Masri celebrating the capture of the base.[83]

Okaidi's appearance in the video was just one indication of his close relationship with ISIS commanders. As noted in Chapter 14, Okaidi had acknowledged that "my relationship with the brothers in ISIS is good" and that "I communicate almost daily with the brothers from ISIS."[84]

The emergence of the video of Okaidi and the ISIS commander celebrating, in the words of the *New York Times*, "like members of a victorious basketball team," proved embarrassing for Ambassador Ford and the Obama administration, given Ford's close relationship with Okaidi.[85]

McClatchy reports that in response to the Menagh video, Ford called Okaidi directly to complain, and that the video had created "a public relations nightmare for the Obama administration, which was trying to show Congress and the American public that it was boosting moderates and isolating extremists on the battlefield." However, as McClatchy notes, "when the importance of the jihadis became undeniable, Obama administration officials were irate."[86]

Launching a U.S. bombing campaign only weeks after the events at Menagh would have led to the black flag of the jihadis flying over Damascus and exposed even further the U.S.'s reliance on al-Qaeda in the war against the Syrian government. For at least some U.S. officials, Chairman of the Joint Chiefs Martin Dempsey among them, this was going too far.

I Too Know Them

Senator John McCain had no such reservations, however, and continued to push for a U.S. bombing campaign in support of al-Qaeda in the wake of the Ghouta attack. During a town hall meeting in McCain's home state of Arizona on September 5, 2013, a Syrian-American Christian woman confronted him on his Syria policy. She implored the senator to end the conflict through "negotiations and diplomacy, not bombs," saying that "we cannot afford to shed more Syrian blood." She explained further:

> I have an 18-year-old cousin [who] just was killed ten days ago by the so-called rebels and al-Qaeda, and they are not Syrian. They are coming to Syria from all over the world to fight… We cannot afford to turn Syria into another Iraq or Afghanistan… We don't want al-Qaeda to take over…
>
> We are the minority Christians who are unfortunately by you and so many in the Senate are just considering us as collateral damage. And I refuse that, because I can trace my family's name to the Bible… From the beginning of humanity we were there, and we refuse to leave and be considered collateral damage.[87]

McCain responded by boasting, "I too have been to Syria, I too know the people who are fighting there, I met them, I know them, and I know who they are," referring to his brief trip across the Turkish border to Syria three months earlier.

During his May 2013 visit, McCain met and was photographed with members of the Northern Storm Brigade, a U.S.-backed armed opposition group based in the city of Azaz.

One of the men with whom McCain was photographed had been implicated in the kidnapping of 11 Lebanese Shiite pilgrims a year before.[88]

A month prior to McCain's visit, *Time* magazine's Patrick Wells embedded with the brigade as it participated in the siege of the Menagh air base alongside the Nusra Front. A Northern Storm commander told Wells that he had fought against U.S. forces in Iraq after the 2003 invasion.[89]

In August, the brigade celebrated the capture of Menagh alongside ISIS and Liwa al-Tawhid.[90] In September, just three months after McCain's visit, the brigade abducted and sold American journalist Steven Sotloff to ISIS.[91] After holding Sotloff captive for a year, ISIS released a video showing one of its members beheading him.

From the Beginning of Humanity

One day before the Syrian-American Christian woman confronted McCain at the town hall meeting in Arizona, the "rebels" he claimed to know so well began a campaign to root out Syria's ancient Christian community in the town of Maaloula. Home to two ancient monasteries, Mar Sarkis and Mar Thecla, Maaloula is one of the last places in the world where Aramaic, thought to be the language of Jesus, is still spoken.

According to legend, Maaloula was founded after Saint Thecla, a noble virgin and disciple of Paul the Apostle, was being pursued by Roman soldiers because of her Christian faith. Thecla came upon a mountain, and after praying, the mountain split open, allowing her to escape through a narrow chasm in the cliffs.

On September 4, 2013, a Jordanian suicide bomber targeted a Syrian army checkpoint protecting the entrance to Maaloula, giving the signal for Nusra and FSA militants to attack the town.[92] The Barnabas Fund, a Christian humanitarian aid group, reported that at least seven Christians were killed and around 15 kidnapped, with bodies of Christians shot dead and left lying in the streets.[93]

Virtually all of the town's 3,000 residents fled, seeking haven in Bab Touma, the Christian quarter of Damascus. A local priest slammed the FSA for posting a video on YouTube allegedly showing its militants defending the churches and Christians in the town. He called the video "pure propaganda," explaining that "the Free Army is free in name only. In fact, it has been a threat to Christians for a long time, saying repeatedly that sooner or later our turn would come." He explained further that "so far, most Muslims are with the Christians," and that the local "sheikh condemned the attack saying that what is happening is against Islam," but "unfortunately, these fighters do not respect local Muslim leaders, who, like us, are powerless in the face of all this hate."[94]

The militants withdrew from Maaloula shortly after the September 4 assault, but invaded the town again three months later, on December 3, this time kidnapping 12 nuns from the Mar Thecla convent, as well as orphans under their foster care. The nuns were among the few who had refused to leave the town after the assault in September.[95] Militants also looted and destroyed rare Christian icons and altars, some of the oldest in the world, while also demolishing the statue of the Virgin Mary that had watched over the town from the top of the cliffs looming above.[96] The nuns were released three months later as part of a prisoner exchange negotiated in part by Qatari officials.[97]

This led journalist Harout Ekmanian to comment later:

> At the same time, we see that there is almost no difference between the group called Free Syrian Army or other jihadist groups and ISIS. For instance, these "moderate" opposition groups burned the churches down, when they entered Kessab. They entered Malula, where there is still an ancient Christian community speaking Aramaic. They destroyed that place too. There are many other examples like these.[98]

Senator McCain and other U.S. officials attempting to orchestrate regime change in Syria of course knew the nature of the men they were supporting, and that, as the Christian woman who confronted McCain warned, al-Qaeda would take over the country if a U.S.-led bombing campaign was unleashed in the wake of the Ghouta massacre. McCain, CIA Director John Brennan, and other U.S. officials nevertheless continued to push for U.S. military intervention.

Go to Hell

On September 9, 2013, just as President Obama and his chief of staff, Denis McDonough, continued the public relations push for war, Secretary of State Kerry gave a press conference in London in which he rhetorically suggested that one way to avert U.S. intervention would be if Assad immediately gave up his entire chemical weapons stock. Russian Foreign Minister Sergei Lavrov seized the opening and suggested to Kerry that the U.S. and Russia arrange to do just that.[99]

Lavrov quickly gained the consent of the Syrian leadership, and after a marathon series of meetings over the coming days, an agreement was reached with Kerry on Saturday, September 14, to facilitate the destruction of Syria's chemical weapons.

This provided Obama the final pretext he needed to resist the hordes and call off a U.S. bombing campaign altogether. Referring the issue to Congress had bought the president time, and now Foreign Minister Lavrov had provided Obama a way out.

In response, the U.S.-backed FSA chief, General Salim Idris, who was just one month removed from massacring Alawites in Latakia alongside ISIS and Nusra, "denounced the initiative." The *New York Times* quoted Idris as saying, "All of this initiative does not interest us. Russia is a partner with the regime in killing the Syrian people."[100] FSA commander Qassem Saaddedine, who had prepared to launch an offensive to take Damascus in concert with the expected Western bombing campaign, was blunt, saying, "Let the Kerry-Lavrov plan go to hell. We reject it, and we will not protect the inspectors."[101]

If Idris and Saaddedine really believed the government had perpetrated the Ghouta atrocity, this was an odd response. From the opposition point of view, the destruction of Syria's chemical weapons would prevent a repeat of such an atrocity. Instead, opposition leaders denounced the initiative because their objective of coming to power under the protection of U.S. bombs had been frustrated.

17. The CIA Doubles Down on Dirty War

The Trap

This of course raises the question: Why would Obama change course during his walk with his chief of staff, Denis McDonough, on the White House lawn on August 30, just one day before a long-planned military assault was set to commence, and instead refer the issue to the U.S. Congress?

Journalist Michael Gordon of the *New York Times* writes that

> the rethink began when the British Parliament voted against participating in the mission, which prompted the president to question his decision to strike without a congressional vote of support — a step that was not required constitutionally, but would provide political cover in case the operation went awry or led to a protracted intervention.[1]

In other words, although many parties were pressuring the president to green-light the intervention, Obama knew that he alone would be blamed if things went wrong. This is possibly why he later told Jeffrey Goldberg of *The Atlantic* that he "was walking into a trap — one laid both by *allies* and by adversaries" (emphasis added), but which he escaped by referring the issue to Congress and later agreeing to the plan to destroy Syria's chemical weapons.[2]

Obama was bitterly criticized as a result. *The Daily Beast* reported that

> the Saudi point man on the Syrian conflict, Prince Bandar bin Sultan, has been angry over the Obama administration's Middle East policies — from the decision to refrain from striking President Bashar al-Assad's forces for their use of sarin nerve gas in August.[3]

Bandar's frustration is unsurprising, given his outsized role in the broader regime change project, and his close management of Liwa al-Islam, which carried out the Ghouta attack.

Elements in the U.K. government working with the Saudis to push for intervention were similarly frustrated. British Ambassador to Saudi Arabia John Jenkins wrote at the time:

> I remember vividly the last week of August 2013, when Assad was going to be punished for stepping over that particular "red line." I was in Riyadh at the time and *involved in seeking, on behalf of the British*

government, senior engagement by the Saudis in an international response, which they were willing to give. The sense of frustration when the U.K. and U.S. stepped back was palpable.[4] (emphasis added)

The *Los Angeles Times* similarly reported that Turkish President Erdoğan "did not hide his displeasure when the recent U.S.-Russian-brokered deal to neutralize Syria's chemical weapons seemed to rule out the prospect of an American bombing campaign against Syria."[5] As noted in Chapter 15, Erdoğan had promised to topple the Syrian government during his visit to Libya in September 2011.

Although he made no public statement to this effect, we can speculate that CIA Director John Brennan was similarly disappointed, given his strong push in the wake of the Ghouta massacre to convince Obama to launch the intervention.

Jeffrey Goldberg notes that Obama was immediately criticized as well by U.S. Senators John McCain and Lindsey Graham, former CIA Director and Secretary of Defense Leon Panetta, former Secretary of State Hillary Clinton, *Foreign Affairs* editor Gideon Rose, Saudi Ambassador to the U.S. Adel al-Jubeir, King Abdallah of Jordan, and Crown Prince Mohammed bin Zayed al-Nahyan of Abu Dhabi.[6]

While speaking with Goldberg about the trap laid for him by his own allies, Obama specifically complained that he

> resented the foreign-policy think-tank complex. A widely held sentiment inside the White House is that many of the most prominent foreign policy think tanks in Washington are doing the bidding of their Arab and pro-Israel funders.[7]

The Devil You Know

Obama's complaint about not only Arab but also pro-Israel think tank funders is crucial to note, given that it was Israeli intelligence which first introduced the concept of the red line regarding chemical weapons use in Syria in 2012 and had supplied much of the false intelligence claiming, at every critical juncture, that the Syrian government had indeed crossed the red line, including immediately after the Ghouta attack itself. In other words, Israeli intelligence was a significant force for advocating Western military intervention in Syria and among those trying to trap Obama.

At first glance, this may seem surprising. Since the beginning of the conflict in 2011, Israeli officials had publicly expressed tacit support for

Assad staying in power. The *Jerusalem Post* claimed on March 23, 2011, that "for all his faults, Assad is the devil we know." The *Post* explained that

> as Israel watches the ongoing demonstrations in Syria against President Bashar Assad, its greatest concern for the moment is the uncertainty that change in Syria would bring to the region. Israel has gotten used to Assad, and he is almost predictable.[8]

The claim that, of all of Israel's borders, "the border with Syria has always been the quietest," was repeated incessantly by Syrian opposition activists, who wished to cast Assad as a friend of Israel and enemy of the Palestinians. Regarding Syria's historical resistance to Israel, opposition activist Robin Yassin-Kassab asked:

> But how resistant was the regime in reality?... The regime policed its own frontier with the occupied Golan Heights so obediently that it remained more peaceful than the borders of states that had signed peace agreements with "the Zionist enemy."[9]

This was merely public posturing, however. Change is exactly what Israel wanted in Syria. But Israeli planners of course realized that any public support for the Syrian opposition would undermine the credibility of the regime change project among Syrians and Muslims broadly, and therefore kept their support for toppling Assad covert.

Israeli interests played a prominent role in the U.S. effort to topple the Syrian government even before 2011. As noted in Chapter 1, support for Israel is a key tenet of neoconservative ideology, and it was neoconservatives in the Bush administration who began the project to target seven countries in five years for regime change, including Syria, Iraq, and Iran, in the wake of 9/11.[10]

U.S. efforts to launch the al-Qaeda-led dirty war on Syria that emerged in 2011 were important for Israel's settler-colonial project because, as Gerald Steinberg of Bar-Ilan University explained during the Second Intifada in 2001: "From an Israeli perspective, the most dangerous threats come from a potential coalition of Arab states and Iran, rather than from the Palestinians alone."[11]

Uri Sagi, Israel's former chief of military intelligence, reiterated this view in September 2013, in the wake of the Ghouta massacre, explaining that "for many years, until the civil war broke out, the Syrians were the last army to pose a serious threat to Israel, and therefore the investment of our intelligence resources in that direction was enormous."[12]

This is an indication that the so-called "Syrian Revolution" was really part of Israel's broader war on the Palestinians and the Axis of Resistance supporting them. The destruction of Yarmouk camp, known as the capital of the Palestinian diaspora, as well as the displacement of its hundreds of thousands of Palestinian refugees in what amounted to a second Nakba, serves as a tragic reminder of this. Israeli planners were supporting the armed groups that invaded Yarmouk in December 2012, including Nusra, but this was not apparent until years later because, as Israeli Defense Minister Moshe Ya'alon explained, it was "not in the rebels' interest to publicize the fact that Israel assists them."[13]

Had Obama green-lit a U.S. attack in August 2013 to "eradicate any military capabilities Assad had," as detailed by Seymour Hersh, Israeli planners would have achieved one of their longest sought-after goals. The incentive for Israel to devote "intelligence resources" toward a false-flag operation in Ghouta in order to blame a sarin attack on Assad was therefore enormous.

The desire to push for regime change in Iran played a role as well, with journalist Yossi Verter writing in *Haaretz* on August 30, 2013, that "from [Israeli Prime Minister Benjamin] Netanyahu's perspective, Assad's ouster might inject the United States with greater confidence to confront Iran."[14]

Syria Is the Keystone

Shortly after the deal to destroy Syria's chemical weapons had been reached, Israel's long-standing preference for regime change in Syria was finally openly acknowledged. In an interview[15] with the *Jerusalem Post*, Israel's outgoing ambassador to the U.S., Michael Oren, explained that "the initial message about the Syrian issue was that *we always wanted [President] Bashar Assad to go*, we always preferred the bad guys who weren't backed by Iran to the bad guys who were backed by Iran" (emphasis added), including if the other "bad guys" were affiliated with al-Qaeda. Oren explained further:

> We understand that they are pretty bad guys… Still, the greatest danger to Israel is by the strategic arc that extends from Tehran to Damascus to Beirut. And we saw the Assad regime as the keystone in that arc. That is a position we had well *before the outbreak of hostilities* in Syria. With the outbreak of hostilities, we continued to want Assad to go. (emphasis added)

Oren also noted Israeli cooperation with Saudi Arabia, which shared an interest with Israel in weakening the "Shiite crescent" as well. Oren remarked that

> in the last 64 years there has probably never been a greater confluence of interest between us and several Gulf States. With these Gulf States we have agreements on Syria, on Egypt, on the Palestinian issue. We certainly have agreements on Iran. This is one of those opportunities presented by the Arab Spring.

This is another indication that the Ghouta false-flag operation was likely carried out not by Liwa al-Islam alone, but by a Safari Club-style coalition of intelligence agencies from multiple countries, whose interests were so aligned as to be indistinguishable, with Saudi intelligence chief Prince Bandar serving as point man for the operation.

Although the false-flag attack in Ghouta did not lead to regime change in Damascus or the complete destruction of Syrian military capabilities (Tel Aviv's maximalist goals), in the end, it was Israel who nevertheless benefited most from the Ghouta massacre.

Syria's chemical weapons were developed in the 1980s as a deterrent to Israeli nuclear capabilities and to any possible large-scale Israeli invasion of Syria resembling the 1982 invasion and occupation of southern Lebanon. This meant that the U.S.-Russian deal to have the Syrian government destroy 1,300 metric tons of chemical warfare agents in the wake of the Ghouta attack was a clear win for Israel. Jeffrey Goldberg reports that the agreement to destroy Syria's chemical weapons "won the president praise from, of all people, Benjamin Netanyahu, the Israeli prime minister," and that it represented "the one ray of light in a very dark region."[16]

In addition, the Syrian government's willingness to give up its chemical weapon deterrent had not resulted in a peace agreement to end the war. Kerry and Lavrov's deal had averted direct U.S. intervention, but U.S. support for the al-Qaeda-dominated insurgency would persist. So long as the bloodshed in Syria continued, this was an acceptable outcome for Israel. Alon Pinkas, a former Israeli consul general in New York, argued, for example, that "this is a playoff situation in which you need both teams to lose, but at least you don't want one to win — we'll settle for a tie... Let them both bleed, hemorrhage to death: that's the strategic thinking here."[17]

Shortly after the Ghouta attack, neoconservative writer Edward Luttwak of the Center for Strategic and International Studies (CSIS) argued in the *New York Times* that such a strategy was in the American interest as well:

There is only one outcome that the United States can possibly favor: an indefinite draw. By tying down Mr. Assad's army and its Iranian and Hezbollah allies in a war against Al Qaeda-aligned extremist fighters, four of Washington's enemies will be engaged in war among themselves and prevented from attacking Americans or America's allies. Maintaining a stalemate should be America's objective. And the only possible method for achieving this is to arm the rebels when it seems that Mr. Assad's forces are ascendant and to stop supplying the rebels if they actually seem to be winning.[18]

In other words, in the view of neoconservatives, it was in America and Israel's interest for the slaughter of Syrians to continue indefinitely via a "stalemate." Despite rejecting direct military intervention, Obama acquiesced to this policy by allowing covert support for the jihadists in Syria to continue.

Al-Qaeda's Air Force

It was in this context that the direct Israeli support for Nusra and other armed opposition groups continued. *Al-Monitor* reported in January 2015 that Israel was assisting the Nusra Front in attacking Syrian army positions in southern Syria near the Golan ceasefire line. According to one activist who supported the armed groups directly, "the battle to capture Quneitra on Sept. 27 [2014] was preceded by coordination and communications between Abu Dardaa, a leader of Jabhat al-Nusra, and the Israeli army to pave the way for the attack." According to an FSA commander who participated in the battle:

The Israeli army provided Abu Dardaa with maps of the border area and the Syrian army's strategic posts in the southern area… During the clashes, the Israelis heavily bombarded many of the regime's posts, shot down a warplane that was trying to impede the progress of the fighters, and targeted other aircraft.[19]

Just days after Nusra's attack on Quneitra, but before Israeli involvement had been reported, Jeffrey White, a former senior U.S. Defense Intelligence Agency analyst with the Washington Institute for Near East Policy (WINEP), a pro-Israel think tank, explained the logic behind Tel Aviv's support for Nusra. He argued on October 2, 2014, that "the risk of empowering an al Qaida affiliate is a small price to pay for Nusra's contributions on the battlefield."[20]

In response, President Assad explained in an interview to *Foreign Affairs* that "whenever we make advances in some place, they [Israel] attack in order to undermine the army. That's why some in Syria joke, how can you say that al-Qaeda doesn't have an air force? They have the Israeli air force."[21]

'We Need Plausible Deniability'

Because the chance for direct U.S. intervention in the wake of the 2013 Ghouta massacre had slipped away and the Syrian army was now ascendant, additional support for al-Qaeda was still needed, at least to restore the stalemate desired by U.S. and Israeli planners. The task of selling this policy to the public fell to former CIA Deputy Director Michael Morell. Because he had retired in August 2013 (just before the Ghouta massacre, and after 33 years in the agency), Morell could now become a public advocate for CIA policies.

In September 2013, Morell spoke at length with the CBS News program *60 Minutes* to argue for more U.S. military aid to armed opposition groups. In the interview, Morell acknowledged that the opposition was dominated by al-Qaeda, in the form of not only the Nusra Front, but also Ahrar al-Sham, which he described as "the two most effective organizations on the battlefield," and that "because they're so good at fighting the Syrians some of the moderate members of the opposition joined forces with them."[22]

Because Morell noted that U.S.-supplied FSA groups had "joined forces" with Ahrar and Nusra, this makes clear that Morell favored arming al-Qaeda, but in a way that would be plausibly deniable. He argued in favor of this by bizarrely suggesting during the *60 Minutes* interview that he was somehow above all concerned about the *threat* from al-Qaeda.

Morell explained:

> I'm concerned because where we're headed right now is toward, I fear, the breakup of the State of Syria [and of the] opportunity for al Qaeda to have a safe haven in Syria that is not dissimilar to the safe haven that it once enjoyed in Afghanistan… The best outcome is a negotiated settlement between the opposition and between the regime that allows for a political transition that keeps the institutions of the state intact… The reason that is important is because it's going to take the institution of the Syrian military and the institutions of the Syrian security services to defeat al Qaeda when this is done.[23]

After detailing these concerns, Morell was asked by *60 Minutes* journalist John Miller whether this required "more or less support than is being provided now" to the al-Qaeda-dominated opposition. Morell answered, "I think it's more."

In other words, to *prevent* the establishment of an al-Qaeda safe haven in Syria in the future, Morell advocated *arming* al-Qaeda in the present.

One week after Morell's *60 Minutes* interview, the results of the U.S. policy he was advocating once again became apparent. McClatchy reported that Katibat al-Nasr, or "the Victory Brigade," an FSA group affiliated with the Hama Military Council, was showing off newly acquired Croatian weapons, including shoulder-fired RPG-27s and RG6 grenade launchers, which the group had acquired via a recent Saudi brokered shipment. McClatchy noted further that the Victory Brigade had been fighting alongside Ahrar al-Sham, and that Ahrar fighters were shown in videos using the same kind of weapons. McClatchy quoted Ali Ankir, a spokesman for Ahrar al-Sham, as explaining: "Of course they share their weapons with us... We fight together."[24]

In 2016, U.S. support for Ahrar al-Sham became apparent after U.S. diplomats shielded the group from being designated as a terrorist group by the UN following a proposal by Russia. This followed a massacre carried out by Ahrar al-Sham in the Alawite town of Zara'a in Hama Province. According to the SOHR, militants from Ahrar al-Sham and the Nusra Front raided homes in the village, killing 19 civilians and kidnapping dozens more.[25]

Russia Today interviewed several residents of Zara'a following the massacre. Ahmad Muhammad al-Qasem explained that

> strangers came to our village. Most of them were foreigners; we understood that they weren't from Syria from the way they looked. They attacked our village, many were killed. My brother is among the dead, his children were wounded. They killed entire families.[26]

Another villager, Munzer Qasem, explained that

> they perpetrated a massacre. I heard of two or three entire families killed. Abu Naval's family was killed. He was an old man and was killed together with his daughters. They were slaughtered in their own house.

In another sign of CIA support for Ahrar al-Sham, the group's spokesman Labib al-Nahhas was allowed to write an op-ed in the *Washington Post* in July 2015.[27] Al-Nahhas was then allowed to visit the U.S. personally in December 2015, despite the group's old links to al-Qaeda, including through Ahrar's founder, Abu Khalid al-Suri, whose death in 2014 was memorialized by al-Qaeda leader Ayman al-Zawahiri.[28]

In October 2013, one month after Michael Morell's *60 Minutes* interview advocating increased arms shipments to the FSA, the *New York Times* reported that Obama administration officials chose to arm what they referred to as Syrian rebels in an off-the-books fashion via the CIA, rather than via a publicly acknowledged program through the Pentagon. This was not only to avoid the legal issues associated with toppling a sovereign government, but also because, in the words of one former senior administration official, "we needed plausible deniability in case the arms got into the hands of Al Nusra," which of course they would.[29]

Morell, who had served as second-in-command at CIA (and even for a time as acting director) from the beginning of the Syria war in 2011 until the eve of the Ghouta massacre in 2013, therefore played a crucial role in laying the foundation for the rise of al-Qaeda in Syria. He also therefore bears significant responsibility, along with previous CIA heads David Petraeus and John Brennan, and Saudi intelligence chief Prince Bandar, for the many atrocities committed in Syria and Iraq by the notorious terror group, whether in the form of Nusra, Ahrar al-Sham, or ISIS, as well as for atrocities committed by allied Salafist militias of the FSA, including most notoriously the massacre of Alawites in Latakia in August 2013.

Exponential Growth

CIA efforts to provide more support to Nusra, Ahrar al-Sham, and FSA groups in the wake of the 2013 Ghouta massacre, as advocated by Morell, were evident not only through the acceleration of U.S. weapons shipments to the al-Qaeda-led insurgency, but also through the ever-expanding flow of jihadists from the Arab world, Europe, and elsewhere, traveling to Syria to join the fight.

In November 2013, just as U.S. planners were maintaining their plausible deniability in arming the Nusra Front, Nick Walsh of CNN reported having witnessed the arrival of large numbers of foreign, fighting-aged men at the Hatay airport outside the Turkish city of Antakya near the Syrian border. Walsh noted that "it is extraordinary to watch this volume of international traffic from countries where al Qaeda has a confirmed and consistent presence into a NATO member state." Walsh spoke with a smuggler helping the jihadists, who explained that in the past few months,

> he's moved about 400 people across the border, and that the rate of people making the crossing has almost tripled since the chemical attacks on the Damascus suburbs in August. And that's just him; there are many other smugglers operating in the area.[30]

This massive increase in the flow of foreign jihadist fighters appears to have been a deliberate effort by U.S., Saudi, and Turkish intelligence to escalate the war in order to compensate for Obama's failure to authorize intervention in the wake of Ghouta. *The Daily Beast* reported in December 2013 that according to Western officials,

> nearly a thousand Saudi jihadists have joined al-Qaeda affiliates in northern Syria in recent months, and they suspect that number will exponentially grow in the coming months… [including] dozens of Saudi jihadists [who] have been allowed to fly out of [the Saudi capital] Riyadh without challenge, several after being released from detention and many of whom were under official travel bans. Those going to fight are not obscure figures: a major in the Saudi border guards was killed in early December in Deir Atieh in Syria; another Saudi jihadist killed fighting in Aleppo was the son of Maj. Gen. Abdullah Motlaq al-Sudairi. Hardline Salafist Saudi clerics have also been heading to Syria without incurring problems from Saudi Arabian authorities.[31]

Abdullah Suleiman Ali of *As-Safir* provided further details, reporting that by late 2013,

> a large number of Saudi jihadists present in Syria are in fact barred from traveling, by virtue of a formal decision issued by the Saudi authorities. These figures include Abdullah bin Qaed al-Otaibi, Badr bin Ajab al-Mqati, Abdulla al-Sudairi, Uqab Mamdouh Marzouki and dozens of others who arrived to Syria despite the travel ban. It is worth mentioning that these Saudis left the kingdom through Riyadh airport, as confirmed by most of them on Twitter… Furthermore, some of them returned back to Saudi Arabia for a short time, in what seemed to be a vacation from jihad, only to return back to Syria again.[32]

Suleiman Ali notes further that those successfully reaching Syria from Saudi Arabia included "senior al-Qaeda members and a large number of those who were banned from traveling, as well as a number of activists and protestors," who traveled to Syria almost immediately after their release from detention in Saudi prisons. Suleiman Ali concludes by asking, "Is it possible that all this happened under the nose of the Saudi authorities?"

As head of the Saudi national security office and Saudi intelligence, Prince Bandar would have been involved in allowing these known al-Qaeda figures and other Saudi extremists to leave the country despite the travel bans.

Despite opposition propaganda that Assad had released jihadists from Sednaya Prison to Islamize the so-called peaceful revolution, in the end it was U.S. and Saudi planners who did so, from prisons in Iraq and Saudi Arabia, respectively.

Washington's support for al-Qaeda-affiliated groups in Syria was further signaled in January 2014 by former Deputy Assistant Secretary of Defense and neoconservative Michael Doran.

Writing in *Foreign Affairs*, the voice of the influential Council on Foreign Relations, Doran asked "whether the fight against al Qaeda is always the strategic priority in the Middle East. It might at times get in the way of other goals, including the efforts to contain Iran and Syria." Doran then urged President Obama to keep Ahrar al-Sham off the designated terror list, despite public confirmation that one of its top leaders, Abu Khalid al-Suri, was an al-Qaeda operative.[33]

The Largest al-Qaeda Safe Haven Since 9/11

It was also no accident that the new wave of jihadi fighters was arriving in Antakya, in Hatay Province, near the Syrian border. As noted in Chapter 16, preparations for attacking Damascus in advance of the Ghouta incident were taking place under the direction of U.S., Qatari, and Turkish intelligence officials from an FSA command center also located in Antakya. It was not only Nick Walsh of CNN watching "this volume of international traffic" of jihadists passing through Antakya, but CIA case officers based in the city as well.

The CIA's partners in Turkish intelligence were in turn busy managing this traffic. In October 2013, the *Wall Street Journal* reported that according to former and current U.S. officials, Turkish intelligence chief Hakan Fidan "acted like a 'traffic cop' that arranged weapons drops and let convoys through checkpoints along Turkey's 565-mile border with Syria."[34]

Al-Monitor reported the same month that Turkish parliament member Mehmet Ali Edipoglu of the country's main opposition party was "overflowing" with reports of Turkish assistance in moving weapons and fighters across the border to radical Islamist groups in Syria.[35] Additionally, Turkish intelligence officers were meeting directly with ISIS commanders. Ahmet Yayala, a former Turkish counterterrorism police officer, said in an interview that Turkish intelligence has "consistently helped ISIS, directly or indirectly," and that in 2014 "we saw the terrorists meeting with our own service. It was extremely upsetting."[36]

One of the Saudi clerics who traveled to Syria in 2013 despite an official travel ban was Abdullah al-Muhaysini, the nephew of a leading Saudi cleric who was the former head of the country's powerful Committee for the Promotion of Virtue and the Prevention of Vice. Muhaysini later became the general religious judge of Jaish al-Fatah, or "the Army of Conquest," a coalition of jihadist groups led by the Nusra Front.[37]

According to David Ignatius of the *Washington Post*, Jaish al-Fatah was created in 2014 at the direction of the intelligence agencies of Turkey, Saudi Arabia, and Qatar. Ignatius explained that "by pumping weapons to Syrian rebels across the Turkish border, the three countries have forged a new opposition coalition known as the Army of Conquest."[38]

As I have detailed elsewhere, the U.S. military played a crucial role in Jaish al-Fatah's conquest of Idlib Province in the spring of 2015 by supplying large numbers of TOW anti-tank missiles to FSA groups fighting with the Nusra-led coalition.[39]

As a result, U.S. official Brett McGurk later expressed concern that Syria's northwest Idlib Province had become "the largest Al Qaeda safe haven since 9/11."[40] In other words, 18 months after former CIA Deputy Director Michael Morell claimed to be concerned about the establishment of an al-Qaeda haven in Syria, the CIA policy Morell advocated had created just that.

18. Syria's Missing

The Caesar Operation

In addition to escalating the war by flooding Syria with jihadists in the wake of the 2013 Ghouta false flag failure, the CIA and its regional allies launched a sophisticated psychological operation, known as the "Caesar photos," to blame the Syrian government falsely for even greater mass atrocities. These Caesar photos later opened the way for U.S. planners to impose even more devastating economic sanctions on Syria in subsequent years, once the U.S.-backed effort to topple the Syrian government through its jihadist proxies had failed.

On January 20, 2014, CNN, *The Guardian*, and *Le Monde* published news about a newly released report claiming to show evidence of "industrial scale killing" by the Syrian government. The report, authored by the U.S. law firm Carter-Ruck, claimed to verify photographic evidence provided by a defected Syrian army photographer who had smuggled 55,000 photographs out of Syria. These photographs allegedly documented the torture and killing of some 11,000 detainees by the Syrian government.[41]

The defected army photographer was given the code-name "Caesar," and his accusations were announced days before a new round of peace negotiations began in Geneva between the Syrian government and opposition. In the wake of Caesar's accusations, the opposition demanded the resignation of the Syrian government, causing the Geneva negotiations to fall apart.

The findings of the report seemed to be confirmed by Human Rights Watch, which conducted a review of the photos and released a report with its own conclusions in December 2015, almost two years later, which stated: "Human Rights Watch determines the photographs to be an authentic record of prisoner deaths in Syrian government facilities."

However, the body of the HRW report contradicted its own conclusion. HRW divided the photos into three categories. As expected, the first category included 28,707 images "of people Human Rights Watch understands to have died in government custody, either in one of several detention facilities or after being transferred to a military hospital."

However, the HRW report notes further that

313

the second category of photographs are images of dead army soldiers or members of the security forces. These photographs were also taken in the morgues of military hospitals…

The third category of photographs taken by the Syrian Military Police can be described as crime scene photographs taken in the aftermath of attacks and cover several categories of incidents including the aftermath of explosions, assassinations of security officers, fires, and car bombs.[42]

In other words, as journalist Rick Sterling points out,

over 46% of the photographs (24,568) [those from category 2 and 3] do not show people "tortured to death" by the Syrian government. On the contrary, they show dead Syrian soldiers and victims of car bombs and other violence. Thus, nearly half the photos show the opposite of what was alleged. These photos, never revealed to the public, confirm that the opposition is violent and has killed large numbers of Syrian security forces and civilians.[43]

Dishonestly, the HRW report then ignored further discussion of categories 2 and 3 of the photographs, stating only that "this report focuses on analyzing the first category of photographs in greater detail."

Further, as mentioned above, the HRW report notes that the first category of photographs consisted of "people Human Rights Watch understands to have died in government custody." However, HRW revealed no details of how they or Carter-Ruck came to understand whether or how many of the victims in these 28,707 photos died in government custody.[44]

Sterling comments that

the photos and the deceased are real, but how they died and the circumstances are unclear. There is strong evidence some died in conflict. Others died in the hospital. Others died and their bodies were decomposing before they were picked up. These photographs seem to document a wartime situation where many combatants and civilians are killed. It seems the military hospital was doing what it had always done: maintaining a photographic and documentary record of the deceased. Bodies were picked up by different military or intelligence branches.[45]

Such activity is expected in periods of conflict. During the height of the sectarian civil war in Iraq in 2005, for example, the *New York Times* reported that in Baghdad

a small window in the morgue is the last hope for people looking for their dead. Holding photographs of the missing, they peer through it to a computer screen where a worker flashes pictures of all the bodies no one has claimed… Some bodies are eventually found by their families, but most languish in the morgue. They are given numbers and, after two months, buried in unmarked graves in two Baghdad cemeteries.[46]

Despite this, HRW and Carter-Ruck simply take for granted that the 28,707 photos in the first category all show victims killed in government custody and portray the simple administrative procedure of documenting these deaths as somehow mysterious and sinister.

Sterling notes further that the Carter-Ruck report itself admits that its analyses of the photos and interviews with Caesar were produced under time constraints, and that Carter-Ruck was contracted by the government of Qatar to issue the report. In other words, the report was funded by a belligerent in the conflict that was also funding armed opposition groups, including jihadists from the Nusra Front. This calls into question the objectivity of the report, especially given that its rushed release occurred just days before the Geneva negotiations, which the armed groups sponsored by Qatar opposed.

Additionally, Sterling points to possible CIA involvement in the origins of the Caesar allegations. Professor David Crane of the Carter-Ruck inquiry team described in an interview with France 24 how Caesar was brought to meet them by "his handler, his case officer."[47] The expression "case officer" usually refers to the CIA, terminology Crane would be familiar with, as he previously worked for the U.S. Defense Intelligence Agency (DIA). This is significant, given the CIA's history in carrying out sophisticated misinformation campaigns.[48]

After reviewing the Carter-Ruck report, Dan Murphy of the *Christian Science Monitor* similarly concluded that

> the report itself is nowhere near as credible as it makes out and should be viewed for what it is: A well-timed propaganda exercise funded by Qatar, a regime opponent who has funded rebels fighting Assad who have committed war crimes of their own.[49]

Despite the lack of credibility of the Caesar allegations, and that the photos demonstrated the violent nature of the U.S.- and Gulf-backed jihadist groups wreaking havoc in the country, the Caesar photos were nevertheless used as the pretext for imposing further crippling sanctions on Syria. The euphemistically named "Caesar Syria Civilian Protection Act" was passed in 2019 by the U.S. Congress and Senate and imposed new sanctions on Syria to strangle the country's economy even further, preventing post-war reconstruction.[50]

Although by 2019 the Syrian army had successfully defended the country against the U.S.-backed jihadist dirty war, these sanctions mean that U.S. planners will continue to punish Syrian civilians for years — possibly even decades — to come as Washington continues to seek regime change, but through different methods.

Syria expert Joshua Landis warned in *Foreign Affairs* that the future Washington has in store for Syria can be anticipated based on the outcome of a previous U.S.-imposed sanctions regime, namely that targeting Iraq in the 1990s. Landis wrote that "U.S. sanctions killed hundreds of thousands of Iraqis. Their effect was gendered, disproportionately punishing women and children. The notion that sanctions work is a pitiless illusion."[51]

Assad's Prisons

While opposition activists sought to blame all deaths documented in the Caesar photos on the Syrian government, Assad's intelligence services were nevertheless responsible for detaining and torturing many Syrians after the war began, including many who disappeared in government prisons and security branches and whose whereabouts were never discovered.

An August 2013 report from the UN's Independent International Commission of Inquiry on the Syrian Arab Republic detailed the abduction, torture, and disappearance of Syrians by various government forces, including Air Force and Military Intelligence, across the country.[1]

The report states that Syrians were abducted from their homes, at checkpoints, in mosques, in hospitals, or following military operations, before being taken to undisclosed locations.

The Commission writes that torture was used in detention centers, security branches, prisons, and hospitals and that interviewees consistently identified Air Force Intelligence as one of the worst perpetrators.

The report cites the case of one detainee, arrested in Daraa city, who "was released from Military Security three weeks later with a broken leg and multiple cigarette burns on his back."

"Detainees in the Al-Fehar Branch in Damascus were held in solitary confinement 'squatting cells,' in which it was impossible to stand upright or lie down. One detainee was held in such conditions for 10 months, beaten daily, suspended by his wrists for 17 days, burned with cigarettes and subjected to electric shocks," the report added.

At checkpoints, men accused of assisting the opposition were often transferred to Military Security and tortured during interrogations. "A man was arrested in January at a checkpoint in Khalidiyeh (Homs). He was detained until his death in June. His body was covered with injuries consistent with extensive beating and whipping," the Commission reported.[2]

Torture also took place at military hospitals, where security and intelligence services operated detention centers, such as within the Abdul Gadir Al-Shagafi Military Hospital in Homs and the Al-Mezzeh Military Hospital in Damascus.

The Commission stated that the bodies of those tortured to death were transferred to hospital morgues. Most bodies were not returned to their families. Some were returned to their family in exchange for a signed statement confirming that the victim had been killed by "terrorists."

"Across the country, families wait — sometimes for extended periods — to know the fate and whereabouts of their relatives," the report states, "leaving families desperate and vulnerable to extortion. Some families pay bribes to those who — often falsely — claimed they could provide information."

One former detainee told the Commission that he was "confronted upon his release by dozens of women thrusting photographs of their male relatives towards him, hoping he might have seen them during his detention."

During a two-month visit to Syria after the fall of the Assad government in December 2024, many Syrians told this author of friends and relatives who were detained by Syrian government forces and either tortured or disappeared.

During a visit to Homs, a taxi driver explained to the author that he had been detained at a checkpoint near Qusayr while seeking to escape the war to Lebanon. But because the soldier at the checkpoint saw that his ID listed his hometown as Rastan, an early center of FSA attacks on the Syrian army, he was detained and held in prison for over a year.

When asked what happened in prison and how he was treated, he simply said, "Too many things to say," before breaking down in tears.

While in a restaurant in Damascus shortly after Assad's fall, this author was present when two employees, a father and his son, emerged from the back room in tears. They told the owner and fellow staff that they had just received word that the names of their three uncles, taken by the government and missing since 2014, had been found in the records at Tishreen military hospital, confirming their deaths.

Sharif, a Kurdish man from Damascus, told this author about his brother Qassem, a bus driver who was detained in 2014 after being accused of transporting militants. Qassem was tortured to death five months later.

Sharif asked bitterly: "Why torture someone like that? If he did something wrong, put him in prison, sure. But to torture and kill him? He is a human being. God created him. Why do that? Many people in Syria have stories like my brother's. Of people taken without questions or answers."

During a visit to Aleppo, an Armenian-Syrian told this author that his good friend, Muhannad, was detained in 2013 after writing a comment against the government on Facebook. He was arrested soon after and taken to the political security branch on Suleimaniyah Street in the city. He was killed under torture a few weeks later, even though he was not involved in opposition activities.

Organ Trade in War

"Organ theft during wars, civil wars, dirty wars, wars involving undisciplined armies is not uncommon," wrote Nancy Scheper-Hughes, chair of Berkeley's doctoral program in medical anthropology and director of Organs Watch, a California-based documentation and research project.

"The demand for fresh organs and tissues… is insatiable," she explained, adding that fresh kidneys from "the brain dead or from those executed with the assistance of trained organ harvesters are the blood diamonds of illicit and criminal trafficking."

Scheper-Hughes highlighted the case of Kosovo, where the organ trade flourished during and immediately after the war between Serbia and the U.S.- and EU-backed Kosovo Liberation Army (KLA) that ended in 1999.

Criminal elements connected to the KLA kidnapped, murdered, and carried out medicalized executions to remove the kidneys of Serbs and other minorities. The victims were held in secret detention sites in Kosovo and across the border in northern Albania.[3]

The first foreign journalist to investigate the KLA role in organ-trafficking was Michael Montgomery, an American who worked as the Balkans correspondent for the London-based *Telegraph*. He found that even a month after the war, "the crimes hadn't stopped."

"At that time, we heard that there were people — Serbs, Roma, some Kosovo Albanians — killed by the Kosovo Liberation Army, and they simply vanished, and it was very strange, and we started looking into that," Montgomery explained.

Though people were being kidnapped, they were not being held for prisoner exchanges with the Serbs, and no ransoms were being demanded. He learned that people were being captured and transferred across the border to Albania to makeshift detention facilities where doctors were present. The captives were then killed and their organs (primarily kidneys) extracted and sent out of the country.

"And we know at the time there was a thriving industry in Istanbul, Turkey for illicit organ transplants. People coming from Israel, from the Middle East, and paying hundreds of thousands of dollars for these kidneys. It seemed like absolute science fiction," he added.[4]

Montgomery's findings prompted further investigation after the war by the United Nations Mission in Kosovo (UNMIK), which found evidence of KLA involvement in the organ trade. Witnesses testified that kidneys were removed during executions and flown to Turkey. However, some witnesses were murdered, forensic data were lost or destroyed, and the investigations were interrupted, Scheper-Hughes adds.[5]

Carla del Ponte, the Chief Prosecutor of the International Criminal Tribunal for the former Yugoslavia, raised the issue of organ-trafficking by elements within the KLA, including its top leadership, in her 2008 book *The Hunt*, in which she detailed her efforts to try Serbian leader Slobodan Milošević for war crimes.

As discussed in Chapter 15, del Ponte was later a member of the UN's Independent International Commission of Inquiry on the Syrian Arab Republic and investigated the March 2013 chemical attack at Khan Assal.

Del Ponte complained that her efforts to investigate KLA war crimes were consistently stifled by U.S. and NATO military officials, which is not surprising given the close support the KLA enjoyed from the CIA.

In 2001, *The Observer* published a report about CIA support for the KLA based on testimony from senior European officers who served with the international peace-keeping force in Kosovo (KFOR), as well as Macedonian and U.S. sources.

One European KFOR battalion commander told the British paper: "The CIA has been allowed to run riot in Kosovo with a private army designed to overthrow Slobodan Milošević. Now he's gone, the U.S. State Department seems incapable of reining in its bastard army."[6]

As journalist Kit Klarenberg details, the KLA also enjoyed support from Osama bin Laden, who was at the same time under indictment in the U.S. for the 1998 bombing of the U.S. embassies in Nairobi, Kenya, and Dar es Salaam, Tanzania.

After establishing a base of operations in Albania, the al-Qaeda chief facilitated a steady flow of jihadists from over half a dozen countries in the Middle East into Kosovo. Fighters from the U.K. also flocked to the battlefield, likely with the assistance of British intelligence, MI6.[7]

According to the *Wall Street Journal*, Ayman al-Zawahiri, the Egyptian doctor and al-Qaeda co-founder, operated terrorist training camps, weapons of mass destruction factories, and money-laundering and drug-trading networks throughout the Balkans, including in Albania and Kosovo. In Albania, the main al-Qaeda training camp included the property of former Albanian premier Sali Berisha, who was then very close to the KLA.[8]

In response to del Ponte's book, the Council on Europe further investigated the organ trade in Kosovo and substantiated her claims. The council issued a report in 2010 stating that the organ trade "developed with the benefit of the chaos prevailing in the region, at the initiative of certain KLA militia leaders linked to organised crime."

The report indicated that abductees were not only handed over to organ-traffickers but were "bought" and "sold." In the process of being moved through transitory detention sites, some abductees "became aware of the ultimate fate that awaited them" and "pleaded with their captors to be spared the fate of being 'chopped into pieces.'" Victims were usually killed by a gunshot to the head, before being operated on to remove one or more of their organs, the report added.[9]

In response to the Council of Europe report, French-Jewish politician and Doctors Without Borders founder Bernard Kouchner vehemently denied the existence of the organ trade in Kosovo.

Kouchner, who was appointed head of UNMIK and governed Kosovo on the UN's behalf from 1999 to 2001, worked closely with KLA leaders, including Hashim Thaci, who later became the Prime Minister and President of Kosovo. Thaci was accused in the Council of Europe report of heading a "mafia-like" Albanian group responsible for smuggling weapons, heroin, and human organs through eastern Europe.[10]

Because of his position at UNMIK during this period, speculation swirled that Kouchner was linked to the organ trade. At best, he was turning a blind eye to the organ-trafficking network run by his friend Thaci and other KLA leaders. At worst, he was directly involved in the organ trade itself.

In response, Kouchner denied that the organ trade was occurring in Kosovo at all and reacted angrily on multiple occasions when confronted by journalists about the issue.

When Voice of America journalist Budimir Ničić asked Kouchner about his alleged role in organ-trafficking in Kosovo, he dismissed the issue entirely, including the evidence presented in the Council of Europe report.

"Organ trade? But you are sick, aren't you? Do I look like someone who would traffic organs? You are insane, to believe all kinds of nonsense like that," Kouchner responded while laughing out loud.

"[T]here was no organ trade. People who talk about things like that are bums and murderers," the UNMIK head added.[11]

Kouchner again reacted angrily when confronted by French journalist Aymeric Caron during a television program on the France 2 channel.

"You are sick… How do you imagine organ trafficking in a country in which hospitals are without electricity?" Kouchner claimed to Caron.[12]

Working under Kouchner at UNMIK was a former British soldier and intelligence officer, James Le Mesurier. As journalist Vanessa Beeley notes, Le Mesurier was responsible for transforming and rebranding the KLA into the Kosovo Protection Corps (KPC), at the same time the KLA was being accused of running cross-border organ-trafficking operations.[13]

The Organ Trade Comes to Syria

Crucially, both Le Mesurier and Kouchner went on to play important roles during the 2011 war in Syria, where the organ trade also flourished.

Doctors Without Borders (or *Médecins Sans Frontières*, MSF), the medical aid group established by Kouchner in the 1970s, provided funding to establish medical battalions for the FSA and Nusra Front in their war against the Syrian army.

As political analyst Tony Cartalucci notes, a press release from the group stated that starting in 2012, MSF had "built a strong and reliable collaboration with medical networks, hospitals and medical points" in Syria, providing them with drugs, medical equipment, and technical support.[14]

During an interview with U.S. National Public Radio (NPR) in August 2013, a member of the group, Stephen Cornish, explained that MSF was equipping makeshift surgical clinics with modern technology and full medical teams to treat not only civilians caught up in the fighting but also opposition militants, including from al-Qaeda. Cornish stated:

> Over the past months, we've had a surgery that was opened inside a cave. We've had another that was opened in a chicken farm, a third one in a house. And these structures, we've tried to outfit them as best as we can with enough modern technology and with full medical teams. They originally were dealing mainly with combatant injuries and people who were — civilians who were directly affected by the conflict. But as the health care system has collapsed, we find more and more civilian needs and other types of needs that need responding.[15]

As noted in Chapter 11, French surgeon and fellow MSF founder Jacques Bérès revealed in August 2012 that he had made three trips to Syria to operate on opposition fighters, including "Jihadists" from the Nusra Front, in Aleppo, Homs, and Idlib.[16]

Kouchner and Bérès also played a key role in promoting regime change in Syria to the French public, where the desire to intervene in Syria was strongest among the Western powers. The "right to intervene" remains "vivid in the French public's mind," the *Washington Post* reported in September 2012, in part because the "concept was pushed onto the international scene" in the 1980s by Kouchner and MSF.[17]

Kouchner and Bérès joined French-Jewish intellectual Bernard Henri Levy to call for international intervention in Syria shortly after Obama issued his "red line" about the use of chemical weapons.

"Enough evasion, we must intervene in Syria!" they wrote in a September 2012 op-ed in *Le Monde*.[18]

In 2014, Kouchner became one of several Western politicians to cross the border from Turkey to visit opposition-held northern Syria for meetings with FSA leaders.[19]

The Role of the White Helmets

In 2011, Kouchner's protégé in Kosovo, James le Mesurier, moved to Turkey to manage civil society projects across the border in Syria. He was working for Analysis Research Knowledge (ARK), the U.K. Foreign and Commonwealth Office contractor which worked to "re-brand" Syria's Salafi-jihadist armed opposition by "softening its image," leaked documents published by The Grayzone revealed.[20]

While working for ARK, le Mesurier founded the White Helmets, a group modeled on the Kosovo Protection Corps that claimed to rescue Syrians killed or injured in Syrian government air strikes.

The group was funded by Mayday Rescue, an NGO based in Istanbul and founded by le Mesurier and other former British soldiers. Mayday provided training, funding, and equipment for the White Helmets, receiving more than €120 million in government funding from countries including Germany, the United Kingdom, the Netherlands, France, and Canada.[21]

The White Helmets became media darlings in the West for publishing videos of its rescue operations claiming to show evidence of potential war crimes committed by Syrian government, and later Russian, forces. Multiple documentaries, including a Netflix film, were made to promote the White Helmets' image as humanitarian saviors.

However, as Vanessa Beeley's reporting showed, the White Helmets enjoyed close ties to Salafi opposition armed groups, including the Nusra Front, and often published videos of staged rescue scenes. Like Kouchner's MSF, le Mesurier's White Helmets played a key role in promoting Western intervention to topple the Syrian government to Western audiences.

These efforts involved participation in staged chemical attacks, including the alleged chlorine attacks in Ltamenah in March 2017, in Khan Sheikhoun in April 2017, and in Douma in April 2018, to induce Western intervention.[22]

A week after the White Helmets published video showing scenes of children being hosed down following the alleged chemical attack in Douma, President Donald Trump ordered the U.S. military — in conjunction with France and the United Kingdom — to launch strikes on Syria in retaliation. The U.S. its allies had "marshaled their righteous power," Trump announced.

However, Beirut-based BBC producer Riam Dalati later wrote on Twitter that "after almost 6 months of investigation, I can prove, without a doubt, that the Douma hospital scene was staged."[23]

Dalati's statement raised questions of how and when the more than 40 victims of the alleged chlorine attack were actually killed, and whether White Helmets members participated in their killing to provide corpses for the staged attack.

When the preliminary investigation of the Organization for the Prohibition of Chemical Weapons (OCPW) into the Douma attack cast doubt on Syrian government responsibility and provided further evidence of possible staging, the leadership of the UN agency intervened to suppress the findings, changing the investigation's conclusions before the final report on the incident was issued.[24]

Perhaps more ominously, the medical and humanitarian work of MSF, and the rescue work of the White Helmets (real or staged), put both groups at the front lines of the conflict and in a position to access the bodies of injured and dead Syrians to harvest their organs.

Like the Kosovo Liberation Army and Kosovo Protection Corps before them, Nusra and the White Helmets were accused of stealing bodies of the dead, and abducting the injured, to take them to Turkey where their organs could be harvested and sold.

Vanessa Beeley reports that according to two residents of East Aleppo, the White Helmets were the "runners" for the organ-traffickers.

"The White Helmet drivers would take the injured or dead bodies to the Turkish border. Many of the injured had light wounds, nothing that needed hospitalization, but the bodies would come back without organs," said Ammar Al-Bakr.

"The bodies, dead and alive, would be inspected in the towns on the borders with Turkey before being taken by Turkish vehicles to the hospitals, but if the injured civilian was a child or young and strong they would be taken directly to the hospital in Turkey because their organs had greater value," explained Salaheddin Azazi.

Mohammad, a Syrian who was a strong opponent of the Assad government and lived in East Aleppo until 2014, told this author that in 2012 and 2013, many Syrians in East Aleppo who were lightly injured in bombings would be taken in ambulances to Turkey and never seen again. He says that many in Aleppo suspected at the time that the reason for this was to take their organs.

Other civilians from Aleppo told Beeley that the threat of organ theft "hung over them" during the five years Nusra and the White Helmets controlled the east of the city.

They said that the Omar Abdulaziz, Al-Quds, and Zarzour hospitals in East Aleppo, all controlled by the opposition, allegedly specialized in organ theft as well.

Beeley stated that she also heard many stories of organ-trafficking from civilians from Eastern Ghouta in the Damascus countryside after the Syrian

Army retook control of it from opposition groups, including from Jaish al-Islam, in 2018.[25]

In early 2014, Hossain Noufel, the head of the forensic pathology department of the Damascus University, told Syrian newspaper *Al-Watan* that there had been more than 18,000 cases of organ-trafficking in opposition-controlled areas in the country's north.[26]

Reports of organ theft in opposition-controlled territory in Syria appeared in the mainstream Western press as well. United Press International (UPI) reported that at least 20 complaints related to the illegal organ trade made their way to the Damascus courts between March 2011 and September 2015, according to the Attorney General of rural Damascus, Ahmad al-Sayyed. He estimated that there had been at least 20,000 cases of illegal organ sales across the country since the start of the war, "especially in border areas where there are no longer any courts or police officers to enforce the laws."

"No such cases were seen before the fighting broke out," UPI added, meaning the illegal organ trade did not exist in Syria before the beginning of the U.S.- and Israeli-led regime change operation.

UPI reported further that according to a Syrian doctor, the organ trade was widespread in areas outside Syrian government control in the northern rural areas of Aleppo and Idlib, near the Turkish border.

"A dermatologist asked me to sell the organs of pro-government detainees in rural Idlib, since, as he put it, they were going to be executed anyway," said the doctor who treated patients in the rural areas around Idlib under Nusra Front control.

"The dermatologist explained to him that there were many buyers who were willing to pay, and that the money would be used to buy much-needed medical equipment and to support the armed opposition groups," UPI wrote.

The doctor said he worried that such operations might lead to innocent people being arrested by so-called rebel groups to harvest their organs. When he refused to participate, he was accused of working for the Syrian government.

After he moved to rural Aleppo, which was under ISIS control, the doctor witnessed cases of organ theft as well.

"The area I moved to was [also] controlled by the Islamic State, and we saw many cases of corpses with missing internal organs, mostly the liver and left kidney. However, I saw one case of a missing bladder," he said.[27]

Reports of ISIS involvement in organ-trafficking emerged in Iraq after the organization conquered large swaths of that country as well. With covert assistance from the U.S. military, Turkish intelligence, and Peshmerga from the Kurdistan Democratic Party (KDP) of Kurdish leader Masoud Barzani, ISIS captured Mosul, Iraq's second-largest city, in June 2014.[28]

Two months later, ISIS and Barzani's Peshmerga collaborated to massacre thousands of Yezidi men and take thousands of Yezidi women and girls as sex slaves during an attack on the nearby Iraqi province of Sinjar.[29]

In December of that year, *Al-Monitor* cited an Iraqi ear, nose, and throat doctor, Siruwan al-Mosuli, as stating that ISIS commanders had hired foreign doctors to run an extensive organ-trafficking system from a hospital in Mosul.

The *Al-Monitor* report claimed ISIS had set up a specialist organ-smuggling division whose sole responsibility is to sell human hearts, livers, and kidneys on the lucrative international black market. Surgeries were performed to extract organs from fallen ISIS fighters, injured civilians, or individuals who were kidnapped. Most of the organs were then smuggled out of Syria and Iraq into neighboring countries, including Turkey, where criminal gangs sold them to international buyers.[30]

A few months later, in February 2015, Iraq's Ambassador to the UN, Mohamed Alhakim, said that ISIS was executing doctors for not harvesting body parts. Alhakim claimed that dozens of bodies with surgical incisions and missing body parts had been found in shallow mass graves near Mosul over the previous few weeks. "We have bodies. Come and examine them. It is clear they are missing certain parts," he told the UN Security Council, pleading for it to investigate the issue.[31]

The UN Human Rights Council did investigate, raising the issue of ISIS' organ trading in a June 2016 report titled "They Came to Destroy: ISIS Crimes Against the Yazidis."

The report stated: "The Commission received testimonies indicating some Yazidi detainees were subjected to medical examinations and treatments unrelated to their conditions, raising concerns about preparation for organ extraction."[32]

However, the issue was largely forgotten, and the above-mentioned passage was later excised from the report, suggesting that some UN officials in Iraq did not wish to draw attention to the issue (like Bernard Kouchner in Kosovo).

More crucially, the UN report omitted the role of Masoud Barzani and the Kurdish Peshmerga in facilitating the genocide of Yezidis. Barzani's goal was to ethnically cleanse Sinjar of its Yezidi population and annex it for inclusion in a future Kurdish state.

Years later, Ali Hussein, a Yezidi from Dohuk, pointed to the threat of organ-trafficking while discussing his efforts to buy the freedom of an 11-year-old Yezidi girl. She had been abducted by ISIS and later sold to a Nusra Front commander who raped her.

In a voice recording from the negotiation played by Hussein for NPR journalist Jane Arraf, the ISIS contact threatened to sell the young girl for her organs if his ransom demand was not met.

"I told you $45,000 from the beginning. I know what they pay in Raqqa. I told you, in Turkey, they would pay $60,000 or $70,000 and take out the girl's organs. But I don't want to do that," the ISIS contact threatened.[33]

The Turkish–Israeli Connection

Just as in Kosovo in the 1990s, it is no accident that in case after case, Turkey is mentioned as the ultimate destination of the trafficked organs.

It is widely recognized that Turkey lies at the center of the international illicit organ trade, and that Israelis are major beneficiaries of it.

In 2011, the *New York Times* reported on the case of a Turkish doctor, Yusuf Sonmez, who was wanted by Interpol for harvesting human organs for an international black-market trafficking ring. Sonmez had performed kidney transplants at the Medicus clinic in Pristina, Kosovo, which was at the center of organ-trafficking allegations involving the KLA a decade before.

The *New York Times* noted that Dr. Sonmez was accused of playing a "major part in the globalization of trade in human kidneys, particularly for matching paid donors with patients from Israel, where for religious reasons there is a shortage of kidney donors and where health insurance plans pay for transplants abroad."[34]

The same year, Bloomberg described the "sprawling global black market in organs," while noting: "Many of the black-market kidneys harvested by these gangs are destined for people who live in Israel." Bloomberg added that one organ-trafficking ring active in Kosovo was led by an Israeli of Turkish descent.[35]

Israelis were also at the center of a network in Turkey working to convince desperate and impoverished Syrian refugees to sell one of their two kidneys.

In May 2022, police teams in the Turkish city of Adana detained five Israelis on allegations of organ-trafficking. The Israelis had provided fake passports to two Syrians who had agreed to sell their kidneys. All seven men had flown from Israel to Turkey one month before to carry out the transplant operations.[36]

Israel's shortage of organ donors has led to the theft of organs of Palestinians killed or abducted by Israeli forces over the long course of the illegal occupation of the West Bank and Gaza.

In 2009, Sweden's largest daily newspaper, *Aftonbladet*, reported testimony that the Israeli army was kidnapping and murdering Palestinians to harvest their organs.

Palestinians claimed that young men from the West Bank and Gaza had been seized by the Israeli army, and their bodies returned to the families with missing organs.

"'Our sons are used as involuntary organ donors,' relatives of Khaled from Nablus said to me, as did the mother of Raed from Jenin as well as the uncles of Machmod and Nafes from Gaza, who all had disappeared for a few days and returned by night, dead and autopsied," wrote Donald Bostrom, the author of the *Aftonbladet* report.

Bostrom also cited an incident of alleged organ theft during the first Palestinian Intifada, or uprising, in 1992. He says that the Israeli army abducted a young man known for throwing stones at Israeli troops in the Nablus area. The young man was shot in the chest, both legs, and the stomach before being taken to a military helicopter, which transported him to an unknown location.

Five nights later, Bostrom said, the young man's body was returned, wrapped in green hospital sheets and "cut-up from his stomach to his chin."[37]

Israel's Channel 2 reported that in the 1990s, specialists at the Abu Kabir Forensic Medicine Institute in Tel Aviv harvested skin, corneas, heart valves, and bones from the bodies of Israeli soldiers, Israeli citizens, Palestinians, and foreign workers without permission from relatives.

The allegations were confirmed by Dr. Yehuda Hiss, former head of Abu Kabir, in an interview she gave to American academic Nancy Scheper-

Hughes (mentioned earlier in this chapter) in 2000. Scheper-Hughes reluctantly released the videotaped interview after Israeli officials denied the accusations in the *Aftonbladet* report, calling them "Anti-Semitic."[38]

Scheper-Hughes later revealed that American peace activist Rachel Corrie was among those whose organs were stolen by doctors at the Abu Khabir institute. In 2003, Corrie was murdered by an Israeli soldier who crushed her to death with a bulldozer as she tried to prevent the demolition of a Palestinian doctor's home in Gaza.[39]

Many analysts were surprised when members of the White Helmets were evacuated to Israel in 2018, as Syrian and Russian forces recaptured territory in southern Syria long occupied by Nusra, ISIS, and the FSA.

The Israeli military evacuated 422 White Helmets and family members, who were then transported to Jordan and given refugee status in Britain, Canada, and Germany.[40]

But such connections between Israel and the White Helmets should not be shocking, given the Israeli role in facilitating organ-trafficking in Turkey and the Israeli military's support for the Nusra Front, with which the White Helmets had a close relationship.

Given the role of the CIA, Israeli intelligence, MI6, and al-Qaeda, as well as Bernard Kouchner, Doctors Without Borders, and James le Mesurier in the U.S.-backed proxy wars in both Kosovo and Syria, it is no surprise that the illicit organ trade reared its ugly head in both theaters.

It is sometimes said that history doesn't repeat itself, but it does rhyme. However, in the cases of Syria and Kosovo, history seems to have repeated itself after all.

Conclusion

In the preceding pages of this book, I have detailed Washington and Tel Aviv's plans for regime change in Syria, with crucial assistance from Riyadh, Doha, Ankara, London, and Paris.

I have given special attention to the August 2013 Ghouta false-flag chemical attack. In my view, the Ghouta massacre was the culmination of a broader regime change effort initiated by neoconservative U.S. planners in the George W. Bush administration starting at least as early as 2001. By 2013, "Operation Timber Sycamore," as the CIA-led regime change effort later came to be known, had a budget of $1 billion per year, the most for any operation in the agency's history.

Because a false-flag chemical attack was needed in order to trigger the Libya-style military intervention desired by U.S., Saudi, French, Turkish, British, and Israeli planners, it is improbable that militants from Liwa al-Islam carried out the horrific massacre and sophisticated psychological operation in Ghouta, which resulted in the murder of hundreds of men, women, and children, on their own.

Instead, the Ghouta false-flag massacre was likely orchestrated by a Safari Club-style coalition of intelligence agencies, with the CIA playing a supervisory role, Saudi intelligence using Liwa al-Islam as a proxy to carry out the massacre, Turkish intelligence helping Nusra and therefore Liwa al-Islam acquire sarin for the rockets, British intelligence orchestrating the psychological operation to produce and distribute videos of the victims, and Israeli intelligence initiating the idea of the red line and fabricating evidence to suggest Assad's guilt in the public mind.

Although evidence for the role of the CIA and allied intelligence agencies in the Ghouta false-flag massacre is only circumstantial, and therefore speculative, it is nevertheless incontrovertible that a Safari Club-style coalition of intelligence agencies, led by the CIA, unleashed a regime change operation targeting Syria, the "sheer energy and meticulous planning" of which was "breathtaking."

As I have shown in the pages of this book, the Timber Sycamore regime change operation involved sparking anti-government protests as part of the so-called Arab Spring, coupled with unleashing al-Qaeda-affiliated Salafist militants to attack Syrian security forces, police, soldiers, and civilians under the cover of these protests and through covert assassinations. It was hoped that unleashing this violence would exploit sectarian cleavages in Syria, trigger a civil war, and open the door to U.S. military intervention to topple the Syrian government for Israel's benefit.

When this maximalist goal failed, and President Obama refused to green-light intervention in the wake of the Ghouta massacre, the Safari-club coalition settled for a less desirable but still acceptable outcome. They continued to flood Syria with weapons and jihadist foreign fighters at least to ensure a "stalemate" between both sides, in which Syrians would continue to be slaughtered for another five years.

As the sectarian Salafist militias, including the Nusra Front, Ahrar al-Sham, ISIS, Liwa al-Tawhid, Saqour al-Sham, Kata'ib Farouq, Ahfad al-Rasoul, and Liwa al-Islam rampaged through Syria, massacring, torturing, looting, and terrorizing everywhere they went, they were doing so under the direction of, and with weapons provided by, their foreign sponsors.

The cyber dissidents, citizen journalists, think tank analysts, media activists, and alleged human rights advocates who covered up these crimes were also doing so at the direction of their well-paying sponsors abroad.

At the same time, the Syrian government committed its own share of crimes in an effort to defeat the foreign-backed Salafist insurgency. Syrian intelligence detained, tortured, and disappeared many civilians suspected of opposing the government or assisting the Salafi armed groups. The Syrian army at times bombed cities and neighborhoods in which the Salafist militants were embedded, without care for the civilians still living there.

But in the end, it was U.S., Saudi, French, British, Turkish, Qatari, and Israeli intelligence that all collaborated to unleash the murder and mayhem suffered by the Syrian people since 2011.

Hundreds of thousands are dead, millions are displaced or live abroad as refugees, and large areas of Syria's major cities lie in ruins.

Crucially, the war left Syria divided, to a large extent on sectarian lines, a long-time goal of Israel and its neoconservative partners in Washington. Sunni-majority Idlib Province remained under the control of Abu Muhammad al-Jolani and his Jihadist fighters from the Nusra Front, formerly of al-Qaeda but now rebranded as Hayat Tahrir al-Sham (HTS). The U.S. military and its Kurdish proxies, the Syrian Democratic Forces (SDF), occupy Kurdish-majority Hasakah Province in the northeast, as well as much of Sunni-majority Raqqa and Deir al-Zour Provinces, the country's crucial energy- and grain-producing regions.

The U.S. was therefore able to maintain leverage against Bashar al-Assad's government in Damascus and deny Syrians the resources they needed to rebuild and function as a society. Crippling U.S.-imposed economic sanctions inflicted further pain and caused many more Syrians to continue to flee the country, but due to utter impoverishment rather than war.

In December 2024, the U.S. and Israel finally achieved their goal of using al-Qaeda to topple Assad's government.

After a two-week lightning offensive launched from Idlib, militants from Jolani's HTS entered Damascus. The Syrian government of Bashar al-Assad had finally fallen.

On December 8, Jolani, the former detainee at Camp Bucca and deputy to ISIS leader Abu Bakr al-Baghdadi, gave a speech from the Umayyad Mosque in the heart of the Syrian capital hailing his "historic" victory.

Less than two weeks later, a high-level U.S. delegation led by U.S. Assistant Secretary of State for Near Eastern Affairs Barbara Leaf met with Jolani in Damascus. Leaf quickly made the U.S. government's previously covert partnership with the former al-Qaeda terrorist leader official by announcing the removal of the long-standing $10 million bounty on his head.

After the Assad government fell, Israel immediately launched one of the largest bombing campaigns in its history, completely destroying the remnants of Syria's military. Israeli forces quickly conquered vast new territory in Syria's Golan Heights, Mount Hermon, and the Yarmouk Basin.

Israeli tanks are now within 20 kilometers of Damascus, while ministers in Prime Minister Benjamin Netanyahu's government call for large swaths of Syria, Lebanon, and Iraq to become part of "Greater Israel."

Many Syrians are hopeful for the future, while others fear that the country is on the brink of another civil war, as HTS militants carry out revenge killings against Alawites and former soldiers, and Turkish proxy forces battle the U.S.-backed Kurds.

At the same time, Christians are now preparing to live under the rule of the same men who burned their monasteries, destroyed their altars, and kidnapped and murdered their nuns and priests.

As a result of the U.S.-initiated dirty war on Syria, virtually every Syrian will have to cope with the trauma resulting from the parents, children, brothers, sisters, and friends they have lost. Because the war criminals in

Washington and Tel Aviv who launched the dirty war on Syria will never be held accountable in this life, we can only pray that they will be held accountable in the next.

Endnotes

Introduction

1 Michael Slackman, "Syrian Leader Blames 'Conspiracy' for Turmoil," New York Times, March 30, 2011. nytimes.com/2011/03/31/world/middleeast/31syria.html.

2 George Baghdadi, "Assad blames 'conspiracy' for Syria unrest," CBS News, January 10, 2012. cbsnews.com/news/assad-blames-conspiracy-for-syria-unrest.

3 Max Fisher, "Straightforward Answers to Basic Questions About Syria's War," *New York Times*, September 18, 2016. nytimes.com/2016/09/19/world/middleeast/syria-civil-war-bashar-al-assad-refugees-islamic-state.html.

4 Robin Yassin-Kassab and Leila al-Shami, *Burning Country: Syrians in Revolution and War* (London: Pluto Press, 2016), pp. 212–3.

5 Shmuley Boteach, "No Holds Barred: Stop the Syrian Genocide or Cancel the Elie Wiesel Lecture," *Jerusalem Post*, November 21, 2016. jpost.com/opinion/no-holds-barred-stop-the-syrian-genocide-or-cancel-the-elie-wiesel-lecture-473285.

6 C.J. Chivers and Eric Schmitt, "Arms Airlift to Syria Rebels Expands, With Aid from C.I.A.," *New York Times*, March 24, 2013. nytimes.com/2013/03/25/world/middleeast/arms-airlift-to-syrian-rebels-expands-with-cia-aid.html.

7 Greg Miller and Karen DeYoung, "Secret CIA program in Syria faces large funding cut," *Washington Post*, June 12, 2015. washingtonpost.com/world/national-security/lawmakers-move-to-curb-1-billion-cia-program-to-train-syrian-rebels/2015/06/12/b0f45a9e-1114-11e5-adec-e82f8395c032_story.html.

8 Patrik Paulov, *Syria's Silenced Voices: Ten Years of War and Terrorism Incited by the West and Its Allies* (Stockholm: Karneval Publishing House, 2019), Chapter 7.

Chapter 1

1 Critical Theory Workshop, "French thought in bad company: The CIA's intellectual world war," Gabriel Rockhill and J. Ponce de Leon, September 30, 2017. youtube.com/watch?v=OAfITSEux3c.

2 Ernesto Sanchez, "Washington's Long History in Syria," *National Interest*, July 12, 2013. nationalinterest.org/commentary/washingtons-long-history-syria-8717.

3 Douglas Little, "1949–1958, Syria: Early experiments in covert action," excerpted from "Cold War and Covert Action: The U.S. and Syria, 1945–1958," *Middle East Journal* (Winter 1990). coat.ncf.ca/our_magazine/links/issue51/articles/51_12-13.pdf.

4 William Blum, *Killing Hope: US Military and CIA Interventions Since World War II* (London: Zed Books, 2004), p. 84.

5 Olivia B. Waxman "The U.S. Intervened in Syria in 1949. Here's What Happened," *Time*, April 13, 2017. time.com/4735438/america-syria-war-coup-history.

6 Ernesto Sanchez, "Washington's Long History in Syria," *National Interest*, July 12, 2013. nationalinterest.org/commentary/washingtons-long-history-syria-8717.

7 Patrick Seale, *Asad: The Struggle for the Middle East* (Berkeley: University of California Press, 1989), pp. 316–7.

8 Itzchak Weismann, "Sa'id Hawwa and Islamic Revivalism in Ba'thist Syria," *Studia Islamica* 85 (1997): 131–54. ou.edu/mideast/Additional pages - non-catagory/Hawwa_Islamic_RevivalismInBaathistSyria_Weismann.pdf.

9 Patrick Seale, *Asad: The Struggle for the Middle East* (Berkeley: University of California Press, 1989), pp. 329–36.

10 "Syria: Muslim Brotherhood Pressure Intensifies," U.S. Defense Intelligence Agency, May 1982. syria360.files.wordpress.com/2013/11/dia-syria-muslimbrotherhoodpressureintensifies-2.pdf.

11 Arwa Khalifa, "On the structure of Salafi organizations in Syria: The Army of Islam as a model," *Al-Jumhuriya*, September 9, 2016. aljumhuriya.net/ar/35519.

12 Flynt Leverett, *Inheriting Syria: Bashar's Trial by Fire* (Washington, D.C.: Brookings Institution Press, 2005), pp. 8–18.

13 David W. Lesch, *Syria: The Fall of the House of Assad* (New Haven: Yale University Press, 2021), p. 11.

14 "American War Generals: General Clark on the Iraq Invasion," National Geographic, September 12, 2014. youtube.com/watch?v=UcWs4TFSjrY.

15 Samer Arabi, "The Attack-Syria Coalition's Neocon Roots," Institute for Policy Studies, October 15, 2012. ips-dc.org/the_attack-syria_coalitions_neocon_roots.

16 Joe Conason, "Seven countries in five years," *Salon*, October 12, 2007. salon.com/2007/10/12/wesley_clark.

17 "The New York Megaphone Interview: Colonel Lawrence Wilkerson," Sander Hicks, February 19, 2014. youtube.com/watch?v=ULAk_u15yZU.

18 Piers Robinson, "The Propaganda of Terror and Fear: A Lesson from Recent History," OffGuardian, March 28, 2020. off-guardian.org/2020/03/28/the-propaganda-of-terror-and-fear-a-lesson-from-recent-history.

19 David W. Lesch, *Syria: The Fall of the House of Assad* (New Haven: Yale University Press, 2021), p. 14.

20 Brad Hoff, "Syrian Christians were Quietly Warned Before the War," Libertarian Institute, November 20, 2021. libertarianinstitute.org/articles/syrian-christians-were-quietly-warned-before-the-war.

21 Christiane Amanpour, "Al-Assad: 'Syria has nothing to do with this crime,'" CNN, October 12, 2005. cnn.com/2005/WORLD/meast/10/12/alassad.transcript.

22 Brad Hoff, "Three Deep State Confessions on Syria," Libertarian Institute, November 7, 2019. libertarianinstitute.org/blog/three-deep-state-confessions-on-syria.

23 Neil King, Jr., "Syria Debate Exposes Iraq Fault Lines," *Wall Street Journal*, December 6, 2005. wsj.com/articles/SB113383235570914692.

24 "A Clean Break: A New Strategy for Securing the Realm," Institute for Advanced Strategic and Political Studies, Study Group on a New Israeli Strategy Toward 2000, 1996, palestineremembered.com/Acre/Articles/Story1351.html.

25 Flynt Leverett, *Inheriting Syria: Bashar's Trial by Fire* (Washington, D.C.: Brookings Institution Press, 2005), p. 151.

26 David Wurmser, "Coping with Crumbling States: A Western and Israeli Balance of Power Strategy for the Levant," Institute for Advanced Strategic and Political Studies, December 1996. scotthorton.org/fairuse/coping-with-crumbling-states-a-western-and-israeli-balance-of-power-strategy-for-the-levant-by-david-wurmser-1996.

27 "The Zionist plan for the Middle East," translated and edited by Israel Shahak, Association of Arab-American University Graduates, Inc. Belmont, Massachusetts, 1982. scribd.com/document/338158548/A-Strategy-for-Israel-in-the-Nineteen-Eighties-Oded-Yinon.

28 Nathan Guttman, "Prominent U.S. Jews, Israel Blamed for Start of Iraq War," *Haaretz*, May 31, 2004. haaretz.com/2004-05-31/ty-article/prominent-u-s-jews-israel-blamed-for-start-of-iraq-war/0000017f-e66f-dea7-adff-f7ff26b20000.

29 Stephen Walt, "I don't mean to say I told you so, but..." *Foreign Policy*, February 8, 2010. foreignpolicy.com/2010/02/08/i-dont-mean-to-say-i-told-you-so-but.

30 Max Boot, "What the Heck Is a 'Neocon'?" *Wall Street Journal*, December 30, 2002. wsj.com/articles/SB104121045871745553.

31 Stephen Walt, "I don't mean to say I told you so, but..." *Foreign Policy*, February 8, 2010. foreignpolicy.com/2010/02/08/i-dont-mean-to-say-i-told-you-so-but.

32 Neil King, Jr., "Syria Debate Exposes Iraq Fault Lines," *Wall Street Journal*, December 6, 2005. wsj.com/articles/SB113383235570914692.

33 Alan Weisman, "'Heroes' in waiting," *Los Angeles Times*, November 28, 2007. latimes.com/archives/la-xpm-2007-nov-28-oe-weisman28-story.html.

34 Salim Abraham, "Farid Ghadry, Syria's Chalabi: From Washington to Damascus," Syria Comment (blog), March 25, 2007. joshualandis.com/blog/farid-ghadry-syrias-chalabi-from-washington-to-damascus-by-salim-abraham.

35 Joshua Landis, "Encouraging Sectarian War as a Means to Bring Down Asad," Syria Comment (blog), December 8, 2006. joshualandis.com/blog/encouraging-sectarian-war-as-a-means-to-bring-down-asad.

36 Brad Hoff, "New Declassified CIA Memo Presents Blueprint for Syrian Regime Collapse," Libertarian Institute, February 14, 2017. libertarianinstitute.org/articles/cia-memo-scenarios-of-syrian-regime-collapse.

37 "Syria: Scenarios of Dramatic Political Change," Central Intelligence Agency, July 30, 1986. cia.gov/library/readingroom/docs/CIA-RDP86T01017R000100770001-5.pdf.

38 "Influencing the SARG in the End of 2006," WikiLeaks, December 13, 2006. wikileaks.org/plusd/cables/06DAMASCUS5399_a.html.

39 Samuel Grove, "Sami Ramadani: Between imperialism and oppression," Counterfire, June 13, 2012. counterfire.org/article/between-imperialism-and-repression. As cited in: Tim Anderson, *The Dirty War on Syria* (Global Research, 2016), p. 97.

40 Robert Naiman, "WikiLeaks Reveals How the US Aggressively Pursued Regime Change in Syria, Igniting a Bloodbath," Truthout, October 9, 2015.

41 "New Intel Syria, Turkey [sic], Israel, Iran. Sid," WikiLeaks, July 23, 2012. wikileaks.org/clinton-emails/emailid/12172.

42 Camille Otrakji, "Ten new year resolution ideas for a healthier American role in Syria and the Middle East in 2015 — Part III of a discussion with Ambassador Robert Ford," The Syria Page, December 31, 2014. creativesyria.com/syriapage/?p=580.

43 David Ignatius, "Careful with Syria," *Washington Post*, November 18, 2005. washingtonpost.com/wp-dyn/content/article/2005/11/17/AR2005111701303.html.

Chapter 2

1 Salim Abraham, "Farid Ghadry, Syria's Chalabi: From Washington to Damascus," Syria Comment (blog), March 25, 2007. joshualandis.com/blog/farid-ghadry-syrias-chalabi-from-washington-to-damascus-by-salim-abraham.

2 Ibid.

3 "Abdul Halim Khaddam: From Vice President of Syria to Exile in Paris," *Al-Sharq al-Awsat*, April 1, 2020. english.aawsat.com/home/article/2210646/exclusive-abdul-halim-khaddam-vice-president-syria-exile-paris.

4 Salim Abraham, "Farid Ghadry, Syria's Chalabi: From Washington to Damascus," Syria Comment (blog), March 25, 2007. joshualandis.com/blog/farid-ghadry-syrias-chalabi-from-washington-to-damascus-by-salim-abraham.

5 Joshua Landis, "Can Bush Bring Down Syrian Regime?" Syria Comment (blog), October 29, 2006. joshualandis.com/blog/can-bush-bring-down-syrian-regime.

6 "UPI: Saudi king meeting Syrian dissidents?" United Press International, October 20, 2006. upi.com/Defense-News/2006/10/20/Saudi-king-meeting-Syrian-dissidents/40281161350493/?ur3=1.

7 Jay Soloman, "To Check Syria, U.S. Explores Bond with Muslim Brothers," *Wall Street Journal*, July 25, 2007. wsj.com/articles/SB118530969571176579.

8 Adam Zagorin, "Syria in Bush's cross hairs," *Time*, December 19, 2006. content.time.com/time/world/article/0,8599,1571751,00.html.

9 Joshua Landis, "Syrian Opposition harmed by Iraq: MB Opens office in D.C.," Syria Comment (blog), April 21, 2007. joshualandis.com/blog/syrian-opposition-harmed-by-iraq-mb-opens-office-in-dc.

10 Ibid.

11 Joshua Landis, "The National Salvation Front Folds," Syria Comment (blog), April 23, 2009. joshualandis.com/blog/the-national-salvation-front-folds.

12 Seymour Hersh, "The 'Redirection,'" *The New Yorker*, February 25, 2007. newyorker.com/magazine/2007/03/05/the-redirection.

13 Ibid.

14 Ibid.

15 State Department Cable, "Influencing the SARG in the end of 2006," WikiLeaks, December 13, 2006. wikileaks.org/plusd/cables/06DAMASCUS5399_a.html.

16 Peter Neumann, "Suspects into Collaborators," *London Review of Books*, April 3, 2014. lrb.co.uk/v36/n07/peter-neumann/suspects-into-collaborators.

17 Borzou Daragahi, "Car bombing in Damascus kills 17," *Los Angeles Times*, September 28, 2008. latimes.com/archives/la-xpm-2008-sep-28-fg-syria28-story.html.

18 "Far from Justice: Syria's Supreme State Security Court," Human Rights Watch, February 2009. hrw.org/sites/default/files/reports/syria0209web.pdf.

19 Kristen Helberg, "The kidnapping of the Douma 4: The Salafist and the human rights activist," Qantara.de, December 12, 2014. en.qantara.de/content/the-kidnapping-of-the-douma-4-the-salafist-and-the-human-rights-activist.

20 "AP: Iraq inmates imposed Islamic justice," NBC News, July 26, 2008. nbcnews.com/id/wbna25865759.

21 Alissa J. Rubin, "U.S. Remakes Jails in Iraq, but Gains Are at Risk," *New York Times*, June 2, 2008. nytimes.com/2008/06/02/world/middleeast/02detain.html.

22 Ghaith Abdul-Ahad, "Al-Qaida turns tide for rebels in battle for eastern Syria," *The Guardian*, July 30, 2012. theguardian.com/world/2012/jul/30/al-qaida-rebels-battle-syria.

23 Craig Whiteside, "Catch and Release in the Land of the Two Rivers," War on the Rocks (blog), December 14, 2018. warontherocks.com/2014/12/catch-and-release-in-the-land-of-two-rivers.

24 Terrence McCoy, "Camp Bucca: The US prison that became the birthplace of Isis," *The Independent*, November 4, 2014. independent.co.uk/news/world/middle-east/camp-bucca-us-prison-became-birthplace-isis-9838905.html.

25 James Gordon Meek and Lee Ferran, "ISIS Leader's Ominous New York Message in Doubt, But US Still on Edge," ABC News, June 16, 2014. abcnews.go.com/Blotter/isis-leaders-ominous-york-message-doubt-us-edge/story?id=24166099.

26 Firas Kilani, "A Caliph Without a Caliphate: The Biography of ISIS's New Leader," *New Lines Magazine*, April 25, 2021. newlinesmag.com/reportage/a-caliph-without-a-caliphate-the-biography-of-isiss-new-leader.

27 Tara John, "Everything we know about ISIS spy chief Abu Muhammad al-Adnani," *Time*, August 4, 2016. time.com/4438388/abu-mohammad-al-adnani-isis-emni-profile/?amp=true.

28 Qassim Abdul-Zahra and Zeina Karam, "AP: Elusive Al-Qaeda leader in Syria stays in shadows," *The Times of Israel*, November 4, 2013. timesofisrael.com/elusive-al-qaeda-leader-in-syria-stays-in-shadows.

29 Anthony Shadid, "In Iraq, Chaos Feared as U.S. Closes Prison," *Washington Post*, March 22, 2009. washingtonpost.com/wp-dyn/content/article/2009/03/21/AR2009032102255_pf.html.

30 Timothy Williams and Omar al-Jawoshy, "Top insurgents escaped prison days after Iraq took over," *New York Times*, July 23, 2010. nytimes.com/2010/07/24/world/middleeast/24iraq.html?ref=iraq.

31 Martin Chulov, "Iraqi officials investigate warden's involvement in al-Qaeda jailbreak," *The Guardian*, July 25, 2010. theguardian.com/world/2010/jul/25/iraq-al-qaida-prison-warden.

32 "AP: Four escape from US custody in maximum-security Baghdad prison," *The National*, September 8, 2010. thenationalnews.com/world/mena/four-escape-from-us-custody-in-maximum-security-baghdad-prison-1.534348.

33 Ryan Teague Beckwith, "Read the CIA Director's Thoughts on the Paris Attacks," *Time*, November 16, 2015. time.com/4114870/paris-attacks-cia-john-brennan.

34 Ian Fisher, "In Rise of ISIS, No Single Missed Key but Many Strands of Blame," *New York Times*, November 18, 2015. nytimes.com/2015/11/19/world/middleeast/in-rise-of-isis-no-single-missed-key-but-many-strands-of-blame.html.

35 "Pgs. 287–93 (291) JW v DOD and State 14-812," U.S. Defense Intelligence Agency, August 12, 2012. judicialwatch.org/documents/pgs-287-293-291-jw-v-dod-and-state-14-812-2.

36 Ibid.

37 Theo Padnos, *Blindfold: A Memoir of Capture, Torture, and Enlightenment* (New York: Scribner, 2021), p. 277.

38 Rania Khalek, "Dispatches: Former Hostage of Al Qaeda in Syria Rejects Jolani's PBS Makeover: 'They Are Lunatics with Guns,'" BreakThrough News, June 9, 2021. youtube.com/watch?v=q3S8MeXOnj4.

39 Rania Abouzeid, "Meet the Islamist Militants Fighting Alongside Syria's Rebels," *Time*, July 26, 2012. world.time.com/2012/07/26/time-exclusive-meet-the-islamist-militants-fighting-alongside-syrias-rebels.

40 Abdullah Suleiman Ali, "As-Safir: Saudi jihadists flow into Syria," Al-Monitor, December 5, 2013. al-monitor.com/pulse/security/2013/12/saudi-fighters-syria-official-silence.html.

41 Thomas Joscelyn, "Al Qaeda's chief representative in Syria killed in suicide attack," *Long War Journal*, February 23, 2014. longwarjournal.org/archives/2014/02/zawahiris_chief_repr.php.

42 Mousab al-Hamadee, "Recalling a Syrian leader who helped jihadis grow prominent in rebellion," McClatchyDC, September 30, 2014. mcclatchydc.com/news/nation-world/world/article24773947.html.

43 Abdullah Suleiman Ali, "As-Safir: Saudi jihadists flow into Syria," Al-Monitor, December 5, 2013. al-monitor.com/pulse/security/2013/12/saudi-fighters-syria-official-silence.html.

44 John Hannah, "Bandar's Return," *Foreign Policy*, April 22, 2011. foreignpolicy.com/2011/04/22/bandars-return.

45 Seymour Hersh, "The 'Redirection,'" *The New Yorker*, February 25, 2007. newyorker.com/magazine/2007/03/05/the-redirection.

46 Charles Harb, "Blowback in Lebanon," *The Guardian*, May 23, 2007. theguardian.com/commentisfree/2007/may/24/comment.syria.

47 Souad Mekhennet and Michael Moss, "A new face of jihad vows attacks on U.S.," *New York Times*, March 16, 2007. nytimes.com/2007/03/16/world/africa/16iht-web-0316profile.4927893.html.

48 Ibid.

49 Ewen MacAskill, Richard Norton-Taylor and Julian Borger, "Bin Laden terror network active in 34 countries," *The Guardian*, September 14, 2001. amp.theguardian.com/world/2001/sep/14/september11.afghanistan1.

50 Chrisopher Davidson, *Shadow Wars: The Secret Struggle for the Middle East* (London: Oneworld Publications, 2016), p. 133.

51 Raffaello Pantucci, "Abu Qatada's Comfortable British Jihad," Jamestown Foundation, *Terrorism Monitor* 6, no. 14 (July 2008). cia.gov/library/abbottabad-compound/C4/C4B547E82874152CD853A695D0F4AFF0_TM_006_014.pdf.

52 Abdel Bari Atwan, "America enabled radical Islam: How the CIA, George W. Bush and many others helped create ISIS," *Salon*, October 18, 2015. salon.com/2015/10/18/america_enabled_radical_islam_how_the_cia_george_w_bush_and_many_others_helped_create_isis.

53 David Samuels, "The New Mastermind of Jihad," *Wall Street Journal*, April 6, 2012. wsj.com/articles/SB10001424052702303299604577323750859163544.

54 Mark Curtis, *Secret Affairs: Britain's Collusion with Radical Islam* (London: Serpent's Tail, 2012), pp. 225–31.

55 Raffaello Pantucci, "British Fighters Joining the War in Syria," Combating Terrorism Center, United States Military Academy at West Point, *CTC Sentinel* 6, no. 2 (February 2013). ctc.usma.edu/british-fighters-joining-the-war-in-syria.

56 Nibras Kazimi, "Zarqawi's Anti-Shia Legacy: Real or Borrowed?" Hudson Institute, November 1, 2006. hudson.org/research/9908-zarqawi-s-anti-shi-a-legacy-original-or-borrowed.

57 William Van Wagenen, "Salafist roots of the Syrian uprising," Libertarian Institute, April 20, 2020. libertarianinstitute.org/articles/the-salafist-roots-of-the-syrian-uprising.

58 Raffaello Pantucci, "British Fighters Joining the War in Syria," Combating Terrorism Center, United States Military Academy at West Point, *CTC Sentinel* 6, no. 2 (February 2013). ctc.usma.edu/british-fighters-joining-the-war-in-syria.

59 Mark Curtis, *Secret Affairs: Britain's Collusion with Radical Islam* (London: Serpent's Tail, 2012), Chapter 12.

60 Michael Meacher, "Britain now faces its own blowback," *The Guardian*, September 9, 2005. theguardian.com/world/2005/sep/10/terrorism.politics.

61 Nick Fielding, "The British Jackal," *Sunday Times* (London) (Republished by the Indian Ministry of External Affairs), April 21, 2002. mea.gov.in/articles-in-foreign-media.htm?dtl/18174/The+British+jackal.

62 Adil Jawad and Kathy Gannon, "AP: Pakistan court overturns conviction in death of Daniel Pearl," ABC News, April 2, 2020. abcnews.go.com/International/wireStory/pakistan-court-overturns-conviction-death-daniel-pearl-69929952.

63 Michael Meacher, "Britain now faces its own blowback," *The Guardian*, September 9, 2005. theguardian.com/world/2005/sep/10/terrorism.politics.

64 Ibid.

65 Nafeez Ahmed, "The circus: How British intelligence primed both sides of the 'terror war,'" Middle East Eye, March 2, 2015. middleeasteye.net/opinion/circus-how-british-intelligence-primed-both-sides-terror-war.

66 Abul Taher, "Call to Arms," *The Guardian*, May 15, 2000. theguardian.com/education/2000/may/16/highereducation.theguardian1.

67 Mark Curtis, *Secret Affairs: Britain's Collusion with Radical Islam* (London: Serpent's Tail, 2012), p. 223.

68 "Supplementary memorandum from Institute for Policy Research & Development (PVE 19A)," by Nafeez Ahmed, UK Parliament, September 2009. publications.parliament.uk/pa/cm200809/cmselect/cmcomloc/memo/previoex/uc19a02.htm#_ftnref36.

69 Martin Banks, "Contacts between the Belgian Islamic radical group, Sharia4Belgium and fellow supporters in rest of Europe has been confirmed," *Brussels Times*, November 17, 2015. brusselstimes.com/35497/contacts-between-the-belgian-islamic-radical-group-sharia4belgium-and-fellow-supporters-in-rest-of-europe-has-been-confirmed.

70 Samira Shackle, "Radical 'IS' preacher on trial," Deutsche Welle, January 11, 2016. dw.com/en/radical-uk-preacher-faces-is-trial/a-18970622.

71 "Radical imam Anjem Choudary on Charlie Hebdo attack," Fox News, February 3, 2017. foxnews.com/video/3976707999001.

72 Jaime Gierson and Shiv Malik, "Preacher Anjem Choudary charged with encouraging support for Islamic State," *The Guardian*, August 5, 2015. theguardian.com/uk-news/2015/aug/05/cleric-anjem-choudary-charged-with-encouraging-support-for-islamic-state.

73 "Press TV: UK planned war on Syria before unrest began: French ex-foreign minister Roland Dumas," Sott.net, June 16, 2013. sott.net/article/262842-UK-planned-war-on-Syria-before-unrest-began-French-ex-foreign-minister-Roland-Dumas.

74 Amandla Thomas-Johnson, and Simon Hooper, "'Sorted' by MI5: How UK government sent British-Libyans to fight Gaddafi," Middle East Eye, November 7, 2018. middleeasteye.net/fr/news/sorted-mi5-how-uk-government-sent-british-libyans-fight-gaddafi-1219906488.

75 Ibid.

76 Arwa Ibrahim, "UK apologises to Libyan dissident Belhaj over rendition," Al Jazeera, May 10, 2018. aljazeera.com/news/2018/5/10/uk-apologises-to-libyan-dissident-belhaj-over-rendition.

77 Sudarsan Raghavan, "These Libyans were once linked to al-Qaeda. Now they are politicians and businessmen," *Washington Post*, September 28, 2017. washingtonpost.com/world/middle_east/these-libyan-ex-militiamen-were-once-linked-to-al-qaeda-now-they-wield-power-in-a-new-order/2017/09/27/8356abf8-97dd-11e7-af6a-6555caaeb8dc_story.html.

78 "Irish Libyans join rebels trying to oust Gadafy," *Irish Times*, August 13, 2011. irishtimes.com/news/irish-libyans-join-rebels-trying-to-oust-gadafy-1.596469.

[79] Tam Hussein, "Mahde al-Harati: A Libyan force multiplier," Syria Comment (blog), September 26, 2017. joshualandis.com/blog/mahdi-al-harati-a-libyan-force-multiplier.

[80] Ali Hashem, "'Irish Sam' Joins Fight in Syria," Al-Monitor, March 11, 2013. al-monitor.com/originals/2013/03/irish-sam-hossam-al-najjar-soldier-libya-syria-book.html.

Chapter 3

[1] Craig Whitlock, "U.S. secretly backed Syrian opposition groups, cables released by WikiLeaks show," *Washington Post*, April 17, 2011. washingtonpost.com/world/us-secretly-backed-syrian-opposition-groups-cables-released-by-wikileaks-show/2011/04/14/AF1p9hwD_story.html.

[2] Jay Soloman, "To Check Syria, U.S. Explores Bond with Muslim Brothers," *Wall Street Journal*, July 25, 2007. wsj.com/articles/SB118530969571176579.

[3] Charlie Skelton, "The Syrian opposition: who's doing the talking?" *The Guardian*, July 12, 2012. theguardian.com/commentisfree/2012/jul/12/syrian-opposition-doing-the-talking.

[4] Craig Whitlock, "U.S. secretly backed Syrian opposition groups, cables released by WikiLeaks show," *Washington Post*, April 17, 2011. washingtonpost.com/world/us-secretly-backed-syrian-opposition-groups-cables-released-by-wikileaks-show/2011/04/14/AF1p9hwD_story.html.

[5] Sarah E. Yerkes and Tamara Cofman Wittes, "The Middle East Partnership Initiative: Progress, Problems, and Prospects," Brookings Institution, November 29, 2004. brookings.edu/research/the-middle-east-partnership-initiative-progress-problems-and-prospects.

[6] Duncan Green, "8 myths about non-violent activism (from a movement that overthrew a dictator)," From Poverty to Power (blog), Oxfam, February 25, 2015. oxfamapps.org/fp2p/8-myths-about-non-violent-activism-from-a-movement-that-overthrew-a-dictator.

[7] Eli Lake, "Why Obama Let Iran's Green Revolution Fail," Bloomberg News, August 24, 2016. bloomberg.com/opinion/articles/2016-08-24/why-obama-let-iran-s-green-revolution-fail.

[8] Carl Gibson and Steve Horn, "Exposed: Globally renowned activists collaborated with intelligence firm Stratfor," Occupy.com, December 2, 2013. occupy.com/article/exposed-globally-renowned-activist-collaborated-intelligence-firm-stratfor#sthash.uyX2lbES.HGgqoj2y.dpbs.

[9] Hugh Macleod and Anna Sofie Flamand, "Tweeting the police state," Al Jazeera, April 9, 2011. aljazeera.com/features/2011/4/9/tweeting-the-police-state.

[10] Ron Nixon., "U.S. Groups Helped Nurture Arab Uprisings," *New York Times*, April 14, 2011. nytimes.com/2011/04/15/world/15aid.html.

[11] David Ignatius, "Innocence abroad: The new world of spyless coups," *Washington Post*, September 22, 1991. washingtonpost.com/archive/opinions/1991/09/22/innocence-abroad-the-new-world-of-spyless-coups/92bb989a-de6e-4bb8-99b9-462c76b59a16.

[12] Ron Nixon., "U.S. Groups Helped Nurture Arab Uprisings," *New York Times*, April 14, 2011. nytimes.com/2011/04/15/world/15aid.html.

[13] "Special Briefing to Announce the Alliance of Youth Movement," James K. Glassman, Under Secretary of State for Public Diplomacy and Public Affairs and Jared Cohen, Policy Planning Staff, Washington, D.C. U.S. Department of State, November 24, 2008. 2001-2009.state.gov/r/us/2008/112310.htm.

14 Timothy Dumas, "Digital Diplomat," *Greenwich Magazine*, April 2011. web.archive.org/web/20150911010241/greenwichmag.com/g/April-2011/Digital-Diplomat.

15 Christina Larson, "State Department Innovator Goes to Google," *Foreign Policy*, September 7, 2010. foreignpolicy.com/2010/09/07/state-department-innovator-goes-to-google.

16 Noemie Emery, "The Great Right Hope, Hillary Clinton?" *The Weekly Standard*, November 19, 2008. cbsnews.com/news/the-great-right-hope-hillary-clinton.

17 Lee Smith, "Shadow Play: Agents of Influence on Egypt Ambassador Pick Robert S. Ford," *Tablet*, April 2, 2010. tabletmag.com/sections/israel-middle-east/articles/shadow-play. As quoted in Camille Otrakji, "A frank look at America's interests, values and mistakes, in Syria," The Syria Page, October 21, 2014. creativesyria.com/syriapage/?p=453.

18 Vijay Prashad, "The Elevation of Jeffrey Feltman," *CounterPunch*, May 25, 2012. counterpunch.org/2012/05/25/the-elevation-of-jeffrey-feltman.

19 David Schenker, "Who Decides on the Levant in Washington?" Washington Institute for Near East Policy, October 6, 2009. washingtoninstitute.org/policy-analysis/who-decides-levant-washington.

20 Rania Khalek, "Robert Kagan and other Neocons are backing Hillary Clinton," *The Intercept*, July 25, 2016. theintercept.com/2016/07/25/robert-kagan-and-other-neocons-back-hillary-clinton.

21 Michael J. Morell, "I Ran the C.I.A. Now I'm Endorsing Hillary Clinton," *New York Times*, August 5, 2016. nytimes.com/2016/08/05/opinion/campaign-stops/i-ran-the-cia-now-im-endorsing-hillary-clinton.html.

22 Jeremy Kuzmarov, "There is Absolutely No Reason in the World to Believe That Bill Clinton Is a CIA Asset — Except for All the Evidence," *CovertAction Magazine*, January 3, 2022. covertactionmagazine.com/2022/01/03/there-is-absolutely-no-reason-in-the-world-to-believe-that-bill-clinton-is-a-cia-asset-except-for-all-the-evidence.

23 Mark Landler and Brian Stelter, "Washington taps into a potent new force in diplomacy," *New York Times*, June 16, 2009. nytimes.com/2009/06/17/world/middleeast/17media.html.

24 Tina Rosenberg, "Revolution U," *Foreign Policy*, February 17, 2011. foreignpolicy.com/2011/02/17/revolution-u-2.

25 Ryan Lizza, "The Consequentialist: How the Arab Spring remade Obama's foreign policy," *The New Yorker*, April 25, 2011. newyorker.com/magazine/2011/05/02/the-consequentialist.

26 Eli Lake, "Why Obama Let Iran's Green Revolution Fail," Bloomberg News, August 24, 2016. bloomberg.com/opinion/articles/2016-08-24/why-obama-let-iran-s-green-revolution-fail.

27 David E. Sanger, James Glanz, and Jo Becker, "Around the World, Distress Over Iran," *New York Times*, November 28, 2010. nytimes.com/2010/11/29/world/middleeast/29iran.html.

28 David Sanger, "The Larger Game in the Middle East: Iran," *New York Times*, April 2, 2011. nytimes.com/2011/04/03/weekinreview/03sanger.html?pagewanted=all.

29 Yasha Levine, *Surveillance Valley: The Secret Military History of the Internet* (New York: Public Affairs Books, 2018), pp. 233–47.

30 Jillian York, "Jacob Appelbaum Presents Tor at Arab Bloggers Workshop 2009," Global Voices, Advox, December 9, 2009. advox.globalvoices.org/2009/12/09/jacob-appelbaum-presents-tor-at-arab-bloggers-workshop-2009.

[31] Efthimia Dilpizoglou, "Jacob Appelbaum in the Middle East in 2009 — the tweets," Project Keep Staring (blog), March 2, 2016. mariatechnosux.wordpress.com/2016/03/02/jacob-appelbaum-in-the-middle-east-in-2009-the-tweets.

[32] Ibid.

[33] Bob Dreyfus, "Al Jazeera's Muslim Brotherhood Problem," *The Nation*, July 10, 2013. thenation.com/article/archive/al-jazeeras-muslim-brotherhood-problem.

[34] "U.S. Department of State Case No. F-2014-20439 Doc No. C05795577 Date: 01/07/2016," WikiLeaks, August 3, 2012. wikileaks.org/clinton-emails/emailid/12166#efmAMoAbj.

[35] "Interactive: Tracking Syria's defections," Al Jazeera, July 30, 2012. aljazeera.com/news/2012/7/30/interactive-tracking-syrias-defections.

[36] Jillian Yorke, "There are other funding options than the USG," Jillian C. Yorke (blog), February 6, 2015. jilliancyork.com/2015/02/06/there-are-other-funding-options-than-the-usg.

[37] David Kushner, "The Darknet: Is the Government Destroying 'the Wild West of the Internet'?" *Rolling Stone*, October 22, 2015. https://www.google.com/url?q=https://web.archive.org/web/20181030211435/https://www.rollingstone.com/politics/politics-news/the-darknet-is-the-government-destroying-the-wild-west-of-the-internet-198271/&sa=D&source=docs&ust=1710439753094680&usg=AOvVaw3c4Ip3dgFcpAKVPrbgsxHZ.

[38] Mark Landler, "Twitter Musings in Syria Elicit Groans in Washington," *New York Times*, June 29, 2010. nytimes.com/2010/06/30/world/30diplo.html.

[39] "1st know [sic] case of a successful social media campaign in Syria," WikiLeaks, September 23, 2009. wikileaks.org/clinton-emails/emailid/1626.

[40] Seth Weintraub, "Google to open 'Google Ideas' global technology think tank," *Fortune*, August 15, 2010. fortune.com/2010/08/15/google-to-open-google-ideas-global-technology-think-tank.

[41] Timothy Dumas, "Digital Diplomat," *Greenwich Magazine*, April 2011. web.archive.org/web/20150911010241/greenwichmag.com/g/April-2011/Digital-Diplomat.

[42] "Google is not what it seems," by Julian Assange, WikiLeaks, October 23, 2014. wikileaks.org/google-is-not-what-it-seems/#ftn81.

[43] Mark Landler, "Secret Report Ordered by Obama Identified Potential Uprisings," *New York Times*, February 16, 2011. nytimes.com/2011/02/17/world/middleeast/17diplomacy.html.

[44] War & Revolution 2010–11 (@WaR2011sl): "Thread: Presidential Study Directive 11 (#PSD11) issued by Obama admin in August 2010, months before 'Arab Spring' uprisings, instructing US agencies (State Dep, CIA, Pentagon etc) to 'prepare for change' in Middle East & North Africa via 'tailored' 'country-by-country' approach," July 28, 2022. twitter.com/WaR2011sl/status/1552624951357743105.

[45] Scott Wilson, "Obama administration prepares for possibility of new post-revolt Islamist regimes," *Washington Post*, March 3, 2011. washingtonpost.com/world/national-security/obama_administration_prepares_for_possibility_of_new_post_revolt_islamist_regimes/2011/03/02/AB9qyfN_story.html.

[46] Christian Chesnot and Georges Malbrunot, *Les Chemins De Damas: Le dossier noir de la relation franco-syrienne* (Paris: Robert Laffont, 2014), p. 190.

[47] David Ignatius, "Obama's low-key strategy for the Middle East," *Washington Post*, March 4, 2011. washingtonpost.com/opinions/obamas_strategy_for_the_middle_east/2011/03/04/A BdEwuN_story.html.

[48] War & Revolution 2010–11 (@WaR2011sl): "Thread: Presidential Study Directive 11 (#PSD11) issued by Obama admin in August 2010, months before 'Arab Spring' uprisings, instructing US agencies (State Dep, CIA, Pentagon etc) to 'prepare for change' in Middle East & North Africa via 'tailored' 'country-by-country' approach," July 28, 2022. twitter.com/WaR2011sl/status/1552624951357743105.

[49] David Ignatius, "Obama's low-key strategy for the Middle East," *Washington Post*, March 4, 2011. washingtonpost.com/opinions/obamas_strategy_for_the_middle_east/2011/03/04/A BdEwuN_story.html.

[50] Radwan Ziadeh, Steven Heydemann, and Karen Farrell, "Syria's Democratic Past: Lessons for the Future," National Endowment for Democracy, January 7, 2010. ned.org/events/syrias-democratic-past-lessons-for-the-future.

[51] Charlie Skelton, "The Syrian opposition: who's doing the talking?" *The Guardian*, July 12, 2012. theguardian.com/commentisfree/2012/jul/12/syrian-opposition-doing-the-talking.

[52] Josh Rogin, "Conservatives call for Obama to intervene in Syria," *Foreign Policy*, February 17, 2012. foreignpolicy.com/2012/02/17/conservatives-call-for-obama-to-intervene-in-syria.

[53] "Murky Alliances: Muslim Brotherhood, the Movement for Justice and Democracy, and the Damascus Declaration," WikiLeaks, July 8, 2009. wikileaks.org/plusd/cables/09DAMASCUS477_a.html.

[54] Robert Ford, "Among Syria's Revolutionaries," *New Lines Magazine*, October 14, 2020. newlinesmag.com/first-person/among-syrias-revolutionaries.

[55] Deutsche Welle staff, Dana Sumlaji, and Wafaa Albadry, "Exclusive: How Syria's hard-line rebels turned against a human rights activist," Deutsche Welle, July 17, 2021. dw.com/en/exclusive-how-syrias-hard-line-rebels-turned-against-a-human-rights-activist/a-58270075.

[56] Zeina Erhaim, "How the Syrian Revolution Was Organized — And How It Unraveled," *New Lines Magazine*, March 16, 2021. newlinesmag.com/essays/how-the-syrian-revolution-was-organized-and-how-it-unraveled.

[57] Ibid.

[58] "Organization Profile," Syrian Center for Media and Freedom of Expression. scm.bz/wp-content/plugins/pdfjs-viewer-shortcode/pdfjs/web/viewer.php?file=https%3A%2F%2Fscm.bz%2Fwp-content%2Fuploads%2F2020%2F07%2FSCM_Profile.pdf&download=true&print=true&openfile=false.

[59] Emily Tamkin, "Who's Afraid of George Soros?" *Foreign Policy*, October 10, 2017. foreignpolicy.com/2017/10/10/whos-afraid-of-george-soros.

[60] Zeina Erhaim, "How the Syrian Revolution Was Organized — And How It Unraveled," *New Lines Magazine*, March 16, 2021. newlinesmag.com/essays/how-the-syrian-revolution-was-organized-and-how-it-unraveled.

[61] Camille Otrakji, "A frank look at America's interests, values and mistakes, in Syria," The Syria Page, October 21, 2014. creativesyria.com/syriapage/?p=453.

[62] Vanessa Beeley, "George Soros: Anti-Syria Campaign Impresario," Wrong Kind of Green, January 21, 2016. wrongkindofgreen.org/2016/01/23/george-soros-anti-syria-campaign-impresario.

63 "Syrian human rights activist Wissam Tarif insists on using real name in CNN interview," CNN, April 23, 2011. youtube.com/watch?v=IKkODkqh96o.

64 Liam Stack and Katherine Zoepf, "Syria Presses Crackdown in Two Cities on Coast," New York Times, April 12, 2011. nytimes.com/2011/04/13/world/middleeast/13syria.html.

65 Nicholas Blanford, "Syria wants to talk to opposition leaders, but there aren't any," Christian Science Monitor, May 3, 2011. csmonitor.com/World/Middle-East/2011/0503/Syria-wants-to-talk-to-opposition-leaders-but-there-aren-t-any.

66 Gabriela M. Keller, "The mysterious militia of the Syrian regime (German)," Die Welt, June 24, 2011. welt.de/politik/ausland/article13447012/Die-geheimnisvolle-Miliz-des-syrischen-Regimes.html.

67 Ed Pilkington, "Avaaz faces questions over role at centre of Syrian protest movement," The Guardian, March 2, 2012. theguardian.com/world/2012/mar/02/avaaz-activist-group-syria.

68 Tara Bahrampour, "3 prominent Syrians resign in protest against deadly crackdown," Washington Post, April 23, 2011. washingtonpost.com/world/syrian-forces-fire-on-crowds-mourning-fridays-scores-of-dead/2011/04/23/AFy49SWE_story.html.

69 "Troops, Backed by Tanks, Move to Quell Dissent in Syrian Towns," New York Times, May 10, 2011. nytimes.com/2011/05/11/world/middleeast/11syria.html.

70 Uri Friedman, "Meet Wissam Tarif, the man updating us on Syria," The Atlantic, April 23, 2011. theatlantic.com/international/archive/2011/04/meet-wissam-tarif-man-updating-us-syria/349932.

71 "Looking for answers in Syria," National Public Radio, May 4, 2011. npr.org/2011/05/04/135995093/looking-for-answers-in-syria.

72 Wissam Tarif, "Witnessing Dera'a's Torment," Institute for War and Peace Reporting, May 12, 2011. iwpr.net/global-voices/witnessing-deraas-torment.

73 Uri Friedman, "Meet Wissam Tarif, the man updating us on Syria," The Atlantic, April 23, 2011. theatlantic.com/international/archive/2011/04/meet-wissam-tarif-man-updating-us-syria/349932.

74 "Press FAQ." Avaaz. secure.avaaz.org/page/en/pressfaq.

75 Will Evans, "Profile: MoveOn.org," National Public Radio, August 4, 2008. npr.org/templates/story/story.php?storyId=92458361.

76 Simon van Zuylen-Wood, "The Great Escape: Has One NGO Been Lying About Its Role in Syria?" The New Republic, May 26, 2012. newrepublic.com/article/103330/syria-avaaz-activist-group-journalism.

77 Nadine Elali and Aline Sara, "NOW Lebanon: Talking to Wissam Tarif: Activism under pressure," The Arab Network for the Study of Democracy, August 9, 2012. ademocracynet.com/index.php?page=articles&id=3181&action=Detail&__cf_chl_jschl_tk__=pmd_ddbea9616f15360f353cab3ed4378e1169a67996-1626552958-0-gqNtZGzNAg2jcnBszQc6.

78 Deborah Amos, "Aid Group's Role in Syria Pushes Limits," National Public Radio, March 14, 2012. npr.org/2012/03/13/148542026/aid-groups-role-in-syria-pushes-limits.

79 Simon van Zuylen-Wood, "The Great Escape: Has One NGO Been Lying About Its Role in Syria?" The New Republic, May 26, 2012. newrepublic.com/article/103330/syria-avaaz-activist-group-journalism.

80 Max Blumenthal, "Behind the Syrian Network for Human Rights: How an opposition front group became Western media's go-to monitor," The Grayzone, June 14, 2019. thegrayzone.com/2019/06/14/syrian-network-for-human-rights-opposition-snhr.

81 Brad Hoff, "Syrian Christians were Quietly Warned Before the War," Libertarian Institute, November 20, 2021. libertarianinstitute.org/articles/syrian-christians-were-quietly-warned-before-the-war.

82 Rania Abouzeid, "Sitting Pretty in Syria: Why Few Go Bashing Bashar," *Time*, March 6, 2011. content.time.com/time/world/article/0,8599,2057067,00.html.

83 Charlie Skelton, "The Syrian opposition: who's doing the talking?" *The Guardian*, July 12, 2012. theguardian.com/commentisfree/2012/jul/12/syrian-opposition-doing-the-talking.

Chapter 4

1 "Syria: A demonstration in front of the Ministry of Interior in the capital, Damascus," BBC Arabic, March 16, 2011. bbc.com/arabic/middleeast/2011/03/110316_syria_prisoners_families.shtml.

2 "The Man behind 'Syria Revolution 2011' Facebook-Page Speaks Out," Syria Comment (blog), April 24, 2011. joshualandis.com/blog/the-man-behind-syria-revolution-2011-facebook-page-speaks-out.

3 "AFP: Internet activists bring the 'Syrian revolution' to the world" (Arabic), France 24, April 29, 2011. france24.com/ar/20110429-syria-cyber-activist-malath-aumran-rami-nakhle-profile-revolution-facebook-twitter.

4 Camille Otrakji, "Ten new year resolution ideas for a healthier American role in Syria and the Middle East in 2015 — Part III of a discussion with Ambassador Robert Ford," The Syria Page, December 31, 2014. creativesyria.com/syriapage/?p=580.

5 "Talking about a Revolution: An Interview with Camille Otrakji," Qifa Nabki, May 2, 2011. qifanabki.com/2011/05/02/camille-otrakji-syria-protests.

6 David W. Lesch, *Syria: The Fall of the House of Assad* (New Haven: Yale University Press, 2021), p. 92.

7 Roger Cohen, "Who Really Brought Down Milosevic?" *New York Times Magazine*, November 6, 2000. nytimes.com/2000/11/26/magazine/who-really-brought-down-milosevic.html.

8 "Syria: The Release of Haitham Mallah in the Framework of a General Presidential Pardon," BBC Arabic, March 8, 2011. bbc.com/arabic/middleeast/2011/03/110308_syriapardon_maleh.

9 Rania Abouzeid, "Sitting Pretty in Syria: Why Few Go Bashing Bashar," *Time*, March 6, 2011. content.time.com/time/world/article/0,8599,2057067,00.html.

10 Rania Abouzeid, "The Syrian Style of Repression: Thugs and Lectures," *Time*, February 27, 2011. content.time.com/time/world/article/0,8599,2055713,00.html.

11 Ibid.

12 Muhammad Jamal Barout, *Syria in the Last Decade: The Dialectic of Stagnation and Reform* (Beirut: Arab Center for Research and Policy Studies, 2012), Chapter 5.

13 Mike Giglio, "Syria: The Republic of Fear," *Newsweek*, April 3, 2011. newsweek.com/syria-republic-fear-66433.

14 Azmi Bishara, *Syria: A Path to Freedom from Suffering* (Beirut: Arab Center for Research and Policy Studies, 2013), Chapter 2.

15 Muhammad Jamal Barout, *Syria in the Last Decade: The Dialectic of Stagnation and Reform* (Beirut: Arab Center for Research and Policy Studies, 2012), Chapter 5.

16 Ibrahim Zabad, *Middle Eastern Minorities: The Impact of the Arab Spring* (New York: Routledge, 2017), pp. 221–3.

17 Muhammad Jamal Barout, *Syria in the Last Decade: The Dialectic of Stagnation and Reform* (Beirut: Arab Center for Research and Policy Studies, 2012), Chapter 5.

[18] "Jared Cohen: The Changing Nature of Political Transitions," Stanford Graduate School of Business, May 23, 2012. youtube.com/watch?v=E9PHRLJaG_Y.

[19] "Democracy on Fire: Twitter, Social Movements, and the Future of Dissent with Wael Ghonim, Zeynep Tufekci, and Marshall Ganz," Institute of Politics Harvard Kennedy School of Government, October 27, 2017. youtube.com/watch?v=1E32NGIY6I4.

[20] Amro Ali, "Saeeds of Revolution; De-Mytholigizing Khaled Saeed," *Jadaliyya*, Arab Studies Institute, June 5, 2012. jadaliyya.com/Details/26148.

[21] "Profile: Egypt's Wael Ghonim," BBC News, February 9, 2011. bbc.com/news/world-middle-east-12400529.

[22] Alex Kantrowitz, "Arab Spring Leader Wael Ghonim on Modern Social Media's Promise and Peril," OneZero, February 25, 2021. onezero.medium.com/arab-spring-leader-wael-ghonim-on-modern-social-medias-promise-and-peril-51d90ce1aa95.

[23] "Revolution in Cairo: Inside the April 6 Movement," PBS, *Frontline*, February 14, 2011. pbs.org/wgbh/pages/frontline/revolution-in-cairo/inside-april6-movement.

[24] "Google is not what it seems," by Julian Assange, WikiLeaks, October 23, 2014. wikileaks.org/google-is-not-what-it-seems/#ftn81.

[25] Google Zeitgeist, "How one Facebook page sparked a revolution," Interview with Wael Ghonim, May 17, 2011. youtu.be/Mqh0e5hX5KY.

[26] Azmi Bishara, *Syria: A Path to Freedom from Suffering* (Beirut: Arab Center for Research and Policy Studies, 2013), Chapter 2, footnote 79.

[27] Ibid., footnote 80.

[28] Kareem Fahim and Hwaida Saad, "A Faceless Teenage Refugee Who Helped Ignite Syria's War," *New York Times*, February 8, 2013. nytimes.com/2013/02/09/world/middleeast/a-faceless-teenage-refugee-who-helped-ignite-syrias-war.html.

[29] Mark MacKinnon, "The Graffiti Kids Who Sparked the Syrian War," *Globe and Mail*, December 2, 2016. theglobeandmail.com/world/article-the-graffiti-kids-how-an-act-of-teenage-rebellion-sparked-the-syrian.

[30] Ibid.

[31] Azmi Bishara, *Syria: A Path to Freedom from Suffering* (Beirut: Arab Center for Research and Policy Studies, 2013), Chapter 2, footnote 83.

[32] Rania Abouzeid, *No Turning Back: Life, Loss, and Hope in Wartime Syria* (New York: W.W. Norton & Company, 2018), p. xxi.

[33] "An Activist's Reflections on the Syrian Uprising: Interview with Abdul-Qader Al-Dhoun," Jadaliyya, Arab Studies Institute, July 29, 2013. vimeo.com/71303394.

[34] Joe Sterling, "Daraa: The spark that lit the Syrian flame," CNN, March 1, 2012. cnn.com/2012/03/01/world/meast/syria-crisis-beginnings/index.html.

[35] Azmi Bishara, *Syria: A Path to Freedom from Suffering* (Beirut: Arab Center for Research and Policy Studies, 2013), Chapter 2.

[36] Aron Lund, "First Days of the Revolution: An Interview with Abdulkader Al Dhon," Carnegie Middle East Center, November 29, 2013. carnegie-mec.org/diwan/53738.

[37] Vivienne Walt, "How Libya's Second City Became the First to Revolt," *Time*, February 22, 2011. content.time.com/time/world/article/0,8599,2052980,00.html.

[38] Muhammad Jamal Barout, *Syria in the Last Decade: The Dialectic of Stagnation and Reform* (Beirut: Arab Center for Research and Policy Studies, 2012), Chapter 5, footnote 236.

[39] Phil Sands, "Syria Conflict: Atef Najib, the Man who Sparked the Uprising," *The National*, March 17, 2014. thenationalnews.com/world/syria-conflict-atef-najib-the-man-who-sparked-the-uprising-1.328020?videoId=5688157736001.

40 "An Activist's Reflections on the Syrian Uprising: Interview with Abdul-Qader Al-Dhoun," Jadaliyya, Arab Studies Institute, July 29, 2013. vimeo.com/71303394.

41 "Deaths During Protests in Deraa, and Clashes with Security Forces in Other Cities" (Arabic), France 24, March 18, 2011. france24.com/ar/20110318-syria-damascus-police-mosque-friday-pray-demonstration-unrest.

42 Jacob Appelbaum (@ioerror), April 23, 2011. twitter.com/ioerror/status/50448585501847552. See also: Efthimia Dilpizoglou, "Jacob Appelbaum in the Middle East in 2009 — the tweets," Project Keep Staring (blog), March 2, 2016. mariatechnosux.wordpress.com/2016/03/02/jacob-appelbaum-in-the-middle-east-in-2009-the-tweets.

43 "Sheikh Ahmed Siyasnah — Hizb Tahrir Lebanon 2012," Jay Tharappel, April 20, 2018. youtu.be/wCmEZ-DQGIw.

44 Firas Choufi, "Hizb Ut-Tahrir in Syria: The regime will cede to the Islamic Caliphate," *Al-Akhbar English*, May 3, 2012. islam.ru/en/content/story/hizb-ut-tahrir-syria-regime-will-cede-islamic-caliphate.

45 Christian Chesnot and Georges Malbrunot, *Les Chemins De Damas: Le dossier noir de la relation franco-syrienne* (Paris: Robert Laffont, 2014), pp. 179–81.

46 Nafeez Ahmed, "The circus: How British intelligence primed both sides of the 'terror war,'" Middle East Eye, March 2, 2015. middleeasteye.net/opinion/circus-how-british-intelligence-primed-both-sides-terror-war.

47 "Mourners of Syrian Protesters Chant for Freedom," Reuters, March 19, 2011. reuters.com/article/us-syria-protest/mourners-of-syrian-protesters-chant-for-freedom-idUSTRE72H88M20110319.

48 "Syria: 4 killed in a demonstration in Daraa and the use of force to disperse demonstrators in Damascus," BBC Arabic, March 18, 2011. bbc.com/arabic/middleeast/2011/03/110317_arrsests_syria.shtml.

49 Rania Abouzeid, "Syria's Revolt: How Graffiti Stirred an Uprising," *Time*, March 22, 2011. content.time.com/time/world/article/0,8599,2060788,00.html.

50 Muhammad Jamal Barout, *Syria in the Last Decade: The Dialectic of Stagnation and Reform* (Beirut: Arab Center for Research and Policy Studies, 2012), Chapter 5.

51 "Leak of the People's Assembly, the intervention of Sheikh Youssef Abu Roumieh, deputy of Daraa, on behalf of Atef Najib," Bashar Alhariri, April 1, 2011. youtube.com/watch?v=PVgt-i8fVm8.

52 Rania Abouzeid, *No Turning Back: Life, Loss, and Hope in Wartime Syria* (New York: W.W. Norton & Company, 2018), pp. 55–7.

53 William Van Wagenen, "A Brief History of the Destruction of Yarmouk," Libertarian Institute, April 3, 2019. libertarianinstitute.org/articles/a-brief-history-of-the-destruction-of-yarmouk.

54 "Libya protests: massacres reported as Gaddafi imposes news blackout," *The Guardian*, February 18, 2011. theguardian.com/world/2011/feb/18/libya-protests-massacres-reported.

Chapter 5

1 Gabe Kahn, "Bloody Syrian Protests Continue," Israel National News, March 21, 2011. israelnationalnews.com/news/143026.

2 Michel Chossudovsky, "Syria: Who is Behind the Protest Movement?" *Kanaan Online*, May 3, 2011. kanaanonline.org/en/2011/05/05/syria-who-is-behind-the-protest-movement.

3 Gabe Kahn, "Bloody Syrian Protests Continue," Israel National News, March 21, 2011. israelnationalnews.com/news/143026.

⁴ Rania Abouzeid, *No Turning Back: Life, Loss, and Hope in Wartime Syria* (New York: W.W. Norton & Company, 2018), pp. 56–61.

⁵ Gail Malone, "Conversations from Syria … Dara'a — the first month, a soldier's story," gailmalone — WordPress, November 9, 2016. gailmalone.wordpress.com/2016/11/09/conversations-from-syria-daraa-the-first-month-a-soldiers-story.

⁶ "Gunfire in Homs," Yzahra, July 15, 2011. youtube.com/watch?v=9vyx-8RrYKQ.

⁷ "Syrian security disperses 'demonstrations of anger' by force," Ikhwan Online, March 18, 2011. ikhwanonline.com/article/80862.

⁸ Theo Padnos, *Blindfold: A Memoir of Capture, Torture, and Enlightenment* (New York: Scribner, 2021), p. 277.

⁹ Rania Khalek, "Dispatches: Former Hostage of Al Qaeda in Syria Rejects Jolani's PBS Makeover: 'They Are Lunatics with Guns,'" BreakThrough News, June 9, 2021. youtube.com/watch?v=q3S8MeXOnj4.

¹⁰ Muhammad Jamal Barout, *Syria in the Last Decade: The Dialectic of Stagnation and Reform* (Beirut: Arab Center for Research and Policy Studies, 2012), Chapter 5.

¹¹ Jamie Tarabay, "For many Syrians, the story of the war began with graffiti in Dara'a," CNN, March 15, 2018. cnn.com/2018/03/15/middleeast/daraa-syria-seven-years-on-intl/index.html.

¹² Muhammad Jamal Barout, *Syria in the Last Decade: The Dialectic of Stagnation and Reform* (Beirut: Arab Center for Research and Policy Studies, 2012), Chapter 5.

¹³ Ibid., Chapter 5, footnote 222.

¹⁴ "Deaths During Protests in Deraa, and Clashes with Security Forces in Other Cities" (Arabic), France 24, March 18, 2011. france24.com/ar/20110318-syria-damascus-police-mosque-friday-pray-demonstration-unrest.

¹⁵ "Reports of a Massacre in Homs" (Arabic), Al Jazeera, April 19, 2011. aljazeera.net/news/2011/4/19/أنباء-عن-مجزرة-في-حمص.

¹⁶ "Damascus Accuses Salafists of Rebellion and a Sit-in Space for Protestors in Homs" (Arabic), *Al-Akhbar*, April 19, 2011. al-akhbar.com/Politics/87186.

¹⁷ Alison Matheson, "Christians under attack from anti-government protesters in Syria," *Christian Post*, May 5, 2011. christianpost.com/news/christians-under-attack-from-anti-government-protestors-in-syria-50104.

¹⁸ Muhammad Jamal Barout, *Syria in the Last Decade: The Dialectic of Stagnation and Reform* (Beirut: Arab Center for Research and Policy Studies, 2012), Chapter 7, including footnotes 459, 460, and 463.

¹⁹ "We Live as in War: Crackdown on Protesters in the Governorate of Homs, Syria," Human Rights Watch, November 11, 2011. hrw.org/report/2011/11/11/we-live-war/crackdown-protesters-governorate-homs-syria.

²⁰ Rania Abouzeid, "Syria's Revolt: How Graffiti Stirred an Uprising," *Time*, March 22, 2011. content.time.com/time/world/article/0,8599,2060788,00.html.

²¹ Joshua Landis, "Western Press Misled — Who Shot the Nine Soldiers in Banyas? Not Syrian Security Forces," Syria Comment (blog), April 13, 2011. joshualandis.com/blog/western-press-misled-who-shot-the-nine-soldiers-in-banyas-not-syrian-security-forces.

²² "Director of Al Jazeera office in Damascus: That is why I resigned" (Arabic), Zaman al-Wasl, May 7, 2011. zamanalwsl.net/news/article/19499.

²³ Roee Nahmias, "Al-Jazeera journalist resigns over 'incitement,'" ynetnews, March 24, 2011. ynetnews.com/articles/0,7340,L-4060180,00.html.

24 Ali Hashem, "Al Jazeera journalist explains resignation over Syria and Bahrain coverage," The Real News Network, March 12, 2012. therealnews.com/stories/ahashempt10319.

25 "Al Jazeera exodus: Channel losing staff over 'bias,'" RT, March 12, 2012. rt.com/news/al-jazeera-loses-staff-335.

26 Kareem Fahim and Hwaida Saad, "A Faceless Teenage Refugee Who Helped Ignite Syria's War," *New York Times*, February 8, 2013. nytimes.com/2013/02/09/world/middleeast/a-faceless-teenage-refugee-who-helped-ignite-syrias-war.html.

27 Muhammad Jamal Barout, *Syria in the Last Decade: The Dialectic of Stagnation and Reform* (Beirut: Arab Center for Research and Policy Studies, 2012), Chapter 6, footnote 385.

28 "Sweid describes details of his meeting with Assad" (Arabic), Al Jazeera, January 13, 2012. aljazeera.net/news/2012/1/13/سويد-يروي-تفاصيل-لقاءاته-مع-الأسد.

29 Azmi Bishara, *Syria: A Path to Freedom from Suffering* (Beirut: Arab Center for Research and Policy Studies, 2013), Chapter 2, footnote 86.

30 Muhammad Jamal Barout, *Syria in the Last Decade: The Dialectic of Stagnation and Reform* (Beirut: Arab Center for Research and Policy Studies, 2012), Chapter 5, footnote 239. Also see "Homs Bayada Demonstration," uploaded by MrSirya75, for video of an early demonstration in Homs where this slogan is repeated: youtube.com/watch?v=aoY6RqeFJyQ.

31 Ibid., Chapter 5, footnote 37.

32 "Deaths During Protests in Deraa, and Clashes with Security Forces in Other Cities" (Arabic), France 24, March 18, 2011. france24.com/ar/20110318-syria-damascus-police-mosque-friday-pray-demonstration-unrest.

33 "Syrian Oppositionist Mamoun Al-Homsi: If the Alawites Do Not Renounce Bashar Al-Assad, We Will Turn Syria into Their Graveyard," Middle East Media Research Institute, December 28, 2011. memri.org/reports/syrian-oppositionist-mamoun-al-homsi-if-alawites-do-not-renounce-bashar-al-assad-we-will.

34 Thomas Pierret, *Religion and State in Syria: The Sunni Ulama from Coup to Revolution* (New York: Cambridge University Press, 2013), p. 237.

35 Muhammad Jamal Barout, *Syria in the Last Decade: The Dialectic of Stagnation and Reform* (Beirut: Arab Center for Research and Policy Studies, 2012), Chapter 5.

36 Nir Rosen, "Islamism and the Syrian uprising," *Foreign Policy*, March 8, 2012. foreignpolicy.com/2012/03/08/islamism-and-the-syrian-uprising.

37 Murad Ali, "Shabiha describe Syrian revolution activists as 'al-'Ara'ara,'" *Al-Bayan*, April 19, 2012. albayan.ae/one-world/arabs/2012-04-19-1.1633702.

38 "Syrian Sunni Cleric Adnan al-Ar'our threatens the Alawites who supported the Syrian regime: We shall mince them in meat grinders and feed their flesh to the dogs," Middle East Media Research Institute, June 26, 2011. memri.org/tv/syrian-sunni-cleric-adnan-al-arour-threatens-alawites-who-supported-syrian-regime-we-shall-mince.

39 Sharmine Narwani, "Syria: The hidden massacre," RT, May 7, 2014. rt.com/op-ed/157412-syria-hidden-massacre-2011.

40 Muhammad Jamal Barout, *Syria in the Last Decade: The Dialectic of Stagnation and Reform* (Beirut: Arab Center for Research and Policy Studies, 2012), Chapter 7, footnotes 399 and 400.

41 Raffaello Pantucci, "British Fighters Joining the War in Syria," Combating Terrorism Center, United States Military Academy at West Point, *CTC Sentinel* 6, no. 2 (February 2013). ctc.usma.edu/british-fighters-joining-the-war-in-syria.

42 "'We've Never Seen Such Horror': Crimes against Humanity by Syrian Security Forces," Human Rights Watch, June 1, 2011. hrw.org/report/2011/06/01/weve-never-seen-such-horror/crimes-against-humanity-syrian-security-forces.

43 "'The Syrian Conundrum and Conflict' as an introductory event to the series 'West Asia Conflicts,' part 1," Centre for Policy Research, October 29, 2019. youtube.com/watch?v=2cnfOiYYlh8&feature=youtu.be.

44 Ibid.

45 "Syria unrest: Twelve killed in Latakia protest," BBC News, March 27, 2011. bbc.com/news/world-middle-east-12873053.

46 Rania Abouzeid, "Arab Spring: Is a Revolution Starting Up in Syria?" *Time*, March 19, 2011. content.time.com/time/world/article/0,8599,2060398,00.html.

47 Patrick Cockburn, "Patrick Cockburn: Whose hands are behind those dramatic YouTube pictures?" *The Independent*, January 15, 2021. independent.co.uk/voices/commentators/patrick-cockburn-whose-hands-are-behind-those-dramatic-youtube-pictures-6289808.html.

48 Mike Giglio, "Syria: The Republic of Fear," *Newsweek*, April 3, 2011. newsweek.com/syria-republic-fear-66433.

49 Josh Wood, "Dissidents from Syria Seek Haven in Lebanon," *New York Times*, April 6, 2011. nytimes.com/2011/04/07/world/middleeast/07iht-m07-syria-dissidents.html.

50 Sarina Rosenthal, "More than 140 Characters: The Man Behind @MalathAumran," Harvard Graduate School of Education, April 23, 2015. canvas.harvard.edu/files/844822/download?download_frd=1.

51 Tara Bahrampour, "A hunted Syrian activist begins his work anew in Washington," *Washington Post*, August 28, 2012. washingtonpost.com/local/a-hunted-syrian-activist-begins-his-work-anew-in-washington/2012/08/28/69e23bba-ed56-11e1-b09d-07d971dee30a_story.html.

52 Ali Ali, "Challenging the Syrian state: using information systems to document human-rights violations," openDemocracy, May 19, 2015. opendemocracy.net/en/opensecurity/challenging-syrian-state-using-information-systems-to-document-human-rights-vio.

53 Anthony Shadid, "Syria Escalates Crackdown as Tanks Go to Restive City," *New York Times*, April 25, 2011. nytimes.com/2011/04/26/world/middleeast/26syria.html.

54 "Deraa: A City Under Dark Siege," Al Jazeera, April 27, 2011. aljazeera.com/indepth/features/2011/04/2011427215943692865.html.

55 Sam Dagher, *Assad or We Burn the Country: How One Family's Lust for Power Destroyed Syria* (New York: Little, Brown and Company — Hachette Book Group, 2019), p. 219.

56 "An Activist's Reflections on the Syrian Uprising: Interview with Abdul-Qader Al-Dhoun," Jadaliyya, Arab Studies Institute, July 29, 2013. vimeo.com/71303394.

57 Muhammad Jamal Barout, *Syria in the Last Decade: The Dialectic of Stagnation and Reform* (Beirut: Arab Center for Research and Policy Studies, 2012), Chapter 5, including footnotes 240 and 241.

58 Ibid.

59 Joshua Landis, "Western Press Misled — Who Shot the Nine Soldiers in Banyas? Not Syrian Security Forces," Syria Comment (blog), April 13, 2011. joshualandis.com/blog/western-press-misled-who-shot-the-nine-soldiers-in-banyas-not-syrian-security-forces.

60 "Syria — Daraa revolution was armed to the teeth from the very beginning," Truth Syria, April 10, 2012. youtube.com/watch?v=VKN-tP4s_uU.

61 Matthew Jones, "The 'Preferred Plan': The Anglo-American Working Group Report on Covert Action in Syria, 1957," *Intelligence and National Security* 19, no. 3 (September 2004): pp. 401–15. researchgate.net/publication/239427177_The_'Preferred_Plan'_The_Anglo-American_Working_Group_Report_on_Covert_Action_in_Syria_1957.

62 "Interview with Flynt Leverett," Scott Horton, *Scott Horton Show*, April 8, 2014. scotthorton.org/interviews/040814-flynt-leverett.

63 Syriana Analysis, "Hamad bin Jassim: we spent $2 trillion to remove Bashar al-Assad," by Kevork Almassian, March 24, 2022. youtube.com/watch?v=56FvWppe_5M.

64 "Qatar 'maybe' supported al-Qaeda in Syria, says former PM," Middle East Eye, October 31, 2017. middleeasteye.net/news/qatar-maybe-supported-al-qaeda-syria-says-former-pm.

65 "Syrian unrest: Inquiry into Hamza al-Khatib's death," BBC News, June 1, 2011. bbc.com/news/world-middle-east-13622959.

66 Hugh Macleod and Annasofie Flamand, "Tortured and killed: Hamza al-Khateeb, age 13," Al Jazeera, May 31, 2011. aljazeera.com/features/2011/5/31/tortured-and-killed-hamza-al-khateeb-age-13.

67 "Crimes of the Syrian regime tortured and killed a child aged less than 13 Khatib terrible," Islamsyra, May 28, 2011. youtube.com/watch?v=J4JN1hx-hSc.

68 Hugh Macleod and Annasofie Flamand, "Tortured and killed: Hamza al-Khateeb, age 13," Al Jazeera, May 31, 2011. aljazeera.com/features/2011/5/31/tortured-and-killed-hamza-al-khateeb-age-13.

69 "The truth about the boy who became a symbol of anti-Syrian uprising," European Council on International Relations, June 1, 2011. europeaninternationalrelation.wordpress.com/2011/06/01/the-truth-about-the-boy-who-become-a-symbol-of-anti-syrian-uprising-hamza-al-khateeb.

70 "The Medical Examiner Interview about Hamza Al-Khateeb," Truth Syria, December 12, 2011. youtube.com/watch?v=7xlRDgVh6Dg.

71 "Interview with Hamza Al-Kateeb's father after he met the president," Truth Syria, December 7, 2011. youtube.com/watch?v=WzsZOxduaVA&list=UUDrnROqHtRoes4MXz_hsgTg&index=2.

72 Hugh Macleod and Annasofie Flamand, "Tortured and killed: Hamza al-Khateeb, age 13," Al Jazeera, May 31, 2011. aljazeera.com/features/2011/5/31/tortured-and-killed-hamza-al-khateeb-age-13.

73 Liz Sly, "Torture of boy reinvigorates Syria's protest movement," *Washington Post*, May 29, 2011. washingtonpost.com/world/middle-east/torture-of-boy-reinvigorates-syrias-protest-movement/2011/05/29/AGPwIREH_story.html.

Chapter 6

1 "Syria: Security Forces Fire on Protesters," Human Rights Watch, March 28, 2011. hrw.org/news/2011/03/28/syria-security-forces-fire-protesters.

2 "Syria unrest: Twelve killed in Latakia protest," BBC News, March 27, 2011. bbc.com/news/world-middle-east-12873053.

3 "The specter of sectarianism surrounded Latakia, and the people set up barricades at the entrances to villages and neighborhoods" (Arabic), *Al-Quds Al-Arabi*, March 27, 2011. alquds.co.uk/شبح-الطائفية-حاصر-اللاذقية-والأهالي-ي.

4 "'The Syrian Conundrum and Conflict' as an introductory event to the series 'West Asia Conflicts,' part 1," Centre for Policy Research, October 29, 2019. youtube.com/watch?v=2cnfOiYYlh8&feature=youtu.be.

5 "As-Safir: What if it is proven that a Lebanese team was involved in the events in Syria?" (Arabic), Lebanon Debate, March 29, 2011. lebanondebate.com/news/44295.

6 Rania Abouzeid, *No Turning Back: Life, Loss, and Hope in Wartime Syria* (New York: W.W. Norton & Company, 2018), pp. 55–61.

7 Anthony Shadid, "Syrian Navy Joins Attack on Key Rebellious Port City," *New York Times*, August 14, 2011. nytimes.com/2011/08/15/world/middleeast/15syria.html?_r=1&hp.

8 "Syrian forces 'shell Latakia' for third day," Al Jazeera, August 15, 2011. aljazeera.com/news/middleeast/2011/08/20118158309760895.html?xif=%C3%83%C2%A2%C3%A2%E2%80%9A%C2%AC%C3%82%C2%9D

9 "An 'exodus' movement from neighborhoods in Latakia and Turkish warnings to Damascus" (Arabic), BBC Arabic, August 15, 2011. bbc.com/arabic/middleeast/2011/08/110815_syria_refugees.

10 "Statement by UNRWA spokesman, Chris Gunness," United Nations Relief and Works Agency, August 15, 2011. unrwa.org/newsroom/official-statements/unrwa-gravely-concerned-about-heavy-gun-fire-refugee-camp-syrian-port.

11 Khaled Yacoub Oweis, "Syria forces hold hundreds in Latakia sports stadium," Reuters, August 17, 2011. reuters.com/article/us-syria-idUSTRE77D0LP20110817.

12 "Latakia doctor says crackdown aims to divide and conquer," *Los Angeles Times*, August 18, 2011. latimesblogs.latimes.com/babylonbeyond/2011/08/syria-latakia-doctor-accuses-regime-of-sectarian-war-.html.

13 "Palestinian Refugees of Syria in Light of the Syrian Revolution," by Tarek Homoud, Palestinian Return Centre, 2012 prc.org.uk/upload/library/files/PRSinLightofSyrianRev.pdf.

14 "Palestinian debate about the bombing of the Raml camp and the displacement of refugees," *Al-Akhbar*, August 15, 2011. al-akhbar.com/Arab/93173.

15 Sharmine Narwani, "Hollywood in Homs and Idlib?" Mideast Shuffle (blog), March 13, 2012. mideastshuffle.com/2012/03/13/hollywood-in-homs-and-idlib.

16 "Palestinian debate about the bombing of the Raml camp and the displacement of refugees," *Al-Akhbar*, August 15, 2011. al-akhbar.com/Arab/93173.

17 Sabr Darwish, "Cities in Revolution, Banias: Al-Bayda, the White City," *SyriaUntold*, May 5, 2011. cities.syriauntold.com/citypdf/Baniyas_en.pdf.

18 Khaled Yacoub Oweis, "Syrian rebel sheikh calls for war on Assad's Alawite heartland," Reuters, July 10, 2013. reuters.com/article/us-syria-crisis-coast/syrian-rebel-sheikh-calls-for-war-on-assads-alawite-heartland-idUSBRE9690PU20130710.

19 Bissam Walid, "This is how the demonstration was documented inside the prison" (Arabic), *SyriaUntold*, October 20, 2016. syriauntold.com/2016/10/20/-وثقت-هكذا المعتقل-داخل-ةالمظاهر.

20 Sabr Darwish, "Cities in Revolution, Banias: Al-Bayda, the White City," *SyriaUntold*, May 5, 2011. cities.syriauntold.com/citypdf/Baniyas_en.pdf.

21 Katherine, "Syrian soldiers shot for refusing to fire on protesters," *The Guardian*, March (pseudonym), theguardian.com/world/2011/apr/12/syrian-soldiers-shot-protest.

22 Ibid.

23 Joshua Landis, "Western Press Misled — Who Shot the Nine Soldiers in Banyas? Not Syrian Security Forces," Syria Comment (blog), April 13, 2011. joshualandis.com/blog/western-press-misled-who-shot-the-nine-soldiers-in-banyas-not-syrian-security-forces.

24 Ibid.

25 Azmi Bishara, *Syria: A Path to Freedom from Suffering* (Beirut: Arab Center for Research and Policy Studies, 2013), Chapter 5, footnote 234.

26 Ibid., Chapter 5, footnote 233.

27 Sabr Darwish, "Cities in Revolution, Banias: Al-Bayda, the White City," *SyriaUntold*, May 5, 2011. cities.syriauntold.com/citypdf/Baniyas_en.pdf.

28 Muhammad Jamal Barout, *Syria in the Last Decade: The Dialectic of Stagnation and Reform* (Beirut: Arab Center for Research and Policy Studies, 2012), Chapter 6, footnote 338.

29 "Security reinforcement in Baniyas and Homs" (Arabic), Al Jazeera, April 10, 2011. aljazeera.net/news/2011/4/10/تعزيز-أمني-في-بانياس-وحمص.

30 Alix Van Buren, "The dean of dissidents speaks, 'The protest will not cease,'" *la Repubblica*, April 12, 2011. repubblica.it/esteri/2011/04/12/news/dissidente_siriano-14823798.

31 "AFP: Deadly shooting in Banias, Syria: witnesses," *Al-Ahram*, April 10, 2011. english.ahram.org.eg/NewsContent/2/8/9739/World/Region/Deadly-shooting-in-Banias,-Syira-witnesses.aspx.

32 Khaled Yacoub Oweis, "Syrian dies of wounds, democracy protest in 5th week," Reuters, April 16, 2011. reuters.com/article/idINIndia-56377820110416.

33 Sabr Darwish, "Cities in Revolution, Banias: Al-Bayda, the White City," *SyriaUntold*, May 5, 2011. cities.syriauntold.com/citypdf/Baniyas_en.pdf.

34 "Nidal Jannoud Killers," srtruth0, May 30, 2011. youtube.com/watch?v=Ew9moHwJKiE.

35 Liam Stack and Katherine Zoepf, "Syria Presses Crackdown in Two Cities on Coast," *New York Times*, April 12, 2011. nytimes.com/2011/04/13/world/middleeast/13syria.html.

36 Ibid.

37 Bissam Walid, "This is how the demonstration was documented inside the prison" (Arabic), *SyriaUntold*, October 20, 2016. syriauntold.com/2016/10/20/هكذا-وثقت-المظاهرة-داخل-المعتقل.

38 Sharmine Narwani, "Questioning the Syrian 'Casualty List,'" *Monthly Review*, February 28, 2012. mronline.org/2012/02/28/narwani280212-html.

39 Muhammad Jamal Barout, *Syria in the Last Decade: The Dialectic of Stagnation and Reform* (Beirut: Arab Center for Research and Policy Studies, 2012), Chapter 6.

40 Katherine Zoepf, "New Grievances Broaden Syria's Protest Movement," *New York Times*, April 13, 2011. nytimes.com/2011/04/14/world/middleeast/14syria.html.

41 Khaled Yacoub Oweis, "Syrian dies of wounds, democracy protest in 5th week," Reuters, April 16, 2011. reuters.com/article/idINIndia-56377820110416.

42 Muhammad Jamal Barout, *Syria in the Last Decade: The Dialectic of Stagnation and Reform* (Beirut: Arab Center for Research and Policy Studies, 2012), Chapter 6.

43 "AP: Student Protest in Syrian Capital Turns Violent," WBUR News, April 11, 2011. wbur.org/news/2011/04/11/syria-2.

44 Khaled Yacoub Oweis, "Deal struck to try to calm restive Syrian city," Reuters, April 13, 2011. reuters.com/article/uk-syria/deal-struck-to-try-to-calm-restive-syrian-city-idUKTRE73D02C20110414.

45 "Demonstrations in As-Suwayda and the army in Baniyas" (Arabic), Al Jazeera, April 15, 2011. aljazeera.net/news/2011/4/15/مظاهرات-بالسويداء-والجيش-ببانياس.

46 "Snipers kill soldier in Banias — Syrian state news agency," *Gulf News*, April 14, 2011. gulfnews.com/news/mena/syria/snipers-kill-soldier-in-banias-syrian-state-news-agency-1.792133.

47 Muhammad Jamal Barout, *Syria in the Last Decade: The Dialectic of Stagnation and Reform* (Beirut: Arab Center for Research and Policy Studies, 2012), Chapter 6.

48 Katherine Marsh, "Syria protests continue as Bashar al-Assad promises reform," *The Guardian*, April 16, 2011. theguardian.com/world/2011/apr/16/bashar-al-assad-syria.

49 Azmi Bishara, *Syria: A Path to Freedom from Suffering* (Beirut: Arab Center for Research and Policy Studies, 2013), Chapter 5, footnote 233.

50 Alix Van Buren, "The dean of dissidents speaks, 'The protest will not cease,'" *la Repubblica*, April 12, 2011. repubblica.it/esteri/2011/04/12/news/dissidente_siriano-14823798.

51 Joshua Landis, "Western Press Misled — Who Shot the Nine Soldiers in Banyas? Not Syrian Security Forces," Syria Comment (blog), April 13, 2011. joshualandis.com/blog/western-press-misled-who-shot-the-nine-soldiers-in-banyas-not-syrian-security-forces.

52 Liam Stack and Katherine Zoepf, "Syria Presses Crackdown in Two Cities on Coast," *New York Times*, April 12, 2011. nytimes.com/2011/04/13/world/middleeast/13syria.html.

Chapter 7

1 Muhammad Jamal Barout, *Syria in the Last Decade: The Dialectic of Stagnation and Reform* (Beirut: Arab Center for Research and Policy Studies, 2012), Chapter 6.

2 Azmi Bishara, *Syria: A Path to Freedom from Suffering* (Beirut: Arab Center for Research and Policy Studies, 2013), Chapter 2.

3 "Syria slashes gas oil subsidy, tripling price," Reuters, May 3, 2008. mobile.reuters.com/article/amp/idUSL0319586220080503.

4 Muhammad Jamal Barout, *Syria in the Last Decade: The Dialectic of Stagnation and Reform* (Beirut: Arab Center for Research and Policy Studies, 2012), Chapter 6.

5 Ibid.

6 Azmi Bishara, *Syria: A Path to Freedom from Suffering* (Beirut: Arab Center for Research and Policy Studies, 2013), Chapter 2.

7 "AFP: Demonstrations in many cities and more deaths despite Assad's announcement of reforms," France 24, March 25, 2011. france24.com/ar/20110325-daraa-syria-clashes-fire-demonstration-police-dead.

8 "Attacking the Officers Club in Homs, and news of 'the dismissal of its governor,'" Zaman al-Wasl, March 26, 2011. zamanalwsl.net/news/article/18956.

9 Azmi Bishara, *Syria: A Path to Freedom from Suffering* (Beirut: Arab Center for Research and Policy Studies, 2013), Chapter 2, footnote 120.

10 Katie Paul, "Syrian Rebels, Regime Offer Dueling Tales of Karm al-Zeitoun Massacre," *The Daily Beast*, March 13, 2012. thedailybeast.com/syrian-rebels-regime-offer-dueling-tales-of-karm-al-zeitoun-massacre?

11 "Syria: New demonstrations… And Daraa receives its governor with a strike. Evening demonstrations in the outskirts of cities… The release of 7 detainees hints at the possibility of amending the emergency, not canceling it" (Arabic), *Al-Jarida*, April 6, 2011. aljarida.com/ext/articles/print/1461895413360812500.

12 Azmi Bishara, *Syria: A Path to Freedom from Suffering* (Beirut: Arab Center for Research and Policy Studies, 2013), Chapter 2.

13 "Activist: Syrian forces kill eight protesters in Homs city" (Arabic), Reuters, April 18, 2011. reuters.com/article/oegtp-syria-hms-mn3-idARACAE73H0IM20110418.

14 Azmi Bishara, *Syria: A Path to Freedom from Suffering* (Beirut: Arab Center for Research and Policy Studies, 2013), Chapter 5.

15 Muhammad Jamal Barout, *Syria in the Last Decade: The Dialectic of Stagnation and Reform* (Beirut: Arab Center for Research and Policy Studies, 2012), Chapter 6, footnote 369.

16 Sharmine Narwani, "Questioning the Syrian 'Casualty List,'" Mideast Shuffle (blog), February 28, 2012. mideastshuffle.com/2012/02/28/questioning-the-syrian-casualty-list.

17 "Procession of the Brigadier Abdu al-Tallawi and his sons and the martyr Ali Badour," dintist78, April 18, 2011. youtube.com/watch?v=9ccK6laVGC4.

18 "Syria: Three officers were killed by gunmen's fire, and security killed four protesters in Homs" (Arabic), *Al Riyadh*, April 20, 2011. alriyadh.com/625218.

19 "We live as in war: Crackdown on Protesters in the Governorate of Homs, Syria," Human Rights Watch, November 11, 2011. hrw.org/report/2011/11/11/we-live-war/crackdown-protesters-governorate-homs-syria.

20 "News of a massacre in Homs" (Arabic), Al Jazeera, April 19, 2021. aljazeera.net/news/2011/4/19/أنباء-عن-مجزرة-في-حمص.

21 Rania Abouzeid, *No Turning Back: Life, Loss, and Hope in Wartime Syria* (New York: W.W. Norton & Company, 2018), pp. 35–7.

22 Christian Chesnot and Georges Malbrunot, *Les Chemins De Damas: Le dossier noir de la relation franco-syrienne* (Paris: Robert Laffont, 2014), pp. 178, 180, 211.

23 John Rosenthal, "Eyewitness to the Syrian Rebellion: Late Father Frans Denounced a Violent 'Opposition, Instigated and Paid by Foreign Interests,'" Centre for Research on Globalization, *Brics Post*, April 19, 2014. globalresearch.ca/eyewitness-to-the-syrian-rebellion-late-father-frans-denounced-a-violent-opposition-instigated-and-paid-by-foreign-interests/5378784.

24 Anne Barnard, "Long a Survivor in Syria, a Dutch Priest Is Slain," *New York Times*, April 7, 2014. nytimes.com/2014/04/08/world/middleeast/dutch-priest-shot-to-death-in-syrian-city-homs.html.

25 "News of a massacre in Homs" (Arabic), Al Jazeera, April 19, 2021. aljazeera.net/news/2011/4/19/أنباء-عن-مجزرة-في-حمص.

26 Ibid.

27 Sharmine Narwani, "Questioning the Syrian 'Casualty List,'" Mideast Shuffle (blog), February 28, 2012. mideastshuffle.com/2012/02/28/questioning-the-syrian-casualty-list.

28 "Procession of the martyr major Iyad Harfoush," RTV Syria, April 19, 2011. youtube.com/watch?v=37B4eH93-OY.

29 "Syria: Three officers were killed by gunmen's fire, and security killed four protesters in Homs" (Arabic), *Al Riyadh*, April 20, 2011. alriyadh.com/625218.

30 Muhammad Jamal Barout, *Syria in the Last Decade: The Dialectic of Stagnation and Reform* (Beirut: Arab Center for Research and Policy Studies, 2012), Chapter 6, footnote 363.

31 Jonathan Littell, *Syrian Notebooks: Inside the Homs Uprising* (New York: Verso Books, 2015), p. 45.

32 Walid al-Faris, *Homs, the Great Siege: Documenting Seven Hundred Days of Siege* (Beirut: Arab Center for Research and Policy Studies, 2015), Chapter 3, part 1.

33 Azmi Bishara, *Syria: A Path to Freedom from Suffering* (Beirut: Arab Center for Research and Policy Studies, 2013), Chapter 2, footnote 136.

34 Radwan Mortada, "Okab Sakr Smuggles Arms, Ignites Civil War in Syria," *Al-Akhbar*, December 1, 2012. uprootedpalestinian.wordpress.com/2012/12/01/hariri-and-sakr-caught-red-handed.

35 Charles Harb, "Blowback in Lebanon," *The Guardian*, May 23, 2007. theguardian.com/commentisfree/2007/may/24/comment.syria.

36 Justin Salhani, "Forgotten, but not gone: Fatah al-Islam still a factor in Lebanon," *Daily Star*, December 6, 2014. dailystar.com.lb/News/Lebanon-News/2014/Dec-06/280102-forgotten-but-not-gone-fatah-al-islam-still-a-factor-in-lebanon.ashx.

37 "Al Jazeera exodus: Channel losing staff over 'bias,'" RT, March 12, 2012. rt.com/news/al-jazeera-loses-staff-335.

38 Ali Hashem, "Al Jazeera journalist explains resignation over Syria and Bahrain coverage," The Real News Network, March 12, 2012. therealnews.com/stories/ahashempt10319.

39 "Syria Broadens Deadly Crackdown on Protesters," *New York Times*, May 8, 2011. nytimes.com/2011/05/09/world/middleeast/09syria.html.

40 "Syria protests: Rights group warns of 'Deraa massacre,'" BBC News, May 5, 2011. bbc.com/news/world-middle-east-13299793.

41 Bilal Y. Saab, "The Syrian spillover and Salafist radicalization in Lebanon, Combating Terrorism Center," United States Military Academy at West Point, *CTC Sentinel* 6, no. 7 (July 2013). ctc.westpoint.edu/the-syrian-spillover-and-salafist-radicalization-in-lebanon-in-lebanon.

42 Ali Hashem, "Al Jazeera journalist explains resignation over Syria and Bahrain coverage," The Real News Network, March 12, 2012. therealnews.com/stories/ahashempt10319.

43 "20 years after 9/11, millions of victims of 'War on Terror': Reflections with Prof: Asad Abu Khalil," The Grayzone, Moderate Rebels Podcast, September 11, 2021. youtube.com/watch?v=Oca3UvG2HPA.

44 Ulrike Putz, "Jihadists Declare Holy War Against Assad Regime," *Der Spiegel*, March 30, 2012. spiegel.de/international/world/foreign-jihadists-declare-war-on-syria-s-assad-a-824875.html.

45 Ulrike Putz, "Christians flee from radical rebels in Syria," *Der Spiegel*, July 25, 2012. spiegel.de/international/world/christians-flee-from-radical-rebels-in-syria-a-846180.html.

46 Peter Galbraith, "A dilemma for Syria's minorities," *Los Angeles Times*, September 8, 2013. latimes.com/opinion/la-xpm-2013-sep-08-la-oe-galbraith-syria-minorities-20130908-story.html.

47 Fatih Gökhan Diler, "'Alevis to the grave, Christians to Beirut' is still a common slogan," *Agos*, October 17, 2016. agos.com.tr/en/article/16756/alevis-to-the-grave-christians-to-beirut-is-still-a-common-slogan.

48 Ulrike Putz, "Christians flee from radical rebels in Syria," *Der Spiegel*, July 25, 2012. spiegel.de/international/world/christians-flee-from-radical-rebels-in-syria-a-846180.html.

49 "AFP: Lebanese Islamist killed in Syria," Al-Arabiya, April 26, 2012. english.alarabiya.net/articles/2012%2F04%2F26%2F210447.

50 Alexandra Sandels and Patrick J. McConnell, "Syria Christian refugees in Lebanon fear Islamist rebels," *Los Angeles Times*, August 22, 2012. latimes.com/world/la-xpm-2012-aug-22-la-fg-syria-christians-20120822-story.html.

51 Ethan Bronner, "Israeli Troops Fire as Marchers Breach Borders," *New York Times*, May 15, 2011. nytimes.com/2011/05/16/world/middleeast/16mideast.html.

52 Isabel Kershner, "Israeli Soldiers Shoot at Protestors on the Syrian Border," *New York Times*, June 5, 2011. nytimes.com/2011/06/06/world/middleeast/06mideast.html.

53 William Van Wagenen, "A Brief History of the Destruction of Yarmouk," Libertarian Institute, April 3, 2019. libertarianinstitute.org/articles/a-brief-history-of-the-destruction-of-yarmouk.

54 Ibid.

55 Roula Hajjar, "Violence at Palestinian camp funerals in Syria leaves 20 dead," *Los Angeles Times*, June 8, 2011. latimes.com/world/la-xpm-2011-jun-08-la-fg-syria-palestinians-20110608-story.html.

56 Khaled Yacoub Oweis, "Pro-Syrian Palestinian group kills 11 refugees: sources," Reuters, June 7, 2011. reuters.com/article/us-syria-palestinians-killings/pro-syrian-palestinian-group-kills-11-refugees-sources-idUSTRE7564MN20110607.

57 Isabel Kershner, "Fighters Shoot Protesters at a Palestinian Camp in Syria," *New York Times*, June 7, 2011. nytimes.com/2011/06/08/world/middleeast/08damascus.html?_r=1&ref=global-home.

58 Nidal Bitari, "Yarmouk Refugee Camp and the Syrian Uprising: A View from Within," *Journal of Palestine Studies* 43, no. 1 (Autumn 2013): pp. 61–78. jstor.org/stable/10.1525/jps.2013.43.1.61.

59 "Yarmouk, the full truth," by Ibrahim al-Ali, Action Group for Palestinians, June 2015. actionpal.org.uk/en/reports/special/yarmouk_truth_en.pdf.

60 "Palestinian Refugees of Syria in Light of the Syrian Revolution," by Tarek Homoud, Palestinian Return Centre, June 2015. prc.org.uk/upload/library/files/PRSinLightofSyrianRev.pdf.

61 Sharmine, Narwani, "Stealing Palestine: Who dragged Palestinians into Syria's conflict?" RT, November 10, 2014. rt.com/op-ed/203907-palestine-syria-shelling-clashes-conflict.

62 Nasser Sharara, "Have defections reached the 'bedroom' of Jibril?" (Arabic), *Al-Akhbar*, December 24, 2012. al-akhbar.com/Arab/80742.

63 Asad Abu al-Khalil, "Flash: what is happening in Yarmuk Camp near Damascus?" Angry Arab Blogspot, June 6, 2011. angryarab.blogspot.com/2011/06/flash-what-is-happening-in-yarmuk-camp.html.

Chapter 8

1 Hala Jaber, "Syria caught in crossfire of extremists," *Sunday Times*, June 26, 2011. thetimes.co.uk/article/syria-caught-in-crossfire-of-extremists-pvb9lslv3wz.

2 Nir Rosen, "Q&A: Nir Rosen on Syria's protest movement," Al Jazeera, February 16, 2012. aljazeera.com/indepth/features/2012/02/20122157654659323.html.

3 "Q&A: Nir Rosen on Syria's armed opposition," Al Jazeera, February 13, 2012. aljazeera.com/features/2012/2/13/qa-nir-rosen-on-syrias-armed-opposition.

4 "Casualty recording in Syria: Interview with Wissam Tarif, Insan Association," Every Casualty Counts, September 15, 2011. everycasualty.org/casualty-recording-in-syria-interview-with-wissam-tarif-insan-association.

5 Hala Jaber, "Syria caught in crossfire of extremists," *Sunday Times*, June 26, 2011. thetimes.co.uk/article/syria-caught-in-crossfire-of-extremists-pvb9lslv3wz.

6 Muhammad Jamal Barout, *Syria in the Last Decade: The Dialectic of Stagnation and Reform* (Beirut: Arab Center for Research and Policy Studies, 2012), Chapter 7, footnotes 459, 460, and 463.

7 Rania Abouzeid, *No Turning Back: Life, Loss, and Hope in Wartime Syria* (New York: W.W. Norton & Company, 2018), pp. 55–61.

8 Joshua Landis, "What Happened at Jisr al-Shagour," Syria Comment (blog), June 13, 2011. joshualandis.com/blog/what-happened-at-jisr-al-shagour.

9 Rania Abouzeid, "Syria's Wounded Refugees: Tales of Massacre and Honorable Soldiers," *Time*, June 12, 2011. content.time.com/time/world/article/0,8599,2077207,00.html.

10 Rania Abouzeid, *No Turning Back: Life, Loss, and Hope in Wartime Syria* (New York: W.W. Norton & Company, 2018), pp. 55–61.

[11] Rania Abouzeid, "In Blow to Opposition, a Dissident Syrian Army Officer is Captured," *Time*, September 15, 2011.
content.time.com/time/world/article/0,8599,2093441,00.html.

[12] "The defection of officers in the Syrian army, translated into English," Al Jazeera, July 5, 2011. youtube.com/watch?v=4elucIT1Kog.

[13] "AP: Syrian defector regime insider from Sunni family," Fox News, July 6, 2012.
foxnews.com/world/syrian-defector-_-regime-insider-from-sunni-family.

[14] Aron Lund, "The Free Syrian Army Doesn't Exist," Syria Comment (blog), March 16, 2013. joshualandis.com/blog/the-free-syrian-army-doesnt-exist.

[15] "Guide to the Syrian rebels," BBC News, December 13, 2013. bbc.com/news/world-middle-east-24403003.

[16] Joseph Holliday, "The Struggle for Syria in 2011," Institute for the Study of War, December 2011. understandingwar.org/report/struggle-syria-2011.

[17] Azmi Bishara, *Syria: A Path to Freedom from Suffering* (Beirut: Arab Center for Research and Policy Studies, 2013), Chapter 5.

[18] Mohammad Abu Rumman, "Islamists, Religion, and the Revolution in Syria," Friedrich Ebert Stiftung, 2013 library.fes.de/pdf-files/bueros/amman/10236.pdf.

[19] Bisam Nasir, "Sarouri Salafism: What is the extent of its presence in the Syrian revolution?" Arabi21, October 8, 2015. arabi21.com/story/864291.

[20] Ibid.

[21] Haytham Mouzahem, "Syrian opposition condemns jihadists targeting Alawite," Al-Monitor, August 14, 2013. al-monitor.com/pulse/originals/2013/08/syria-opposition-alawite-massacres-sectarianism.html.

[22] Hassan Hassan, "Muhammad Surur and the normalisation of extremism," *The National*, November 13, 2016. thenationalnews.com/opinion/muhammad-surur-and-the-normalisation-of-extremism-1.214695.

[23] Mohammad Abu Rumman, "Islamists, Religion, and the Revolution in Syria," Friedrich Ebert Stiftung, 2013 library.fes.de/pdf-files/bueros/amman/10236.pdf.

[24] C.J. Chivers, "Behind the Black Flag: The Recruitment of an ISIS Killer," *New York Times*, December 20, 2015. nytimes.com/2015/12/21/world/middleeast/isis-recruitment-killer-hassan-aboud.html.

[25] Ibid.

[26] Yasin Raed al-Halabi, "The leader of the Daoud Brigade after his defection from the Islamic Front leads the battles of ISIS in the countryside of Aleppo" (Arabic), *Al-Quds Al-Arabi*, August 15, 2014. alquds.co.uk/%EF%BB%BFالج-عن-انشقاقه-بعد-داوءلوا-قائد.

[27] "The commander of the Sham Hawks Brigade, Ahmed Issa al-Sheikh: I was not in Sednaya — And our battle with the 'state' is a battle of deterrence and we will not accept its guardianship," Zaman al-Wasl, January 27, 2014.
zamanalwsl.net/news/article/45949.

[28] Sarah Birke and Katie Paul, "Inside Syria's Fracturing Rebellion," *The New Republic*, August 29, 2012. newrepublic.com/article/106748/hed.

[29] Ibid.

[30] Asher Berman, "Rebel groups in Jabal al-Zawiya," Institute for the Study of War, July 26, 2012.
understandingwar.org/sites/default/files/Backgrounder_RebelGroupsJebelAlZawiyah_31July.pdf.

[31] Wael Essam, "Is the Islamic State in Syria an extension of the Syrian revolution's factions?" (Arabic), *Al-Quds Al-Arabi*, May 8, 2015. alquds.co.uk/%EF%BB%BF-هل تنظيم-الدولة-الإسلامية-في-سوري.

32 Aron Lund, "Syrian Jihadism," *UI Brief* No. 13, Swedish Institute of International Affairs, September 14, 2012. sultan-alamer.com/wp-content/uploads/77409.pdf.

33 Yasin Raed al-Halabi, "The leader of the Daoud Brigade after his defection from the Islamic Front leads the battles of ISIS in the countryside of Aleppo" (Arabic), *Al-Quds Al-Arabi*, August 15, 2014. alquds.co.uk/%EF%BB%BFالجـ-عن-انشقاقه-بعد-داود-لواء-قائد.

34 C.J. Chivers and Karam Shoumali, "Hassan Aboud, an ISIS Commander, Dies from Battlefield Wounds," *New York Times*, March 17, 2016. nytimes.com/2016/03/18/world/middleeast/hassan-aboud-an-isis-commander-dies-from-battlefield-wounds.html.

35 "Syria protests: Rights group warns of 'Deraa massacre,'" BBC News, May 5, 2011. bbc.com/news/world-middle-east-13299793.

36 Report of the independent international commission of inquiry on the Syrian Arab Republic United Nations Human Rights Council, November 23, 2011. daccess-ods.un.org/access.nsf/Get?Open&DS=A/HRC/S-17/2/Add.1&Lang=E.

37 Sharmine Narwani, "Syria: The hidden massacre," RT, May 7, 2014. rt.com/op-ed/157412-syria-hidden-massacre-2011.

38 Sharmine Narwani, "Questioning the Syrian 'Casualty List,'" Mideast Shuffle (blog), February 28, 2012. mideastshuffle.com/2012/02/28/questioning-the-syrian-casualty-list.

39 Michael Doran and Salman Sheikh, "Getting Serious in Syria," Brookings Institution, July 29, 2011.

40 Jared Cohen, "Tech for Change," Think with Google (blog), October 2012. thinkwithgoogle.com/future-of-marketing/digital-transformation/tech-for-change.

41 Fabrice Balanche, "Syria: From Non-Religious and Democratic Revolution to ISIS," *Hérodote* (January 2016). hoover.org/sites/default/files/fabrice_balanche_herodote.pdf.

42 Michael Pizzi and Nuha Shabaan, "Sunni vs. Sunni: Pro-revolution Sunnis lament Assad backers," Syria Direct, June 21, 2013. syriadirect.org/sunni-vs-sunni-pro-revolution-sunnis-lament-assad-backers.

43 Camille Otrakji, "Ten new year resolution ideas for a healthier American role in Syria and the Middle East in 2015 — Part III of a discussion with Ambassador Robert Ford," The Syria Page, December 31, 2014. creativesyria.com/syriapage/?p=580.

44 Michael Pizzi and Nuha Shabaan, "Sunni vs. Sunni: Pro-revolution Sunnis lament Assad backers," Syria Direct, June 21, 2013. syriadirect.org/sunni-vs-sunni-pro-revolution-sunnis-lament-assad-backers.

45 "Q&A: Nir Rosen on Syria's armed opposition," Al Jazeera, February 13, 2012. aljazeera.com/features/2012/2/13/qa-nir-rosen-on-syrias-armed-opposition.

46 Azmi Bishara, *Syria: A Path to Freedom from Suffering* (Beirut: Arab Center for Research and Policy Studies, 2013), Chapter 5.

47 Rania Abouzeid, *No Turning Back: Life, Loss, and Hope in Wartime Syria* (New York: W.W. Norton & Company, 2018), p. 74.

48 Walid al-Faris, *Homs, the Great Siege: Documenting Seven Hundred Days of Siege* (Beirut: Arab Center for Research and Policy Studies, 2015), Chapter 1, part 2.

49 Ammar Abd al-Hamid, "The Shredded Tapestry: The State of Syria Today," Foundation for Defense of Democracies, September 25, 2012. fdd.org/analysis/2012/09/25/the-shredded-tapestry-the-state-of-syria-today.

50 "AP: Syrian defector regime insider from Sunni family," Fox News, July 6, 2012. foxnews.com/world/syrian-defector-_-regime-insider-from-sunni-family.

51 Ammar Abd al-Hamid, "The Shredded Tapestry: The State of Syria Today," Foundation for Defense of Democracies, September 25, 2012. fdd.org/analysis/2012/09/25/the-shredded-tapestry-the-state-of-syria-today.

52 Rania Abouzeid, *No Turning Back: Life, Loss, and Hope in Wartime Syria* (New York: W.W. Norton & Company, 2018), p. 100.

53 Walid al-Faris, *Homs, the Great Siege: Documenting Seven Hundred Days of Siege* (Beirut: Arab Center for Research and Policy Studies, 2015), Chapter 6, part 4.

54 David Enders, "Rare inside view of Syria's rebels finds a force vowing to fight on," McClatchyDC, April 23, 2012. mcclatchydc.com/news/nation-world/world/article24728275.html.

55 James Bay, "Up close with the Free Syrian Army," Al Jazeera, May 9, 2012. aljazeera.com/features/2012/5/9/up-close-with-the-free-syrian-army.

56 Wael Essam, "Is the Islamic State in Syria an extension of the Syrian revolution's factions?" (Arabic), *Al-Quds Al-Arabi*, May 8, 2015. alquds.co.uk/%EF%BB%BF-هل-تنظيم-الدولة-الإسلامية-في-سوري.

57 Malek al-Abdeh, "Rebels, Inc.," *Foreign Policy*, November 21, 2013. foreignpolicy.com/2013/11/21/rebels-inc.

58 Nir Rosen, "Armed defenders of Syria's revolution," Al Jazeera, September 27, 2011. aljazeera.com/features/2011/09/27/armed-defenders-of-syrias-revolution.

59 "Syria: Summary Killings and Other Abuses by Armed Opposition Groups," Amnesty International, March 14, 2013. amnesty.org/en/documents/MDE24/008/2013/en.

60 Azmi Bishara, *Syria: A Path to Freedom from Suffering* (Beirut: Arab Center for Research and Policy Studies, 2013), Chapter 2, footnote 136.

61 "Assassination of a nuclear engineer by unknown persons in Homs" (Arabic), Al Bawaba, September 28, 2011. albawaba.com/ar/-أخبار/اغتيال-مهندس-نووي-بيد-مجهولين-في-حمص-394248.

62 Azmi Bishara, *Syria: A Path to Freedom from Suffering* (Beirut: Arab Center for Research and Policy Studies, 2013), Chapter 11.

63 Ibid., Chapter 2, part 1.

64 "The martyr Amran Daweek after the security forces were done with him," Ugarit News, May 24, 2011. youtube.com/watch?v=caAd9dgfAP4.

65 "Syria: 'Dozens killed' as thousands protest in Hama," BBC News, June 4, 2011. bbc.com/news/world-middle-east-13642917.

66 "Who is Major General Muhammad Mufleh, and where is he now? Find out the reasons behind his disappearance" (Arabic), *Ad-Diyar*, February 13, 2018. alkawthartv.ir/news/122571.

67 Ben Taub, "The Assad Files: Capturing the top-secret documents that tie the Syrian regime to mass torture and killings," *The New Yorker*, April 18, 2016. newyorker.com/magazine/2016/04/18/bashar-al-assads-war-crimes-exposed.

68 Dan Murphy, "Syrians stage mass protest in Hama today," *Christian Science Monitor*, July 1. 2011. csmonitor.com/World/Backchannels/2011/0701/Syrians-stage-mass-protest-in-Hama-today-VIDEO.

69 "U.S. ambassador in Hama to support Syria protesters," Reuters, July 7, 2011. reuters.com/article/us-syria-usa/u-s-ambassador-in-hama-to-support-syria-protesters-idUSTRE7665OJ20110707.

70 Camille Otrakji, "Ten new year resolution ideas for a healthier American role in Syria and the Middle East in 2015 — Part III of a discussion with Ambassador Robert Ford," The Syria Page, December 31, 2014. creativesyria.com/syriapage/?p=580.

71 Ibid.

[72] Nir Rosen, "Assad's Alawites: The guardians of the throne," Al Jazeera, October 10, 2011. aljazeera.com/indepth/features/2011/10/20111010122434671982.html.

[73] Anthony Shadid, "In scarred Syria city, a vision of a life free from Dictators," *New York Times*, July 19, 2011. nytimes.com/2011/07/20/world/middleeast/20hama.html?referringSource=articleShare.

[74] James Harkin, "The incredible story behind the Syrian protest singer everyone thought was dead," *GQ Magazine*, December 7, 2016. gq-magazine.co.uk/article/syria-civil-war.

[75] "The martyr Ibrahim Qashoush, who was slaughtered at the hands of the security forces and the shabiha, and his body was thrown into the Orontes at Bab al-Nahr" (Arabic), Hama al-Akhbariya, July 5, 2011. youtube.com/watch?v=uBzk8WZZxzg.

[76] James Harkin, "The incredible story behind the Syrian protest singer everyone thought was dead," *GQ Magazine*, December 7, 2016. gq-magazine.co.uk/article/syria-civil-war.

[77] "Amnesty International reveals shocking new evidence of extreme brutality in Syria — Mutilated body of abducted 18-year-old woman killed in horrific circumstances," Amnesty International, September 23, 2011. amnestyusa.org/press-releases/amnesty-international-reveals-shocking-new-evidence-of-extreme-brutality-in-syria-mutilated-body-of-abducted-18-year-old-woman-killed-in-horrific-circumstances.

[78] "AP: Syria: Woman Held by Security Is Beheaded, Rights Group Says," *New York Times*, September 23, 2011. nytimes.com/2011/09/24/world/middleeast/syria-woman-held-by-security-is-beheaded-rights-group-says.html.

[79] "Rights groups admit Syria 'identity mistake,'" Al Jazeera, October 6, 2011. aljazeera.com/news/2011/10/6/rights-groups-admit-syria-identity-mistake.

[80] Nada Bakri, "Syrian Woman Says Reports of Her Death Were Mistaken," *New York Times*, October 5, 2011. nytimes.com/2011/10/06/world/middleeast/woman-believed-killed-by-syrian-forces-turns-up-on-tv.html.

[81] Hugh MacLeod, "Zeinab al-Hosni: A Syrian murder mystery," *GlobalPost*, October 25, 2011. theworld.org/stories/2011-10-25/zeinab-al-hosni-syrian-murder-mystery.

[82] Hala Jaber, "Syria caught in crossfire of extremists," *Sunday Times*, June 26, 2011. thetimes.co.uk/article/syria-caught-in-crossfire-of-extremists-pvb9lslv3wz.

[83] Nir Rosen, "Syria: The revolution will be weaponized," Al Jazeera, September 23, 2011. aljazeera.com/indepth/features/2011/09/2011923115735281764.html.

[84] "First foreign troops in Syria back Homs rebels. Damascus and Moscow at odds," DEBKAfile, February 8, 2012. debka.com/first-foreign-troops-in-syria-back-homs-rebels-damascus-and-moscow-at-odds.

[85] Raven Clabough, "Possible U.S. Involvement in Covert Warfare in Syria," *The New American*, March 7, 2012. thenewamerican.com/possible-us-involvement-in-covert-warfare-in-syria.

[86] Jonathan Littell, *Syrian Notebooks: Inside the Homs Uprising* (New York: Verso Books, 2015), p. 137.

[87] Nir Rosen, "The Battle for Homs," Al Jazeera, February 9, 2012. aljazeera.com/news/middleeast/2012/02/20122101097421319.html.

[88] Nick Thompson, "Homs: Bloody winter in Syria's revolution capital," CNN, February 7, 2012. cnn.com/2011/12/16/world/meast/syria-homs-profile/index.html.

[89] Katie Paul, "A Syrian Rebel's Firsthand Report on the Fighting and Bombing in Homs," *The Daily Beast*, February 28, 2012. thedailybeast.com/a-syrian-rebels-firsthand-report-on-the-fighting-and-bombing-in-homs?ref=scroll.

[90] "Syria: Summary Killings and Other Abuses by Armed Opposition Groups," Amnesty International, March 14, 2013. amnesty.org/en/documents/MDE24/008/2013/en.

[91] Sharmine Narwani, "Homs Opposition: Al Farouq Battalion is Killing Us," Mideast Shuffle (blog), May 14, 2012. mideastshuffle.com/2012/05/13/homs-opposition-al-farouq-battalion-is-killing-us.

[92] Bernard, "The State Department Lies With Its Satellite Pictures Of Syria - No Artillery 'Deployed,'" Moon of Alabama (blog), February 11, 2012. moonofalabama.org/2012/02/lying-with-pictures.html.

[93] Sharmine Narwani, "High tech trickery in Homs," Mideast Shuffle (blog), February 14, 2012. mideastshuffle.com/2012/02/14/high-tech-trickery-in-homs.

[94] "Reuters: France demands inquiry into journalist's death in Homs," France 24, January 12, 2012. france24.com/en/20120112-france-demands-probe-killing-french-journalist-homs.

[95] Philippe Gélie, "Syria: France suspects 'manipulation,'" *Le Figaro*, January 12, 2012. lefigaro.fr/international/2012/01/12/01003-20120112ARTFIG00687-syrie-la-france-soupconne-une-manipulation.php.

[96] Georges Malbrunot, "Jacquier aurait été victime d'une bavure des insurgés," *Le Figaro*, January 20, 2012. lefigaro.fr/international/2012/01/20/01003-20120120ARTFIG00667-jacquier-aurait-ete-victime-d-une-bavure-des-insurges.php.

[97] Jonathan Littell, "In Homs we are all wading in blood," *The Guardian*, February 21, 2012. theguardian.com/world/2012/feb/21/homs-snipers-target-anyone.

[98] Joan Nassivera, "Government Is Said to Kill 200 in Attack in Syrian City," *New York Times*, February 3, 2012. nytimes.com/2012/02/04/world/middleeast/syrian-government-said-to-kill-200-in-attack-in-homs.html.

[99] William Van Wagenen, "Is there a Western plot to overthrow Assad?" Libertarian Institute, June 21, 2017. libertarianinstitute.org/articles/western-plot-overthrow-assad.

[100] "Syria Assad: Army massacres 'scores' in city of Homs," BBC News, February 4, 2012. bbc.com/news/world-middle-east-16883911.

[101] Flavius Mihaies, "Christians Face Total Purge From Syria," *Newsweek*, January 10, 2016. newsweek.com/christians-face-purge-syria-413463.

Chapter 9

[1] "Syrian Army Drives Rebels From Embattled City," National Public Radio, March 1, 2012. npr.org/2012/03/01/147742477/syrian-army-drives-out-rebels-in-embattled-city.

[2] Jonathan Littell, *Syrian Notebooks: Inside the Homs Uprising* (New York: Verso Books, 2015), p. 91.

[3] Ibid., p. 131.

[4] Wael Essam, "Is the Islamic State in Syria an extension of the Syrian revolution's factions?" (Arabic), *Al-Quds Al-Arabi*, May 8, 2015. alquds.co.uk/%EF%BB%BF-هل تنظيم-الدولة-الإسلامية-في-سوري.

[5] Paul Conroy, *Under the Wire: Marie Colvin's Final Assignment* (Philadelphia: Weinstein Books, 2013), Chapter 6.

[6] "Transcript: Marie Colvin's final CNN interview," CNN, February 22, 2012. cnn.com/2012/02/26/world/syria-marie-colvin/index.html.

[7] Paul Conroy, *Under the Wire: Marie Colvin's Final Assignment* (Philadelphia: Weinstein Books, 2013), Chapter 9.

[8] "Red Cross pushes to rescue wounded in Homs," Al Jazeera, February 25, 2012. aljazeera.com/news/2012/2/25/red-cross-pushes-to-rescue-wounded-in-homs.

[9] "What Is Edith Bouvier's Role in Sarkozy's 'Humanitarian Corridors' Plans?" Moon of Alabama (blog), February 26, 2012. moonofalabama.org/2012/02/what-is-edith-bouviers-role-in-sarkozys-humanitarian-corridors-plans.html.

10 Christian Chesnot and Georges Malbrunot, *Les Chemins De Damas: Le dossier noir de la relation franco-syrienne* (Paris: Robert Laffont, 2014), pp. 204–7.

11 "How Avaaz Is Sponsoring Fake War Propaganda from Syria," Moon of Alabama (blog), March 3, 2012. moonofalabama.org/2012/03/avaaz-sponsoring-fake-reporting-from-syria.html.

12 "The Veto: Exposing CNN, Al Jazeera, Channel 4, western media propaganda war in Syria," by Rafiq Lutf, Abdul Mun'aim Arnous and Vanessa Beeley, none, none, March 21, 2019. youtube.com/watch?v=5VMTfkP0jSQ.

13 Patrick Cockburn, "Whose hands are behind those dramatic YouTube pictures?" *The Independent*, January 15, 2012. independent.co.uk/voices/commentators/patrick-cockburn-whose-hands-are-behind-those-dramatic-youtube-pictures-6289808.html.

14 Sharmine Narwani, "Stratfor Challenges Narratives on Syria," Mideast Shuffle (blog), December 20, 2011. factsandarts.com/current-affairs/stratfor-challenges-narratives-syria.

15 Patrick Seale, "In Syria, this is no plan for peace," *The Guardian*, May 27, 2012. theguardian.com/commentisfree/2012/may/27/syria-no-plans-peace.

16 Ian Cobain, Alice Ross, Rob Evans, and Mona Mahmood, "How Britain funds the 'propaganda war' against Isis in Syria," *The Guardian*, May 3, 2016. theguardian.com/world/2016/may/03/how-britain-funds-the-propaganda-war-against-isis-in-syria.

17 "Syrian activists decry 'massacre' in Houla," Al Jazeera, May 26, 2012. youtube.com/watch?v=Am2byWvHTLI.

18 Stephanie Nebehay, "Most Houla victims killed in summary executions: U.N.," Reuters, May 29, 2012. reuters.com/article/us-syria-un-idUSBRE84S10020120529.

19 "Response to massacre in Syria urged," *Daily Star*, May 25, 2012. dailystar.co.uk/news/response-massacre-syria-urged-18540034?int_source=amp_continue_reading&int_medium=amp&int_campaign=continue_reading_button.

20 "AP: Dozens of children killed in new Syria attack," *The Times*, May 26, 2012. timesonline.com/story/news/nation-world/2012/05/26/dozens-children-killed-in-new/18432680007.

21 "Syria massacre in Houla condemned as outrage grows," BBC News, May 27, 2012. bbc.com/news/world-middle-east-18224559.

22 Hannah Furness, "BBC News uses 'Iraq photo to illustrate Syrian massacre,'" *The Telegraph*, May 27, 2012. telegraph.co.uk/culture/tvandradio/bbc/9293620/BBC-News-uses-Iraq-photo-to-illustrate-Syrian-massacre.html.

23 "Syria 'massacre' sparks international outrage," France 24, May 26, 2012. france24.com/en/20120526-syria-un-monitors-arrive-scene-massacre-houla-homs-province-syrian-observatory-human-rights.

24 John Rosenthal, "General Mood: 'Two Versions' of the Houla Massacre," PJ Media, June 26, 2012. pjmedia.com/blog/john-rosenthal/2012/06/26/general-mood-two-versions-of-the-houla-massacre-n9828.

25 "Q&A General Mood to the Press PT2," UNSMIS, June 15, 2012. youtube.com/watch?v=UOTJdHTloLg.

26 John Rosenthal, "General Mood: 'Two Versions' of the Houla Massacre," PJ Media, June 26, 2012. pjmedia.com/blog/john-rosenthal/2012/06/26/general-mood-two-versions-of-the-houla-massacre-n9828.

[27] Rainer Hermann, "Neue Erkenntnisse zu Getoeteten Von Hula: Abermals Massaker in Syrien," *Frankfurter Allgemeine Zeitung*, June 7, 2012. faz.net/aktuell/politik/neue-erkenntnisse-zu-getoeteten-von-hula-abermals-massaker-in-syrien-11776496.html.

[28] Christoph Reuter and Abd al-Kadher Adhun, "Searching for the Truth Behind the Houla Massacre," *Der Spiegel*, July 23, 2012. spiegel.de/international/world/a-look-back-at-the-houla-massacre-in-syria-a-845854.html.

[29] John Rosenthal, "The Houla Massacre Redux," *National Review*, June 15, 2012. nationalreview.com/corner/houla-massacre-redux-john-rosenthal.

[30] Patrick Cockburn, "Syria After the Massacre," *CounterPunch*, May 28, 2012. counterpunch.org/2012/05/28/syria-after-the-massacre.

[31] Alex Thomson, "Spooks view on Syria: what WikiLeaks revealed," Channel 4 News, August 28, 2013. channel4.com/news/by/alex-thomson/blogs/syria-spooks-wikileaks-military.

[32] Alan J. Kuperman, "Obama's Libya Debacle: How a Well-Meaning Intervention Ended in Failure," *Foreign Affairs*, March/April 2015. foreignaffairs.com/articles/libya/2019-02-18/obamas-libya-debacle.

Chapter 10

[1] Qassim Abdul-Zahra and Zeina Karam, "AP: Elusive Al-Qaeda leader in Syria stays in shadows," *The Times of Israel*, November 4, 2013. timesofisrael.com/elusive-al-qaeda-leader-in-syria-stays-in-shadows.

[2] "Abu Muhammad al-Jolani, Leader of the Fateh al-Sham Front" (Arabic), Al Jazeera, July 26, 2015. aljazeera.net/encyclopedia/2015/7/26/أبو-محمد-الجولاني.

[3] Al Jazeera, "Today's meeting — Abu Muhammad al-Jolani: Al-Nusra and the future of Syria" (Arabic), December 13, 2013. youtube.com/watch?v=DIr1HoHJlQA.

[4] Al Jazeera, "Without Borders — Abu Muhammad al-Julani, Emir of the Nusra Front" (Arabic), May 27, 2015. youtube.com/watch?v=-hwQT43vFZA.

[5] William Van Wagenen, "Did Assad Deliberately Release Islamist Prisoners to Militarize and Radicalize the Syrian Uprising?" Libertarian Institute, February 22, 2018. libertarianinstitute.org/articles/assad-deliberately-release-islamist-prisoners-militarize-radicalize-syrian-uprising.

[6] Aaron Zelin, "Tunisian foreign fighters in Iraq and Syria," Washington Institute for Near East Policy, 2018 washingtoninstitute.org/media/1250.

[7] Abdullah Suleiman Ali, "As-Safir: Saudi jihadists flow into Syria," Al-Monitor, December 5, 2013. al-monitor.com/pulse/security/2013/12/saudi-fighters-syria-official-silence.html.

[8] Ibid.

[9] "Syria says twin suicide bombings in Damascus kill 44," BBC News, December 23, 2011. bbc.com/news/world-middle-east-16313879.

[10] Joshua Landis, "Suicide Bombing Changes Nature of the Syrian Revolution," Syria Comment (blog), December 23, 2011. joshualandis.com/blog/suicide-bombing-changes-nature-of-the-syrian-revolution.

[11] "Syria unrest: Damascus blast and clashes kill many," BBC News, January 7, 2012. bbc.com/news/world-middle-east-16437865.

[12] "Abu Muhammad al-Jolani, Leader of the Fateh al-Sham Front" (Arabic), Al Jazeera, July 26, 2015. aljazeera.net/encyclopedia/2015/7/26/أبو-محمد-الجولاني.

[13] "AFP: Unknown Islamist group claims suicide attacks in Syria," Al-Arabiya, February 29, 2012. english.alarabiya.net/articles/2012/02/29/197781.

14 "AFP: Jihadists, weapons moving from Iraq to Syria: Baghdad," *Al-Ahram*, February 11, 2012. english.ahram.org.eg/News/34267.aspx.

15 Ghaith Abdul-Ahad, "Al-Qaida turns tide for rebels in battle for eastern Syria," *The Guardian*, July 30, 2012. theguardian.com/world/2012/jul/30/al-qaida-rebels-battle-syria.

16 Ibid.

17 Theo Padnos, *Blindfold: A Memoir of Capture, Torture, and Enlightenment* (New York: Scribner, 2021), pp. 276–9.

18 Guardian, "Owen Jones meets Theo Padnos — 'Western hawks are responsible for my Syria torture,'" by Owen Jones, January 13, 2017. youtube.com/watch?v=iE1dAXb4P8Y.

19 Ghaith Abdul-Ahad, "Al-Qaida turns tide for rebels in battle for eastern Syria," *The Guardian*, July 30, 2012. theguardian.com/world/2012/jul/30/al-qaida-rebels-battle-syria.

20 Ibid.

21 Seymour Hersh, *The Killing of Osama bin Laden* (New York: Verso Books, 2017), pp. 65–6.

22 "Libyan fighters join 'free Syrian army' forces," Al Bawaba, November 29, 2011. albawaba.com/news/libyan-fighters-join-free-syrian-army-forces-403268.

23 Tam Hussein, "Mahde al-Harati: A Libyan force multiplier," Syria Comment (blog), September 26, 2017. joshualandis.com/blog/mahdi-al-harati-a-libyan-force-multiplier.

24 Hadeel al-Shalchi and Maggie Michael, "AP: Libyan hero plays down Islamic militant past," *Houston Chronicle*, September 2, 2011. houstonchronicle.com/news/nation-world/article/Libyan-hero-downplays-Islamic-militant-past-2153714.php.

25 Jamie Merrill, "UK admits contact with Libyan group linked to Manchester bomber," Middle East Eye, April 6, 2018. middleeasteye.net/fr/news/revealed-uk-government-communications-groups-linked-manchester-bomber-53000913.

26 Tam Hussein, "Mahde al-Harati: A Libyan force multiplier," Syria Comment (blog), September 26, 2017. joshualandis.com/blog/mahdi-al-harati-a-libyan-force-multiplier.

27 Mary Fitzgerald, "The Syrian Rebels Libyan Weapon," *Foreign Policy*, August 9, 2012. foreignpolicy.com/2012/08/09/the-syrian-rebels-libyan-weapon.

28 "Interview: Libyan — Syrian revolutionary Mahdi al-Harati," *Al-Sharq al-Awsat*, October 5, 2012. eng-archive.aawsat.com/theaawsat/features/interview-libyan-syrian-revolutionary-mahdi-al-harati.

29 Tam Hussein, "Mahde al-Harati: A Libyan force multiplier," Syria Comment (blog), September 26, 2017. joshualandis.com/blog/mahdi-al-harati-a-libyan-force-multiplier.

30 Oliver Duggan, "First British fighter killed in Syria named as Ibrahim al-Mazwagi," *The Independent*, March 3, 2013. independent.co.uk/news/world/middle-east/first-british-fighter-killed-in-syria-named-as-ibrahim-almazwagi-8518517.html.

31 Paul Christian, "University of Hertfordshire in Hatfield graduate was in same militant group as 'Jihadi John,'" *Welwyn Hatfield Times*, March 2, 2015. whtimes.co.uk/news/university-of-hertfordshire-in-hatfield-graduate-was-in-same-militant-5518040.

32 Jenny Stanton, "Jihadi John's Migrant Mujahideen," *Daily Mail*, February 28, 2015. dailymail.co.uk/news/article-2972260/Jihadi-John-s-Migrant-Mujahadeen-boasted-slaughter-filmed-training-shopping-cereal-fanatical-band-brothers-infamous-executioner-went-Syria-fight-ISIS-three-dead.html.

[33] Jeremy Bender, "One of ISIS's top commanders was a 'star pupil' of US-special forces training in the country of Georgia," *Business Insider*, September 17, 2015. businessinsider.in/One-of-ISIS-top-commanders-was-a-star-pupil-of-US-special-forces-training-in-the-country-of-Georgia/articleshow/49005048.cms.

[34] Paul Christian, "University of Hertfordshire in Hatfield graduate was in same militant group as 'Jihadi John,'" *Welwyn Hatfield Times*, March 2, 2015. whtimes.co.uk/news/university-of-hertfordshire-in-hatfield-graduate-was-in-same-militant-5518040.

[35] Naina Bajekal, "ISIS mass beheading video took 6 hours to film and multiple takes," *Time*, December 9, 2014. time.com/3624976/isis-beheading-technology-video-trac-quilliam.

[36] Alexandra Topping, Josh Halliday, and Nishaat Ismail, "Who is Mohammed Emwazi? From shy, football-loving boy to Isis killer," *The Guardian*, November 13, 2015. theguardian.com/uk-news/2015/mar/02/who-is-mohammed-emwazi-from-lovely-boy-to-islamic-state-executioner.

[37] Victoria Ward, "Cleric said to be behind Tunisian beach massacre is living on benefits in Britain," *The Telegraph*, July 6, 2015. telegraph.co.uk/news/worldnews/islamic-state/11720000/Cleric-said-to-be-behind-Tunisian-beach-massacre-is-living-in-benefits-in-Britain.html.

[38] Alexandra Topping, Josh Halliday, and Nishaat Ismail, "Who is Mohammed Emwazi? From shy, football-loving boy to Isis killer," *The Guardian*, November 13, 2015. theguardian.com/uk-news/2015/mar/02/who-is-mohammed-emwazi-from-lovely-boy-to-islamic-state-executioner.

[39] Dan Murphy, "British government made 'Jihadi John' torture prisoners. Really?" *Christian Science Monitor*, February 26, 2015. csmonitor.com/World/Security-Watch/Backchannels/2015/0226/British-government-made-Jihadi-John-torture-and-kidnap-prisoners-Really.

[40] Nico Hines, "Why Did Britain Let 'Jihadi John' Go Free?" *The Daily Beast*, February 26, 2015. thedailybeast.com/why-did-britain-let-jihadi-john-go-free.

[41] Duncan Gardham and Richard Spillett, "Suspected terrorist stopped at Heathrow with a guide to jihad walks free after intelligence services 'refuse to hand over evidence,'" *Daily Mail*, June 1, 2015. dailymail.co.uk/news/article-3105884/Terror-suspect-Bherlin-Gildo-freed-intelligence-services-refuse-hand-evidence.html.

[42] Richard Norton-Taylor, "Terror trial collapses after fears of deep embarrassment to security services," *The Guardian*, June 1, 2015. theguardian.com/uk-news/2015/jun/01/trial-swedish-man-accused-terrorism-offences-collapse-bherlin-gildo.

[43] Duncan Gardham and Richard Spillett, "Suspected terrorist stopped at Heathrow with a guide to jihad walks free after intelligence services 'refuse to hand over evidence,'" *Daily Mail*, June 1, 2015. dailymail.co.uk/news/article-3105884/Terror-suspect-Bherlin-Gildo-freed-intelligence-services-refuse-hand-evidence.html.

[44] "ISIS Militants Charged with Deaths of Americans in Syria," United States Attorney's Office, Eastern District of Virginia, October 7, 2020. justice.gov/usao-edva/pr/isis-militants-charged-deaths-americans-syria.

[45] Duncan Gardham and Richard Spillett, "Suspected terrorist stopped at Heathrow with a guide to jihad walks free after intelligence services 'refuse to hand over evidence,'" *Daily Mail*, June 1, 2015. dailymail.co.uk/news/article-3105884/Terror-suspect-Bherlin-Gildo-freed-intelligence-services-refuse-hand-evidence.html.

[46] Nafeez Ahmed, "The circus: How British intelligence primed both sides of the 'terror war,'" Middle East Eye, March 2, 2015. middleeasteye.net/opinion/circus-how-british-intelligence-primed-both-sides-terror-war.

47 Raffaello Pantucci, "British Fighters Joining the War in Syria," Combating Terrorism Center, United States Military Academy at West Point, *CTC Sentinel* 6, no. 2 (February 2013). ctc.usma.edu/british-fighters-joining-the-war-in-syria.

48 "Bakri Says Training UK Islamists for 'Jihad' in Syria at Lebanon Camp," *An-Nahar*, November 25, 2012. naharnet.com/stories/en/62207.

49 Ibid.

50 Raffaello Pantucci, "British Fighters Joining the War in Syria," Combating Terrorism Center, United States Military Academy at West Point, *CTC Sentinel* 6, no. 2 (February 2013). ctc.usma.edu/british-fighters-joining-the-war-in-syria.

51 Ruth Michaelson, "The curious case of Moaezzem Begg," *Foreign Policy*, October 9, 2014. foreignpolicy.com/2014/10/09/the-curious-case-of-moazzem-begg.

52 Ian Cobain and Randeep Ramesh, "Moazzam Begg was in contact with MI5 about his Syria visits, papers show," *The Guardian*, October 2, 2014. theguardian.com/world/2014/oct/02/moazzam-begg-contact-mi5-agents-papers.

53 Numan Abd al-Wahid, "Did Moazzam Begg meet and/or train 'Jihadi John' in Syria with the collusion of British Intelligence?" Colonial Karma (blog), March 2, 2015. churchills-karma.com/2015/03/02/did-moazzam-begg-meet-andor-train-jihadi-john-in-syria-with-the-collusion-of-british-intelligence.

54 Jamie Merrill, "UK admits contact with Libyan group linked to Manchester bomber," Middle East Eye, April 6, 2018. middleeasteye.net/fr/news/revealed-uk-government-communications-groups-linked-manchester-bomber-53000913.

55 Adam Entous, Nour Malas, and Margaret Coker, "A Veteran Saudi Power Player Works to Build Support to Topple Assad," *Wall Street Journal*, August 25, 2013. wsj.com/articles/SB10001424127887323423804579024452583045962.

56 Mark Mazzetti, Robert F. Worth, and Michael R. Gordon, "Obama's Uncertain Path Amid Syria Bloodshed," *New York Times*, October 22, 2013. nytimes.com/2013/10/23/world/middleeast/obamas-uncertain-path-amid-syria-bloodshed.html.

57 Michael R. Gordon, *Degrade and Destroy: The Inside Story of the War Against the Islamic State, from Barack Obama to Donald Trump* (New York: Farrar, Straus and Giroux, 2022), Chapter 3.

58 Douglas Laux and Ralph Pezzullo, *Left of Boom: How a Young CIA Case Officer Penetrated the Taliban and al-Qaeda* (New York: St Martin's Press, 2016), pp. 280–1.

59 Aaron Maté, "'Al Qaeda Is on Our Side': How Obama/Biden Team Empowered Terrorist Networks in Syria," Real Clear Investigations, April 20, 2022. realclearinvestigations.com/articles/2022/04/20/al_qaeda_is_on_our_side_how_obamabiden_officials_helped_create_a_safe_haven_for_terrorists_in_syria_827477.html.

60 Adam Entous, Nour Malas, and Margaret Coker, "A Veteran Saudi Power Player Works to Build Support to Topple Assad," *Wall Street Journal*, August 25, 2013. wsj.com/articles/SB10001424127887323423804579024452583045962.

61 Mark Mazzetti and Matt Apuzzo, "U.S. Relies Heavily on Saudi Money to Support Syrian Rebels," *New York Times*, January 23, 2016. nytimes.com/2016/01/24/world/middleeast/us-relies-heavily-on-saudi-money-to-support-syrian-rebels.html.

62 Jack Shafer, "The CIA and Riggs Bank," *Slate*, January 7, 2005. slate.com/news-and-politics/2005/01/the-cia-and-riggs-bank.html.

63 Aaron Good, Ben Howard, and Peter Dale Scott, "The Twenty Year Shadow of 9/11 (Part 2): Why Did Key U.S. Officials Protect the Alleged 9/11 Plotters?" *CovertAction Magazine*, September 13, 2021. covertactionmagazine.com/2021/09/13/the-twenty-year-shadow-of-9-11-part-2-why-did-key-u-s-officials-protect-the-alleged-9-11-plotters.

Chapter 11

1 Karen DeYoung and Liz Sly, "Syrian rebels get influx of arms with gulf neighbors' money, U.S. coordination," *Washington Post*, May 15, 2012. washingtonpost.com/world/national-security/syrian-rebels-get-influx-of-arms-with-gulf-neighbors-money-us-coordination/2012/05/15/gIQAds2TSU_story.html.

2 Andrew Osborn, "How 'Damascus Volcano' erupted in Assad's stronghold," Reuters, July 20, 2012. reuters.com/article/us-syria-crisis-damascus/how-damascus-volcano-erupted-in-assads-stronghold-idUSBRE86J17E20120720.

3 Martin Chulov and Ian Black, "Leading Syrian regime figures killed in Damascus bomb attack," *The Guardian*, July 18, 2012. theguardian.com/world/2012/jul/18/syrian-regime-figures-bomb-attack.

4 Neil MacFarquhar, "Syrian Rebels Land Deadly Blow to Assad's Inner Circle," *New York Times*, July 18, 2012. nytimes.com/2012/07/19/world/middleeast/suicide-attack-reported-in-damascus-as-more-generals-flee.html.

5 Andrew Osborn, "How 'Damascus Volcano' erupted in Assad's stronghold," Reuters, July 20, 2012. reuters.com/article/us-syria-crisis-damascus/how-damascus-volcano-erupted-in-assads-stronghold-idUSBRE86J17E20120720.

6 Neil MacFarquhar and Dalal Mawad, "Syria Hardens Its Response to Rebels in Damascus Clashes," *New York Times*, July 17, 2012. nytimes.com/2012/07/18/world/middleeast/syria-hardens-response-to-clashes-in-damascus.html.

7 "Syrian troops take Midan neighborhood from rebels," *Christian Science Monitor*, July 20, 2012. csmonitor.com/World/Latest-News-Wires/2012/0720/Syrian-troops-retake-Midan-neighborhood-from-rebels.

8 Layla M., "Has Assad won the first round in the battle For Damascus?" Al-Monitor, July 24, 2012. al-monitor.com/originals/2012/al-monitor/did-assad-win-the-first-round-in.html.

9 Aron Lund, "Into the Tunnels: The Rise and Fall of Syria's Rebel Enclave in the Eastern Ghouta," The Century Foundation, December 21, 2016. tcf.org/content/report/into-the-tunnels.

10 Joshua Landis, "Zahran Alloush, his ideology and beliefs," Syria Comment (blog), December 15, 2013. joshualandis.com/blog/zahran-alloush.

11 William Van Wagenen, "Did Assad Deliberately Release Islamist Prisoners to Militarize and Radicalize the Syrian Uprising?" Libertarian Institute, February 22, 2018. libertarianinstitute.org/articles/assad-deliberately-release-islamist-prisoners-militarize-radicalize-syrian-uprising.

12 Aron Lund, "The Syrian Rebel Who Tried to Build an Islamist Paradise," *Politico Magazine*, March 31, 2017. politico.com/magazine/story/2017/03/the-syrian-rebel-who-built-an-islamic-paradise-214969.

13 "Far from Justice: Syria's Supreme State Security Court," Human Rights Watch, February 2009. hrw.org/sites/default/files/reports/syria0209web.pdf.

14 Kristen Helberg, "The kidnapping of the Douma 4: The Salafist and the human rights activist," Qantara.de, December 12, 2014. en.qantara.de/content/the-kidnapping-of-the-douma-4-the-salafist-and-the-human-rights-activist.

15 "Protestors march in Syria as president names new prime minister," CNN, April 3, 2011. cnn.com/2011/WORLD/meast/04/03/syria.unrest/index.html.

16 "Zahran Alloush, the leader of an organized army, has been under the surveillance since 1987" (Arabic), Khaleej Online, December 25, 2015. alkhaleejonline.net/-زهران/سياسة. علوش-قائد-جيش-منظم-كان-تحت-الأنظار-منذ-1987.

17 Zaman 9

18 "Syrian Islamic brigades unite with regional support in anticipation of a political solution," *Al-Hayat*, October 6, 2013. samanews.ps/ar/post/173810.

19 Anne Barnard, "Powerful Syrian Rebel Leader Reported Killed in Airstrike," *New York Times*, December 25, 2015. nytimes.com/2015/12/26/world/middleeast/zahran-alloush-syria-rebel-leader-reported-killed.html.

20 "Tentative Jihad: Syria's Fundamentalist Opposition," International Crisis Group, October 12, 2012. crisisgroup.org/middle-east-north-africa/eastern-mediterranean/syria/tentative-jihad-syria-s-fundamentalist-opposition.

21 Zeina Erhaim, "How the Syrian Revolution Was Organized — And How It Unraveled," *New Lines Magazine*, March 16, 2021. newlinesmag.com/essays/how-the-syrian-revolution-was-organized-and-how-it-unraveled.

22 Ghadi Francis, *My Pen and My Pain: 100 Days in Syria* (Beirut: Dar al Saqi, 2012), p. 259.

23 Kristen Helberg, "The kidnapping of the Douma 4: The Salafist and the human rights activist," Qantara.de, December 12, 2014. en.qantara.de/content/the-kidnapping-of-the-douma-4-the-salafist-and-the-human-rights-activist.

24 Ibid.

25 "Tentative Jihad: Syria's Fundamentalist Opposition," International Crisis Group, October 12, 2012. crisisgroup.org/middle-east-north-africa/eastern-mediterranean/syria/tentative-jihad-syria-s-fundamentalist-opposition.

26 Patrick Cockburn, Robert Fisk, and Kim Sengupta, *Syria, Descent into the Abyss, An Unforgettable Anthology of Contemporary Reporting* (London: Independent Print Limited, 2014), p. 166.

27 Martin Chulov and Nour Ali, "Syria violence spreads to commercial capital Aleppo," *The Guardian*, August 12, 2011. theguardian.com/world/2011/aug/12/syria-violence-spreads-aleppo.

28 Neil MacFarquhar, "2 Security Complex Car Bombings Kill Dozens, Syria Says," *New York Times*, February 10, 2012. nytimes.com/2012/02/11/world/middleeast/blasts-in-aleppo-syria-homs-violence-said-to-continue.html.

29 "AFP: Unknown Islamist group claims suicide attacks in Syria," Al-Arabiya, February 29, 2012. english.alarabiya.net/articles/2012/02/29/197781.

30 Abd al-Rahman al-Haj, "Salafism and Salafism in Syria: From Reform to Jihad," Al Jazeera, May 20, 2013. studies.aljazeera.net/ar/reports/2013/05/2013520105748485639.html.

31 Ammar Abd al-Hamid, "The Shredded Tapestry: The State of Syria Today," Foundation for Defense of Democracies, September 25, 2012. fdd.org/analysis/2012/09/25/the-shredded-tapestry-the-state-of-syria-today.

32 Brian Murphy and Zeina Karam, "AP: Qatar faces backlash among rebel groups in Syria," *The Times of Israel*, April 24, 2013. timesofisrael.com/qatar-faces-backlash-among-rebel-groups-in-syria.

33 "Liwaa al-Tawhid Brigade," Terrorism Resource and Analysis Consortium (TRAC), n.d. trackingterrorism.org/group/liwaa-al-tawhid-brigade.

34 "The martyrdom of the commander of the Tawhid Brigade, Abdul Qadir al-Saleh," El-Dorar Al-Shamiya, November 18, 2013. eldorar.com/node/34161.

35 "The commander of the Tawhid Brigade, one of the most prominent leaders of the armed opposition in Syria, was killed," Euronews, November 18, 2013. arabic.euronews.com/2013/11/18/syria-militant-leader-dies-in-aleppo.

36 C.J. Chivers, "A Rebel Commander in Syria Holds the Reins of War," *New York Times*, January 1, 2013. nytimes.com/2013/02/02/world/middleeast/the-saturday-profile-hajji-marea-a-rebel-commander-in-syria-holds-reins-of-war.html.

37 Joshua Landis, "Syria's Top Five Insurgent Leaders," Syria Comment (blog), October 1, 2013. joshualandis.com/blog/biggest-powerful-militia-leaders-syria.

38 Luke Harding and Martin Chulov, "Syrian rebels fight Assad troops in Aleppo," *The Guardian*, July 22, 2012. theguardian.com/world/2012/jul/22/syrian-rebels-fight-aleppo.

39 "Who is Major General Muhammad Mufleh, and where is he now? Find out the reasons behind his disappearance" (Arabic), *Ad-Diyar*, February 13, 2018. alkawthartv.ir/news/122571.

40 Al- / "This is how the head of the Military Intelligence branch in Aleppo, Muhammad al-Mufleh, escaped and was killed after he handed over its 'security keys' to the Turks!?" (Arabic), *Al-Haqiqa*, September 7, 2012.
syriathepromise.wordpress.com/2012/09/07/هكذا-فرّ-رئيس-فرع-المخابرات-العسكرية-ف.

41 Radwan Mortada, "The 'battle of liberation' knocks on the doors of Aleppo," *Al-Akhbar*, May 28, 2013. al-akhbar.com/Arab/51573.

42 Martin Chulov, "Syrian rebels fight on for Aleppo despite local wariness," *The Guardian*, August 21, 2012. theguardian.com/world/2012/aug/21/syrian-rebels-aleppo-local-hostility.

43 James Foley, "Syria: Rebels losing support among civilians in Aleppo," *GlobalPost*, October 16, 2012. theworld.org/stories/2012-10-16/syria-rebels-losing-support-among-civilians-aleppo.

44 Robert F. Worth, "Aleppo after the fall," *New York Times Magazine*, May 24, 2017. nytimes.com/2017/05/24/magazine/aleppo-after-the-fall.html.

45 Rania Abouzeid, *No Turning Back: Life, Loss, and Hope in Wartime Syria* (New York: W.W. Norton & Company, 2018), pp. 170–1.

46 "The martyrdom of the commander of the Tawhid Brigade, Abdul Qadir al-Saleh," El-Dorar Al-Shamiya, November 18, 2013. eldorar.com/node/34161.

47 Firas Namus, "Liwa Tawhid in Syria: The Nusra Front are our brothers" (Arabic), Al Jazeera, December 21, 2012. aljazeera.net/news/2012/12/21/لواء-التوحيد-بسوريا-جبهة-النصرة.

48 Justin Vela and Liz Sly, "In Syria, group suspected of al-Qaeda links gaining prominence in war to topple Assad," *Washington Post*, August 19, 2012. washingtonpost.com/world/middle_east/in-syria-group-suspected-of-al-qaeda-links-gaining-prominence-in-war-to-topple-assad/2012/08/19/c7cffd66-ea22-11e1-9ddc-340d5efb1e9c_story.html.

49 "US funded FSA kills together with ISIL and Jabhat al-Nusra," Hands Off Syria, October 5, 2014. youtube.com/watch?v=NMlnxu1zrNk.

50 Robert Ford, "Among Syria's Revolutionaries," *New Lines Magazine*, October 14, 2020. newlinesmag.com/first-person/among-syrias-revolutionaries.

51 Martin Chulov, "Syrian rebels fight on for Aleppo despite local wariness," *The Guardian*, August 21, 2012. theguardian.com/world/2012/aug/21/syrian-rebels-aleppo-local-hostility.

52 "Syria: 'Half the fighters I treated were jihadists,' says French doctor," France 24, September 11, 2012. france24.com/en/20120911-foreign-jihadists-syria-doctors-without-borders-aleppo-jacques-beres.

53 Patrick Cockburn, Robert Fisk, and Kim Sengupta, *Syria, Descent into the Abyss, An Unforgettable Anthology of Contemporary Reporting* (London: Independent Print Limited, 2014), p. 219.

54 Hermoine Macura, "Kidnapped Priest Killed, Chopped Up by ISIS as 'Christians Become a Form of Currency' in Mid-East War, Says Aid to the Church in Need," *Christian Post*, August 12, 2015. christianpost.com/news/kidnapped-priest-killed-chopped-up-by-isis-as-christians-become-a-form-of-currency-in-mid-east-war-says-aid-to-the-church-in-need-142658.

55 "AFP: Christians hold out in Syria's Aleppo despite jihadist threat," *Daily Mail*, November 26, 2014. dailymail.co.uk/wires/afp/article-2850680/Christians-hold-Syrias-Aleppo-despite-jihadist-threat.html.

56 Martin Chulov, "Syrian rebels fight on for Aleppo despite local wariness," *The Guardian*, August 21, 2012. theguardian.com/world/2012/aug/21/syrian-rebels-aleppo-local-hostility.

57 James Foley, "Syria: Rebels losing support among civilians in Aleppo," *GlobalPost*, October 16, 2012. theworld.org/stories/2012-10-16/syria-rebels-losing-support-among-civilians-aleppo.

58 Steven Sotloff, "In Aleppo, Bread Lines and Disenchantment with the FSA," *Syria Deeply* (blog), The New Humanitarian, February 5, 2013. deeply.thenewhumanitarian.org/syria/articles/2013/02/05/in-aleppo-bread-lines-and-disenchantment-with-the-fsa.

59 Karen Leigh, "In Syria, Kidnapping Becomes a 'Big-Money Business,'" *Syria Deeply* (blog), The New Humanitarian, June 6, 2013. deeply.thenewhumanitarian.org/syria/articles/2013/06/06/in-syria-kidnapping-becomes-a-big-money-business.

60 Patrick Cockburn, Robert Fisk, and Kim Sengupta, *Syria, Descent into the Abyss, An Unforgettable Anthology of Contemporary Reporting* (London: Independent Print Limited, 2014), pp. 178–80, 199, 209.

61 Ibid., pp. 347–8.

62 James Foley, "Syria: Rebels losing support among civilians in Aleppo," *GlobalPost*, October 16, 2012. theworld.org/stories/2012-10-16/syria-rebels-losing-support-among-civilians-aleppo.

63 "AP: Syria 'suicide bombers' kill 34 and injure 120 in Aleppo," *The Guardian*, October 3, 2012. amp.theguardian.com/world/2012/oct/03/syria-suicide-bombs-34-aleppo.

64 James Foley, "Syria: Rebels losing support among civilians in Aleppo," *GlobalPost*, October 16, 2012. theworld.org/stories/2012-10-16/syria-rebels-losing-support-among-civilians-aleppo.

65 Steven Sotloff, "In Aleppo, Bread Lines and Disenchantment with the FSA," *Syria Deeply* (blog), The New Humanitarian, February 5, 2013. deeply.thenewhumanitarian.org/syria/articles/2013/02/05/in-aleppo-bread-lines-and-disenchantment-with-the-fsa.

66 Edward Dark, "How We Lost the Syrian Revolution," Al-Monitor, May 28, 2013. al-monitor.com/originals/2013/05/syria-revolution-aleppo-assad.html.

67 Liz Sly, "Islamic law comes to rebel-held areas of Syria," *Washington Post*, March 19, 2013. washingtonpost.com/world/middle_east/islamic-law-comes-to-rebel-held-syria/2013/03/19/b310532e-90af-11e2-bdea-e32ad90da239_story.html.

68 Theo Padnos, *Blindfold: A Memoir of Capture, Torture, and Enlightenment* (New York: Scribner, 2021), p. 193.

69 James Harkin, "Is this the Syrian dungeon where beheaded U.S. and British hostages were caged by ISIS? Pictures show factory basement 'where half-starved westerners were held in darkness,'" *Daily Mail*, December 19, 2014. dailymail.co.uk/news/article-2871180/Is-Syrian-dungeon-U-S-British-hostages-caged-ISIS-beheaded-Chilling-pictures-factory-basement-half-starved-westerners-held-darkness.html.

70 Theo Padnos, *Blindfold: A Memoir of Capture, Torture, and Enlightenment* (New York: Scribner, 2021), p. 341.

71 "The boy killed for an off-hand remark about Muhammad - Sharia spreads in Syria," BBC News, July 2, 2013. bbc.com/news/world-middle-east-23139784.

72 Nu'man Abd al-Wahid, "How Yassin-Kassab Portrayed the Jihadi Capture of Aleppo as 'Liberation,'" Colonial Karma (blog), April 18, 2019. churchills-karma.com/2019/04/18/how-yassin-kassab-portrayed-the-jihadi-capture-of-aleppo-as-liberation.

Chapter 12

1 Rod Nordland, "Al Qaeda Taking Deadly New Role in Syria's Conflict," *New York Times*, July 24, 2012. nytimes.com/2012/07/25/world/middleeast/al-qaeda-insinuating-its-way-into-syrias-conflict.html?_r=1&bl.t

2 "Al-Jarba's proposal to form a 'national army' faces widespread criticism" (Arabic), *Al-Quds Al-Arabi*, August 14, 2013. alquds.co.uk/2-ان-يواجه-وطني-جيش-تشكيل-الجربا-اقتراح.

3 "AP: Qatar faces backlash among rebel groups in Syria," *The Times of Israel*, April 24, 2013. timesofisrael.com/qatar-faces-backlash-among-rebel-groups-in-syria.

4 Nicholas Heras, "Alwiya Ahfaad ar-Rasool: A Growing Force in the Syrian Armed Opposition," Fair Observer, May 19, 2013. fairobserver.com/region/middle_east_north_africa/alwiya-ahfaad-ar-rasool-growing-force-syrian-armed-opposition.

5 "How did (Saddam al-Jamal) become the most prominent Syrian ISIS leader?" (Arabic), Orient News, May 17, 2018. orient-news.net/ar/news_show/149019.

6 Joshua Landis, "Syria's Top Five Insurgent Leaders," Syria Comment (blog), October 1, 2013. joshualandis.com/blog/biggest-powerful-militia-leaders-syria.

7 "The Liberation of Hamdan Airport" (Arabic), Abo Yazn Albokmal, November 17, 2012. youtube.com/watch?v=R91nnJ_I2DY.

8 "Nas' full interview with the leader of ISIS, Saddam al-Jamal" (Arabic), NAS News, January 24, 2019. youtube.com/watch?v=DzqSXdmSWg4&feature=youtu.be.

9 "Who Are Syria's Big Five Insurgent leaders?" *The Syrian Observer*, October 2, 2013. syrianobserver.com/EN/features/34504/who_are_syrias_big_five_insurgent_leaders.html.

10 Basma Atassi, "Syrian fighter defects to Qaeda-linked group," Al Jazeera, December 16, 2013. aljazeera.com/indepth/features/2013/12/syrian-fighter-defects-qaeda-linked-group-201312158517493207.html.

11 Matthew Acton, "ISIS leader responsible for infamous execution of downed pilot who was burned alive in a cage is captured," *Daily Mail*, May 15, 2018. dailymail.co.uk/news/article-5730125/ISIS-leader-responsible-pilot-burned-alive-cage-captured.html.

12 "Drug Addicts Yesterday, Daesh Emirs Today: Firas al-Salman, 'Abu Ahmed al-Bukamal'" (Arabic), Deir Ezzor 24, 2015. deirezzor24.net/داعش-أمراء-الأمس-حشاشو-سلسلة/ اليوم.

13 David Enders, "With Syria's eastern oilfields in rebel hands, a brisk business in pirated crude grows," McClatchyDC, November 21, 2012. mcclatchydc.com/news/nation-world/world/article24740638.html.

14 David Enders, "Rebels flying black Islamist flag seize artillery base in Syria's Deir al Zour province," McClatchyDC, November 22, 2012. mcclatchydc.com/article24740659.html.

15 "The Free Army: There is no place for 'PKK' fighters in Ras al-Ayn," *Al Joumhouria*, January 23, 2013. aljoumhouria.com/ar/news/51824.

16 "Turkey urges recognition of Syrian opposition," Al Jazeera, November 15, 2012. aljazeera.com/news/2012/11/15/turkey-urges-recognition-of-syrian-opposition.

17 Roy Gutman and McClatchy Foreign Staff, "Kurdish-Nusra battle becoming war within a war in northern Syria," McClatchyDC, July 23, 2013. mcclatchydc.com/news/nation-world/world/article24751405.html.

18 Omar Hossino and Kinda Kanbar, "How Michel Kilo Negotiated a Tenuous Truce in Ras Al Ayn," *Syria Deeply* (blog), The New Humanitarian, March 5, 2013. deeply.thenewhumanitarian.org/syria/articles/2013/03/05/how-michel-kilo-negotiated-a-tenuous-truce-in-ras-al-ayn.

19 "The Free Army: There is no place for 'PKK' fighters in Ras al-Ayn," *Al Joumhouria*, January 23, 2013. aljoumhouria.com/ar/news/51824.

20 Susannah George, "In Syria, Two Opponents of The Regime Fight Each Other," National Public Radio, January 24, 2013. npr.org/sections/thetwo-way/2013/01/23/170096518/in-syria-two-opponents-of-the-regime-fight-each-other.

21 "AFP: Dead in clashes between the Kurds and the armed opposition near the border with Turkey" (Arabic), France 24, January 19, 2013. france24.com/ar/20130119--قتلى-اشتباكات بين-مسلحين-معارضين-أكراد-في-منطقة-سورية-حدودية-تركيا-رأس-العين.

22 Tim Arango, "Wider Chaos Feared as Syrian Rebels Clash with Kurds," *New York Times*, December 6, 2012. nytimes.com/2012/12/07/world/middleeast/wider-chaos-feared-as-syrian-rebels-and-kurds-clash.html.

23 "AP: Recent-Ras al-Ayn," Associated Press, March 26, 2013. aparchive.com/metadata/youtube/d55561c5653e88e6b77f30166a1f6def.

24 Jenan Moussa and Harold Doornbos, "The Civil War Within Syria's Civil War," *Foreign Policy*, August 28, 2013. foreignpolicy.com/2013/08/28/the-civil-war-within-syrias-civil-war.

25 "Clashes between Kurdish fighters and the Free Syrian Army in the border city of Ras al-Ain topple truce" (Arabic), *Al-Sharq al-Awsat*, January 19, 2013. archive.aawsat.com/details.asp?section=4&issueno=12471&article=713728#.YBbaBOipHqY.

26 Elie Hanna, Youssef Sheikho, "Syria's Kurds United: The Ankara Project will not pass" (Arabic), *Al-Akhbar*, February 2, 2020. al-akhbar.com/Arab/45617.

27 Patrice Taddonio, "Flashback: How US-Backed Kurds Defeated ISIS in Kobani, Syria," PBS, *Frontline*, October 9, 2019. pbs.org/wgbh/frontline/article/flashback-how-us-backed-kurds-defeated-isis-in-kobani-syria.

28 "Kilo praises the Turkish role in the Syrian crisis" (Arabic), Anatolia Agency, February 17, 2013. aa.com.tr/ar/archive/273671/كيلو-يشيد-بالدور-التركي-في-الأزمة-السورية.

29 Marlin Dick, "A sect in the Middle: Syria's Alawites endure considerable resentment," *Daily Star*, October 6, 2012. dailystar.com.lb/News/Middle-East/2012/Oct-06/190351-a-sect-in-the-middle-syrias-alawites-generate-considerable-resentment.ashx#ixzz28edAP9AX.

30 Mariam Karouny, "Syria's Islamist rebels join forces against Assad," Reuters, October 11, 2012. reuters.com/article/us-syria-crisis-rebels/syrias-islamist-rebels-join-forces-against-assad-idUSBRE89A0Y920121011.

31 Ibid.

32 "Syrian Islamic Liberation Front (SILF) /Syrian Liberation Front," Global Security. globalsecurity.org/military/world/para/silf.htm.

33 Aron Lund, "The Free Syrian Army Doesn't Exist," Syria Comment (blog), March 16, 2013. joshualandis.com/blog/the-free-syrian-army-doesnt-exist.

34 "Guide to the Syrian rebels," BBC News, December 13, 2013. bbc.com/news/world-middle-east-24403003.

35 Neil MacFarquhar and Hwaida Saad, "Rebel Groups in Syria Make Framework for Military," *New York Times*, December 7, 2012. nytimes.com/2012/12/08/world/middleeast/rebel-groups-in-syria-make-framework-for-military.html.

36 "Profile: Syrian National Council chairman George Sabra," BBC News, November 13, 2012. bbc.com/news/world-middle-east-20312255.

37 Abdallah Suleiman Ali, "Noose tightens around Jabhat al-Nusra," Al-Monitor, March 18, 2015. al-monitor.com/pulse/security/2015/03/syria-clamp-down-jabhat-al-nusra.html.

38 Hassan Hassan, "How the Muslim Brotherhood Hijacked Syria's Revolution," *Foreign Policy*, March 13, 2013. foreignpolicy.com/2013/03/13/how-the-muslim-brotherhood-hijacked-syrias-revolution.

39 Ben Norton, "Leaked docs expose massive Syria propaganda operation waged by Western govt contractors and media," The Grayzone, September 23, 2020. thegrayzone.com/2020/09/23/syria-leaks-uk-contractors-opposition-media.

40 United States Defense Intelligence Agency (DIA) Memo, U.S. Defense Intelligence Agency, August 12, 2020. judicialwatch.org/wp-content/uploads/2015/05/Pg.-291-Pgs.-287-293-JW-v-DOD-and-State-14-812-DOD-Release-2015-04-10-final-version11.pdf.

41 Tim Arango, Anne Barnard, and Hwaida Sadd, "Syrian Rebels Tied to Al Qaeda Play Key Role in War," *New York Times*, December 8, 2012. nytimes.com/2012/12/09/world/middleeast/syrian-rebels-tied-to-al-qaeda-play-key-role-in-war.html.

42 Rania Abouzeid, "Interview with Official of Jabhat al-Nusra, Syria's Islamist Militia Group," *Time*, December 25, 2012. world.time.com/2012/12/25/interview-with-a-newly-designated-syrias-jabhat-al-nusra.

43 David Enders and Hannah Allam, "Head of new U.S.-backed Syrian coalition endorses al Qaida-linked rebel faction," McClatchyDC, December 12, 2012. mcclatchydc.com/paywall/subscriber-only?resume=24741589&intcid=ab_archive.

44 Firas Nuhas, "Liwa al-Tawhid in Syria: Jabhat al-Nusra are our brothers," Al Jazeera, December 21, 2012. aljazeera.net/news/2012/12/21/لواء-التوحيد-بسوريا-جبهة-النصرة. <bp: URL>>

45 Sahib Anjarini, "As-Safir: The Story of Al-Tawhid Brigade: Fighting for Sharia in Syria," Al-Monitor, October 22, 2013. al-monitor.com/pulse/security/2013/10/syria-opposition-islamists-tawhid-brigade.html#ixzz6Xt2CBUac.

46 Umberto Bacchi, "Syria Civil War: US Diplomatic Double-Speak Holds Clear Dangers," *International Business Times*, December 12, 2012. ibtimes.co.uk/syria-national-coalition-al-nursa-414172.

47 "After America's terrorism announcement, the street declares 'victory to Nusra' and the 'Free [Army]' unites with it" (Arabic), Zaman al-Wasl, December 11, 2012. zamanalwsl.net/news/article/33772.

48 Khaled Jakob Oweis, "Al Qaeda grows powerful in Syria as endgame nears," Reuters, December 19, 2012. reuters.com/article/us-syria-crisis-qaeda/al-qaeda-grows-powerful-in-syria-as-endgame-nears-idUSBRE8BJ06B20121220.

49 "Army of Islam executes dozens of youth in Eastern Ghouta" (Arabic), Al-Quds Al-Arabi, May 11, 2015. alquds.co.uk/%EF%BB%BFجيش-الاسلام-ينفذ-أحكام-الإعدام-على.

50 Nado Bakos, "Terrorist group fills power vacuum among Syria rebels," CNN, January 10, 2013. cnn.com/2013/01/09/opinion/bakos-syria-al-qaeda/index.html.

51 Tim Arango, Anne Barnard, and Hwaida Sadd, "Syrian Rebels Tied to Al Qaeda Play Key Role in War," New York Times, December 8, 2012. nytimes.com/2012/12/09/world/middleeast/syrian-rebels-tied-to-al-qaeda-play-key-role-in-war.html.

52 C.J. Chivers and Eric Schmitt, "Arms Airlift to Syria Rebels Expands, With Aid from C.I.A.," New York Times, March 24, 2013. nytimes.com/2013/03/25/world/middleeast/arms-airlift-to-syrian-rebels-expands-with-cia-aid.html.

53 David E. Sanger, "Rebel Arms Flow Is Said to Benefit Jihadists in Syria," New York Times, October 14, 2012. nytimes.com/2012/10/15/world/middleeast/jihadists-receiving-most-arms-sent-to-syrian-rebels.html.

54 "Syrian rebels say Americans, Britons helped train them," McClatchyDC, December 14, 2012. mcclatchydc.com/news/nation-world/world/article24741685.html.

55 David S. Cloud and Raja Abdulrahman, "U.S. has secretly provided arms training to Syria rebels since 2012," Los Angeles Times, June 21, 2013. latimes.com/world/middleeast/la-xpm-2013-jun-21-la-fg-cia-syria-20130622-story.html.

56 "AP: 'Master plan' underway to help Syria rebels take Damascus with U.S.-approved airlifts of heavy weapons," CBS News, March 28, 2013. cbsnews.com/news/ap-master-plan-underway-to-help-syria-rebels-take-damascus-with-us-approved-airlifts-of-heavy-weapons.

57 Eliot Higgins, "Evidence of Jabhat al-Nusra with Croatian Weapons," Brown Moses (blog), March 23, 2013. brown-moses.blogspot.com/2013/03/evidence-of-jabhat-al-nusra-with.html.

58 Zeina Karam, "Rebels seize air defense base in southern Syria," Washington Post, March 23, 2013. washingtonpost.com/world/rebels-seize-air-defense-base-in-southern-syria/2013/03/23/8c7854a8-93ea-11e2-8ea1-956c94b6b5b9_story.html.

59 Mark Mazzetti, Michael R. Gordon, and Mark Landler, "U.S. Is Said to Plan to Send Weapons to Syrian Rebels," New York Times, June 13, 2013. nytimes.com/2013/06/14/world/middleeast/syria-chemical-weapons.html.

60 Phil Sands and Suha Maayeh, "Syrian rebels get arms and advice through secret command centre in Amman," The National, December 27, 2013. thenationalnews.com/world/syrian-rebels-get-arms-and-advice-through-secret-command-centre-in-amman-1.455590.

61 "Students reported killed in Syria air attack," Al Jazeera, September 29, 2013. aljazeera.com/news/2013/9/29/students-reported-killed-in-syria-air-attack.

62 "Special arms for Syria rebels fall into Nusra hands," Daily Star, October 4, 2013. dailystar.com.lb/News/Middle-East/2013/Oct-04/233502-special-arms-for-syria-rebels-fall-into-nusra-hands.ashx.

63 David D. Kirkpatrick, "Qatar's Support of Islamists Alienates Allies Near and Far," *New York Times*, September 7, 2014. nytimes.com/2014/09/08/world/middleeast/qatars-support-of-extremists-alienates-allies-near-and-far.html.

64 Phil Sands and Suha Maayeh, "Islamist militants' secret role in Syrian rebels' successes," *The National*, January 5, 2014. thenationalnews.com/world/islamist-militants-secret-role-in-syrian-rebels-successes-1.250042.

65 Mark Hosenball, "Congress secretly approves U.S. weapons flow to 'moderate' Syrian rebels," Reuters, January 27, 2014. reuters.com/article/us-usa-syria-rebels/congress-secretly-approves-u-s-weapons-flow-to-moderate-syrian-rebels-idUSBREA0Q1S320140127.

66 David Enders and Hannah Allam, "Head of new U.S.-backed Syrian coalition endorses al Qaida-linked rebel faction," McClatchyDC, December 12, 2012. mcclatchydc.com/paywall/subscriber-only?resume=24741589&intcid=ab_archive.

Chapter 13

1 Liz Sly and Karen DeYoung, "In Syria, new influx of weapons to rebels tilts the battle against Assad," *Washington Post*, February 23, 2013. washingtonpost.com/world/in-syria-new-influx-of-weapons-to-rebels-tilts-the-battle-against-assad/2013/02/23/a6bf2bc0-7dfb-11e2-9073-e9dda4ac6a66_story.html?utm_term=.86703499ea09.

2 Neil MacFarquhar and Dalal Mawad, "Syria Hardens Its Response to Rebels in Damascus Clashes," *New York Times*, July 17, 2012. nytimes.com/2012/07/18/world/middleeast/syria-hardens-response-to-clashes-in-damascus.html.

3 Khaled Yacoub Oweis and Mariam Karouny, "Syrian rebels fight close to heart of Damascus," Reuters, February 6, 2013. reuters.com/article/us-syria-crisis-damscus/syrian-rebels-fight-close-to-heart-of-damascus-idUSBRE9150BD20130206.

4 "AP: 'Master plan' underway to help Syria rebels take Damascus with U.S.-approved airlifts of heavy weapons," CBS News, March 28, 2013. cbsnews.com/news/ap-master-plan-underway-to-help-syria-rebels-take-damascus-with-us-approved-airlifts-of-heavy-weapons.

5 Nidal Bitari, "Yarmouk Refugee Camp and the Syrian Uprising: A View from Within," *Journal of Palestine Studies* 43, no. 1 (Autumn 2013): pp. 61–78. jstor.org/stable/10.1525/jps.2013.43.1.61.

6 Anaheed al-Hardan, "Uncertain fate for Palestinians in Syria," *Electronic Intifada*, July 12, 2012. electronicintifada.net/content/uncertain-fate-palestinians-syria/11490.

7 Ibid.

8 Sharmine, Narwani, "Stealing Palestine: Who dragged Palestinians into Syria's conflict?" RT, November 10, 2014. rt.com/op-ed/203907-palestine-syria-shelling-clashes-conflict.

9 "AFP: Palestinians join revolt: Activists, FSA," *Al-Ahram*, July 18, 2012. english.ahram.org.eg/News/48062.aspx.

10 Sharmine, Narwani, "Stealing Palestine: Who dragged Palestinians into Syria's conflict?" RT, November 10, 2014. rt.com/op-ed/203907-palestine-syria-shelling-clashes-conflict.

11 Ibid.

12 "Suqur al-Sham, Brigade Daoud, the bombing of the Ricarda checkpoint," Rishad al-'awadhi, July 13, 2012. youtube.com/watch?v=qsQNkjgC5F4.

13 "AP: Mohammed Rafeh, 30; actor killed by Syrian rebels," *Boston Globe*, November 5, 2012. bostonglobe.com/metro/obituaries/2012/11/05/prominent-syrian-born-palestinian-actor-mohammed-rafeh-kidnapped-killed/m8gNEcnKnLPRtSCB9UFp5K/story.html.

14 "Syria: Summary Killings and Other Abuses by Armed Opposition Groups," Amnesty International, March 14, 2013. amnesty.org/en/documents/MDE24/008/2013/en.

15 Ibid.

16 "Massacre in Tadamon: how two academics hunted down a Syrian war criminal," *The Guardian*, April 27, 2022. theguardian.com/world/2022/apr/27/massacre-in-tadamon-how-two-academics-hunted-down-a-syrian-war-criminal.

17 Ibid.

18 "Two Palestinians tell the new Arab how they knew their son in the video of the Solidarity massacre" (Arabic), Al-Araby Al-Jadeed, May 2, 2022. alaraby.co.uk/video/قصة-إنسان/فلسطينيان-يرويان-للعربي-الجديد-كيف-عرفا-ابنهما-بفيديو-مجزرة-التضامن.

19 "AFP: Palestinians join Syria revolt: Activists, FSA," *Al-Ahram*, July 18, 2012. english.ahram.org.eg/News/48062.aspx.

20 "Syria crisis: UN mission given 30 day extension – Friday 20," *The Guardian*, July 2012," theguardian.com/world/middle-east-live/2012/jul/20/syria-crisis-rebels-seize-borders-live.

21 Anas Zarzar, "The Displaced Persons of Khan Eshieh Camp: Chapters from the Tragedy of the Syrian Crisis" (Arabic), *Al-Akhbar*, September 3, 2012. al-akhbar.com/Arab/74977.

22 Anas Zarzar, "The tragedy of displacement is being renewed… and there is a consensus to keep it as a 'safe area'" (Arabic), *Al-Akhbar*, July 31, 2012. al-akhbar.com/Arab/73335.

23 "AFP: Palestinians join Syria revolt: Activists, FSA," *Al-Ahram*, July 18, 2012. english.ahram.org.eg/News/48062.aspx.

24 Anas Zarzar, "The people of Yarmouk: who will drag us into the conflict?" (Arabic), *Al-Akhbar*, August 7, 2012. al-akhbar.com/Arab/73709.

25 Sharmine, Narwani, "Stealing Palestine: Who dragged Palestinians into Syria's conflict?" RT, November 10, 2014. rt.com/op-ed/203907-palestine-syria-shelling-clashes-conflict.

26 Naser Sharara, "Have the defections reached Ahmed Jibril's 'bedroom'?" (Arabic), *Al-Akhbar*, December 24, 2012. al-akhbar.com/Arab/80742.

27 "204 dead and the FSA attacks the Damascus police" (Arabic), Al Jazeera, July 20, 2012. aljazeera.net/news/2012/7/20/204-قتلى-و-الحر-يهاجم-شرطة-دمشق.

28 "Massacre: 20 Palestinians killed during the bombing of Yarmouk camp in the capital Damascus" (Arabic), *Al-Arab*, August 3, 2012. alarab.com/Article/475749.

29 Patrick Strickland, "Nusra and ISIS targeting, assassinating Palestinian leaders in Yarmouk," *Syria Deeply* (blog), The New Humanitarian, August 17, 2015. deeply.thenewhumanitarian.org/syria/articles/2015/08/17/nusra-and-isis-targeting-assassinating-local-palestinian-leaders-in-yarmouk.

30 Anas Zarzar, "The people of Yarmouk: who will drag us into the conflict?" (Arabic), *Al-Akhbar*, August 7, 2012. al-akhbar.com/Arab/73709.

31 Yousef Diab, "Mortar Massacre in Yarmouk Camp in Damascus Kills 20 Palestinians and Wounds 25" (Arabic), *Al-Sharq al-Awsat*, August 4, 2012. archive.aawsat.com/details.asp?section=4&issueno=12303&article=689371#.Y5td71H MK5d.

32 Damien Cave and Dalal Mawad, "Deadly Attack on Refugee Camp in Syria Could Shift Palestinian Allegiances to Rebels," *New York Times*, August 3, 2012. nytimes.com/2012/08/04/world/middleeast/syria-assault-palestinian-camp-damascus.html.

33 Ibid.

34 Rod Nordland and Dalal Mawad, "Palestinians in Syria Are Reluctantly Drawn Into Vortex of Uprising," *New York Times*, June 30, 2012. nytimes.com/2012/07/01/world/middleeast/palestinians-in-syria-drawn-into-the-violence.html.

35 "Syria rebels bring fight to pro-Assad Palestinians," Reuters, October 31, 2012. reuters.com/article/syria-crisis-palestinians/syria-rebels-bring-fight-to-pro-assad-palestinians-idUSL5E8LV1I220121031.

36 Nidal Bitari, "Yarmouk Refugee Camp and the Syrian Uprising: A View from Within," *Journal of Palestine Studies* 43, no. 1 (Autumn 2013): pp. 61–78. jstor.org/stable/10.1525/jps.2013.43.1.61.

37 Mustafa al-Harash, "Yarmouk Camp: Suffering, Destruction and Intractable Crisis" (Arabic), Institute for Palestine Studies, June 13, 2014. palestine-studies.org/sites/default/files/uploads/files/Al Harsh Yarmouk.pdf.

38 Nour Samaha, "The Defenders of Yarmouk," *Foreign Policy*, May 4, 2015. foreignpolicy.com/2015/05/04/inside-the-ruins-of-yarmouk-refugee-camp-syria.

39 Whitney Webb, "The Intercept withheld NSA doc that may have turned course of war," MintPress News, October 30, 2017. mintpressnews.com/intercept-withheld-nsa-doc-that-may-have-altered-course-of-syria-war/233757.

40 Carol Morello, "Syrian official calls for negotiated settlement to war," *Washington Post*, December 16, 2012. washingtonpost.com/world/middle_east/at-yarmouk-refugee-camp-in-syria-fighting-intensifies/2012/12/16/b4edde1a-4798-11e2-b6f0-e851e741d196_story.html?noredirect=on&utm_term=.9e7d48e4501c.

41 An Employee of the *New York Times* in Syria and Anne Barnard, "A Syrian Airstrike Kills Palestinian Refugees and Costs Assad Support," *New York Times*, December 16, 2012. nytimes.com/2012/12/17/world/middleeast/syrian-airstrike-kills-palestinian-refugees.html.

42 Hania Mourtada and Rick Gladstone, "Syria Warns Refugees Not to Aid Rebels," *New York Times*, December 17, 2012. nytimes.com/2012/12/18/world/middleeast/syria-warns-palestinians-not-to-aid-rebels-as-camp-residents-flee.html.

43 Martin Chulov, "Palestinians flee to Lebanon after jet bombs Syria's largest refugee camp," *The Guardian*, December 18, 2012. theguardian.com/world/2012/dec/18/syria-palestinian-refugees-flee-yarmouk.

44 Jonathan Steele, "How Yarmouk refugee camp became the worst place in Syria," *The Guardian*, March 5, 2015. theguardian.com/news/2015/mar/05/how-yarmouk-refugee-camp-became-worst-place-syria.

45 Anas Zarzar and Marah Mashi, "Yarmouk Battles: A Bloody Day Leads to FSA Control," *Al-Akhbar*, December 17, 2012. al-akhbar.com/Arab/80377.

46 Ibid.

47 "Yarmouk Camp: Wide-spread flight, and new fears in Baba Amr" (Arabic), *Al-Akhbar*, December 18, 2012. al-akhbar.com/node/173906.

48 Ibid.

49 Ibid.

50 Nidal Bitari, "Yarmouk Refugee Camp and the Syrian Uprising: A View from Within," *Journal of Palestine Studies* 43, no. 1 (Autumn 2013): pp. 61–78. jstor.org/stable/10.1525/jps.2013.43.1.61.

51 Alison Tahmizian Meuse, "The conversation: Forgotten and under siege in Damascus's [sic] Yarmouk Refugee Camp," *Syria Deeply* (blog), The New Humanitarian, March 15, 2013. deeply.thenewhumanitarian.org/syria/articles/2013/03/15/the-conversation-forgotten-and-under-siege-in-damascuss-yarmouk-refugee-camp.

52 "Israel Reportedly Providing Direct Aid, Funding to Syrian Rebels," *Haaretz*, June 19, 2017. haaretz.com/israel-news/2017-06-19/ty-article/israel-reportedly-providing-direct-aid-to-syrian-rebels/0000017f-f06c-d223-a97f-fdfdfef50000.

53 Asa Winstanley, "Israel may be arming Al-Qaeda in Syria," Middle East Monitor, January 30, 2015. middleeastmonitor.com/20150130-israel-may-be-arming-al-qaeda-in-syria.

54 Yaroslav Trofimov, "Al Qaeda a lesser evil? Syria War Pulls U.S., Israel Apart," *Wall Street Journal*, March 12, 2015. wsj.com/articles/al-qaeda-a-lesser-evil-syria-war-pulls-u-s-israel-apart-1426169708.

55 Nour Samaha, "The curious case of Israel, al-Nusra and 'Facebook Spy,'" Al Jazeera, April 27, 2015. aljazeera.com/news/2015/4/27/the-curious-case-of-israel-al-nusra-and-facebook-spy.

56 Raphael Ahren, "Israel acknowledges it is helping Syrian rebel fighters," *The Times of Israel*, June 29, 2015. timesofisrael.com/yaalon-syrian-rebels-keeping-druze-safe-in-exchange-for-israeli-aid.

57 "Statement by the commissioner-general on Palestine Refugees trapped inside Yarmouk," United Nations Relief and Works Agency, December 20, 2013. unrwa.org/newsroom/official-statements/statement-commissioner-general-palestine-refugees-trapped-inside.

58 "Insight-Syria uses red tape, threats to control U.N. aid agencies," Reuters, December 15, 2013. reuters.com/article/syria-crisis-aid/insight-syria-uses-red-tape-threats-to-control-u-n-aid-agencies-idUSL5N0JL1E020131215.

59 "Crossroads of Crisis: Yarmouk, Syria, and the Palestine Refugee Predicament," United Nations Relief and Works Agency, February 25, 2014. unrwa.org/newsroom/official-statements/crossroads-crisis-yarmouk-syria-and-palestine-refugee-predicament.

60 Qassem Qassem, "Letters of Sababa and Handhala" (Arabic), *Al-Akhbar*, December 23, 2013. al-akhbar.com/Palestine/62429.

61 Jonathan Steele, "How Yarmouk refugee camp became the worst place in Syria," *The Guardian*, March 5, 2015. theguardian.com/news/2015/mar/05/how-yarmouk-refugee-camp-became-worst-place-syria.

62 "Insight-Syria uses red tape, threats to control U.N. aid agencies," Reuters, December 15, 2013. reuters.com/article/syria-crisis-aid/insight-syria-uses-red-tape-threats-to-control-u-n-aid-agencies-idUSL5N0JL1E020131215.

63 "Commander of the Omariya Covenant Brigade: Dozens of martyrs and wounded in shelling on Yarmouk camp" (Arabic), Ma'an News, January 16, 2014. maannews.net/news/665792.html.

64 Anne Barnard, "Islamic State Seizes Palestinian Refugee Camp in Syria," *New York Times*, April 4, 2015. nytimes.com/2015/04/05/world/middleeast/islamic-state-seizes-palestinian-refugee-camp-in-syria.html.

65 Janine di Giovani, "Under Siege in Yarmouk," *Newsweek*, May 6, 2015. newsweek.com/under-siege-yarmouk-328807.

Chapter 14

1 "4 dead in the Free Army battle to take over Taftanaz airport" (Arabic), Al Jazeera Mubasher, January 2, 2013. aljazeeramubasher.net/news/miscellaneous/2013/1/2/4-قتلى-في-معركة-الجيش-الحر-للسيطرة-على.

2 Rania Abouzeid, "Ground War: Syria's Rebels Prepare to Take a Province from Assad," *Time*, February 7, 2013. world.time.com/2013/02/07/ground-war-syrias-rebels-prepare-to-take-a-province-from-assad.

3 "Statement of the start of the al-Bunyan al-Marsous battle to liberate Idlib" (Arabic), Markaz Tawthiq al-Thuwra al-Suriya, December 26, 2012. youtube.com/watch?v=KH3LzGWNMcM.

4 "4 dead in the Free Army battle to take over Taftanaz airport" (Arabic), Al Jazeera Mubasher, January 2, 2013. aljazeeramubasher.net/news/miscellaneous/2013/1/2/4-قتلى-في-معركة-الجيش-الحر-للسيطرة-على.

5 "We manage all internal battles in a central operations room… and the coalition must accelerate the formation of the government" (Arabic), *Okaz*, January 6, 2013. okaz.com.sa/article/534043.

6 Babak Dehganpisheh, "Rebel fighters, mostly Islamists, seize key Syrian air base," *Washington Post*, January 11, 3013. washingtonpost.com/world/middle_east/rebel-fighters-mostly-islamists-seize-key-syrian-air-base/2013/01/11/f46c7b1c-5bf4-11e2-beee-6e38f5215402_story.html.

7 Andrew Tabler, Jeffrey White, and Aaron Zelin, "Fallout from the Fall of Taftanaz," Washington Institute for Near East Policy, January 14, 2013. washingtoninstitute.org/policy-analysis/fallout-fall-taftanaz.

8 Babak Dehganpisheh, "Rebel fighters, mostly Islamists, seize key Syrian air base," *Washington Post*, January 11, 3013. washingtonpost.com/world/middle_east/rebel-fighters-mostly-islamists-seize-key-syrian-air-base/2013/01/11/f46c7b1c-5bf4-11e2-beee-6e38f5215402_story.html.

9 Rania Abouzeid, "Ground War: Syria's Rebels Prepare to Take a Province from Assad," *Time*, February 7, 2013. world.time.com/2013/02/07/ground-war-syrias-rebels-prepare-to-take-a-province-from-assad.

10 "The story of the control of the Taftanaz military airport" (Arabic), Al Jazeera, January 19, 2013. aljazeera.net/amp/news/2013/1/19/قصة-السيطرة-ة-على-مطار-تفتناز-العسكري.

11 Yasin Raed al-Halabi, "The leader of the Daoud Brigade after his defection from the Islamic Front leads the battles of ISIS in the countryside of Aleppo" (Arabic), *Al-Quds Al-Arabi*, August 15, 2014. alquds.co.uk/%EF%BB%BFالج-انشقاقه-عن-بعد-داوود-لواء-قائد.

12 Phil Sands and Suha Maayeh, "Islamist militants' secret role in Syrian rebels' successes," *The National*, January 5, 2014. thenationalnews.com/world/islamist-militants-secret-role-in-syrian-rebels-successes-1.250042.

13 Babak Dehganpisheh, "Rebel fighters, mostly Islamists, seize key Syrian air base," *Washington Post*, January 11, 3013. washingtonpost.com/world/middle_cast/rebel-fighters-mostly-islamists-seize-key-syrian-air-base/2013/01/11/f46c7b1c-5bf4-11e2-beee-6e38f5215402_story.html.

14 Steve Lalla, "Resistance is not Futile: A Brief History of Lebanon's Hezbollah," *CounterPunch*, January 15, 2021. counterpunch.org/2021/01/15/resistance-is-not-futile-a-brief-history-of-lebanons-hezbollah.

15 "AFP: Syria sends extra troops after rebels seize Idlib," *Al-Ahram*, October 10, 2012. english.ahram.org.eg/NewsContent/2/8/55206/World/Region/Syria-sends-extra-troops-after-rebels-seize-Idlib-.aspx.

16 "Jamal Maaruf Taunts Afif Suleiman," Syria Survey (blog), November 21, 2012. syriasurvey.blogspot.com/2012/11/jamal-maaruf-taunts-afif-suleiman.html.

17 "AFP: Syria truce 'violated' as clashes erupt at base: watchdog," *Hürriyet Daily News*, October 26, 2012. hurriyetdailynews.com/syria-truce-violated-as-clashes-erupt-at-base-watchdog-33298.

18 "3 tanks destroyed in the battle to liberate Idlib" (Arabic), El-Dorar Al-Shamiya, January 19, 2013. eldorar.com/node/448.

19 Rania Abouzeid, "Ground War: Syria's Rebels Prepare to Take a Province from Assad," *Time*, February 7, 2013. world.time.com/2013/02/07/ground-war-syrias-rebels-prepare-to-take-a-province-from-assad.

20 Rania Abouzeid, "How Syria's Rebels Aren't Winning the War: The Anatomy of a Battle," *Time*, May 20, 2013. world.time.com/2013/05/20/how-syrias-rebels-arent-winning-the-war-the-anatomy-of-a-battle.

21 Rania Abouzeid, "Syria's Many Militias: Inside the Chaos of the Anti-Assad Rebellion," *Time*, March 5, 2013. world.time.com/2013/03/05/syrias-many-militias-inside-the-chaos-of-the-anti-assad-rebellion.

22 "AP: Even as rebels capture key cities, their drive through northern Syria slows as ammo and supplies run low," *NY Daily News*, March 5, 2021. nydailynews.com/news/world/rebels-drive-northern-syria-slows-ammo-supplies-run-article-1.1279932.

23 Hania Mourtada and Rick Gladstone, "Assad's Forces Break Through Rebel Blockade of Military Bases," *New York Times*, April 15, 2013. nytimes.com/2013/04/16/world/middleeast/assad-loyalists-breach-rebels-blockade-of-military-bases.html.

24 Jonathan Dupree, "Syria Update: Regime Breaks Siege of Wadi al-Deif," Institute for the Study of War, April 18, 2013. understandingwar.org/backgrounder/syria-update-regime-breaks-siege-wadi-al-deif.

25 "We manage all internal battles in a central operations room... and the coalition must accelerate the formation of the government" (Arabic), *Okaz*, January 6, 2013. okaz.com.sa/article/534043.

26 "After America's terrorism announcement, the street declares 'victory to Nusra' and the 'Free [Army]' unites with it" (Arabic), Zaman al-Wasl, December 11, 2012. zamanalwsl.net/news/article/33772.

27 "Al-Akaidi returns to lead the military in Syria" (Arabic), *Enab Baladi*, October 4, 2017. enabbaladi.net/archives/176444.

28 "Liberation of Menagh Military Airport, legend of the airports in Syria" (Arabic), El-Dorar Al-Shamiya, August 11, 2013. eldorar.com/node/19808.

29 Nicolas Tenzer, "War of Extermination in Syria," Australian Outlook (blog), Australian Institute of International Affairs, October 13, 2016. internationalaffairs.org.au/australianoutlook/syria-war-of-extermination.

30 Jett Goldsmith, "The casualties of Obama's Syria policy," Middle East Eye, August 22, 2016. middleeasteye.net/fr/node/55947.

31 "More than 370,000 people are thought to be killed since the rise of Syrian revolution," Syrian Observatory for Human Rights, February 23, 2016. syriahr.com/en/44437.

32 Paul D. Shinkman, "Dempsey: Syrian No-Fly Zone Wouldn't Work," *U.S. News & World Report*, April 30, 2013. usnews.com/news/articles/2013/04/30/dempsey-syrian-no-fly-zone-wouldnt-work.

33 Rania Abouzeid, "How Islamist Rebels in Syria Are Ruling a Fallen Provincial Capital," *Time*, March 23, 2013. world.time.com/2013/03/23/how-islamist-rebels-in-syria-are-ruling-a-fallen-provincial-capital.

34 "Civilians plead with Syrian fighters," Al Jazeera, October 3, 2012. aljazeera.com/news/2012/10/3/civilians-plead-with-syrian-fighters.

35 "Syria's rebels: We have captured Raqqa," *Daily Star*, March 5, 2013. dailystar.com.lb/News/Middle-East/2013/Mar-05/208857-syrias-rebels-we-have-captured-raqqa.ashx#axzz2Mccn0NE4.

36 "Syria crisis: Raqqa governor held by rebels 'as city falls,'" BBC News, March 5, 2013. bbc.com/news/world-middle-east-21666913.

37 Khalid al-Ghalli, "The story of the fall of Raqqa to ISIS" (Arabic), Irfaa Sawtak, May 17, 2017. irfaasawtak.com/articles/2017/05/17/قصة-سقوط-الرقة-في-يد-داعش.

38 "Syria's rebels: We have captured Raqqa," *Daily Star*, March 5, 2013. dailystar.com.lb/News/Middle-East/2013/Mar-05/208857-syrias-rebels-we-have-captured-raqqa.ashx#axzz2Mccn0NE4.

39 Matthew Barber, "The Raqqa Story: Rebel Structure, Planning, and Possible War Crimes," Syria Comment (blog), April 3, 2013. joshualandis.com/blog/the-raqqa-story-rebel-structure-planning-and-possible-war-crimes.

40 Sarah Birke, "How ISIS Rules," *New York Review of Books*, December 9, 2014. nybooks.com/daily/2014/12/09/how-isis-rules.

41 Khaled Yacoub Oweis, "Syria opposition says captures eastern city of Raqqa," Reuters, March 4, 2013. reuters.com/article/us-syria-crisis-city/syria-opposition-says-captures-eastern-city-of-raqqa-idUSBRE92310920130304.

42 "How Did Raqqa Fall to the Islamic State of Iraq and Syria?" *SyriaUntold*, January 13, 2014. syriauntold.com/2014/01/13/how-did-raqqa-fall-to-the-islamic-state-of-iraq-and-syria.

43 "Syria's rebels: We have captured Raqqa," *Daily Star*, March 5, 2013. dailystar.com.lb/News/Middle-East/2013/Mar-05/208857-syrias-rebels-we-have-captured-raqqa.ashx#axzz2Mccn0NE4.

44 "The 'liberated' Syrian city of Raqqa avoids chaos, gains visitors," Al-Arabiya, March 31, 2013. english.alarabiya.net/en/News/middle-east/2013/03/31/The-liberated-Syrian-city-of-Raqqa-avoids-chaos-gains-visitors.html.

45 Rania Abouzeid, "How Islamist Rebels in Syria Are Ruling a Fallen Provincial Capital," *Time*, March 23, 2013. world.time.com/2013/03/23/how-islamist-rebels-in-syria-are-ruling-a-fallen-provincial-capital.

46 Zeina Karam, "Power Struggle Underway in rebel-held Syrian town," Associated Press, June 26, 2013. apnews.com/article/30c2df60b70e44d6811091b6bb54ae5e.

47 David Remnick, "The Tragic Legacy of Raqqa is Being Slaughtered Silently," *The New Yorker*, October 21, 2017. newyorker.com/news/as-told-to/the-tragic-legacy-of-raqqa-is-being-slaughtered-silently/amp.

48 Qassim Abdul-Zahra and Zeina Karam, "AP: Elusive Al-Qaeda leader in Syria stays in shadows," *The Times of Israel*, November 4, 2013. timesofisrael.com/elusive-al-qaeda-leader-in-syria-stays-in-shadows.

49 Khalid al-Ghalli, "The story of the fall of Raqqa to ISIS" (Arabic), Irfaa Sawtak, May 17, 2017. irfaasawtak.com/articles/2017/05/17/قصة-سقوط-الرقة-في-يد-داعش.

50 Theo Padnos, "My Captivity," *New York Times Magazine*, October 29, 2014. nytimes.com/2014/10/28/magazine/theo-padnos-american-journalist-on-being-kidnapped-tortured-and-released-in-syria.html.

51 William Van Wagenen, "Why Does Assad Buy Oil From ISIS?" Libertarian Institute, August 27, 2017. libertarianinstitute.org/articles/assad-buy-oil-isis. Prominent Nusra commander Sultan Atwi noted that "Nusra won huge money from oil wells and gas stations." See: "'Abu Maria: The Nusra leader behind the split with IS in Syria?' Prominent Nusra commander Sultan Atwi noted that 'Nusra won huge money from oil wells and gas stations,'" Middle East Eye. middleeasteye.net/features/abu-maria-nusra-leader-behind-split-syria.

52 "Syrian rebels seek control over oilfields," *Financial Times*, April 25, 2013. ft.com/content/d8821326-ab2c-11e2-8c63-00144feabdc0.

53 Vivienne Walt, "Syria's Opposition Hopes to Win the War by Selling Oil," *Time*, May 1, 2013. world.time.com/2013/05/01/can-syrias-rebellion-win-the-war-by-selling-oil.

54 "Syrian rebels seek control over oilfields," *Financial Times*, April 25, 2013. ft.com/content/d8821326-ab2c-11e2-8c63-00144feabdc0.

55 Vivienne Walt, "Syria's Opposition Hopes to Win the War by Selling Oil," *Time*, May 1, 2013. world.time.com/2013/05/01/can-syrias-rebellion-win-the-war-by-selling-oil.

56 "FSA spokesman: 'We will commit to any deal to invest in oil if air cover is provided,'" Syria Direct, April 25, 2013. syriadirect.org/news/fsa-spokesman-%e2%80%98we-will-commit-to-any-deal-to-invest-in-oil-if-air-cover-is-provided%e2%80%99.

57 "Deir Ezzor: 'ISIS' is approaching the oil fields" (Arabic), *As-Safir*, April 16, 2014.

58 Julian Borger and Mona Mahmood, "EU decision to lift Syrian oil sanctions boosts jihadist groups," *The Guardian*, May 19, 2013. theguardian.com/world/2013/may/19/eu-syria-oil-jihadist-al-qaida.

59 "Inside ISIS Inc. The Journal of a barrel of oil," *Financial Times*, February 29, 2016. ig.ft.com/sites/2015/isis-oil.

60 Khalid al-Ghalli, "The story of the fall of Raqqa to ISIS" (Arabic), Irfaa Sawtak, May 17, 2017. irfaasawtak.com/articles/2017/05/17/قصّة-سقوط-الرقة-في-يد-داعش.

61 Deborah Amos, "As Rebels Fight Rebels, Grim Reports from a Syrian City," National Public Radio, January 8, 2014. keranews.org/2014-01-08/as-rebels-fight-rebels-grim-reports-from-a-syrian-city.

62 Zeina Karam, "Power Struggle Underway in rebel-held Syrian town," Associated Press, June 26, 2013. apnews.com/article/30c2df60b70e44d6811091b6bb54ae5e.

63 Wael Essam, "'Al-Quds al-Arabi' narrates the reasons for the sudden fall of Raqqa in the hands of the Islamic State… the relationship between Jabhat al-Nusra and 'ISIS' in the city… from a solid alliance to a relentless war" (Arabic), *Al-Quds Al-Arabi*, January 30, 2014. alquds.co.uk/القدس-العربي-تروي-أسباب-سقوط-الرقة-بش.

64 Mariam Karouny, "Syria's 'bride of the revolution' mourns freedom in al Qaeda's grip," Reuters, December 5, 2013. reuters.com/article/us-syria-crisis-qaeda-raqqa/syrias-bride-of-the-revolution-mourns-freedom-in-al-qaedas-grip-idUSBRE9B40XB20131205.

65 Sarah Birke, "How ISIS Rules," *New York Review of Books*, December 9, 2014. nybooks.com/daily/2014/12/09/how-isis-rules.

66 Wael Sawah, "Has the Syrian Revolution Been Hijacked by Islamists?" *The Syrian Observer*, August 16, 2020. syrianobserver.com/EN/features/34917/weekend_has_the_syrian_revolution_been_hijacked_by_islamists.html.

67 Rania Abouzeid, *No Turning Back: Life, Loss, and Hope in Wartime Syria* (New York: W.W. Norton & Company, 2018), p. 173.

68 Ibid.

69 "FSA hopes seized border post will help civilians escape violence," *The National*, July 22, 2012. thenationalnews.com/world/mena/fsa-hopes-seized-border-post-will-help-civilians-escape-violence-1.591769.

70 Rania Abouzeid, "In Syria, the Rebels Have Begun to Fight Among Themselves," *Time*, March 26, 2013. world.time.com/2013/03/26/in-syria-the-rebels-have-begun-to-fight-among-themselves.

71 Ibid.

72 Muhammad Iqbal Belu, "The War of the Crossings: Battles between the Islamic State and the Farouq Brigades" (Arabic), Orient News, July 4, 2013. orient-news.net/ar/news_show/4229.

[73] Jamie Dettmer, "Lawlessness Spreading in Rebel-held Syria," Voice of America, March 28, 2013. voanews.com/world-news/middle-east-dont-use/lawlessness-spreading-rebel-held-syria.

[74] Malek al-Abdeh, "Rebels, Inc.," *Foreign Policy*, November 21, 2013. foreignpolicy.com/2013/11/21/rebels-inc.

[75] "Syria: Brigade Fighting in Homs Implicated in Atrocities," Human Rights Watch, May 13, 2013. hrw.org/news/2013/05/13/syria-brigade-fighting-homs-implicated-atrocities.

[76] Chris Hughes and Sam Webb., "Mirror, "Al-Qaeda 'cannibal' Abu Sakkar who ate Syrian soldier's heart in gruesome video killed in combat," *Mirror*, April 6, 2016. mirror.co.uk/news/world-news/al-qaeda-cannibal-abu-sakkar-7698125.

[77] Rania Abouzeid, *No Turning Back: Life, Loss, and Hope in Wartime Syria* (New York: W.W. Norton & Company, 2018), p. 173.

[78] Ibid.

[79] Nicholas Heras, "Kata'ib al-Farouq al-Islamiya: A Key Armed Opposition Group in the Battle to Cut Assad Off from Damascus," Jamestown Foundation, *Terrorism Monitor* 11, no. 8 (September 2013). jamestown.org/program/kataib-al-farouq-al-islamiya-a-key-armed-opposition-group-in-the-battle-to-cut-assad-off-from-damascus.

[80] Robin Yassin-Kassab and Leila al-Shami, *Burning Country: Syrians in Revolution and War* (London: Pluto Press, 2016), p. 127.

[81] "Syria in Crisis: Suhair al-Atassi," Carnegie Middle East Center, April 1, 2013. carnegie-mec.org/diwan/48619?lang=en.

[82] Mark Tomass, *The Religious Roots of the Syrian Conflict: The Remaking of the Fertile Crescent* (New York: Palgrave Macmillan, 2016), p. 171.

[83] "US funded FSA kills together with ISIL and Jabhat al-Nusra," Hands Off Syria, October 5, 2014. youtube.com/watch?v=NMlnxu1zrNk.

[84] Ibid.

[85] Zeina Khodr, "Meeting al-Qaeda in Syria," Al Jazeera, July 9, 2013. aljazeera.com/features/2013/7/9/meeting-al-qaeda-in-syria.

[86] James Harkin, *Hunting Season: James Foley, ISIS, and the Kidnapping Campaign That Started a War* (Little, Brown and Company – Hachette Book Group, 2015), p. 107.

[87] David S. Cloud and Raja Abdulrahman, "U.S. has secretly provided arms training to Syria rebels since 2012," *Los Angeles Times*, June 21, 2013. latimes.com/world/middleeast/la-xpm-2013-jun-21-la-fg-cia-syria-20130622-story.html.

[88] Joanna Paraszczuk, "Syria Analysis: Which Insurgents Captured Menagh Airbase — & Who Led Them?" EA WorldView, August 7, 2013. eaworldview.com/2013/08/syria-feature-which-insurgents-captured-the-menagh-airbase.

[89] "Statement on the Formation of the Supreme Military Council Command of Syria," Carnegie Middle East Center, December 15, 2012. carnegie-mec.org/diwan/50445?lang=en.

[90] "Syrian T-55 Hit by Concourse Missile," Military.com, July 8, 2013. military.com/video/operations-and-strategy/antitank-weapons/syrian-t-55-hit-by-concourse-missile/2534632071001. See: "Syria Rebels Deploy Concourse Missiles Against Dictator's Army Checkpoint," Syria Today, October 20, 2013. youtube.com/watch?v=T-8nhHZKhgk.

[91] Luis Martinez, "U.S. Ambassador Makes Secret Crossing Into Syria to Briefly Meet With Rebels," ABC News, May 10, 2013. abcnews.go.com/blogs/politics/2013/05/us-ambassador-makes-secret-crossing-into-syria-to-briefly-meet-with-rebels.

92 Michael R. Gordon, *Degrade and Destroy: The Inside Story of the War Against the Islamic State, from Barack Obama to Donald Trump* (New York: Farrar, Straus and Giroux, 2022), Chapter 3.

93 Robert Ford, "Among Syria's Revolutionaries," *New Lines Magazine*, October 14, 2020. newlinesmag.com/first-person/among-syrias-revolutionaries.

94 "Syria conflict: US Senator John McCain visits rebels," BBC News, May 27, 2013. bbc.com/news/world-us-canada-22683261.

95 Dana El Baltaji, "Syria Rebels Threaten to Wipe Out Shiite, Alawite Towns," Bloomberg News, May 21, 2013. bloomberg.com/news/articles/2013-05-21/syria-rebels-threaten-to-wipe-out-shiite-alawite-towns. For the full *Al-Arabiya* interview, see "Colonel Zakaria reveals for the first time the facts and secrets of the battle of Al-Qusayr," International News, May 20, 2013. youtube.com/watch?v=6tW5-yI4YaM.

96 Kevin Jon Heller, "Rebels in Syria Threaten Genocide Against the Shia," Opinio Juris, May 28, 2013. opiniojuris.org/2013/05/28/rebels-in-syria-threaten-genocide-against-the-shia.

97 Dana El Baltaji, "Syria Rebels Threaten to Wipe Out Shiite, Alawite Towns," Bloomberg News, May 21, 2013. bloomberg.com/news/articles/2013-05-21/syria-rebels-threaten-to-wipe-out-shiite-alawite-towns.

98 Mark Mazzetti, Robert F. Worth, and Michael R. Gordon, "Obama's Uncertain Path Amid Syria Bloodshed," *New York Times*, October 22, 2013. nytimes.com/2013/10/23/world/middleeast/obamas-uncertain-path-amid-syria-bloodshed.html.

99 Thomas Hegghammer and Aaron Y. Zelin, "How Syria's Civil War Became a Holy Crusade," Washington Institute for Near East Policy, July 7, 2013. washingtoninstitute.org/policy-analysis/how-syrias-civil-war-became-holy-crusade.

100 "Al-Qaradawi: Al-Assad is a prisoner of his sect, and Syria is more ahead of the revolts than its neighbors" (Arabic), *Al-Ahram*, March 25, 2011. gate.ahram.org.eg/News/53398.aspx.

101 "Al-Qaradhawi issues a fatwa to kill millions of Syrians, whether combatants or civilians," UsaDegage, December 16, 2012. youtube.com/watch?v=ZgVF0t2mfsE&feature=youtu.be.

102 "Thus al-Qaradhawi incited the killing of al-Bouti," 24.ae, March 28, 2013. youtube.com/watch?v=jpMIa1ACn1g.

103 Hania Mourtada and Anne Barnard, "Dozens of Shiites Reported Killed in Raid by Syria Rebels," *New York Times*, June 12, 2013. nytimes.com/2013/06/13/world/middleeast/syria.html.

104 "Reports of 'massacre' in eastern Syria," Al Jazeera, June 12, 2013. aljazeera.com/news/2013/06/12/reports-of-massacre-in-eastern-syria.

105 "Syria rebels 'kill Shia residents of eastern village,'" BBC News, June 12, 2013. bbc.com/news/world-middle-east-22870776.

106 Fernande van Tets, "Syria: 60 Shia Muslims massacred in rebel 'cleansing' of Hatla," *The Independent*, June 13, 2013. independent.co.uk/news/world/middle-east/syria-60-shia-muslims-massacred-rebel-cleansing-hatla-8656301.html.

107 Ibid.

108 "Liwa al-Tawhid threatens to transfer the battle to Lebanon and calls for attacking two Shiite villages in Syria" (Arabic), *Al-Quds Al-Arabi*, May 29, 2013. alquds.co.uk/-لواء‎ التوحيد-يهدد-بنقل-المعركة-إلى-لبن.

[109] "Syrian civil war: Bashar al-Assad's forces take strategic town of Qusayr," Australian Broadcasting Corporation, June 5, 2013. abc.net.au/news/2013-06-05/syrian-army-overruns-rebels-forces-in-qusayr/4735618.

[110] Mark Mazzetti, Robert F. Worth, and Michael R. Gordon, "Obama's Uncertain Path Amid Syria Bloodshed," *New York Times*, October 22, 2013. nytimes.com/2013/10/23/world/middleeast/obamas-uncertain-path-amid-syria-bloodshed.html.

[111] Glenn Thrush and Reid Epstein, "Obama's forced hand on Syria," *Politico*, June 13, 2013. politico.com/story/2013/06/president-obama-syria-chemical-weapons-092782.

[112] "U.S. sending Patriot missiles to Jordan, may remain beyond drills," Reuters, June 4, 2013. reuters.com/article/us-jordan-us-syria/u-s-sending-patriot-missiles-to-jordan-may-remain-beyond-drills-idUSBRE95315R20130604.

[113] Josh Rogin, "Top Democrat endorses Syria no-fly zone," *Foreign Policy*, March 19, 2013. foreignpolicy.com/2013/03/19/top-democrat-endorses-syria-no-fly-zone.

[114] Burgess Everett, "McCain, Graham call for no-fly zone," *Politico*, June 14, 2022. politico.com/story/2013/06/syria-no-fly-zone-092766.

[115] Dexter Filkins, "The Thin Red Line: Inside the White House debate over Syria," *The New Yorker*, May 6, 2013. newyorker.com/magazine/2013/05/13/the-thin-red-line-2.

Chapter 15

[1] Mark Landler, "Obama Threatens Force Against Syria," *New York Times*, August 20, 2012. nytimes.com/2012/08/21/world/middleeast/obama-threatens-force-against-syria.html.

[2] Mark Mazzetti, Robert F. Worth, and Michael R. Gordon, "Obama's Uncertain Path Amid Syria Bloodshed," *New York Times*, October 22, 2013. nytimes.com/2013/10/23/world/middleeast/obamas-uncertain-path-amid-syria-bloodshed.html.

[3] Adam Entous, Siobhan Gorman, and Cassell Bryan-Low, "Networks of Spies Aid Syria Gas Probe," *Wall Street Journal*, August 23, 2013. wsj.com/articles/networks-of-spies-aid-syria-gas-probe-1377300693.

[4] Charles Glass, "Tell Me How This Ends: America's muddled involvement with Syria," *Harper's Magazine*, March 27, 2018. harpers.org/archive/2019/02/american-involvement-in-syria.

[5] Howard LaFranchi, "Hillary Clinton floats a Syria no-fly zone. How real an option for US?" *Christian Science Monitor*, August 13, 2012. csmonitor.com/USA/Foreign-Policy/2012/0813/Hillary-Clinton-floats-a-Syria-no-fly-zone.-How-real-an-option-for-US.

[6] Ibid.

[7] Zaid Jilani, "In secret Goldman Sachs speech Hillary Clinton admitted a no-fly zone would 'kill a lot of Syrians,'" *The Intercept*, October 10, 2016. theintercept.com/2016/10/10/in-secret-goldman-sachs-speech-hillary-clinton-admitted-no-fly-zone-would-kill-a-lot-of-syrians.

[8] Salim Abraham, "Farid Ghadry, Syria's Chalabi: From Washington to Damascus," Syria Comment (blog), March 25, 2007. joshualandis.com/blog/farid-ghadry-syrias-chalabi-from-washington-to-damascus-by-salim-abraham.

[9] "Syrian opposition groups call for no-fly zone," Australian Broadcasting Corporation, September 29, 2011. abc.net.au/pm/content/2011/s3329018.htm.

[10] "Syria's Homs under a military siege, activists say," CNN, December 24, 2011. edition.cnn.com/2011/12/24/world/meast/syria-unrest/index.html.

11 "Syrian doctors speaks of horrors faced by civilians," Al Jazeera, April 1, 2012. youtube.com/watch?v=sYttYiOXkVw.

12 Azmi Bishara, *Syria: A Path to Freedom from Suffering* (Beirut: Arab Center for Research and Policy Studies, 2013), Chapter 5.

13 Hillary Clinton Email Archive, "H: MEMO, SYRIA ON THE EDGE. SID," WikiLeaks, June 19, 2011. wikileaks.org/clinton-emails/emailid/12602.

14 "GlobalPost: Qaddafi apparently sodomized after capture," CBS News, October 24, 2011. cbsnews.com/news/globalpost-qaddafi-apparently-sodomized-after-capture.

15 "AFP: Erdogan visits Libya as NTC and pro-Gaddafi forces clash," France 24, September 16, 2011. france24.com/en/20110916-libya-turkey-erdogan-visit-ntc-forces-clash-pro-gaddafi-resistance-sirte-bani-walid.

16 "Moazzem Begg: Syria's honor and betrayal," 5 Pillars, November 9, 2019. youtube.com/watch?v=CUB1VYFUhus&feature=youtu.be.

17 Christopher Phillips, *The Battle for Syria: International Rivalry in the New Middle East* (Llandysul, Wales: Gomer Press Ltd, 2016), p. 171.

18 Georges Malbrunot, "Bachar el-Assad a sauvé son pouvoir, mais règne sur un champ de ruines," *Le Figaro*, December 16, 2020. lefigaro.fr/international/bachar-el-assad-a-sauve-son-pouvoir-mais-regne-sur-un-champ-de-ruines-20201216.

19 Christian Chesnot and Georges Malbrunot, *Les Chemins De Damas: Le dossier noir de la relation franco-syrienne* (Paris: Robert Laffont, 2014), p. 192.

20 Ibid., p. 183.

21 "French Philosopher Bernard Henri Levy: What was done in Libya can be done in Syria," Middle East Media Research Institute, July 27, 2012. memri.org/player/clip/12513/1/1.

22 Alain Gresh, "France's new Neocons," *Le Monde*, November 20, 2013. mondediplo.com/outsidein/france-s-new-neocons.

23 "France's Hollande too passive on Syria- Bernard: Henri Levy," Reuters, August 3, 2012. reuters.com/article/us-syria-crisis-france-idUSBRE8720F420120803.

24 "Des Syriens demandent réparation à Fabius," *Le Figaro*, October 12, 2014. lefigaro.fr/flash-actu/2014/12/10/97001-20141210FILWWW00263-des-syriens-demandent-reparation-a-fabius.php.

25 Nu'man Abd al-Wahid, *Debunking the Myth of America's Poodle: Great Britain Wants War* (London: Zero Books, 2020).

26 "France, U.K. Have Differing Motives for Intervening in Libya," *Forbes*, March 29, 2011. forbes.com/sites/energysource/2011/03/29/france-u-k-have-differing-motives-for-intervening-in-libya.

27 Richard Spencer, "Britain drew up plans to build 100,000-strong Syrian rebel army," *The Telegraph*, July 4, 2014. telegraph.co.uk/news/worldnews/middleeast/syria/10947773/Britain-drew-up-plans-to-build-100000-strong-Syrian-rebel-army.html.

28 Simon Walters, "Ex-Army head: PM is to blame for rise of ISIS: Damning accusation by Chief of Staff in explosive new Cameron biography," *Daily Mail*, August 29, 2015. dailymail.co.uk/news/article-3215566/Ex-Army-head-PM-blame-rise-ISIS-Damning-accusation-Chief-Staff-explosive-new-Cameron-biography.html.

29 Ammar Abd al-Hamid, "The Shredded Tapestry: The State of Syria Today," Foundation for Defense of Democracies, September 25, 2022. fdd.org/analysis/op-eds/2012/09/25/the-shredded-tapestry-the-state-of-syria-today.

30 Rania Abouzeid, "Syria's Secular and Islamist Rebels: Who Are the Saudis and the Qataris Arming?" *Time*, September 18, 2012. world.time.com/2012/09/18/syrias-secular-and-islamist-rebels-who-are-the-saudis-and-the-qataris-arming.

31 Eric Schmitt and David E. Sanger, "Hints of Syrian Chemical Push Set Off Global Effort to Stop It," *New York Times*, January 7, 2013. nytimes.com/2013/01/08/world/middleeast/chemical-weapons-showdown-with-syria-led-to-rare-accord.html.

32 Ilan Ben Zion, "Stop Assad before he uses chemical weapons, Syria's opposition leader implores international community," *The Times of Israel*, December 7, 2012. timesofisrael.com/syrian-opposition-chief-implores-international-community-to-act-not-talk-against-assad.

33 Seymour Hersh, "Whose Sarin?" *London Review of Books*, December 19, 2013. lrb.co.uk/the-paper/v35/n24/seymour-m.-hersh/whose-sarin.

34 Alistair Dawber, "'Chemical weapons were used on Homs': Syria's military police defector tells of nerve gas attack," *The Independent*, December 26, 2012. independent.co.uk/news/world/middle-east/chemical-weapons-were-used-on-homs-syria-s-military-police-defector-tells-of-nerve-gas-attack-8431380.html.

35 Raffi Khatchadourian, "The Case of Agent 15: Did Syria Use a Nerve Agent?" *The New Yorker*, January 16, 2013. newyorker.com/news/news-desk/the-case-of-agent-15-did-syria-use-a-nerve-agent.

36 Josh Rogin, "Exclusive: Secret State Department cable: Chemical weapons used in Syria," *Foreign Policy*, January 25, 2013. foreignpolicy.com/2013/01/15/exclusive-secret-state-department-cable-chemical-weapons-used-in-syria.

37 Raffi Khatchadourian, "The Case of Agent 15: Did Syria Use a Nerve Agent?" *The New Yorker*, January 16, 2013. newyorker.com/news/news-desk/the-case-of-agent-15-did-syria-use-a-nerve-agent.

38 Elise Labott, "U.S.: Syria didn't use chemical weapons in Homs incident," CNN, January 6, 2013. security.blogs.cnn.com/2013/01/16/u-s-syria-didnt-use-chemical-weapons-in-homs-incident.

39 Elaine M. Grossman, "Why Doubts Are Growing About An Alleged Syrian Chemical Attack," Yahoo News, January 29, 2013. news.yahoo.com/why-doubts-growing-alleged-syrian-chemical-attack-162949465--politics.html.

40 Adam Entous, Siobhan Gorman, and Cassell Bryan-Low, "Networks of Spies Aid Syria Gas Probe," *Wall Street Journal*, August 23, 2013. wsj.com/articles/networks-of-spies-aid-syria-gas-probe-1377300693.

41 Michael R. Gordon, "Consulate Supported Claim of Syria Gas Attack, Report Says," *New York Times*, January 15, 2013. nytimes.com/2013/01/16/world/middleeast/consulate-said-to-support-claim-of-syrian-gas-attack.html?ref=michaelrgordon&_r=0.

42 Eric Schmitt and David E. Sanger, "Hints of Syrian Chemical Push Set Off Global Effort to Stop It," *New York Times*, January 7, 2013. nytimes.com/2013/01/08/world/middleeast/chemical-weapons-showdown-with-syria-led-to-rare-accord.html.

43 Oliver Holmes and Erika Solomon, "Alleged chemical attack kills 25 in northern Syria," Reuters, March 19, 2013. reuters.com/article/us-syria-crisis-chemical/alleged-chemical-attack-kills-25-in-northern-syria-idUSBRE92I0A220130319.

44 Vanessa Beeley, "'Aleppo Media Centre' Funded by French Foreign Office, EU and US," 21st Century Wire, September 20, 2016. 21stcenturywire.com/2016/09/20/exclusive-aleppo-media-centre-funded-by-french-foreign-office-eu-and-us.

45 "Syrians trade Khan al-Assal chemical weapons claims," BBC News, March 19, 2013. bbc.com/news/world-middle-east-21841217.

46 Anne Barnard, "Syria and Activists Trade Charges on Chemical Weapons," *New York Times*, March 19, 2013. nytimes.com/2013/03/20/world/middleeast/syria-developments.html.

47 Martin Chulov, "Syria attacks involved chemical weapons, rebels and regime claim," *The Guardian*, March 19, 2013. theguardian.com/world/2013/mar/19/syria-rocket-attacks-chemical-weapons.

48 "Final Report." United Nations Mission to Investigate Allegations of the Use of Chemical Weapons in the Syrian Arab Republic, December 13, 2013. unoda-web.s3.amazonaws.com/wp-content/uploads/2013/12/report.pdf.

49 Adam Larson, "The Ghouta Massacre's Sarin Myth, Brightly Lit: Exploring Kafr Batna's... Rebel Gas Chambers?" Monitor on Massacre Marketing (blog), May 4, 2013. libyancivilwar.blogspot.com/2016/01/was-syria-chemical-weapons-probe.html.

50 "Soil sample proves chemical weapons used in Syria," *The Times of Israel*, April 13, 2013. timesofisrael.com/soil-sample-proves-chemical-weapons-used-in-syria.

51 Rick Gladstone and Eric Schmitt, "Syria Faces New Claim on Chemical Arms," *New York Times*, April 18, 2013. nytimes.com/2013/04/19/world/middleeast/Syria.html.

52 "Ban appoints Swedish scientist to lead probe into alleged chemical weapons use in Syria," United Nations, March 26, 2013. news.un.org/en/story/2013/03/435562.

53 "Soil sample proves chemical weapons used in Syria," *The Times of Israel*, April 13, 2013. timesofisrael.com/soil-sample-proves-chemical-weapons-used-in-syria.

54 "Syria Is Waiting Investigation Team into Khan al-Assal Incident, Demands Credible Information on Other Claims," Syrian Arab News Agency, May 1, 2013. sana.sy/eng/22/2013/05/01/480100.htm.

55 "Final Report." United Nations Mission to Investigate Allegations of the Use of Chemical Weapons in the Syrian Arab Republic, December 13, 2013. unoda-web.s3.amazonaws.com/wp-content/uploads/2013/12/report.pdf.

56 Leslie Gelb, "Leslie H. Gelb: Obama is Right on Chemical Warfare in Syria," *The Daily Beast*, April 27, 2013. thedailybeast.com/leslie-h-gelb-obama-is-right-on-chemical-warfare-in-syria.

57 Adam Larson, "The Ghouta Massacre's Sarin Myth, Brightly Lit: Exploring Kafr Batna's... Rebel Gas Chambers?" Monitor on Massacre Marketing (blog), May 4, 2013. libyancivilwar.blogspot.com/2016/01/was-syria-chemical-weapons-probe.html.

58 "Syria: Chemical weapons used by rebels came from Turkey," *The Times of Israel*, April 27, 2013. timesofisrael.com/syrian-official-chemical-weapons-used-by-rebels-came-from-turkey.

59 Barton Gellman, "U.S. Spied on Iraq Via U.N.," *Washington Post*, March 2, 1999. washingtonpost.com/wp-srv/inatl/daily/march99/unscom2.htm.

60 "Syrian rebels call on world to put words to action," CBS News, April 26, 2013. cbsnews.com/news/syrian-rebels-call-on-world-to-put-words-to-action.

61 Mohammed Sergie and Karen Leigh, "Evidence of Nerve Gas in Aleppo Deaths," ABC News, April 17, 2013. abcnews.go.com/International/evidence-nerve-gas-aleppo-deaths/story?id=18977091.

62 Anthony Lloyd, "Revealed: tragic victims of Syria's nerve gas war," *The Times*, April 26, 2013. thetimes.co.uk/article/revealed-tragic-victims-of-syrias-nerve-gas-war-zncnccbx3nw.

63 Case Consortium @ Columbia, "Just Enough Alarm: *GlobalPost* and the Syrian Chemical Attack Story," *Columbia School of Journalism Case Consortium*, 2014. ccnmtl.columbia.edu/projects/caseconsortium/casestudies/148/casestudy/files/global/148/Global Post final2.pdf.

64 Tracey Shelton, "Syria: The horrific chemical weapons attack that probably wasn't a chemical weapons attack," *GlobalPost*, April 30, 2013. theworld.org/dispatch/news/regions/middle-east/syria/130430/syria-chemical-weapons-attack-aleppo-sheikh-maqsoud-april-13-assad-obama-fsa.

65 Eliot Higgins, "Three Chemical Weapon Specialist Answer Questions About Chemical Weapons In Syria," Brown Moses (blog), May 21, 2013. brown-moses.blogspot.com/2013/05/three-chemical-weapon-specialist-answer.html.

66 Kit Klarenberg, "British intelligence operative's involvement in Ukraine crisis signals false flag attacks ahead," The Grayzone, March 24, 2022. thegrayzone.com/2022/03/24/british-intelligence-ukraine-false-flag.

67 Anthony Lloyd, "Revealed: tragic victims of Syria's nerve gas war," *The Times*, April 26, 2013. thetimes.co.uk/article/revealed-tragic-victims-of-syrias-nerve-gas-war-zncnccbx3nw.

68 Christiane Amanpour, "American doctor gives 'proof of chemical weapon use' to U.S.," CNN, April 29, 2013. amanpour.blogs.cnn.com/2013/04/29/american-doctor-gives-proof-of-chemical-weapon-use-to-u-s.

69 Eli Lake, "The president who allowed genocide — what Syrians say of Obama," *New York Post*, September 27, 2016. nypost.com/2016/09/27/the-president-who-allowed-genocide-what-syrians-say-of-obama.

70 Max Blumenthal, "'Al Qaeda's MASH unit': How the Syrian American Medical Society is selling regime change and driving the US to war," The Grayzone, April 12, 2018. thegrayzone.com/2018/04/12/al-qaedas-mash-unit-how-the-syrian-american-medical-society-is-selling-regime-change-and-driving-the-us-to-war.

71 Julian Perry Robinson, "Alleged use of chemical weapons in Syria," *Harvard Sussex Program Occasional Paper*, June 26, 2013. sussex.ac.uk/Units/spru/hsp/occasional papers/HSPOP_4.pdf.

72 Anthony Deutsch, "'Evidence' of Syrian chemical weapon use not up to U.N. standard," Reuters, April 26, 2013. reuters.com/article/syria-crisis-chemical-weapons/evidence-of-syrian-chemical-weapon-use-not-up-to-u-n-standard-idUSL6N0DD2F320130426.

73 Ibid.

74 "U.S. intelligence believes Syria's Assad used chemical weapons 'on a small scale' by Anne Gearan and Craig Whitlock," *Washington Post*, April 25, 2013. washingtonpost.com/world/middle_east/us-intelligence-agencies-assad-used-chemical-weapons-on-a-small-scale/2013/04/25/208346aa-adc0-11e2-98ef-d1072ed3cc27_story.html.

75 The Editorial Board, "Were Chemical Weapons Used in Syria?" *New York Times*, April 24, 2013. nytimes.com/2013/04/25/opinion/were-chemical-weapons-used-in-syria.html.

76 "Final Report." United Nations Mission to Investigate Allegations of the Use of Chemical Weapons in the Syrian Arab Republic, December 13, 2013. unoda-web.s3.amazonaws.com/wp-content/uploads/2013/12/report.pdf.

77 "Syria conflict: BBC shown 'signs of chemical attack,'" BBC News, May 16, 2013. bbc.com/news/world-middle-east-22549861.

78 Ibid.

79 Tracey Shelton and Erin Cunningham, "Turkish doctors: No nerve gas in Syrian victims' blood," *Anchorage Daily News*, May 5, 2013. adn.com/nation-world/article/turkish-doctors-say-no-nerve-gas-syrian-victims-blood/2013/05/06.

80 Christophe Ayad, "Syrie: Paris et Londres affirment avoir des preuves de l'utilisation de gaz sarin," *Le Monde*, June 4, 2013. lemonde.fr/proche-orient/article/2013/06/04/laurent-fabius-confirme-l-utilisation-de-gaz-sarin-en-syrie_3424140_3218.html.

[81] "AFP: Video: Doctors record 'chemical attacks' in Syria," Al-Arabiya, June 2, 2013. english.alarabiya.net/News/middle-east/2013/06/01/Doctors-record-chemical-attacks-in-Syria.

[82] Ibid.

[83] "Syrian doctors speaks of horrors faced by civilians," Al Jazeera, April 1, 2012. youtube.com/watch?v=sYttYiOXkVw.

[84] Robert Stuart, "Complaint to the BBC regarding Panorama's 'Saving Syria's Children,'" Australians for Reconciliation in Syria, July 2, 2014. australiansforreconciliationinsyria.org/complaint-to-the-bbc-regarding-panoramas-saving-syrias-children.

[85] Anne-Marie Slaughter, "Obama should remember Rwanda as he weighs action in Syria," *Washington Post*, April 26, 2013. washingtonpost.com/opinions/obama-should-remember-rwanda-as-he-weighs-action-in-syria/2013/04/26/08f77c20-ae8a-11e2-8bf6-e70cb6ae066e_story.html.

[86] Bill Keller, "Syria Is Not Iraq," *New York Times*, May 5, 2013. nytimes.com/2013/05/06/opinion/keller-syria-is-not-iraq.html.

[87] Damien Mcelroy, "UN accuses Syrian rebels of chemical weapons use," *The Telegraph*, May 6, 2013. telegraph.co.uk/news/worldnews/middleeast/syria/10039672/UN-accuses-Syrian-rebels-of-chemical-weapons-use.html.

[88] Tony Cartalucci, "NATO's War on Syria Just Got Dirtier," Centre for Research on Globalization, December 10, 2013. globalresearch.ca/natos-war-on-syria-just-got-dirtier/5361103. (Screenshots of emails between Matthew VanDyke and Eliot Higgins are contained in this article.)

[89] Seymour Hersh, "The Red Line and the Rat Line," *London Review of Books*, April 17, 2014. lrb.co.uk/the-paper/v36/n08/seymour-m.-hersh/the-red-line-and-the-rat-line.

[90] Jean-Philippe Rémy, "Chemical warfare in Syria," *Le Monde*, May 27, 2013. lemonde.fr/proche-orient/article/2013/05/27/chemical-war-in-syria_3417708_3218.html.

[91] Matthew Schofield, "Chemical Weapons Experts Still Skeptical About US Claim That Syria Used Sarin," McClatchyDC, June 15, 2013. mcclatchydc.com/news/nation-world/world/article24750067.html.

[92] Anne Barnard, "Syria and Activists Trade Charges on Chemical Weapons," *New York Times*, March 19, 2013. nytimes.com/2013/03/20/world/middleeast/syria-developments.html.

[93] Jean-Philippe Rémy, "Des analyses confirment l'ampleur de l'usage de sarin en Syrie," *Le Monde*, June 28, 2013. lemonde.fr/proche-orient/article/2013/06/28/des-analyses-confirment-l-ampleur-de-l-usage-de-sarin-en-syrie_3438187_3218.html.

[94] "Final Report." United Nations Mission to Investigate Allegations of the Use of Chemical Weapons in the Syrian Arab Republic, December 13, 2013. unoda-web.s3.amazonaws.com/wp-content/uploads/2013/12/report.pdf.

[95] "Briefing note on the Integrity Initiative," by Paul McKeigue, David Miller, Jake Mason, and Piers Robinson, Working Group on Syria Propaganda and Media, December 21, 2018. syriapropagandamedia.org/working-papers/briefing-note-on-the-integrity-initiative.

[96] Haley Bissegger, "Timeline: How President Obama handled Syria," *The Hill*, September 15, 2013. thehill.com/policy/international/182367-timeline-how-president-obama-handled-syria.

[97] Glenn Thrush and Reid Epstein, "Obama's forced hand on Syria," *Politico*, June 13, 2013. politico.com/story/2013/06/president-obama-syria-chemical-weapons-092782.

[98] Ben Rhodes, "Inside the White House During the Syrian 'Red Line' Crisis," *The Atlantic*, June 3, 2018. theatlantic.com/international/archive/2018/06/inside-the-white-house-during-the-syrian-red-line-crisis/561887.

[99] Dan Roberts, "US says it will arm Syrian rebels following chemical weapons tests," *The Guardian*, June 14, 2014. theguardian.com/world/2013/jun/13/syria-chemical-weapons-us-confirm.

[100] C.J. Chivers, Eric Schmitt, and Mark Mazzetti, "In Turnabout, Syria Rebels Get Libyan Weapons," *New York Times*, June 21, 2013. nytimes.com/2013/06/22/world/africa/in-a-turnabout-syria-rebels-get-libyan-weapons.html.

[101] Mark Hosenball, Phil Stewart, "Exclusive: Congress delaying U.S. aid to Syrian rebels — sources," Reuters, July 8, 2013. reuters.com/article/us-usa-syria-arms-idUSBRE96713N20130708.

[102] Mark Landler and Thom Shanker, "Pentagon Lays Out Options for U.S. Military Effort in Syria," *New York Times*, July 22, 2013. nytimes.com/2013/07/23/world/middleeast/pentagon-outlining-options-to-congress-suggests-syria-campaign-would-be-costly.html.

[103] Dan Roberts, "US says it will arm Syrian rebels following chemical weapons tests," *The Guardian*, June 14, 2014. theguardian.com/world/2013/jun/13/syria-chemical-weapons-us-confirm.

[104] "Chemical weapons trigger U.S. aid to Syrian rebels," *Columbus Dispatch*, June 14, 2013. eu.dispatch.com/story/news/military/2013/06/14/chemical-weapons-trigger-u-s/23380852007.

[105] "On-the-Record Conference Call by Deputy National Security Advisor for Strategic Communications Ben Rhodes on Syria," The White House Office of the Press Secretary, June 13, 2013. obamawhitehouse.archives.gov/the-press-office/2013/06/13/record-conference-call-deputy-national-security-advisor-strategic-commun.

[106] "AP: Syrian regime used chemical weapons twice in Aleppo: U.S. letter," CTV News, June 14, 2013. ctvnews.ca/world/syrian-regime-used-chemical-weapons-twice-in-aleppo-u-s-letter-1.1326064.

[107] Matthew Schofield, "Chemical Weapons Experts Still Skeptical About US Claim That Syria Used Sarin," McClatchyDC, June 15, 2013. mcclatchydc.com/news/nation-world/world/article24750067.html.

[108] Edith Lederer, "Russia accuses West of inventing chemical weapons claims," *The Times of Israel*, July 12, 2013. timesofisrael.com/russia-accuses-west-of-inventing-chemical-weapons-claims.

Chapter 16

[1] "AP: UN inspectors arrive in Damascus on chemical probe," *The Times of Israel*, August 18, 2013. timesofisrael.com/un-inspectors-arrive-in-damascus-on-chemical-probe.

[2] "Syria chemical attack: What we know," BBC News, September 24, 2013. bbc.com/news/world-middle-east-23927399.

[3] "AP: Obama aide says U.S. lacks 'irrefutable' evidence Syria's Assad used chemical weapons," PennLive, September 8, 2013. pennlive.com/midstate/2013/09/obama_aid_says_us_lacks_irrefu.html.

[4] Mark Mazzetti, Robert F. Worth, and Michael R. Gordon, "Obama's Uncertain Path Amid Syria Bloodshed," *New York Times*, October 22, 2013. nytimes.com/2013/10/23/world/middleeast/obamas-uncertain-path-amid-syria-bloodshed.html.

5 Adam Entous, Sam Dagher, and Siobhan Gorman, "U.S., Allies Prepare to Act as Syria Intelligence Mounts," *Wall Street Journal*, August 27, 2013. wsj.com/articles/SB10001424127887324906304579039342815115978.

6 "United Nations Mission to Investigate Allegations of the Use of Chemical Weapons in the Syrian Arab Republic: Report on the Alleged Use of Chemical Weapons in the Ghouta Area of Damascus on 21 August 2013," United Nations, September 13, 2013. un.org/zh/focus/northafrica/cwinvestigation.pdf.

7 "Syria conflict: 'Chemical attacks kill hundreds,'" BBC News, August 21, 2013. bbc.com/news/world-middle-east-23777201.

8 Adam Entous, Sam Dagher, and Siobhan Gorman, "U.S., Allies Prepare to Act as Syria Intelligence Mounts," *Wall Street Journal*, August 27, 2013. wsj.com/articles/SB10001424127887324906304579039342815115978.

9 Kimberly Dozier, "US says 'very little doubt' Assad behind chemical attack," *The Times of Israel*, August 25, 2013. timesofisrael.com/us-official-says-very-little-doubt-assad-behind-chemical-attack.

10 Gareth Porter, "In Rush to Strike Syria, U.S. Tried to Derail U.N. Probe," Inter Press Service, August 27, 2013. ipsnews.net/2013/08/in-rush-to-strike-syria-u-s-tried-to-derail-u-n-probe.

11 Adam Entous, Sam Dagher, and Siobhan Gorman, "U.S., Allies Prepare to Act as Syria Intelligence Mounts," *Wall Street Journal*, August 27, 2013. wsj.com/articles/SB10001424127887324906304579039342815115978.

12 Harriet Sherwood, "Israeli intelligence 'intercepted Syrian regime talk about chemical attack,'" *The Guardian*, August 28, 2013. theguardian.com/world/2013/aug/28/israeli-intelligence-intercepted-syria-chemical-talk.

13 Adam Entous, Sam Dagher, and Siobhan Gorman, "U.S., Allies Prepare to Act as Syria Intelligence Mounts," *Wall Street Journal*, August 27, 2013. wsj.com/articles/SB10001424127887324906304579039342815115978.

14 Ben Rhodes, "Inside the White House During the Syrian 'Red Line' Crisis," *The Atlantic*, June 3, 2018. theatlantic.com/international/archive/2018/06/inside-the-white-house-during-the-syrian-red-line-crisis/561887.

15 Kimberly Dozier, "AP sources: Intelligence on weapons no 'slam dunk,'" Associated Press, August 30, 2013. apnews.com/article/c2ad647bc3c248f286ad4d186f1ba9d2.

16 Ben Rhodes, "Inside the White House During the Syrian 'Red Line' Crisis," *The Atlantic*, June 3, 2018. theatlantic.com/international/archive/2018/06/inside-the-white-house-during-the-syrian-red-line-crisis/561887.

17 Isabelle Lasserre, "Syrie: l'opération anti-Assad a commence," *Le Figaro*, August 22, 2013. lefigaro.fr/international/2013/08/22/01003-20130822ARTFIG00438-syrie-l-operation-anti-assad-a-commence.php.

18 Ibid.

19 Christian Chesnot and Georges Malbrunot, *Les Chemins de Damas: Le dossier noir de la relation franco-syrienne* (Paris: Robert Laffont, 2014), p. 255.

20 "Obama warned on Syria intel," Consortium for Independent Journalism, *Consortium News*, September 6, 2013. consortiumnews.com/2013/09/06/obama-warned-on-syrian-intel.

21 Richard Spencer, "Britain drew up plans to build 100,000-strong Syrian rebel army," *The Telegraph*, July 4, 2014. telegraph.co.uk/news/worldnews/middleeast/syria/10947773/Britain-drew-up-plans-to-build-100000-strong-Syrian-rebel-army.html.

22 Erika Solomon, "Syrian rebels plan raids to exploit Western strikes — commander," Reuters, August 31, 2014. reuters.com/article/uk-syria-crisis-rebels-strike/syrian-rebels-plan-raids-to-exploit-western-strikes-commander-idUKBRE97U06520130831.

23 Patrick McDonnell and Shashank Bengali, "Syrian rebels allege new gas attack," *Los Angeles Times*, August 21, 2013. latimes.com/world/la-fg-syria-poison-gas-20130822-story.html.

24 Noah Shachtman, "Exclusive: Intercepted Calls Prove Syrian Army Used Nerve Gas, U.S. Spies Say," *Foreign Policy*, August 27, 2013. foreignpolicy.com/2013/08/27/exclusive-intercepted-calls-prove-syrian-army-used-nerve-gas-u-s-spies-say.

25 Kimberly Dozier and Zeina Karam, "AP: Doubts linger over Syria gas attack evidence," *The Times of Israel*, September 8, 2013. timesofisrael.com/doubts-linger-over-syria-gas-attack-evidence.

26 Rick Gladstone and C.J. Chivers, "Forensic Details in U.N. Report Point to Assad's Use of Gas," *New York Times*, September 16, 2013. nytimes.com/2013/09/17/world/europe/syria-united-nations.html.

27 Eliot Higgins, "Sy Hersh's Chemical Misfire," *Foreign Policy*, December 9, 2013. foreignpolicy.com/2013/12/09/sy-hershs-chemical-misfire.

28 Rick Gladstone and C.J. Chivers, "Forensic Details in U.N. Report Point to Assad's Use of Gas," *New York Times*, September 16, 2013. nytimes.com/2013/09/17/world/europe/syria-united-nations.html.

29 C.J. Chivers, "New Study Refines View of Sarin Attack in Syria," *New York Times*, December 28, 2013. nytimes.com/2013/12/29/world/middleeast/new-study-refines-view-of-sarin-attack-in-syria.html.

30 Seymour Hersh, "Whose Sarin?" *London Review of Books*, December 19, 2013. lrb.co.uk/the-paper/v35/n24/seymour-m.-hersh/whose-sarin.

31 Michael Kobs, Chris Kabusk, and Adam Larson, "Ghouta Sarin Attack: Review of Open-Source Evidence," Rootclaim, n.d. rootclaim-media.s3.amazonaws.com/syria2013evidence.pdf.

32 Seymour Hersh, "Whose Sarin?" *London Review of Books*, December 19, 2013. lrb.co.uk/the-paper/v35/n24/seymour-m.-hersh/whose-sarin.

33 "Obama warned on Syria intel," Consortium for Independent Journalism, *Consortium News*, September 6, 2013. consortiumnews.com/2013/09/06/obama-warned-on-syrian-intel.

34 Mark Landler, David E. Sanger, and Thom Shanker, "Obama Set for Limited Strike on Syria as British Vote No," *New York Times*, August 29, 2013. nytimes.com/2013/08/30/us/politics/obama-syria.html.

35 Glenn Thrush, "Obama's Obama," *Politico Magazine*, January/February 2016. politico.com/magazine/story/2016/01/denis-mcdonough-profile-213488.

36 Seymour Hersh, "The Red Line and the Rat Line," *London Review of Books*, April 17, 2014. lrb.co.uk/the-paper/v36/n08/seymour-m.-hersh/the-red-line-and-the-rat-line.

37 Glenn Thrush, "Obama's Obama," *Politico Magazine*, January/February 2016. politico.com/magazine/story/2016/01/denis-mcdonough-profile-213488.

38 Kimberly Dozier and Zeina Karam, "AP: Doubts linger over Syria gas attack evidence," *The Times of Israel*, September 8, 2013. timesofisrael.com/doubts-linger-over-syria-gas-attack-evidence.

39 Patrick McDonnell and Shashank Bengali, "Syrian rebels allege new gas attack," *Los Angeles Times*, August 21, 2013. latimes.com/world/la-fg-syria-poison-gas-20130822-story.html.

40 "Jared Cohen: The Changing Nature of Political Transitions," Stanford Graduate School of Business, May 23, 2012. youtube.com/watch?v=E9PHRLJaG_Y.

41 "Statement by the President on Syria," The White House Office of the Press Secretary, August 31, 2013. obamawhitehouse.archives.gov/the-press-office/2013/08/31/statement-president-syria.

42 "U.S.: Proven link of Assad to gas attack lacking," ABC News, September 8, 2013. abc13.com/archive/9240433.

43 Ben Hubbard and Hwaida Saad, "Images of Death in Syria, but No Proof of Chemical Attack," New York Times, August 21, 2013. nytimes.com/2013/08/22/world/middleeast/syria.html.

44 Patrick McDonnell and Shashank Bengali, "Syrian rebels allege new gas attack," Los Angeles Times, August 21, 2013. latimes.com/world/la-fg-syria-poison-gas-20130822-story.html.

45 "Syria conflict: 'Chemical attacks kill hundreds,'" BBC News, August 21, 2013. bbc.com/news/world-middle-east-23777201.

46 Ian Cobain, Alice Ross, Rob Evans, and Mona Mahmood, "How Britain funds the 'propaganda war' against Isis in Syria," The Guardian, May 3, 2016. theguardian.com/world/2016/may/03/how-britain-funds-the-propaganda-war-against-isis-in-syria.

47 Ben Norton, "Leaked docs expose massive Syria propaganda operation waged by Western govt contractors and media," The Grayzone, September 23, 2020. thegrayzone.com/2020/09/23/syria-leaks-uk-contractors-opposition-media.

48 Nicholas Watt, Rowena Mason and Nick Hopkins, "Blow to Cameron's authority as MPs rule out British assault on Syria," The Guardian, August 30, 2013. theguardian.com/politics/2013/aug/30/cameron-mps-syria.

49 "Syria crisis: Incendiary bomb victims 'like the walking dead,'" BBC News, August 29, 2013. bbc.com/news/av/world-23892594.

50 Robert Stuart, "Analysis of the 30 September 2013 BBC Panorama documentary 'Saving Syria's Children' and related BBC News reports," Fabrication in BBC Panorama. bbcpanoramasavingsyriaschildren.wordpress.com.

51 Ibid.

52 "Syria Crisis: Cameron loses Commons vote on Syria action," BBC News, August 30, 2013. bbc.com/news/uk-politics-23892783.

53 "'You Can Still See Their Blood': Executions, Indiscriminate Shootings, and Hostage Taking by Opposition Forces in Latakia Countryside," Human Rights Watch, October 2013. hrw.org/sites/default/files/reports/syria1013_ForUpload.pdf.

54 Ruth Sherlock, "Syrian rebels accused of sectarian murders," The Telegraph, August 11, 2013. telegraph.co.uk/news/worldnews/middleeast/syria/10236362/Syrian-rebels-accused-of-sectarian-murders.html.

55 Anne Barnard, "Syrian Civilians Bore Brunt of Rebels' Fury, Report Says," New York Times, October 11, 2013. nytimes.com/2013/10/11/world/middleeast/syrian-civilians-bore-brunt-of-rebels-fury-report-says.html.

56 Rania Abouzeid, "On Syria's front lines: A night in the field clinic: Scrambling to save lives in the Syrian conflict," Al Jazeera, August 28, 2013. america.aljazeera.com/articles/2013/8/28/a-night-in-the-fieldclinic.html.

57 Rania Abouzeid, No Turning Back: Life, Loss, and Hope in Wartime Syria (New York: W.W. Norton & Company, 2018), p. 233.

58 Ibid.

59 Vanessa Beeley, "One family talks about terrorist massacre in Ballouta August 2013," Vanessa Beeley (blog), November 3, 2018. patreon.com/posts/syria-one-family-22489877.

60 Greg Miller, "CIA ramping up covert training program for moderate Syrian rebels," *Washington Post*, October 2, 2013. washingtonpost.com/world/national-security/cia-ramping-up-covert-training-program-for-moderate-syrian-rebels/2013/10/02/a0bba084-2af6-11e3-8ade-a1f23cda135e_story.html.

61 Denis O'Brien, PhD, *Murder in the Sun Morgue: A Critique of the Sarin Myth and a Cyber-Investigation of the Ghouta Massacre* (Penury Press, 2014). scribd.com/document/230748990/Murder-in-the-SunMorgue.

62 Adam Larson, "The Ghouta Massacre's Sarin Myth, Brightly Lit: Exploring Kafr Batna's... Rebel Gas Chambers?" Monitor on Massacre Marketing (blog), May 22, 2014. libyancivilwar.blogspot.com/2014/11/the-ghouta-massacres-sarin-myth.html.

63 "Who is Responsible for Chemical Attacks in Syria? Guest Blog by Professor Paul McKeigue (Part 2)," Tim Hayward (blog), August 31, 2017. timhayward.wordpress.com/2017/08/31/who-is-responsible-for-chemical-attacks-in-syria-guest-blog-by-professor-paul-mckeigue-part-2.

64 Joshua Landis, "Zahran Alloush, his ideology and beliefs," Syria Comment (blog), December 15, 2013. joshualandis.com/blog/zahran-alloush.

65 "AFP: Syrian rebels using caged civilian captives as 'human shields': Dozens of men and women believed to be Alawites being held in metal cages as 'human shields' in Damascus suburb, local activists report," *The Telegraph*, November 2, 2015. telegraph.co.uk/news/worldnews/middleeast/syria/11971269/Syrian-rebels-using-caged-pro-Assad-captives-as-human-shields.html.

66 "Jaish al-Islam to leave Douma in return for releasing prisoners," Reuters, April 8, 2018. reuters.com/article/us-mideast-crisis-syria-ghouta-negotiati/jaish-al-islam-to-leave-douma-in-return-for-releasing-prisoners-idUKKBN1HF09Z?edition-redirect=uk.

67 Mona Mahmoud, "UN inspectors ordered out by regime after 90 minutes — doctors," *The Guardian*, August 26, 2013. theguardian.com/world/2013/aug/26/un-chemical-weapons-syria-90-minutes.

68 "Angela Kane on Syria chemical attack victims and autopsies," Human Rights Investigations, October 6, 2013. humanrightsinvestigations.org/2013/10/06/angela-kane-on-syria-chemical-attack-victims-and-autopsies.

69 Adam Larson, "The Ghouta Massacre's Sarin Myth, Brightly Lit: Exploring Kafr Batna's... Rebel Gas Chambers?" Monitor on Massacre Marketing (blog), May 22, 2014. libyancivilwar.blogspot.com/2014/11/the-ghouta-massacres-sarin-myth.html.

70 "United Nations Mission to Investigate Allegations of the Use of Chemical Weapons in the Syrian Arab Republic: Report on the Alleged Use of Chemical Weapons in the Ghouta Area of Damascus on 21 August 2013," United Nations, September 13, 2013. un.org/zh/focus/northafrica/cwinvestigation.pdf.

71 Sharmine Narwani and Radwan Mortada, "Questions Plague UN Report on Syria," Mideast Shuffle (blog), September 30, 2013. mideastshuffle.com/2013/09/30/questions-plague-un-report-on-syria.

72 Robert Parry, "NYT Replays Its Iraq Fiasco in Syria," Consortium for Independent Journalism, *Consortium News*, December 20, 2013. consortiumnews.com/2013/12/20/nyt-replays-its-iraq-fiasco-in-syria.

73 Gareth Porter, "New Data Raise Further Doubt on Official View of August 21 Gas Attack in Syria," Truthout, April 29, 2014. truthout.org/articles/new-data-raise-further-doubt-on-official-view-of-aug-21-gas-attack-in-syria.

74 Ibid.

75 "Final Report." United Nations Mission to Investigate Allegations of the Use of Chemical Weapons in the Syrian Arab Republic, December 13, 2013. unoda-web.s3.amazonaws.com/wp-content/uploads/2013/12/report.pdf.

76 Seymour Hersh, "Whose Sarin?" *London Review of Books*, December 19, 2013. lrb.co.uk/the-paper/v35/n24/seymour-m.-hersh/whose-sarin.

77 "Syria: Reported chemical weapons use," UK Joint Intelligence Organization, August 29, 2013.
assets.publishing.service.gov.uk/government/uploads/system/uploads/attachment_dat a/file/235094/Jp_115_JD_PM_Syria_Reported_Chemical_Weapon_Use_with_annex.p df.

78 Mehdi Hassan, "Syria: Chemical Weapons Expert Jean Pascal Zanders Says Gas Might Not Be Sarin, Urges Caution," *Huffington Post*, August 30, 2013. huffingtonpost.co.uk/2013/08/30/syria-sarin-claims_n_3843049.html.

79 Patrick McDonnell and Shashank Bengali, "Syrian rebels allege new gas attack," *Los Angeles Times*, August 21, 2013. latimes.com/world/la-fg-syria-poison-gas-20130822-story.html.

80 Hillary Clinton Email Archive, "SPOT REPORT 02/12/II," Email from Jake Sullivan to Hillary Clinton, WikiLeaks, February 12, 2022. wikileaks.org/clinton-emails/emailid/23225#efmAGIAHu.

81 United States Defense Intelligence Agency (DIA) Memo, U.S. Defense Intelligence Agency, August 12, 2020. judicialwatch.org/wp-content/uploads/2015/05/Pg.-291-Pgs.-287-293-JW-v-DOD-and-State-14-812-DOD-Release-2015-04-10-final-version11.pdf.

82 Anne Barnard and Eric Schmitt, "As Foreign Fighters Flood Syria, Fears of a New Extremist Haven," *New York Times*, August 8, 2013. nytimes.com/2013/08/09/world/middleeast/as-foreign-fighters-flood-syria-fears-of-a-new-extremist-haven.html.

83 Robert Ford, "Among Syria's Revolutionaries," *New Lines Magazine*, October 14, 2020. newlinesmag.com/first-person/among-syrias-revolutionaries.

84 "US funded FSA kills together with ISIL and Jabhat al-Nusra," Hands Off Syria, October 5, 2014. youtube.com/watch?v=NMlnxu1zrNk.

85 Anne Barnard and Eric Schmitt, "As Foreign Fighters Flood Syria, Fears of a New Extremist Haven," *New York Times*, August 8, 2013. nytimes.com/2013/08/09/world/middleeast/as-foreign-fighters-flood-syria-fears-of-a-new-extremist-haven.html.

86 "Warnings of jihadists among Syria's rebels came early," McClatchyDC, August 14, 2013. mcclatchydc.com/news/nation-world/national/national-security/article31018362.html.

87 "Syrian Woman Rips Into McCain At Town Hall For His Support For Bombing Syria 9 5 2013," Susan Duclos, September 5, 2013. youtube.com/watch?v=8x_vusWz33c.

88 Erika Solomon, "U.S. Senator McCain pictured with Syrian rebel kidnapper: paper," Reuters, May 30, 2013. reuters.com/article/world/us-senator-mccain-pictured-with-syrian-rebel-kidnapper-paper-idUSBRE94T0V3.

89 Patrick Wells, "The Northern Storm: Inside A Syrian Rebel Group," *Time*, April 9, 2013. youtube.com/watch?v=YqgTXYM128A.

90 Joanna Paraszczuk, "Syria Analysis: Which Insurgents Captured Menagh Airbase & Who Led Them?" *EA World View*, August 7, 2013. ea-worldview.com/2013/08/syria-feature-which-insurgents-captured-the-menagh-airbase.

91 Josh Rogin, "Obama Administration and Sotloff Family Battle Over Blame for Journalist's Kidnapping," *The Daily Beast*, September 22, 2014. thedailybeast.com/obama-administration-and-sotloff-family-battle-over-blame-for-journalists-kidnapping.

92 "Syrian rebels to retreat from Christian town of Maaloula," France 24, September 11, 2013. france24.com/en/20130911-syrian-rebels-withdraw-christian-town-maaloula.

93 "Siege of Maaloula highlights threat to Syria's Christians: Help them today," Institute for Palestine Studies, September 13, 2013. barnabasfund.org/UK/News/Archives/Siege-of-Maaloula-highlights-threat-to-Syrias-Christians-help-them-today.html (archive link: web.archive.org/web/20131204115948/barnabasfund.org/UK/News/Archives/Siege-of-Maaloula-highlights-threat-to-Syrias-Christians-help-them-today.html).

94 "Maaloula: Christians flee village where people still speak the language of Jesus," AsiaNews, September 6, 2013. asianews.it/news-en/Maaloula:-Christians-flee-village-where-people-still-speak-the-language-of-Jesus-28942.html.

95 Umberto Bacchi, "Syria Nun Kidnapping: Greek Orthodox Patriarch Urges Release of Maaloula Sisters," *International Business Times*, December 3, 2013.

96 Daniele Rocchi, "Syria: the challenge faced by the Christian population of Maaloula, where there's no more time to look back," Servizio Informazione Religiosa, June 18, 2019. agensir.it/mondo/2019/06/18/syria-the-challenge-faced-by-the-christian-population-of-maaloula-where-theres-no-more-time-to-look-back.

97 "Syria crisis: Nuns freed by rebels arrive in Damascus," BBC News, March 10, 2014. bbc.com/news/world-middle-east-26510202.

98 Fatih Gökhan Diler, "'Alevis to the grave, Christians to Beirut' is still a common slogan," *Agos*, October 17, 2016. agos.com.tr/en/article/16756/alevis-to-the-grave-christians-to-beirut-is-still-a-common-slogan.

99 Kirit Radia, Nick Schifrin, Dana Hughs, "Syria 'Welcomed' Russian Proposal to Destroy Its Chemical Weapons,'" ABC News, September 9, 2013. abcnews.go.com/International/syria-welcomed-russian-proposal-destroy-chemical-weapons/story?id=20198655.

100 Michael R. Gordon, "U.S. and Russia Reach Deal to Destroy Syria's Chemical Arms," *New York Times*, September 14, 2013. nytimes.com/2013/09/15/world/middleeast/syria-talks.html.

101 Warren Strobel and Mariam Karouny, "U.S., Russia agree on Syria weapons, Obama says force still option," Reuters, September 13, 2013. reuters.com/article/us-syria-crisis/u-s-russia-agree-on-syria-weapons-obama-says-force-still-option-idUSBRE98A15720130914.

Chapter 17

1 Michael R. Gordon, *Degrade and Destroy: The Inside Story of the War Against the Islamic State, from Barack Obama to Donald Trump* (New York: Farrar, Straus and Giroux, 2022), Chapter 3.

2 Jeffrey Goldberg, "The Obama doctrine," *The Atlantic*, April 2016. theatlantic.com/magazine/archive/2016/04/the-obama-doctrine/471525.

3 Jaime Detmer, "Syria's Saudi Jihadist Problem," *The Daily Beast*, December 16, 2013. thedailybeast.com/syrias-saudi-jihadist-problem.

4 John Jenkins, "Syria's world war: how the West allowed Russian and Iran to take control," *The New Statesman*, September 8, 2016. newstatesman.com/world/2016/09/syria-s-world-war-how-west-allowed-russian-and-iran-take-control.

5 Patrick McDonnell, "Turkey is alarmed by extremist militants in Syria border area," *Los Angeles Times*, November 10, 2013. latimes.com/world/la-fg-turkey-border-radicals-20131110-story.html.

6 Jeffrey Goldberg, "The Obama doctrine," *The Atlantic*, April 2016. theatlantic.com/magazine/archive/2016/04/the-obama-doctrine/471525.

7 Ibid.

8 Yaakov Katz, "For all his faults, Assad is the devil we know," *Jerusalem Post*, March 23, 2011. jpost.com/middle-east/for-all-his-faults-assad-is-the-devil-we-know.

9 Robin Yassin-Kassab and Leila Al-Shami, *Burning Country: Syrians in Revolution and War* (London: Pluto Press, 2016), p. 214.

10 Joe Conason, "Seven countries in five years," *Salon*, October 12, 2007. salon.com/2007/10/12/wesley_clark.

11 Gerald M. Steinberg, "Israel looks over the horizon: Responding to the threats of weapons proliferation," Jerusalem Center for Public Affairs, *Jerusalem Letter*, July 1, 2001. jcpa.org/jl/vp457.htm.

12 Ronen Bergman, "The Spies Inside Damascus: The Mossad's secret war on the Syrian WMD machine," *Foreign Policy*, September 20, 2013. foreignpolicy.com/2013/09/20/the-spies-inside-damascus.

13 Raphael Ahren, "Israel acknowledges it is helping Syrian rebel fighters," *The Times of Israel*, June 29, 2015. timesofisrael.com/yaalon-syrian-rebels-keeping-druze-safe-in-exchange-for-israeli-aid.

14 Ilan Ben Zion, "And now we play the waiting game," *The Times of Israel*, August 30, 2013. timesofisrael.com/and-now-we-play-the-waiting-game.

15 Herb Keinon, "Israel wanted Assad gone since start of Syria civil war," *Jerusalem Post*, September 17, 2013. jpost.com/Syria-Crisis/Oren-Jerusalem-has-wanted-Assad-ousted-since-the-outbreak-of-the-Syrian-civil-war-326328.

16 Jeffrey Goldberg, "The Obama doctrine," *The Atlantic*, April 2016. theatlantic.com/magazine/archive/2016/04/the-obama-doctrine/471525.

17 Jodi Rudoren, "Israel Backs Limited Strike Against Syria," *New York Times*, September 5, 2013. nytimes.com/2013/09/06/world/middleeast/israel-backs-limited-strike-against-syria.html.

18 Edward N. Luttwak, "In Syria, America Loses if Either Side Wins," *New York Times*, August 24, 2013. nytimes.com/2013/08/25/opinion/sunday/in-syria-america-loses-if-either-side-wins.html.

19 Khaled Atallah, "Are Israel, Jabhat al-Nusra coordinating on attacks in Syria?" Al-Monitor, January 14, 2015. al-monitor.com/originals/2015/01/syria-opposition-daraa-israel-communication-nusra.html.

20 Hannah Allam and Jonathan Landay, "U.S., anti-Assad rebels in Syria remain at odds over role of al-Qaeda," McClatchyDC, October 2, 2014. mcclatchydc.com/news/nation-world/national/national-security/article24774124.html.

21 Lazar Berman, "Assad: Israel operates as al-Qaeda's air force," *The Times of Israel*, January 26, 2015. timesofisrael.com/assad-israel-operates-as-al-qaedas-air-force.

22 Bill Gertz, "Former CIA leader: Syria's Islamist Rebels Gaining Power," *Washington Free Beacon*, September 13, 2013. freebeacon.com/national-security/former-cia-leader-syrias-islamist-rebels-gaining-power.

23 "Ex-CIA official fears Syria could become al Qaeda safe haven," CBS News, September 13, 2013. youtube.com/watch?v=gha3AlrAwe0.

[24] David Enders, "Rebel cooperation in Syrian town shows challenge of isolating Islamists," McClatchyDC, September 25, 2013. mcclatchydc.com/news/nation-world/world/article24745666.html#storylink=cpy.

[25] "Insurgents seize Syrian Alawite village, killing 19: Observatory," Reuters, May 13, 2016. reuters.com/article/us-mideast-crisis-syria-village-idUSKCN0Y41ME.

[26] "Syrian villagers describe massacre by militant group spared from UN terror blacklist," RT, May 13, 2016. rt.com/news/342983-syria-zara-carnage-alsham/amp.

[27] Labib Al Nahhas, "The deadly consequences of mislabeling Syria's revolutionaries," Washington Post, July 10, 2015. washingtonpost.com/opinions/the-deadly-consequences-of-mislabeling-syrias-revolutionaries/2015/07/10/6dec139e-266e-11e5-aae2-6c4f59b050aa_story.html.

[28] Hannah Allam, "Syrian rebel whose group is linked to al Qaida visited U.S.," McClatchyDC, May 21, 2015. mcclatchydc.com/news/nation-world/national/national-security/article78962527.html.

[29] Mark Mazzetti, Robert F. Worth, and Michael R. Gordon, "Obama's Uncertain Path Amid Syria Bloodshed," New York Times, October 22, 2013. nytimes.com/2013/10/23/world/middleeast/obamas-uncertain-path-amid-syria-bloodshed.html.

[30] Nick Paton Walsh, "The secret jihadi smuggling route through Turkey," CNN, November 5, 2013. edition.cnn.com/2013/11/04/world/europe/isis-gaining-strength-on-syria-turkey-border/index.html.

[31] Jaime Detmer, "Syria's Saudi Jihadist Problem," The Daily Beast, December 16, 2013. thedailybeast.com/syrias-saudi-jihadist-problem.

[32] Abdullah Suleiman Ali, "As-Safir: Saudi jihadists flow into Syria," Al-Monitor, December 5, 2013. al-monitor.com/pulse/security/2013/12/saudi-fighters-syria-official-silence.html.

[33] Michael Doran, "The Good and Bad of Ahrar al-Sham," Foreign Affairs, January 23, 2014. foreignaffairs.com/articles/syria/2014-01-23/good-and-bad-ahrar-al-sham.

[34] Adam Entous and Joe Parkinson, "Turkey's Spymaster Plots Own Course on Syria," Wall Street Journal, October 10, 2013. wsj.com/articles/SB10001424052702303643304579107373585228330.

[35] Fehim Tastekin, "Radical Groups Operate on Turkey's Border," Al-Monitor, October 17, 2013. al-monitor.com/originals/2013/10/jihadist-syria-border-turkey-radical-groups.html.

[36] Jefferson Morley, "What Did Turkey Know About Baghdadi's Hideout?" The New Republic, October 30, 2019. newrepublic.com/article/155504/turkey-know-baghdadis-hideout.

[37] Ali Hashem, "Iranian official says prominent Saudi jihadist 'man in control' in Syria," Al-Monitor, May 11, 2016. al-monitor.com/originals/2016/05/syria-saudi-cleric-mohaysini-rise-new-bin-laden.html.

[38] David Ignatius, "A new cooperation on Syria," Washington Post, May 12, 2015. washingtonpost.com/opinions/a-new-cooperation-on-syria/2015/05/12/bdb48a68-f8ed-11e4-9030-b4732caefe81_story.html.

[39] William Van Wagenen, "Ambassador Ford Lied About Giving TOW Missiles to Al-Qaeda in Syria," Libertarian Institute, June 1, 2022. libertarianinstitute.org/articles/ambassador-ford-lied-about-giving-tow-missiles-to-al-qaeda-in-syria.

[40] Ben Hubbard, "In a Syria Refuge, Extremists Exert Greater Control," New York Times, August 13, 2017. nytimes.com/2017/08/13/world/middleeast/idlib-syria-displaced-militants.html.

41 "A Report into the credibility of certain evidence with regard to Torture and Execution of Persons Incarcerated by the current Syrian regime," Carter-Ruck and Co. Solicitors of London, January 20, 2014. static.guim.co.uk/ni/1390226674736/syria-report-execution-tort.pdf.

42 "If the Dead Could Speak: Mass Deaths and Torture in Syria's Detention Facilities," Human Rights Watch, December 16, 2015. hrw.org/report/2015/12/16/if-dead-could-speak/mass-deaths-and-torture-syrias-detention-facilities.

43 Rick Sterling, "The Caesar Photo Fraud that Undermined Syrian Negotiations," *CounterPunch*, March 4, 2016. counterpunch.org/2016/03/04/the-caesar-photo-fraud-that-undermined-syrian-negotiations.

44 "If the Dead Could Speak: Mass Deaths and Torture in Syria's Detention Facilities," Human Rights Watch, December 16, 2015. hrw.org/report/2015/12/16/if-dead-could-speak/mass-deaths-and-torture-syrias-detention-facilities.

45 Rick Sterling, "The Caesar Photo Fraud that Undermined Syrian Negotiations," *CounterPunch*, March 4, 2016. counterpunch.org/2016/03/04/the-caesar-photo-fraud-that-undermined-syrian-negotiations.

46 Sabrina Tavernise, "End of the Line for Families of Baghdad's Missing: The City Morgue," *New York Times*, May 20, 2005. nytimes.com/2005/05/20/world/middleeast/end-of-the-line-for-families-of-baghdads-missing-the-city.html.

47 "David M. Crane, Co-author of a report on Syrian prisoners," France 24, May 15, 2014. france24.com/en/20140315-interview-david-michael-crane-co-author-report-on-syrian-prisoners-torture-killing-assad-regime.

48 "Former CIA Agent John Stockwell Talks about How the CIA Worked in Vietnam and Elsewhere," Witness to War, September 29, 2017. youtube.com/watch?v=NK1tfkESPVY.

49 Dan Murphy, "Syria smoking gun report merits a careful read," *Christian Science Monitor*, January 21, 2014. csmonitor.com/World/Security-Watch/Backchannels/2014/0121/Syria-smoking-gun-report-warrants-a-careful-read.

50 "Caesar Syria Civilian Protection Act," U.S. Department of State, June 17, 2020. 2017-2021.state.gov/caesar-syria-civilian-protection-act//index.html.

51 Joshua Landis and Steven Simon, "The Pointless Cruelty of Trump's New Syria Sanctions," *Foreign Affairs*, August 17, 2020. foreignaffairs.com/articles/syria/2020-08-17/pointless-cruelty-trumps-new-syria-sanctions.

Chapter 18

1 United Nations Human Rights Council, "Report of the Independent International Commission of Inquiry on the Syrian Arab Republic," August 16, 2013. refworld.org/reference/countryrep/unhrc/2013/en/97249.

2 Ibid.

3 Nancy Scheper-Hughes, "Organ Trafficking During Times of War and Political Conflict," International Affairs Forum. ia-forum.org/Files/HDSQLC.pdf.

4 Marija Ristic, "Kosovo Organ-Trafficking: How the Claims were Exposed." *Balkan Insight*, September 4, 2015. balkaninsight.com/2015/09/04/kosovo-organ-trafficking-how-the-claims-were-exposed-09-04-2015-1.

5 Nancy Scheper-Hughes, "Organ Trafficking During Times of War and Political Conflict," International Affairs Forum. ia-forum.org/Files/HDSQLC.pdf.

6 Peter Beaumont, Ed Vulliamy and Paul Beaver, "'CIA's bastard army ran riot in Balkans' backed extremists,'" *The Guardian*, March 11, 2001. theguardian.com/world/2001/mar/11/edvulliamy.peterbeaumont.

[7] Kit Klarenberg, "How Britain and America Backed Kosovo Jihadists," *Global Delinquents*, April 24, 2022. kitklarenberg.com/p/how-britain-and-america-backed-jihadists.

[8] Marcia Christoff Kurop, "Al Qaeda's Balkan Links," *Wall Street Journal*, November 1, 2001. wsj.com/articles/SB1004563569751363760.

[9] Dick Marty, "Inhuman treatment of people and illicit trafficking in human organs in Kosovo," European Parliament Assembly, Committee on Legal Affairs and Human Rights, January 7, 2011. scp-ks.org/sites/default/files/public/coe.pdf.

[10] Paul Lewis, "'Kosovo PM is head of human organ and arms ring,' Council of Europe reports," *The Guardian*, December 14, 2010. theguardian.com/world/2010/dec/14/kosovo-prime-minister-llike-mafia-boss.

[11] Bojana Barlovac, "French FM calls reporter 'sick' for organ trafficking question," *Balkan Insight*, March 3, 2010. balkanin-sight.com/2010/03/03/french-fm-calls-reporter-sick-for-organ-trafficking-question.

[12] Douglas Hand, "Kouchner again reacts violent at mention of organ trafficking in Kosovo," *In Serbia*, January 6, 2015. inserbia.info/kouchner-again-reacts-violent-at-mention-of-organ-trafficking-in-kosovo.

[13] Vanessa Beeley, "The White Helmets, alleged organ traders and child kidnappers, should be condemned not condoned," Russia Today, January 22, 2019. rt.com/op-ed/449431-syria-white-helmets-organ-traders.

[14] Tony Cartalucci, "'Doctors' behind Syrian chemical weapons claims are aiding terrorists," Global Research, August 25, 2013. globalre-search.ca/doctors-behind-syrian-chemical-weapons-claims-are-aiding-terrorists/5346870.

[15] "Doctor: 'We Truly Are Failing the Syrian People,'" National Public Radio, May 17, 2013. npr.org/2013/05/17/184845130/doctor-we-truly-are-failing-the-syrian-people.

[16] "Syria: 'Half the fighters I treated were jihadists,' says French doctor," France 24, September 11, 2012. france24.com/en/20120911-foreign-jihadists-syria-doctors-without-borders-aleppo-jacques-beres.

[17] Edward Cody, "From France, an urge to intervene in Syria," *Washington Post*, September 10, 2012. washing-tonpost.com/world/middle_east/from-france-an-urge-to-intervene-in-syria/2012/09/10/4c83c936-fb24-11e1-8adc-499661afe377_story.html.

[18] Jacques Bérès, Mario Bettati, André Glucksmann, Bernard Kouchner, Bernard-Henri Lévy, "Assez de dérobades, il faut intervenir en Syrie!" *Le Monde*, October 22, 2012. lemonde.fr/idees/article/2012/10/22/assez-de-derobades-il-faut-intervenir-en-syrie_1779116_3232.html.

[19] "Syria Tells UN That McCain, Former Diplomats Visited Illegally," Reuters, January 5, 2015. reuters.com/article/world/syria-tells-un-that-mccain-and-former-diplomats-visited-illegally-idUSKBN0KE1P2.

[20] Ben Norton, "Leaked docs expose massive Syria propaganda operation waged by Western govt contractors and media," The Grayzone, September 23, 2020. thegrayzone.com/2020/09/23/syria-leaks-uk-contractors-opposition-media.

[21] Shannon Van Sant, "Death in Istanbul: The Untold Story of Syria's White Helmets," *Politico*, April 19, 2023. politico.eu/article/white-helmets-james-le-mesurier-death-emma-winberg-untold-story-syria-war-mayday-rescue.

[22] Paul McKeigue, David Miller, Jake Mason, Piers Robinson, "How the OPCW's investigation of the Douma incident was nobbled," School for Policy Studies, June 26, 2019. syriapropagandamedia.org/how-the-opcws-investigation-of-the-douma-incident-was-nobbled.

[23] Vanessa Beeley, "Real 'obscene masquerade': How BBC depicted staged hospital scenes as proof of Douma chemical attack," Russia Today, February 16, 2019. rt.com/op-ed/451623-bbc-staged-footage-douma-chemical-attack.

24 Paul McKeigue, David Miller, Piers Robinson, "Briefing note on the final report of the OPCW Fact-Finding Mission on the alleged chemical attack in Douma in April 2018," School for Policy Studies, April 11, 2019. syriapropagandamedia.org/working-papers/briefing-note-on-the-final-report-of-the-opcw-fact-finding-mission-on-the-alleged-chemical-attack-in-douma-in-april-2018.

25 Vanessa Beeley, "The White Helmets, alleged organ traders & child kidnappers, should be condemned not condoned," Russia Today, January 22, 2019. rt.com/op-ed/449431-syria-white-helmets-organ-traders.

26 "Organ trafficking adds up to Syrians' suffering," Alalam News, March 25, 2014. en.alalam.ir/news/1579147.

27 Ahmad Haj Hamdo, "The underbelly of Syria's war: a thriving trade in human organs," United Press International, May 12, 2016. upi.com/Top_News/World-News/2016/05//The-underbelly-of-Syrias-war-a-thriving-trade-in-human-organs/5301462896201.

28 William Van Wagenen, "Made in America: The ISIS conquest of Mosul," *The Cradle*, July 2, 2024: thecradle.co/articles/made-in-america-the-isis-conquest-of-mosul.

29 William Van Wagenen, "Masoud Barzani: The Butcher of Sinjar," *The Cradle*, July 25, 2024: thecradle.co/articles/masoud-barzani-the-butcher-of-sinjar.

30 John Hall, "UN urged to investigate ISIS's bloody trade in human organs after Iraqi ambassador reveals doctors are being executed for not harvesting body parts," *Daily Mail*, February 18, 2015. dailymail.co.uk/news/article-2958220/UN-urged-investigate-ISIS-s-bloody-trade-human-organs-Iraqi-ambassador-reveals-doctors-executed-not-harvesting-body-parts.html.

31 Ibid.

32 United Nations Human Rights Council, "'They came to destroy': ISIS Crimes Against the Yazidis," June 15, 2016. ohchr.org/sites/default/files/Documents/HRBodies/HRCouncil/CoISyria/A_HRC_32_CRP.2_en.pdf.

33 Jane Arraf, National Public Radio, "Yazidis tell their stories about life under ISIS," March 14, 2019. npr.org/2019/03/14/703287508/yazidis-tell-their-stories-about-life-under-isis.

34 Doreen Carvajal, "Trafficking Investigations Put Surgeon in Spotlight," *New York Times*, February 10, 2011. ny-times.com/2011/02/11/world/europe/11organ.html.

35 Michael Smith, Daryna Krasnolutska and David Glovin, "Organ Gangs Force Poor to Sell Kidneys for Desperate Israelis," Bloomberg News, November 1, 2011. bloomberg.com/news/articles/2011-11-01/organ-gangs-force-poor-to-sell-kidneys-for-desperate-israelis.

36 "Israeli organ trafficking network busted in Adana during transplants," *Daily Sabah*, May 3, 2024. dailysabah.com/turkiye/israeli-organ-trafficking-network-busted-in-adana-during-transplants/news.

37 Morten Berthelsen and Barak Ravid, "Top Sweden Newspaper Says IDF Kills Palestinians for Their Organs," *Haaretz*, August 18, 2009. haaretz.com/2009-08-18/ty-article/top-sweden-newspaper-says-idf-kills-palestinians-for-their-organs/0000017f-db4a-db22-a17f-fffb257c0000.

38 Ian Black, "Doctor admits Israeli pathologists harvested organs without consent," *The Guardian*, December 21, 2009. theguardian.com/world/2009/dec/21/israeli-pathologists-harvested-organs.

39 Nancy Scheper-Hughes, "Organ Trafficking During Times of War and Political Conflict," International Affairs Forum. ia-forum.org/Files/HDSQLC.pdf.

[40] Ben Hubbard, "Israel Aids Evacuation From Syria of Hundreds of 'White Helmets' and Families," *New York Times*, July 22, 2018.
nytimes.com/2018/07/22/world/middleeast/israel-white-helmets-syria.html.

Acknowledgments

This book would not have been possible without the guidance and support of many individuals. I am especially grateful to Scott Horton, the Director of the Libertarian Institute, who first gave me the opportunity to publish my analyses of the Syrian war. Without his encouragement, I would never have thought to write this book. The decades Scott has devoted to antiwar activism and his encyclopedic knowledge of the so-called Terror Wars have made him a major role model for me.

I would like to extend a special thanks to the book's editor, Ben Parker, who has spent countless hours bringing the book to fruition. Thanks as well to Mike Dworski and Grant F. Smith for their assistance in preparing this book for publication. I wish to extend a huge thank you to Andrew Zehnder, who did an amazing job designing the book's cover.

I also wish to thank journalist Sharmine Narwani, whose courageous on-the-ground reporting from Syria and questioning of the mainstream media narrative on Syria was an inspiring example to me.

Finally, I wish to thank Kevork Almassian, who has provided me with amazing encouragement over the years. I have learned so much from his analysis and research exposing the U.S./Israeli effort to destroy Syria, despite facing significant dangers to himself.

The Libertarian Institute

Check out the Libertarian Institute at LibertarianInstitute.org. It's Scott Horton, Sheldon Richman, Laurie Calhoun, James Bovard, Ted Galen Carpenter, Kyle Anzalone, Keith Knight and the best libertarian writers and podcast hosts on the Internet. We are a 501(c)(3) tax-exempt charitable organization. EIN 83-2869616.

Help support our efforts. Visit LibertarianInstitute.org/donate or:

The Libertarian Institute
612 W. 34th St.
Austin, TX, 78705

Check out all of our other great books at LibertarianInstitute.org/books:

Provoked: How Washington Started the New Cold War with Russia and the Catastrophe in Ukraine by Scott Horton

Hotter Than the Sun: Time to Abolish Nuclear Weapons by Scott Horton

Enough Already: Time to End the War on Terrorism by Scott Horton

Fool's Errand: Time to End the War in Afghanistan by Scott Horton

Diary of a Psychosis: How Public Health Disgraced Itself During Covid Mania by Thomas E. Woods, Jr.

Last Rights: The Death of American Liberty by James Bovard

Questioning the COVID Company Line: Critical Thinking in Hysterical Times by Laurie Calhoun

Domestic Imperialism: Nine Reasons I Left Progressivism by Keith Knight

Voluntaryist Handbook by Keith Knight

Israel, Winner of the 2003 Iraq Oil War by Gary Vogler

The Fake China Threat and Its Very Real Danger by Joseph Solis-Mullen

The Great Ron Paul: The Scott Horton Show Interviews 2004–2019

No Quarter: The Ravings of William Norman Grigg, edited by Tom Eddlem

Coming to Palestine by Sheldon Richman

What Social Animals Owe to Each Other by Sheldon Richman

Keep a look out for more great titles to be published in 2025 and 2026.